slow wine

A YEAR
IN THE LIFE
OF THE
VINEYARDS
AND WINES
OF THE USA

slow wine

A YEAR IN THE LIFE OF THE VINEYARDS AND WINES OF THE USA

2025

ALL RIGHTS RESERVED

Copyright © 2025 Slow Food Promozione S.r.l. SB.

Authors:
Giancarlo Gariglio, **Editor-in-chief**
Deborah Parker Wong, **National Editor**
Pam Strayer, **Managing Editor**

California
Contributing editors:
Heidi Dickerson, Darlene Hayes, Charles Kelly, Jaime Knee, Allison Levine, Laurie Love, Cindy Rynning, Fred Swan, Amber Turpin, Mary Beth Vierra

Oregon
Contributing editors:
Nancy Croisier, Neal D. Hulkower, Ph.D., Ellen Landis, Annie McKay

Washington
Contributing editors:
Jusden Aumand, Nancy Croisier, Annie McKay

New York
Contributing editor:
Laura Winter Falk

Interns: Stella Shi

Book Design: Francesco Perona

Cover Design: Alice Iuri and Mauro de Toffol / theWorldofDot

The opinions expressed in this manuscript are solely the opinions of the author. The author has represented and warranted full ownership and/or legal right to publish all the materials in this book.
This book may not be reproduced, transmitted, or stored in whole or in part by any means, including graphic, electronic, or mechanical without the express written consent of the publisher except in the case of brief quotations embodied in critical articles and reviews.

Published by Slow Food Promozione S.r.l. SB
Via Mendicità Istruita, 14 – 12042 Bra (CN)—ITALY

ISBN: 978-88-947332-2-8

INDEX

Introduction	5
Slow Food Manifesto for good, clean and fair wine	6
How to read the guide	11
TOP Wine Awards	13
Winery Awards	21
Index of wineries	239
Index of places	242

CALIFORNIA — 25

North Coast - **Napa**	26
North Coast - **Sonoma**	47
North Coast - **Mendocino & Other**	78
North Coast - **San Francisco Bay Area**	94
Santa Cruz Mountains	99
Central Coast - **Monterey & Other**	111
Central Coast - **San Luis Obispo**	114
Central Coast - **Santa Barbara County**	130
South Coast	158
Inland Valleys and Sierra Foothills	162

OREGON — 165

Willamette Valley	166
Southern Oregon	197
Columbia Gorge	200

WASHINGTON — 205

NEW YORK — 219

Finger Lakes	220
Finger Lakes - Cayuga	222
Finger Lakes - Seneca	223
Long Island	228

INTRODUCTION

Two themes we identified in 2023 - climate resilience and diversity in all its many forms – continued to dominate the discussions during our visits with 380 wineries in 2024.

Wineries are embracing more and more regenerative farming practices. That means changing rootstocks, going no till, and planting heat tolerant varieties. Or, it can mean going organic, to better retain moisture in the soil. Energy is another accelerating, ecofriendly direction—as wineries grow their solar power arrays and put new electric tractors into service.

Diversity in the people growing grapes and making wine is another theme. Korean and Indian families are now winery owners, bringing with them new food and wine pairings, and black and Hispanic wine professionals are working in greater numbers in positions of authority. In addition, many young winemakers are emerging, adventurously buying wine grapes from far and wide.

Varieties grown in the U.S. are also diversifying with new releases of Aglianico, Carricante, Fiano, Falanghina, Godello, Gouais Blanc, Nero d'Avola and others. At the same time, more historic vineyards and iconic wineries are getting time to shine, with growing recognition for the cultural and sensory delights they bring.

New regions are also gaining ground-the SLO Coast, York Mountain (outside Paso), and San Benito County are but a few of the places where wine growers are exploring new expressions.

Thanks to the stellar team work of this year's 16 field coordinators, the 2025 guide includes returning wineries and dozens of newcomers who have joined the Slow Wine community.

We're grateful to our writers and to all the wineries we visited this year, as well as to our many readers and supporters. To the producers—thank you for sharing your wines, your practices and your insights with us so we can produce an annual guide that promotes transparency, dialog and delight.

Pam Strayer
Managing Editor, US

Deborah Parker Wong
National Editor, US

SLOW WINE COALITION

A COLLABORATIVE WINE NETWORK

Slow Food®
Slow Wine Coalition

The Slow Food Manifesto for good, clean and fair wine

The Manifesto for good, clean and fair wine is born from Slow Food's experience over the years, a long-standing relationship in which wine has played a crucial role, thanks to the passionate involvement of wine experts, winemakers and technicians.

Through the production and consumption of wine made according to the Manifesto, we aim to positively influence the future of viticulture, by breaking the ties from the use of chemicals and monocultures, and re-establishing our connection to biodiversity across terroirs and regions.

For some years now, vanguard vignerons from across the globe have understood and communicated that we must change course. This change, however, cannot happen by acting alone. For this reason, we are calling on wine lovers and professionals alike to come together and play a fundamental role in the promotion and consumption of wines with strong environmental, ethical and social values. This is important now, more than ever, as we navigate a period of economic and ecological reconstruction.

Through this interaction with other actors in the network, winemakers themselves will have the opportunity to be exposed to other fundamental subjects such as education to conscious consumption, the centrality of a narration focused on what is really important to tell (and to know) about each wine and the territory from which it comes from, as well as recognizing the right value of one's product.

Please consider - The wineries in this guide are inspired by the spirit of the Manifesto but it does not serve as the criteria for being listed in the guide.

SLOW FOOD MANIFESTO
FOR GOOD, CLEAN AND FAIR WINE

Wineries must grow a **minimum 70% of the grapes used in the production of their wine** themselves.
Exceptions are given for regions in which widespread sourcing is common, e.g. Madeira, Napa Valley, the south of Spain, etc.

Wineries **may not use chemically synthesized fertilizers**, herbicides, or anti-botrytis fungicides.

A conscious and sustainable **approach to the use of environmental resources** in winemaking must be applied. Dependence on irrigation systems must be limited and should only aim to avoid critical water-stress conditions.

Winery buildings, should they need to be constructed, must respect their environmental surroundings. Management, upkeep and eventual restauration of extant buildings should take **sustainability into account.**

Wineries should not utilize techniques like reverse osmosis or other physical methods of must concentration. Furthermore, the addition of RCGM (rectified concentrated grape must) or sugar (according to the country of production) is not permitted, with the exception of sparkling wines or wines where these practices fall under traditional techniques. Oak chips used to aromatize wines are also prohibited.

Permitted levels of sulfites should not exceed the limits listed under the European Union's regulations for organic wine.

 The wines must **show terroir and reflect their place of origin.** It is for this reason that we encourage the use of indigenous yeasts, as well as scientific research to isolate native yeasts which can then be replicated and used by the winery or other winemakers of the same area and geographical denomination.

 The wines **must be free of any winemaking defects**, as they tend to homogenize the wines and stamp out any regional identity.

 Wineries should actively engage and **collaborate with the entire surrounding farming community** in order to strengthen and enhance the agricultural system of the area. In this vein, the winery must maintain a principled relationship with its associates, as well as its employees, fostering personal and professional growth. It is moreover important that the winery cooperates and shares knowledge with other producers, avoiding unfair competition.

 Sustainable winemakers **encourage biodiversity** through practices such as: alternating vineyards with hedges and wooded areas; soil management practices that include grass and green manure and exclude, in any case, bare soil, with potential exceptions for short, seasonal periods; the protection of pollinating insects and useful fauna through the use of insecticides which are allowed in organic farming, where such interventions are necessary, and in any case avoiding their use during the flowering of the vine and of other herbaceous species present in the vineyard; the breeding of animals with respect for their welfare and the production of manure on the farm, as well as the production of compost from pruning residues and other organic materials.

THE FIRST-EVER UNIVERSITY DEDICATED SOLELY TO GASTRONOMIC SCIENCES

Located in Piedmont, at the heart of gastronomic excellence, UNISG was founded by Slow Food and offers a unique, innovative educational model. Backed by over 150 companies in the agri-food sector, it combines interdisciplinary courses, hands-on learning, and study trips around the globe.

Undergraduate degree in:
Food Sciences and Cultures

MSc in:
Food Industry Management

Master in:
New Food Thinking
World Food Studies
Food Communication & Marketing
Agroecology and Food Sovereignty

Hybrid Master in:
Local Food Policy

Bite into our courses!

@UNISG

@unisg_official

HOW TO READ THE GUIDE

THE WINERY

BOTTLE — Symbol awarded to wineries whose bottles represented excellent average quality at our tastings.

COIN — Symbol awarded to wineries whose bottles are good value for money.

SNAIL — Symbol awarded to a winery that we recognize for the way it interprets Slow Food values (sensory perceptions, territory, environment, identity) and also offers good value for money.

A winery which, either on the premises or in the immediate vicinity, offers food and refreshments.

A winery which, either on the premises or in the immediate vicinity, offers hospitality.

Prices — The prices indicated represent the suggested retail price as listed by the wineries.

THE WINES

TOP WINE — The finest bottles from a sensory point of view.

SLOW WINE — Top Wines that, beyond their outstanding sensory quality, demonstrate terroir-related values such as history and identity, as well as offering good value for money. The attribution of this accolade implies the absence of any chemical herbicides in the vineyard. The Slow Wine accolade also considers value for money, taking into account the time and place of production.

EVERYDAY WINE — Top Wines retailing up to 30 $.

Wine type
- White wine
- Rosé wine
- Red wine
- Sparkling white wine
- Sparkling rosé wine
- Sparkling red wine
- Dessert wine
- Orange wine

Type of ageing
- Stainless steel
- Concrete
- Small barrels
- Large casks
- Amphora

The data regarding viticultural and enological practices were provided by the producers.

Slow Wine Guide USA features only wines that producers have verified are herbicide free. However, we do not verify that all the wines a producer makes meet the standard of the Slow Wine Manifesto for good, clean and fair wine.

TOP WINE AWARDS

California

NORTH COAST - **NAPA**

26 **Howell Mountain ADAMVS**
 Cabernet Sauvignon 2019
 ADAMVS

27 **Stags Leap District Black Label**
 Cabernet Sauvignon 2021
 Baldacci Family Vineyards

28 **Spring Mountain District Cain Five 2021** SLOW WINE
 Cain Vineyard And Winery

29 **Napa Valley Founding Brothers Red 2021**
 Cathiard Vineyard

30 **Napa Valley Pritchard Hill**
 Cabernet Sauvignon 2021
 Chappellet

30 **Oak Knoll Unoaked Chardonnay 2022** EVERYDAY WINE
 Clif Family Winery

31 **Napa Valley Kronos Vineyard**
 Cabernet Sauvignon 2021 SLOW WINE
 Corison

31 **St. Helena Estate Sauvignon Blanc 2023**
 Crocker & Starr

33 **Oakville East Block Cabernet Franc 2019**
 Detert Family Vineyards

33 **Napa Valley Dominus 2021** SLOW WINE
 Dominus/Napanook

34 **St. Helena J. Leducq Cabernet Sauvignon 2021**
 Ehlers Estate

34 **Napa Valley Chockablock**
 Red Blend 2021 EVERYDAY WINE
 Elizabeth Rose

35 **Napa Valley Sauvignon Blanc 2023** EVERYDAY WINE
 Frog's Leap

35 **Napa Valley Estate Cabernet Sauvignon 2021**
 Gallica

36 **Yountville Single Vineyard**
 Cabernet Sauvignon 2020 SLOW WINE
 Ghost Block

36 **Napa Valley Fumé Blanc 2022** SLOW WINE
 Grgich Hills Estate

37 **Oak Knoll District Quartz Creek Vineyard**
 Chardonnay 2022 SLOW WINE
 Heitz Cellar

37 **Carneros Hyde Vineyard Chardonnay 2021**
 Hyde de Villaine - HdV

38 **Oakville Vine Hill Ranch**
 Cabernet Sauvignon 2019 SLOW WINE
 Keplinger Wines

38 **California Gemina White Blend 2023** SLOW WINE
 Massican

39 **Howell Mountain**
 Cabernet Sauvignon 2021 SLOW WINE
 Neal Family Vineyards

40 **Napa Valley Yount Mill**
 Vineyard Sémillon 2021 SLOW WINE
 Newfound Wines

40 **Oakville Oakville Ranch**
 Red Wine 2021
 Oakville Ranch

41 **Napa Valley Opus One 2021**
 Opus One

42 **Oakville Merlot 2021** SLOW WINE
 Paradigm

42 **Mount Veeder Incubo**
 Cabernet Sauvignon 2021 SLOW WINE
 Pott Wines

43 **Rutherford Quintessa**
 Bordeaux Blend 2021
 Quintessa

43 **Los Carneros Scintilla Sonoma**
 Vineyard Abraxas 2019 SLOW WINE
 Robert Sinskey Vineyards

44 **Mount Veeder Estate Leslie's Blend 2019**
 Rudd Estate

44 **Napa Valley Brothers Vineyard**
 Cabernet Sauvignon 2021
 Snowden Vineyards

45 **St. Helena Napa Valley Spottswoode Estate**
 Cabernet Sauvignon 2021 SLOW WINE
 Spottswoode Estate Vineyard & Winery

45 **Rutherford Estate Chardonnay 2022**
 Staglin Family Vineyard

46 **Stags Leap District Fay Vineyard**
 Cabernet Sauvignon 2021 SLOW WINE
 Stags Leap Wine Cellars

46 **Napa Valley Las Flores**
 Cabernet Sauvignon 2018 SLOW WINE
 Volker Eisele Family Estate

47 **Napa Valley Cabernet Sauvignon 2022** SLOW WINE
 ZD Wines

NORTH COAST - **SONOMA**

48 California The Red Herring 2023 ● EVERYDAY WINE
Accenti Wines

48 Oakville Oakville Ranch Grenache 2021 ● SLOW WINE
Á Deux Têtes

49 Sonoma Valley Redshift Rosé 2022 ● SLOW WINE
Abbot's Passage

49 Sonoma County Bordeaux Blend Acaibo 2017 ● SLOW WINE
Acaibo

51 Contra Costa Evangelho Heritage Blend 2022 ● SLOW WINE
Bedrock Wine Co.

51 Sonoma Mountain Obsidian Point Cabernet Sauvignon 2021 ●
Benziger Family Winery

53 Cucamonga Valley Lopez Vineyard Monga Zin 2021 ● SLOW WINE
Carol Shelton Wines

53 El Dorado County Fenaughty Vineyards ViBES! Picpoul 2023 ○ EVERYDAY WINE
CARY Q WINES

54 Russian River Valley Las Cimas Vineyard Refosco 2022 ●
Comunitá

54 Santa Cruz Mountains Black Ridge Vineyard Red Wine 2021 ●
Cormorant Cellars

55 Sonoma Coast Chardonnay 2022 ○
County Line Vineyards

55 Sonoma Valley Rossi Ranch Valeria Amphora Red Field Blend 2019 ● SLOW WINE
Dane Cellars

56 Dry Creek Valley Hawk Mountain Estate Sangiovese 2021 ●
DaVero Farms & Winery

57 Russian River Valley DuMOL Estate Pinot Noir 2022 ● SLOW WINE
DuMOL

57 Redwood Valley pink lemonade Field Blend 2023 ⊛ EVERYDAY WINE
Emme Wines

58 Sonoma Coast Freestone Estate Pinot Noir 2022 ● SLOW WINE
Ernest Vineyards

59 Sonoma Valley Fission Cabernet Sauvignon 2020 ●
Far Mountain

61 California Neon Vermentino 2023 ○ EVERYDAY WINE
Guthrie Family Wines

61 Mendocino County Carignane 2022 ●
Horse & Plow

62 Mendocino County Yorkville Highlands Lost Hills Arneis 2023 ○
Idlewild

62 Russian River Valley Olivet Grange Pinot Gris 2022 ○
Inman Family Wines

63 Sonoma County Las Cimas Vineyard Aligoté 2023 ○
Jolie-Laide Wines

63 Petaluma Gap Panther Ridge Pinot Noir 2021 ●
Joseph Jewell

64 Moon Mountain District Estate Cabernet Sauvignon 2020 ● SLOW WINE
Kamen Estate Wines

64 Moon Mountain District Trinity Ridge Vineyard Cabernet Sauvignon 2021 ● SLOW WINE
Lasseter Family Winery

65 Sonoma Coast The Pivot Vineyard Pinot Noir 2022 ●
Littorai Wines

65 Sonoma Mountain van der Kamp Vineyard Pinot Meunier 2023 ●
Marchelle Wines

66 Russian River Valley Diana's Vineyard Pinot Noir 2022 ●
Merriam Vineyards

67 Lodi Sauvignon Blanc 2023 ○ EVERYDAY WINE
Monte Rio Cellars

67 Moon Mountain District Cabernet Sauvignon 2021 ● SLOW WINE
Moon Hollow

68 Russian River Valley Wildcard Wine-Cider Blend 2022 ⊛ EVERYDAY WINE
North American Press

68 Sonoma Hillsides Syrah 2022 ● SLOW WINE
Pax Wines

69 Russian River Hillside Vineyard Old Vines Pinot Noir 2019 ● SLOW WINE
Porter Creek Vineyards

69 Dry Creek Valley Barbera Reserve 2022 ● SLOW WINE
Preston Farm & Winery

70 Dry Creek Valley Fig Tree Vineyard Sauvignon Blanc 2022 ○ SLOW WINE
Quivira Vineyards

70 Sonoma Coast Harrison Grade Estate Syrah 2021 ● SLOW WINE
Radio-Coteau

71 Carneros Estate Chardonnay 2021 ○
Ram's Gate Winery

72 Santa Cruz Mountains Peter Martin Ray Chardonnay 2021 ○
Read Holland

72 Mendocino Testa Vineyard Boaz 2022 ●
Ruth Lewandowski Wine

73 Sonoma Valley Sparkling Mission 2023 ⊛ SLOW WINE
Scribe

73 Sonoma Coast Day One Pinot Noir 2021 ● SLOW WINE
Senses Wines

74 Moon Mountain District Cabernet Sauvignon 2019 ● SLOW WINE
Stone Edge Farm

75 Cabernet Sauvignon 2021
Surveyor

75 Sonoma Valley Kitty Face Grenache Blanc 2023
The Grenachista

76 Russian River Valley Estate Grenache Noir 2021
Two Shepherds

76 Mendocino County Alder Spring Sparkling Pinot Noir 2018
Under the Wire

77 Dry Creek Valley Barbera 2022
Unti Vineyards

78 Sonoma Valley Rossi Homage Blanc 2022 SLOW WINE
Winery Sixteen 600

NORTH COAST
MENDOCINO & OTHER

80 Mendocino County Girasole Pinot Blanc 2022 EVERYDAY WINE
BARRA of Mendocino

81 Potter Valley Blue Quail Pinot Gris 2023 SLOW WINE
Blue Quail and McFadden Winery

81 Mendocino County Single Vineyard The Butler Red Blend 2020
Bonterra Organic Estates

82 Anderson Valley Hacienda Sequoia Vineyard Pinot Noir 2022
Brashley Vineyards

82 Mendocino County Estate Viognier 2021 SLOW WINE
Campovida

83 Terroir 95470 Sangiovese 2015 EVERYDAY WINE
Chance Creek Vineyards

84 Lake County High Valley Rosé 2023 EVERYDAY WINE
Clay Shannon

84 Lake County Sparkling Brut Rosé Nonvintage
Cricket Farms

85 Anderson Valley Dach Vineyard Chardonnay 2022 SLOW WINE
Domaine Anderson

85 Mendocino Ridge Radiolaria Estate Pinot Noir 2022 SLOW WINE
Drew Family Wines

87 Anderson Valley Handley Estate Vineyard Blanc de Blanc 2019
Handley Cellars

88 Mendocino Ridge Sauvignon Blanc 2022 SLOW WINE
Mariah Vineyards

89 Mendocino County Bricarelli Ranch Nero d'Avola 2021
Martha Stoumen Wines

89 Redwood Valley Chardonnay 2022 EVERYDAY WINE
Mia Bea Wines

90 Anderson Valley Première Reserve Chardonnay 2022 EVERYDAY WINE
Navarro Vineyards & Winery

90 High Valley Mother Vine Rosé 2023 SLOW WINE
OVIS

90 High Valley Betsy's Vineyard Petit Sirah 2019
OVIS

91 Anderson Valley Pinot Noir 2021
Pennyroyal Farm

91 Mendocino County Pétillant Naturel 2018 EVERYDAY WINE
Powicana Farm

92 Hopland Rosé of Merlot 2022 EVERYDAY WINE
Terra Savia

93 Potter Valley Vecino Vineyard The Hatchling Sauvignon Blanc 2023
Unturned Stone

NORTH COAST
SAN FRANCISCO BAY AREA

94 Santa Maria Valley Bien Nacido Vineyard Syrah 2021
Covenant Wines

95 California Vineyard Select Zinfandel 2022 EVERYDAY WINE
Dashe Cellars

96 Lake County Remi Sauvignon Blanc 2023
Ettellia

97 Populis Reversée Red Wine 2023 EVERYDAY WINE
Les Lunes Wine

99 Clement Hills Vermentino 2023 EVERYDAY WINE
Terah Wine Co.

SANTA CRUZ MOUNTAINS

100 Santa Cruz Mountains Whole Cluster Estate Pinot Noir 2022
Alfaro Family Vineyard & Winery

100 Santa Cruz Mountains Regan Vineyard Estate La Vita Red Blend 2019
Bargetto Winery

101 Ben Lomond Mountain Estate Cabernet Sauvignon 2021 SLOW WINE
Beauregard Vineyards

101 Chalone Rodnick Farm Vineyard Chenin Blanc 2022
Big Basin Vineyards

102 Santa Cruz Mountains George's Vineyard Estate Cabernet Sauvignon 2017 SLOW WINE
Cooper-Garrod

103 Santa Cruz Mountains Estate Pinot Noir 2022
Ferrari Ranch Wines

103 Santa Cruz Mountains Lester Vineyard Pinot Noir 2019
House Family Vineyards

104 Santa Cruz Mountains Francisco Estate Pinot Noir 2021
Lester Estate Wines

104 Santa Cruz Mountains Cabernet Sauvignon 2022
Madson Wines

TOP WINE AWARDS

105 **Santa Cruz Mountains Chaine d'Or Vineyard Cabernet Sauvignon 2019** ●
Maison Areion

106 **Santa Cruz Mountains Spring Ridge Vineyard Bee Block Estate Chardonnay 2019** ○
Neely Wine

106 **Santa Cruz Mountains Mt. Eden Clone Estate Pinot Noir 2021** ●
Regan Vineyards Winery

107 **Santa Cruz Mountains Mt. Pajaro Pinot Noir 2021** ● SLOW WINE
Rhys Vineyards

107 **Dry Creek Valley Lytton Springs Zinfandel 2022** ● SLOW WINE
Ridge Vineyards

108 **Santa Cruz Mountains Le Boeuf Vineyard Chardonnay 2022** ○
Sandar & Hem Winery

108 **Santa Cruz Mountains Zayante Vineyard Zinfandel 2021** ● SLOW WINE
Santa Cruz Mountain Vineyard

109 **Santa Cruz Mountains Lester Family Vineyard Pinot Noir 2021** ●
Sante Arcangeli Family Wines

109 **Cienaga Valley Wirz Vineyard Cabernet Pfeffer 2022** ● SLOW WINE
Ser Winery

110 **Santa Cruz Mountains Alloy Bordeaux Blend 2013** ●
Silver Mountain Vineyards

110 **Santa Cruz Mountains Hidden Springs Chardonnay 2019** ○ SLOW WINE
Storrs Winery & Vineyards

111 **Santa Cruz Mountains Wild Yeast Estate Pinot Noir 2021** ●
Windy Oaks Estate

CENTRAL COAST
MONTEREY & OTHER

112 **Mokelumne River Bourboulenc 2022** ○
Acquiesce Winery & Vineyards

112 **Mt. Harlan Ryan Vineyard Pinot Noir 2021** ● SLOW WINE
Calera

113 **Cienega Valley Terraces Estate Pinot Gris 2022** ○
Eden Rift Vineyards

113 **Cienega Valley Eden Rift Pinot Noir 2022** ●
Seabold Cellars

114 **San Benito County Benitoite Red Blend 2022** ● EVERYDAY WINE
Stirm Wine Co.

CENTRAL COAST
SAN LUIS OBISPO

115 **Paso Robles Adamo Red Rhone Blend 2017** ● SLOW WINE
AmByth Estate

116 **Paso Robles Willow Creek District Blend #2 2022** ● SLOW WINE
Cairjn Wine Cellars

116 **Templeton Gap District Sagrantino 2021** ●
Clesi Winery

117 **Central Coast The Source Syrah 2021** ● SLOW WINE
Copia Vineyards & Winery

117 **Central Coast Hyperbole Pinot Noir 2022** ●
Cordant Winery

118 **SLO Coast Pinot Noir 2023** ● EVERYDAY WINE
Dunites Wine Co.

118 **Willow Creek District Estate Cabernet Sauvignon Reserve 2021** ● SLOW WINE
Dunning Vineyards

119 **Highlands District Shell Creek Valdigue 2023** ●
Field Recordings Wine

119 **Paso Robles Alma Paso 2023** ● SLOW WINE
Four Lanterns Winery

120 **Willow Creek District Chopping Block GSM 2020** ●
Fulldraw Vineyard

120 **Paso Robles Adelaida District Luna Matta Vineyard Nebbiolo 2020** ●
Giornata Wines

121 **Adelaida District Block 22 Syrah 2021** ●
Halter Ranch

121 **Adelaida District Sisu Red Rhone Blend 2021** ●
kukkula

122 **Central Coast GSM 2021** ●
Lindquist Family Wines

122 **Willow Creek District Meso Cabernet Sauvignon 2021** ● SLOW WINE
LXV Wine

123 **Understory Red Rhone Blend 2021** ●
MAHA

123 **Paso Robles Willow Creek and Geneseo Fog Catcher 2021** ●
Niner Wine Estates

124 **Paso Robles Templeton Gap Reckoning 2019** ● SLOW WINE
Onx

124 **Carmel Valley Massa Vineyard Cabernet Sauvignon 2023** ●
Outward Wines

125 **SLO Coast Chardonnay 2022** ○
Phelan Farm

125 **Estrella District Cavern Select Rosé 2023** ◉ EVERYDAY WINE
Robert Hall Winery

126 **San Benito County Family Ties Montepulciano 2021** ●
San Rucci Winery

126 **SLO Coast Creekside Chardonnay 2022** ○ SLOW WINE
Stolo Vineyards

127 **Adelaida District Esprit de Tablas 2021** ● SLOW WINE
Tablas Creek Vineyard

127 Santa Barbara County Kick On Ranch
Clone 239 Riesling 2021 ○
Tatomer

128 Willow Creek District Homestead Hill Vineyard
Grenache 2022 ●
Thacher Winery & Vineyard

128 Willow Creek District Best Day Rosé 2023 ❋
Thibido Winery

129 Santa Maria Valley Ranchos Ontiveros Vineyard
Godello 2022 ○
Verdad Wine Cellars

129 Three Syrah 2022 ●
Villa Creek Cellars

CENTRAL COAST
SANTA BARBARA COUNTY

130 Amador County Shake Ridge Ranch Grenache 2022 ●
A Tribute to Grace

131 Santa Barbara County Gamay 2023 ● SLOW WINE
âmevive

131 Sta. Rita Hills Rosé of Syrah 2023 ❋ EVERYDAY WINE
Ampelos Cellars

132 Santa Ynez Valley Sauvignon Blanc 2023 ○ SLOW WINE
Beckmen Vineyards

133 Santa Maria Valley Bien Nacido Estate
Pinot Noir 2022 ● SLOW WINE
Bien Nacido

133 Paicines Paicines Ranch Grenache 2023 ● SLOW WINE
Camins 2 Dreams

134 Santa Barbara County Scotty-Boy! Klong Bursts &
Fizz Fuzz Pet Nat of Pinot Grigio 2022 ❋
Central Coast Group Project / Scotty Boy / L'Arge d'Oor

135 Sta. Rita Hills Mourvedre 2022 ●
Clementine Carter Wines

136 Santa Ynez Valley Cuvée Constantine
Red Rhone Blend 2021 ●
Demetria Estate

136 Santa Barbara County Sangiovese 2022 ● EVERYDAY WINE
Disko Wines

137 Sta. Rita Hills Sous Le Chêne Pinot Noir 2023 ●
Domaine de la Côte

137 Sta. Rita Hills Sanford & Benedict Vineyard
Pinot Noir 2022 ●
Dragonette Cellars

138 Ballard Canyon Kimsey Syrah 2021 ●
Dusty Nabor Wines

138 Santa Ynez Valley White Barn Vineyard
Sauvignon Blanc 2023 ○ EVERYDAY WINE
Eislynn Wines

142 Santa Maria Valley Presqu'ile Vineyard
Holus Bolus Syrah 2022 ●
Joy Fantastic & Holus Bolus

142 Los Olivos Dogged Vine Vineyard To Market
Grenache 2022 ●
Kings Carey Wines

143 Alisos Canyon Nebbiolo 2019 ●
L.A. Lepiane Wines

143 SLO Coast Pinot Noir 2023 ● EVERYDAY WINE
Land of Saints Wine Company

144 Ballard Canyon Estate
Malvasia Bianca 2023 ○ EVERYDAY WINE
Larner Vineyard & Winery

144 Santa Ynez Valley Cabernet Franc 2023 ●
Lieu Dit

145 Santa Barbara County Clos Mullet
Cabernet Franc 2022 ●
Lo-Fi Wines

145 Los Olivos District Ballard Adobe Vineyard
Sauvignon Blanc 2023 ○
Luna Hart

146 Santa Barbara County Grenache Blanc 2023 ○
Mallea Wines

146 Sta. Rita Hills Estate Chardonnay 2023 ○
Melville

147 Santa Maria Valley Rancho Ontiveros Vineyard
Pinot Noir 2021 ●
Native9

148 Ballard Canyon Bella Vista Vineyard Nancy's
Cuvee 2021 ●
Piazza Family Wines

148 Arroyo Grande Rim Rock Vineyard Syrah 2022 ●
Piedrasassi

149 Santa Barbara County Pocket
Full of Stones 2022 ○ SLOW WINE
Roark Wine Company

150 Alisos Canyon Nolan Ranch Vineyard
Clairette Blanche 2023 ○ EVERYDAY WINE
RZN Wines

151 Sta. Rita Hills Radian Vineyard Pinot Noir 2020 ●
SAMsARA Wine Co.

151 Sta Rita Hills Patterson Vineyard Chardonnay 2022 ○
Sandhi Wines

152 Santa Barbara County Grenache Rose 2022 ❋
Shokrian Vineyard

152 Los Olivos District Pet Nat Rosé 2023 ❋
Solminer

153 Santa Maria Valley Belle of the Ball
Chardonnay 2022 ○
Solomon Hills Estate

153 Sta. Rita Hills 943 Pinot Noir 2021 ●
Spear Vineyards & WInery

154 Ballard Canyon Unfiltered
Sauvignon Blanc 2023 ○ EVERYDAY WINE
Stolpman Vineyard

155 Alisos Canyon Martian Ranch Gamay Noir 2023 ●
Story of Soil Wine

155 Sta. Rita Hills Spear Vineyard Grenache 2020 ●
tercero wines

156 Sta. Rita Hills Mae Estate Pinot Noir 2022 ●
Tyler Winery

TOP WINE AWARDS

157 Los Olivos District Malvasia Biana 2023 ○
Vega Vineyard & Farm

158 Los Angeles County Rock Farms Vineyard Zee Rosso
Bubbles Primitivo Pet Nat 2023 ⊛   SLOW WINE
Wildflower Winery

SOUTH COAST

159 San Diego County Encounter
Sauvignon Blanc 2021 ⊛   EVERYDAY WINE
Charlie & Echo

159 San Bernardino Okneski Vineyard Zinfandel 2023 ●
Herrmann York

160 Santa Ynez Valley Défier Merlot 2021 ●
J. Brix Wines

160 Cucamonga Valley Chiara 2023 ○   SLOW WINE
Los Angeles River Wine Co.

161 San Diego County Grenache 2022 ●
Los Pilares

161 Ventura County Estate Red Blend 2020 ●
Ojai Mountain Vineyard

INLAND VALLEYS AND SIERRA FOOTHILLS

163 Sierra Foothills Barbera d'Amador 2022 ●   EVERYDAY WINE
Andis Wines

163 Mokelumne River Las Cerezas Vineyard
Albariño 2023 ○
Bokisch Vineyards

164 Fiddletown Easton "E" Zinfandel 2015 ●   SLOW WINE
Terre Rouge/Easton Wines

164 El Dorado County Camino Alto Vineyard
Mind Over Matter 2023 ○   EVERYDAY WINE
The End of Nowhere

Oregon

WILLAMETTE VALLEY

166 Yamhill-Carlton Abbott Claim Vineyard
Pinot Noir 2021 ●
Abbott Claim

167 Eola-Amity Hills Antikythera
Pinot Noir 2022 ●   SLOW WINE
Antica Terra

167 Willamette Valley Juel Pinot Noir 2022 ●   SLOW WINE
Antiquum Farm

169 Chehalem Mountains Creta
Pinot Noir 2022 ●   SLOW WINE
Beckham Estate Vineyard

169 Yamhill-Carlton Estate Reserve
Pinot Noir 2019 ●   SLOW WINE
Belle Pente Vineyard & Winery

170 Ribbon Ridge Le Pre du Col Vineyard Pinot Noir 2022 ●
Bergström Wines

170 Eola-Amity Hills Aeolian Estate
Pinot Noir 2022 ●   SLOW WINE
Bethel Heights Vineyard

171 Eola-Amity Hills Viola Auxerrois 2023 ○
Björnson Vineyard

172 Ribbon Ridge Les Dijonnais Pinot Noir 2022 ●
Brick House Wines

172 Eola-Amity Hills Rastaban Pinot Noir 2022 ●   SLOW WINE
Brooks Wine

173 Eola-Amity Hills Estate Pinot Noir 2021 ●   SLOW WINE
Bryn Mawr Vineyards

173 Willamette Valley Benjamin Vineyard Pinot Noir 2021
2021 ●   SLOW WINE
Celestial Hill Vineyard

174 Laurelwood District Chehalem Estate
Pinot Noir 2022 ●   SLOW WINE
Chehalem Winery

175 Willamette Valley Life Pinot Noir 2019 ●   SLOW WINE
Cooper Mountain Vineyards

175 Dundee Hills Reserve Pinot Noir 2021 ●
Cramoisi Vineyard

176 Tualatin Hills Whole Cluster
Pinot Noir 2022 ●   SLOW WINE
David Hill Vineyards and Winery

176 Applegate Valley Four Diamonds Farm
Nero d'Avola 2022 ⊛   EVERYDAY WINE
Day Wines

177 Ribbon Ridge Clos Gallia Estate
Pinot Noir 2022 ●   SLOW WINE
Domaine Divio

177 Dundee Hills Cuvée Laurène
Pinot Noir 2022 ●   SLOW WINE
Domaine Drouhin Oregon

178 Columbia Gorge
The Tango Tempranillo 2017 ●   SLOW WINE
Dominio IV

178 Eola-Amity Hills Björnson Vineyard
Pinot Noir 2022 ●   SLOW WINE
Élevée Winegrowers

179 Eola-Amity Hills Summum Chardonnay 2022 ○
Evening Land Vineyards

179 Eola-Amity Hills Le Puits Sec Vineyard
Pinot Noir 2022 ●   SLOW WINE
Evesham Wood

180 Chehalem Mountains La Belle Promenade
Pinot Noir 2021 ●   SLOW WINE
Flâneur Wines

180 Eola-Amity Hills Temperance Hill Vineyard
Pinot Noir Heritage No. 20 2022 ●
Goodfellow Family Cellars

181 Eola-Amity Hills Temperance Hill Vineyard
Pinot Noir 2022 ●
Granville Wine Co.

181 Willamette Valley Croft Vineyard
Pinot Noir 2022 ●   SLOW WINE
Haden Fig

182 **Dundee Hills La Colina Vineyard Pinot Noir 2022** ● SLOW WINE
J.C. Somers Vintner

182 **Willamette Valley Vespidae Pinot Noir 2022** ● SLOW WINE
J.K. Carriere

183 **Chehalem Mountains Cuvée Karen Ann Pinot Noir 2021** ●
Jachter Family Wines

184 **Willamette Valley Steiner Block Pinot Gris 2022** ○ SLOW WINE
King Estate Winery

184 **Chehalem Mountains Cuvée Giselle Pinot Noir 2022** ●
Lachini Vineyards

185 **Yamhill-Carlton Eocene Rosé 2023** ◐ SLOW WINE
Lafayette and White Cellars

185 **Willamette Valley Thea's Selection Pinot Noir 2022** ● SLOW WINE
Lemelson Vineyards

186 **Eola-Amity Hills Estate Pinot Noir 2022** ● SLOW WINE
Lingua Franca

186 **Chehalem Mountains Hi-Tone Pinot Noir 2021** ● SLOW WINE
Longplay Wine

188 **McMinnville Asha Pinot Noir 2013** ● SLOW WINE
Maysara Winery

188 **Dundee Hills Nysa Vineyard Pinot Noir 2022** ●
Nicolas-Jay

189 **Mount Pisgah Estate Pinot Noir 2022** ● SLOW WINE
Open Claim Vineyards

189 **Willamette Valley Retina Pinot Noir 2022** ● SLOW WINE
Ratio:Wines

190 **Willamette Valley Unmet Desire Pinot Noir 2022** ● SLOW WINE
Remy Wines

190 **Yamhill-Carlton Résonance Vineyard Pinot Noir 2021** ● SLOW WINE
Résonance

191 **Ribbon Ridge RR Estate Reserve Riesling 2016** ○ SLOW WINE
Ridgecrest

191 **Yamhill-Carlton Roots Estate Racine Pinot Noir 2021** ●
Roots Wine Co.

192 **Eola-Amity Hills Zéphirine Pinot Noir 2022** ● SLOW WINE
Roserock Drouhin Oregon

192 **Laurelwood District Flora's Reserve Pinot Noir 2022** ● SLOW WINE
Ruby Vineyard & Winery

193 **Dundee Hills Rosé of Pinot Noir 2023** ◐ SLOW WINE
Sokol Blosser Winery

193 **Willamette Valley Estates Pinot Noir 2022** ● SLOW WINE
Soter Vineyards

194 **Yamhill-Carlton Shea Vineyard Pinot Noir 2021** ● SLOW WINE
St. Innocent Winery

194 **Dundee Hills Estate Reserve Pinot Noir 2021** ● SLOW WINE
Stoller Family Estate

195 **Dundee Hills The Eyrie South Block Reserve Pinot Noir 2019** ●
The Eyrie Vineyards

195 **Yamhill-Carlton La Crête Chardonnay 2021** ○ SLOW WINE
WillaKenzie Estate

196 **Dundee Hills Imprint Pinot Noir 2022** ●
Winderlea Vineyard & Winery

196 **McMinnville YH J Block Pinot Noir 2019** ● SLOW WINE
Youngberg Hill

SOUTHERN OREGON

197 **Applegate Valley Syrah 2020** ● SLOW WINE
Cowhorn Vineyard & Garden

198 **Rogue Valley Alto Pinot Noir 2022** ● SLOW WINE
DANCIN

198 **Umpqua Valley 50th Anniversary Pinot Noir 2017** ● SLOW WINE
HillCrest Vineyard

199 **Applegate Valley Mae's Vineyard Syrah 2019** ● SLOW WINE
Quady North

199 **Applegate Valley Estate Syrah 2022** ● SLOW WINE
Troon Vineyard

200 **Rogue Valley Rosé of Grenache 2023** ◐ SLOW WINE
Upper Five Vineyard

COLUMBIA GORGE

201 **Mosier Hills Trousseau 2023** ●
Analemma Wines

Washington

207 **Columbia Valley Rivercrest Vineyard Organic Pinot Noir 2023** ● EVERYDAY WINE
Badger Mountain Vineyard

207 **Red Mountain Coda 2022** ● EVERYDAY WINE
Cadence Winery

208 **Walla Walla Valley Eleanor Estate Red Wine 2021** ●
Caprio Cellars

208 **Walla Walla Valley Hors Categorie Syrah 2021** ● SLOW WINE
Cayuse Vineyards & Bionic Wines

210 **Columbia Gorge Estate Syrah 2021** ● SLOW WINE
Domaine Pouillon

210 **Walla Walla Valley Sconni Block Estate BFM 2021** ●
Dusted Valley

211 **Red Mountain Hedges Cabernet Franc 2021** ● SLOW WINE
Foundry Vineyards

211 Lake Chelan Burning Desire Estate Cabernet Franc 2021
Hard Row to Hoe Vineyards

212 Red Mountain La Haute Cuvée Cabernet Sauvignon 2019
Hedges Family Estate

212 Walla Walla Valley Fiddleneck Vineyard Grenache 2021 — SLOW WINE
Horsepower Vineyards

213 Columbia Gorge Hi Hill Vineyard Blanc de Noirs 2022
Lushington Wines

214 Walla Walla Valley Red Blend Seven Hills 2021
Pepperbridge Winery

215 Columbia Gorge Pear Ridge Vineyard Perpetual Cuvee
Pét Project

215 Oak Ridge Skin-Contact Gewürztraminer 2022 — SLOW WINE
Savage Grace

216 Columbia Gorge Gamay Noir 2022 — SLOW WINE
Syncline

217 Yakima Valley Dead Poplar Vineyard Grenache 2022
Upsidedown Wines

217 Naches Heights Estate Sagrantino 2018 — SLOW WINE
Wilridge Vineyard, Winery & Distillery

New York

FINGER LAKES

220 Finger Lakes Brut 2020 — EVERYDAY WINE
Dr. Konstantin Frank Winery

221 Finger Lakes Ingle Vineyard Blaufrankisch 2023
Heron Hill Winery

221 Finger Lakes Shale Creek Chardonnay 2023
Living Roots Wine & Co

FINGER LAKES - CAYUGA

222 Cayuga Lake Sauvignon Blanc 2023 — EVERYDAY WINE
Buttonwood Grove Winery

223 Cayuga Lake Concrete Diamond Pinot Noir Gewurztraminer Co-ferment 2023 — EVERYDAY WINE
Six Eighty Cellars

FINGER LAKES - SENECA

224 Seneca Lake Cabernet Sauvignon 2023
Damiani Wine Cellars

224 Finger Lakes Element Chardonnay 2017
Element Winery

225 Cayuga Lake Higgins Vineyard Reserve Estate Pinot Noir 2021 — SLOW WINE
Heart & Hands Wine Company

225 Seneca Lake HJW Bio Riesling 2020 — SLOW WINE
Hermann J. Wiemer Vineyard

226 Seneca Lake Estate Dry Riesling 2023
Hillick & Hobbs

226 Seneca Lake Dry Riesling 2020 — EVERYDAY WINE
Ravines Wine Cellars

227 Seneca Lake Sparkling Riesling Sekt Extra Brut 2019 — SLOW WINE
Red Tail Ridge Winery

227 Seneca Lake Estate Vineyard Riesling 2022 — SLOW WINE
Silver Thread Vineyard

228 Seneca Lake SSV Teinturier Dry Rosé 2023 — EVERYDAY WINE
Standing Stone Vineyards

LONG ISLAND

229 Long Island Meditazione Orange Wine 2018
Channing Daughters Winery

229 Long Island Lifeforce Sauvignon Blanc 2023
Macari Vineyards

230 Long Island White Horse Selection Antonov Sauvignon Blanc 2021
Wölffer Estate Vineyard

WINERY AWARDS

California

NORTH COAST - **NAPA**

🐌 Snail
- 26 ADAMVS
- 28 Burgess Cellars
- 29 Cathiard Vineyard
- 30 Clif Family Winery
- 31 Corison
- 33 Dominus/Napanook
- 35 Frog's Leap
- 35 Gallica
- 36 Ghost Block
- 36 Grgich Hills Estate
- 39 Neal Family Vineyards
- 40 Oakville Ranch
- 41 Oakville Winery
- 42 Paradigm
- 43 Quintessa
- 43 Robert Sinskey Vineyards
- 44 Rudd Estate
- 44 Snowden Vineyards
- 46 Volker Eisele Family Estate
- 47 ZD Wines

🍾 Bottle
- 27 Baldacci Family Vineyards
- 28 Cain Vineyard And Winery
- 30 Chappellet
- 32 Dana Estates | Onda
- 32 David Arthur Vineyards
- 33 Detert Family Vineyards
- 34 Ehlers Estate
- 37 Heitz Cellar
- 37 Hyde de Villaine - HdV
- 38 Keplinger Wines
- 40 Newfound Wines
- 45 Spottswoode Estate Vineyard & Winery
- 45 Staglin Family Vineyard
- 46 Stags Leap Wine Cellars

$ Coin
- 34 Elizabeth Rose

NORTH COAST - **SONOMA**

🐌 Snail
- 48 Á Deux Têtes
- 49 Acaibo
- 52 Canihan Wines
- 56 DaVero Farms & Winery
- 64 Kamen Estate Wines
- 64 Lasseter Family Winery
- 67 Moon Hollow
- 69 Porter Creek Vineyards
- 69 Preston Farm & Winery
- 74 Small Vines
- 74 Stone Edge Farm
- 78 Winery Sixteen 600

🍾 Bottle
- 51 Bedrock Wine Co.
- 54 Cormorant Cellars
- 55 Dane Cellars
- 56 Darling Wines
- 57 DuMOL
- 58 Enfield Wine Co.
- 58 Ernest Vineyards
- 59 Far Mountain
- 63 Jolie-Laide Wines
- 68 Pax Wines
- 70 Quivira Vineyards
- 71 Ram's Gate Winery
- 72 Read Holland
- 75 Surveyor
- 76 Under the Wire

$ Coin
- 52 Birdhorse
- 53 Carol Shelton Wines
- 55 County Line Vineyards
- 61 Guthrie Family Wines
- 61 Horse & Plow

NORTH COAST - **MENDOCINO & OTHER**

🐌 Snail
- 81 Blue Quail and McFadden Winery
- 84 Clay Shannon

85 Domaine Anderson
90 OVIS

🍾 Bottle
85 Drew Family Wines

💲 Coin
81 Bonterra Organic Estates
83 Chance Creek Vineyards
93 Unturned Stone

NORTH COAST - **SAN FRANCISCO BAY AREA**

🍾 Bottle
95 Dashe Cellars
95 Donkey & Goat

💲 Coin
97 Les Lunes Wine

SANTA CRUZ MOUNTAINS

🐌 Snail
102 Cooper-Garrod
107 Rhys Vineyards

🍾 Bottle
101 Beauregard Vineyards
101 Big Basin Vineyards
102 Birichino
103 Ferrari Ranch Wines
104 Lester Estate Wines
104 Madson Wines
105 Maison Areion
108 Sandar & Hem Winery
108 Santa Cruz Mountain Vineyard
109 Sante Arcangeli Family Wines
110 Silver Mountain Vineyards
111 Windy Oaks Estate

💲 Coin
100 Alfaro Family Vineyard & Winery
100 Bargetto Winery
105 Margins Wine

CENTRAL COAST - **MONTEREY & OTHER**

🍾 Bottle
112 Calera

💲 Coin
114 Stirm Wine Co.

CENTRAL COAST - **SAN LUIS OBISPO**

🐌 Snail
121 Halter Ranch
125 Phelan Farm

🍾 Bottle
122 Lindquist Family Wines
127 Tablas Creek Vineyard
127 Tatomer

CENTRAL COAST - **SANTA BARBARA COUNTY**

🐌 Snail
137 Domaine de la Côte
139 Folded Hills
140 Grimm's Bluff
141 J. Dirt

🍾 Bottle
130 A Tribute to Grace
132 Au Bon Climat
134 Chanin Wine
142 Joy Fantastic & Holus Bolus
142 Kings Carey Wines
147 Montemar Winery
148 Piedrasassi
149 Refugio Ranch Vineyards
150 Roblar Winery & Vineyards
151 Sandhi Wines
156 The Brander Vineyard

💲 Coin
136 Disko Wines
139 Entity of Delight
143 Land of Saints Wine Company
145 Lo-Fi Wines
154 Storm Wines

SOUTH COAST

💲 Coin
159 Charlie & Echo
159 Herrmann York
160 J. Brix Wines
161 Los Pilares

INLAND VALLEYS AND SIERRA FOOTHILLS

💲 Coin
164 The End of Nowhere

Oregon

WILLAMETTE VALLEY

 Snail

- 167 Antica Terra
- 167 Antiquum Farm
- 169 Beckham Estate Vineyard
- 169 Belle Pente Vineyard & Winery
- 172 Brick House Wines
- 175 Cooper Mountain Vineyards
- 177 Domaine Drouhin Oregon
- 182 J.K. Carriere
- 183 Johan Vineyards
- 185 Lemelson Vineyards
- 187 Lumos Wine Co.
- 188 Maysara Winery
- 189 Open Claim Vineyards
- 190 Résonance
- 193 Soter Vineyards
- 195 The Eyrie Vineyards
- 196 Youngberg Hill

 Bottle

- 166 Abbott Claim
- 168 Authentique Wine Cellars
- 170 Bergström Wines
- 170 Bethel Heights Vineyard
- 171 Big Table Farm
- 172 Brooks Wine
- 177 Domaine Divio
- 178 Dominio IV
- 179 Evesham Wood
- 180 Flâneur Wines
- 182 J.C. Somers Vintner
- 184 King Estate Winery
- 186 Lingua Franca
- 188 Nicolas-Jay
- 192 Roserock Drouhin Oregon
- 192 Ruby Vineyard & Winery
- 193 Sokol Blosser Winery
- 195 WillaKenzie Estate
- 196 Winderlea Vineyard & Winery

$ Coin

- 171 Björnson Vineyard
- 176 David Hill Vineyards and Winery
- 181 Haden Fig
- 186 Longplay Wine
- 191 Ridgecrest

SOUTHERN OREGON

 Snail

- 197 Cowhorn Vineyard & Garden

- 199 Troon Vineyard
- 200 Upper Five Vineyard

COLUMBIA GORGE

 Snail

- 201 Analemma Wines

 Bottle

- 202 EST

Washington

 Snail

- 209 Domaine Magdalena
- 217 Wilridge Vineyard, Winery & Distillery

 Bottle

- 208 Caprio Cellars
- 208 Cayuse Vineyards & Bionic Wines
- 212 Hedges Family Estate
- 215 Savage Grace
- 216 Syncline

$ Coin

- 207 Badger Mountain Vineyard
- 216 Tagaris Winery

New York

FINGER LAKES - CAYUGA

$ Coin

- 222 Buttonwood Grove Winery

FINGER LAKES - SENECA

 Snail

- 225 Hermann J. Wiemer Vineyard
- 227 Red Tail Ridge Winery

 Bottle

- 226 Hillick & Hobbs
- 227 Silver Thread Vineyard

LONG ISLAND

 Bottle

- 229 Channing Daughters Winery

WINERY AWARDS

CALIFORNIA

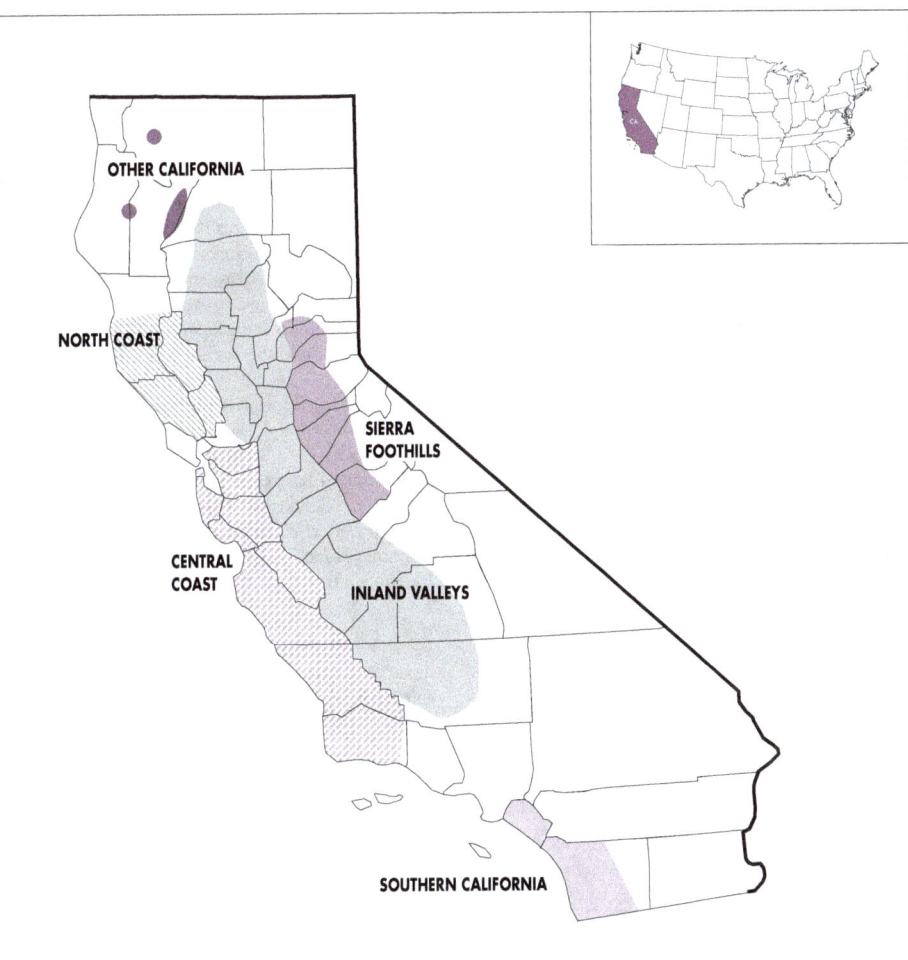

- 26 North Coast - **Napa**
- 47 North Coast - **Sonoma**
- 78 North Coast - **Mendocino & Other**
- 94 North Coast - **San Francisco Bay Area**
- 99 **Santa Cruz Mountains**
- 111 Central Coast - **Monterey &** Other
- 114 Central Coast - **San Luis Obispo**
- 130 Central Coast - **Santa Barbara County**
- 158 **South Coast**
- 162 **Inland Valleys and Sierra Foothills**

NORTH COAST
NAPA

🐌 Snail

26 ADAMVS
28 Burgess Cellars
29 Cathiard Vineyard
30 Clif Family Winery
31 Corison
33 Dominus/Napanook
35 Frog's Leap
35 Gallica
36 Ghost Block
36 Grgich Hills Estate
39 Neal Family Vineyards
40 Oakville Ranch
41 Oakville Winery
42 Paradigm
43 Quintessa
43 Robert Sinskey Vineyards
44 Rudd Estate
44 Snowden Vineyards
46 Volker Eisele Family Estate
47 ZD Wines

🍾 Bottle

27 Baldacci Family Vineyards
28 Cain Vineyard And Winery
30 Chappellet
32 Dana Estates | Onda
32 David Arthur Vineyards
33 Detert Family Vineyards
34 Ehlers Estate
37 Heitz Cellar
37 Hyde de Villaine - HdV
38 Keplinger Wines
40 Newfound Wines
45 Spottswoode Estate Vineyard & Winery
45 Staglin Family Vineyard
46 Stags Leap Wine Cellars

$ Coin

34 Elizabeth Rose

ANGWIN

ADAMVS

501 White Cottage Road N - tel. (707) 965-0555
www.adamvs.com - info@adamvs.com

 With land stewardship as their priority, the estate continually evolves farming practices that further wine quality.

PEOPLE - An elite Howell Mountain producer, owner Denise Adams promoted Amy Particelli to general manager, following the departure of winemaker Alberto Bianchi who returned to his native Italy. Viticulturist Guiseppe Tumbarello (who joined the winery team in 2023) and a team of five have brought all farming in house. Biodynamic practices have expanded with a new "chateau" to house sheep on the property and 12 tons of manure from eight Hereford cows contributing to soil health.

VINEYARDS - Howell mountain's shallow red clay and volcanic soils were the inspiration for the winery's Latin name which means "red soil." The steep, mountainous 80 acre property has 20 acres under vine with seven more currently in development. The team grafted Blocks 1 and 2 to Sauvignon Blanc (to double its production) and to Cabernet Franc. They also started braiding the canopy of Block 10, a technique suited to low vigor, balanced areas.

WINES - Although a drought year, 2019 was a very high quality, uniform vintage without heat spikes. The resulting wines show concentration, depth, and structure which are the makings of an ageworthy vintage.

🔝 Howell Mountain ADAMVS Cabernet Sauvignon 2019 ● 486 cases; 400 $ - 🛢 - Characteristic of mountain fruit from a drought year. Deeply colored with rich aromas of blackberries, blueberries, black plums and sandalwood. Full bodied with the addition of black cherries and red plums scented with nutmeg, cinnamon and black pepper through a firm finish.

Howell Mountain TÉRES Cabernet Sauvignon 2019 ● 783 cases; 135 $ - 🛢 - Deeply opaque to a narrow ruby lip, showing signature dark mountain fruit aromas of blackberry, mulberry, black currant, black cherry and toast. Full bodied and youthful with tightly wound dark fruit over a firm tannin backbone and peppery finish. Hold for five to seven.

acres 27 - cases 2,000
Fertilizers biodynamic compost, manure
Plant protection biodynamic preparations, organic
Weed control animal grazing, mechanical
Yeasts selected indigenous yeasts
Grapes 100% owned
Certification biodynamic, organic

NAPA

ASHES AND DIAMONDS

4130 Howard Lane - tel. (707) 666-4777
www.ashesdiamonds.com - info@ashesdiamonds.com

PEOPLE - Forward thinking proprietor Kashy Khaledi (an executive at Capitol Records, MTV and other brands) came from a Napa wine family but had a vision for a new voice in Napa. He brought in an LA architect to design the chic, modernist winery and hired winemaker rockstars Steve Matthiasson and Diane Snowden-Seysses. A tech-centric and Millennial crowd has embraced the winery.

VINEYARDS - The winery champions varieties not usually focused on in Napa–Sémillon for the Blanc, Sangiovese for a dark rosé, and Cabernet Franc. These come from sites using only organic materials or from the Oak Knoll District estate (Merlot and Cab Franc) which is certified organic. Single vineyard Cabs from Oakville, Atlas Peak and the Santa Cruz Mountains each showcase varied terroir and a wide spectrum of flavors.

WINES - The new director of winemaking, Sam Barron, oversees the cellar. Championing minimal intervention wines, the winery has three zero zero (nothing added) natural wines among its offerings.

Oak Knoll District Chardonnay 2022 ⬤ 90 cases; 50 $ - Aged five months in oak barrels (20% new). A vervy take on Chardonnay, this zero zero wine is low alcohol (at 12%). Some skin contact puts it between an orange wine and a purely white one. Pretty quince, lemon and delicate citrus notes.

Napa Valley Rosa 2023 ⬤ 600 cases; 45 $ - A deeper darker take on the winery's regular rosé, this one's uniquely packed with crunchy red fruit–a zero zero "fruit punch" of a wine. The blend is Sangiovese (79%) and Cabernet Franc (21%). Matthiasson ferments the grapes on the skins for five days.

Diamond Mountain District Cabernet Sauvignon II 2022 ⬤ 450 cases; 125 $ - Aged months in French oak (37% new). From a site with volcanic soils, Diane Snowden-Seysses' take on Cabernet sees 23 days of maceration. It's nuanced, delicate and complex.

acres 25 - cases 11,000
Fertilizers compost, cover crops, organic fertilizer
Plant protection sulfur, copper, organic
Weed control mechanical, manual
Yeasts spontaneous fermentation, commercial cultured yeasts
Grapes purchase 61%
Certification some of the vineyards are certified organic

NAPA

BALDACCI FAMILY VINEYARDS

6236 Silverado Trail - tel. (707) 944-9261
www.baldaccivineyards.com - info@baldaccivineyards.com

PEOPLE - Real estate developer Thomas and wife Brenda Baldacci purchased their 29 acre Stags Leap District property in 1998 and later bought two more vineyards. Their son Michael Baldacci came aboard in 2012 and was promoted to winemaker in 2018. Their diverse vineyard locations enable them to make everything from Chardonnay and Pinot Noir to Cabernet and even an estate grown Brut sparkling wine.

VINEYARDS - They have three Napa Valley vineyards, each in a different region–Stags Leap District, Calistoga and Carneros–ranging from the southernmost part of Napa to the northernmost, with a mountain site as well. They certified the Stags Leap site organic in 2024 and use only organically approved materials on their 17 acre Stella Knight vineyard in Calistoga (partially in the Diamond Mountain region) and their 23 acre Honey B Vineyard in the Carneros (Chardonnay and Pinot Noir).

WINES - Classically styled wines, predominantly Cabernet Sauvignon, approachable in their youth, yet maintaining complexity and stamina to age.

Stags Leap District Black Label Cabernet Sauvignon 2021 ⬤ 1,042 cases; 125 $ - Aged 22 months in French oak (75% new). Highlights the appellation, with the classic aromas of mint and chocolate and the velvet gloved, blue fruit palate and subtle yet focused finish.

Calistoga Stella Knight Vineyard Cabernet Sauvignon 2021 ⬤ 725 cases; 125 $ - Aged 22 months in French oak (75% new). Calistoga site is cooler than their others, shade from trees at the base of Diamond Mountain. Aromas of dark chocolate, walnut and spice, with a concentrated midpalate. This wine is full bodied and textural, yet velvety.

Diamond Mountain District Cabernet Sauvignon 2021 ⬤ 94 cases; 175 $ - From seven rows that arc through Diamond Mountain appellation. The oak profile is heavier, with more depth to the finish and chalky tannins. Built to age.

acres 45 - cases 14,000
Fertilizers organic fertilizer
Plant protection organic
Weed control animal grazing, mechanical, manual
Yeasts spontaneous fermentation, commercial cultured yeasts
Grapes purchase 15%
Certification some of the vineyards are certified organic

NAPA

BURGESS CELLARS

2921 Silverado Trail - tel. (707) 963-4766
www.burgesscellars.com - concierge@burgesscellars.com

 A new team has taken over the reins of this classic winery, upgrading farming to organic and regenerative standards and a new approach to estate wines.

PEOPLE - The former home of Souverain winery, the original Burgess hillside site is historic as the place where celebrated vintners Mike Grgich and Warren Winiarski cut their teeth. (Both went on to win the 1976 Paris Tasting). In 2020 Lawrence Wine Estates purchased the property, which immediately burned to the ground in the Glass Fire, prompting a move to a new valley floor location while they pivoted toward new eco-friendly practices. Julia Wildt is the estate director.

VINEYARDS - Macy Stubstad oversees the four estate sites, including three in the Oak Knoll District on the valley floor, in addition to the original 27 acre Burgess vineyard (renamed Sorenson) on an eastern hillside. The Cab vines on the 33 acre western Oak Knoll District Quartz Creek site were planted in 2018. Surrounding the winery, the two acre Clos Abeille features Zobeck's beloved sheep, chickens, and pollinator gardens.

WINES - Meghan Zobeck (formerly of Screaming Eagle and Melka Atelier) became winemaker in 2020. She uses gentle extractions coupled with minimal oak use (20-35% new on reds) and occasionally foudre, puncheon and amphora.

Napa Valley Promiscua Cabernet Sauvignon 2021 ● 2,142 cases; 125 $ - 🝆 - Aged 22 months in French oak (20% new). A blend of Oak Knoll valley floor and Sorenson hillside fruit. Lean, with complex red fruit and herbal notes.
Oak Knoll District Quartz Creek Cabernet Sauvignon 2021 ● 88 cases; 175 $ - 🝆 - Aged for 22 months in French oak barrique (30% new). From vines planted in 2018 (clones 685, 412 and 169) on the valley floor.
Napa Valley Sorenson Cabernet Sauvignon 2021 ● 1,000 cases; 250 $ - 🝆 - Vine age ranges from four to 50 years. Classic markers for this historic vineyard include crisp blue and red fruit, savory herbal aromatics of rosemary and thyme, and a subtle oak signature of earthy graphite.

---

acres 80 - cases 3,678
Fertilizers compost, biodynamic compost, cover crops, manure, organic fertilizer, synthetic fertilizer
Plant protection sulfur, biodynamic preparations, organic
Weed control animal grazing, mechanical
Yeasts selected indigenous yeasts
Grapes 100% owned
Certification some of the vineyards are certified organic, converting to organic

ST. HELENA

CAIN VINEYARD AND WINERY

3800 Langtry Road - tel. (707) 963-1616
www.cainfive.com - winery@cainfive.com

PEOPLE - For more than three decades, Howell's winemaking and winegrowing practices have distinguished the Spring Mountain estate. The 2019 Bell Fire hit it hard, destroying the tasting room and winery but not the spirit and determination of the team. Chris Howell, winegrower and co-GM, and vineyard manager Ashley Anderson-Bennett have rehabilitated the vines that survived to produce the 2021 vintage.

VINEYARDS - The 500 acre estate sits along the crest of the Mayacamas Range from 1,400-2,100 feet. Its 90 planted acres (certified organic) grow surviving vines from 1987, 1998 and 2003. Shallow, weathered sedimentary soils comprised of sandstone, shale and clay are naturally devigoring and vines are terraced across bowls and swales. The elevation results in cooler days and warmer nights. Cain buys fruit from Napa growers for its non-estate wines. Some wines (not featured here) may be grown with herbicide.

WINES - The complexity and varied aspects of the terroir and Howell's finesse with mountain fruit are a rarity captured in the estate wines. The winery is known for waiting to release its Cain Five vintages only when the wines reach their optimal drinking window.

TOP Spring Mountain District Cain Five 2021 SLOW WINE ● Bordeaux Blend; 300 cases; 200 $ - 🝆 - Aged in French oak (30% new). Their only all estate wine is an unspecified blend of Cabernet Sauvignon, Merlot, Cabernet Franc, Malbec and Verdot Deep and dark fruited with firm, resolved tannins and fresh, persistent layers.
Spring Mountain Cain Five 2011 ● Cabernet Sauvignon, Cabernet Franc, Merlot; 3,500 cases; 155 $ - 🝆 - The coolest of three successive vintages reaching an optimal drinking window. Garrigue-scented black currant and prune with "al dente" tannins and notes of tobacco and umami.

---

acres 90 - cases 144,000
Fertilizers biodynamic compost, organic fertilizer
Plant protection organic
Weed control mechanical
Yeasts spontaneous fermentation
Grapes purchase 75%
Certification some of the vineyards are certified organic

NAPA

CANTADORA | OLIVIA BRION

tel. (707) 234-8156
www.oliviabrion.com - info@oliviabrion.com

PEOPLE - When Kira Ballotta used to analyze wineries for an San Francisco bank's mergers and acquisitions, she didn't think she would get bitten by the wine bug. But it led to washing barrels at Olivia Brion in 2011, working in enology at Alpha Omega and by 2022, owning both the Olivia Brion label and a newer one, Cantadora. Her bottle labels feature celebrated women of Yesterday (Olivia Brion) and today (Cantadora).

VINEYARDS - Ballotta buys from growers ranging from Santa Cruz and Sonoma to the Sacramento Delta and the Sierras. She says all are practicing or certified organic. In Amador County, Grenache and Tempranillo come from Ann Kraemer's celebrated Shake Ridge Ranch (impeccably farmed but not certified organic). Chardonnay comes from Napa's Steve Matthiasson Linda Vista vineyard (certified organic) in the Oak Knoll District.

WINES - Ballotta makes only tiny lots, ranging from 100 to 150 cases on average, using neutral oak.

Clarksburg Olivia Brion Taquine White Blend 2022 ⬤ 250 cases; 32 $ - 🛢 - Aged 9 months in neutral French oak. A novel, 50/50 blend of Italian varieties Falanghina and Cortese (grown in the Sacramento Delta). Fragrant aromatics.

Sierra Foothills Olivia Brion Les Vagabondes Tempranillo 2019 ⬤ 115 cases; 40 $ - 🛢 - Aged 21 months in neutral French oak. From top quality fruit grown at Shake Ridge Ranch in Amador County.

Amador County Olivia Brion Mon Amour Interdit Grenache-Syrah 2022 ⬤ 100 cases; 40 $ - 🛢 - Aged 21 month in neutral French oak. A 50/50 blend of Grenache and Syrah, all from Shake Ridge Ranch grapes. Chillable, lighter style red with red fruits. Delicate and nuanced.

acres 0 - cases 1,000
Fertilizers compost, cover crops, organic fertilizer
Plant protection sulfur, copper, organic
Weed control mechanical
Yeasts spontaneous fermentation
Grapes purchase 100%
Certification some of the vineyards are certified organic

ST. HELENA

CATHIARD VINEYARD

1978 Zinfandel Lane - tel. (707) 302-5503
www.cathiardvineyard.com - hospitality@cathiardvineyard.com

 Dedicated to Bordeaux varieties, this extraordinary French family is bringing French flair, organic farming and outstanding wines even in its first Napa vintages.

PEOPLE - Celebrated Bordeaux vintners Florence and Daniel Cathiard bought the former Flora Springs estate in Rutherford in 2020. In Bordeaux, they're famous as the owners of the famed Chateau Smith Haut-Lafitte (SHL). In Napa, Justine Labbé is general manager and head winemaker, with SHL winemaker Fabien Teitgen and Michel Rolland as consultants. The team is transitioning to organic certification and dry farming.

VINEYARDS - With 200 acres of forests on upper terraces and a wide variety of soils (volcanic and sedimentary), stretching like an accordion between valley floor and mountain elevations (200 to 1,200 feet), the estate offers tremendous complexity. Four acres of Merlot is being replanted to Cabernet Sauvignon and Cab Franc. They are adding 1.2 acres of Sauvignon Blanc on a terrace above for future white wines SHL is known for.

WINES - Their second vintage, 2021 was a dry year with low yields, small berries, and concentrated tannins. The wines show freshness and pure fruit.

🔝 Napa Valley Founding Brothers Red 2021 ⬤ 1,200 cases; 225 $ - 🛢 - Aged 16-18 months in French oak (50% in new barrels and 20% in foudres). From 25 year old vines, a blend of Cabernet Sauvignon (59%), Merlot (32%), and Cab Franc (9%). Its black fruits are focused, elegant and ageworthy.

Napa Valley Hora Red 2021 ⬤ 2,500 cases; 125 $ - 🛢 - Aged 14 months in French oak (40% new). From 19 year old, valley floor vines. A blend of Cabernet Sauvignon (55%), Merlot (35%) and Malbec (10%). Fresh and approachable in its youth, with red fruits and silky tannins.

Napa Valley Cabernet Sauvignon 2021 ⬤ 700 cases; 395 $ - 🛢 - Aged 18-20 months in French oak (80% new). 100% Cabernet. From the oldest hillside vines (36 year old). Embodies finesse. Find dark fruits, chocolate, and spice in the aromas and flavors, with a long finish of cassis and dried herbs. Made for cellaring.

acres 60 - cases 5,000
Fertilizers compost, cover crops
Plant protection sulfur, organic
Weed control mechanical
Yeasts spontaneous fermentation, commercial cultured yeasts
Grapes 100% owned
Certification some of the vineyards are certified organic, converting to organic

ST. HELENA

CHAPPELLET

1581 Sage Canyon Road - tel. (707) 963-7445
www.chappellet.com - concierge@chappellet.com

PEOPLE - Founded by Donn and Molly Chappellet in 1967, this iconic Pritchard Hill winery remains family owned and committed to producing world class, Bordeaux variety wines from their hilltop site in the Vaca Mountains. They're also dedicated to maintaining the diverse, natural ecosystem that surrounds them. Andrew Opatz, director of vineyard operations, has been at Chappellet since 2007. Phillip Corallo-Titus has been the winemaker for more than 30 years.

VINEYARDS - The oldest vines date to 1999 and were certified organic in 2007. Soils are young, very well drained volcanics with flat to steep grades and 360° of exposure. They grow eight clones of Cabernet, plus Cab Franc, Malbec, Petit Verdot and three rare acres of Chenin Blanc. Surrounded by 536 acres of wild lands, pest control in the vines comes from bird and owl boxes and releases of beneficial insects. (Other wines, not featured here, may be grown with herbicide.)

WINES - The power of Napa Valley mountain Cabernet Sauvignon portrayed with nuance and balance.

🔝 **Napa Valley Pritchard Hill Cabernet Sauvignon 2021** ● 3,000 cases; 325 $ - 🍷 - Vineyard and barrel selection of the estate's best grapes. Mouth-filling, rich velvet, bold flavors: blackberry, black cherry, plum, cassis, dark chocolate, mineral, charcoal, espresso. Extremely long. Ageworthy yet very accessible.
Napa Valley Hideaway Vineyard Cabernet Sauvignon 2021 ● 1,500 cases; 175 $ - 🍷 - 100% Cabernet from 1,425 feet. Very complex, intense: tangy purple and black fruit, raisin, spice, espresso, black olive, mineral, dark chocolate, charcoal. Full body, plush grainy velvet. Luxurious yet well balanced
Napa Valley Signature Cabernet Sauvignon 2021 ● 12,300 cases; 95 $ - 🍷 - A 50-50 blend of estate and purchased fruit (from the Vaca mountains south of Chappellet). Medium+ body, plush, integrated tannins. Black fruit, dark red cherry, violets and unsweetened chocolate. Satisfying.

acres 104 - cases 45,000
Fertilizers compost, cover crops, organic fertilizer, synthetic fertilizer
Plant protection sulfur, synthetic pesticides, organic
Weed control animal grazing, mechanical, manual
Yeasts commercial cultured yeasts
Grapes purchase 40%
Certification some of the vineyards are certified organic

ST. HELENA

CLIF FAMILY WINERY

709 Main Street - tel. (707) 968-0625
www.cliffamily.com - wineryexperience@cliffamily.com

Marking 20 years in 2024, the winery relentlessly pursues and achieves organic farming and sustainability goals.

PEOPLE - Sustainability minded, this year winemaker Laura Barrett introduced lighter weight glass bottles, eliminated foil capsules and replaced screw caps with biodegradable agglomerated corks. The winery achieved B Corp Certification in 2023 making it the third in Napa Valley to receive this recognition. Their Sip & Support monthly fundraising program benefits 12 local nonprofit partners each year. Chef Magnus Young offers a 100% plant based tasting menu in the Enoteca.

VINEYARDS - Barrett works with vineyard manager Erik Dodd to refine the estate's farming practices. The estate vineyards (certified organic) grow nine grape varieties on their 90 acres in the Oak Knoll AVA, using regenerative practices. They have additional vineyards on Howell Mountain. They buy grapes from growers using only organic approved materials. Sheep, barn owls and songbird boxes contribute to vine and soil health.

WINES - The Valle di Sotto vineyard in Oak Knoll is recognized as a cooler site where marine influences help maintain acidity.

🔝 **Oak Knoll Unoaked Chardonnay 2022** EVERYDAY WINE ○ 680 cases; 38 $ - 🍷 - Whole cluster pressing and no malolactic fermentation prior to four months in stainless steel barrels define the style showing ripe pear, Meyer lemon and stone fruit with a bright, fruity finish.
Oak Knoll Valle di Sotto Zinfandel 2022 ● 737 cases; 75 $ - 🍷 - Aged 14 months in French oak (13% new). Newly planted Zinfandel is a rarity now in Napa Valley. This Valle di Sotto shows dark cherry and brown spice aromas with red fruit evolving to black licorice through the finish.
Napa Valley Proprietary Red 2021 ● 912 cases; 125 $ - 🍷 - Aged 22 months in French oak (80% new). A blend of Cabernet Sauvignon (81%), Cabernet Franc (8%), Malbec (6%) and Petit Verdot (5%). From Oak Knoll. Lush flavors of baked bread and blackberry pie underscored with tobacco, cocoa and toffee with a hint of dried herbs.

acres 90 - cases 15,000
Fertilizers compost, cover crops, organic fertilizer
Plant protection sulfur, copper, organic
Weed control animal grazing, mechanical, manual
Yeasts commercial cultured yeasts
Grapes purchase 10%
Certification some of the vineyards are certified organic

ST. SAINT HELENA

CORISON

987 Saint Helena Highway - tel. (707) 963-8026
www.corison.com - visit@corison.com

 An iconic Napa Valley winery, dedicated to making beloved, outstanding, classic Cabernet Sauvignon.

PEOPLE - Cathy Corison's career began in 1979 working for Napa icons Chappellet Vineyard and Staglin Family. She created her own label in 1987. Her husband, William Martin, found the Kronos Vineyard, which they bought in 1995, and designed the winery barn. Their daughters Grace and Rose work with them. Grace led the effort to become certify both of their vineyards organic, achieved in 2023.

VINEYARDS - They have two estate vineyards—Kronos, famed for its gnarled, historic vines (in front of the winery) and Sunbasket. Both are west of Highway 29 in the St. Helena AVA. Kronos' 50 year old vines sit on phylloxera resistant St. George rootstock. A decade ago, Corison bought Sunbasket, from which they'd sourced fruit for 15 years. Planted by André Tchelistcheff in the early 1950's, it's on the St. Helena Mayacamas bench. Gewürztraminer comes from Alta Vista Vineyard on Moon Mountain.

WINES - Cathy says, "I love the 2021s. Cabernet can produce so many fruit flavors—red to blue to black. A season like this puts all those flavors in the glass at the same time."

Napa Valley Kronos Vineyard Cabernet Sauvignon 2021 SLOW WINE ● 350 cases; 225 $ - - Elegant intensity, fantastic persistence of juicy fruit. Aromas of red and black fruit, spice, vanilla, wood. Mouth-filling black cherry, dusty earth, and savory dried herb. Fine grain texture.

Napa Valley Sunbasket Cabernet Sauvignon 2021 ● 200 cases; 225 $ - - On the nose, chewy blackberry, chocolate and graphite. Engaging, evolving palate. Round, soft attack with dark fruit, savory mineral. Fine, chewy tannins carry the midpalate. Gentle waves of acidity for the long finish.

Napa Valley Cabernet Sauvignon 2021 ● 1,975 cases; 125 $ - - Fresh and balanced. Generous aromas of black currant, gravel, caramel, vanilla, and mocha. Long palate with black currant, black cherry, mineral buoyed by acidity, and framed by dusty texture.

acres 19 - cases 2,500
Fertilizers cover crops, organic fertilizer
Plant protection sulfur, organic
Weed control mechanical
Yeasts selected indigenous yeasts, commercial cultured yeasts
Grapes purchase 40%
Certification some of the vineyards are certified organic

ST. HELENA

CROCKER & STARR

700 Dowdell Lane - tel. (707) 967-9111
www.crockerstarr.com - reservations@crockerstarr.com

PEOPLE - A celebrated Napa winery, Crocker & Starr produces Bordeaux varieties on an historic site. Founding winemaker Pam Starr previously made wine at Spottswoode. In 2022, she hired Julie Robertson as winemaker. Ecofriendly measures include installing solar panels in 2023 and being Napa Green certified in both the vineyard and winery. Robertson joined the Napa Valley Zero Waste Committee to reduce waste in their own operations and throughout the region.

VINEYARDS - They use only organic approved materials on the Napa Green certified estate. The vineyard team is experimenting with no till, regenerative practices on two blocks, hoping to promote vine longevity. Their new cover crop brings in pollinators and beneficials. Adventurously, they are piloting Pierce's disease resistant hybrid wine grapes (Ambulo Blanc and Paseante). After planting 400 olive trees in 2023, in 2024, they released their first estate olive oil.

WINES - New this year: Ambulo Blanc hybrid was harvested for the first time in 2023. It's currently in barrel.

TOP **St. Helena Estate Sauvignon Blanc 2023** ○ 912 cases; 52 $ - - Whole cluster pressed. Fermented in concrete egg (31%), French oak barrique and puncheon (23%), and stainless steel (46%). A very aromatic wine with notes of mango and guava, with a weighted midpalate.

Napa Valley Red Blend of Cabernet Franc 2020 ● 376 cases; 72 $ - - Aged 22 months in oak. A Cabernet Franc dominant blend (64%) with Cabernet Sauvignon (36%). Aromas of dark red fruits, blackberry, violets, tobacco and a savory herbal note. Elegant with silky tannins.

Napa Valley Rock Loam Clay RLC Cabernet Sauvignon 2021 ● 482 cases; 85 $ - - Aged 22 months in French oak (65% new). From diverse soils (rock, loam, clay). A classic Cab with sandalwood, red plum, mulberry, briary, tobacco leaf and cocoa notes. On the palate, the wine is dense and rich but fresh with smooth velvet tannins.

acres 80 - cases 4,500
Fertilizers compost, cover crops, manure, organic fertilizer
Plant protection sulfur, organic
Weed control animal grazing, mechanical, manual
Yeasts spontaneous fermentation, selected indigenous yeasts, commercial cultured yeasts
Grapes 100% owned
Certification none

ST. HELENA

DANA ESTATES | ONDA

P.O. Box 153
www.danaestates.com - inquiries@danaestate.com

PEOPLE - An iconic producer, the winery embodies elegance and precision both in the thoughtfully designed architecture and attention to detail in every step. In 2005, Hi Sang Lee, a Korean real estate and wine magnate (and a passionate collector of Bordeaux and Cabernet) bought an historic 1883 ghost winery in St. Helena, hired renowned wine country architect Howard Backen to renovate it and brought in wine consultant Philippe Melka to create the winery and caves.

VINEYARDS - The DANA label makes single vineyard wines from each of the three certified organic estate vineyards–Helms (8 acres on the valley floor in Rutherford), Hershey (35 acres at 1,800' on Howell Mountain) and Lotus (5 acres on rocky soils at 1,200' in Vaca Mountains on the east side of Napa Valley). The Onda wines feature the Crystal Springs estate vineyard in an area below Howell Mountain, (which is on the path to becoming its own appellation).

WINES - Chris Cooney makes the wines, which rank among the region's most renowned. The style of each wine is complex, layered and extremely elegant and precise.

Napa Valley Onda Cabernet Sauvignon 2019 ● 1,929 cases; 300 $ - ⌨ - Cabernet Sauvignon blended with Cabernet Franc (2%) and Petit Verdot (1%). Precise and focused on the palate with black cherries, cassis, blackberries, plum, and currants. Embodies purity and elegance.

Napa Valley Onda Cabernet Sauvignon 2015 ● 1,278 cases; 375 $ - ⌨ - Blended with Merlot (5%) and Petit Verdot (3%). Black cherry and plum on the nose with a bit of baking spice, opening to cassis and blackberries and a hint of violet on the palate. Stunning.

Rutherford Helms Vineyard DANA Cabernet Sauvignon 2021 ● 312 cases; 829 $ - ⌨ - Aged in French oak (100% new). From vines planted in 1997 and 1998 on gravelly loam soils. A drought year vintage with low yields. Blackberries, cassis and plums shine through. A vibrant, laser focused wine.

acres 48 - cases 2,000
Fertilizers compost, biodynamic compost, cover crops
Plant protection sulfur, organic
Weed control mechanical
Yeasts spontaneous fermentation, selected indigenous yeasts
Grapes 100% owned
Certification some of the vineyards are certified organic

ST. HELENA

DAVID ARTHUR VINEYARDS

210 Long Ranch Road - tel. (707) 963-5190
www.davidarthur.com - info@davidarthur.com

PEOPLE - The winery's storied history begins with Don Long, a Palo Alto butcher turned grocer, who bought nearly 1,000 acres of cattle ranch on Pritchard Hill in the 1960's. There was no road to the property and it was a long hike. Fast forward to 1985: his youngest son David decided to make wine, hiring the now legendary Heidi Peterson Barrett as consultant. She in turn later recommended Nile Zacherle, who has now made the wines since 2008.

VINEYARDS - At 1,100+ feet of elevation, the estate vines (certified organic) grow on low vigor, shallow, volcanic soils. Adjacent sagebrush contributes to the terroir. Zacherle considers himself as much a winegrower as a winemaker and pays meticulous attention to the nuances of vineyard blocks. In addition to Cabernet Sauvignon, the winery grows and makes Nebbiolo and Sangiovese. (Some wines, not featured here, may be grown with herbicide.)

WINES - The winemaking is straight ahead with little intervention. Oak use varies depending on vintage and specific blocks.

Napa Valley Three Acre Cabernet Sauvignon 2019 ● 640 cases; 165 $ - ⌨ - Aged 20 months in French oak. The block features clone 337, which yield small, thick-skinned berries. Blended with Petit Verdot (4%). Full bodied with aromas of blackberry and cassis. Notes of black tea, cocoa and bay laurel. On the palate, notes of blackberry compote and toasted oak.

Napa Valley Old Vine Cabernet Sauvignon 2021 ● 188 cases; 275 $ - ⌨ - Aged in French oak (100% new). From vines planted in the 1970s. Blended with Petit Verdot (6%). On. the nose and palate, rich notes of cassis and blackberry. The texture is velvety. One for the cellar.

Napa Valley Elevation 1147 Cabernet Sauvignon 2021 ●
142 cases; 300 $ - ⌨ - The flagship wine. On the nose, currants, blackberries and herbaceous notes of fresh pine needles. On the palate, dark cherry, cassis and wild blueberry. A long, textured finish. Cellarworthy.

acres 19 - cases 3,000
Fertilizers compost, cover crops
Plant protection sulfur, synthetic pesticides, organic
Weed control mechanical
Yeasts spontaneous fermentation
Grapes purchase 20%
Certification some of the vineyards are certified organic

OAKVILLE

DETERT FAMILY VINEYARDS

P.O. BOX 374 - tel. (707) 799-1220
www.detert.com - info@detert.com

PEOPLE - The Detert family's fortuitous To Kalon holdings date back to Hedwig Detert, who, when widowed, sold the family's Guenoc Ranch in Lake County and bought a portion of the then unknown To Kalon vineyard in Oakville from Caroline Stelling, Martin Stelling's widow, in 1954. Today it is hallowed ground. The property was later divided between two of her heirs. One portion is owned by Detert's three great grandsons—Tom Garrett, John Garrett and Bill Cover. Tom makes the wines.

VINEYARDS - While most of To Kalon is planted to Cabernet Sauvignon, Stelling first planted this site to Cabernet Franc in 1949, said to be the first planted in Napa Valley. Replanted in 1979, it is now some of the oldest Cabernet Franc in Napa. The vines grow in cobble in an alluvial fan, famously rich in minerals and rocks. The prized East Block grows seven acres of 1979 vines. The family sells two thirds of their coveted fruit to other wineries, including Mondavi, their neighbor.

WINES - Complex, elegant Napa Cab Franc from a distinctive site shows the differences in vine age in two contrasting bottlings.

Oakville East Block Cabernet Franc 2019 ● 200 cases; 225 $ - ▣ - A showstopper from 1979 vines. Striking aromas and notes of cassis. Elegant with black cherry and cassis on the palate. Beautifully layered.

Oakville Cabernet Franc 2021 ● 195 cases; 125 $ - ▣ - The blend is Cabernet Franc (85%) and Cabernet Sauvignon (15%). Vibrant and intense with aromas of dark berries and fruits. Plush and satisfying.

Oakville Cabernet Sauvignon 2021 ● 300 cases; 125 $ - ▣ - Blended with Cabernet Franc (3 percent). Elegant and refined with typical Napa notes of black cherry and dark chocolate. Complex with a long finish.

acres 28 - cases 700
Fertilizers n/a
Plant protection sulfur, synthetic pesticides
Weed control mechanical
Yeasts n/a
Grapes 100% owned
Certification none

YOUNTVILLE

DOMINUS/NAPANOOK

2570 Napa Nook Road - tel. (707) 944-8954
www.dominusestate.com - info@dominusestate.com

 Dry farmed vineyards enable it to harvest flavors from the earth transparently, resulting in world famous wines.

PEOPLE - Christian Moueix founded the iconic Dominus Estate in 1982 with Robin Lail and Marcia Smith, owners of the Napanook Vineyard. (George Yount planted Napa's first vines on that site in 1838.) Famed for winemaking and estate ownership in Bordeaux, he is very active in technical aspects at Dominus. Tod Mostero, director of viticulture and winemaking and a Napa Green board member, has led day to day activities since 2007. A full time viticultural team farms the estate.

VINEYARDS - The dry farmed vineyard at the foot of the Mayacamas is slightly sloping. Planted 90 percent to Cabernet Sauvignon with Cabernet Franc and Petit Verdot, it is certified both organic and Napa Green sustainable. Adapting for climate change, Dominus recently changed their treatment of cover crops, leading to dramatic decreases in soil temperature and increases in retained moisture. They have also been adjusting row direction and trellising.

WINES - Oak is limited to 20-40 percent new. Minimal intervention with very specific, targeted actions as needed.

Napa Valley Dominus 2021 SLOW WINE ● 3,700 cases; 359 $ - ▣ - Aged in oak (40% new). A youthful powerhouse with a pretty nose that loves air. Even more savory than the Napanook, the extremely long palate is loaded with iron and graphite, dry earth, spice, a scattering of dry leaves, and chewy black cherry. Very fine, grainy and chalky tannins are at the fore now. Those and plenty of acidity and fruit promise a very long life.

Napa Valley Napanook 2021 ● 3,000 cases; 95 $ - ▣ - Notes of perfectly ripe blackcurrant and black cherry, hints of dark mineral and briary blackberry. The palate is savory-forward—dry herb, earth, mineral with spice—with a mix of dark fruits and dark red cherry. Medium-plus body with fine, grainy texture. Powerful and ageworthy.

acres 112 - cases 10,000
Fertilizers compost, cover crops
Plant protection organic
Weed control animal grazing, mechanical, manual
Yeasts selected indigenous yeasts
Grapes 100% owned
Certification organic

ST. HELENA

EHLERS ESTATE

3222 Ehlers Lane - tel. (707) 963-5972
www.ehlersestate.com - info@ehlersestate.com

PEOPLE - The historic 1886 stone winery got a makeover from the celebrated Backen & Backen architecture firm, reopening in late 2023. With former winemaker Laura Diaz Munos' departure to Mondavi, Adam Casto joined the team as winemaker in 2023. He's spent 10 years at Gandona Estate on Pritchard Hill and has worked with Philippe Melka. The winery is owned by a French-American foundation that donates its profits to medical research.

VINEYARDS - In 2023, the winery hired vineyard manager Dominick Bianco to bring the farming in house. He and Casto are replanting 40 percent of the estate. Casto is trialing new vineyard architecture. In the cellar, the winery added smaller tanks (to isolate blocks) and upgraded wastewater treatment with a new eco-efficient Biofiltro vermicompost system.

WINES - Casto is reframing the winery portfolio to highlight the estate fruit in relation to the planting and location.

● **St. Helena J. Leducq Cabernet Sauvignon 2021** ● 600 cases; 120 $ - ⊞ - Named for the founder, this single block bottling showcases grapes sourced solely from a small volcanic hill on the estate. On the nose, pomegranate, dried oregano, crushed dried rose petal, wood shavings and cocoa. An evolving palate of blueberry and mint.

St. Helena Cabernet Sauvignon 1886 2021 ● 4,000 cases; 160 $ - ⊞ - Deep color of dark red velvet, savory and spiced, with red cassis and paprika on the nose. Complex and structured palate of cooked berries, spice rub and hibiscus. Ageworthy.

St. Helena Estate Cabernet Franc 2021 ● 850 cases; 80 $ - ⊞ - Bing cherry, crushed herbs, rose and wet stone on the nose, with brambly red berry fruit, violet, red pepper umami in the mouth. The tannins are soft for the youth of the vintage.

---

acres 40 - cases 7,000
Fertilizers compost, organic fertilizer
Plant protection sulfur, organic
Weed control mechanical, manual
Yeasts spontaneous fermentation, commercial cultured yeasts
Grapes purchase 20%
Certification some of the vineyards are certified organic

OAKVILLE

ELIZABETH ROSE

7830-40 St. Helena Highway - tel. (800) 848-9630
www.ghostblockwine.com - drinkcab@ghostblockwine.com

PEOPLE - A value brand in Napa? Elizabeth Rose is just that. The brand is run by Morgaen Hoxsey Pickett and Kendall Hoxsey Onysko who represent the fifth generation of their family in Napa. Back in 1938, the family bought 1,000 acres in Oakville and Yountville after Prohibition. The brand recently signed a deal with Whole Foods, which will carry some of their wines. The company has 21 houses on their vast property and provide houses for workers—a rarity in Napa.

VINEYARDS - In 1992, their 558 acres of estate vines were among the first to be certified organic in Napa. They grow 19 different wine grape varieties in two appellations: Yountville and Oakville. They are the only growers of a rare variety called Flora. They've also recently planted Pinotage, a cross between Pinot and Cinsault, and a half acre of Albarino. Their vast composting facility, which provides all their compost, takes up an acre of their land.

WINES - Jeff Onysko, Kendall's husband, makes the wine. The wines all feature screwtops.

● **Napa Valley Chockablock Red Blend 2021** EVERYDAY WINE ● 1,650 cases; 30 $ - ⊞ - A blend of Cabernet Sauvignon (69%), Merlot (17%), and Malbec (15%), aged in neutral oak for 12 months. Offers up red cherry and black plum notes.

Yountville Flora 2022 ○ 35 cases; 25 $ - 🍶⊞ - This fun and exotic variety is one to try. A 1938 cross between Semillon and Gewürztraminer, it pairs well with Thai or Mexican food. It's stirred on the lees every two weeks. Off dry with notes of apple, peach, and honey. Refreshing and novel.

Napa Valley Rosé 2023 ● 290 cases; 25 $ - 🍶 - A popular and bold rosé wine that sells out early. It's a blend of Syrah (49%), Cinsault (40%) and Grenache (11%). Find strawberry and stone fruit notes. Crisp and refreshing.

---

acres 58 - cases 4,000
Fertilizers compost, cover crops
Plant protection organic
Weed control mechanical
Yeasts commercial cultured yeasts
Grapes 100% owned
Certification organic

RUTHERFORD

FROG'S LEAP

8815 Conn Creek Road - tel. (707) 963-4704
www.frogsleap.com - ribbit@frogsleap.com

 A green role model in Napa, they honor agricultural traditions and ecological priorities while making beautiful wines.

PEOPLE - Organic pioneers in Napa (certified in 1997), John and Rory Williams run the iconic winery known for its ecofriendly practices, fairly priced fine wines and worker fairness. Their track record–solar since 2005, a LEED certified tasting room in 2006, adding biodiversity and other climate friendly practices–speaks for itself. Promoting from within, Pablo Polanco, their cellarmaster for 30 years, is the winemaker with his daughter Xochilt as assistant winemaker.

VINEYARDS - Grapes come from 200 acres of their own dry farmed estates in Rutherford along with growers' certified organic vineyards from Carneros to St. Helena and Mendocino. Uniquely, they also dry farm heritage grapes like Petite Sirah and Valdiguié (nicknamed Napa Gamay). Father and son live side by side on the Rossi site, their crown jewel, in two Victorian houses by a vintage winery and water tower.

WINES - Balanced, pure and nuanced wines. New: Treasured best blocks from Rossi go into limited release wines.

Napa Valley Sauvignon Blanc 2023 EVERYDAY WINE O 15,500 cases; 30 $ - ⬜ - A mainstay of the winery's production for decades and a popular restaurant wine. Five percent fermented and aged in cement eggs. The rest is stainless steel aged 6 months sur lie. Crisp, refreshing and complex with tension and depth.

Rutherford Williams Rossi Merlot 2019 ● 500 cases; 80 $ - ⬛ - Aged 32 months in French oak (some new). Best blocks. Merlot (87%) Cabernet Sauvignon (10%) and Cabernet Franc (3%). Plush–berries and plums–and delicious.

Rutherford Williams Rossi Cabernet Sauvignon 2019 ● 500 cases; 125 $ - ⬛ - Aged 32 months in new French oak (100%). Best blocks. Cabernet with Cab Franc (5%). Vines planted in 2008 and 2010. Blackberry and raspberry fruits with an herbal-floral streak.

---

acres 200 - cases 50,000
Fertilizers compost, cover crops
Plant protection organic
Weed control mechanical
Yeasts spontaneous fermentation, commercial cultured yeasts
Grapes purchase 25%
Certification organic

ST. HELENA

GALLICA

2300 Vallejo Street - tel. (707) 963-1096
www.gallicawine.com - info@gallicawine.com

 An all star. Dedicated to making elegant and nuanced wines.

PEOPLE - One of Napa Valley's most respected winemakers, Rosemary Cakebread has worked 40+ vintages in Napa, focusing primarily on Cabernet from Oakville, Rutherford, and St. Helena. After ten years as the winemaker at Spottswoode, she created her own brand, Gallica. Its first vintage was 2007. She's known for delicate, graceful wines that are aged in little to no new oak. Nate Kane is the estate vineyard manager.

VINEYARDS - Gallica uses only grapes from celebrated, certified organic vineyards. Her tiny St. Helena estate has old vine Cabernet Sauvignon and Petite Sirah. Oakville Ranch in the Vaca Mountains (Oakville AVA) and the historic Rossi Ranch in Sonoma Valley are farmed by renowned viticulturalist Phil Coturri. On red volcanic soils, Oakville is renowned for Cab. Rossi excels in Rhones. As of 2023, Albariño is from Terra Alta in Lodi's Clements Hills AVA.

WINES - Cakebread says 2021 and 2023 were among the five best vintages she's seen, with perfect growing conditions and great acidity in the wines.

Clements Hills Lodi Terra Alta Vineyard Albariño 2023 O 250 cases; 38 $ - ⬜ - Absolutely gorgeous—ripe nectarine, tropical fruit, peach, citrus blossoms, sweet citrus, and mineral. The palate shows effortless grace, sensuous viscosity and silky texture.

St. Helena Estate Rosé 2023 ● 100 cases; 38 $ - ⬜ - Soft nose of flowers, stone fruit, red cherry, strawberry, raspberry, vanilla. Fresh and lightly chalky palate: tart red fruit, orange pith, mineral, drying herb. Refreshing, enough intensity and texture to stand up to food.

Napa Valley Estate Cabernet Sauvignon 2021 ● 125 cases; 210 $ - ⬛ - Bursting with rich black currant and black cherry, mocha, dry leaves, caramel and subtle spice. Savory palate of dark mineral, grilled black fruit, espresso, dark chocolate, well-toasted wood, and caramel. Very fine, persistent tannins. Well balanced and quite long. Superb.

---

acres 2 - cases 1,500
Fertilizers compost, cover crops
Plant protection sulfur, organic
Weed control mechanical
Yeasts spontaneous fermentation
Grapes purchase 90%
Certification organic

OAKVILLE

GHOST BLOCK

7830-40 St. Helena Highway - tel. (800) 848-9630
www.ghostblockwine.com - drinkcab@ghostblockwine.com

 An Italian family–committed to organics–maintains their heritage and preserves old Zin vines in Cab country as well as making fine Cab themselves.

PEOPLE - An old Italian family's fifth generation daughters oversee the largest organic vineyard in Napa, producing a wide range of wines across three brands. The Pelissa family bought land in 1938 and in 1993, their descendants acquired the 9th bonded winery in the state. The fifth generation–Kendall Hoxsey Onysko and Morgaen Hoxsey Pickett–manage the company today. Twenty one houses on the property provide housing for their workers, a rarity in Napa.

VINEYARDS - Certified organic since 1995, the family owns 558 acres of prized Oakville and Yountville holdings next to famed Cab producers Opus One and To Kalon. Their historic Pelissa vineyard boasts some of the last Zinfandel vines in Oakville. Adventurously they are replacing a half acre of Cab with Albarino. New vineyard tours offer visitors a chance to go into the vines with experienced winegrowers.

WINES - Kristi Koford makes the wines, using 50-80 percent of new French oak on the prized Cabs. New this year: a late harvest wine.

TOP Yountville Single Vineyard Cabernet Sauvignon 2020 SLOW WINE ● 800 cases; 140 $ - 🛢 - Aged 24 months in French oak (80% new). Arom the prized Ghost Block vineyard, their crown jewel. A dry year, the vintages was marked by low yield and high concentration. Complex with black fruits–black cherry, black currant, blackberry. Best cellared or decanted.
Oakville Estate Cabernet Sauvignon 2021 ● 4,400 cases; 95 $ - 🛢 - Aged 24 months in French oak (60% new). Grown on the Rock Cairn vineyard in Oakville (77%) and Ghost Block in Yountville (23%). Vine age: up to 35 years old. Elegant, it's composed of Cabernet Sauvignon (96%), with Malbec and Petit Verdot. Velvety with black fruits and plums.
Yountville Late Harvest Semillon-Sauvignon Blanc 2021 ● 100 cases; 50 $ - 🍷 - A late harvest blend of Sauvignon Blanc (82%) and Semillon (18%). Flavors of honey, vanilla, and dried stone fruit.

acres 58 - cases 4,000
Fertilizers compost, cover crops
Plant protection sulfur, organic
Weed control mechanical
Yeasts commercial cultured yeasts
Grapes 100% owned
Certification organic

RUTHERFORD

GRGICH HILLS ESTATE

1829 St. Helena Highway - tel. (707) 963-2784
www.grgich.com - info@grgich.com

 In addition to its world class wines and green leadership, the winery is making wine from the rare, original Zinfandel Crljenak Kastelanski (Tribidrag) clone it has lovingly preserved.

PEOPLE - Croatian born Mike (or Miljenko) Grgich (1923-2023) left a legacy the world will not forget, even after his passing at the age of 100. His win at the historic 1976 Tasting of Paris set Napa on a new course in the global story of wine. Austin Hills (of Hills Bros. Coffee) co-founded the winery with him. Mike's daughter Violet Grgich is president. Mike's nephew Ivo Jeramaz manages production. Violet continues the philanthropic traditions her immigrant parents started.

VINEYARDS - Certified regenerative organic in 2023, Jeramaz is blazing a pioneering trail in educating his peers about the economics of organic and benefits of no till. Crimping cover crop in the vine rows increases fertility and water retention. The portfolio of five estate vineyards covers the best regions for each variety, with Cabernet in Rutherford and Yountville, and Chardonnay in the Carneros.

WINES - Their three tiers delineate top wines from widely distributed, more affordable wines, providing consumers with a variety of price points. All are first rate in quality.

TOP Napa Valley Fumé Blanc 2022 SLOW WINE ○ 9,405 cases; 34 $ - 🛢 - Aged six months on the lees in neutral oak. Juicy, crisp and refreshing. Contains 80 percent Musque clone, known for its vibrant aromatics. Bright lime and citrus on the palate.
Napa Valley Miljenko's Chardonnay 2021 ○ 974 cases; 60 $ - 🛢 - From the "King of Chardonnay." Fermented in large oak casks with minimal oak and no malo. Lively with citrus aromas and green apple on the nose, the citrus follows through on the vibrant, complex palate. Bright acidity.
Carneros Cabernet Franc 2020 ● 522 cases; 88 $ - 🛢 - Aged 20 months in oak (43% new). Blended with Cabernet Sauvignon (14%). Currants, plums and red berries on the gorgeous palate. Freshness and complexity. Integrated tannins.

acres 366 - cases 65,000
Fertilizers compost, biodynamic compost, cover crops
Plant protection sulfur, biodynamic preparations, organic
Weed control mechanical
Yeasts spontaneous fermentation
Grapes 100% owned
Certification organic, regenerative

ST. HELENA

HEITZ CELLAR

436 St. Helena Highway - tel. (707) 963-3542
www.heitzcellar.com - info@heitzcellar.com

PEOPLE - Winemaker Brittany Sherwood joined Heitz in 2012 and credits David Heitz with defining a classic style and his father, Joe, for Napa Valley's first vineyard-designated Cabernet Sauvignon from Martha's Vineyard. Founded in 1961, the winery was sold to Gaylan Lawrence in 2018. Working with assistant winemaker Sam Dhiman and cellarmaster Erik Griffin, Sherwood has new wines from Spring Valley vineyard in the bottle awaiting release.

VINEYARDS - Viticulturist Mark Neal farms Martha's Vineyard and the remainder of the estate farming has been outsourced to a trio vineyard management companies under the direction of Macy Stubstad, who has joined as director of vineyard operations. The 50-acre Quartz Creek vineyard in Oak Knoll has rare quartzite amid clay loam series soils while the 132-acre Trailside vineyard in eastern Rutherford is well-drained volcanic and gravelly clay loam.

WINES - With a renewed emphasis on the '70s, Sherwood makes fresh and fruit-focused aromatics a priority and has reduced the percentage of new oak used in the wines.

● Oak Knoll District Quartz Creek Vineyard Chardonnay 2022 SLOW WINE O 800 cases; 85 $ - ⦿ - Aged for 15 months in large casks (20% new) with regular battonage. Harmonious and balanced showing lemon and white tree fruits with a nutty secondary note through a bright, intense finish. Youthful with potential for greater expression.
Napa Valley Lot C-91 Cabernet Sauvignon 2019 ● 3,000 cases; 120 $ - ⦿ - 24 months in new and neutral barrels and 1 year in bottle. Voluminous aromas of dried mint and star anise unfurling with layers of red and black fruit spiced with clove and cocoa nibs.
Rutherford Trailside Vineyard Cabernet Sauvignon 2018 ● 2,500 cases, 200 $ - ⦿ - 36 months in new and neutral barrels. A melange of red fruits scented with the garrigue markers of the vineyard. Tannins are fine and plush, quite ready to enjoy.

acres 425 - cases 35,000
Fertilizers compost, cover crops, manure
Plant protection sulfur, copper, organic
Weed control animal grazing, mechanical
Yeasts spontaneous fermentation, selected indigenous yeasts, commercial cultured yeasts
Grapes 100% owned
Certification organic

NAPA

HYDE DE VILLAINE - HDV

588 Trancas Street - tel. (707) 251-9121
www.hdvwines.com - nate@hdvwines.com

PEOPLE - HdV is a partnership between two revered wine families—the Hydes of Napa Valley and de Villaines of Burgundy—which celebrates its 25th anniversary next year. Burgundy native Guillaume Boudet makes the wines. Retired from the iconic Domaine de la Romanée Conti in Burgundy, Aubert de Villaine continues to travel to Napa and consult on HdV winemaking at least twice a year.

VINEYARDS - Grapes are from specially selected, reserve clones in the Hyde vineyard (in the Carneros), grown and custom farmed for HdV. New Pinot and Chardonnay blocks, planted in 2019-20, haven't been used in the wines yet. In 2022, drought reduced yields to roughly half of average. The 2023 vintage was a cool and super wet one. It replenished the water table, offered generous yields, and resulted in a harvest three weeks later than the 10 year average.

WINES - HdV wines are made with neutral, cultured yeasts and aged with very restrained use of new oak.

● Carneros Hyde Vineyard Chardonnay 2021 O 1,000 cases; 85 $ - ⦿ - Aged in both concrete eggs (18 months), small barrel (15% new) and foudre. Lithe and graceful with beautiful, fine silky texture. Appetizing aromas and juicy palate of pear, yellow apple, pineapple, baking spice and oak. Very long, mineral finish.
Los Carneros Ygnacia Pinot Noir 2021 ● 200 cases; 130 $ - ⦿ - Aged in French oak (15% new). Marvelous aromatic intensity. Dark flowers, black cherry, tea, spice, and wild berries. Lightly chewy tannins.
Carneros Californio Syrah 2019 ● 350 cases; 85 $ - ⦿ - Aromas of meaty black plum, black cherry, dried beef, spice, accents of red cherry and vanilla. The palate adds espresso, toasted wood, and mineral. Great balance between fruit, savory elements, and measured tannins. No whole cluster.

acres 0 - cases 2,000
Fertilizers organic fertilizer
Plant protection synthetic pesticides, organic
Weed control mechanical
Yeasts commercial cultured yeasts
Grapes purchase 100%
Certification none

NAPA

KEPLINGER WINES

926 Franklin Street - tel. (707) 815-7824
www.keplingerwines.com - tyson@keplingerwines.com

PEOPLE - Voted winemaker of the year by the prestigious Vinous in 2023, Napa legend Helen Keplinger and her husband DJ Warner founded their own winery in Napa in 2006 and quickly established an impressive reputation. Keplinger's resume includes stints working with Heidi Barrett and making cult wines for other brands. Her own label allows her to make the wines she loves.

VINEYARDS - Though she makes a nuanced Napa Cab—some have received 100 point scores—Keplinger's love of Rhone varietals is one thing that separates her from others in Napa. It leads her to buy grapes from renowned growers in Sonoma (the Uvalde family) and in the Sierra Foothills (Goldbud and Shake Ridge Ranch). In Napa, she waited years to get Cab from Napa's celebrated Oakville Ranch (certified organic) and Vine Hill, both in Oakville. Worth the wait.

WINES - Keplinger's elegant and distinctive wines showcase a unique voice. Think purity and expressiveness.

● Oakville Vine Hill Ranch Cabernet Sauvignon 2019 SLOW WINE ● 300 cases; 225 $ - 🍷 - From a celebrated Oakville vineyard. A glorious superstar of a wine, with a palate of black currant, cassis and so much more. Silky tannins. Lay it down.

Amador County Lithic GSM 2013 ● 250 cases; 85 $ - 🍷 - Aged 18 months in French oak (15% new). Partial whole cluster (30%). Grown at Shake Ridge Ranch on quartz, basalt, and shale. Delicate with beautiful balance. Dark fruited with cherry, blackberry and garrigue.

Russian River Valley El Diablo Grenache 2021 ● 100 cases; 85 $ - 🍷 - From sandy loam soils farmed by Ulises Valdez Jr. Ribbons of flavor and blue fruits unfurl as in a kaleidoscope of strawberries, crushed stones and rose on the palate.

acres 0 - cases 1,600
Fertilizers compost, cover crops
Plant protection sulfur, organic
Weed control mechanical, manual
Yeasts spontaneous fermentation
Grapes purchase 100%
Certification some of the vineyards are certified organic

ST. HELENA

MASSICAN

P.O. Box 86
www.massican.com - hello@massican.com

PEOPLE - Massican begins in Sicily. Time there helped Dan Petroski, top former Napa Cab winemaker at Larkmead, realize the profundity of white wines and decided to produce Mediterranean white wines grown in California. He sold the company to Gallo in 2023, setting it on a mission to grow under his helm to 50,000 cases a year within five years. To lower its carbon footprint, the winery switched to lighter weight bottles (468 grams) with 50 percent recycled glass.

VINEYARDS - Petroski named his label after Monte Massico, the southern Italy site known for producing the Grand Cru of ancient times. The brand buys all of its fruit. (Some wines, not featured here, are grown with synthetic herbicide). The wines featured here come from organically grown blocks. Petroski is working with the other vineyards to transition to organic farming. He lists the vineyards and the percentage of organic grapes in each bottle on the website's "about" section.

WINES - Petroski has a deft hand in the cellar. Believing that wine is food, he also sponsors cooking classes on Instagram and publishes a cookbook chapter by chapter on Massican's website.

● California Gemina White Blend 2023 SLOW WINE ○ 1,500 cases; 38 $ - 🥂 - Aged in French oak (40%) and stainless steel. The blend is Greco (60%), Falanghina (23%) and Fiano (17%). Crisp and nuanced with lemon and lime on the palate.

Napa Valley Hyde Chardonnay 2023 ○ 547 cases; 60 $ - 🍷 - Barrel fermented and aged in neutral French oak. From the Musque clone of Chardonnay planted in 1992. Light bodied with subtle citrus flavors.

acres 0 - cases 10,000
Fertilizers compost, cover crops, organic fertilizer, synthetic fertilizer
Plant protection sulfur, synthetic pesticides, copper, organic
Weed control mechanical
Yeasts spontaneous fermentation, commercial cultured yeasts
Grapes purchase 100%
Certification none

ANGWIN

NEAL FAMILY VINEYARDS

716 Liparita Avenue - tel. (707) 965-2800
www.nealvineyards.com - info@nealvineyards.com

 A pioneer who has mastered the art of organic farming, Neal's been a leading role model for a new generation of organic wine growers and led his own winery to new heights.

PEOPLE - When it comes to organic farming, second generation Napa grower and vintner Mark Neal is the O.G. He runs his own vineyard management company, founded by his dad in 1968. He farms Martha's Vineyard, one of Napa's Grand Cru sites. Certified organic (since 1984!) and biodynamic (since 2021), he was the first in Napa to receive Regenerative Organic certification (in 2022). The 2024 harvest marks Mark's 58th harvest in Napa and his 41st organic harvest.

VINEYARDS - Neal prides himself on his 22 clones of Cabernet which give complexity to the wines. He farms 17 acres in Rutherford (originally planted by his father Jack) and 12.5 acres on Howell Mountain, purchased in 1990, for its sunny microclimate and red volcanic Aiken soil. To double his crop, he's interplanted a wide variety of climate friendly whites (Assyrtiko, Vermentino and more) on the Rutherford property between the Cabernet vines.

WINES - Certified winemaking is as important to Neal as is his farming. He certifies all wines "Made with Organic Grapes," a high standard prohibiting commonly used additives.

Howell Mountain Cabernet Sauvignon 2021 SLOW WINE
975 cases; 125 $ - Aged 22 months in French oak barrels (75% new). Built to age. The clonal blend adds complexity. Elegant and expressive with pure fruit. Watch it evolve after cellaring. From a great vintage.
Napa Valley Cabernet Sauvignon 2021 2,482 cases; 48 $ - Aged 18 months in French oak (20% new). A blend of valley and mountain fruit. On the palate, find red and black fruit, followed by a persistent dark fruit note on the finish. A great value.
Rutherford Vermentino 2023 O 1,300 cases; 42 $ - Aged four months in French oak (20% new) and puncheons. Subtler than the 2022. Aromas of citrus and flowers lead to juicy nectarine and lemon on the palate.

acres 27 - cases 3,500
Fertilizers biodynamic compost, cover crops
Plant protection sulfur, biodynamic preparations, organic
Weed control animal grazing, mechanical
Yeasts spontaneous fermentation, commercial cultured yeasts
Grapes 100% owned
Certification biodynamic, organic, regenerative

NAPA

NEOTEMPO

Silverado Trail
www.neotempo.wine

PEOPLE - The husband and wife team of Iranian born Kia Behnea and South Africa native Tracy Borman bought their Silverado property in 2011 after successful careers in tech in Silicon Valley. Devoted to addressing climate change, Behnea has reinvented the wine bottle, creating a carbon saving hexagonal bottle that greatly reduces carbon shipping emissions and launched an AI enabled precision viticulture company Scout. Veteran Napa winemaker Tony Biagi makes the wines.

VINEYARDS - Initially farmed by Napa organic vineyard manager Mark Neal, who planted three different ENTAV clones of Cabernet (412, 338, and 685) in 2012. Organic icon Phil Coturri is farming and now uses Scout to oversee the vines. The estate sits just outside the Oak Knoll AVA on the east side of Napa Valley. Grenache comes from Lasseter's Justi Creek (certified organic) in Sonoma Valley, which Coturri also farms. Neotempo is now planting cuttings from the Sonoma estate in Napa.

WINES - The Grenache "rosé" is a decidedly different and refreshing take. Biagi's practiced hand in making Cabernet expertly blends vineyard components to create a rich, decadent, elegant and very complex Cabernet.

Sonoma Valley Sensoria Love Grenache Rosé 2022
93 cases; 80 $ - Golden yellow, rose gold in color from just two hours on the skins. High acid. White strawberries with lemon accents with pleasing, slightly tart notes. Utterly unique.
Napa Valley Kiatra Estate Cabernet Sauvignon 2022
407 cases; 250 $ - Aged 18 months in French oak (80% new). From four separate picks selected for phenolic ripeness. On the nose, red and black fruits–raspberries, black cherries and spices. On the palate, concentrated black cherries, blackberries, cassis and a hint of cinnamon. Decant if you must drink it now, but best cellared.

acres 3 - cases 600
Fertilizers cover crops
Plant protection sulfur, organic
Weed control mechanical, manual
Yeasts commercial cultured yeasts
Grapes purchase 20%
Certification organic

ST. HELENA

NEWFOUND WINES

1200 Oak Avenue - tel. (727) 686-0526
www.newfoundwines.com - audra@newfoundwines.com

PEOPLE - Napa based, Audra and Matt Naumann started their brand in 2016, purchasing their 40 acre High View Vineyard, ranch and winery in El Dorado County in the Sierra Foothills. Matt worked with Failla, a renowned producer, in different roles for a decade. Both he and Audra have spent 20 years in the industry. The couple sources from spectacular sites and their small lot wines are sought after and showcased by sommeliers nationwide.

VINEYARDS - Sourcing from several organic sites in Mendocino, Mt. Veeder, the Sierra Foothills and Napa Valley, they await their first harvest from their own five acres of planted vines at 2,100 feet overlooking the middle fork of the Consumnes River. The soils are a combination of granitic, Aiken and volcanic on southwest facing slopes of up to 20 degrees. There they've planted dry farmed, head trained Grenache, Semillon and Syrah.

WINES - A philosophy of nature led farming drives the winemaking ethos of using native yeast, whole cluster pressing, and bottling unfined and unfiltered.

Napa Valley Yount Mill Vineyard Sémillon 2021 SLOW WINE O 250 cases; 35 $ - ⊞ - Expressive old vine Semillon that undergoes 22 months aging. Profound intensity and balance at 12% showing lemongrass, flinty minerality, chamomile tea and a lithe texture.

Sonoma Coast Placida Vineyard Grenache 2022 ● 102 cases; 55 $ - ⊞ - The second vintage from this coastal site planted to the Alban 2 clone. Spicy white pepper and lush, ripe dark cherries expressive of a warmer growing season.

Amador County Shake Ridge Ranch Mourvedre 2022 ● 130 cases; 65 $ - ⊞ - Aged for 14 months in 600 L barrels. Showing savory, almost meaty notes of thyme, dark cherry and darker, umami driven fruits with a leaner 12.5% body.

acres 5 - cases 1,000
Fertilizers compost, cover crops, organic fertilizer
Plant protection sulfur, copper, organic
Weed control mechanical
Yeasts spontaneous fermentation
Grapes purchase 100%
Certification some of the vineyards are certified organic

NAPA

OAKVILLE RANCH

7781 Silverado Trail - tel. (707) 944-9665
www.oakvilleranch.com - info@oakvilleranch.com

 Great wines, great farming. Ecofriendly, it promotes biodiversity, native habitats, and wildlife–and makes stellar wines.

PEOPLE - In 1989, Mary and Bob Miner (co founder of Oracle) purchased a weekend getaway estate with tennis court, pool and vineyards–and became growers. After Bob's death in 1994, Mary hired Phil Coturri to convert the vineyards to organic and began using 15 percent of the grapes for an estate label. They sell most grapes to legendary producers (who have made 100 point wines from the site). Shelia Gentry is the general manager. Jennifer Rue makes the wines.

VINEYARDS - Coturri oversees the celebrated vineyards (certified organic) which grow on red volcanic soils surrounded by mountain garrigue.. The estate has 70 acres planted on a 370 acre site at 500-1,000 feet in the Vaca Range. The team continues to work towards regenerative practices, such as flattening (or crimping), rather than mowing cover crops. They are committed to biodiversity preserving wild grass, native meadows and woodlands.

WINES - The Cabernet Sauvignon showcases the diversity of clones. They also grow Cab Franc (Robert's favorite), a bit of Chardonnay (Mary's favorite) and a few rows of Grenache (Phil's favorite).

Oakville Oakville Ranch O Red Wine 2021 ● 50 cases; 225 $ - ⊞ - One each of the best barrels of Cabernet Sauvignon and Cabernet Franc in top years. 2021 is sensuous with a fine grained texture, gorgeous black currant and an intricate weave of red fruit, dark flowers and mountain herb.

Napa Valley Cabernet Sauvignon 2021 ● 302 cases; 125 $ - ⊞ - Generous aromas of caramel, black currant, toasted wood, dry currant leaf, black plum, and dark flowers. Full bodied. Fine grain texture, extremely long flavors of mocha, caramel, dark flowers, black fruit and savory mineral.

Napa Valley Robert's Cabernet Franc 2021 ● 103 cases; 140 $ - ⊞ - Elegant nose of purple berries, red currant and ripe, crushed raspberries. Fine grained and velvety tannins frame the full bodied fruit. Excellent, mountain Cabernet Franc.

acres 70 - cases 750
Fertilizers compost, cover crops
Plant protection sulfur, organic
Weed control mechanical
Yeasts commercial cultured yeasts
Grapes 100% owned
Certification organic

OAKVILLE

OAKVILLE WINERY

7830-40 St. Helena Highway - tel. (800) 848-9630
www.ghostblockwine.com - drinkcab@ghostblockwine.com

 A family run winery with certified organic vines, some of which date back to 1998. The winery provides houses on site for workers.

PEOPLE - The descendants of the Pelissa family farm 558 acres of vines organically, selling most of their grapes, but keeping about 10 percent for their own three wine brands. (Ghost Block is their top brand; Elizabeth Rose is their value brand). Fifth generation Pelissa family sisters Morgaen Hoxsey Pickett and Kendall Hoxsey Onysko run the winery today. 2024 marks the family's 121st harvest. A new vineyard tour enables visitors to tour the vines with an experienced wine grower.

VINEYARDS - Locals nicknamed the Pelissa family's vast acreage in Yountville and Oakville "the Pelissa Hills," for its size. The vineyards span five generations of family history, from the Zinfandel era to the modern Cab era. Once this was the site of the legendary Georges de Latour Private Reserve. Today the family preserves 18 acres of old clone Zinfandel vines to honor previous generations, paying homage to their Italian roots.

WINES - The Zinfandel and Cabernet offer a taste of Napa history. Lynn Watanabe makes the wines. New this year: A rosé of Cab Franc.

Oakville Cabernet Franc Rose 2023 ● 80 cases; 35 $ - ▢ - A winery only wine. Aromas of strawberry, cherry, pomegranate, and cranberry, with peach and pink grapefruit flavors, leading to a refreshing finish with white pepper notes.

Oakville Zinfandel 2021 ● 1,000 cases; 35 $ - ⊞ - From 20 year old vines. Aged 12 months in neutral oak. Aromas of cherry and pomegranate, spices, with fine-grained tannins. A piece of history. This deep ruby color wine has aromas of ripe strawberry, cherry, pomegranate and hibiscus flower.

Oakville Cabernet Sauvignon 2021 ● 1,400 cases; 75 $ - ⊞ - Aged 24 months in French oak (50% new). From dry farmed vines as old as 1998, it includes a variety of clones including the legendary BV-7 clone. Notes of blackberry, black cherry and cassis on the palate. A long finish.

acres 58 - cases 2,300
Fertilizers compost, cover crops
Plant protection organic
Weed control mechanical
Yeasts commercial cultured yeasts
Grapes 100% owned
Certification organic

OAKVILLE

OPUS ONE

7900 St. Helena Highway - tel. (707) 944-9442
www.opusonewinery.com - info@opusonewinery.com

PEOPLE - Almost hidden amidst the Oakville terrain, the iconic winery completed a major renovation in 2020 and has significantly expanded its hospitality programs. Now a joint venture between Baron Philippe de Rothschild S.A. and Constellation Brands, Opus One was founded in 1978 by Robert Mondavi and Baron Philippe de Rothschild. Winemaker Michael Silacci has been at the helm since 2001. Kimberlee Marinelli was appointed assistant winemaker and viticulturist in 2023.

VINEYARDS - Marinelli is responsible for all aspects of carbon capture, agroecology, and regenerative farming for the estate's four certified organic vineyards. Seventy percent are in the To Kalon Vineyard. Thirty percent are on the To Kalon fan. The five traditional Bordeaux grape varieties are planted on Bale clay loam and gravel. The winery and vineyard were the first to achieve Napa Green Gold level certification and the estate pursues more than 100 sustainable practices.

WINES - Classic Bordeaux winemaking that defies the Napa stereotype is achieved through meticulous viticultural and cellar practices, producing this iconic wine.

TOP Napa Valley Opus One 2021 ● 25,000 cases; 365 $ - ⊞ - Aged 19.5 months in new French oak, a blend of Cabernet Sauvignon (93%,) Cabernet Franc (4%), Petit Verdot (2%), Merlot (8.5%) and Malbec (.5%) that is reflective of the estate. Lifted aromas of cassis and dark cherry and brown spice. Dense and creamy with fine, tannins, balanced acidity and notes of black tea and licorice through the finish. Hold.

Napa Valley Overture 2021 ● 6,000 cases; 160 $ - ⊞ - With 19.5 months in new French oak, a blend of Cabernet Sauvignon (89%), Cabernet Franc (4%), Petit Verdot (4%) and Merlot (3%) that shows aromas of red fruit and bright, juicy flavors of black currant, blueberry and fraises du bois with mocha emerging on the finish. Supple in texture with fine tannins.

acres 170 - cases 30,000
Fertilizers compost, cover crops
Plant protection sulfur, organic
Weed control mechanical
Yeasts spontaneous fermentation
Grapes 100% owned
Certification organic

OAKVILLE

PARADIGM

1277 Dwyer Road - tel. (707) 944-1683
www.paradigmwinery.com - info@paradigmwinery.com

 Civic minded, this exceptional Napa winery consistently works for the good of the community while making affordably priced (for Napa), top tier wines.

PEOPLE - Deeply rooted in Napa, vintners Ren and Marilyn Harris are among the local leaders who made Napa what it is today. Marilyn, 81 (a descendant of the Pelissa family, Napa's largest organic growers; see Ghost Block listing), and Ren, 82, founded key community organizations. In 2024, they appointed Jake Pickett, husband of Morgaen Hoxsey (also of the Pelissa family), as the new general manager. They are also part of the 1% for the Planet organization.

VINEYARDS - Certified organic in 2021, the gravelly soils on the west side of the acclaimed Oakville appellation grow Cabernet Sauvignon as well as Zinfandel, Cabernet Franc and Merlot. They added a bit more Cab Franc in 2024. They also grow 147 olive trees and sell organic estate olive oil. The property is uniquely positioned between the Mayacamas and Yountville Hills where ocean influences create cooler temperatures and beneficial airflow.

WINES - Superstar Heidi Barrett's handpicked collaborator (for 18 years), Mark Fasi is now the winemaker. The two will continue to work together on blending. After aging in oak (typically 40% new), the wines are bottle aged before release. The wines couple bright fruit with balanced acidity. Bottle labeled: "Ingredients: Organic Grapes."

Oakville Merlot 2021 SLOW WINE ● 89 cases; 603 $ - ⊞ - A blend of Merlot (99%) and Cabernet Sauvignon (1%). Aged 22 months in French oak (50%). Find ripe plum with velvety, silky tannins. Lush, round, rich and ready to drink–or age.
Oakville Cabernet Franc 2021 ● 370 cases; 98 $ - ⊞ - A complex weave of blueberries, herbs and cardamom on the nose with opulent blueberries on the palate.
Oakville Cabernet Sauvignon 2021 ● 4,300 cases; 98 $ - ⊞ - Scheduled for release in winter 2025.

acres 48 - cases 6,500
Fertilizers compost, cover crops
Plant protection organic
Weed control mechanical
Yeasts commercial cultured yeasts
Grapes 100% owned
Certification organic

NAPA

POTT WINES

2272 Mt Veeder Road - tel. (707) 967-9378
www.pottwine.com - claire@pottwine.com

PEOPLE - A top Napa winemaker and sought after consultant, Aaron Pott calls himself a "defrocked biodynamicist." He introduced the practices at Quintessa and Chateau La Tour Figeac, but then adapted them in non-standard ways to better suit specific properties. At harvest he and his wife Claire get help from the 14 person crew Aaron uses at the five properties he consults for. He has plans to build his own winery and open it in 2025.

VINEYARDS - The tiny estate vineyard is high up in the Mount Veeder AVA on a steep slope planted with reds that lands at a small, level area planted to Viognier. The vineyard has never seen chemicals. Nearby, Pott farms his neighbor's Lagier-Meredith's 4.5 acres, now virtually part of his estate. He makes and sprays five to eight different, herbal teas including his own concoctions with agave and kelp. He also gets grapes from client sites.

WINES - He has a unique, discernible style across the sites. The Viognier sees time in clay amphora. Reds ferment in 1.25 ton, Burgundian, open top, wood fermenters with manual punch downs. Cab Franc is a favorite.

Mount Veeder Incubo Cabernet Sauvignon 2021 TOP SLOW WINE ● 140 cases; 195 $ - ⊞ - Aged 20 months in French oak (50% new). Ripe dark fruit on the nose lead to a complex and powerful, yet relaxed, palate with more dark fruit wrapped in spicy leaves and loads of beautifully soft tannins.
Mount Veeder Space & Time Cabernet Franc Blend 2021 ● 125 cases; 195 $ - ⊞ - Fabulous Cab Franc. Full flavored and nearly full bodied. Red fruit, flowers, aromatic spice and wood with just enough of Mount Veeder's famous tannins (extremely soft, powdery).
Mount Veeder Lagier-Meredith Vineyard Syrah 2022 ● 180 cases; 90 $ - ⊞ - Classic aromas/flavors of beef, plum, blackberry, black licorice, spice and mineral. Full bodied, intense, very long. Co-fermented with 5% whole-cluster Viognier at the bottom of each vat. Wonderful stuff.

acres 5 - cases 1,200
Fertilizers compost, cover crops, manure
Plant protection sulfur, organic
Weed control none
Yeasts spontaneous fermentation
Grapes 100% owned
Certification organic

RUTHERFORD

QUINTESSA

1601 Silverado Trail S - tel. (707) 286-2730
www.quintessa.com - carly.imhof@quintessa.com

 Biodynamic practices under the guidance of biodiversity expert Olga Barbosa are guiding the redevelopment of 35 acres.

PEOPLE - Named in refence to the five elements—earth, air, fire, water and spirit (essence)—Chilean born vintners Valeria and Agustin Huneeus founded the winery in 1989, and celebrated their 35th year in 2024. Winemaker Rebekah Wineburg is now in her 10th vintage. Wineburg collaborates with consulting geologist Brenna Quigley and Chilean biodiversity and vineyards expert Olga Barbosa to learn the full potential of the pristine 280 acre estate.

VINEYARDS - The estate began biodynamic farming practices in 1996, achieved organic certification in 2019, following with biodynamic certification in 2021 during former estate director Rodrigo Soto's tenure. Longtime vineyard manager Martin Galvan makes all the biodynamic preparations. A terroir study of the property identified five terroir units that are now being managed precisely. Sheep and a herd of five cows graze the estate.

WINES - Wineburg is laser focused on terroir and adept in her well considered use of oak.

Rutherford Quintessa Bordeaux Blend 2021 ● Bordeaux Blend; 10,000 cases; 250 $ - ⊞ - Aged 22 months in new French Oak (65%), neutral oak (32%) and terracotta amphora (3%) this small vintage shows lifted floral aromas, red and black currants, well integrated oak as sous bois and star anise with notes of bay leaf and characteristic fine, resolved tannins.

---

acres 160 - cases 10,000
Fertilizers compost, biodynamic compost, cover crops, organic fertilizer
Plant protection sulfur, biodynamic preparations, organic
Weed control animal grazing, mechanical
Yeasts spontaneous fermentation
Grapes 100% owned
Certification biodynamic, organic

NAPA

ROBERT SINSKEY VINEYARDS

4059 Old Sonoma Road - tel. (707) 944-9090
www.robertsinskey.com

 A risk taker, founder Robert Marshall Sinskey, MD, was among the first wave of Pinot Noir growers in the Carneros beginning in 1986. His son Robert carries it forward.

PEOPLE - Napa's Pinot Noir powerhouse is forging a new path, making closer connections between the worlds of food and wine with its new farm and culinary programs. Vintner Rob Sinskey and his wife and chef Maria bought a farm in the Carneros (with orchards, gardens, sheep and goats) where they will host tastings. They promise that a culinary mecca is in the making.

VINEYARDS - Kari Flores oversees their four vineyards (spanning Napa and Sonoma counties) with a flock of sheep that resides on the property year-round. The sheep mow and fertilize the vineyards and prevent erosion. The winery also grow olives, fruits and nuts alongside its vines. Certified organic since 2001, the winery is one of the few in Napa that is all estate and all organic in the vines. That is especially unique in the cool climate Carneros.

WINES - Jeff Virnig has been the winemaker since 1991. Pinot Noir is the main event. Alsatians are also a standout.

Los Carneros Scintilla Sonoma Vineyard Abraxas 2019 SLOW WINE ○ 2,150 cases; 36 $ - 🍷 - A beautiful Alsatian blend that's become a Sinskey classic. It unfolds a ribbon of flavors. Riesling brings focus, Gewürztraminer texture and snap, while Pinot Blanc offers melon notes and Pinot Gris orange and peach. A floral gem. It's brilliant with food.
Los Carneros Pinot Noir 2018 ● 6,250 cases; 55 $ - ⊞ - Aged in French oak (30% new). A selection from multiple estate vineyards. Martini and Swan clones predominate. Floral aromas and flavors of cranberry, bing cherry and earth notes.
Napa Valley Marcien 2015 ● 1,340 cases; 110 $ - ⊞ - Aged two years in barrel (30% new) and nine in bottle. Complex and fruity, it beautifully integrates its Cab Franc, Cabernet Sauvignon and Merlot components, offering a palate of black cherry, plum and cassis.

---

acres 150 - cases 12,000
Fertilizers compost, cover crops
Plant protection sulfur, organic
Weed control animal grazing, mechanical
Yeasts spontaneous fermentation, commercial cultured yeasts
Grapes 100% owned
Certification organic

OAKVILLE

RUDD ESTATE

500 Oakville Crossroad - tel. (707) 944-8757
www.ruddwines.com - info@ruddwines.com

 An Oakville classic, known for its Howard Backen designed architecture, fine farming, beautiful gardens and impressive wines.

PEOPLE - Leslie Rudd bought the Oakville property in 1996 to create a multi-generational family business. After his death in 2018, his daughter Samantha, who trained at Chateaux Margaux and Spottswoode, assumed the helm. She appointed estate enologist Natalie Bath as winemaker in 2020. Oscar Henquet is the estate director. To foster greater knowledge and involvement, all employees participate in vineyard activities. Their second label is called Crossroads.

VINEYARDS - Under former vineyard director Macy Substad, the original Oakville estate was certified organic. The newer, Mount Veeder acreage is also certified organic now. The vineyard team uses biodynamic sprays and other ecofriendly practices. Rudd is switching from sheep to Wagyu cattle for weed control. The cows do less damage to the cover crop, provide better fertilizer and compact the soil less.

WINES - Fermentation and aging vessels include small oak barrels (new and neutral), concrete, stainless steel and amphorae.

TOP Mount Veeder Estate Leslie's Blend 2019 ● 250 cases; 295 $ - 🍷 - Aged in French oak (53% new). A stellar blend. Complex, intense, savory but well fruited with superbly integrated oak. Intense aromas and flavors of dark plum and berry fruit, kalamata olive, spice and dry herb. Very long finish.

Oakville Estate Red Cabernet Sauvignon 2020 ● 750 cases; 295 $ - 🍷 - Aged in French oak (45% new). A refined nose and bold palate of dusty earth, poached black and red fruit, spice, espresso and toasted wood. Full bodied with a plethora of very fine, grippy tannins.

Mount Veeder Crossroads Mountain Blend 2019 ● 200 cases; 90 $ - 🍷 - This first vintage of Crossroads Mountain is an excellent display of the soft, plush, powdery tannins Mount Veeder is known for. Generous red and black cherry, earth, dark spice, toasty oak, and espresso swaddled in thick, luxurious cashmere.

acres 63 - cases 5,000
Fertilizers compost, cover crops
Plant protection sulfur, biodynamic preparations
Weed control animal grazing, mechanical
Yeasts spontaneous fermentation
Grapes 100% owned
Certification organic

ST. HELENA

SNOWDEN VINEYARDS

490 Taplin Road - tel. (707) 963-4292
www.snowdenvineyards.com - office@snowdenvineyards.com

 For its transition away from chemicals in the vines and for its recognition of the importance of surrounding forests and biodiversity.

PEOPLE - The Snowden family owns and manages the 160 acre property the previous generation bought in 1955 as a rural retreat. Third generation Diana Snowden Seysses, the winemaker, graduated from UC Davis in 2001 and married a French vintner. Since 2003, she's been enologist at his family's winery, Domaine Dujac, in Burgundy. She took over winemaking at Snowden in 2005 and now commutes between Burgundy and Napa.

VINEYARDS - The estate is in the Vaca range, at 500+ feet between Howell Mountain and Pritchard Hill (above the Auberge du Soleil resort). It's a historic vineyard on the crest which, in 1891, had 60 planted acres. The Snowden's returned 52 previously planted acres to natural habitat. Now 137 acres are fields or forest (oak, madrone, bay and fir), preserving a balance with nature. Dujac transitioned the estate to organic farming and certification, achieved in 2024.

WINES - Aiming for a restrained style, Snowden Seysses typically picks 2-3 weeks before most of the valley. She's dialed new oak down from 75% to 30%. All reds ferment with wild yeast and are unfined.

TOP Napa Valley Brothers Vineyard Cabernet Sauvignon 2021 ● 400 cases; 110 $ - 🍷 - The flagship Cabernet. Full bodied and rich with syrupy black fruit, cassis, floral nuances, and touches of bramble and damp herb. Plenty of sophisticated yet firm tannins give the wine shape. Outstanding.

Napa Valley The Ranch Cabernet Sauvignon 2021 ● 795 cases; 70 $ - 🍷 - Wonderful black currant, blackberry jam, boysenberry, earth, black cherry and a touch of dark spice. Lithe in the mouth with velvety tannins and a juicy, mineral finish.

Napa Valley Lost Vineyard Merlot 2022 ● 208 cases; 45 $ - 🍷 - Very refined, balanced, easy to drink. Gentle tannins frame the fruit without getting in the way. Red flowers, red and black cherry, red berries, wet clay, white pepper and raw beef.

acres 23 - cases 2,500
Fertilizers compost, cover crops, organic fertilizer
Plant protection sulfur, organic
Weed control mechanical
Yeasts spontaneous fermentation, commercial cultured yeasts
Grapes 100% owned
Certification organic

ST. HELENA

SPOTTSWOODE ESTATE VINEYARD & WINERY

1902 Madrona Avenue - tel. (707) 963-0134
www.spottswoode.com - estate@spottswoode.com

PEOPLE - A Napa legend and organic pioneer, founder Mary Novak (1932-2016) began replanting the vineyard to Cabernet in 1973, launching the estate's modern era, and later passing the baton to her daughters. Beth joined in 1987 and is a respected evangelist for environmental causes. Lindy took on national marketing. Aron Weinkauf has been head winemaker since 2011. Ever ecofriendly, the winery is Napa Green certified sustainable, True Zero Waste certified and a B Corp.

VINEYARDS - The historic estate near downtown St. Helena is certified organic, regenerative organic (silver), and biodynamic. Sheep, goats, pigs and chickens are part of the estate farming program. Their new 20 acre planting in Knights Valley will include Bordeaux variety reds and Alicante Bouschet as well as Sauvignon Blanc. In Napa, they're conducting a small climate pilot growing Mediterranean varieties (Assyrtiko, Falanghina, Marselan, Touriga Nacional and more).

WINES - Harvest is timed for freshness rather than maximum ripeness. Red wines are aged mostly in French oak barrels (up to 50% new).

St. Helena Napa Valley Spottswoode Estate Cabernet Sauvignon 2021 SLOW WINE ● 3,700 cases; 285 $ - Aged 20 months in oak (62% new). The 40th vintage of this wine is intense but well mannered, lithe yet laced with firm, light grained tannins. Ripe black currant and black cherry, spice, mineral, dark chocolate and dry herb with balancing acidity. Very long finish.

Napa Valley Lyndenhurst Cabernet Sauvignon 2021 ● 2,900 cases; 110 $ - Aged 20 months in oak (new 35%). From the estate vineyard and six others. (Two are certified organic, and the others using organic practices). Blueberry, ripe black currant, dusty earth on nose and again on the palate along with blackberry, spice, dark mineral, a whisper of oak. Flavorful and textured.

acres 42 - cases 10,815
Fertilizers compost, cover crops, organic fertilizer
Plant protection biodynamic preparations, synthetic pesticides, organic
Weed control animal grazing, mechanical
Yeasts commercial cultured yeasts
Grapes purchase 50%
Certification some of the vineyards are certified organic, some of the vineyards are certified biodynamic, regenerative

RUTHERFORD

STAGLIN FAMILY VINEYARD

P.O. Box 680 - tel. (707) 963-3994
www.staglinfamily.com - info@staglinfamily.com

PEOPLE - Family owned and operated since 2005, Shannon Staglin, daughter of founders Shari and Garen, now manages the estate. It's always had a top winemaker at the helm. Director of winemaking Fredrik Johansson has been there 16 years. Michel Rolland consults. Longtime assistant winemaker Matt Peterson was promoted to head winemaker. Staglin runs on solar energy and donates all profits from its second wine, Salus, to One Mind, a brain health nonprofit.

VINEYARDS - Certified organic in 2005, the estate was planted by Andre Tchelistcheff in the 1960s with Cabernet cuttings from Beaulieu Vineyards. In addition, Staglin is one of only two Rutherford producers making estate Chardonnay. Nestled against the hills, the vineyard gets plenty of morning and midday light, but is shielded from harsh afternoon sun. This allows a longer, cooler growing season, yielding well developed tannins and complex flavors.

WINES - Rich and structured, the wines love bottle age. The second label, the more affordable Salus, is made from younger vines and ready to drink upon release.

Rutherford Estate Chardonnay 2022 ○ 400 cases; 175 $ - Aged in 10 months in French oak (42% new) and concrete egg (8%). From vines planted in 1990s. Textured, ageworthy Chardonnay. Just ripe yellow apple, lemon and cinnamon on the nose, and on the juicy palate, along with mineral and nutmeg. Excellent now, will be even better in three years.

Rutherford Estate Cabernet Sauvignon 2020 ● 1,500 cases; 325 $ - Aged 27 months in French oak (49% new). Picked pre-heat wave (and avoiding the worst of the 2020 fire). After extensive sorting and testing, they released a wine full of their typical mocha, caramel, spice, gently baked black currant, and tangy rhubarb notes on nose and palate. Extremely long with loads of soft, gently grainy velvet texture.

acres 48 - cases 3,000
Fertilizers compost, cover crops
Plant protection sulfur, copper, organic
Weed control mechanical
Yeasts spontaneous fermentation, commercial cultured yeasts
Grapes 100% owned
Certification organic

NAPA

STAGS LEAP WINE CELLARS

5766 Silverado Trail - tel. (707) 261-6427
www.stagsleapwinecellars.com - Reservations@slwc.com

PEOPLE - This iconic Napa estate, famous for its winning role in the landmark 1976 Tasting of Paris, is now solely owned by founder Warren Winiarski's friends, the Antinori family (part owners from 2007-2023). Marcus Notaro has been the winemaker since 2013, providing a consistent hand in the cellar. After selling the winery in 2007, Winiarski devoted himself to philanthropy in his retirement years—funding environmental causes in Napa—before his death in 2024.

VINEYARDS - Long time vineyard director Kirk Grace retired in 2023, leaving the vines under the care of his handpicked successor, Guillermo Perez, who Grace hired in 2020. With full support from senior management, Perez is converting all 500 acres of the Napa estate vineyards to organic certification. The first wave included 148 acres—including the estate's crown jewels, the renowned 36 acre S.L.V. and 61 acre Fay vineyards. They were Regenerative Organic Certified in November 2024.

WINES - Historically considered on par with Bordeaux's classed growths, balanced oak integration creates structured, ageworthy, classic wines.

TOP Stags Leap District Fay Vineyard Cabernet Sauvignon 2021 SLOW WINE ● 3,178 cases; 200 $ - 🍷 - Aged 21 months French oak (85% new). A site with a fabled history, it was the first planting of Cab in the now famed Stags Leap District. A blend of Cabernet Sauvignon (98%) and Cabernet Franc (2%) with floral and anise aromas, dark cherry fruit and boysenberry.

Stags Leap District SLV Cabernet Sauvignon 2021 ● 2,310 cases; 250 $ - 🍷 - Aged 21 months in French oak (100% new). Aromas of dark red and black currants with boysenberries, blackberries and cassis.

Stags Leap District Cask Cabernet Sauvignon 2021 ● 1,900 cases; 325 $ - 🍷 - Aged 22 months in French oak (100% new). A best barrels selection from the volcanic soils at both Fay and S.L.V. vineyards. Fay's aromas coupled with SLV's structure and dark fruit. Black and blue fruits lead to a richly flavored midpalate.

acres 253 - cases 120,000
Fertilizers compost, cover crops, organic fertilizer, synthetic fertilizer
Plant protection sulfur, synthetic pesticides, organic
Weed control mechanical
Yeasts spontaneous fermentation, selected indigenous yeasts
Grapes purchase 40%
Certification some of the vineyards are certified organic, regenerative, converting to organic

ST. HELENA

VOLKER EISELE FAMILY ESTATE

3080 Lower Chiles Valley Road - tel. (707) 965-9485
www.volkereiselefamilyestate.com - info@volkereiselefamilyestate.com

 In an upgraded tasting setting, this green leader beautifully preserves its history and showcases its exceptional, organically grown wines and legacy.

PEOPLE - Celebrating the 50th anniversary of the estate, Alexander, winegrower and his wife Catherine Eisele, marketing director, carry forward the family run winery established by his parents, German born Volker (1937-2015) and Liesel Eisele. The older couple bought the land in 1974 and raised their family there. Growers first, they then became vintners. Molly Lippitt's made the wines since 2014. Volker is revered for his political leadership in protecting Napa's agricultural land from development.

VINEYARDS - Organically farmed for 50 years (and certified since 1997), the estate is at 900-1,100 feet in the rural Chiles Valley, making it significantly cooler than the Napa valley floor and promoting a longer growing season. Led by father and son Jose and Pedro Nevarez, the dedicated, six person vineyard crew is full time.

WINES - Bringing her experience from working with legends Julien Fayard, Philipe Melka, and Heidi Barrett, Lippitt deftly showcases the site's inherent balance of fruity and savory characters.

TOP Napa Valley Las Flores Cabernet Sauvignon 2018 SLOW WINE ● 100 cases; 90 $ - 🍷 - Aged 22 months in French oak (55% new). A unique single block, where the crew noticed that the mustard blooms more brightly. Juicy red and black fruit (cherry, currants) and cassis. Robust, textured tannins and great length. Sumptuous, ageworthy and exceptional.

Napa Valley Terzetto 2019 ● 240 cases; 90 $ - 🍷 - Aged 22 months in French oak (60% new). Catherine aptly describes this as "German engineering," because Volker wanted to show off, as a grower, that he could grow and ripen (simultaneously) equal parts of Cabernet Franc, Cabernet Sauvignon and Merlot to co-ferment them. Full bodied with flavors of red plum, red and black currant, red cherry and hints of creamy oak and spice.

acres 60 - cases 5,000
Fertilizers compost, cover crops
Plant protection sulfur, organic
Weed control mechanical
Yeasts commercial cultured yeasts
Grapes 100% owned
Certification organic

NAPA

ZD WINES

8383 Silverado Trail - tel. (707) 963-5188
www.zdwines.com - info@zdwines.com

 The winery buys grapes only from certified organic growers, setting a precedent—and improving wine quality.

PEOPLE - Third generation family winemaker Brandon deLeuze celebrates his 20th vintage this year at one of Napa Valley's pioneering wineries founded in 1969. DeLeuze works with cellar master Greg Chouinard who has made the last eight vintages and senior winemaker Chris Pisani. Winery chef Jill deLeuze Billeci works with produce from the culinary garden for the tasting room's pairing menus.

VINEYARDS - The winery transitioned its growers to organic certification in 2018, a commitment that was 20 years in the making. A third of ZD's total grape sourcing comes from estate vineyards—3.2-acres in Rutherford planted to Cabernet Sauvignon and 15 acres of Chardonnay (replanted to Wood clone) and 14 acres of Pinot Noir (667 and Hanzell) in the Carneros. They are solar powered and use owl boxes and goats. Both estate vineyards have been certified organic since 1999.

WINES - ZD's Chardonnay style, one that forgoes ML and relies on long, cool barrel fermentation, was perfected in the early '70s and prevails. The reds are increasingly complex and savory.

Napa Valley Cabernet Sauvignon 2022 SLOW WINE
6,100 cases; 78 $ - Aged in American oak (15% new). Black raspberry, red currant and sous bois building to an expansive midpalate of red and black fruits, mulberry, dark chocolate and pretty spice that lift through the finish.

Napa Valley Sauvignon Blanc 2023 O 1,900 cases; 37 $ - A complex aging regime of American Oak barrels (48%), stainless steel barrels (33%) and concrete tanks (19%). Fresh nectarine, green apple and ripe lemon aromas with perfect weight in the mouth and waves of peaches and ripe citrus.

California Chardonnay 2023 O 18,000 cases; 44 $ - Aged 10 months in American oak. Barrel fermented. This multiple AVA wine has lush flavors of tropical fruit compote and rich notes of vanilla and creme brulee.

---

acres 34 - cases 30,000
Fertilizers compost, cover crops
Plant protection sulfur, organic
Weed control animal grazing, mechanical
Yeasts commercial cultured yeasts
Grapes purchase 75%
Certification organic

NORTH COAST
SONOMA

🐌 Snail

48 Á Deux Têtes
49 Acaibo
52 Canihan Wines
56 DaVero Farms & Winery
64 Kamen Estate Wines
64 Lasseter Family Winery
67 Moon Hollow
69 Porter Creek Vineyards
69 Preston Farm & Winery
74 Small Vines
74 Stone Edge Farm
78 Winery Sixteen 600

🍾 Bottle

51 Bedrock Wine Co.
54 Cormorant Cellars
55 Dane Cellars
56 Darling Wines
57 DuMOL
58 Enfield Wine Co.
58 Ernest Vineyards
59 Far Mountain
63 Jolie-Laide Wines
68 Pax Wines
70 Quivira Vineyards
71 Ram's Gate Winery
72 Read Holland
75 Surveyor
76 Under the Wire

$ Coin

52 Birdhorse
53 Carol Shelton Wines
55 County Line Vineyards
61 Guthrie Family Wines
61 Horse & Plow

SANTA ROSA

ACCENTI WINES

1160 Hopper Ave #B - tel. (707) 339-1491
www.accentiwines.com - info@accentiwines.com

PEOPLE - Established in 2018, Accenti Wines is a collaboration between James and Lorenza Allen. The two met while studying winemaking in France. James, born in Missouri, and Lorenza, born in Alba, Italy, draw on their shared and different experiences to make wine. They have started exploring Albariño and, after making rosé from Grenache, they have started making a red wine from Grenache.

VINEYARDS - James and Lorenza farm three little vineyards around Napa Valley, which they call Three Gardens. Grenache comes from The Doctor Vineyard in Alexander Valley. Three acres grow nine year old head trained Grenache with a little Viognier, Syrah, and Mourvedre (which they co-ferment). Verdelho comes from Contra Costa, Merlot from Sonoma, and Carignan from Mendocino in the Redwood Valley.

WINES - Their winemaking goal is to produce food friendly wines that are fresh, vibrant, fruit forward and with moderate alcohol.

⊙ California The Red Herring 2023 EVERYDAY WINE ⊙ 88 cases; 30 $ - ⊞ - Aged in neutral oak. Verdelho juice fermented on the skins of freshly pressed Grenache (90%), Syrah, Mourvèdre, and Viognier. A very unique, crushable, fresh, mineral driven red wine. A bright cherry red color with aromas of both a white wine and a red wine.
Napa Valley Three Gardens Cabernet Sauvignon 2021 ⊙ 135 cases; 64 $ - ⊙ - Picked on early side. 25% whole cluster. Foot tread and punch down, then fermented in tank and aged in neutral barrel. A savory nose with dark red and black fruits mixed with leather, tar, and sweet spice. Medium bodied with textured tannins and juicy acidity.
California Orange Flamingo Verdelho 2023 ⊙ 70 cases; 29 $ - ⊞ - Notes of white peach and chamomile flowers and round on the palate with a soft texture that leaves your mouth watering.

acres 6 - cases 1,000
Fertilizers compost, cover crops, organic fertilizer
Plant protection sulfur
Weed control mechanical
Yeasts spontaneous fermentation
Grapes purchase 60%
Certification some of the vineyards are certified organic

SONOMA

Á DEUX TÊTES

589 1st Street - tel. (707) 721-1805
www.winerysixteen600.com - info@winerysixteen600.com

 A magnificent Franco-American collaboration, with legendary partners operating at the height of their powers, yielding great wines.

PEOPLE - The name means two heads are better than one. The label is the love child of renowned organic vineyard manager Phil Coturri and the now late Rhone winemaking consultant Philippe Cambie (who was much mourned when he died in 2021). The two Grenache geeks succeeded in their quest to show the heights northern California Grenache could achieve. Rhone based Isabel Gassier, who assisted Cambie, now carries on the winemaking with Phil's son, Sam Coturri.

VINEYARDS - Coturri's crusaded for Grenache in northern California for years, sourcing for this label from renowned vineyards (all certified organic) that he farms on both sides of the Mayacamas. The historic Rossi Ranch (nicknamed "To Kalon for Grenache") in Sonoma Valley has light volcanic ash and obsidian shards. (Over decades, Coturri has restored this historic site.) He also planted a few rows of Grenache at Oakville Ranch, in Napa's Vaca Mountains (on red, volcanic soils).

WINES - Gassier and Coturri use extended maceration, pushing extraction to the edge, to create balanced, complex, ageworthy wines with depth and concentration.

⊙ TOP Oakville Oakville Ranch Grenache 2021 SLOW WINE ⊙ 500 cases; 105 $ - ⊞ - Mourvedre's in the blend. It has a cherry red rim and stunning cherry and red fruit notes, the distinctive licorice note, and impressive depth and concentration.
Sonoma Valley Rossi Ranch Grenache 2021 ⊙ 500 cases; 105 $ - ⊞ - Grown on the cooler of the two sites, it's more austere than its Napa mountain grown sibling. Rimmed with garnet edges, it offers ethereal cherry and spice notes, along with the characteristic Cambie licorice note and a long finish.
Sonoma Valley Rosé 2022 ⊙ 60 cases; 59 $ - ⊞ - A perennial favorite. Not your ordinary California rosé, it's filled with ribbons of flavors that unfold. Nuanced and complex. An intensely aromatic nose and great balance of fruit and acidity. Swoonworthy.

acres n/a - cases 1,000
Fertilizers compost, cover crops
Plant protection sulfur, organic
Weed control animal grazing, mechanical
Yeasts spontaneous fermentation
Grapes 100% owned
Certification organic

GLEN ELLEN

ABBOT'S PASSAGE

777 Madrone Road - tel. (707) 939-3017
www.abbotspassage.com - info@abbotspassage.com

PEOPLE - Katie Bundschu, sixth generation member of a prominent wine family, is the first in her family to make wine in Glen Ellen, over the hill from her family's Gundlach Bundschu Rhinefarm (founded in 1858). She started Abbot's Passage in 2015 to do her own thing, and in 2020, the family purchased the historic Valley of the Moon winery as her base. The new setting, best described as farmhouse chic, is both casual and elegant.

VINEYARDS - The estate's majestic, head trained old vines (planted in 1940), surrounding the tasting room, are a highlight. They were certified regenerative organic in 2023. Some were grafted over to Carignane, Mourvedre and Petite Sirah to make this a more complex field blend. The team also buys grapes from Steel Plow and Cassata (both certified organic) in Sonoma Valley as well as other growers.

WINES - Co-fermentation is a stylistic hallmark. Winemaker Joe Uhy co-ferments the wines in neutral oak, using partial whole cluster for some to add texture and complexity. They also have a new sparkling wine.

TOP **Sonoma Valley Redshift Rosé 2022** SLOWWINE ● 548 cases; 28 $ - 🍷 - From the old vines Zinfandel on the estate. Aromatic and crisp, its novel red berry flavors shine on the midpalate and finish. Distinctive.
Sonoma Valley Points Unknown Red Rhone Blend 2021 ● 345 cases; 65 $ - ⊞ - From the Steel Plow vineyard. The blend is Grenache (57%), Mourvedre (22%) and Syrah (21%). Find cranberry and red fruits with spice on the palate. Low to medium tannins let the fruit lead.
Sonoma Valley Estate Vineyard Makeshift Red Blend 2021 ● 448 cases; 45 $ - ⊞ - Their best seller. Partial whole cluster on the Zin (20%). A unique estate blend of their old vine, estate Zinfandel (62%), Petite Sirah (23%) and the Portuguese grape Souzao (15%). Red fruits predominate, with an underlying bass note of dark fruits from the Petite Sirah.

acres 40 - cases 5,000
Fertilizers compost, cover crops, organic fertilizer, synthetic fertilizer
Plant protection sulfur, synthetic pesticides, organic
Weed control mechanical
Yeasts spontaneous fermentation, commercial cultured yeasts
Grapes purchase 70%
Certification some of the vineyards are certified organic

HEALDSBURG

ACAIBO

10603 Chalk Hill Road - tel. (707) 791-0943
www.acaibo.com - pascal@acaibo.com

 The Lurtons are part of a growing French colony of leading organic producers from the Bordeaux who are creating top quality Sonoma wines that deliver excellent value.

PEOPLE - Organic and biodynamic pioneers in Bordeaux, Claire Villars-Lurton and Gonzague Lurton built their Sonoma winery in 2014. Each had previously inherited and run family estates in Bordeaux–three in Margaux (Chateau Durfort-Vivens, Chateau Ferriere, and Chateau Gurgue) and one in Pauillac (Chateau Haut-Bages Liberal). Nicolas Vonderheyden is the technical director with Éric Boissenot as winemaking consultant. Pascal Guerlou manages the winery and sales for GC Lurton Estates USA.

VINEYARDS - The Lurtons' Trinité Estate is in the Chalk Hill AVA, between the cool Russian River at the west, the warm Alexander Valley at the northeast and Knights Valley. The vines grow in a natural amphitheater. Twelves acres were grafted over to Bordeaux varieties. The vines were planted in 1998 and grow at 750 feet elevation on hillsides and varied microclimates on clay loam and compacted ash soils.

WINES - The wines are made in a style described as a correct meeting of California and Bordeaux with marked freshness and plush tannins.

TOP **Sonoma County Bordeaux Blend Acaibo 2017** SLOWWINE ● 1,100 cases; 80 $ - ⊞ - Aged 16 months in French oak (65% new). A blend of Cabernet Sauvignon (75%), Merlot (13%) and Cabernet Franc (12%). Their winery's premier cru, it's a selection of the best blocks. On the palate, black currant, black cherries, tobacco and cloves wrapped in supple, generous tannins.
Sonoma County Bordeaux Blend Amaino 2017 ● 400 cases; 60 $ - - A Merlot dominant blend composed of Merlot (63%), Cabernet Sauvignon (29%), and Petite Sirah (8%). Plums, dark cherries, and ripe red fruit with silky tannins and a long finish.
Sonoma County Merlot 2019 ● 50 cases; 45 $ - - Ages 15 months in French oak (10% new). Blackberries, dark cherries, cocoa on the nose and palate with silky tannins. Well balanced.

acres 24 - cases 1,300
Fertilizers compost, biodynamic compost, cover crops, organic fertilizer
Plant protection sulfur, biodynamic preparations, organic
Weed control mechanical
Yeasts spontaneous fermentation
Grapes 100% owned
Certification none

NAPA

ADASTRA

2545 Las Amigas Road - tel. (707) 255-4818
www.adastrawines.com - info@adastrawines.com

PEOPLE - Owners Chris and Naomi Thorpe established their Carneros estate vineyard in 1984. Their son in law, Edwin Richards, became GM in 1995. That was also the first vintage of Adastra's own branded wines, then made by celebrated winemaker Pam Starr. Edwin took over winemaking in 2016. The majority of Adastra's sales are direct to consumer, especially through their wine club.

VINEYARDS - Farmed organically since 2002, the 33 acre ranch was certified in 2005. It is also certified Napa Green. The wines, all estate, are from four clones of Merlot, five of Chardonnay, six of Pinot Noir and a single clone of Syrah. Due to drought, yields were low in 2021 and 2022. 2023 saw a return to normalcy. Re-seeding of their cover crop began in 2024.

WINES - Adastra wines reflect their source in the Napa Valley side of Carneros with rich, flavorful and rounded takes on cool climate varieties, such as Chardonnay, Pinot Noir and Syrah.
Los Carneros Chardonnay 2022 ○ 70 cases; 44 $ - ⊞ - Fermented and aged 16 months in French oak (37% new). Full bodied and creamy with very fine, silky texture. Just ripe yellow apple, mineral, spice, and poached pear lightly coated in butter and caramel, accented by oak.
Los Carneros Pinot Noir 2022 ● 81 cases; 52 $ - ⊞ - Aged 15 months in French oak (66% new). Supple and soft with full body and very fine grained texture on the warm palate. Generous aromas and flavors of gently poached strawberry, raspberry, red cherry, sandalwood, spice, dried herb, toasty wood and dark mineral.
Los Carneros Syrah 2022 ● 125 cases; 52 $ - ⊞ - Rich, full-bodied Syrah with dense plum and black cherry, earth, black pepper and dried thyme. Lightly grippy texture. 15 months in 50% new French oak

acres 12 - cases 1,100
Fertilizers organic fertilizer
Plant protection organic
Weed control mechanical
Yeasts spontaneous fermentation, commercial cultured yeasts
Grapes 100% owned
Certification organic

HEALDSBURG

AMISTA VINEYARDS

3320 Dry Creek Road - tel. (707) 431-9200
www.amistavineyards.com/ - info@amistavineyards.com

PEOPLE - Former chemist Michael Farrow (1943-2023) fell in love with winemaking in the mid 1990's, at first making it in his garage. In 1999, he and his wife Vicky bought their Dry Creek Valley dream property. Mike was the first winemaker. They hired Ashley Herzberg in 2011 to the role of head winemaker. She persuaded them to move to organic farming, transitioning with their vineyard manager, Paco Mendoza. Slow Wine enthusiast Brian Shapiro is the estate director.

VINEYARDS - Amidst a sea of neighbors growing Zinfandel, the property was once planted entirely to Chardonnay (Wente and Dijon clones). The winery was a leader in a Dry Creek restoration project started in 2015, helping to create spawning habitat to support endangered trout and salmon. Solar panels over their tasting room's outdoor terrace provide power. The vines were certified organic in 2024.

WINES - Devoted to Rhones and sparkling wines (and sometimes a combination of both), Herzberg makes both still and traditional method sparkling wines.
Dry Creek Valley Blanc de Blanc 2022 ⊛ 458 cases; 50 $ - ⎔ - A crisp and refreshing Brut with a kiss of lemon on the palate. Caseworthy. One of the only organically grown Blanc de Blancs in California.
Dry Creek Valley Rosé Sparkling Syrah 2021 ❋ 386 cases; 58 $ - ⎔ - Brut Nature. Dried strawberries on the nose open to red currants and berries on the palate in a delicious fizz. Zero dosage.
Dry Creek Valley Tres GSM Red Rhone Blend 2022 ● 279 cases; 55 $ - ⊞ - Aged 10 months in neutral oak. The blend is equal parts Grenache, Syrah and Mourvedre, with the Mourvedre adding a bass note to the symphony of spice, black cherry and red fruit. Well integrated.

acres 21 - cases 3,000
Fertilizers compost, cover crops
Plant protection sulfur, organic
Weed control mechanical, manual
Yeasts spontaneous fermentation, commercial cultured yeasts
Grapes 100% owned
Certification organic

SONOMA

BEDROCK WINE CO.

414 1st Street E - tel. (707) 364-8763
www.bedrockwineco.com - chris@bedrockwineco.com

PEOPLE - Winemakers and proprietors Morgan Twain Peterson MW (Master of Wine) and Chris Cottrell are dedicated to preserving, promoting and enjoying old vine wines. They focus on head trained, dry farmed, legacy vineyards. Morgan is descended from Zin royalty–his father Joel famously started Ravenswood. On Bedrock's podcast Chris and Morgan talk about the vineyards they work with, providing the inside story on the wines they make.

VINEYARDS - They buy grapes from 25 growers spanning from Mendocino in the north, the Sierra foothills on the east, and the Santa Maria Valley in the south. In addition, the Petersons own the historic, 111 acre Bedrock vineyard (organic certified; regenerative certification in process) on the valley floor in Glen Ellen. In Lodi, the farm the 10 acre Kathusha vineyard and own or lease the historic Evangelo vineyard. Note: Some wines (not featured here) are grown with herbicide.

WINES - Transparency is the goal. No fancy footwork, just minimal intervention. They also make sparkling wine under their other label, Under the Wire.

TOP Contra Costa Evangelho Heritage Blend 2022
SLOW WINE ● 500 cases; 45 $ - 🍷 - A field blend of Zinfandel, Carignan, Mataro (Mourvedre), and a few others planted in 1890s on the famous Delhi sands that define the Sacramento River delta area. Delicate cherries. Food friendly.
Sonoma Valley The Bedrock Heritage Red 2022 ● 750 cases; 48 $ - 🍷 - The flagship wine–they call it their O.G.– comes from 33 acres of vines first planted in 1888. The field blend (of 30 different varieties) grows on red, cobbly soils in the historic Sonoma Valley Bedrock vineyard. Bright, light. Red fruits. A classic.
Sonoma Valley Ode to Lucien Mourvèdre Blend 2021 ● 150 cases; 46 $ - 🍷 - Aged in a combination of Stockinger foudre and 600-liter demi-muids. Almost entirely from 1880s plantings the home ranch. 40% whole cluster. Very dialed back and lightweight. Dark cherries. Dark black fruits on the midpalate.

acres 151 - cases 5,700
Fertilizers compost, cover crops, organic fertilizer, synthetic fertilizer
Plant protection sulfur, synthetic pesticides, organic
Weed control mechanical
Yeasts spontaneous fermentation
Grapes purchase 80%
Certification some of the vineyards are certified organic

GLEN ELLEN

BENZIGER FAMILY WINERY

1883 London Ranch Road - tel. (707) 935-3000
www.benziger.com - buywine@benziger.com

PEOPLE - Benziger was the first winery in Sonoma County to produce a certified Biodynamic wine, in 2001. Now in its forty third year, it has 24 years of biodynamic certification to its credit. Winemaker Lisa Amaroli, who has been making wine for over 25 vintages, admits to having a soft spot for their Sonoma coast vineyards which produce biodynamic Pinot Noir and Chardonnay.

VINEYARDS - Vineyard manager Jerry Mackling oversees the estate vines which provide eight percent of the fruit. They are dry farmed. The team is adept at spotting symptomatic vines and taking preemptive measures to maintain balance. The estate has insectaries that act as "insect superhighways," radiating throughout the vineyard to keep pests under control. They also rotate their resident flock of sheep until bud break to manage weeds. (Some of the wines, not featured here, may be grown with herbicide.)

WINES - Amaroli believes that a gentle hand is required when natural fermentation is used and relies on early picking decisions for freshness.

TOP Sonoma Mountain Obsidian Point Cabernet Sauvignon 2021 ● 405 cases; 83 $ - 🍷 - From the mountain's volcanic soils. Showing aromas of black fruit, violet and rich cocoa moving to blackberry and pomegranate with tannins building through the finish.
Sonoma Mountain Paradiso de Maria Sauvignon Blanc 2023 ○ 364 cases; 43 $ - 🥂 - Whole cluster pressed with a small percentage fermented in French oak. Notes of grapefruit followed by a melange of citrus flavors showing Meyer lemon and lime zest which keep the finish lively.
Sonoma Valley Tribute Bordeaux Blend 2021 ● 1,149 cases; 100 $ - 🍷 - A blend of Cabernet Sauvignon (63%), Cabernet Franc (12%), Merlot (10%), Malbec (10%), and Petit Verdot (5%). Aromas of sweet earth and marionberries. Black cherries, plum, clove and milk chocolate coat fine, layered tannins. Balanced and ageworthy.

acres 85 - cases 137,000
Fertilizers compost, biodynamic compost, cover crops
Plant protection sulfur, biodynamic preparations, synthetic pesticides
Weed control animal grazing, mechanical
Yeasts spontaneous fermentation, commercial cultured yeasts
Grapes purchase 92%
Certification biodynamic, organic, some of the vineyards are certified organic, some of the vineyards are certified biodynamic

VINEBURG

BIRDHORSE $

P.O. Box 28 - tel. (707) 532-4231
www.birdhorsewines.com - birdhorsewines@gmail.com

PEOPLE - Corinne Rich and Katie Rouse met at U.C. Davis when they were both getting master's degrees in viticulture. Following a harvest in South Africa, they created their wine label in 2019. They make classically styled wines, showcasing lesser known regions and varieties. They have grown production this year, purchased their first concrete egg and gotten married. They also support the queer community with a fundraiser wine.

VINEYARDS - Birdhorse works with eight vineyard sites all around the state, seeking out lesser known regions and growers who use little to no synthetic chemicals in the vineyards, thus aligning with Birdhouse's mission and beliefs. They are hyper selective and try to have long term relationships with all of their growers. Both The Bench in Lodi and the Poor Ranch in Mendocino are certified organic.

WINES - The Birdhorse ethos is that terroir expression should not be limited to only well known varieties.

Contra Costa County Verdelho 2023 ○ 250 cases; 27 $ - ⓦ - Last vintage from this site. More rainfall in 2023 led to better balance in the vines, achieving their ideal ripeness. Bright tropical, green leaf and pear aromas, with a lush, long lasting palate full of salinity and citrus.

Clements Hills Vermentino 2023 ○ 100 cases; 28 $ - ⓦ - Ripeness from sunshine and an ethereal lightness from the sandy soil. The winemaking is kept simple, resulting in a bright, crystalline hued wine with aromas of white peach and lime. Crisp flavors of juicy citrus, tart green apple and lots of varietal character.

Mendocino County Carignan 2022 ● 60 cases; 32 $ - ⓦ - Dusty red soils lead to concentration and fruit power. Partial whole cluster (30%) Light bodied with aromas of iron, violet, paprika. Fruit forward with flavors of cranberry, cocoa powder and violet pastille candy.

acres 0 - cases 1,000
Fertilizers compost, biodynamic compost, cover crops, organic fertilizer
Plant protection sulfur, organic
Weed control animal grazing, mechanical
Yeasts spontaneous fermentation
Grapes purchase 100%
Certification some of the vineyards are certified organic

SONOMA

CANIHAN WINES

1340 Napa Road - tel. (415) 990-9270
www.canihanwines.com - bill@canihanwines.com

 A dedicated, small family owned operation making organically grown wines for 25 years in Sonoma on the valley floor near the Carneros.

PEOPLE - Winemaker Bill Canihan's estate and label are a tribute to his Swiss born grandfather's dream of having a winery in California. Canihan's father, Bill Canihan Sr., bought the 20 acre property in 1973 from a Basque farmer, planting its first vines in 1998. Tastings take place in an historic barn on the vineyard site–a very authentic setting that is uncommon these days.

VINEYARDS - Dry farmed, the vineyard sit on the flats in Sonoma Valley bordering the cool Carneros region. The vines are a field blend of four Pinot Noir Dijon clones–115, 667, 777 and 828–along with 2A, Masson, Pommard, Swan, and Wadenswil, bringing clonal variety to the wines. Rafael Oseguera manages the vines.

WINES - Handcrafted with minimal intervention. In the works: a Blanc de Noir, their first sparkling wine.

Sonoma Coast Pinot Noir 2018 ● 228 cases; 70 $ - ⓦ - Aged 16 months in French oak (22% new). Cold soaked for five days. Aromas of cherries, rose and strawberries followed by the same on the palate. From an exceptional vintage.

Sonoma Coast Pinot Noir 2019 ● 252 cases; 55 $ - ⓦ - Aged 16 months in French oak (30% new). From eight clones. Layers of rose, Bing cherries, ripe blackberries with dried violet and Earl Gray tea notes.

Sonoma Coast Exuberance Syrah 2018 ● 300 cases; 70 $ - ⓦ - Cofermented with Viognier (4%). Aged 16 months in French oak (25% new). Red fruits, plums and hay scents on the nose. On the palate, black cherries, red fruits, and herbaceous notes.

acres 15 - cases 1,500
Fertilizers compost, cover crops
Plant protection sulfur, organic
Weed control mechanical
Yeasts spontaneous fermentation
Grapes 100% owned
Certification organic

SANTA ROSA

CAROL SHELTON WINES $

3354-B Coffey Lane - tel. (707) 575-3441
www.carolsheltonwines.com - info@carolshelton.com

PEOPLE - A renowned winemaker known for ZinZ fandel, pioneering Carol Shelton established her own winery in 2000. A 1978 graduate of U.C. Davis in viticulture and winemaking, she made wine for 17 years before starting the winery with her husband and business partner Mitch Mackenzie. After surviving fires that burned her house and some vineyards she buys from, she carries on and is part of the renaissance celebrating old vines with the Historic Vineyard Society.

VINEYARDS - Shelton works with 14 vineyards. Two are historic and certified organic. The Wild Thing Zin—half of her production—come from 65 year old vines at Cox Vineyard in Mendocino. 2020 is the last vintage made. (The owner died). Shelton has been a consistent purchaser of grapes from the 106 year old José Lopez Vineyard (inland from LA), where 18 inch high, dry farmed, bush vines grow in pure sand. Some wine (not featured here) may be grown with herbicide.

WINES - Shelton buys many grapes from historic sites, keeping precious old vines in the ground and showcasing their delicate flavors.

⊙ Cucamonga Valley Lopez Vineyard Monga Zin 2021 SLOW WINE ● 914 cases; 28 $ - ⊞ - Aged in American oak barrels (10% new). The blend is Zinfandel (95%), with a dollop of Touriga Nacional and Rose of Peru (Mission). A creamy mouthful of deep black cherry fruit, berries and bright cherry with a long, lush finish. Super concentrated. Three days of cold soak, 10 days on skins, A classic.

Mendocino County Cox Vineyard Wild Thing Old Vine Zinfandel 2020 ● 8,000 cases; 20 $ - ⊞ - Last call, vineyard sold. Blend: Zinfandel (76%), Carignane (10%), Petite Sirah (9%), and mixed reds (Malbec, Grenache Noir, Cab+). Also available in half bottles. ($13). Labeled: Ingredients: Organic Grapes. A four day cold soak and a 23 day maceration bring out the complex, jammy fruit and mouth coating flavors: black cherry, ripe plum and raspberry.

acres 0 - cases 15,000
Fertilizers compost, cover crops, manure, organic fertilizer, synthetic fertilizer
Plant protection sulfur, synthetic pesticides, copper
Weed control animal grazing, mechanical
Yeasts spontaneous fermentation, commercial cultured yeasts
Grapes purchase 100%
Certification some of the vineyards are certified organic

SANTA ROSA

CARY Q WINES

1160 Hopper Ave. #B - tel. (305) 586-6666
www.caryqwines.com - cary@caryqwines.com

PEOPLE - Now in her 11th vintage, Miami native Cary Quintana is an Hispanic winemaker of Cuban heritage. Quintana cut her teeth working in Berkeley's Gilman District, a natural wine enclave. After excelling at co-ferments and blends, she's turned her focus to single varieties. Hyper environmentally conscious, she uses a minimalistic approach and sources from iconic vineyards. Aging vessels will vary according to vintage.

VINEYARDS - In 2023 Quintana began working with Fenaughty Vineyards which is known for its elegant acidity. In the Sierra Foothills, at 2,700 feet, the site is composed of Aiken Volcanic clay loam farmed by Chuck Mansfield of Goldbud Farms in El Dorado. She buys Mourvedre from Shake Ridge Ranch which has a mix of volcanic soils including quartz, basalt, shale and soapstone at 1,750 feet in Amador County. Other grapes come from a certified organic site (Terra Alta) in Lodi's Clements Hill.

WINES - Quintana's style shows freshness and a vibrancy that's undeniable. Her wines were featured in the Shake Ridge Ranch tasting for the inaugural Terra Madre Americas masterclasses in 2024.

Amador County Shake Ridge Ranch Hollis Mourvedre 2022 ● 75 cases; 38 $ - ⊙ - Aged in in neutral French oak. Partial whole cluster (25%). Picked early for freshness and showing floral aromatics of violet and lavender with savory dark berries and making it ideal for gastronomic pairings.

⊙ El Dorado County Fenaughty Vineyards ViBES! Picpoul 2023 EVERYDAY WINE ○ 100 cases; 28 $ - ⌑ - Direct press releases zippy citrus and golden apple aromatics and flavors of honeysuckle, bright lemon and saline mineral around a structure so characteristic of this variety.

acres 0 - cases 175
Fertilizers compost, cover crops
Plant protection sulfur, organic
Weed control mechanical
Yeasts spontaneous fermentation
Grapes purchase 100%
Certification organic

HEALDSBURG

COMUNITÁ

2201 Westside Road - tel. (707) 433-2222
www.comunitawines.com - info@comunitawines.com

PEOPLE - Comunitá means "community" in Italian, a community started by David Drummond and winemaker Sam Bilbro to celebrate their love affair with wines of northeast Italy. After a career in Silicon Valley as a Google senior attorney, Drummond retired at 61 and purchased a 500 acre ranch in 2018. Launched in 2024, the brand has five wines inspired by Alto Adige and Friuli, including a ramato style Pinot Grigio, Refosco, Schioppettino, and two blends.

VINEYARDS - In the 1990s and early 2000's, previous owners planted Cabernet Sauvignon, Pinot Noir and Zinfandel on the site. Under the new leadership, the team grafted 46 Italian grape varieties to the vines, mostly from northern Italy. In 2020, they began using only organic approved materials and regenerative practices, including permanent cover crops, sheep grazing in spring and crimping instead of tilling. They also planted four insectary hedge rows to attract beneficial insects.

WINES - Marrying Italian grape varieties to California's climate, Drummond says, "...tradition is simply an experiment that worked."

⦿ **Russian River Valley Las Cimas Vineyard Refosco 2022** ● 100 cases; 45 $ - 🍷 - Aged 11 months in neutral puncheon. Whole cluster, lightly foot tread. Violets, forest floor, and ripe red and black fruit aromas, with grippy, drying tannins and waves of bold acidity.

Russian River Valley Las Cimas Vineyard Monte Regio 2022 ○ 100 cases; 45 $ - 🍷 - Monte Regio is Italian for Monterey where David Drummond grew up. The blend is Ribolla Gialla (34%), Riesling (34%), Friulano (23%), and Malvasia Bianca (9%). A wine that is fresh and mineral with salty floral aromas, a waxy midpalate, and textured acidity.

Russian River Valley Las Cimas Vineyard Pinot Grigio 2023 ◉ 100 cases; 35 $ - 🍷 - The wine is a blood orange color and has notes of blood orange and stemmed roses. Light and fresh with a persistent midpalate weight.

acres 70 - cases 500
Fertilizers compost, cover crops, manure, organic fertilizer
Plant protection sulfur, organic
Weed control animal grazing, mechanical, manual
Yeasts spontaneous fermentation
Grapes 100% owned
Certification none

WINDSOR

CORMORANT CELLARS

1200 American Way - tel. (707) 836-3730
www.cormorantcellars.com - info@cormorantcellars.com

PEOPLE - U.C. Davis educated winemaker Charles Gilmore has made wine for big name companies—including C. K. Mondavi and Fetzer—for decades, honing his skills. His own label, launched in 2018, is where he gets to play, experiment and perfect his techniques. He's drawn to Sauvignon Blanc and whites in general—four out of his six current releases are whites—but his newly released reds are impressive. He leans in on authenticity in both grapes and winemaking.

VINEYARDS - Gilmore seeks out top growers and chooses to work only with organically grown grapes. Three of his five vineyard sources are certified organic–Martorana and Preston Vineyards in nearby Dry Creek Valley and Zabala in Arroyo Seco. His other growers–Fenaughty Vineyard in El Dorado County and Black Ridge Vineyard in the Santa Cruz Mountains–use only organic approved materials.

WINES - Classic, hands off winemaking showcases fruit purity. That means minimal intervention, minimal oak and great attention paid to the getting growers with the best fruit.

⦿ **Santa Cruz Mountains Black Ridge Vineyard Red Wine 2021** ● n.a.; 47 $ - 🍷 - Aged in neutral oak. A blend of Merlot (72%), Cabernet Sauvignon (24%) and Petit Verdot (4%). Black cherry and plum made more complex by the blend. No added sulfites. Elegant, balanced and extremely well priced.

Arroyo Seco Zabala Vineyard Gamay Noir 2023 ● n.a.; 33 $ - 🍷 - Partial whole cluster (20%). Light bodied. Red cherry, black raspberry, cherry pie flavors. Balance and freshness. A wine that makes you want another glass.

El Dorado Fenaughty Vineyard Vermentino 2023 ○ 70 cases; 28 $ - 🍷 - Whole cluster, barrel fermented, neutral oak. From grapes grown by a legendary grower, Ron Mansfield. Citrus notes coat the tongue in this expressive white wine with body and texture. Crisp acidity.

acres 0 - cases 1,000
Fertilizers compost, cover crops, organic fertilizer
Plant protection sulfur, organic
Weed control mechanical
Yeasts spontaneous fermentation
Grapes 100% owned
Certification some of the vineyards are certified organic

SEBASTOPOL

COUNTY LINE VINEYARDS $

2040 Barlow Lane - tel. (707) 823-2578
www.countylinevineyards.com - info@countylinevineyards.com

PEOPLE - Named for the winery team's travels—buying fruit in Mendocino to take back to Sonoma. Acclaimed vintner Eric Sussman of Radio Coteau (see separate listing) created this affordably priced label to make everyday wines from well grown grapes vinified in a pure style. A third of the fruit comes from Radio Coteau, partly making it a sort of second label from Radio Coteau. The brand began making a rosé in 2003 and expanded. Its new Orfin Lotts offshoot makes natural wines.

VINEYARDS - The brand buys most of its grapes from 10 different growers. Radio Coteau estate fruit (certified biodynamic) supplies a third of the grapes. Many of the wines come from the same vineyards Radio Coteau buys from. Pinot Noir for their signature Elke Rosé comes from Boonville in Anderson Valley. The Syrah and Zinfandel are from certified organic vineyards in the Sonoma Coast. Chardonnay comes from West Sonoma County.

WINES - The winemaking is minimal intervention, producing restrained, lower alcohol wines that pair well with food.

⊙ Sonoma Coast Chardonnay 2022 ○ 122 cases; 36 $ - ⊞ - Aged in concrete, neutral French oak and stainless steel. Whole cluster. Natural acidity and tension, driven by fruit and minerality from the site as well as the aging vessels. Aromas of white pepper, stone fruit and white blossoms. It is round yet zippy with flavors of apple peel and ripe pear.

Sonoma Coast Pinot Noir 2022 ● 356 cases; 36 $ - ⊞ - Partially foot trod. Fruit forward wine with aromas of leather and cherry followed by cranberry, pink peppercorn and strawberry on the palate.

Sonoma Coast Syrah 2022 ● 148 cases; 36 $ - ⊙ - Aged in 500L French oak puncheons. A savory palate of black pepper, thyme and espresso. Full bodied, evolving over time.

---

acres 22 - cases 4,000
Fertilizers compost, cover crops, organic fertilizer
Plant protection organic
Weed control mechanical, manual
Yeasts spontaneous fermentation
Grapes purchase 50%
Certification some of the vineyards are certified organic, some of the vineyards are certified biodynamic

GLEN ELLEN

DANE CELLARS

14300 Arnold Drive - tel. (707) 529-5856
www.danecellars.com - bart@danecellars.com

PEOPLE - Winemaker Bart Hansen learned his craft in the Sonoma Valley community on his way to establishing his own artisanal brand. Beginning in 1986, he worked his way up in winemaking positions at Kenwood, Benziger Family Winery and Lasseter Family Vineyards before focusing full time on his own brand in 2018. His charming tasting room, across the street from the popular Jack London Village, is in an historic redwood tank. Hansen is also one of the hosts of highly entertaining The Wine Makers Podcast.

VINEYARDS - With a background of working in organic and biodynamic wineries, Hansen prefers organically farmed grapes. Red Rhones come from the renowned Rossi Ranch (certified organic) farmed by Phil Coturri. Zinfandel comes from historic, dry farmed, head trained vines at Rancho Aqua Caliente (certified organic) planted in 1940's. Other sources include Beltane Ranch and Lazy Dog Vineyards.

WINES - Transparent winemaking that showcases the fruit purity and site, creating vibrant wines.

⊙ Sonoma Valley Rossi Ranch Valeria Amphora Red Field Blend 2019 SLOW WINE ● n.a.; 60 $ - ⊙ - Aged 24 months in amphora. A blend of Grenache (68%) and Mourvedre (32%). From vines planted at the renowned Rossi Ranch in Kenwood. After blending, one lot was aged in amphora and another barrel aged. This one is the amphora. Aromatic and elegant.

Sonoma Valley Zinfandel 2020 ● n.a.; 48 $ - ⊞ - Aged 19 months in neutral French oak. Partial whole cluster (15%). Clarity in a bottle. Red fruits in harmony.

Sonoma Valley Malbec 2020 ● n.a.; 60 $ - ⊞ - Aged 18 months in neutral French oak. From vines planted in 2002. A rich, red with plum flavors and a glorious balance of fruit and acid.

---

acres 0 - cases 3,000
Fertilizers compost, cover crops, organic fertilizer
Plant protection sulfur, synthetic pesticides, organic
Weed control mechanical
Yeasts spontaneous fermentation
Grapes purchase 100%
Certification some of the vineyards are certified organic

SONOMA

DARLING WINES

27 E Napa Street Suite A - tel. (707) 758-9393
www.darlingwines.com - tom@darlingwines.com

PEOPLE - College sweethearts Tom and Ashley Darling did not think they would be in the wine business. But after a fluke opportunity to buy some special Syrah grapes from the Petaluma Gap in 2016, their lives changed. They produce mostly single vineyard bottlings and were recently featured by Jancis Robinson. They are getting broader distribution around the state, including Los Angeles, and in some Michelin starred restaurants—Aubergine, Commis and the French Laundry.

VINEYARDS - Focusing on Chardonnay, Pinot Noir and Syrah, they buy from 13 vineyards, using fruit from coastal North Coast vineyards as well as the Santa Cruz Mountains. The Petaluma Gap La Cruz Vineyard site, planted by Ted Lemon, is no till, applies only recycled water and uses sheep for weed control. Unsprayed for 20 years, a new five acre lease at Saint Marks vineyard in Russian River Valley is a special no till site.

WINES - The red wines are often made using whole clusters to emphasize aromatics and to express lighter, fresher, brighter, savory and floral components.

Petaluma Gap Azaya Vineyard Pinot Noir 2022 ● 100 cases; 60 $ - ⌧ - Darling manages the farming on this site. Partial whole cluster (50%). Aromas of forest and dried strawberry, with a savory, saline, elderberry and puckery palate.

Sonoma Coast Turnstone Vineyard Pinot Noir 2022 ● 60 cases; 50 $ - ⌧ - From a site at 240 feet of elevation in the Sebastopol hills with Goldridge loam soils. Very light bodied. Stewed and spiced plum, cocoa and crushed herbs on the nose. High acid. Cranberry, black tea and orange zest on the palate.

Sonoma Coast Den Chosta Syrah 2022 ● 175 cases; 48 $ - ⌧ - "Den Chosta" means Irish "up the coast," a nod to Darling's Irish heritage. Partial whole cluster (75%). Aromatic and easy drinking. Dried fig, cocoa, baking spice and anise on the nose. Tight tannins. Cranberry, soy sauce, cedar wood, iron and blueberry on the palate.

---

acres 5 - cases 2,000
Fertilizers compost, biodynamic compost, cover crops, organic fertilizer
Plant protection sulfur, biodynamic preparations, synthetic pesticides, organic
Weed control animal grazing, mechanical, manual
Yeasts spontaneous fermentation
Grapes purchase 90%
Certification none

HEALDSBURG

DAVERO FARMS & WINERY

766 Westside Road - tel. (707) 431-8000
www.davero.com - hello@davero.com

 For its dedication to biodynamic and regenerative farming and employing practices that mimic nature on their living farm. Great wines result.

PEOPLE - A Dry Creek green pioneer, Israeli born Rea Prince, a soil biome specialist, now leads the winery that founder Ridgely Evers envisioned as a diversified, certified biodynamic farm, specializing in climate appropriate Italian cultivars, which hold the heat and retain acidity. Soil focused, the team includes Jared Minori as farm manager with Michael Presley as soilkeeper. The team offers educational events on regenerative farming to the community.

VINEYARDS - Their Dry Creek estate and their Lodi grower partner Vino Farms, both certified organic and biodynamic, specialize in Italian varieties, including Sagrantino, Fiano, Barbera and Moscato Bianco among many. Ancestral Korean and Jewish methods have increased soil organic matter one percent a year. The estate integrates animals, gardens and olive trees along with the vines. They grow the only Pallagrello Bianco planted outside Caserta, Italy.

WINES - The core belief in soil health and neutral vessels yields wines of varietal purity.

TOP Dry Creek Valley Hawk Mountain Estate Sangiovese 2021 ● 150 cases; 80 $ - ⌧ - Brunello style richness, complexity, texture and finesse. Powdered, firm tannins layer on juicy blue to raspberry acidity and a touch of clove, finishes with tannin grip.

Dry Creek Valley Estate Valladares Vineyard Fiano 2022 ○ 50 cases; 70 $ - ⌧ - High acidity and rich alcohol combine for a surprisingly delicate mouthfeel. The fresh palate is intense of lemon sucker with salty tension, finishing powdery dry.

Dry Creek Valley Hawk Mountain Estate Sagrantino 2016 ● 100 cases; 90 $ - ⌧ - The flagship wine. A complex of fruit—bright cranberry and rhubarb, fresh plum and ripe blackberry—with Indian spice hints. Mature yet still fresh fruit tannins beautifully coat the mouth and maintain energy.

---

acres 16 - cases 3,800
Fertilizers compost, biodynamic compost, cover crops
Plant protection sulfur, biodynamic preparations, organic
Weed control animal grazing, mechanical, manual
Yeasts spontaneous fermentation
Grapes purchase 50%
Certification some of the vineyards are certified organic, some of the vineyards are certified biodynamic, converting to organic

WINDSOR

DUMOL

1400 American Way - tel. (707) 837-7910
www.dumol.com - winery@dumol.com

PEOPLE - An iconic Chardonnay and Pinot Noir producer, it's led by renowned viticulturalist/winemaker Andy Smith, who partners with philanthropists Laurie and Jeffrey Ubben (he's a successful hedge fund manager) in ownership. (The Ubben's also own the popular Little Saint restaurant in Healdsburg.) In 2024, Smith added estate vineyard management to his job title and promoted long time assistant winemaker Jenna Davis to winemaker.

VINEYARDS - After bringing farming in house under Smith, they now have a vineyard team of 20. The dry farmed estate vines (mostly in Green Valley) are in the first stages of official organic certification, following years of organic farming. The estates are high density plantings (like many in Burgundy). Note: Some wines (not featured here) are farmed with herbicide. On their newest estate—the 22 acre Galante Vineyard—the team's begun by first replanting eight acres.

WINES - Meticulous attention to detail—matching clone, soil type, whole cluster, pressing, cooperage, barrel size and aging protocols to varietal and site—yields superb wines.

🔴 Russian River Valley DuMOL Estate Pinot Noir 2022 SLOW WINE ● 800 cases; 120 $ - 🍷 - Aged 17 months in French oak (40% new). A flagship wine from 20 year old, high density plantings (Calera selections) on Goldridge and clay soils. Black berries and dark cherry carry through from the nose to the palate. Stunning.

Sonoma Coast MacIntyre Estate Pinot Noir 2022 ● 748 cases; 100 $ - 🍷 - Aged 14 months in French oak (33% new). Grown on sandy soils on the coolest estate site. Tiny berries. Red and black fruit aromas, with savory notes. On the palate, translucent wild berry fruits. A long lingering finish.

Russian River Valley Estate Chardonnay 2022 ○ 720 cases; 90 $ - 🍷 - Aged 11 months in French oak cigar barrels (25% new). Citrus oil on the nose, with grapefruit and more on the palate. Vibrant.

acres 90 - cases 3,000
Fertilizers compost, cover crops, organic fertilizer, synthetic fertilizer
Plant protection sulfur, synthetic pesticides, organic
Weed control mechanical
Yeasts spontaneous fermentation
Grapes purchase 30%
Certification converting to organic

SEBASTOPOL

EMME WINES

6780 McKinley Street #170
www.emmewines.com - info@emmewines.com

PEOPLE - Rosalind Reynolds approaches winemaking with all of the precision and attention one would expect from someone who thought their original post-collage path led to medical school. Instead, she fell for wine and winemaking. She works closely with a few growers in and around Sonoma County, and her focus is on grapes that were more popular a generation or two ago, especially Colombard and Carignan.

VINEYARDS - While farming a small vineyard of her own, most of the grapes in Rosalind's wines come from three family owned vineyards, in particular one in Mendocino County's Redwood Valley owned by the Ricetti family, the source most of the grapes for the wines featured here. The Ricetti vineyard's eighty year old vines are head trained and dry farmed on gravelly loam soils, and the vineyard is certified organic.

WINES - Focuses on a lighter interpretation of historic California grapes with strong structure and bright fruit at an affordable price.

🔴 Redwood Valley pink lemonade Field Blend 2023 EVERYDAY WINE ◐ 390 cases; 26 $ - 🍷 - Aged in neutral barriques for five+ months. A field blend of all the varieties planted at Ricetti Vineyard picked separately. Red and black raspberries, ripe red currants, lemon, spice and warm blossoms. Lower alcohol (11%).

Redwood Valley amando el sol White Blend 2023 ○ 150 cases; 28 $ - 🥚🏺🍷 - A small portion of each variety was aged in either a concrete egg (Colombard) or neural oak (Chardonnay). Rich, ripe flavors of peaches and apricots, sweet lemon and grapefruit. Great backbone and structure from the cooler climate Colombard.

Redwood Valley for you, anything Carignan 2022 ● 190 cases; 28 $ - 🍷 - Aged sur lie in neutral oak barriques for five months. Partially foot trod grapes from dry farmed old vines. Notes of ripe cherries, plum skin, warm grass, spice and an undertone of bramble.

acres 1 acre - cases 1,800
Fertilizers organic fertilizer
Plant protection sulfur, organic
Weed control mechanical, manual
Yeasts spontaneous fermentation
Grapes purchase 95%
Certification some of the vineyards are certified organic

SANTA ROSA

ENFIELD WINE CO.

1160b Hopper Avenue - tel. (707) 287-4514
www.enfieldwine.com - info@enfieldwine.com

PEOPLE - Winemaker John Lockwood creates wines from vineyards with distinctive voices. He harvested with Littorai (in Sonoma County) and Bodega Melipal (in Argentina) and worked the vineyards at Failla (in Sonoma County) for five years before bootstrapping his own brand with his wife Amy Seese Longwood. His strong viticultural background leads him to fascinating sites. Enfield wines always offer excellent value.

VINEYARDS - Enfield buys grapes from vineyards farmed from sustainably to "way beyond organic." Grapes come from four wildly diverse AVAs, ranging from Chalone in the central coast (Brosseau is certified organic) to Fort Ross-Seaview in northern Sonoma as well as the celebrated Shake Ridge Ranch in Amador County's Sierra Foothills. Some of the wines (not featured here) may be grown with herbicide.

WINES - He picks early and makes wines that are full flavored. Expect balance, complexity and, usually, minerality.

Fort Ross-Seaview Waterhorse Ridge Cabernet Sauvignon 2022 ● 140 cases; 65 $ - ⊞ - Overflowing flavors of black currant, blueberry, roasted chestnut, dark chocolate, and dark flowers. Medium+ body, refreshing acidity, youthful but friendly tannins. 13.8% alcohol.

Napa Valley Hennessey Ridge Cabernet Sauvignon 2022 ● 75 cases; 90 $ - ⊞ - The inaugural Enfield Hennessy Ridge is stellar, old school Cabernet that drinks well now but will blossom in the cellar. Medium+ body with light, grainy tannins well balanced by flavors of dark fruit, mineral, and dry tobacco. 12.4% alcohol.

Fort Ross-Seaview Waterhorse Ridge Cabernet Franc 2022 ● 75 cases; 38 $ - ⊞ - Delicious, Chinon style Cabernet Franc that opens to appetizing notes of red and purple fruit, mulberry leaf, coffee, graphite and dark mineral. Complex, intense, and evolving. 100% whole cluster. 13.3% alcohol.

acres 40 - cases 3,500
Fertilizers compost, cover crops, organic fertilizer
Plant protection sulfur, synthetic pesticides, organic
Weed control mechanical
Yeasts spontaneous fermentation
Grapes purchase 67%
Certification some of the vineyards are certified organic

HEALDSBURG

ERNEST VINEYARDS

320 Center Street - tel. (707) 687-9176
www.ernestvineyards.com - hello@ernestvineyards.com

PEOPLE - Inspired by their love of cool climate wines from the foggy coast of west Sonoma, Erin Brooks and husband Todd Gottula, owners of Grand Cru Custom Crush, founded the label in 2012. They hired Joseph Ryan as their winemaker and partner. The team opened an elegant, new tasting room on Healdsburg Plaza in 2023. There they offer visitors tastes, glasses and bottles of their understated, single vineyard Chardonnay and Pinot from cold sites.

VINEYARDS - Chardonnay and Pinot Noir come primarily from their certified organic Sonoma Coast and West Sonoma Coast estates—Cleary Ranch, Michael Valentine and Joyce vineyards. They also buy from Alder Springs (farmed only with organic materials) in Mendocino. They recently acquired two new sites in Occidental and Freestone Ridge for future vintages and are working toward getting a new Freestone-Occidental AVA which would be part of the West Sonoma Coast.

WINES - Showcases the delicate, subtleties of cool climate Chardonnay and Pinot Noir made with a light hand in the cellar. The Pinot's are typically fermented 1/3 whole cluster and aged in oak (less than 40% new).

TOP Sonoma Coast Freestone Estate Pinot Noir 2022 SLOW WINE ● 420 cases; 58 $ - ⊞ - Aged in oak (35% new). Partial whole cluster (33%). From two adjacent estate vineyards. Vibrant with rich, darker fruit notes in a satisfying balance. Midpalate of cherry and a hint of cola. True to the vintage.

Sonoma Coast Freestone Estate Chardonnay 2022 ○ 180 cases; 52 $ - ⊞ - Aged in French oak (35% new). Gossamer, translucent, whisper light lemon on the palate leads to a lingering lime finish.

Mendocino County Alder Springs Petite Arvine 2022 ○ 130 cases; 42 $ - ⊞ - Aged in French oak (35% new). A Swiss varietal that is uncommon in the U.S. A standout variety for its rarity and complexity. Asian pears and tropical fruits with an appealing underlying hint of varietal sweetness.

acres 34 - cases 4,500
Fertilizers cover crops, organic fertilizer
Plant protection organic
Weed control mechanical
Yeasts spontaneous fermentation
Grapes purchase 40%
Certification some of the vineyards are certified organic

SONOMA

EXTRADIMENTIONAL WINE CO. YEAH

27 E. Napa Street, Suite E
www.winecoyeah.com - yeah@winecoyeah.com

PEOPLE - The free spirited husband and wife team of winemaker Hardy Wallace and Kate Graham specialize in unconventional blends and want to take wine lovers "outside the known universe," as their eclectic label's name suggests. Wallace made natural wines at his former label, Dirty & Rowdy Wine Co., from 2010-2021. His favorite grape—Mourvedre—is his new label's star. The couple opened a downtown Sonoma tasting room off the Plaza in 2023.

VINEYARDS - Wallace buys fruit from more than 15 appellations. Favorites for Mourvèdre include the old vine Evangelho Vineyard in Contra Costa County and the high altitude Shake Ridge Ranch in Amador County's Sierra Foothills, as well as Carignan and Zinfandel from Contra Costa County, Dry Creek Valley in Sonoma and other sites in Mendocino.

WINES - The highly original blends are made in tiny lots—around 100 cases or so for each—meaning that wines come and go in short order.

Chalone Mountain Echoes Orange Wine 2022 ◉ 115 cases; 45 $ - 🍾 - A cloudy, novel Chardonnay blend with 45 days of skin contact showing apricot, citrus blossom, fennel and chamomile with tart tangerine, orange bitters, green tea and fresh apricot on the palate.

Contra Costa County Mind Left Body Mourvedre 2022 ● 125 cases; 47 $ - 🍾 - Blend includes Zinfandel (15%) and Chardonnay (10%). Aromas of raspberry, violet, sandalwood, amber and cinnamon. On the palate, balanced with elegant raspberry leaf tea, tart cherry and incense.

California Partial Eclipse Red Blend 2022 ● 97 cases; 55 $ - 🍾 - Mourvèdre blend with Carignane, Petite Sirah, Primitivo and Zinfandel. Aromas of cherry pipe tobacco, potpourri, mulberry and cedar and a vibrant, rich palate of tart cherry, boysenberry, blueberry, redwood duff and orange oil.

acres 0 - cases 1,500
Fertilizers compost, cover crops, synthetic fertilizer
Plant protection sulfur, synthetic pesticides
Weed control mechanical
Yeasts spontaneous fermentation
Grapes purchase 100%
Certification some of the vineyards are certified organic

SONOMA

FAR MOUNTAIN

www.farmountainwine.com - heights@farmountainwine.com

PEOPLE - Husband and wife vintners Rodrigo Soto and Mai Errazuriz started their own wine brand specializing in dry farmed, old vines growing on under the radar sites above the town of Sonoma. Their first vintage was 2019. Soto was the former estate director at Napa's prestigious Quintessa winery and an early days biodynamic pioneer at Benziger in Glen Ellen as well as in his native Chile. He makes the wines. The beautiful labels done by renowned artist Tom Killion depict the vineyard sites.

VINEYARDS - The wines come from two old vine, dry farmed vineyards on Bald Mountain (which may become part of the Moon Mountain AVA). The Chardonnay site was planted in 1972 to heritage California clones. The soils are fractured basalt rock. Cabernet comes from Alta Vista vineyard on steep hillsides where 50+ year old, dry farmed vines grow on terraces at 1,000-1,200 feet of elevation. The soils are red clay loam.

WINES - Restrained oak (30% or less) and aging (one year) let the taste of the terroir shine through in balanced, intriguing and complex wines.

🔝 Sonoma Valley Fission Cabernet Sauvignon 2020 ● 1,500 cases; 80 $ - 🍾 - Aged 12 months in French oak (27% new). Dark fruits, blackberries, cherries and herbs reflect the garrigue of the mountain site. Moderate tannins. Integrated and balanced as well as novel, subtle and compelling.

Sonoma Valley Myrna Chardonnay 2020 ○ 1,500 cases; 60 $ - 🍾 - Aged 12 months in French oak (18% new). From heritage California clones. Whole cluster pressed. Barrel fermented with lees contact throughout aging. Well structured. Lean with Meyer lemon and pears. Crisp acidity.

acres 0 - cases 3,000
Fertilizers n/a
Plant protection sulfur, synthetic pesticides, copper
Weed control n/a
Yeasts spontaneous fermentation
Grapes purchase 100%
Certification none

ALAMEDA

FEST WINE CO.

P.O. Box 1757 - tel. (510) 290-7079
www.festwineco.com - michael@festwineco.com

PEOPLE - Now in their seventh vintage, the husband and wife team of Michael and Stacey Schriefer founded their tiny label Fest in 2019. A native of Bremen, Germany, Michael trained at U.C. Davis and worked as a laboratory technician at Trinchero Family Estates for seven years. "Fest" in German means a celebration among families, neighbors or friends. The couple make their wines at a custom crush facility in Healdsburg.

VINEYARDS - The two buy fruit from two vineyards. The Pigasus vineyard, at 850 feet, courses over 10 acres of rolling hills at the western edge of Sonoma Mountain. The Pinot Noir blocks consist of two clones: Pommard and 777. The van der Kamp Vineyard was originally planted in 1952 making it one of the oldest continuously operated Pinot Noir vineyard in California. The 25 acre vineyard sits at 1,500 feet on the northern aspect of Sonoma Mountain.

WINES - Classic, high elevation Pinot Noir that's sheer and savory with minimal extraction and optimal flavor. There's a juicy sapidity and lithe texture to these superbly crafted vintages.

Sonoma Mountain van der Kamp Vineyard Pinot Noir 2022 ● 100 cases; 56 $ - ⊞ - The combination of old heritage clones and a handful of local and suitcase clones show expressive red cherry, raspberry and red plum with hints of savory herbs, tea leaf and subtle spice.

Sonoma Mountain van der Kamp Vineyard Pinot Noir 2021 ● 60 cases; 54 $ - ⊞ - After tasting all the 2021's made from van der Kamp, Schriefer used 30 percent whole cluster for a style that shows pomegranate, strawberry and is delicately spiced with nutmeg and vanilla. The 2022 was a warmer vintage at 13.6.

Sonoma Mountain Pigasus Vineyard Pinot Noir 2021 ● 60 cases; 46 $ - ⊞ - With half Pommard and half 777 clones, there's more forward cherry and cranberry fruit here with lean, savory notes of mushroom and forest floor.

acres 0 - cases 100
Fertilizers cover crops, organic fertilizer
Plant protection sulfur, organic
Weed control animal grazing, mechanical
Yeasts spontaneous fermentation, commercial cultured yeasts
Grapes purchase 100%
Certification none

SONOMA

GLORIA FERRER

23555 Arnold Drive - tel. (866) 845-674
www.gloriaferrer.com - info@gloriaferrer.com

PEOPLE - One of the biggest Cava producers in the world, the Barcelona based Ferrer family, who own the sparkling wine giant Freixenet, started their first American winery in 1982 in the Carneros. Today it's led by general manager Melanie Shafer with winemaker Kyle Altomare and vineyard director Brad Kurtz. New on the horizon: estate grown Malvasia Bianca, for both still and sparkling wines. Visitors can enjoy a variety of tapas, a seafood platter and even churros at the tasting room, popular for its vistas.

VINEYARDS - The producer has two sites: Home (204 acres) and Circle Bar (127 acres). The team is working on organic certification, expected in 2025. They're also implementing more soil health and biodiversity projects, including adding native plant hedgerows as insectaries. A large replanting project is underway, preparing to meet the challenges of climate change by using biochar, drought tolerant rootstock and winter sheep grazing (to avoid tractor passes and soil compaction).

WINES - Compelling bubbles made in a wide variety of styles from dry (Extra Brut) to sweet (Demi-Sec), along with a growing selection of still wines.

Carneros NV Vista Brut Nonvintage ⊛ 1,500 cases; 52 $ - ⌒ - Aged 3.5 years. A mainstay made from Pinot Noir (98%). Features aromas and flavors of cranberry, white nectarine and Bing cherry, finishing with a bright note of red apple.

Carneros Alquimia Rosé 2019 ⊛ 1,000 cases; 62 $ - ⌒ - A blend of Pinot Noir (60%) and Chardonnay (40%). This dry sparkler captivates with vibrant raspberry, tangerine and passionfruit flavors. Three hours of skin contact give it its rosy hue.

Carneros Cuvée Rosé 2017 ⊛ 800 cases; 94 $ - ⌒ - Their top of the line bottling. A creamier wine that spends five years en tirage and a minimum of one year in cork. The blend is Pinot Noir (55%) and Chardonnay (45%) with 13 grams/L of dosage. Elegant and floral.

acres 331 - cases 60,000
Fertilizers compost, cover crops, organic fertilizer
Plant protection sulfur, organic
Weed control mechanical
Yeasts commercial cultured yeasts
Grapes 100% owned
Certification converting to organic

SONOMA

GUTHRIE FAMILY WINES $

tel. (707) 307-3614
www.guthriefamilywines.com - blair@guthriefamilywines.com

PEOPLE - Making high end Napa Cab for Stewart Cel€lars is his day job, but New Zealand native Blair Guthrie makes wines on the very opposite side of the spectrum for his own label, preferring a low intervention style. He likes making affordably priced, high quality wines, including Rhones. His background in graphic design informs the unique bottle art. He buys only organically grown fruit, which means expanding to other varieties as well.

VINEYARDS - Describing himself as one of the "small guys convincing the small vineyards to go organic, in baby steps," he leases and farms three acres of Gamay that he grafted on a conventional site. There he uses only organic approved materials. He buys white Rhones from Lodi–Picpoul Blanc and Vermentino–from certified organic growers-and reds–Carignan–from Dogali Vineyard (certified organic) in the Pine Mountain-Cloverdale Peak AVA.

WINES - Picked early to maintain fresh acidity. The wines are fresh, acid driven, and aromatic. Minerality is a signature of his wine style.

● California Neon Vermentino 2023 EVERYDAY WINE ○ 250 cases; 28 $ - 🍷 - A crystal, golden hue, with aromas of green everything–herbs, ferns and lemongrass. Flavor notes of Asian pear, lime zest and green almond. Lovely acidity and juicy salinity.

Lodi Picpoul Blanc 2023 ○ 150 cases; 28 $ - 🍷 - Incredibly zippy aroma, lemon zest and curd and some sea breeze minerality, with a hint of ripe stone fruit and lime leaf. Saline, pineapple and coriander on the palate, floral yet savory.

Mendocino Galaxy Carbonic Carignan 2023 ● 250 cases; 28 $ - 🍷 - A Beaujolais. style wine, and one of his signature wines. From dry farmed old vines. Fermented whole cluster, with carbonic maceration for a week. A super light red with aromas of alpine herb, amaro, black cherry and pepper. Juicy candied flavors of twizzlers and strawberries.

acres 4 - cases 2,000
Fertilizers compost, cover crops
Plant protection sulfur, organic
Weed control mechanical, manual
Yeasts spontaneous fermentation
Grapes purchase 80%
Certification some of the vineyards are certified organic, some of the vineyards are certified biodynamic

SEBASTOPOL

HORSE & PLOW $

1272 Gravenstein Highway N - tel. (707) 827-3486
www.horseandplow.com - suzanne@horseandplow.com

PEOPLE - Wines certified as "Made with Organic GraGpes" have been the north star of established winemakers Chris Condos and Suzanne Hagins since launching in 2008. Their central focus is making small lot, site specific wines from many varietals, but they also produce cider from local heritage apples. On the horizon: a brandy (already aging three years) and Vermentino along with Assyrtiko, Grüner Veltliner and more. Community minded, the offer live music on Sundays. Half of wine sales are to locals.

VINEYARDS - Sourcing fruit only from certified organic vineyards in the North Coast, the two support small family growers. Cox Vineyard's 100 year-old Carignan, in the steep hills above Ukiah, has been certified for 35 years, supplying early picks for rosé and later for reds. Bill Canihan grows cool climate Syrah in Carneros that Chris co-ferments with Canihan's Viognier. The Syrah also plays a role in their popular red blend.

WINES - Their vivid and fresh wines come from using only organic fruit, no cellar additives, traditional methods and low sulfur with the goal of pure, clean flavors.

● Mendocino County Carignane 2022 ● 200 cases; 32 $ - 🍷 - Partial whole cluster (25%). Their flagship wine. Savory black pepper and deep raspberry aromas welcome dried herbs, flowers, minerality and dark berried medium acidity ends with a touch of chalky tannins.

Mendocino County Rosé of Carignane 2023 ◐ 600 cases; 22 $ - 🍷 - Whole cluster, direct press. Light salmon in color. Yellow rose, white pepper and ginger aromatics lead to a lively, ultra juicy grapefruit core wrapped in acidity, finishing long with an orange peel note.

Sonoma Coast Syrah 2018 ● 100 cases; 38 $ - 🍷 - De-stemmed Syrah and with 5 percent whole Viognier. Plums, black fruit and spice on the nose carries to the palate. Long finish of deep blue fruit, plum skins and tannin grip.

acres 0 - cases 4,000
Fertilizers compost, biodynamic compost, cover crops, manure, organic fertilizer
Plant protection sulfur, biodynamic preparations, organic
Weed control animal grazing, mechanical, manual
Yeasts spontaneous fermentation, selected indigenous yeasts, commercial cultured yeasts
Grapes purchase 100%
Certification organic

HEALDSBURG

IDLEWILD

132 Plaza Street - tel. (707) 385-9310
www.idlewildwines.com - info@idlewildwines.com

PEOPLE - Fourth generation winemaker Sam Bilbro focuses on Piemontese grapes. In 2024, Overshine Wine Company (owned by former Google attorney David Drummond) bought the brand. Now the managing partner, Sam oversees the business. There are 11 single varietal wines, as well as the Flora & Fauna "table wines" label which include a white, red, rose, and sparkling. The duo have planted Brachetto, Pelaverga, Rucche and 50+ more at Drummond's Las Cimas in Healdsburg.

VINEYARDS - Sam owns and manages Lost Hills Ranch, which his father planted in 2001, in the Yorkville Highlands AVA in Mendocino. The high elevation site sits at 1,200+ feet. Soils are fractured sandstone with schist and quartz. (Bilbro managed Fox Hill vineyard, planted to Italian varietals, which was sold to Chris Brockway in 2023. It became certified organic in 2024.) Drummond owns Las Cimas in the Russian River Valley, a steep and rocky site growing Italian varieties.

WINES - With a focus on Piemontese grapes, Idlewild makes true to varietal wines from California that are food friendly and balanced. They also have another brand, Comunita, launched in 2024.

● Mendocino County Yorkville Highlands Lost Hills Arneis 2023 ○ 250 cases; 36 $ - 🍷🛢 - Aged five months in 50/50 stainless steel and neutral oak. Stone fruit, almond, and white flower aromas but minerality takes the lead. Delicate acidity coats the mouth. A salty mineral finish.

North Coast Flora and Fauna Rosé 2023 ● 1,200 cases; 25 $ - 🍷🛢 - Barbera, Dolcetto and Nebbiolo (30% each) with Grignolino (10%). A copper peach color, the wine is structured and savory with notes of blood orange and orange skin tannins, textured acidity and a juicy finish.

Mendocino County Yorkville Highlands Lost Hills Ranch Barbera 2021 ● 300 cases; 48 $ - 🛢 - Aged 12 months in neutral barrel. Whole cluster (75%) with the remainder destemmed for fruit density. Fresh and electric with dense red fruit aromas, mineral graphite notes, and smooth tannins.

---

acres 86 - cases 7,000
Fertilizers compost, organic fertilizer
Plant protection sulfur, organic
Weed control mechanical, manual
Yeasts spontaneous fermentation
Grapes purchase 20%
Certification some of the vineyards are certified organic

SANTA ROSA

INMAN FAMILY WINES

3900 Piner Road - tel. (707) 293-9576
www.inmanfamilywines.com - info@inmanfamilywines.com

PEOPLE - Since 2002, Kathleen Inman's overseen her vines and made wines under her own winery, aided by her daughter, Ashley (marketing), and her sister Diana (accounting and compliance). Kathleen's new frontier in 2024 is making a new Pinot Gris/white Pinot Noir Blend and a Blanc de Noir in 2024. She's now put in a new well and water treatment system and uses recycled green bottles for her sparkling wines.

VINEYARDS - Inman farms her Olivet Grange vineyard with organic inputs, composts with food scraps, and is no till. She welcomes local wildlife who spread their manure. She buys 20 percent of the grapes she uses, purchasing Pinot Noir from Pratt Vine Hill in the Russian River Valley since they started in 2013. She buys a small amount of old vine Grenache (unsprayed) from Sceales Vineyard in Alexander Valley.

WINES - Honoring her 40 years of happy marriage to her husband Simon, she continues making her Endless Crush Rosé.

● Russian River Valley Olivet Grange Pinot Gris 2022 ○ 67 cases; 40 $ - 🍷 - Aged in neutral barrels with lees stirring. Pretty aromatic nose with notes of peach, melon, wet stone, and salinity. Lovely mouthfeel with richness on the midpalate, tartness on the finish and vibrant acidity.

Russian River Valley Endless Crush Rosé of Pinot Noir 2023 ● 455 cases; 40 $ - 🍷 - A delicate baby pink color with aromas of watermelon, strawberry, and honeysuckle, the wine has intense, electric acidity and a long finish, making you want more.

Russian River Valley OGV Estate Pinot Noir 2021 ● 625 cases; 75 $ - 🛢 - Aged in French oak (20% new). Partial whole cluster. Vibrant with notes of cherries, raspberries, pomegranate, blackberry and baking spices. On the palate, juicy red fruit notes and spic with balanced tannins and acid.

---

acres 8.3 - cases 3,800
Fertilizers compost, cover crops, organic fertilizer
Plant protection sulfur, synthetic pesticides, organic
Weed control mechanical, manual
Yeasts spontaneous fermentation, commercial cultured yeasts
Grapes purchase 20%
Certification none

SONOMA

JOLIE-LAIDE WINES

21684 Eighth Street East, Suite 400 - tel. (707) 501-7664
www. jolielaidewines.com - info@jolielaidewines.com

PEOPLE - Scott and Jenny Schultz's indie winery is celebrated for its love of whole cluster, foot stomped winemaking and for offbeat varietals—Mondeuse and Trousseau Gris, for example. Scott formerly worked with Pax Mahle. Jenny has a degree in winemaking from U.C. Davis. The couple produce close to 20 wines each year. They moved to a large new warehouse space in Sonoma's Eighth Street district, home to an enclave of wineries, where they offer tastings.

VINEYARDS - The winery buys grapes from more than 20 sites across the state. Las Cimas Vineyard in the Russian River Valley grows old vine Aligoté, Gamay, Mondeuse, Poulsard and Trousseau on complex Franciscan soils. A rare Scheurebe, planted in the 1970's by a renowned German winemaker, is a new wine for them, coming from St. Helena in Napa Valley.

WINES - The house style often involves foot trodding and partial carbonic maceration, keeping aromatics high but tannins low, with texture coming from whole cluster fermentations.

Chalone Mélon de Bourgogne 2023 ◯ 450 cases; 32 $ - 🍷 - Loire inspired, it's fresh and bright. Aromas of fragrant white blossoms, green apple and pear, fern fronds, saline and minerality on the palate, soft texture with a hit of acidity.

🔝 Sonoma County Las Cimas Vineyard Aligoté 2023 ◯ 200 cases; 45 $ - 🍷 - From Las Cimas Vineyard in Sonoma County and Siletto (certified organic) in San Benito County. Vibrant with aromas of citrus blossom and lemongrass. Silky, elegant in the mouth with flavors of apple peel, melon rind and wet stone.

Yorkville Highlands Hawks Butte Vineyard Syrah 2021 ● 225 cases; 55 $ - 🍷 - A light, ethereal Syrah. Aromas of seaweed, currant, black olive and soil with flavor notes of smoke, granite, plum and spice. Medium bodied and elegant.

acres 0 - cases 6,500
Fertilizers compost, cover crops
Plant protection sulfur, organic
Weed control mechanical, manual
Yeasts spontaneous fermentation
Grapes purchase 100%
Certification some of the vineyards are certified organic

FORESTVILLE

JOSEPH JEWELL

6542 Front Street - tel. (707) 820-1621
www.josephjewell.com - info@josephjewell.com

PEOPLE - Raised in Humboldt County and living in Sonoma County, Adrian Manspeaker has big love for both regions. At Joseph Jewell, which is named after his middle name, Adrian celebrates both with single vineyard designates. In 2023, with a huge crop, he increased production by 1,500 cases. The 2024 vintage may be as big. Adrian is also the winemaker at Raymond Burr Winery in Sonoma and at Panther Creek in Petaluma.

VINEYARDS - Adrian buys grapes from 11 vineyards—five in Humboldt and six in Sonoma. In Humboldt, Ryan, Phelps, and Elk Prairie farm organically. In Sonoma, Raymond Burr does not use herbicides. Grist and Panther Ridge are certified organic. In Sonoma all of the vineyards have different soils, ranging from Josephine (loam, silty, sandy, fractured shales) to Goldridge (silty sandy loam) to rocks and dark soils. In Humboldt, the soils are more similar with sandy, fractured tone and shale.

WINES - Made with minimal intervention, Joseph Jewell wines express the diverse vineyards in Sonoma and Humboldt counties.

🔝 Petaluma Gap Panther Ridge Pinot Noir 2021 ● 144 cases; 55 $ - 🍷 - Aged 18 months in French oak (33% new). A blend of Calera and 115 clones. Notes of dark red fruits, minerality, and graphite, with intense tannins resulting from Petaluma Gap winds.

Humboldt County Ryan Vineyard Pinot Noir 2021 ● 144 cases; 45 $ - 🍷 - Aged 18 months in French oak (25% new). Aromas of wild red fruits, violets, and a mild herbaceous mint, due to pennyroyal grown in the vineyard. Wild and intense yet smooth tannins and a fresh fruit lift on the finish.

Dry Creek Valley Grist Zinfandel 2021 ● 200 cases; 45 $ - 🍷 - Aged 18 months in barrel (25% new). A "Pinot-esque" style Zinfandel. Very pretty aromatics with red fruit, floral, and white pepper notes. Bright and lifted with plum skin tannins and good acidity.

acres 0 - cases 4,000
Fertilizers compost, biodynamic compost, cover crops, manure, organic fertilizer
Plant protection sulfur, biodynamic preparations, copper
Weed control mechanical, manual
Yeasts spontaneous fermentation
Grapes purchase 100%
Certification some of the vineyards are certified organic

SONOMA

KAMEN ESTATE WINES

111 B East Napa St. - tel. (707) 938-7292
www.kamenwines.com - info@kamenwines.com

 An organic pioneer on Moon Mountain paying meticulous attention to farming and winemaking.

PEOPLE - New York City native and Hollywood screenwriter Robert Kamen (who wrote The Karate Kid as well as the Taken films) found his piece of heaven in a 280-acre parcel of in the rugged southern Mayacamas in 1979. Working with organic winegrower extraordinaire Phil Coturri, he planted vines and sold grapes. In 1996, he became a top tier vintner, releasing his first estate wines in 1999. Mark Herold is the winemaker.

VINEYARDS - The vines (certified organic) sit on volcanic soil at 1,100-1,500 feet in mountainous terrain above Sonoma Valley. While most of the site is planted to Cabernet, smaller blocks grow Cabernet Franc, Grenache, Petite Sirah, Sauvignon Blanc and Syrah. In 2008, the team developed an almost impossible to plant 14-acre section of volcanic rock—now named the Lava Block—which consists of chunks of hardened lava, now making an extraordinary wine.

WINES - Herold deftly crafts Cabernet Sauvignon from mountain vines into world class wines.

● Moon Mountain District Estate Cabernet Sauvignon 2020 SLOW WINE ● 1,350 cases; 125 $ - "Less extracted than previous vintages," the winery says, and also about half as many cases in this vintage (due to fires). A glorious representation of Moon Mountain at its best with blackberry, cherry and currant notes. Well balanced and definitely ageworthy though it is very appealing now.
Moon Mountain Writer's Block Red Blend 2021 ● 400 cases; 75 $ - A blend of Cabernet Sauvignon, Petite Sirah and Syrah. A deep, rich red blend with compelling aromas of blackberries, dark cherries and pomegranates followed by abundant black and purple fruit flavors. Balanced and complex.
Moon Mountain District Lava Block Cabernet Sauvignon 2021 ● 420 cases; 205 $ - A complex, elegant and opulent blockbuster. From 15 year old vines. Bountiful aromatics. On the palate, dark, luscious, black and purple fruits and spice box in balance. One for the cellar.

acres 43 - cases 4,000
Fertilizers compost
Plant protection sulfur, organic
Weed control mechanical
Yeasts commercial cultured yeasts
Grapes 100% owned
Certification organic

GLEN ELLEN

LASSETER FAMILY WINERY

1 Vintage Lane - tel. (707) 933-2814
www.lasseterfamilywinery.com - jenifer@lfwinery.com

 Organic farming, field blends and thoughtful winemaking express Bordeaux, Rhone and old Italian varieties.

PEOPLE - In 1993, John and Nancy Lasseter acquired the historic property originally founded by a French winemaker in 1894. The 95 acre-estate on the outskirts of Glen Ellen combines three adjacent parcels that were formerly parts of Ranchos Vallejo and Los Guilicos and was expanded in 2017 to Moon Mountain. Danielle Langlois, who had worked with Phil Coturri and Mark Herold, joined in 2018 as winemaker and works with consulting winemaker Tony Biagi.

VINEYARDS - Organic vineyard guru Phil Coturri oversees the estate vines using sheep for weed control. He's also trialing crimping in Heritage Blocks at Justi Creek planted to century old Zinfandel in a field blend with rare varieties. Syrah, Grenache and Mourvèdre grow to the east of Calabasas Creek on the Creekside Blocks and the newest vineyard, 9 acre Trinity Ridge, sits at 2,000 feet in the Moon Mountain District with 107 different soil types.

WINES - Langlois has a light touch with whites and roses and lets the nature of the estate's powerful mountain fruit fully express itself.

● Moon Mountain District Trinity Ridge Vineyard Cabernet Sauvignon 2021 SLOW WINE ● 245 cases; 150 $ - Aged in French oak (100% new). This high elevation, cool site shows lush, dark fruit with cedar, blackberry and black pepper cloaking generous tannins. Notes of mesquite and coyote brush emerge through the finish.
Sonoma Mountain Trinity Ridge Sauvignon Blanc 2022 ○ 145 cases; 60 $ - Aged 10 months in a French oak egg barrel (45% new). Phelps and Musque clones are barrel fermented for a honeyed, peaches and cream expression that is bright and mineral.
Sonoma Valley Chemin de Fer Rhone Blend 2021 ● Red Rhone Blend; 400 cases; 65 $ - Aged 14 months in French oak (42% new). Whole cluster. The blend is Grenache (67%), Mourvedre(26%) and Syrah (7%). Earthy black cherry, black raspberry and cranberry flavors, rich and dense with dried thyme through the finish.

acres 58 - cases 5,000
Fertilizers compost, cover crops
Plant protection sulfur, organic
Weed control animal grazing, mechanical, manual
Yeasts spontaneous fermentation, commercial cultured yeasts
Grapes 100% owned
Certification organic

SEBASTOPOL

LITTORAI WINES

788 Gold Ridge Road - tel. (707) 823-9586
www.littorai.com - info@littorai.com

PEOPLE - One of California's most acclaimed vintners, Dijon educated Ted Lemon gained notoriety as the first American in 1984 to be a vineyard manager in Burgundy. In 1994, he and his wife established Littorai in 1993 with purchased fruit. Both had strong winery backgrounds. They began purchasing and leasing vineyards in 2000 and built their straw bale winery in 2008. Fine wine legends, the Lemons are role models for biodiversity as well as biodynamics.

VINEYARDS - They are deeply biodynamic in practice (though they are not Demeter certified) and grow their own plants for biodynamic sprays, graze cows and sheep, integrate chickens and more. Their estate vineyards provide half the winery's fruit –The Pivot (at the winery), The Haven (west of Occidental), and One Acre (Anderson Valley). They also partner with eight leased vineyards in the cool climates of West Sonoma Coast and Mendocino's Anderson Valley. These are farmed to Ted's specs.

WINES - Ecofriendly in farming as well as their operations, they are solar powered. Oak aging is restrained (up to 25% new). The wines are made to age.

Sonoma Coast The Pivot Vineyard Pinot Noir 2022 573 cases; 100 $ - Vivid nose of tangy red cherry, raspberry, and rose petal sprinkled with brown spice. Mouthwatering palate with very fine, framing tannins and more red cherry, raspberry, and rose petal, but also dark mineral, oak, vanilla. Very long, cherry-skin finish.
Russian River Valley Mays Canyon Chardonnay 2022 150 cases; 105 $ - A lovely nose of pear, yellow apple, spice, oak, dusty mineral. A more savory palate with delicate texture and flavors of mineral, salted pear, dry meadow. Refreshing acidity. Long, lemon mineral finish.
Sonoma Coast Hirsch Vineyard Pinot Noir 2022 197 cases; 105 $ - Black cherry and a hint of basil foreshadow flavors of dark mineral, black cherry, bitter orange, savory dried herb. Great balance among all aspects and light, chewy texture guarantee a long life for this wine.

acres 40 - cases 3,500
Fertilizers compost, cover crops, organic fertilizer
Plant protection sulfur, biodynamic preparations, organic
Weed control mechanical
Yeasts spontaneous fermentation
Grapes purchase 67%
Certification some of the vineyards are certified organic

SEBASTOPOL

MARCHELLE WINES

2095 Gravenstein Hwy North - tel. (707) 953-9463
www.marchellewines.com - info@marchellewines.com

PEOPLE - Known in the industry as the "vine whisperer" and "cellar magician" for resuscitating vineyards, superstar Greg La Follette launched this tiny under the radar brand focused on old vines in 2001 with Kevin Lee, a friend and Silicon Valley marketer, who's the co-founder and managing partner. La Follette was mentored under the legendary winemaker André Tchelistcheff and has had a storied career at La Crema, Hartford, Flowers Winery and more.

VINEYARDS - Old vine Chardonnay and Pinot Noir predominate. Planted to Pinot Noir, Harmony Lane, the estate vineyard, sits below a ridgeline at 800 feet, at the edge of the marine layer. They also buy from Mendocino, Napa and Sonoma (Wes Cameron, 1965; van der Kamp, 1952; Betty Ann, 1900), as well as Lodi (Bechthold, 1886) and Santa Maria Valley (Bien Nacido, 1973). Some wines (not featured here) are farmed with herbicides.

WINES - Evan Damiano is the winemaker. They make wines in a custom crush facility in Sebastopol.

Sonoma Mountain van der Kamp Vineyard Pinot Meunier 2023 70 cases; 54 $ - Aged six months in neutral oak. Carbonic fermentation. Vines date back to 1952 and sit at 1,800 feet elevation with lots of wind. In color, a dark rosé. Fragrant aromas of ripe cherries, wild raspberry, roses, and dried herbs and textured with savory notes.
Santa Maria Valley Bien Nacido L Block Chardonnay 2021 100 cases; 50 $ - Aged 18 months on the lees in neutral oak. From own rooted vines planted in 1973. Barrel fermented. Vibrant with stone fruit and honeysuckle notes, bright acidity and a fresh saline finish.
Sonoma Mountain van der Kamp vineyard Pinot Noir 2022 70 cases; 70 $ - Aged 18 months in neutral oak. Made in small, one ton vats and sent to barrel with a little residual sugar. Pinot Meunier (8%) added. Graceful and elegant with lots of red fruit aromas and vibrant acidity.

acres 3 - cases 900
Fertilizers compost, biodynamic compost, cover crops, organic fertilizer
Plant protection sulfur, organic
Weed control mechanical, manual
Yeasts spontaneous fermentation
Grapes purchase 80%
Certification some of the vineyards are certified organic

HEALDSBURG

MERRIAM VINEYARDS

11650 Los Amigos Road - tel. (707) 433-4032
www.merriamvineyards.com - info@merriamvineyards.com

PEOPLE - Estate manager Evan Merriam runs the winery that his New England based parents Peter Merriam (a passionate wine lover) and Diana started when they first bought vineyards in 2000 and a winery soon after. The late great "Amigo Bob" Cantisano (1951-2020), a famous organic consultant, helped the family adopt organic farming and certification. Today William Weese is the winemaker. Their new tasting room and stylish, dog friendly (leashes required) hospitality grounds opened in 2023.

VINEYARDS - Uniquely located on the east side of the Russian River Valley, the estate was first certified organic in 2012. Today two of their three estates still are. They grow both Burgundian (certified organic vines; 5 clones of Pinot) and Bordeaux vines (not certified). They are experimenting with no till on some blocks under vineyard consultant Steve Domenichelli's "less is more" approach. Some wines (not featured here) are grown with herbicide.

WINES - The winery is one of the few certified organic wineries in Sonoma, enabling it to label its organically grown estate wines as "Made with Organic Grapes," a high standard that guarantees a certain level of purity.

● Russian River Valley Diana's Vineyard Pinot Noir 2022 ● 300 cases; 56 $ - ⊞ - Aged in French oak (30% new). A four clone blend. A floral bouquet amplifies a gorgeous rose filled palate with blue and red fruit, deep powdery tannins and juicy acidity. Pomegranate on the polished finish.
Russian River Valley Three Sons Pinot Noir 2021 ● 30 cases; 84 $ - ⊞ - Aged 18 months in French oak (100% new). A blend of three clones, each grown on its own one acre block. Blended after barrel aging. Plums, blackberries and baking spices.
Russian River Valley Danielle's Vineyard Fumé Blanc 2022 ○ 175 cases; 42 $ - ⊞ - Aged 12 months in French oak (35% new) including four months sur lie. With head trained Semillon (10%). A medium rich body of lemon oil and grapefruit.

acres 46 - cases 3,000
Fertilizers compost, cover crops, organic fertilizer, synthetic fertilizer
Plant protection synthetic pesticides, copper, organic
Weed control mechanical
Yeasts spontaneous fermentation, commercial cultured yeasts
Grapes purchase 10%
Certification some of the vineyards are certified organic

SEBASTOPOL

MERRY EDWARDS

2959 Gravenstein Hwy N - tel. (707) 823-7466
www.merryedwards.com - taste@merryedwards.com

PEOPLE - Edwards, one of California's first women winemakers, started this iconic Russian River Valley label in 1996 and sold it in 2019 to French Champagne house Louis Roederer. Edwards handpicked her successor, Heidi van der Mehden, already renowned for her winemaking with Cab rockstar Richard Arrowood, and she became the winemaker in 2018. Solar panels provide most of the power and bee friendly plants dot the landscaping.

VINEYARDS - One of the six estates—the flagship Meredith (20 acres), planted in 1996 on Goldridge soil—is converting to organic certification. (Some of the wines, not featured here, may be grown with herbicide.) Edwards' favorite Clone 37 is planted on all of the estates. Fertilizing mushroom compost comes from a neighboring farm. Roederer's 12 acre Dach Vineyard in Anderson Valley, certified organic and biodynamic, also provides grapes.

WINES - While Edwards' style leaned into bold phenolics (achieved with Clone 37, bigger fermenters and 50+% new oak) that still provide structure, the wines are moving toward greater freshness and balance.

Anderson Valley Dach Vineyard Pinot Noir 2022 ● 320 cases; 75 $ - ⊞ - Aged 10 months in French oak (54% new). Multiple heritage clones. Red fruit, plum and blueberry aromas and flavors.
Russian River Valley Coopersmith Vineyard Pinot Noir 2022 ● 280 cases; 70 $ - ⊞ - Aged 10 months in French oak (58% new). 100 percent Clone 37. Opens with signature cocoa and chocolate aromas followed by red and blue fruits on the palate.
Russian River Valley Meredith Estate Pinot Noir 2021 ● 1,400 cases; 90 $ - ⊞ - Aged in French oak (55% new). The flagship wine from a mix of clones. A bold Pinot Noir with Bing cherry on the nose and black cherry and dark chocolate on the palate. Finishes long.

acres 79 - cases 28,000
Fertilizers compost, cover crops, manure, organic fertilizer
Plant protection sulfur, biodynamic preparations, synthetic pesticides, copper, organic
Weed control mechanical
Yeasts commercial cultured yeasts
Grapes purchase 35%
Certification some of the vineyards are certified organic, some of the vineyards are certified biodynamic, converting to organic

SEBASTOPOL

MONTE RIO CELLARS

6780 McKinley Street Ste 170 - tel. (917) 589-6838
www.monteriocellars.com - info@monteriocellars.com

PEOPLE - A former restaurant owner and New York sommelier, Patrick Cappiello moved to Sonoma after meeting winemaker Pax Mahle who became his best friend and mentor. In 2017 he came to work harvest and then in 2018 made the first vintage of his Monte Rio Cellars where he focuses on heritage grapes and more. He describes himself on Instagram (where he has 37,000 followers) as a "natural winemaker (that uses SO2)." Jesus Aleman is the assistant winemaker.

VINEYARDS - He buys from about 15 vineyards, mostly in Lodi, for value and vine age, scouring the area for organic growers. Vino Farms' Craig Ledbetter has 50 acres of Sangiovese and Vermentino (certified organic and biodynamic). Likewise, fourth generation Nico Teresi has 65 acres of Petite Sirah and Zin (certified organic) and is adding Southern Italian varieties. Jessie's Grove has 124-year old Carignan planted in 1900. Cappiello also farms a small vineyard in Lodi planted to Flame Tokay from the 1860s.

WINES - Focused on heritage vineyards. Cappiello produces handcrafted naturally made wines with tension and texture.

Lodi Sauvignon Blanc 2023 EVERYDAY WINE ○ 800 cases; 24 $ - Fermented half in tank and half neutral barrique. Picked twice and blended before bottling. Sancerre style. Mineral driven with subtle citrus notes. Alive and vibrant on the palate with electric acidity and lots of texture.
Clement Hills The Bench Vermentino 2023 ◉ 700 cases; 24 $ - Aged four months in neutral oak. Fermented 30 days on the skins with gentle daily punchdowns. An orange wine that is a clementine orange in color with notes of tangerines, orange blossoms and citrus, textured tannins and a juicy finish.
Clement Hills River's Edge Vineyard Sangiovese 2022 ● 800 cases; 24 $ - Aged in old barrique. Whole cluster. Biodynamic fruit. Fermented in tank. A wine with beautiful floral notes and an elegant finish.

acres 205 - cases 8,000
Fertilizers compost, biodynamic compost, cover crops, manure, organic fertilizer
Plant protection sulfur, biodynamic preparations, organic
Weed control animal grazing, mechanical
Yeasts spontaneous fermentation
Grapes purchase 100%
Certification some of the vineyards are certified organic, converting to biodynamic

SONOMA

MOON HOLLOW

481 First Street West - tel. (707) 744-4777
www.moonhollow.com - info@moonhollow.com

 An emerging producer from Moon Mountain making exceptional estate wines from organic vines.

PEOPLE - After selling their social media network Bebo in 2008, in 2011 founders Xochi, a Bay Area native, and English born Michael Birch bought a sprawling 360 acre former Arabian horse facility in Sonoma. The first estate wine was released in 2017. Organic vineyard manager Phil Coturri oversees it and French born sommelier Christophe Tassan (formerly at The Battery) is the manager. Their new downtown tasting room, designed by hipster decorator Ken Fulk, opened in 2024.

VINEYARDS - The mountain property, now 720 acres, sits on a majestic site with sweeping views. The 18 acres of vines grow in thin volcanic soils yielding small berries. Two thirds is planted to Cabernet Sauvignon, on three different rootstalks. It grows 12 Cabernet clones Coturri selected from other estates with similar soils. They also raise vegetables, fruit, chickens and Kune Kune pigs on the property–hence the logo featuring a pig.

WINES - The renowned Mark Herold, a Moon Mountain veteran, makes the superbly crafted wines from classic Bordeaux and Rhone varieties.

Moon Mountain District Cabernet Sauvignon 2021 SLOW WINE ● 1,200 cases; 120 $ - Aged 22 months in French oak (66% new). The flagship Cab is blended with Cabernet Franc (12%). On the lighter side of Cab. Its 12 different clones give it multiple layers of black fruit, spice notes, and tiny herbaceous notes from mountain garrigue. Very elegant.
Moon Mountain District Syrah 2021 ● 125 cases; 85 $ - Aged 22 months in French oak (33% new). Vibrant cherry notes shine through in this complex, balanced wine. Exceptional.
Moon Mountain District Grenache 2020 ● 450 cases; 80 $ - Aged 22 months in French oak (33% new). Tablas Creek clones. Cofermented with Mourvedre (15%). A pure voice of silky red fruits, including raspberries and strawberries, with spices, sings in this head turning wine.

acres 18 - cases 2,000
Fertilizers compost, cover crops
Plant protection sulfur, organic
Weed control mechanical
Yeasts commercial cultured yeasts
Grapes 100% owned
Certification organic

SANTA ROSA

NORTH AMERICAN PRESS

Sonoma County - PO Box 2833 - tel. (805) 704-1224
www.northamericanpress.wine - matt@northamericanpress.com

PEOPLE - Winegrower Matt Niess has a vision for understanding time and place in a vineyard that goes beyond exploring how traditional European grape varieties express themselves in North American terroir. He works exclusively with varieties that have indigenous North American grape genetics in their makeup. That includes wild hybrids discovered along Sonoma County's backroads and deliberate crosses meant to exploit the unique characters of North American natives.

VINEYARDS - Matt farms a small vineyard growing grafts of wild grapes discovered nearby. He also works with hybrid grapes including from Buffalo Creek, located at 5,500 feet in the Carson Range (granitic soils) and a small plot of Baco Noir on the Sonoma Coast. He believes these varieties can be farmed more naturally, without sprays, as they have evolved with the local environment, an ethos reflected in vineyards he works with as well as his own.

WINES - Unexpected fruit sources expand the notion of what great North American wine can be.

TOP Russian River Valley Wildcard Wine-Cider Blend 2022 EVERYDAY WINE 150 cases; 23 $ - Aged in neutral oak for six months. A co-fermentation of wild hybrid grapes and dry farmed, certified organic Gravenstein apples. The blend was fermented before finishing in bottle and left undisgorged. A tart, refreshing blend of ruby grapefruit, raspberry, red currant, lemon zest, fresh thyme and touch of nutmeg.

Sonoma Coast The Rebel Baco Noir 2023 75 cases; 33 $ - Aged nine months in neutral oak. A European/North American hybrid. Tart and full bodied with soft, supple tannins and flavors of black currant, blackberry black and red raspberries, red plum skin, sour orange and a touch of cayenne pepper.

Nevada The Maker 75 cases; 31 $ - Aged six months in neutral oak. A textured blend of Brianna and LaCrosse hybrid grapes. Rich notes of sweet lemon, grapefruit peel, ripe nectarine, muskmelon, white currant and lemongrass.

acres 5 - cases 5000
Fertilizers none
Plant protection none
Weed control mechanical, manual
Yeasts spontaneous fermentation
Grapes purchase 60%
Certification none

SEBASTOPOL

PAX WINES

6780 McKinley Street, Suite 170 - tel. (707) 310-2743
www.paxwines.com - pam@paxwines.com

PEOPLE - Founded in 2000, acclaimed vintners Pax and Pam Mahle champion unsung varieties that now enchant their fans. Initially captivated by Chenin Blanc and North Coast grown Syrah (their flagship varieties), they've added to their repertoire, seeking out and bringing to life vibrant and elegant expressions of Gamay, Mondeuse, Mourvedre and Trousseau Gris as well as their flagship varieties. They make the wines in Sebastopol's trendy Barlow District, where their casual tasting room is located.

VINEYARDS - Sourcing is all over the place—from the vast reaches of Sonoma itself and north to Mendocino, south to Lodi and east to high elevation sites in Amador County and El Dorado counties in the Sierra Foothills. The range of microclimates and soils offers tremendous diversity.

WINES - Pure fruit and balanced wines with an authentic voice that perfectly frames the grapes from these choice sites.

TOP Sonoma Hillsides Syrah 2022 SLOW WINE 650 cases; 60 $ - The top of the line Syrah in a lineup it's hard to choose from. Plush and nuanced from sites ranging from steep and rocky to sand. Balanced, dense and powerful with elegance and grace.

Sonoma Coast Rancho Coda Gamay 2022 98 cases; 38 $ - Aged 10 months in neutral oak. The vineyard's new name is Las Cimas Ranch. Whole cluster (100%). Partial carbonic maceration. Concentrated dark cherry and black plums with delicate tannins. A scene stealer.

Russian River Trousseau Gris 2022 1,200 cases; 30 $ - Fermented in concrete. Grown at the Fanucchi Wood Vineyard. Refreshing and rare. Vibrant, juicy and versatile. Caseworthy.

acres 0 - cases 6,000
Fertilizers compost, biodynamic compost, cover crops
Plant protection sulfur, organic
Weed control mechanical
Yeasts spontaneous fermentation
Grapes purchase 100%
Certification none

HEALDSBURG

PORTER CREEK VINEYARDS

8735 Westside Road - tel. (707) 433-6321
www.portercreekvineyards.com - info@portercreekvineyards.com

 One of the state's best Pinot and Chardonnay producers, here winegrower and winemaker are one and the same, making nuanced wines overdeliver.

PEOPLE - Die hard fans and sommeliers alike love this classic, family owned and run producer. It's as close to Burgundy in farming and winemaking as the Russian River Valley gets. George Davis purchased the land in 1978. Second generation Alex Davis, a true vigneron, runs the estate. His daughter, third generation Fiona Davis, is currently studying viticulture and enology at Cal Poly.

VINEYARDS - The hillside estate contains some of the oldest Pinot Noir and Chardonnay vines in the Russian River (dating back to 1978 and 1981 respectively) and they are still producing. The vines were first certified organic and biodynamic in 2003. This year Davis planted an acre of Syrah on the estate. New plantings are high density. The winery installed ecofriendly solar arrays and uses an electric Monarch tractor.

WINES - Schooled in Old World style by Burgundian masters (Georges Roumier), Dijon educated Davis uses classic techniques. New oak use is around 30%.

Russian River Hillside Vineyard Old Vines Pinot Noir 2019 SLOWWINE ● 281 cases; 92 $ - From vines planted in 1973. Red fruits and rose petals and a bit of dark red fruit shining through. The long, silky finish that comes from old vines. Outstanding.
Russian River Valley Fiona Hill Vineyard Pinot Noir 2021 ● 475 cases; 65 $ - The flagship Pinot Noir is grown on steep hillsides, digging its roots into hard clay topsoil underlain by fractured bedrock. In the mouth, soft tannins frame notes of wild berry and forest floor.
Russian River Valley Haley Marie Vineyard Viognier 2021 O 296 cases; 45 $ - Davis has been making Viognier from other sources for 20 years, until planting his own in 2015. This vintage is the inaugural, all estate, single vineyard Viognier. Rich yet nuanced, it's elegant, offering up mango, pear and nectar.

acres 22 - cases 4,000
Fertilizers compost, biodynamic compost, manure
Plant protection sulfur, biodynamic preparations, organic
Weed control mechanical
Yeasts spontaneous fermentation
Grapes purchase 20%
Certification some of the vineyards are certified organic, some of the vineyards are certified biodynamic

HEALDSBURG

PRESTON FARM & WINERY

9282 W Dry Creek Road - tel. (707) 433-3372
www.prestonfarmandwinery.com - mail@prestonvineyards.com

 One of the classics. A winner for farming, wine, people and community.

PEOPLE - Lou and Suan Preston have created an agragrian paradise devoted to farming both food and wine and creating community. They grow more than 200 crops and sell veggies, olive oil and lamb sausages at the local farmers market and their on site farm store. They also teach summer camp kids about agriculture and have U-pick strawberries and pumpkins in season. Grayson Hartley makes the wines. Some wines are foot trod.

VINEYARDS - A poster child for regenerative agriculture, the winery grows Dry Creek's climate appropriate varieties—Rhones and Zinfandel—and treasures a few blocks of 100+ year old, head trained Carignane and Zinfandel. It's adventurously planted Italian varieties including Barbera, Nero d'Avola, Ribolla Gialla, Schioppettino, Tocai Friulano and Vermentino. All are dry farmed and certified organic.

WINES - The winery as well as the vineyards is certified organic enabling them to put "Made with Organic Grapes" on the label, a higher standard than for most wines.

Dry Creek Valley Barbera Reserve 2022 SLOWWINE ● 50 cases; 65 $ - Foot trod and aged longer in large foudres, these special blocks produced a wine of great depth and complexity. The regular Barbera ($42), with raspberry and cherry cola on the nose and red fruits on the palate, is also excellent.
Dry Creek Valley Cinsault 2022 ● 439 cases; 40 $ - From dry farmed vines planted in 1990. A juicy go to wine with cherry pie flavors made more complex with darker fruit undertones along with herbal and savory notes in the mix. Also delicious served chilled.
Dry Creek Valley White Wine 2022 O White Blend; 140 cases; 42 $ - A blend of Sauvignon Blanc (50%) Ribolla Gialla (25%), and Friulano (25%). The Sauvignon is skin fermented. On the nose, ripe apricot and pear juice with citrus and stone fruits on the palate. Complex and vibrant.

acres 63 - cases 8,000
Fertilizers biodynamic compost, cover crops
Plant protection biodynamic preparations, organic
Weed control animal grazing, mechanical
Yeasts spontaneous fermentation
Grapes 100% owned
Certification organic

HEALDSBURG

QUIVIRA VINEYARDS

4900 W Dry Creek Road - tel. (707)431-8333
www.quivirawine.com - info@quivirawine.com

PEOPLE - A green farming pioneer, it's celebrated eco-friendly, agrarian values and wines since 2004 when it was first certified organic. It went solar in 2005. Current owners Pete and Terri Kight continue the 40+ year long stewardship established first by the Wendts (who started the winery in 1981), but will be passing the baton on to a future owner soon. (The winery is for sale.) It's best known for Rhônes, renowned rosé, Sauvignon Blanc and that Dry Creek favorite, Zinfandel.

VINEYARDS - The organic farm is home to cows, pigs, chickens, bees, olive trees and vegetable gardens (featuring plants from Slow Food's Ark of Taste list of endangered varieties). Winemaker Hugh Chappelle builds wine complexity through massal selections of multiple clones. For climate resilience, he's focused on late ripening grapes that can hang through late summer heat—Cinsault, Grenache, Semillon, Syrah and Vermentino.

WINES - Long time winemaker Hugh Chapelle has been an essential guiding force since 2010, making expressive, balanced wines that delicately showcase fruit purity.

🔵 **Dry Creek Valley Fig Tree Vineyard Sauvignon Blanc 2022** SLOW WINE ⭘ 1,465 cases; 32 $ - 🔘 - Musque clone (30%). One of three Sauvignon Blancs from this Sauvignon Blanc loving producer. Highly aromatic nose of guava and blossoms. Ripe grapefruit on the palate, followed by a lengthy finish. Outstanding year after year.

Dry Creek Valley Wine Creek Ranch Rosé 2023 ● 1,100 cases; 32 $ - 🔘 - A perennial favorite, Grenache (53%) dominates the blend, partnered with Petite Sirah (22%), Counoise (14%), Mourvèdre (7%) and Primitivo (4%). Notes of guava, passion fruit, tart strawberry and pink grapefruit. Vibrant and refreshing.

Dry Creek Valley Wine Creek Ranch Grenache 2021 ● 200 cases; 45 $ - 🔘 - Partial whole cluster, aged in foudres. Red fruit driven with a juicy palate of pomegranate, raspberry, strawberry and dark cherries. Very versatile for food pairings.

acres 68 - cases 18,500
Fertilizers compost, biodynamic compost, manure, organic fertilizer
Plant protection sulfur, organic
Weed control mechanical
Yeasts spontaneous fermentation, selected indigenous yeasts
Grapes purchase 20%
Certification some of the vineyards are certified organic

SEBASTOPOL

RADIO-COTEAU

2040 Barlow Lane - tel. (707) 823-2578
www.radiocoteau.com - clientservices@radiocoteau.com

PEOPLE - Winegrower Eric Sussman's vision was to create an integrated community of people and nature. This philosophy is amply demonstrated by his estate farm which is home to poultry, goats, fruit trees, uncultivated wild lands and an extensive vegetable garden, the produce of which is shared with winery and vineyard workers.

VINEYARDS - Farmed since 1892, the 42 acre ranch (certified biodynamic) sits at 800 feet along a ridge above the town of Occidental. At this elevation, morning fogs burn away early, followed by long hours of sun and cool ocean breezes. Rich, well draining Goldridge loam sits atop water retaining clay allowing the vineyard to be farmed without irrigation. Non estate vineyards occupy spots nearby with similar soils, but varying climactic conditions.

WINES - A deft communion of traditional European winemaking practices and Sonoma Coast fruit.

🔵 **Sonoma Coast Harrison Grade Estate Syrah 2021** SLOW WINE ● 140 cases; 70 $ - 🔘 - Aged 20 months in 500 L neutral puncheons. Partial whole cluster (20%). Rich and spicy with notes of ripe black plum, black cherry and black pepper. Smooth and ripe with perfect subtle balance.

Sonoma Coast Dusty Lanes Syrah 2021 ● 140 cases; 68 $ - 🔘 - Aged 20 months in large format neutral oak. Darker and more brooding than the Harrison Grade, with more black fruit notes (black cherry, blueberry, black raspberry) and much more of the spicy black pepper that Rhone style Syrah is known for.

Sonoma Coast Estate Riesling 2022 ⭘ 216 cases; 50 $ - 🔘 - Aged 10 month in Austrian 600L neutral barrels. Whole cluster pressed. Ripe and bright and at the same time quite delicate. Warm, ripe aromas and flavors of lemon, lime, pear, peach, nectarine and white flowers supported by balancing acidity.

acres 22 - cases 4,000
Fertilizers compost, biodynamic compost, cover crops, organic fertilizer
Plant protection sulfur, biodynamic preparations, organic
Weed control mechanical
Yeasts spontaneous fermentation
Grapes purchase 50%
Certification some of the vineyards are certified organic, some of the vineyards are certified biodynamic

SEBASTOPOL

RAEN

6780 McKinley Avenue - tel. (707) 633-3016
www.raenwinery.com - info@raenwinery.com

PEOPLE - Now an acclaimed West Sonoma Pinot Noir producer, Carlo and Dante Mondavi founded RAEN (Research in Agriculture and Enology) in 2013. After joining as assistant winemaker in 2017, New Zealand native Melanie McIntyre became winemaker in 2023. Inspired by Monarch butterflies, Carlo Mondavi raises awareness for eco-friendly farming by donating proceeds from a rosé released annually on Earth Day to the Xerces Society and Sonoma County Wildlife Rescue.

VINEYARDS - Carlo Mondavi has taken a leading role in the Monarch electric tractor parent company and the team here uses one at their Freestone Occidental vineyard (certified organic). Described as "where the ocean meets the forest," the estate is a release site for bobcats and foxes by Sonoma County Wildlife. RAEN farms six West Sonoma Coast vineyards (some leased) at elevations from 600 to 1,200 feet. 2022 marks the tenth vintage from the seven acre Sonoma Coast estate.

WINES - Minimal intervention, whole cluster (90-100%) and predominately neutral oak (with just 10 to 12% new) lets the sites shine through.

Fort Ross-Seaview Lady Marjorie Chardonnay 2022 O 1,500 cases; 68 $ - ⊞ - The second vintage for this whole cluster pressed Chardonnay that's a showcase of intensity and persistence with layers of ripe citrus, crisp stone fruits and saline minerality.

North Coast Monarch Challenge Rosé 2023 ● 500 cases; 30 $ - 🍷⊞ - The eighth bottling made to fundraise for saving Monarch butterflies. A true coastal rose with racy acidity and a vibrant melange of stone fruit, blond raspberries and pink grapefruit.

Freestone Occidental Bodega Vineyard Pinot Noir 2022 ● 200 cases; 130 $ - ⊞ - 100% whole cluster. A reflection of the coastal redwood forest that rings the site, whole cluster amplifies aromas of alpine strawberries, and damp sous bois. The flavors move to darker red and black raspberry with notes of resinous, piney herbs and blood orange.

acres 18 - cases 3,800
Fertilizers compost, cover crops
Plant protection sulfur, organic
Weed control mechanical
Yeasts spontaneous fermentation
Grapes purchase 50%
Certification some of the vineyards are certified organic

SONOMA

RAM'S GATE WINERY

28700 Arnold Drive - tel. (707) 721-8700
www.ramsgatewinery.com - concierge@ramsgatewinery.com

PEOPLE - Co-owner of the winery since 2011, O'Neill Vintners & Distillers founder and CEO Jeff O'Neill bought out his partners in 2024 to become the sole owner. The move also launched his company's new luxury wine division. In 2022, O'Neill became a certified B corp. General manager and winemaker Joe Nielsen assumed the helm in 2018, joined by assistant winemaker Rachel Bordes, a Cal Poly graduate, in 2020. The winery offers a five course wine and food pairing.

VINEYARDS - Ram's Gate sits at the gateway to Sonoma Valley overlooking the vast wetlands of the Napa Sonoma Marsh and the San Pablo Bay. The team is replanting Chardonnay and Pinot Noir clones—Chardonnay to the Wente clone and Pinot Noir to heritage clones Calera and Mt. Eden. They conserve water, reducing irrigation and collecting rainwater. Sheep help with weeding and falcons with pest control. Some wines (not featured here) may be grown with herbicide.

WINES - The estate is Increasingly recognized for its Chardonnay. Nielsen's quest for quality—terroir is emerging in the estate wines—as well as upgraded hospitality show the winery has raised the bar for Sonoma's luxury tier.

⊙ Carneros Estate Chardonnay 2021 O 312 cases; 76 $ - ⊞ - Aged 11 months in French oak (25% new). Wente clone (63%) with Mt. Eden and Robert Young for the balance. Youthful with notes of lychee, kiwi and chai spice.

Carneros Estate Pinot Blanc 2022 O 500 cases; 40 $ - 🍷 - Aged six months in neutral French oak (86%). Etude and Beringer clones contribute notes of apricot, wheatgrass and wildflower honey with some added texture from the dry vintage.

Carneros Estate Pinot Noir 2021 ● 357 cases; 85 $ - ⊞ - Aged 16 months in French oak (34% new). Partial whole cluster. A blend of Massal (57%) and Clone 828 (43%) from older vines. A concentrated, ageworthy vintage.

acres 28 - cases 10,000
Fertilizers compost, cover crops, organic fertilizer
Plant protection sulfur, synthetic pesticides
Weed control animal grazing, mechanical
Yeasts spontaneous fermentation, commercial cultured yeasts
Grapes purchase 65%
Certification some of the vineyards are certified organic

SANTA ROSA

READ HOLLAND

1160 Hopper Avenue, Ste B - tel. (707) 721-2401
www.readhollandwines.com - info@readholland.com

PEOPLE - A collaboration with the Read family and winemaker Ashley Holland, the brand was inspired by their mutual love of Pinot Noir from Anderson Valley's Deep End, an area known for its cool climate and unique flavors. Holland honed her craft during four harvests in Marlborough (think "University of Sauvignon Blanc" as she describes it), did stints in Uruguay and worked at Three Sticks in Sonoma. Beyond Pinot, they make heritage and old vine Chardonnay, Riesling and Sauvignon Blanc.

VINEYARDS - The label buys fruit from small growers living on their vineyard sites who prioritize organic practices. Pinot clones vary from Pommard at two Deep End sites—Conzelman and Romani—to 115 at Bevel (next to Savoy) and Mt. Eden (head trained, dry farmed) in the Santa Cruz Mountains. At the historic Upton (certified organic) in Redwood Valley, planted in 1969, the original three person crew farms the Sauvignon Blanc vines. Some wines, not featured here, are grown with herbicide.

WINES - Holland seeks character over polish in elegant wines, like hard pressing Chardonnay skins to capture flavor, long cold malo ferments, and Stockinger barrels to let Pinot Noir shine.

⊙ Santa Cruz Mountains Peter Martin Ray Chardonnay 2021 ○ 110 cases; 60 $ - ⊞ - Beautifully alive and satin graceful. Mt. Eden clone. Nose of lemon verbena and sea salt opens to a palate lithe and long with lemon drop sucker hinted with saline and phenolic texture. Unfined, unfiltered.
Mendocino Upton Vineyard Sauvignon Blanc 2023 ○ 250 cases; 30 $ - ⊞ - Dry farmed, concrete fermented. Lovely nose of lime blossom and nettle. Fresh acidity on rich palate of lemon balm, finishes long with grapefruit and sweet herb.
Anderson Valley Deep End Pinot Noir 2021 ● 392 cases; 60 $ - ⊞ - Aged in French oak (27% new). Partial whole cluster (35%). Warm spices and earth on the nose. Herbaceous deep cherry acidity, juicy raspberry and bright, brandied cherries wrap the tannic structure, destined for suppleness.

acres 0 - cases 800
Fertilizers compost, cover crops, organic fertilizer, synthetic fertilizer
Plant protection sulfur, organic
Weed control mechanical, manual
Yeasts spontaneous fermentation, commercial cultured yeasts
Grapes purchase 100%
Certification some of the vineyards are certified organic

HEALDSBURG

RUTH LEWANDOWSKI WINE

132 Plaza Street - tel. (707) 385-1797
www.ruthlewandowskiwines.com - evan@ruthlewandowskiwines.com

PEOPLE - Natural winemaker Evan Lewandowski began in 2012, initially with the intention of making wine in his home state of Utah. He believes that the world needs intentionally made, affordably priced, weeknight wine, and his cuvee wines have become wildly popular among natural wine aficionados, featuring a range of varieties—Arneis, Barbera, Cortese, Dolcetto, Mission, Muscat, Nebbiolo, Souzao, Tinta Roriz and Touriga Nacional.

VINEYARDS - Lewandowski buys most of the grapes from Fox Hill Vineyard (certified organic), which fellow natural winemaker Chris Brockway (of Broc Wines) purchased in 2023. Seven additional sites include Lost Hills (owned by Chris Bilbro), historic Testa (certified organic) in Calpella and Rorick in Calaveras County.

WINES - The range extends from entry level wines to unique, single vineyard designates. Zero zero wines—nothing added or taken away—are just one of the many styles.

⊙ Mendocino Testa Vineyard Boaz 2022 ● 320 cases; 42 $ - ⋓ ⊞ - A co-ferment of Charbono (2019) and old vine Grenache (1912) and Carignan (1947). Very aromatic with baking spice, Earl Grey tea, dark chocolate and cedar. Distinct plum and brambles on the palate, with a nice lingering finish.
Mendocino Fox Hill Vineyard Chilion Cortese 2021 ○ 285 cases; 35 $ - ⊞ ⊙ - Zero zero. Aromatic and bright, with woodsy, apricot and oregano on the nose, plus a ton more juicy and dried apricot on the lush yet tension filled palate.
Mendocino Fox Hill Vineyard L. Stone Sangiovese 2021 ● 530 cases; 45 $ - ⋓ ⊞ ⊙ - An homage honoring Lewandowski's time in Brunello Montalcino. Notes of morello cherry, allspice, oregano and salted black licorice. Fresh and earthy with high toned fruit, showcasing the prettiness of the varietal.

acres 0 - cases 6,500
Fertilizers compost, cover crops
Plant protection sulfur, organic
Weed control animal grazing, mechanical, manual
Yeasts spontaneous fermentation
Grapes purchase 100%
Certification organic

SONOMA

SCRIBE

2100 Denmark Street - tel. (707) 939-1858
www.scribewinery.com - frontdesk@scribewinery.com

PEOPLE - Adam and Andrew Mariani transformed a crumbling 1858 hacienda built by the German immigrant Dressler brothers into a fashionable, picturesque, Instagrammable destination, enhanced by an impressive culinary program run by their sister Kelly, a chef who trained at Slow Food in Italy. Kelly's cooking videos are posted on the winery's website. Gustavo Sotelo-Miller is the winemaker.

VINEYARDS - On their estate below Arrowhead Mountain, south of the town of Sonoma, they grow Burgundian wines as well as classic German varieties that Geisenheim immigrant Emil Dressler first planted here in the 1850's—including Riesling and Sylvaner—in what was once called the Rhine Farm. Notably Scribe has also planted to acres of the Mission grape, an historic variety the Spanish missionaries relied upon. (Some wines, not featured here, may be grown with herbicide.)

WINES - The winemaking experiments with new takes on classics, like a skin fermented Chardonnay, a sparkling Mission wine, and a white pressed Pinot Noir rosé.

Sonoma Valley Sparkling Mission 2023 SLOW WINE n.a.; 54 $ - Once a peasant wine grape, Mission was the first wine grape early missionaries planted in California. As a still wine, unless in expert hands, it verges on rusticity. As a sparkler, though, it's transformed. This effervescent one delivers a delicious fizz of strawberry, cranberry and rhubarb with a tiny hint of sweetness.

Sonoma Valley Estate Riesling 2023 O 1,100 cases; 46 $ - Aged five months in stainless steel and concrete. In 1858, Emil Dressler brought the first Riesling cuttings to America and planted them on the estate site in 1858. Replanting it here was an homage. A delicate wine with subtle charms, displaying stone fruit notes. A beautiful finish.

Sonoma Valley Skin Fermented Chardonnay 2022 O n.a.; 44 $ - Fermented on skins for up to 90 days in concrete eggs. Skin contact brings out bergamot and orange blossom in a textured wine with an intriguing balance of fruit and acidity.

acres 53 - cases 15,000
Fertilizers cover crops, organic fertilizer, synthetic fertilizer
Plant protection sulfur, synthetic pesticides, copper, organic
Weed control mechanical
Yeasts spontaneous fermentation, commercial cultured yeasts
Grapes purchase 50%
Certification none

OCCIDENTAL

SENSES WINES

P.O. BOX 171 - tel. (707) 874-8550
www.senseswines.com - hello@senseswines.com

PEOPLE - Founded in 2011 by three childhood friends, Christopher Strieter, Max Thieriot and Myles Lawrence-Briggs, Senses' estate vineyards are located in the West Sonoma Coast and Russian River Valley AVAs. The renowned Thomas Rivers Brown makes the wines with assistant winemaker Derek Flegal who joined in 2018. Strieter was instrumental in organizing the region's growers to create the West Sonoma Coast appellation which was approved in May 2022.

VINEYARDS - The winery's portfolio has expanded considerably through sourcing from as many as nine vineyards in addition to their estate: B.A. Thieriot which is planted to five acres of mixed Chardonnay clones and 3.5 acres of Pinot Noir; Hillcrest, known as 'Day One', three acres of Pinot Noir (Calera, 828, Swan & 115), and Bodega Thieriot which is nine acres of Calera Pinot Noir planted in 2016. The winery did not produce red wines in 2020. Valdez & Sons Vineyard Management farms the estate vineyards.

WINES - Distinctly cool climate in character, the wines from these sought after sites are recognizable for their intensity, focus and purity.

Sonoma Coast Day One Pinot Noir 2021 SLOW WINE 345 cases; 135 $ - Aged 10 months in French oak (30% new). Complex floral and sous bois aromas, layers of bright cherry and berries, youthful and exuberant with fine-grained tannins and green peppercorn spice; lithe and long.

West Sonoma Coast Bodega Pinot Noir 2021 320 cases; 135 $ - Aged 12 months in French oak (100% new). Aromas of lavender and red cherries moving to crisp pomegranate, black cherries with notes of ferrous earth and toast.

West Sonoma Coast Chardonnay B.A. Thieriot 2021 O 225 cases; 135 $ - Aged 14 months in French oak (30% new). Aromas of citrus and baked pears, lean and shy as tasted pre release with white stone fruit and young pineapple flavors and pronounced acidity.

acres 24 - cases 6,000
Fertilizers organic fertilizer
Plant protection synthetic pesticides
Weed control mechanical
Yeasts spontaneous fermentation
Grapes purchase 65%
Certification none

SEBASTOPOL

SMALL VINES

1600 Barlow Lane - tel. (707) 823-0886
www.smallvines.com - info@smallvines.com

 Putting farming and devotion to terroir first, their vibrant Chardonnays and Pinot Noirs are among the finest in Sonoma, demonstrating the region's potential in the hands of skilled grower-vintners.

PEOPLE - Acclaimed vintners Paul and Kathryn Sloan farmed for others, waiting for the opportunity to buy their own estate, and in 2007 landed the dream site in Green Valley that Paul had tried to lease for years. Their The Barlow Homestead (TBH) winery is housed in a former apple barn, surrounded by orchards and vines.

VINEYARDS - Meticulous farmers, their six dry farmed estates offer varied terrain expressed in each of their nuanced wines. They look for coastal influences and low vigor soil for high density spacing, planting 3,630 vines to the acre. The technique is practiced in Burgundy but rare in the U.S. . They farm using only organic approved materials. Their largest site, the 12 acre TBH, grows 5 Pinot clones (Calera, Swan, Pommard and more) on a windy knoll on Goldridge soils.

WINES - High density plantings increase fruit intensity (with smaller berries and thicker skin), creating wines of greater concentration. In the cellar, classic winemaking results in exceptional elegance, vivid fruit purity and depth.

Sonoma Coast Chardonnay 2022 ○ 175 cases; 55 $ - ▦ - Barrel fermented and aged 8 months in French oak (20% new) on lees. Wente and Mt. Eden clones. Whole cluster (100%). Vibrant, with bright acidity and depth. A clear citrus voice enlivens from entry to finish.
Sonoma Coast TBH Chardonnay 2022 ○ 155 cases; 75 $ - ▦ - Barrel fermented and aged in French oak (14% new). A selection of specific clusters from TBH. Captivating stone fruit and citrus lead to a saline finish.
Sonoma Coast TBH Pinot Noir 2022 ● 127 cases; 150 $ - ▦ - Aged 12 months in French oak (18% new) on lees. Delicious blue and red fruits with a hint of herbaceousness on the palate end with a cherry flourish.

---

acres 20 - cases 3,000
Fertilizers biodynamic compost, cover crops
Plant protection sulfur, biodynamic preparations, organic
Weed control mechanical, manual
Yeasts spontaneous fermentation
Grapes 100% owned
Certification none

GLEN ELLEN

STONE EDGE FARM

5700 Cavedale Road - tel. (707) 935-6520
www.stoneedgefarm.com - concierge@stoneedgefarm.com

 A pioneering, organic producer harnessing a talented A-list team of Moon Mountain aficionados, making celebrated wines.

PEOPLE - Proprietors Mac and Leslie McQuown and team know Moon Mountain well. This is their second go at making renowned wines from the region. Former (and founding) Stone Edge winemaker Jeff Baker, a Moon Mountain legend, passed the winemaking baton to Spanish born Alejandro Zimman in 2018 who has grown the winery's reputation for producing exceptional wines.

VINEYARDS - Superstar organic vineyard expert Phil Coturri has been the longstanding viticulturalist here. The estate has two sites-one high on Moon Mountain and one down in Sonoma Valley. At 1,800 feet of elevation, the 18 acre Silver Cloud Vineyard is the Bordeaux variety workhorse, growing 75 percent of the fruit. The McQuown's also have a 16 acre organic farm and vines at their family residence, with a solar microgrid and zero carbon footprint.

WINES - Zimman's renowned for his first growth Bordeaux style wines made here from Coturri's outstanding fruit.

🔝 **Moon Mountain District Cabernet Sauvignon 2019**
SLOW WINE ● Cabernet Sauvignon; 581 cases; 150 $ - ▦ - Finesse, complexity and refined character. Aromas of wet stone, plum, chocolate, and a palate that is savory and silky, with cassis, bay leaf and an elegant finish.
Sonoma Valley Cabernet Sauvignon 2019 ● 970 cases; 150 $ - ▦ - A blend of mountain (43%) and valley (57%) fruit, fermented by block. Aromas of mocha, tobacco, forest floor, dried blueberry and oregano, with flavors of black pepper, jerky, black licorice and juniper.
Moon Mountain District Sauvignon Blanc 2022 ○ 497 cases; 50 $ - ▦ - A Bordeaux white. It's Sauvignon Blanc with Sémillon (23%). Barrel fermented. Tropical on the nose, full of passionfruit and spice, followed by a burst of juicy citrus, lime curd and nuttiness on the palate.

---

acres 24 - cases 4,500
Fertilizers compost, cover crops, manure
Plant protection organic
Weed control mechanical, manual
Yeasts spontaneous fermentation, commercial cultured yeasts
Grapes 100% owned
Certification organic

HEALDSBURG

SONOMA

SURVEYOR

THE GRENACHISTA

100 Montage Way - tel. (707) 342-3806 - (707) 979-9000
www.montage.com/healdsburg - jennifer.chiesa@montage.com

21684 8th Street East, Suite 450 - tel. (805) 704-0779
www.thegrenachista.com - casey@crgraybehlwines.com

PEOPLE - Sonoma all star Jesse Katz (Aperture Cellars) was hired in 2016 to create the vineyards and wine for this private label for the luxurious Montage Healdsburg resort. Overseeing viticulture as well as winemaking from the ground up, he planted the vineyard in 2019, creating small blocks throughout the resort's 258 acres, positioned to provide picturesque vineyard views.

VINEYARDS - The resort property is set on eastern hills with volcanic soils in the heart of Alexander Valley. The vines grow in high density in meter by meter spacing, which requires tending by hand. The vines grows all five Bordeaux reds—Cabernet Franc, Cabernet Sauvignon, Malbec, Merlot and Petit Verdot—as well as Sauvignon Blanc. Rows are labeled with custom metal signs identifying each planted variety as an educational feature for guests.

PEOPLE - The winery name explains it all. Casey Graybehl seeks out Grenache anywhere he can find it in northern California. With Grenache Blanc, he makes a still wine and two pet nats. With Grenache Noir, he makes a rosé, a pet nat, a carbonic, a blend, and four, soon to be five, vineyard designates. And, in 2024 he made a white wine from Grenache Gris thanks to David Mounts who grafted budwood in 2023 in Dry Creek. Casey makes all of his Grenache wines in 500L neutral puncheons.

VINEYARDS - Casey farms the 1.5 acre Kitty Face Vineyard, named by his young daughter, purchased in 1999 and planted to Grenache Blanc and farms by hand. In 2023, Casey added Placer Digging Vineyard, a new vineyard in the Sierra Foothills. He continues to source from Alder Springs in Mendocino. In Sonoma, Mathis has shifted to regenerative and Algerfield, where he gets Grenache for rosé, is working towards organic. Some wines, (not featured here), may be grown with herbicide.

WINES - Katz's attention to details—high density plantings, for instance—and meticulous winemaking create expressive wines of finesse.

WINES - Highlighting the versatility and unique characteristics Grenache, the terroir-driven wines are fresh, vibrant, and expressive.

TOP **Cabernet Sauvignon 2021** ● 300 cases; 135 $ - 🛢 - Small berried grapes fermented on skins for three weeks. Focused with incredible richness and concentration with aromas of cocoa nib, blueberry and chocolate mint. Espresso, crushed dried herbs and black fruit flavors.

Alexander Valley Rosé 2023 ◐ 300 cases; 75 $ - 🛢 - Aged six months in French oak (33% new). A blend five Bordeaux varietals. Whole cluster adds texture. Bright and lively with lush red berry and floral aromatics. Crisp flavors of citrus, cranberry and subtle spice.

Sonoma County Sauvignon Blanc 2021 ○ 300 cases; 84 $ - 🛢 - Aged on lees for 16 months. Lush aromatics of white peach and melon. Tropical sorbet and lemongrass flavors. A rich, textured wine, with creaminess on the midpalate and enough acidity to create tension and layered complexity.

TOP **Sonoma Valley Kitty Face Grenache Blanc 2023** ○ 80 cases; 34 $ - 🥚🛢 - Fermented in concrete egg and neutral barrels. Whole cluster. Very pretty nose of stone fruit, flowers, pear, citrus blossoms. Elegant and delicate acidity with a lovely textured roundness on the palate thanks to the concrete aging.

Sonoma Valley Kitty Face Carbonic Grenache Blanc 2023 ○ 80 cases; 28 $ - 🛢 - Uniquely carbonic, sealed in tank for 10 days, pressed and fermented into neutral barrels and stainless steel drums. Aromas of ripe yellow apples, apple skins, and peach tea. Savory juiciness. Tastes like peach tea.

Mendocino County Alder Spring Grenache Noir 2022 ● 110 cases; 46 $ - 🛢 - Aged in 500-liter puncheons (one new, one neutral). Whole cluster. Black raspberry, cranberry, bramble, herbal and forest floor aromas and juicy tannins with a touch of vanilla and spice on the finish

acres 15.5 - cases 900
Fertilizers compost, cover crops
Plant protection sulfur, organic
Weed control mechanical, manual
Yeasts spontaneous fermentation
Grapes 100% owned
Certification none

acres 1.5 - cases 1,000
Fertilizers compost, biodynamic compost, cover crops, manure
Plant protection sulfur, biodynamic preparations, synthetic pesticides
Weed control animal grazing, mechanical, manual
Yeasts spontaneous fermentation
Grapes purchase 90%
Certification none

WINDSOR

TWO SHEPHERDS

7763 Bell Road - tel. (415) 613-5731
www.twoshepherds.com - william@twoshepherds.com

PEOPLE - The year 2025 marks the 15th anniversary of Two Shepherds which was started in 2010. The Two Shepherds, William Allen and Karen Daenen, have grown their flock. They welcomed two more Nigerian dwarf goats for a total of five. And they added two new Kune Kune pigs who are herbivores and help with weed control. These new animals join the three donkeys, six chickens, three cats and two dogs who make up their menagerie and are honored on the cans of Natty Pets Sparkling Orange Picpoul.

VINEYARDS - The couple farms a high density planting of Grenache Gris and Grenache. They also buy grapes from vineyards ranging from Sonoma to Madera on to San Benito County and Lodi. Allen seeks out vineyards using organic approved materials. Siletto Vineyard in San Benito is certified organic. Their Lodi Vermentino comes from certified biodynamic vines.

WINES - William produces wines that are fresh with vibrant acidity as well as ageworthy.

TOP **Russian River Valley Estate Grenache Noir 2021** ● 144 cases; 38 $ - ⊞ - Aged seven month in neutral oak. Spends five months on lees before blending. Partial whole cluster (25%). Elegant and savory nose with aromas of raspberry and black cherry, juicy acidity and delicately textured tannins.

Dunnigan Hills Centime Skin Fermented White Blend 2022 ⊙ 600 cases; 34 $ - ⊞ - Aged 10 months neutral oak. Picpoul (25%) from Dunnigan Hills with Vermentino (60%) and Albarino (15%) from Lodi. Grapes crushed and on skins for 12 days. Aromas of grapefruit, tangerine and ginger. With soft textured tannins and fleshy acidity.

Dunnigan Hills Windmill Vineyard Natty Pets Sparkling Orange Picpoul 2023 ⊙ 450 cases; 9 $ - 🍶 ⊞ - Aged in neutral barrel. Fermented on skins (75%) and in stainless steel (25%). Blended and slowly micro-carbonated for five days. The color of cantaloup with citrus and red apple notes and light carbonation.

acres 1.5 - cases 4,000
Fertilizers compost, biodynamic compost, cover crops, manure, organic fertilizer
Plant protection sulfur, biodynamic preparations, organic
Weed control animal grazing, mechanical, manual
Yeasts spontaneous fermentation
Grapes purchase 90%
Certification some of the vineyards are certified organic, some of the vineyards are certified biodynamic

SONOMA

UNDER THE WIRE

414 1st Street E - tel. (707) 343-1478
www.underthewirewines.com - info@underthewirewines.com

PEOPLE - Morgan Twain-Peterson MW (Master of Wine) and Chris Cottrell are more famous for their Bedrock wines, but the two are sparkling wine geeks and uniquely make single vineyard designate sparkling wines (rather than the blended sparkling wines Champagne is famous for). They make the wines at Cruse Wine Co. in Petaluma. The winery offers tastings along with caviar pairings at their tasting room in downtown Sonoma in the historic General Joseph Hooker House.

VINEYARDS - Grapes come from all over wine country including Sonoma Valley, Napa's Wild Horse Valley AVA, and northern Mendocino County. Recent selections have highlighted Chuy Vineyard in Moon Mountain, Hirsch Vineyard on the Sonoma Coast. Heron Lake in Napa, Brosseau (certified organic) in the Chalone AVA in Monterey County, and Alder Springs in Laytonville (Mendocino County). Note: Some wines (not featured here) are grown with herbicide.

WINES - The wines are made via the traditional method, en tirage for three years, followed by two years in bottle. They use traditional varieties—Chardonnay and Pinot Noir—as well as unconventional ones, including old vine Zinfandel (from their Bedrock estate) and a rare, old vine, white field blend in Napa.

TOP **Mendocino County Alder Spring Sparkling Pinot Noir 2018** ⊙ 120 cases; 52 $ - ⊞ - A distinctive voice shines through, showcasing wild, savory flavors, and red fruit with herbal notes. The vines are now gone. The wine spent 36 months en tirage, with 1 gram of dosage, and was disgorged in March 2023.

Carneros Sangiacomo Vineyard Sparkling Chardonnay 2018 ⊙ 150 cases; 52 $ - ⊞ - From vines planted in 1982 (and no longer in the ground). Three years on the lees. 2 grams of dosage. Citrus and pear with a unique pineapple note on the finish. Delicious.

acres n/a - cases 1,000
Fertilizers compost, cover crops, organic fertilizer, synthetic fertilizer
Plant protection sulfur, synthetic pesticides, organic
Weed control mechanical, manual
Yeasts spontaneous fermentation
Grapes purchase 80%
Certification some of the vineyards are certified organic

HEALDSBURG

UNTI VINEYARDS

4202 Dry Creek Road - tel. (707) 433-5590
www.untivineyards.com - info@untivineyards.com

PEOPLE - Its close knit team is an integral part of Unti's success. Father and son George and Mick Unti planted their first vines in the 1990s and started making wine in 1997. Jason Valenti took over as winemaker in 2015 and the same team of seven people has worked with them for over 20 years. Their focus is on Rhone and Italian varieties which are ideally suited to the climate of the Dry Creek Valley.

VINEYARDS - Unti has seen a lot of success with Vermentino and is in the process of planting more. When old blocks in the vineyard need to be replanted, they replant or graft with Vermentino. They have 4.5 acres of Vermentino which includes the Rolle Clone from Tablas Creek, a Sardinian clone, and a Ligurian clone. The young block of Barbera planted in 2018 has come into production. After tasting the 2022 vintage, they knew it could stand on its own and bottled it as a Barbera Superiore.

WINES - Unti takes an approach that is both modern (sorting techniques, temperature controlled tanks, and hygiene) and traditional (native yeasts, variety of aging vessels and blocking malolactic fermentation in order to retain acidity).

● Dry Creek Valley Barbera 2022 ● 850 cases; 35 $ - Aged 15 months in French oak barrels (33% new). A blend of two Barbera clones from blocks planted in 1998 and 2018. Dark red fruit aromas with an herbaceous note. Juicy acidity washes over the moderate tannins.

Dry Creek Valley Vermentino 2023 O 620 cases; 38 $ - A blend of three Vermentino clones. Expressive floral aromas. Vibrant and juicy with mouthwatering acidity.

Dry Creek Valley Grenache 2022 ● 275 cases; 38 $ - Aged 14 months in neutral oak. Grenache (75%) with Syrah (25% with some whole cluster added for depth). Pretty raspberry and floral aromas with notes of white pepper. Medium bodied and balanced. Delicate tannins with a touch of spice on the finish.

acres 60 - cases 8,500
Fertilizers compost, cover crops, organic fertilizer
Plant protection sulfur, organic
Weed control mechanical, manual
Yeasts spontaneous fermentation
Grapes 100% owned
Certification none

SONOMA

WARD FOUR WINES

21684 Eighth Street East - tel. (202) 538-1808
www.wardfourwines.com - justin@wardfourwines.com

PEOPLE - Winemaker/owner Justin Trabue makes wines that reflect her way of being in the world–warm, joyful and gracious. The winery is named for the Washington D.C. area where she was raised, and many of her wines are inspired by family members. Justin's goal is to take well grown grapes and bring out something unexpected in the wines they make.

VINEYARDS - With no vineyard of her own, Justin buys from small, family owned operations that honor ethical labor guidelines. She also seeks out growers whose farming practices follow those of certified organic growers–using cover crops and organic fertilizers and manual weed management. Some of the vineyards, including Grist vineyard, are certified organic.

WINES - The wines are bold in attitude yet playful and delicate in their nuanced aromas and flavors.

Contra Costa Cecchini Ranch Muscat Blanc 2023 ◎ 61 cases; 36 $ - Nine days of skin contact give this wine a lovely texture to complement powerful floral notes of honeysuckle, jasmine and orange blossom all balanced by bright lychee, dried apricot and very ripe pear.

Contra Costa Favalora Vineyard Barbera 2023 ● 52 cases; 40 $ - Smooth and silky with notes of blueberry yogurt, black raspberry, sun dried tomato, tomato leaf and oregano with perfectly balanced acid and tannin.

Dry Creek Valley Grist Vineyard Petite Syrah 2022 ● 35 cases; 60 $ - Aged 16 months in barrel (one neutral, one new). Certified organic grapes grown on iron rich soil. A rich, juicy wine with notes of fig, black plum, elderflower, dates, black olive, dark fruits and a touch of cayenne pepper.

acres 0 - cases 125
Fertilizers compost, cover crops, organic fertilizer
Plant protection sulfur, organic
Weed control none, manual
Yeasts spontaneous fermentation
Grapes purchase 100%
Certification some of the vineyards are certified organic

SONOMA

WINERY SIXTEEN 600

589 1st Street W - tel. (707) 721-1805
www.winerysixteen600.com - sam@winerysixteen600.com

 A superstar for its under the radar, small lot wines recognized for their world class quality.

PEOPLE - In 2007, organic vineyard manager extraordinaire Phil Coturri founded his wine label with his son Sam to make wine from sites Phil farms. (They also have another label, A Deux Tetes, a Franco-American collaboration.) The Coturri's devotion to the Grateful Dead, irreverent love of life (and wine), and huge library of vinyl records have made their brand especially popular with younger wine drinkers as well as wine lovers of all ages.

VINEYARDS - Though he's planted and farmed dozens of acclaimed Cabernet sites in Napa (Mayacamas, Oakville Ranch) and on Moon Mountain, Phil Coturri's heart belongs to Rhone varieties. Grapes come from sites he farms for their owners–the historic Rossi Ranch in Sonoma Valley, vines on Moon Mountain (a region Coturri helped to develop) and Oakville Ranch in Napa (which he farms).

WINES - Three A-list winemakers are on board–Alejandro Zimman, Erich Bradley and Rhone native Isabel Gassier–bringing out the complexity and purity of the sites.

Sonoma Valley Rossi Homage Blanc 2022 SLOW WINE
○ 264 cases; 42 $ - 🍷 - Roussanne (80%), Grenache Blanc (15%) and Clairette Blanche (5%). A tribute to vineyard owner Val Rossi. Fragrant and filled with vibrant fruit–apple, pear, peach, Asian pear and honeysuckle. Exceptional in bottle or can.

Moon Mountain District Liquid Sky Cabernet Sauvignon 2021 ● 25 cases; 250 $ - 🍷 - From a 6 acre site near Phil's house on a steep, rocky slope. A stunning example of Moon Mountain terroir in the masterful hands of maestro Alejandro Zimman. Magnums only. One for the ages.

Moon Mountain District Estate Zinfandel 2021 ● 100 cases; 50 $ - 🍷 - From historic Moon Mountain vines (Monte Rosso clones) surrounding Phil's house. Luscious, mouthcoating cherry and dark fruit. More than the sum of its parts.

---

acres 1.5 - cases 2,500
Fertilizers compost, cover crops
Plant protection sulfur
Weed control animal grazing, mechanical
Yeasts spontaneous fermentation
Grapes purchase 90%
Certification organic

NORTH COAST
MENDOCINO & OTHER

🐌 Snail
81 Blue Quail and McFadden Winery
84 Clay Shannon
85 Domaine Anderson
90 OVIS

🍾 Bottle
85 Drew Family Wines

$ Coin
81 Bonterra Organic Estates
83 Chance Creek Vineyards
93 Unturned Stone

HOPLAND

ALTA ORSA WINES

1850 Duncan Springs Road - tel. (707) 540-4311
www.orsawines.com - martin@orsawines.com

PEOPLE - A native of Columbia, winemaker Martin Bernal-Hafner fell in love with wine, wine culture and wine community working harvest in the Rhone Valley at M. Chapoutier. As part of a seven year tutelage under vintner Paul Hobbs, he traveled to Argentina and onward to Sonoma. In 2019, he teamed up with Roger Peng, businessman extraordinaire, and together they founded Orsa Wine to make wine on the historic, old vine Topel vineyard high above Hopland. Ricardo Garcia is also a partner.

VINEYARDS - On a 160 acre property, Martin farms no till on eight acres of deep rooted vines hugging steep slopes on terraced rows on a northwest facing hillside. Using only organic approved materials, he plants cover crops—crimson clover, peas, and hairy vetch—and uses sheep to control weeds in order to grow Cabernet Sauvignon, Chardonnay, Merlot, and Pinot Noir.

WINES - Martin crafts "farming forward" wines, constantly tasting each of the estate blocks.

Mendocino County AO Reserve Cabernet 2019 ● 220 cases; 45 $ - ⊞ - Aged 2 years in neutral oak. Enticing aromas of spice and berry, rich full with blackberry jam and hint of vanilla. Lingering finish pairs with smoky grilled meat. Lovely wine.

Mendocino County AO Estate Hillside Cuvée 2019 ● 112 cases; 36 $ - ⊞ - Aged two years in French oak (30% new). A blend of Cab with Merlot (20%). Fermented in small tanks. Dense, clear crimson with aromas that fill the nose with salty meat and a touch of allspice, with fruit-rich, mouth-filling tannins and a lingering finish.

Mendocino County AO Estate Soil Series Cabernet Sauvignon 2019 ● 50 cases; 55 $ - ⊞ - Two years in the barrel releases classic Cabernet aromas of bright plum along with savory tea and cloves, a rolling complex mouthful and a lovely long finish.

acres 8 - cases 1,000
Fertilizers compost, cover crops, manure
Plant protection sulfur
Weed control animal grazing
Yeasts spontaneous fermentation
Grapes purchase 30%
Certification none

YORKVILLE

ARTEVINO

20799 CA-128 - tel. (707) 895-3001
www.artevinowine.com - contact@artevinowine.com

PEOPLE - A descendent of Portuguese fruit ranchers in Los Gatos, Tom Rodrigues inherited a passion for wine. Also a renowned artist, his stained glass got him gigs at Skywalker Ranch and designing wine labels, including for Far Niente. His baseball art is in the Baseball Hall of Fame. In 2001, he bought property with vines on Maple Creek near Yorkville. Here he combines his passions for Art Nouveau labels and wine.

VINEYARDS - On his tiny Yorkville Highlands estate near the headwaters of the Russian and Navarro Rivers (with warm days and cool nights), the vines sit above 800 feet. The soils are composed of schist, sandstone, and other sedimentary and metamorphic rocks. Due to climate change, Rodrigues may let the grapes hang until October. Instead of brix, he checks the grape seeds and waits until seeds are brown not green.

WINES - More hang time means fuller rich flavors in addition to longer aging. "Get your fruit ripe and the rest is easy," he says.

Yorkville Highlands Estate Chardonnay 2020 ○ 290 cases; 48 $ - ⓠ - Aged 11 months, in new French oak and neutral oak (25%). Knock your socks off aromas of apple butter and poached pear precede a round mouthful of deliciousness, with a crisp finish. SF Chronicle double gold medal winner.

Yorkville Highlands Estate Flora 2021 ○ 40 cases; 32 $ - 🍷 - An orange wine, skin fermented Flora, the variety that is a cross of Sémillon and Gewürztraminer. Two days on skins give it a light peachy hue. Fermented and aged in neutral oak for 11 months. A bright mouthful of subtle ripe pear and a hint of butterscotch on the finish.

Yorkville Highlands Estate Merlot 2018 ● 220 cases; 42 $ - ⊞ - Intoxicating wet earth, blue flowers, sweet tobacco and leather welcome a complex, light, lithe plum and boysenberry palate with lovely full tannin grip. Purple velvet in a glass.

acres 7 - cases 1,000
Fertilizers compost, manure
Plant protection sulfur
Weed control mechanical
Yeasts spontaneous fermentation, commercial cultured yeasts
Grapes 100% owned
Certification none

REDWOOD VALLEY

BARRA OF MENDOCINO

7051 N State Street - tel. (707) 485-0322
www.barraofmendocino.com - info@barraofmendocino.com

PEOPLE - An organic powerhouse in Redwood Valley, the late Charlie Barra founded it. A legend, his first harvest was in 1946. His wife Martha oversees three vineyards, a winery, event center and custom crush facility (certified organic). Winemaker Randy Meyer joined the team in 2020, after working at Korbel for decades. They have two brands–Girasole ("sunflower" in Italian) which is fresh, light and vegan, and Barra which is classic varietals, aged in oak.

VINEYARDS - Vineyard foreman Roberto Gonzalez oversees three certified organic estates. Soils are Redvine, Pinole and Talmage with sandy loam and moderate amounts of clay. Elevations range from 700 to 900 feet with great drainage in the valley and more temperature variation on hillsides. Notably, Martha and Roberto made biochar from their own vine cuttings to enhance the soil using it and pomace for replanting new varietals and clones.

WINES - Randy uses gentle extraction techniques to achieve balance. All of the wines are labeled "Made with Organic Grapes," meaning sulfites and additives are restricted.

Mendocino County Girasole Pinot Blanc 2022 EVERYDAY WINE - 1,764 cases; 16 $ - A golden hued wine. Aged in stainless steel for 90 days. Find citrus highlights accented by a hint of honeysuckle loll on the palate of this refreshing, fruit forward white.

Mendocino County Barra Reserve Pinot Noir 2022 - 900 cases; 26 $ - Ruby colored, brilliant berry aromas and hint of sandalwood. Radiant palate of concentrated plum, black cherry, and touch of vanilla. Double Gold winner at SF Chronicle wine competition..

Mendocino County Barra Reserve Cabernet Sauvignon 2021 - 520 cases; 28 $ - A great value for a food friendly Cabernet. Swirling releases black currant aromas and a fruit forward, pleasant earthiness. Finishes with a hint of vanilla.

acres 275 - cases 20,000
Fertilizers compost, cover crops
Plant protection sulfur, copper
Weed control mechanical, manual
Yeasts commercial cultured yeasts
Grapes 100% owned
Certification organic

BOONVILLE

BEE HUNTER WINE

Anderson Valley - 14077 Hwy 128 - tel. (707) 895-3995
www.beehunterwine.com - beehunterwine@gmail.com

PEOPLE - In 2017 Andy and Ali DuVigneaud joined forces in Anderson Valley to create the Bee Hunter brand. An Anderson Valley native, Andy had pursued interests in computer science and architecture before finding his passion for winemaking after a stint at Navarro Vineyards. He makes the Bee Hunter wines at Lichen Estate. Ali worked at Handley Cellars tasting room before she and Andy opened their own in Boonville.

VINEYARDS - Always "be(e) huntin'" is the moniker and motto of Andy and Ali who taste and research varietals from hidden sustainable, organic or biodynamic vineyards in Mendocino and Sonoma counties. Their focus is on single vineyard designates, including Sauvignon Blanc, Syrah and Zinfandel.

WINES - Though focused on Pinot Noir, they make a wide variety of wines, including a Brut sparkling wine.

Anderson Valley Lichen Estate Pinot Noir 2018 - 300 cases; 80 $ - Aged 32 months in French oak (25% new). Dark magenta, with sweet tart aromas of dried plums and figs. Rich fruitiness on the palate balanced with low tannins.

Anderson Valley Wentzel Vineyard Pinot Noir 2017 - 175 cases; 80 $ - From Dijon clones. Grown at nearly 800 feet near Philo. A bright fruit nose, lingering berry flavors with a hint of tannin and a smooth finish.

Anderson Valley Broken Leg Vineyard Syrah 2016 - 200 cases; 80 $ - Aged three years in oak (33% new). Grown on a small steep vineyard above Philo. Lees aging without racking. Plummy, fruit rich with a hint of leather in the middle and a long finish.

acres 0 - cases 2,000
Fertilizers cover crops, organic fertilizer
Plant protection sulfur, copper, organic
Weed control manual
Yeasts spontaneous fermentation
Grapes purchase 100%
Certification some of the vineyards are certified organic

HOPLAND

BLUE QUAIL AND MCFADDEN WINERY

Potter Valley - 13275 S Highway 101 - tel. (707) 744-8463
www.mcfaddenfarm.com - info@mcfaddenfarm.com

 In 1983, he built his own hydroelectric powerhouse, avoiding the use of fossil fuels. That was just the beginning of his ecofriendly approach. He also sell his grassfed beef from the farm in the tasting room.

PEOPLE - Guinness McFadden, now 86, is a renowned community leader, organic vintner and grower on the beloved Potter Valley acreage he's farmed since 1970. A New Yorker by birth and a decorated Navy veteran (with a stint in Vietnam), he found a passion for wine in Europe, while at Stanford dissed becoming part of the corporate world, instead heading to the country (and its lifestyle) to raise kids, make herb blends, garlic and bay wreaths and grow vines and make wine.

VINEYARDS - At 1,100 feet of elevation, sandwiched between hot Ukiah and the higher and cooler Lake County, the vineyards sit at the headwaters of the Russian River's east fork. Certified organic since 1990, he is a grower, but after seeing his grapes win awards in wines, he was inspired to make his own wine. Now he keeps 50 percent of the fruit. Foreman José Medina has overseen the vines for 52 years.

WINES - "Growing wine, not grapes" is his motto. Pricing makes these wines extraordinary values, especially the often sold out sparkling wine.

Potter Valley Blue Quail Pinot Gris 2023 SLOW WINE
○ 1,293 cases; 18 $ - 🍷 - Extraordinary. Stainless fermented. Made Alsatian style highlighting minerality, plus aromas of nectarine, Golden Delicious apples with a palate full of cooked quince and citrus hint, finishing with spring blossoms and a faint sweetness.

Potter Valley Blue Quail Chardonnay 2022 ○ 4,185 cases; 18 $ - 🍷 - Whole cluster pressed, fermented in stainless. Golden hued, viscous, fruity mouthfeel with apricot, peaches, and a hint of characteristic flint.

Potter Valley Blue Quail Sauvignon Blanc 2022 ○ 6,255 cases; 18 $ - 🍷 - Whole cluster pressed, fermented in stainless. Luscious fruit forward aromas of honeydew and guava fuse with soft minerality on a Meyer lemon zest and grapefruit blossom finish.

acres 160 - cases 14,000
Fertilizers compost, cover crops
Plant protection sulfur, organic
Weed control mechanical, manual
Yeasts commercial cultured yeasts
Grapes 100% owned
Certification organic

HOPLAND

BONTERRA ORGANIC ESTATES $

12901 Old River Road - tel. (707) 671-0063
www.bonterra.com - elizabeth.archer@bonterraorganic.com

PEOPLE - An organic trailblazer, the Chilean owned winery has deep roots in Mendocino and has continued the ecofriendly culture its Fetzer family founders imbued in it when it was founded in 1987. Continuing to up its eco friendly and green goals, the company is a certified B Corp. Veteran winemaker Jeff Cichocki retired in 2024. Margaret Leonardi-Pruett makes both the estate and non-estate wines. Sebastian Donoso now makes the single vineyard wines.

VINEYARDS - Joseph Brinkley and Todd Madden manage the Mendocino estate vineyards where 20 percent of the wine comes from. The estate farming is no till and grazed by sheep in spring. These vines are certified Regenerative Organic at the silver level. For the non-estate wines, which are 80 percent of production, grapes come from certified organic growers throughout California. On the bottle, 80 percent of the wines are now California appellated.

WINES - All of the wines are certified "Made with Organic Grapes," which means there are strict limits on additives, low sulfites and rigorous winemaking standards.

Mendocino County Single Vineyard The Butler Red Blend 2020 ● 2,000 cases; 50 $ - 🛢 - Aged 14 months in French oak (12% new). A Syrah dominant blend (63%) with Petite Syrah (18%), Mourvedre (12%), Grenache (6%) and Viognier (1%). Smooth, rich, bursting with boysenberry and ripe plum with a hint of smoked meat.

Mendocino County Bonterra Single Vineyard The Roost Chardonnay 2022 ○ 2,000 cases; 35 $ - 🛢 - Aged 10 months on lees in French oak (15% new). Dijon clone. Whole cluster. On the palate, honeysuckle, magnolia, nutmeg and subtle cinnamon.

Mendocino County Bonterra Estate Collection Sauvignon Blanc 2023 ○ 10,000 cases; 20 $ - 🛢 - From Dooley Creek Ranch. Luscious, with notes of honeydew melon, citrus and grapefruit. Long lasting finish.

acres 850 - cases 550,000
Fertilizers compost, cover crops, organic fertilizer
Plant protection sulfur, copper
Weed control animal grazing, mechanical, manual
Yeasts commercial cultured yeasts
Grapes purchase 80%
Certification regenerative

PHILO

BRASHLEY VINEYARDS

7000 Highway 128 - tel. (707) 510-7360
www.brashleyvineyards.com - ashley@brashleyvineyards.com

PEOPLE - After falling for the charms of Anderson Valley, in 2018 Ashley and Bram Palm of upstate New York bought a home with two acres of planted vines in Anderson Valley's Deep End. In 2019 Ashley went from grower to vintner, buying the Brutocao winery with its eight acre Bevel vineyard and hiring winemaker Ashley Holland. They're upping production of their popular white Pinot. Coming releases include a Vin Gris and their first sparkling Blanc de Noir.

VINEYARDS - They have two estate vineyards. Travis Foote oversees the dry farmed Pommard vines on their two acre Hacienda Sequoia in the Deep End which sit on sandstone soils. Greg Ardzrooni oversees the Bevel site (next to the renowned Savoy vineyard, which he also manages) planted to 115 and 777. With the team, Holland converted to using only organic approved materials and no-till farming, building mulch and organic matter for water retention as well as reducing soil compaction and disturbance.

WINES - Longer cold soaks with non-saccharomyces yeasts avoid the need to sulfur. Holland strives for vivacity and exuberance in style, lighter vessels and lees stirring, no settling, for a touch of palate richness.

TOP Anderson Valley Hacienda Sequoia Vineyard Pinot Noir 2022 ● 120 cases; 70 $ - ⊞ - A stunningly poised interplay of elements. Supple, with fresh raspberry richness backed by concentration of black fruit and baking spice. Remarkable.

Anderson Valley Bevel Vineyard White Pinot Noir 2022 ○ 145 cases; 50 $ - ⛊ ⛐ ⊞ - Beautiful textural complexity. Lime and blossom open to silken creamy texture enlivened with lemon balm acidity. Finish is mineral seashell and sweet green herb.

Anderson Valley Bevel Vineyard Pinot Noir 2022 ● 200 cases; 68 $ - ⊞ - Clones 115 and Pommard lead the mix. Bright cranberry and juicy blueberry hinted with lavender flower reflect against talc-like tannins.

acres 10.2 - cases 850
Fertilizers compost, cover crops, organic fertilizer
Plant protection sulfur, organic
Weed control mechanical, manual
Yeasts spontaneous fermentation
Grapes purchase 10%
Certification none

HOPLAND

CAMPOVIDA

13601 Old River Road - tel. (707) 400-6300
www.campovida.com - hello@campovida.com

PEOPLE - In 2011, eco-minded Anna Bueselinck and Gary Breen purchased the historic Valley Oaks property, moving from Oakland to Mendo for the lifestyle. The site was once home to local Pomos, followed by immigrant farmers, and then the Fetzer family winery. Within a year, they made their first wine, Viognier, and won Gold at the SF Chronicle competition. Thus began wholehearted investments in their tasting room, modern event space and two acres of spectacular, historic gardens.

VINEYARDS - The couple bought the rest of the Valley Oaks estate, expanding their holdings from 20 to 100 planted acres (certified organic) on the 150 acre property. On its gravelly loam soil, they grow Cabernet Sauvignon, Chardonnay, Grenache, Nebbiolo, Sangiovese, Viognier and Zinfandel. Current releases include grapes they bought from local growers, including dry farmed Nero D'Avola and Zinfandel from Chiarito and Cabernet and Grenache from biodynamic certified Dark Horse.

WINES - Winemaker Wells Guthrie (previously with Copain) makes the minimal intervention wines in small lots. Rarities include Nebbiolo, Nero D'Avola and a sparkling wine.

TOP Mendocino County Estate Viognier 2021 SLOW WINE ○ 190 cases; 40 $ - ⊞ - Fermented in stainless and aged in neutral French oak. Pale gold hue with floral aromas and complex flavors of peach and honeysuckle, with a crisp satisfying finish.

Mendocino County Estate Rosé di Grenache 2022 ⦿ 75 cases; 40 $ - ⛊ - A classic summer wine one can pour year round. Pink hue. Complex flavors from pomelo and rose petals to peach and a hint of dark cherry.

Mendocino County Estate Sangiovese Riserva 2018 ● 250 cases; 44 $ - ⊞ - From their "Ancestors Block," five acres planted in 1992. A velvety potpourri of dried cherries, roast peppers, with a hint of leather and a mouth savoring long finish.

acres 100 - cases 1,000
Fertilizers compost, cover crops, manure
Plant protection sulfur, copper, organic
Weed control animal grazing, mechanical, manual
Yeasts selected indigenous yeasts
Grapes 100% owned
Certification some of the vineyards are certified organic, some of the vineyards are certified biodynamic

REDWOOD VALLEY

CESAR TOXQUI CELLARS

7301 North State Street - tel. (707) 391-8411
www.toxqui.com - ctoxqui@att.net

PEOPLE - Cesar Toxqui grew up around grapevines in Puebla, Mexico (where Spaniards planted vines in the 1500's). At 16, he moved to Ukiah, got a job on a bottling line and came under the tutelage of winemaker Jess Tidwell. Finding he was good at winemaking, he got a degree in viniculture and made wine at home. Winning Best of Class at Lake Co. Home Winemaker Fest in 2004-5 spurred him and his wife Ruth to start a "mom and pop" boutique winery in Redwood Valley.

VINEYARDS - Cesar says he buys only organically farmed wineries, including Filligreen Farm in Anderson Valley (certified biodynamic) and Benedetti Vineyards and Champi Vineyards in Redwood Valley (said to use only organic approved materials). He works closely with the farmers throughout the season and harvest.

WINES - He punches down open top fermenters twice daily, extending maceration to extract flavor and color, and uses traditional methods, including native yeasts, to "make wines as nature intended," he says.

Redwood Valley Chardonnay 2020 O 300 cases; 22 $ - Aged two years in neutral French oak. From Champi vineyard. Light amber with a nutty aroma, and apricot and citrus flavors with a fresh finish.
Anderson Valley Pinot Noir 2021 ● 75 cases; 48 $ - From biodynamic certified grapes at Filligreen Farm in Anderson Valley. Pommard clone. Lighter color extracted from whole berry fermentation and a clean bright aroma and flavor.
Redwood Valley Merlot 2019 ● 150 cases; 34 $ - Aged three years in neutral French oak. From Benedetti Vineyard. Blend includes a bit of Cabernet and Sangiovese. At 16.5%, the alcohol is softened by an elegant smoothness of soft tannins and ripe fruit.

acres n/a - cases 2,500
Fertilizers compost
Plant protection sulfur, organic
Weed control mechanical
Yeasts commercial cultured yeasts
Grapes purchase 10%
Certification some of the vineyards are certified organic

REDWOOD VALLEY

CHANCE CREEK VINEYARDS $

9154 Colony Drive - tel. (707) 710-7438
www.bockwineandspirits.com - lou.bock@bockwineandspirits.com

PEOPLE - When Lou Bock, a student of Alan Chadwick at U.C. Santa Cruz, committed to planting, mowing, pruning and harvesting his rocky benchland vineyard, he named it for Thomas McGuane's book "An Outside Chance." A former Peace Corps volunteer, cattle rancher, and potter who wound up a vintner and homesteader, Lou feels like he is in a McGuane story—where the luck of the draw is all important…You make the most of what you get. The wines are made at Graziano.

VINEYARDS - It's all about "the grapes and the vineyards," says Bock. In 1980, Lou cleared old, untended vines from his high acid, benchland soil. These days, in springtime, he herds his lambs between the vines to mow and, at harvest, gently picks 12 acres of prized Sauvignon Blanc, along with a half acre of Viognier, and two acres of Sangiovese. The latter is a rare clone, Il Poggione, from Montalcino.

WINES - "Lou's grapes are so good, we try not to screw them up," says winemaker Alexandra Graziano, who, with Chasen Boatright, shepherds Lou's grapes into his two labels—Chance Creek and Terroir 95470.

TOP Terroir 95470 Sangiovese 2015 EVERYDAY WINE ● 250 cases; 20 $ - Great value for Super Tuscan like style, like Sangiovese Grosso into the coveted Italian Brunello. The Sangiovese (93%) pops with wild cherry, while Cabernet Sauvignon (4%) adds a hint of cassis, and Syrah (3%) broadens the finish.
Redwood Valley Chance Creek Strictly Sauvignon Blanc 2023 O 200 cases; 20 $ - Aged six to nine months in neutral barrels. A post drought harvest netted only two tons an acre. Pink grapefruit, green apple, and honeysuckle dance across palate. There's velvety mouthfeel and satisfying complexity.
Redwood Valley Terroir 95470 Sauvignon Blanc 2022 O 300 cases; 20 $ - Barrel fermented in neutral oak. Blended with Viognier (10%). A satisfying mouthful, highlighted with zesty citrus and lychee fresh finish.

acres 14 - cases 1,000
Fertilizers cover crops, organic fertilizer
Plant protection sulfur, organic
Weed control animal grazing, mechanical, manual
Yeasts commercial cultured yeasts
Grapes 100% owned
Certification organic

LAKEPORT

CLAY SHANNON

4350 Thomas Drive - tel. (707) 281-6370
www.shannonfamilyofwines.com - info@shannonridge.com

 Now a North Coast organic powerhouse, their sheep centered, closed-loop farming and organic certification are setting a new standard in the region.

PEOPLE - A green pioneer making waves, Shannon won the 2021 California Green Medal Environment Award. Shannon turned his first Lake County vineyards in 1996 into today's 2,500 acres. Of six labels, the all organic Clay Shannon label showcases varieties from high elevation slopes. Joy Merrilees, vice president of production, oversaw the conversion to organic farming (2022) of the High Valley blocks and makes certified "Made with Organic Grapes" wines.

VINEYARDS - The estate is one of the largest certified organic vineyards in the U.S. Its regenerative closed loop farming system uses 1,000 sheep as hooved vineyard hands, leverages chickens for fertilizer and makes worm casting tea from pomace compost, adding the tea to their irrigation system to build soil microbes and up micronutrients. They are also trying a no-touch vineyard, raising wires to allow sheep to sucker, shoot thin and mow year round.

WINES - Volcanics, UV intensity, and winds raise acidity, tannins and concentration, even in whites. A touch of extra ripeness balances tannins for wines that punch well above their price point in character and acidity.

⊕ **Lake County High Valley Rosé 2023** EVERYDAY WINE
2,530 cases; 30 $ - 🍷 - In a Southern Rhône style opens with aromas of cantaloupe, blood orange skin and blossom with tangerine and gentle warmth, finishing dry with a touch of tannin.

Lake County Long Valley Ranch Pinot Noir 2022 ● 206 cases; 45 $ - 🍽 - Clone 777 from the coolest site, Long Valley Ranch. Nose of light raspberry, cherry and earth echo on the palate with berry cola, baking spice, wild herbs and pleasingly light tannins.

Lake County The Barkley Cabernet Sauvignon 2021 ●
16,000 cases; 45 $ - 🍽 - Deep blackberry and black cherry are accented by licorice, tobacco, sweet blue florals and black pepper. Sweet tannins from an early-pressed, easy to enjoy Cabernet.

---

acres 1,200 - cases 99,000
Fertilizers compost, manure
Plant protection sulfur, organic
Weed control animal grazing, mechanical
Yeasts spontaneous fermentation, commercial cultured yeasts
Grapes 100% owned
Certification organic

LAKEPORT

CRICKET FARMS

4350 Thomas Drive - tel. (707) 281-6370
www.shannonfamilyofwines.com - info@shannonridge.com

PEOPLE - An organically grown, sparkling wine brand, Cricket Farms is named after owner Angie Shannon's border collie Cricket. Wines are low in alcohol at 10.5%. The sustainably farmed Lake County ranch is home to working vineyard sheep, grazing chickens, and 150 year old pear trees whose blossoms are on the label. Launched with sparkling Brut and Brut Rosé, Cricket plans to release still versions of low alcohol Chenin Blanc and Viognier in the future. Joy Merrilees is vice president of production.

VINEYARDS - Owned by Shannon Family of Wines, the vines grow at 1,500 to 2,300 feet using a closed loop regenerative farming system. Sheep control weeds, fertilize soils and perform leafing work. Fertilization comes from chicken manure, farm compost and a newly added worm compost tea. Adding a sparkling wine to the portfolio moves part of the harvest earlier, reducing fertilizer and water needs and saving farmer passes in the heat. All are part of Shannon's vision for full circle sustainable farming.

WINES - Grapes are picked early at high acidity and low brix (17.5), lightly pressed, and fermented dry. Secondary fermentation is via Charmat method with 10 g/l dosage. The resulting profile is balanced fruit sweetness, crisp mouthfeel and a dry finish. The wines are also certified "Made with Organic Grapes."

⊕ **Lake County Sparkling Brut Rosé Nonvintage** ⊛ ; 2,500 cases; 38 $ - 🍷 - An unconventional blend of Zinfandel (65%), Mourvedre (45%) and Chardonnay (1%). A nose of ripe apples opens to flavors of cherry and black and red berries. Expressive acidity on the creamy palate finishes distinctly dry with hints of tart pineapple.

Lake County Sparkling Brut Nonvintage ⊛ 2,500 cases; 38 $ - 🍷 - Made from Chardonnay. White peach and blossom nose with juicy white peach palate in creamy bubbles.

---

acres 35 - cases 5,000
Fertilizers compost, manure
Plant protection sulfur, organic
Weed control animal grazing, mechanical
Yeasts spontaneous fermentation, commercial cultured yeasts
Grapes 100% owned
Certification organic

PHILO

DOMAINE ANDERSON

9201 CA-128 - tel. (707) 895-3626
www.domaineanderson.com - info@domaineanderson.com

 In a constant state of evolution, the winery exemplifies the rewards of progressive conversion to organic and biodynamic certification.

PEOPLE - Winemaker Darrin Low and the viticultural team continually push for optimized growing conditions for the estate. Michael Boer, a fifth generation grower from Mendocino, joined the team in 2024 as vineyard manager, working under director of vineyard operations Bob Gibson. As chair of the 2024 Anderson Valley Pinot Noir Festival technical conference, Low continually promotes awareness that prioritizes the health of the valley.

VINEYARDS - Regenerative practices continue to advance with the production of in house compost that incorporates biochar to further carbon sequestration, increase organic matter and build up the microbial activity and structure in the soil. Low has added 1.5 acres of Fairhills Vineyard, an organic certified parcel in the Deep End of the valley, to the 2022 estate Chardonnay. These acres were included in the estate's total organic certified acres in 2024.

WINES - 2022 marked the end of three drought vintages. There's an intensity and balance to the wines that reveals the power and elegance of the terroir.

Anderson Valley Dach Vineyard Chardonnay 2022
110 cases; 55 $ - Dach has never tasted better, showing a distinct expression of site that elevates it above the estate Chardonnay. Flinty aromas of pomelo and yuzu pith with fresh, delicious intensity that sings through the precise finish.
Anderson Valley Estate Chardonnay 2022 750 cases; 40 $ - Aged 10 months in French oak (21% new). There's toasted almond and a bright mineral expression underlying lush flavors of ripe citrus, mango and tangerine peel.
Anderson Vally Estate Pinot Noir 2021 710 cases; 55 $ - Aged 16 months in neutral oak. Bouncy, ripe cherry and raspberry fruit. Well integrated secondary notes of black tea and sous bois are woven through the juicy, expressive fruit and generous finish.

acres 53 - cases 2,400
Fertilizers compost, organic fertilizer
Plant protection sulfur, biodynamic preparations, organic
Weed control animal grazing, mechanical
Yeasts spontaneous fermentation, commercial cultured yeasts
Grapes 100% owned
Certification organic, some of the vineyards are certified biodynamic

ELK

DREW FAMILY WINES

31351 Philo Greenwood Road - tel. (707) 877-1771
www.drewwines.com - molly@drewwines.com

PEOPLE - Twenty years ago, when Jason was vineyard manager at Navarro, he and Molly Drew bought an organic apple orchard with a view of the Pacific Ocean. Jason had worked at world class Napa and Santa Barbara wineries and holds degrees in agroecology from U.C. Santa Cruz and oenology from in Australia's Adelaide University. Molly has expertise in label design. Their Faîte De Mer Farm (made by sea) sits above the fogline just 3.3 miles from the coast.

VINEYARDS - Their certified organic Mendocino Ridge site (minimum 1,200 elevation), cool yet with sun above the coastal fog, doesn't experience the diurnal temperature swings of their valley counterparts. The dense sandstone soils have clay, iron and shale. Lighter sandy and rocky soils evoke their ocean floor origins and contain radiolarian chert and quartz. They grow Chardonnay and Pinot and buy Syrah and other grapes from Mendocino Ridge neighbors.

WINES - The wines show an elegance unique to the cool, high altitude Mendocino Ridge climate, whether sourced from their estate vines or from other nearby ridgetop vines.

Mendocino Ridge Radiolaria Estate Pinot Noir 2022
100 cases; 70 $ - Aged 11 months in French oak (30% new). Grown on Mendocino's most westward site. Partial whole cluster. Black cherry, wild raspberry and savory mushroom, with mountain herbs and lingering herbaceousness on the finish.
Mendocino Ridge Radiolaria Estate Chardonnay 2022 150 cases; 60 $ - Aged 11 months in oak (15% new). From Wente and two Dijon clones. Lively with aromas of citrus and lemon curd. A luscious mouthful–rich with minerality. A lingering finish.
Mendocino Ridge Field Selections Pinot Noir 2022
150 cases; 80 $ - A wine from a cold spring vintage grown in mature vineyards on clay and shale. Lively, bright flavors of plum, forest huckleberry. A classic.

acres 10 - cases 2,000
Fertilizers compost, cover crops, manure
Plant protection sulfur, synthetic pesticides, organic
Weed control animal grazing, mechanical
Yeasts spontaneous fermentation
Grapes purchase 50%
Certification some of the vineyards are certified organic

HOPLAND

DUNCAN PEAK

14500 Mountain House Road - tel. (916) 664-8413
www.duncanpeakwines.com - info@duncanpeakwines.com

PEOPLE - Starting in 2020, Chinese born Jane Jiang (winemaker) and brother Max Luo (marketing and export) began managing the historic Duncan Peak Vineyard their family (fine wine distributors) purchased in 2014 with ambitious export plans. They revitalized the now organic vineyard while Jane studied winemaking at U.C. Davis and interned in leading wineries. Their consulting winemaker, Kale Anderson, was the youngest winemaker to win a 100 point score from Robert Parker.

VINEYARDS - Jane manages the vines (certified organic). Underground springs and a seasonal reservoir water the deep well drained soils of rich clay loam. Sheep graze in spring. The oldest Cabernet vines were planted in 1984. The estate is also home to wild turkeys and deer. Migrating cranes visit their pond.

WINES - Five pressed and free run lots are fermented separately to express unique profiles and complexity. Different yeast strains complement what is naturally occurring.

Mendocino County Chronicle Reserve Red 2022 ● 309 cases; 54 $ - ⊞ - Aged 18 months in French oak (30% new). Blended with Petite Sirah (17%). Rose petals and red berries waft from the glass, where rich red cherry with a touch of vanilla combine in silky elegance.

Mendocino County MAX Cabernet Sauvignon 2022 ● 50 cases; 82 $ - ⊞ - Aged 18 months in French oak (some new). Second vintage. Some old vines. Richly smooth dark wine with lush mouthfeel. Black currant and cherry rich legs linger with a hint of burnt caramel.

Mendocino County MAX Reserve Blend Cabernet Sauvignon 2021 ● 112 cases; 82 $ - ⊞ - A low yield vintage create beautifully vibrant ruby color, and concentrated flavors of jammy berries, a hint of green pepper, and silky tannins. MAX on the label refers to Jane's brother and co-proprietor.

acres 7 - cases 500
Fertilizers cover crops, manure
Plant protection sulfur
Weed control animal grazing, mechanical
Yeasts commercial cultured yeasts
Grapes purchase 10%
Certification some of the vineyards are certified organic

HOPLAND

ETTORE

14160 Mountain House Road - tel. (707) 744-1114
www.ettore.wine - contact@ettore.wine

PEOPLE - In 2018, Italian Swiss vigneron Ettore Biraghi, a European winemaking maverick, invested in Mendocino where he found all natural winemaking talent. Sofia Rivier, an Argentinian with a degree in agronomy, met Ettore in Switzerland where she attained a masters in viticulture and enology. She manages the vineyard and crafts the wine at both Ettore and Terra Savia. Ettore uses his Purovino, a trademarked scientific method, to eliminate sulfites.

VINEYARDS - The vines, shared with the label Terra Savia, grow Cabernet, Chardonnay and Merlot in the Sanel Valley, where cool Pacific winds are kept at bay. Warm days and cool nights offer perfect ripening. The vines were planted in 1991, 1995 and 1998. Ettore credits the soil's marine sediment and volcanic deposits for creating minerality as well as layers of flavors.

WINES - The PurovinoTM method replaces sulfur both in the cellar and during the production of the wines all of which complete malolactic conversion for stability.

Mendocino Chardonnay Pure 2019 ○ 1,430 cases; 28 $ - ⎕ - Different flavor profiles—tropical fruit, peach, spice, and pineapple—come from four tons of grapes. "Super fun to blend," says Sofia. Light golden, fruit forward, with a complex smooth rich mouthfeel.

Mendocino County Merlot Zero 2019 ● 413 cases; 35 $ - ⎕ - Dark red color with floral aromas like red roses and purple violets. Bright fruit flavors mingle black currant and blueberry accented with a touch of licorice at the end and a lingering finish.

Mendocino County Cabernet Sauvignon Signature 2019 ● 807 cases; 52 $ - ⊞ - Aged 18 months in French oak barrels. Deep red color. A complex texture that balances oak structure with complexity of cassis, juniper, and plum, unctuously lolling on the palate.

acres 29 - cases 1,500
Fertilizers compost, cover crops
Plant protection sulfur
Weed control mechanical, manual
Yeasts commercial cultured yeasts
Grapes 100% owned
Certification organic

REDWOOD VALLEY

FREY VINEYARDS

14000 Tomki Road - tel. (800) 760-3739
www.freywine.com - katrina@freywine.com

PEOPLE - After the disastrous Redwood Complex Fire in 2017, which destroyed their winery and family homes, no added sulfite wines powerhouse Frey's back with a new, ecofriendly, fire resistant metal winery. They have four generations and 40 years of organic and biodynamic winemaking under their belt. Matriarch Beba, age 100 and mother of 12, lives with most of the family on 1,000 acres at the Russian River headwaters. Jonathan Frey and Todd Boek make the wines.

VINEYARDS - Derek Dahlen oversees the vines. Their biodynamic home ranch (Demeter certified) sits on Redvine, clay soil and gravelly benchland. There they use traditional biodynamic preparations made with chamomile, dandelion, nettle, oak bark and yarrow along with horn silica sprays from quartz. They recycle water via worm composters. Cows, goats, sheep and chickens graze among vines. In addition, they buy nearly half the grapes from certified organic growers in California.

WINES - Yeasts vary. On USDA certified "Organic Wines," they use certified organic yeast. Demeter certified "Biodynamic Wines" use only native. New this year: an orange wine.
Redwood Valley Estate Orange Beard 2023 ⊚ 1,394 cases; 14 $ - 🍷 - A blend of Muscat (30%) and Pinot Grigio (70%) with brief skin contact. Carnelian in color. Aromas of orange blossoms, tangerine and honeyed tropical fruit.
Redwood Valley Estate Biodynamic Field Blend 2022 ● 5,190 cases; 18 $ - 🍷 - Aged eight months with oak staves. Cabernet, for structure and tannins, blended with Merlot for longevity and graceful fruitiness, and Petite Sirah for stand out color. Earthy and redolent of blackberry and olallieberry, with a hint of cocoa nib.
Redwood Valley Estate Biodynamic Syrah 2021 ● 229 cases, 20 $ - 🍷 - Marigold and sunflower aromas. A mouthful of boysenberry, black olives, clove, cocoa and slight salty finish. Lush.

acres 350 - cases 160,000
Fertilizers compost, cover crops
Plant protection biodynamic preparations
Weed control mechanical, manual
Yeasts spontaneous fermentation, commercial cultured yeasts
Grapes purchase 45%
Certification biodynamic, organic

PHILO

HANDLEY CELLARS

Anderson Valley - 3151 Highway 128 - tel. (707) 895-3876
www.handleycellars.com - handley.lulu@gmail.com

PEOPLE - Born in 1962, Lulu Handley, raised by the late, organic pioneer Milla Handley (1951-2020), is coming into her own at the helm, while raising toddlers, with support from husband Scott Handley. Winemaker Randy Schock has made the wines for 20 years. As ecofriendly measures, they eliminated foil capsules, printed their logo on taint-free composite corks and get 75 percent of power from solar. They are transitioning to lower weight bottles.

VINEYARDS - Milla, the first woman winemaker and one of the early vintners in Anderson Valley, (1982) was the first be to be organically certified in the region in 2005. Sustainability minded, the year round vineyard crew uses tea from worm castings for fertigation. An aeration system with beneficial bacteria added to the reservoir creates natural habitat for water wildlife. They also buy grapes from local growers with whom they have long standing relationships.

WINES - They are masters of the region's aromatic whites. Minimal impacts create subtle and elegant expressions of each varietal.
🔝 Anderson Valley Handley Estate Vineyard Blanc de Blanc 2019 ⊛ 400 cases; 62 $ - 🍷 - Whole cluster press. No dosage. Three years on tirage. Tiny taut, fruity, crisp bubbles Stone fruit, almond, and lemon verbena complement long creamy finish.
Anderson Valley Handley Pinot Noir Rosé 2023 ● 224 cases; 28 $ - 🍷 - "Best Pinot grapes ever," says Lulu. Whole cluster pressed. Racked in stainless to preserve fruit. Lees stirred in neutral oak. Aromas of berries and watermelon, creamy strawberries and a hint of melon on the palate. Fruit forward finish.
Anderson Valley Estate Chardonnay 2021 ○ 427 cases; 32 $ - 🍷 - Aged 10 months in French oak (20% new). Picked in September for "beautiful" acid. 30% goes through malolactic. Complex with aromas of apple, pear and hint of caramel; crisp finish.

acres 20 - cases 9,000
Fertilizers compost, cover crops, organic fertilizer
Plant protection sulfur, synthetic pesticides, organic
Weed control mechanical, manual
Yeasts commercial cultured yeasts
Grapes purchase 50%
Certification some of the vineyards are certified organic

BOONVILLE

LICHEN ESTATE

Anderson Valley - 11001 County Road 151 - tel. (707) 895-7949
www.lichenestate.com - info@lichenestate.com

PEOPLE - In 2005, Douglas Stewart, an experienced wine entrepreneur, built his first winery, Breggo Cellar, near Boonville. After selling the Breggo brand in 2009, he kept his vineyard and created Lichen to showcase organically farmed, minimal intervention wines. A third of his production is sparkling wine which he makes onsite. The winery has offers lodging in a cottage or an Airstream.

VINEYARDS - When Doug purchased the 203 acre ranch in 2000, it had been a sheep ranch for 150 years. Eight years later, he planted the alluvial, loamy soil vineyard in meter by meter spacing. He uses underground watering lines to keep weeds down and allow mower access in the early stages of the vineyard. Permanent cover crops grow in between the vine rows. Various rootstocks are matched to soil and clone. He is resuming organic certification.

WINES - Uniquely he makes a white Pinot Noir and a (sparkling) Blanc de Blanc of Pinot Gris.

Anderson Valley Estate Grand Cuvée Brut Rosé 2017 239 cases; 95 $ - Made in house from start to finish. It spends 54 months en tirage. A touch of still Pinot Noir added at disgorging. Another year under cork. Aromas of dried mango and papaya blend into peach and watermelon with a lingering finish and hint of candied ginger.

Anderson Valley Estate Pinot Gris 2022 O 300 cases; 35 $ - Multiple lots blended in different proportions create a fruit forward wine. Light honey color with aromas of orange blossom, a viscous mouthful loaded with stone fruit and a lovely citrus finish.

Anderson Valley Estate Pinot Noir 2021 ● 350 cases; 49 $ - Aged 18 months in oak puncheons (20% new). Aromas of dried floral and raspberry. Bright ripe cherry with hints of cola and nutmeg.

acres 7 - cases 2,500
Fertilizers cover crops, manure, organic fertilizer
Plant protection sulfur, copper, organic
Weed control animal grazing, mechanical
Yeasts spontaneous fermentation, commercial cultured yeasts
Grapes 100% owned
Certification converting to organic

MANCHESTER

MARIAH VINEYARDS

Mendocino Ridge - 33525 Mountain View Road - tel. (707) 291-6559
www.mariahvineyards.com - wine@mariahvineyards.com

PEOPLE - In 1979, Dan and Vicky Dooling bought 90 acres in Mendocino County on a ridgetop with an ocean view. They planted grapes in 1980, built a house, raised four children and created a small winery off the grid with solar energy, biodiesel generator and a tractor. They named it for the ever present coastal wind. It's now run by daughter Nicole and her Swiss born spouse Michael Frey. It was the first winery certified in Savory Institute's Global Land to Market regenerative program.

VINEYARDS - At 2,400 feet overlooking the Pacific Ocean, the dry farmed, no till vineyard in the unique Mendocino Ridge AVA (1,200 elevation minimum) is surrounded by a biodiverse forest ecosystem. This high elevation, cool climate vineyard, above the fog line, produces coveted Chardonnay, Pinot Noir, Primitivo, Sauvignon Blanc and Zinfandel. They report they use only organic approved materials.

WINES - The current wines were made by ENA winemaker Eglantine Chauffour. Nicole and Michael are starting a new brand called Dirt Wine set to launch in 2025 with winemaker Joanna Wells-Castorani (of Model Farm wines).

TOP Mendocino Ridge Sauvignon Blanc 2022 SLOW WINE O 56 cases; 32 $ - 45% malolactic. Light lemon color. Bright citrus and applesauce settles in to a complex balance of grass and dried fruit on the palate with refreshing finish.

Mendocino Ridge Pinot Noir 2022 ● 66 cases; 42 $ - Clear ruby color and elegant mouthfeel saturated with tart cherry, porcini mushroom, and soft tannins. A delicate finish.

Mendocino Ridge Primitivo 2021 ● 88 cases; 30 $ - Aged 10 months neutral oak. Earthy with wild huckleberries on the nose. Easy tannins and dried berries loaded with brilliantly balanced texture and lush mouthfeel.

acres 30 - cases 200
Fertilizers compost, cover crops
Plant protection sulfur, biodynamic preparations, copper, organic
Weed control mechanical
Yeasts spontaneous fermentation
Grapes 100% owned
Certification none

SEBASTOPOL

MARTHA STOUMEN WINES

6780 McKinley Street, #170 - tel. (707) 309-6500
www.marthastoumen.com - info@marthastoumen.com

PEOPLE - One of the "cool kids" into under the radar varieties, after ten years leading her own natural-esque wine brand, Stoumen is finetuning her business. Making wines at Pax Mahle's winery in Sebastopol, she works with Tim Lyons as her assistant. Most of her wines are small lot except for her affordably priced, chilled red wine Post Flirtation (3,600 cases), a Zin-Carignane blend, which is the largest production in her line-up.

VINEYARDS - Stoumen buys grapes from more than eight vineyards under contracts that specify no herbicide use. At the sole site she farms—head trained and dry farmed Bricarelli Vineyard in Ukiah Valley—she is exploring regenerative, no till practices—roller crimping. In Mendocino, she buys grapes from Ricetti and Venturi (both certified organic). Elsewhere she buys Syrah from Grist (certified organic) in Dry Creek Valley, Vermentino comes from Vino Farms in Lodi (certified biodynamic).

WINES - Stoumen produces low intervention wines with a focus on lesser known varieties and regions. New: putting ingredients labels on some of her wines.

● **Mendocino County Bricarelli Ranch Nero d'Avola 2021** ● 333 cases; 48 $ - ⊞ ⓠ - Aged in neutral oak and puncheon for 20 months. Aromas of wild red and black fruits with pretty floral notes.
Contra Costa County Solo Act 2022 ○ 216 cases; 37 $ - ⊞ - Aged for eight months in neutral oak. Blend of Roussanne (39%), Marsanne (35%) and Muscat Blanc (26%). A co-fermented field blend. Aromas of apricot juice and wildflowers. Soft, round, and delicate on the palate, with a saline finish.
Redwood Valley Honeymoon 2022 ○ 280 cases; 39 $ - ⊞ - Colombard (55%) and Chardonnay (45%) from Ricetti Vineyard. The Colombard bush vines were planted in 1948. Barrel fermented for texture and layers. On the nose, citrus, stone fruit and floral notes. On the palate, notes of honey and very bright acidity.

---

acres 5 - cases 6,000
Fertilizers compost, biodynamic compost, cover crops, organic fertilizer
Plant protection sulfur, biodynamic preparations, organic
Weed control mechanical, manual
Yeasts spontaneous fermentation
Grapes purchase 85%
Certification some of the vineyards are certified organic, some of the vineyards are certified biodynamic

REDWOOD VALLEY

MIA BEA WINES

P.O. Box 731 - tel. (707) 485-8606
www.miabeawines.com - info@miabeawines.com

PEOPLE - The late Pete Barra's family has grown grapes in Redwood Valley for 100+ years. He purchased the property in 1967 and planted grapes first sold in 1970. He was one of the original growers for Fetzer and then Bonterra. In 2014, after Beatriz, his wife of 57 years, passed, daughters Cyndi, Lori, and Christina launched Mia Bea, the name of Pete's beloved fishing boat. The rose on the label memorializes those Pete tended and picked for his wife and daughters.

VINEYARDS - When Pete planted Chardonnay, Petite Sirah and Pinot Noir, his daughters were old enough to assist (albeit reluctantly) with clearing the land. The grapes thrive on the rolling sandy loam and Redvine soils. Today the sisters embrace their farming heritage with tastings that take place next to the vineyards.

WINES - Ukiah based winemaker Chris Nelson makes the wines with a light touch in the cellar.

● **Redwood Valley Chardonnay 2022** EVERYDAY WINE ○ 259 cases; 24 $ - ⓠ - Whole cluster pressing and 24 hour cold settling. Rich fruit flavors of unoaked Chardonnay.
Redwood Valley Pinot Noir Rosé 2022 ◐ 128 cases; 24 $ - ⓠ - A red rose on the label hints at the flavor to come from this lightly pressed Pinot Noir, with floral aromas in a swirl of bright blush color. A crisp fruity mouthfeel and pleasant finish.
Redwood Valley Pinot Noir 2022 ● 245 cases; 26 $ - ⓠ - Aged eight months in neutral French oak (75%) and new American oak (25%). After destemming, whole clusters soak for three days. Lovely floral aromas, berry rich with silky tannins and bright lingering finish.

---

acres 28 - cases 900
Fertilizers manure
Plant protection sulfur, organic
Weed control mechanical, manual
Yeasts selected indigenous yeasts, commercial cultured yeasts
Grapes 100% owned
Certification organic

PHILO

NAVARRO VINEYARDS & WINERY

Anderson Valley - 5601 CA-128 - tel. (707) 895-3606
www.navarrowine.com - sales@navarrowine.com

PEOPLE - Deborah Cahn and Ted Bennett left the Bay Area in the 1970s to purchase land near Philo with a mission to grow Alsatian style grapes and make wines they love. The 1974 was their first vintage. It was one of the first wineries in the Valley. Now their children Sarah and Aaron are the official proprietors. Jim Klein has made the wines since 1992. They are well priced, high quality wines.

VINEYARDS - On their 935 acre ranch, nestled up the slopes and along the fertile valley, 91 vineyard acres grow grapes. Soils are loamy, clay and gravelly loam. Baby doll sheep keep down weeds. Cover crops enhance fertility. All vineyard and winery workers are full time and live in the Valley. They also buy grapes from local growers. Some wines (not featured here) may be grown with herbicide.

WINES - Wines are punched down by hand to minimize harsh tannins and keep the mouthfeel soft. Large barrels are often used. Uniquely they make a very popular Alsatian white wine blend, Edelzwicker.

TOP Anderson Valley Première Reserve Chardonnay 2022 EVERYDAY WINE ○ 1,186 cases; 33 $ - ⊞ - Aged 10 months in French oak on the lees. Golden color. Lemon blossom and melon. A note reminiscent of cream soda. Finishes long and satisfying.

Anderson Valley Navarro Gewürztraminer 2022 ○ 2,472 cases; 28 $ - ⊞ - Destemmed and fermented in French oak ovals. Deliciously dry, with ginger and rose petal scents interspersed among lychee and orange with a crisp mouthfeel and classic spicy finish.

Anderson Valley Methode á l'Ancienne Pinot Noir 2021 ● 2,224 cases; 39 $ - ⊞ - Aged 10 months in French oak (33% new). Methode á l'Ancienne means hand punchdown. Rich ruby color. Fruit driven notes of cranberry and pomegranate. Balanced mouthfeel.

---

acres 91 - cases 39,000
Fertilizers compost, cover crops, organic fertilizer, synthetic fertilizer
Plant protection sulfur, synthetic pesticides, copper
Weed control animal grazing, mechanical, manual
Yeasts selected indigenous yeasts, commercial cultured yeasts
Grapes purchase 35%
Certification none

LAKEPORT

OVIS

4350 Thomas Drive - tel. (707) 281-6780
www.shannonfamilyofwines.com - info@shannonridge.com

 A Lake County green pioneer, its 1,000 acre, regenerative, organic estate, makes top tier wines and preserves newly discovered historic Cinsault.

PEOPLE - Shannon Family's high end label, Ovis ("shes ep" in Latin) pays homage to its woolly sheep—an essential part of its vineyard crew. Joy Merrilees is vice president of production, In 2014, the team discovered that an old vine with only two leaves left (obscured by scrub for 100+ years) was a rare Cinsault, dating back to 1870 in Croatia, brought by the Ogulin family settlers. It's now inspired its own bottling—Mother Vine.

VINEYARDS - Farming regeneratively, the team relies on its 1,000 sheep (in the vines year round) for tilling, mowing and fertilizing. It also composts and is transitioning to drought resistant rootstock. It supports biodiversity, leaving 60 percent of the land for wildlife. Following its historic Cinsault discovery, Ovis collaborated with Guillaume Nursery to propagate buds and has now planted 700 acres of the historic selection to make a Mother Vine rosé

WINES - Solar intensity, winds and native cover crops (bringing aromatics of bay laurel, tarwood and vetch) create exciting, layered wines, All are certified "Made with Organic Grapes," a high standard.

TOP High Valley Mother Vine Rosé 2023 SLOW WINE ● 700 cases; 38 $ - ⌂ - A blend of Grenache (62%) and the historic Cinsault (38%). Herbal scrub and floral aromatics lead to a palate of concentrated tart raspberry and lime, with a silky texture, tannin grip and a remarkably long finish of salted cantaloupe and lime. Incredible.

TOP High Valley Betsy's Vineyard Petit Sirah 2019 ● 556 cases; 60 $ - ⊞ - Deepest purple. Lush blue fruit and wild botanicals on the nose welcome plush, ripe fruit, followed by tannins tinged with fresh herbal notes. Hedonistic.

High Valley Cabernet Sauvignon 2019 ● 2,500 cases; 60 $ - ⊞ - Aged 18 months in barrel and 18 in bottle. Deep and complex. Tobacco and cassis lead to dried fruits and smooth body layered with structured tannins sparked by juicy acidity.

---

acres 904 - cases 4.856
Fertilizers compost, manure
Plant protection sulfur, organic
Weed control animal grazing, mechanical
Yeasts spontaneous fermentation, commercial cultured yeasts
Grapes 100% owned
Certification organic

BOONVILLE

PENNYROYAL FARM

Anderson Valley - 14930 CA-128 - tel. (707) 895-2410
www.pennyroyalfarm.com - info@pennyroyalfarm.com

PEOPLE - Proprietor Sarah Cahn Bennett is the daughter of iconic Anderson Valley vintners Deborah Cahn and Ted Bennett, who run Navarro Vineyards in Philo (started in 1974). Her parents have owned the former Boonville hayfield Pennyroyal now sits on since 1987. In 2008, Sarah, now general manager of Navarro, developed it into a vineyard. With 96 dairy goats and 26 dairy sheep, Pennyroyal is also known for its creamery where it makes five styles of cheese.

VINEYARDS - The Pennyroyal soils of alluvial sand and clay grow Pinot Noir and Sauvignon Blanc. The vines are Fish Friendly certified. By using a modern V-top trellis, each vine can be suckered by Babydoll Southdown sheep. The sheep are also responsible for composted manure that fertilizes the no till vines. Dairy sheep's milk is made into cheeses to accompany the wines. Grapes also come from Navarro vines.

WINES - Jim Klein, the winemaker at Navarro since 1992, also makes the Pennyroyal wines, using a light touch in the cellar.

🔝 **Anderson Valley Pinot Noir 2021** ● 557 cases; 47 $ - 🏠 - Aged 10 months in French oak (33% new). Ruby colored with aromas of tart berries and rich spices and a lingering fruit-rich finish.
Anderson Valley Pinotrio 2022 ○ 651 cases; 33 $ - 🏠 - This one of a kind wine blends three Pinots—Blanc (40%), Noir (40%), and Gris (20%). Stunning texture and myriad complexity of flavors include dried apple, honeysuckle, citrus and a nutty finish.
Anderson Valley Sauvignon Blanc 2023 ○ 624 cases; 30 $ - 🏠 - Aged four months in 1,600-gallon, neutral French oak ovals. Light golden with crisp mouthfeel. On the palate, hints of lemon and honeydew, and a long finish.

acres 23 - cases 550
Fertilizers compost, cover crops, organic fertilizer, synthetic fertilizer
Plant protection sulfur, synthetic pesticides, copper
Weed control animal grazing, mechanical, manual
Yeasts selected indigenous yeasts, commercial cultured yeasts
Grapes 100% owned
Certification none

REDWOOD VALLEY

POWICANA FARM

3350 Road B - tel. (760) 840-0918
www.powicanafarm.com - powicana@gmail.com

PEOPLE - When French born proprietors Zoubeida and Rémi Sajak moved to a ridgetop overlooking Redwood Valley in 2013, they settled in to make natural wine by hand from Petite Sirah grapes. Their first release in 2015 won a double gold. They participate in RAW Wine events around the country. Living the dream, with their two sons, the property is populated with olive trees, chickens, ducks, geese, pigs and dogs.

VINEYARDS - At 900 feet, Redvine sandy clay loamy soil translates to the word "Powicana" in the local Pomo dialect. Inspired by Masanobu Fukuoka, vines are dry farmed and no till vineyard. It produces 18 tons an acre with superb quality fruit. They've been certified organic since 2019. Growing only one varietal, they creatively vinify it numerous ways.

WINES - Charming labels featuring art from their sons adorn the bottles of sparkling, house, reserve and port Petite Sirah.

🔝 **Mendocino County Pétillant Naturel 2018** EVERYDAY WINE
Petite Sirah; 600 cases; 18 $ - 🏠 - Pale pink pet nat comes in bottles with attached corks, which hold tight during fermentation as light refreshing bubbles develop like first made by French monks in the 1500's. Flora and ripe peach mingle with low alcohol and a bright finish.
Redwood Valley Petite Sirah Fuego! 2017 ● 225 cases; 36 $ - 🏠 - The year deadly fires swept Redwood Valley (2017), the family had to run for their lives. As winds changed, they returned to harvest with lots of help. Whole cluster and a year of aging in neutral oak produced dark red, full-bodied structure with tannins. Best decanted.
Redwood Valley Petite Sirah Blue Dog 2018 ● 400 cases; 36 $ - 🏠 - Classic Petite Sirah. Intense inky color. Violet and cedar aromas, and a mouthful of dense red fruit, hints of cacao and black pepper.

acres 7 - cases 600
Fertilizers biodynamic compost, cover crops
Plant protection biodynamic preparations
Weed control animal grazing, mechanical, manual
Yeasts spontaneous fermentation
Grapes 100% owned
Certification organic

HOPLAND

TERRA SAVIA

14160 Mountain House Road - tel. (707) 744-1114
www.terrasavia.com - mktevents@terrasavia.com

PEOPLE - Aptly named Terra Sávia, which means "wise earth," it's run by an international cast that includes owners Dominican born Yvonne Hall and Swiss born Jurg Fischer along with olive oil maestro Carlo Suarez (who is from Mexican heritage). Argentinian winemaker Sofia Rivier rounds out the group. All enjoy an organic lifestyle, growing organic vegetables, olives and wine grapes. They host winery events throughout the year to share the fruits of all their labor.

VINEYARDS - The 29 acre Sanel Valley vineyard (certified organic since 2013) sits on gravely, loamy benchland soils, nestled against Duncan Peak. It grows Cabernet Sauvignon, Chardonnay, Merlot, Petit Verdot and Pinot Noir. Most were planted by legendary local vintner, Jim Milone, who retired from Terra Savia a year ago.

WINES - Respecting the fruit and manipulating it with little intervention to showcase what the varietals can do is the goal. The winery is also certified organic, enabling the wines to be labeled "Made with Organic Grapes."

● Hopland Rosé of Merlot 2022 EVERYDAY WINE ● 115 cases; 23 $ - ⌑ - Pressed for quick skin contact, the juice cold settles in stainless for a month. Deep salmon color and aromas of strawberries, a bit of pomegranate and a mouthful ranging from raspberry to cherry, fruity but not sweet.

Hopland Merlot 2018 ● 413 cases; 25 $ - ⓜ - Aged 18 months in French oak (25% new). Destemmed and soaked in tanks for two days. Yeast added and pumped over several times a day for two weeks. Deep ruby with slight purple hue previews lush layers of dark currant, blackberry, and cherry are laced with cardamom and anise.

acres 29 - cases 5,000
Fertilizers compost, cover crops
Plant protection sulfur
Weed control mechanical, manual
Yeasts commercial cultured yeasts
Grapes 100% owned
Certification organic

REDWOOD VALLEY

TESTA VINEYARDS

9001 B North State Street - tel. (707) 485-9051
www.testaranch.com - info@testaranch.com

PEOPLE - Maria Testa Martinson, great granddaughter of Mendocino viticulture pioneers, Gaetano Testa and Battista Garzini, knew when she started making wine in 2010 that she wanted to preserve her Italian heritage. Testa wines are Simply White, Simply Black and Rose (named for a beloved aunt). They have a huge cellar club following, host popular events (such as My Big Fat Wedding) and opened a new coffee shop and tasting room. They also rent their historic home for parties.

VINEYARDS - Six generations have farmed the Testa vineyards. Once a redwood forest, some family vineyards were planted 112 years ago on upland benches where Redvine and loamy soils were perfect for Italian grapes. Testa grows sought after old vine Carignane and Charbono along with Barbera, Grenache, Petite Sirah and, of course, the local Italian standby, Zinfandel.

WINES - Just like her Nonno (Gaetano Testa), Maria, working with winemaker Chris Nelson, makes wine to be fruity and not overbearing "so it tastes good with everything; food, friends and family."

Redwood Valley Rosé 2022 ● 400 cases; 25 $ - ⌑ ⓜ - Home Ranch Primitivo, Carignane and Petite Sirah. Light and refreshing. Medium salmon colored from a couple of hours on the skin. Lovely. 10% ABV.

Redwood Valley Simply White 2022 ○ 400 cases; 25 $ - ⌑ - A novel field blend of Chardonnay (70%), Sauvignon Blanc (29%) and Muscat fermented. Crisp pale golden wine with mouthful reminiscent of pear, nectarine and floral with a cleansing finish.

Redwood Valley Testa Coro Mendocino 2017 ● 78 cases; 50 $ - ⊞ - Aged three years in barrel. Coro, which means "chorus in Italian," is a regional Zin blend program. Testa's blend is old vine Zin (54%) and Carignane (30%) with Syrah (10%) and Petite Sirah (6%). Full bodied, with complex notes of cherry, dusty cocoa, smoke and herbs.

acres 100 - cases 3,323
Fertilizers compost, cover crops, manure
Plant protection sulfur
Weed control mechanical, manual
Yeasts spontaneous fermentation
Grapes 100% owned
Certification organic

UKIAH

TRINAFOUR

143 A Clara Avenue - tel. (707) 228-5440
www.trinafourcellars.com - alexmacgregor@sbcglobal.net

PEOPLE - Paying tribute to his Scottish Heritage, evidenced by the name and MacGregor tartan on the label, Alex MacGregor named his brand for the estate in Trinafour, Scotland, where his grandfather was gamekeeper. A Canadian by birth with a degree in marketing and finance, Alex became interested in wine when traveling in France and Spain, then working in restaurants. He previously worked with renowned consultant David Ramey to raise the bar on Mendocino wine quality.

VINEYARDS - A Mendocino winemaker since 2002, Alex knows vineyards with the best grapes and varieties. French Colombard comes from 230 vines at 75 year old Casa Verde Vineyard on an alluvial soil bench in east Redwood Valley foothills. From Lolonis, another historic vineyard on a bench at the eastern base of Redwood Valley foothills, he buys a smattering of Semillon among red vines. Both vineyards are dry farmed, head pruned, and hand hoed.

WINES - With heartfelt admiration for grape growers, Alex likes texture and mouthfeel and keeping acid at bay while being true to the varietal in his winemaking. From whole cluster pressing to tasting from the barrels he decides when to bottle.
Mendocino County Casa Verde Vineyard French Colombard 2023 O 50 cases; 28 $ - 🍽 - Harvested in October, cluster pressed, spontaneously fermented and settled into neutral oak for six months. A round mouthful like white Burgundy, with Anjou pear and lemon grass.
Mendocino County Lolonis Vineyard Semillon 2023 O 50 cases; 28 $ - 🍽 - Waiting for native malolactic fermentation to finish was worth it. This food friendly Semillon has the essence of hay and straw, with a round mouthful like Sauvignon Blanc, and its own zippy finish of Bosc pear and sweet pea shoots.

acres 0 - cases 300
Fertilizers compost, cover crops
Plant protection sulfur, organic
Weed control mechanical
Yeasts selected indigenous yeasts
Grapes purchase 100%
Certification organic

SANTA ROSA

UNTURNED STONE $

116 Lincoln Street - tel. (415) 613-9292
www.unturnedstonewine.com - erin@unturnedstonewine.com

PEOPLE - Erin Mitchell and Randy Czech grew up together, but came to wine separately. Erin worked in wine retail and distribution in Seattle in the '90's, and Randy took up winegrowing in California in the early 2000's. The swirling world of wine brought them back together in 2009, and in 2010 they made their first wine together under their new label. Now, with some farming in house and collaboration with likeminded growers, they make seven or more bottlings each year.

VINEYARDS - They farm a small plot in Dry Creek Valley, where they've learned through experimentation and slow progress how to bring back productivity and resilience to a field of struggling vines. They also selectively purchase fruit from organically farmed sites in Sonoma and Mendocino Counties, including inland vineyards and esteemed coastal vineyards.

WINES - Single vineyard designates are the way for them to express individual sites they choose to work with.
🔝 Potter Valley Vecino Vineyard The Hatchling Sauvignon Blanc 2023 O 230 cases; 25 $ - 🍽 - Made with the aromatic Sauvignon Musqué clone. Tropical white blossom and lychee aromas. Bitter almond, peach, white pepper, lush and full yet with lasting acidity on the palate.
Dry Creek Valley Adel's Vineyard The Blush White Zinfandel 2023 ◐ 105 cases; 25 $ - 🍽 - This bright "Barbie-pink" wine is an unapologetic but dry take on classic California White Zinfandel. A nose of watermelon and red hots candy, lush, thirst quenching on the palate full of red berry and cherry slushie.
Fort Ross-Seaview Waterhorse Ridge Spider Chase Cabernet Sauvignon 2018 ● 190 cases; 50 $ - 🍽 - A field blend of all five Bordeaux varieties. Paprika, berries, coffee, cocoa and lilac on the nose. A palate of jerky, licorice, blackberry, salted dried cherry and peppercorn with high acidity.

acres 1 acre - cases 1,200
Fertilizers compost, cover crops, organic fertilizer
Plant protection sulfur, organic
Weed control mechanical, manual
Yeasts spontaneous fermentation
Grapes purchase 90%
Certification some of the vineyards are certified organic

NORTH COAST
SAN FRANCISCO BAY AREA

 Bottle

95 Dashe Cellars
95 Donkey & Goat

$ Coin

97 Les Lunes Wine

BERKELEY

COVENANT WINES

1102 Sixth Street - tel. (510) 559-9045
www.covenantwines.com - wine@covenantwines.com

PEOPLE - An urban winery, it makes fine, kosher wines. The late Leslie Rudd, a prominent Napa vintner, and former winemaker Jeff Morgan founded it in 2003. Jonathan Hajdu, who started working with Jeff in 2004, is the current winemaker. Sagie Kleinlerer is the managing director. The winery is doubling from 8,000 to 15,000 square feet. Morgan is expanding into spirits, making wine based brandy, sherry, vodka, tequila/mezcal, and whiskey, all produced in Berkeley and made with local products.

VINEYARDS - They buy grapes from sites from the north coast, Lodi and the central coast. Some of the vineyards are certified organic (including Bengier in Napa's Oak Knoll District and Mettler Vineyard in Lodi). They say Scopus in Glen Ellen is working towards organic certification. Some wines (not featured here) may be grown with herbicide.

WINES - All Covenant wines are certified kosher which means that the production crew at the winery is Sabbath observant.

● Santa Maria Valley Bien Nacido Vineyard Syrah 2021 ● 100 cases; 80 $ - 🛢 - Aged 18 months in French oak (75% new). The destemmed grapes undergo a native fermentation in tank. Lush and voluptuous with blackberry, dark cherry, and earthy notes and an elegant finish.

Lodi Mettler Family Vineyard Red C Viognier 2023 ○ 300 cases; 28 $ - 🛢 - Inspired by the Israeli Viognier they last made in 2021. The wine is fresh, floral, and fruity with a full-bodied mouthfeel and bright acidity.

Napa Valley Solomon Lot 70 Cabernet Sauvignon 2022 ● 200 cases; 200 $ - 🛢 - Aged in French oak (75% new). Grown by Steve Matthiasson at the Bengier Vineyards (certified organic). A best barrel selection. Elegant with a purity of flavor. Aromas of dark fruit and cedar with an herbaceous note and cocoa dusted tannins that are firm but soft.

acres 0 - cases 8,000
Fertilizers compost, cover crops, organic fertilizer
Plant protection sulfur, organic
Weed control animal grazing, mechanical
Yeasts spontaneous fermentation
Grapes purchase 100%
Certification some of the vineyards are certified organic

ALAMEDA

DASHE CELLARS

1951 Monarch Street, Hangar 25 - tel. (510) 452-1800
www.dashecellars.com - info@dashecellars.com

PEOPLE - Husband and wife winemakers Mike and Anne Dashe founded their urban winery in 1996. They're renowned for old vine wines, chiefly Zinfandels. Mike's mentor was Paul Draper of Ridge, for whom he worked from 1989 to 1998. Anne, a Brittany native, came from the University of Bordeaux. Their casual, urban outpost winery in Alameda (near Spirits Alley) features a year round colony of blue herons and spectacular bayside views of the San Francisco Bay and skyline.

VINEYARDS - After scouring wine country for choice vineyards for years, the two make a wide assortment of varieties from special spots. A specialty is historic Zinfandel, especially from Louvau's 100 year old vines. Other varieties come from Heringer in the Delta and Oakley's Del Barba Vineyard in Contra Costa County. (Some wines [not featured here] are grown with herbicide.)

WINES - The wines thoroughly overdeliver for price and quality. They're made with traditional winemaking techniques Draper advocated for–old vines, little new oak, native yeast and nothing else, save for minimal amounts of sulfur.

⦿ California Vineyard Select Zinfandel 2022 EVERYDAY WINE ● 2,931 cases; 28 $ - Ⓜ - An incredible wine for the money. A red blend of mostly Zin, with a winning combination of Teroldego (8%) and Tannat (7%), giving it a whole other vibe. The vines are 60 years old. It's juicy, rich and mouthfilling with complex flavors, including a bass note of dark fruit from the Tannat.

Dry Creek Valley Reserve Zinfandel 2022 ● 500 cases; 38 $ - Ⓜ - Their flagship wine. Aged 18 months in French oak puncheons (25% new). The blend is Zinfandel (76%), Petite Sirah (20%) and Grenache (4%). Luscious blackberry and raspberry with a cherry liqueur finish. Elegant.

Clarksburg Heringer Vineyard Concrete Cuvee Chenin Blanc 2023 ○ 800 cases; 26 $ - 🍶 - Half is aged in a 500 gallon, concrete egg and half in stainless steel tank. Beautifully textured. Find pear and stone fruit on the palate. Finishes long.

acres 0 - cases 7,500
Fertilizers compost, cover crops
Plant protection sulfur, synthetic pesticides
Weed control n/a
Yeasts spontaneous fermentation
Grapes purchase 100%
Certification none

BERKELEY

DONKEY & GOAT

1340 5th Street - tel. (510) 868-9174
www.donkeyandgoat.com - dgorders@donkeyandgoat.com

PEOPLE - Natural winemakers par excellence, Donkey & Goat launched in 2004, becoming one of the first major natural wine producers in the U.S. Their tasting room in a warehouse district is the anchor tenant of the popular Drinks District, a cluster of natural wineries in Berkeley. Connor Bockman joined as the winemaker in 2022. In a new move, they recently started farming a Pinot Noir vineyard themselves in Sebastopol.

VINEYARDS - Working with about nine sites, they parptner with growers for access to whole, dedicated blocks. Their regulars include Brosseau (certified organic) in Chalone, Fenaughty Vineyard in El Dorado, Filigreen Farm in Anderson Valley (certified biodynamic), Calleri Vineyard in San Benito (certified organic) and Testa (certified organic) in inland Mendocino. Their award winning pet nat of Grenache Gris comes from Gibson Ranch in Mendocino.

WINES - The portfolio encompasses an eclectic array of varieties, sites and styles ranging from biodynamic Pinot Gris bubbles to under the radar Cabernet Pfeffer and carbonic Carignane.

San Benito Calleri Vineyard Falanghina 2023 ○ 186 cases; 36 $ - Ⓜ - Balanced between ripeness and acid tension, it is briny and herbal, with orange blossom on the nose and a palate of salted pink grapefruit, bitter almond and a lingering finish.

Anderson Valley Filigreen Farm Ramato Pinot Gris 2022 ◐ 298 cases; 35 $ - 🍶 Ⓜ - This "rosé of autumn" is full of orange fleshed melon, orange blossom and copper on the nose with a dried stone fruit and savory, lingering palate. Refreshing with juicy acidity.

Russian River Dommen Vineyard Pinot Meunier 2023 ● 284 cases; 38 $ - Ⓜ - A light bodied, translucent red from old vines. On the nose, cranberry and crushed herbs with flavor notes of wet granite, cherry, dried sage, iron, juniper and raspberry. Can also be served chilled.

acres 1 acre - cases 3,000
Fertilizers compost, biodynamic compost, cover crops, manure, organic fertilizer
Plant protection sulfur, biodynamic preparations, organic
Weed control animal grazing, mechanical, manual
Yeasts spontaneous fermentation
Grapes purchase 98%
Certification some of the vineyards are certified organic, some of the vineyards are certified biodynamic

RICHMOND

ETTELLIA

1387 Marina Way South, #500 - tel. (407) 687-2466
www.etteilla.wine - etteilla.wine@gmail.com

PEOPLE - Owner/winemakers Noelle Vandendriessche and Anne Disabato teamed up just after college, connected in part by their love for and interest in agriculture. After working harvests in South Africa and Australia, they spent a season with noted Sonoma County winemaker Tony Cotturi, who became a good friend and mentor. They are building a winery that embraces and celebrates community.

VINEYARDS - Along with farming four acres of Pinot Noir in the town of Sonoma, Noelle and Anne have developed long term relationships with a few vineyards in nearby counties. White grapes come from the deep, volcanic soils of Lake County's Stone House Cellars and reds from old vines planted on the stony loam of Testa Vineyards in the Redwood Valley.

WINES - Etteilla makes wines that are fresh and dynamic reflections of time and place in the vineyard.

Lake County Remi Sauvignon Blanc 2023 ⊚ 210 cases; 30 $ - ⊞ - Aged eight months in neutral oak. Light skin contact (three days). A surprising combination of tropical fruit aromas and flavors, including pineapple, mango and spicy white pepper.

Lake County Le Chaos | Cider-Sauvignon Blanc 2023 ⊛ 130 cases; 30 $ - 🍾 - A co-fermentation of Gravenstein apple juice (60%) with Sauvignon Blanc (40%) (some whole clusters), bottled as a pet nat and later disgorged. Full of floral aromas and bright flavors of apple and pear skin, fresh green herbs, lemon peel, juicy quince and just ripe apricot with an intriguing texture of lees time.

Redwood Valley The Set Carignan 2022 ● 125 cases; 38 $ - ⓦ - Aged 11 months in neutral oak. From 90 year old vines. Carbonic maceration. on half. Light and flinty with notes of red raspberry and pomegranate and subtle ripe notes of orange blossom and spice.

acres 4 - cases 1,100
Fertilizers none
Plant protection biodynamic preparations, organic
Weed control manual
Yeasts spontaneous fermentation
Grapes purchase 70%
Certification none

RICHMOND

EVERWILD WINES

1401 Marina Way South - tel. (530) 559-4542
www.everwildwines.com - everwildwines@gmail.com

PEOPLE - Winemaker/owner Talia St. Clair grew up in a plant and food loving family in the mountains outside of Sacramento. It was those memories that drew her to winemaking after an early career in the film industry where she met partner Austin Hobart. Together they are exploring how wine can connect them to nature and community. They are members of the Richmond Wine Collective.

VINEYARDS - Talia and Austin work exclusively with small family owned vineyards who see their farming as a labor of love and whose priority is good stewardship of the land. This includes Hartwick Vineyard in Lodi (planted by the current owner's grandfather), Sentinel Oak in Amador County and Chance Creek in Mendocino's Redwood Valley (certified organic).

WINES - All the wines are zero-zero, with as few inputs as possible resulting in wines that are bright with acid with unexpected flavors.

Lodi Cosima Orange Muscat 2022 ○ 48 cases; 32 $ - ⊞ - Aged 10 months in neutral oak. Notes of orange blossom, honey, ripe yellow plum, lemon grass, candied ginger and salt with enough acid to keep all the ripeness in balance.

Redwood Valley Manna From Heaven Sauvignon Blanc 2023 ⊚ 110 cases; 32 $ - ⊞ - Aged seven months in neutral oak. Skin contact (30 days) creates texture and a little astringency to complement notes of sour orange juice, ginger and cilantro stems.

Amador County Pense Pour Toi-Même Syrah 2023 ● 110 cases; 32 $ - ⊞ - Aged eight months in neutral oak. An unconventional blend of Syrah (50%) and Viognier (50%). Bright acids with notes of sweet cherry, strawberry and watermelon.

acres 0 - cases 1,000
Fertilizers compost, cover crops, manure, organic fertilizer
Plant protection sulfur, organic
Weed control animal grazing, mechanical, manual
Yeasts spontaneous fermentation
Grapes purchase 100%
Certification some of the vineyards are certified organic

ORINDA

LES LUNES WINE $

13 Cascade Lane - tel. (707) 320-7857
www.leluneswine.com - contact@leluneswine.com

PEOPLE - Natural winemakers Diego Roig and Shaunt Oungoulian met at UC Davis when they were both getting their master's degrees in viticulture and enology. After trips in France, in 2014, they each returned to California at the same time and started their winery's two low intervention brands–Les Lunes (from vineyards they farm), and Populis (a negotiant brand). The latter is an homage to organic growers mostly in Lodi, Mendocino and the Sierra Foothills.

VINEYARDS - Using only organically approved materials is a baseline. They work with about 20 different vineyards growing several varieties, and farm about half of those sites themselves. For Les Lunes, they lease land from vineyard owners who give them full operational control, converting the vines to organic farming. Growers for their Populis label are typically trusted, multi-generational farmers.

WINES - Experimenting with carbonic is common for the winemakers, as they love the aromatics that result. The style is fresh and pure.

TOP **Populis Reversée Red Wine 2023** EVERYDAY WINE ● 609 cases; 24 $ - ▦ ◎ - Made via the reverse saignée technique. Super aromatic and floral, with green cardamom, pipe tobacco and boysenberry on the nose, and flavor notes of leather, slate and dried strawberry. Typically served chilled.

Redwood Valley Lolonis Vineyard Macerated Chardonnay 2023 ○ 213 cases; 27 $ - ▦ ◎ - This half carbonic, half traditional. Aromas of orange blossom, honeysuckle, apricot, peach, creme brulee. Flavor notes of bitter almond, tropical fruit and juicy acidity.

Mendocino County Zinfandel 2022 ● 210 cases; 32 $ - ▦ ◎ - Partial whole cluster (25%). Old vines. Aromas of wet earth, black raspberry, wild strawberries and a hit of funk. Flavor notes of slate and raspberry with firm tannic structure.

acres 40 - cases 8,000
Fertilizers compost, cover crops, organic fertilizer
Plant protection sulfur, organic
Weed control none, mechanical, manual
Yeasts spontaneous fermentation
Grapes purchase 50%
Certification some of the vineyards are certified organic, converting to biodynamic

RICHMOND

MISCREANT WINES

1401 Marina Parkway South - tel. (631) 513-6157
www.miscreant-wines.com - miscreantwines@gmail.com

PEOPLE - Kathleen McKevney and Jasmine Shevick spent years teaching at the primary grade level before taking the plunge and working on their first vintage. They make natural wines as part of the Richmond Wine Collective. Their approach is to think about what they want to express stylistically while relishing the experience of being students of the process.

VINEYARDS - The two want keep their approach as local as possible, seeking out smaller family owned farms with whom they can develop long term relationships. They are currently working with the Castanon vineyard in Mendocino's Redwood Valley and Rough and Ready vineyards in the Sierra foothills of Nevada County.

WINES - Produces natural wines with a lighter, brighter take on classic European grape varieties.

Mendocino Right Time, Right Place Zinfandel 2022 ◎ 60 cases; 22 $ - ⌀ - Six days of skin contact gives this rosé a deep hue, but the flavors are light and bright with notes of orange peel, red currant, apple skin, tart red plum and spice.

Nevada County Marsanne/Roussanne Blend 2023 ◎ 45 cases; 27 $ - ▦ - Skin contact fermentation gives this wine a distinct spiciness (clove and nutmeg) and a well rounded texture; tart with notes of baked pear, thyme and roasted almonds.

Mendocino Fool's Red Zinfandel 2022 ● 30 cases; 25 $ - ▦ - Aged nine months in neutral oak. A lighter expression of Zinfandel. Tart with notes of raspberry, cranberry, red cherry and a whiff of cigar box and tobacco.

acres 0 - cases 220
Fertilizers n/a
Plant protection n/a
Weed control mechanical
Yeasts spontaneous fermentation
Grapes purchase 100%
Certification some of the vineyards are certified organic

RICHMOND

PURITY WINES

1401 Marina Parkway South - tel. (510) 295-5442
www.puritywine.net - Purity.wine@gmail.com

PEOPLE - Winemaker/owner Noel Diaz and his wife Barrie Quan spent decades in food and hospitality before starting Purity Wines in 2013, and that sense of welcoming service imbues everything they do. Making the transition from sommelier to winemaker was an easy one for Noel as it allows him to continue to create a community and express his experimental artist's soul through wine.

VINEYARDS - Purity wine works exclusively with vineyards that are either certified organic or biodynamic or which are farmed with those principles in mind, particularly rejecting synthetic inputs and relying on creating a healthy environment for the vines. Examples include Hartwick Vineyard in Lodi and Starry Night Vineyard in Calaveras County.

WINES - Purity focuses on making natural wines that are tart, textured and food friendly. Some are zero zero wines.

Lodi Yummo Muscat Pet Nat 2022 ⊛ 150 cases; 28 $ - ⎕ - This pét nat of Orange Muscat is partially treaded by foot then pressed slowly for a little more skin contact. Tart and tangy with notes of orange blossom, orange rind, lemon, stone fruit, mango and green plum and a round texture from the residual lees.

Madera Glory Hole Grenache Blanc 2023 O 110 cases; 28 $ - ⎕ - Foot trod, whole cluster fruit were fermented on the skins for seven days to create an explosive texture; notes of cinnamon, nutmeg, dried apricot, just ripe nectarine and plum skin.

Sierra Foothills Bay Laurel Mourvedre 2017 ● 100 cases; 28 $ - ⌸ - Aged 18 months in new oak. Foot trod, whole cluster. Notes of black plum, black cherry, blackberry, blueberry, black raspberry and clove graced by subtle notes of leather, tobacco and vanilla.

acres 0 - cases 1,500
Fertilizers compost, cover crops, manure
Plant protection sulfur
Weed control animal grazing, mechanical
Yeasts spontaneous fermentation
Grapes purchase 100%
Certification some of the vineyards are certified organic

RICHMOND

SUBJECT TO CHANGE WINES

1387 Marina Way S, #500 - tel. (510) 214-2338
www.subjecttochangewine.com - hello@subjecttochangewine.com

PEOPLE - Natural winemaker Alex Pomerantz is prop active about land stewardship, seeking out family owned vineyards employing organic practices and encouraging them stay on that path or to take the next steps toward biodynamics. He certified his winery organic in 2024 and plans to make certified wines in the future. He makes many single vineyard wines.

VINEYARDS - He works only with certified organic or certified biodynamic vineyards, including many in Mendocino's Redwood Valley and Ciapusci in Yorkville. The climate there is cooler than many of the surrounding areas and has dry farmed, old vines vineyards on sloping red, rocky soils.

WINES - Embraces a wide range of styles ranging from sparkling whites to bold reds to herbal vermouths, all subject to the winemaker's creed of nothing added, nothing taken away. Some are zero zero.

Mendocino Coastview Vineyard Bang Bang Chardonnay 2020 O 144 cases; 38 $ - ⓜ - Barrel fermented and aged in neutral oak. From vines planted in the 1960s. Tart flavors of just ripe stone fruit and minerals.

Mendocino Open Hand Ranch FKA! Field Blend 2022 ● 741 cases; 26 $ - ⓜ - Fermented and aged in a 500L foudre. A field blend of Chardonnay, Pinotage (whole cluster) and Merlot. Light, fresh and tart with notes of red and black plums, black currant, blackberry and blueberry.

Mendocino Ridge Ciapusci Vineyard Lunatic Old Vine Zinfandel 2021 ● 430 cases; 50 $ - ⓜ - Aged 11 months in neutral oak. Whole cluster. Very old vine zinfandel (planted 1870). Simultaneously deep and light with notes of tart, dark fruit (blackberry, blueberry, black plum), tea and black pepper and an acid/tannin structure for aging.

acres 0 - cases 5,000
Fertilizers compost, biodynamic compost, cover crops, organic fertilizer
Plant protection biodynamic preparations, organic
Weed control manual
Yeasts spontaneous fermentation
Grapes purchase 100%
Certification some of the vineyards are certified organic, some of the vineyards are certified biodynamic

RICHMOND

TERAH WINE CO.

425 S 3rd Street - tel. (831) 200-5194
www.terahwineco.com - terah@terahwineco.com

PEOPLE - A gay, Palestinian-American, Terah Bajjalieh studied finance and business and then worked in mortgage lending and trading commodities. She left finance and started studying wine in 2010. She got her master's in winemaking and viticulture in Montpelier in 2015. She returned to the U.S. in 2018 to work with Constellation Brands and in 2020 started Terah Wine Co. In 2024, the U.S. State Department poured her wines for an event focused on Arab American relations.

VINEYARDS - Terah is very hands on and selects vineyards that use only organic approved materials. Organically certified sources in San Benito include Paicines Ranch Vineyard and Siletto Vineyard and, in Lodi, The Bench Vineyard in Clement Hills and Rivers Edge Vineyard in Mokelumne River. Other vineyards include Besson Vineyard, Castro Valley Ranch, Enz Vineyard, Lost Slough Vineyard and the renowned Shake Ridge Ranch (in Amador County).

WINES - Bajjalieh makes wines with a focus on quality and balance with minimal intervention. Approachable yet complex wines showcasing the unique characteristics of the vineyards and the varieties.

Clement Hills Vermentino 2023 EVERYDAY WINE ○ 150 cases; 28 $ - 🍷 - Vibrant, bright and zippy with bold citrus notes, tingling acidity and a textured midpalate. Super fresh.

Mokelumne River Sangiovese 2023 ● 150 cases; 32 $ - Aged 10 months in neutral French oak. Aromas of cherry and strawberry with mineral notes and a hint of meatiness, the wine is medium bodied.

Amador County Shake Ridge Ranch Barbera 2023 ● 128 cases; 40 $ - Aged 10 months in neutral puncheons and barrels. Whole cluster fermentation. Nose pops with aromas of wild strawberry, cherry, raspberry, and roses. Underneath are subtle notes of brown spices, chocolate, and earth. Medium bodied with textured tannins and a long finish.

acres 0 - cases 1,500
Fertilizers compost, cover crops, manure, organic fertilizer
Plant protection sulfur, organic
Weed control animal grazing, mechanical, manual
Yeasts spontaneous fermentation
Grapes purchase 100%
Certification some of the vineyards are certified organic

SANTA CRUZ MOUNTAINS

🐌 Snail
102 Cooper-Garrod
107 Rhys Vineyards

🍾 Bottle
101 Beauregard Vineyards
101 Big Basin Vineyards
102 Birichino
103 Ferrari Ranch Wines
104 Lester Estate Wines
104 Madson Wines
105 Maison Areion
108 Sandar & Hem Winery
108 Santa Cruz Mountain Vineyard
109 Sante Arcangeli Family Wines
110 Silver Mountain Vineyards
111 Windy Oaks Estate

$ Coin
100 Alfaro Family Vineyard & Winery
100 Bargetto Winery
105 Margins Wine

WATSONVILLE

ALFARO FAMILY VINEYARD & WINERY $

420 Hames Road - tel. (831) 728-5172
www.alfarowine.com - mail@alfarowine.com

PEOPLE - This family owned producer founded in 1997 is now into its second generation. In 2019, Ryan Alfaro took over winemaking from his parents, Mary Kay and Richard Alfaro. Three full time employees who have been there for decades also live onsite. Richard has farmed 28 vintages with their agricultural lead, Jose Antonio. Their primary bottlings showcase Chardonnay and Pinot Noir from their Corralitos estate.

VINEYARDS - They have two estates. Planted about 14 years ago, the original 44 acre estate grows Chardonnay, Merlot, Pinot Noir, Syrah and two acres of Grüner Veltliner. They recently grafted over some Cabernet Franc and Cabernet Sauvignon, the first to plant it on the western side of the Santa Cruz Mountains AVA. All of it is dry farmed, hand weeded and unsprayed. They also acquired the historic, 56 acre Trout Gulch Vineyard. Richard farmed it for the last 13 years.

WINES - Ryan is intent on preserving tradition, yet brings a gentle touch, producing lighter bodied wines with more stem inclusion.

Santa Cruz Mountains Whole Cluster Estate Pinot Noir 2022 ● 45 cases; 48 $ - 🍷 - A new wine, intended to be made from a different vineyard each year. This year it is Alfaro's grapes. Whole cluster. Lightly extracted and aromatic, the wine is floral and full of spice and black cherry.

Santa Cruz Mountains Lindsay Paige Vineyard Chardonnay 2022 ○ 144 cases; 35 $ - 🍷 ⓜ - Their richest Chardonnay, this comes from own-rooted vines in the oldest vineyard. Lovely white flower aromas. Concentrated, it is nutty and round.

Santa Cruz Mountains Trout Gulch Vineyard Sparkling Chardonnay 2022 ⊛ 150 cases; 50 $ - 🍷 - Their first sparkling since 2016. Youthful and fruit driven, the goal was a less yeasty sparkling. He made it the same way as he would the still wine, picked slightly earlier. Vivacious and fresh, with juicy green apple.

---

acres 64 - cases 9,000
Fertilizers compost, cover crops, organic fertilizer
Plant protection organic
Weed control mechanical, manual
Yeasts spontaneous fermentation, selected indigenous yeasts
Grapes 100% owned
Certification none

SOQUEL

BARGETTO WINERY $

3535 N Main Street - tel. (831) 475-2258
www.bargetto.com - jbargetto@bargetto.com

PEOPLE - Bargetto Winery is one of the oldest continuously operated wineries in the US, founded in 1933 by two brothers who emigrated to Santa Cruz from Piedmont, Italy. Today, the winery is run by the third generation. John Bargetto is director of winemaking and manages the vineyard and winemaking with winemaker Bobby Graviano. Regan Vineyards Winery, a second brand from Bargetto, makes premium bottlings from the Regan Vineyard (see separate entry).

VINEYARDS - The estate vineyard, Regan, is seven miles inland from the Monterey Bay in the Corralitos area and is planted to seven different grape varieties and clones. Regan Vineyard and Bargetto Winery have been certified sustainable by the CSWA since 2017. (This certification does not limit herbicides or fungicides). Most of the plantings are Italian varietals. Soil is loamy clay.

WINES - Bargetto's wines bring an Italian sensibility to the cool climate terroir of the Santa Cruz Mountains.

Santa Cruz Mountains Regan Vineyard Estate La Vita Red Blend 2019 ● 364 cases; 65 $ - 🍷 - A luxurious, rare blend of northern Italian varietals: Refosco (37%), Nebbiolo (32%) and Dolcetto (31%). Complex Old World style with cedar, tobacco and clove from wood aging and muted red fruits–cherry, huckleberry, plum–plus black tea, earth, herbs and minerals. Ageworthy. Portion of the proceeds donated to Community Bridges Pajaro Relief Fund.

Santa Cruz Mountains Regan Vineyard Reserve Chardonnay 2022 ○ 296 cases; 40 $ - 🍷 - Nicely integrated French oak qualities (vanilla, incense) round out fruit notes of lemon zest, yellow apple, unripe pineapple and yuzu. Fresh salinity on the finish shows the terroir.

---

acres 40 - cases 30,000
Fertilizers compost, biodynamic compost, cover crops, manure
Plant protection sulfur, synthetic pesticides
Weed control animal grazing, mechanical, manual
Yeasts spontaneous fermentation, commercial cultured yeasts
Grapes purchase 10%
Certification none

BONNY DOON

BEAUREGARD VINEYARDS

10 Pine Flat Road - tel. (831) 425-7777
www.beauregardvineyards.com - tastingroom@beauregardvineyards.com

PEOPLE - Beauregard Ranch was purchased by Amos Beauregard in 1945. Bud, Amos's son, farmed it for a lifetime until his son Jim assumed management of the vineyard. Importantly, Jim established Ben Lomond Mountain AVA in 1982, the only sub-AVA in the Santa Cruz Mountains. Jim manages the estate vineyards plus hundreds of other vineyard acres within the AVA. Jim's son, Ryan is the winemaker and also owns the Bald Mountain estate vineyard.

VINEYARDS - The three Ben Lomond Mountain AVA estates each have different microclimates and soils. The 12 acre Beauregard Ranch Vineyard is above the fog at 1,800 feet elevation on sandy loam. The 16 acre Coast Grade Vineyard, planted to Pinot Noir, sits at the fogline at 1,300 feet on limestone. The 40 acre Bald Mountain Vineyard sits below the fogline with heavy coastal influence, contains rare sandy Zayante soil and is transitioning to organic farming.

WINES - Since 2000, Ryan Beauregard produces wines that show the flavor of the land he grew up in and typicity of varietals.

TOP Ben Lomond Mountain Estate Cabernet Sauvignon 2021 SLOW WINE ● 250 cases; 75 $ - 🍷 - Aged in French oak (50% new). An outstanding Santa Cruz Mountains Cab from an historic high elevation vineyard in the heart of Ben Lomond Mountain. Ripe black fruit (currants, dark cherry, plum) with savory notes of cedar, tobacco, redwood, earth, and oak spice. Ageworthy.

Ben Lomond Mountain Bald Mountain Vineyard Estate Chardonnay 2022 ○ 350 cases; 68 $ - 🍷 - Aged in French oak (20% new). Complex and balanced. Expresses its terroir with lemon, pear, white mushroom, sea spray and oyster shell. Medium plus acidity, and a long finish.

Ben Lomond Mountain Coast Grade Vineyard Carbonica Pinot Noir 2023 ● 200 cases; 65 $ - 🍷 - Made in concrete egg using carbonic maceration, the wine is very aromatic with bright, crunchy red fruits and floral notes, low tannin, and good acidity. Fresh, fruity, and enjoyable now.

acres 60 - cases 5,000
Fertilizers organic fertilizer
Plant protection sulfur, synthetic pesticides
Weed control mechanical
Yeasts spontaneous fermentation
Grapes 100% owned
Certification none

BOULDER CREEK

BIG BASIN VINEYARDS

830 Memory Lane - tel. (831) 515-7278
www.bigbasinvineyards.com - bradley@bigbasinvineyards.com

PEOPLE - A classic Santa Cruz Mountains winery deep in the redwoods, it suffered badly in the 2020 CZU Lightning Complex fires which burned 86,000 acres and destroyed vintner Bradley Brown's home and parts of the vineyards. In the years since, the team has been rebuilding both the winery and parts of the vineyard. In 2022, they opened a tasting Santa Cruz tasting room. Eco-minded, Brown experiments with corks and glass to avoid synthetics in contact with wine.

VINEYARDS - Edna Valley Rhone Rock star John Alban, a role model for growing Rhones on mountainsides, mentored Brown when Brown was creating the estate vineyard on this historic site in the redwoods. The Big Basin estate was certified organic in 2012. Brown also buys fruit from the Santa Cruz Mountains and Gabilan Mountains. The latter appellation is defined by elevation, at 1,500 feet and above, and Brown was pivotal in establishing it. The AVA was approved in 2022.

WINES - Aromatic complexity is key. Brown primarily ferments Pinot Noir and Syrah whole cluster and uses a basket press on all the red wines.

TOP Chalone Rodnick Farm Vineyard Chenin Blanc 2022 ○ 130 cases; 44 $ - 🍷 - This star Chenin site has diurnal cool nights, warm days, low mildew pressure and sits on decomposed granite and Calcarea shale. All contribute to this varietal. The wine has ripping acidity with floral and mineral notes.

Santa Cruz Mountains Old Corral Pinot Noir 2021 ● 252 cases; 65 $ - 🍷 - A young estate wine. The whole cluster tannin still apparent, it will gain quite a bit of texture and body over the next few years. It is aromatic, with crushed herbs and site specific spice notes.

Santa Cruz Mountains Sixty-Two Terraces Syrah 2021 ● 130 cases; 60 $ - 🍷 - From two estate acres planted in 2008 on steep terraces (62 in all). Made 100% whole cluster, foot trod and almost no pumping, with nothing added at all. The wine is inky purple, full of black pepper and lilac and savory, with high tannins.

acres 10 - cases 4,200
Fertilizers compost, cover crops, manure, organic fertilizer
Plant protection organic
Weed control animal grazing, mechanical, manual
Yeasts spontaneous fermentation
Grapes purchase 60%
Certification some of the vineyards are certified organic

SANTA CRUZ

BIRICHINO

204 Church Street - tel. (831) 425-4811
www.birichino.com - alex@birichinovino.com

PEOPLE - Malvasia Bianca brought former Bonny Doon workers Alex Krause and John Locke together when they learned that Bonny Doon told the grower it would cease Malvasia production. The two bought the same Malvasia grapes and grew from there. Today they're known as a powerhouse producer of acclaimed, artisanal wines. The irreverent duo chose to name their brand Birichino. In Italian, it means "naughty." New: wine in cans—a still Malvasia, a Malvasia pet nat and a Vin Gris.

VINEYARDS - Grapes come from 21 choice vineyard sites throughout California, some planted as far back as the 1880's and 1910's. They buy Cabernet Pfeffer and old vine Zinfandel from the legendary Enz vineyard, Melon de Bourgogne and Pinot Noir from Rodnick Farm (certified organic) and Sémillon from Yount Mill (certified organic). A new release is a first vintage of Coastview Chardonnay, grown on a spectacular site at 2,200 feet in the Gabilan Mountains.

WINES - They have eclectic and refined taste in varieties and sites and tend toward high acid, aromatic wines.

Yountville Yount Mill Vineyard Semillon 2022 O 220 cases; 28 $ - 🍷🍴 - Inspired by a similar bottling from Forlorn Hope. Bottled unfiltered, the wine is zesty, citrusy and almost like crushed crystals, yet velvety and lush.
Lime Kiln Valley Enz Vineyard Old Vine Mourvedre 2022 ● 100 cases; 40 $ - 🍴🍽 - The Gabilans is one of their favorite mountain ranges. From vines planted in 1922 on this legendary site. A very pretty Mourvedre. It is light red and aromatic, with pomegranate notes. On the palate, wet stone, floral, vegetal and mineral characteristics.
Santa Cruz Mountains Peter Martin Ray Vineyard Cabernet Sauvignon 2021 ● 75 cases; 80 $ - 🍴🍽 - One of three grand cru vineyards they work with. Small clusters. Extremely aromatic and elegant, savory, herbal and unjammy, with raspberry seed characteristics. Ageworthy.

acres 0 - cases 15,500
Fertilizers compost, cover crops, organic fertilizer
Plant protection sulfur, biodynamic preparations, synthetic pesticides, organic
Weed control animal grazing, mechanical, manual
Yeasts spontaneous fermentation
Grapes purchase 100%
Certification some of the vineyards are certified organic

SARATOGA

COOPER-GARROD

22645 Garrod Road - tel. (408) 867-7116
www.garrodfarms.com - winery@garrodfarms.com

 A rare jewel established in 1893 with plantings by Martin Ray certified organic in 2011.

PEOPLE - David Garrod established Garrod Farms in 1893. Originally planted to prunes and apricots, the land was converted to horse stables in 1962. George Cooper married into the family in 1941 and, after a 30 year career as a NASA test pilot, took up winemaking. Since 1996, his son Bill (now winemaker) and Doris Cooper and their children have run the winery. In 2024, CSWA, a sustainability program Bill helped found, honored the winery with its Green Medal Award for its community contributions.

VINEYARDS - Martin Ray provided the first cuttings of Cabernet Sauvignon and helped George Cooper and Jan Garrod plant the vineyard in 1972. Today they have six vineyards (certified CSWA sustainable in 2010 and certified organic in 2011). They dry farm, growing eight varietals, including Cabernet Sauvignon, Chardonnay, Merlot, Pinot Noir, Syrah and Viognier.

WINES - Varietal bottlings are labeled Cooper-Garrod Estate, and blends are labeled Test Pilot, each named after an aircraft that George flew.

TOP Santa Cruz Mountains George's Vineyard Estate Cabernet Sauvignon 2017 SLOWWINE ● 144 cases; 47 $ - 🍽 - Aged 22 months in French oak. From the two acre George's Vineyard, named for the founder, this elegant high elevation Cab offers flavors of cherries, plums, cassis, mint, brown spices and cigar box.
Santa Cruz Mountains Test Pilot F-86 Sabre Jet Bordeaux Blend 2018 ● 120 cases; 45 $ - 🍽 - Aged 10 months in French oak (25% new). A blend of Cabernet Sauvignon (75%), Cabernet Franc (15%) and Merlot (10%). Round and fleshy with dark cherry and plums, dark chocolate and cedar, earth, and leather.
Santa Cruz Mountains Randall Grahm Clone Viognier 2023 O 120 cases; 46 $ - 🍷 - Fresh peaches, apricots, and honeysuckle notes fill the nose and palate. From the two acre Finley estate vineyard planted in 1998 to a clone named after Rhône Ranger Randall Grahm.

acres 28 - cases 2,000
Fertilizers compost, cover crops
Plant protection sulfur, organic
Weed control mechanical, manual
Yeasts spontaneous fermentation
Grapes 100% owned
Certification organic

CORRALITOS

FERRARI RANCH WINES

65 Magnifico Vita Lane - tel. (408) 667-4506
www.ferrariranchwines.com - info@ ferrariranchwines.com

PEOPLE - Dave and Liz Ferrari purchased their hillsit de Corralitos vineyard in 2016, with Pinot Noir vines planted 43 years ago. Santa Cruz Mountains viticulture consultant Prudy Foxx, who uses sustainable, organic, and holistic farming practices, farms this unique old vine site. Ross Reedy deftly leads the winemaking.

VINEYARDS - Ferrari Ranch's Pinot Noir vines grow 40 feet deep in terraced, dry farmed, west facing soils at 700 feet. The steep slopes have a gradient between 20-50%. The soils are deep colluvial, sand and gravel with ancient dune deposits. Redwoods surround the vineyard.

WINES - The winemaking is handcrafted in very small lots honoring the vineyard heritage and keeping the natural expression of it front and center.

Santa Cruz Mountains Estate Pinot Noir 2022 ● 148 cases; 62 $ - 🍷 - A pale ruby with garnet hues in the glass, this Pinot has chocolate, cherry, cinnamon, cranberry, peach, and rose petal on the nose. On the palate are flavors of sour cherry, chocolate, cinnamon stick, redwood, and firm tannins.
Santa Cruz Mountains Estate Rosé of Pinot Noir 2023 ○ 62 cases; 28 $ - 🍷 - Delicate and youthful, the wine is pale salmon in the glass with aromas and flavors of raspberry, white peach, white cherry and a clean crisp finish.
Santa Clara Valley Estate Rosé of Zinfandel 2023 ○ 34 cases; 24 $ - 🍷 - This refreshing, fruit forward, dry rosé gives aromas and flavors of a late summer farmer's market with wild blackberry, strawberry, Santa Rosa plum and pink amaryllis.

acres 12 - cases 413
Fertilizers compost, cover crops, organic fertilizer
Plant protection organic
Weed control mechanical, manual
Yeasts commercial cultured yeasts
Grapes 100% owned
Certification none

SARATOGA

HOUSE FAMILY VINEYARDS

13336 Old Oak Way - tel. (800) 975-7191
www.housefamilyvineyards.com - info@housefamilyvineyards.com

PEOPLE - In 1998, David House purchased the 73 acre property in Saratoga, on the east side of the Santa Cruz Mountains AVA. He and his family live on the property and work the vineyards. House planted vines over three periods: 1998, 2000, and 2004. The first 12 vintages were made by Jeff Patterson of Mount Eden Vineyards. Jim Cargill, Dave's son-in-law, manages winemaking and operations. Jonathan Goodling is the vineyard manager.

VINEYARDS - Old Oak Vineyard, the estate, is 900 feet elevation located in the "Chaine d'Or" part of the Santa Cruz Mountains. The steep 25 degree vineyard is planted on east facing slopes. Vines are tended by hand, harvested by hand, and sustainably farmed. They also buy grapes from other select vineyards.

WINES - While House's vineyard management is very high touch. The winemaking is low touch—minimal intervention.

Santa Cruz Mountains Lester Vineyard Pinot Noir 2019 ● 75 cases; 65 $ - 🍷 - This elegant fruit-forward Pinot Noir tastes of dark cherry, plum, red raspberry with lovely floral aromas balanced by savory qualities of brown spice, earth, and minerality.
Santa Cruz Mountains Estate Cabernet Sauvignon 2020 ● 675 cases; 84 $ - 🍷 - From the estate's steep vineyard, the wine shows ripe black and red fruit qualities along with mint, leather, tobacco, dried meat, pie crust, herbs, and brown spices from oak aging (24 months in 40% new French oak).
Monterey County Coastview Vineyard Syrah 2020 ● 284 cases; 62 $ - 🍷 - A small amount of Viognier (2%) was co-fermented in the blend and gives the wine a lifted, vibrant quality. Blackberry, bay laurel, roasted meat, dark chocolate, and herbs with good acidity and minerality on the finish. Complex and food-friendly.

acres 10 - cases 4,000
Fertilizers compost, manure, organic fertilizer
Plant protection sulfur, synthetic pesticides, copper, organic
Weed control mechanical, manual
Yeasts spontaneous fermentation, selected indigenous yeasts
Grapes purchase 40%
Certification none

APTOS

LESTER ESTATE WINES

2000 Pleasant Valley Road - tel. (831) 728-3793
www.lesterestatewines.com - info@lesterestatewines.com

PEOPLE - Dan and Patty Lester purchased Deer Park Ranch, a 200 acre property in Corralitos, in 1988. In 2014, Lesters' daughter Lori Lester Johnson and her husband Steve Johnson took over after Dan passed away. They developed a unique approach, hiring top winemakers in the region—John Benedetti, Emiddio Justin Massa, Ross Reedy and Dan Person—to make their wines using different clones and wine styles.

VINEYARDS - Local viticultural consultant Prudy Foxx manages the vineyard. Lester estate vineyard has an excellent reputation for growing premium Chardonnay, Syrah and eight different clones of Pinot Noir. They sell most of their fruit to other wineries. Facing southwest, the gently sloped vineyard is on an ancient seabed with alluvial fans and diverse terroir. Foxx supports and promotes vineyard and soil health.

WINES - The wines reflect Lester's unique vineyard terroir, clonal diversity, and are named for the personality of their winemakers.

TOP ● Santa Cruz Mountains Francisco Estate Pinot Noir 2021 ● 140 cases; 57 $ - 🍷 - Previously called Heritage and renamed Francisco in honor of the late Frank Cates. Made by John Benedetti from Vosne Romanée clones. Ripe red fruit, rose, five spice and licorice and tertiary notes of leather, tobacco and earth.
Santa Cruz Mountains Traviso Estate Pinot Noir 2021 ● 190 cases; 57 $ - 🍷 - Aged 11 months in French oak (25% new). Highly aromatic with dark cherry, rose, raspberry, juniper, and brown spices. Ripe tannins and a long finish. Made by Ross Reedy (winemaker for Ferrari Ranch Wines and Truett Hurst.)
Santa Cruz Mountains Estate Chardonnay 2022 O 98 cases; 45 $ - 🍷 - Citrus, pineapple, crème brulée, sandalwood and a touch of vanilla balance bright acidity and a round texture. Robert Young clones. Made by John Benedetti.

acres 15 - cases 1,000
Fertilizers compost, cover crops, manure, organic fertilizer
Plant protection synthetic pesticides, copper, organic
Weed control mechanical
Yeasts spontaneous fermentation, selected indigenous yeasts, commercial cultured yeasts
Grapes 100% owned
Certification none

SANTA CRUZ

MADSON WINES

328 Ingalls Street, Suite G - tel. (831) 345-9834
www.madsonwines.com - info@madsonwines.com

PEOPLE - Started in 2016, the Madson team consists of Cole Thomas, founder/winemaker, and Ken Swegles and Abbey Chrystal—viticulturists and partners. Cole found his wine passion working for Jeff Emery of Santa Cruz Mountain Vineyard. Prior to that, he was an organic vegetable farmer and manager of the Demeter Seed Library. Ken and Abbey live on and farm the Ascona vineyard. Madson Wines pledges to operate 100% carbon neutral, or sequester an equal amount of greenhouse gases as they emit.

VINEYARDS - They do not own vineyards outright, but Madson Wines leases and farms 11.5 acres of vineyards. They also consult directly with sourced vineyards, most of which are in the Santa Cruz Mountains. All use sustainable farming practices, and some use regenerative farming practices.

WINES - A leader in natural wine in the AVA using no fining or filtration, neutral oak, and mostly 100% whole cluster, the wines are clean and vibrant with a purity of fruit and are made to age.

TOP ● Santa Cruz Mountains Cabernet Sauvignon 2022 ● 65 cases; 75 $ - 🍷 - A blend of three vineyards, varying elevations, and different clones. Classic cool-climate Santa Cruz Mountains Cab with cassis and blackberry, redwood, tobacco, and black pepper. The wine has good structure, ripe fruit, and chalky tannin. Aged 18 months in neutral oak, unusual for California Cabernet.
Santa Cruz Mountains Toyon Vineyard Pinot Noir 2022 ● 98 cases; 60 $ - 🍷 - Toyon vineyard is on a southwestern slope three miles from the ocean. An ethereal Pinot. Notes of red cherry, strawberry, sarsaparilla, baking spice, mushroom, earth and soft tannins.
Santa Cruz Mountains Red Tail Vineyard Syrah 2022 ● 48 cases; 48 $ - 🍷 - Bright ruby with violet hues, this beautiful and ageworthy wine bursts with blackberry, dark cherry, sage, meat, and pepper flavors.

acres 0 - cases 2,800
Fertilizers compost, biodynamic compost, cover crops, manure, organic fertilizer
Plant protection sulfur, biodynamic preparations
Weed control animal grazing, mechanical, manual
Yeasts spontaneous fermentation
Grapes purchase 60%
Certification none

WOODSIDE

MAISON AREION

140 Sunrise Drive - tel. (707) 327-9170
www.maison-areion.com - nicolas@maison-areion.com

PEOPLE - Nicolas Vonderheyden is owner, viticulturist and winemaker of this tiny artisanal winery. He grew up on his family's estate, Château Monbrison in Margaux. With a master's degree from the University of Bordeaux, he worked vineyards around the globe. In 2015, Nicolas took over Chaine d'Or Vineyards. In Greek mythology, Areion is a horse with a gift of speech and honors Nicolas' sister who survived a traumatic brain injury and then competed at the 2024 Paris Paralympics.

VINEYARDS - Historic Chaine d'Or Vineyards in the northern part of the Santa Cruz Mountains is just under two acres at 1,400 feet. It was planted in 1987 with Chardonnay (50%), Cabernet Sauvignon (40%) and small amounts of other Bordeaux grapes. Nicolas implemented sustainable and organic farming practices, improved soil and canopy management, and eliminated herbicides and insecticides. The vineyard is converting to organic certification, anticipated in 2026.

WINES - Aged in neutral oak barrels with no filtering, there is minimal settling before bottling.

● Santa Cruz Mountains Chaine d'Or Vineyard Cabernet Sauvignon 2019 ● 90 cases; 52 $ - ⊞ - Cab blended with Merlot (15%) shows its terroir signature. With blackberry, black cherry, mountain fruit, redwood, graphite and mocha. The wine has velvety tannins and a lingering finish.
Santa Cruz Mountains Chaine d'Or Vineyard Chardonnay 2021 ○ 150 cases; 31 $ - ◌ - Age sur lie in amphora (60%) and French oak (40%). Whole cluster. The wine is similar to an "orange" wine. Flavors of evolved apple and peach notes, tree nuts and earth with good acidity and a soft mouthfeel.
Santa Cruz Mountains Tarwater Creek Vineyards Pinot Noir 2021 ● 45 cases; 45 $ - ⊞ - Aged in a combination of new acacia, neutral French oak, stainless and amphora. This subtle yet concentrated wine shows its unique terroir grown on at 1,030 feet among old growth redwoods 9.5 miles from the ocean. Cherry, raspberry, blood orange, redwood and saline notes.

acres 1.8 - cases 350
Fertilizers compost, cover crops, organic fertilizer
Plant protection organic
Weed control mechanical, manual
Yeasts spontaneous fermentation
Grapes purchase 20%
Certification converting to organic

SANTA CRUZ

MARGINS WINE $

402 Ingalls Street, Suite 18 - tel. (925) 413-2654
www.marginswine.com - megan@marginswine.com

PEOPLE - Natural winemaker Megan Bell started her label, with the help of crowdfunding, at the age of 25 to showcase varieties and vineyards that sit on the "margins." She was featured in a new film Living Wine, of a very tough harvest in 2020. Bell opened her tiny "cubby" tasting room in Santa Cruz in early 2024. She now sells three wines for $24 each, with a goal of making more accessibly priced bottles.

VINEYARDS - Bell likes lesser known varieties, including dry farmed Barbera from Zayante in the Santa Cruz Mountains, Muscat Blanc from Cecchini in Contra Costa County, and Assyrtiko from Paicines Ranch (certified organic) in San Benito County. (Paicines uses sheep year round in the vines, thanks to six foot high trellises, allowing them to mow and fertilize year round.) Bell also has an estate site deep in the Santa Cruz Mountains, co-managed with owner Larry Makjavich.

WINES - Bell's pulled back on maceration time, making reds in a much lighter style than before. In 2022 she added back in some heavier wines to find a better balance in her label.

Clarksburg Wilson Vineyard Chenin Blanc 2023 ○ 150 cases; 29 $ - ⊞ - Made from whole cluster fruit and fermented in old barrels, this vintage of the signature wine is fresh, full of zippy acid, yet juicy and bright with melon characteristics.
San Benito County Paicines Ranch Vineyard Grenache 2023 ● 125 cases; 27 $ - ⊞ - Only the third harvest from this young vineyard, the vintage is different compared to previous, with more complexity and structure. The bright, pink hued wine is brambly and fun, full of wild strawberry on the nose with great salinity and mouthfeel.
San Benito County Calleri Vineyard Barbera 2022 ● 100 cases; 30 $ - ⊞ - A surprising top seller. Balanced and fruity, light and bright yet masquerading as a big red. Notes of plumb and dark fruit with nice acidity.

acres 2 - cases 2,500
Fertilizers compost, cover crops, organic fertilizer
Plant protection sulfur, organic
Weed control animal grazing, mechanical
Yeasts spontaneous fermentation
Grapes purchase 85%
Certification some of the vineyards are certified organic

CALIFORNIA — SANTA CRUZ MOUNTAINS

PORTOLA VALLEY

NEELY WINE

575 Portola Road - tel. (650) 206-3213
www.neelywine.com - lucy@neelywine.com

PEOPLE - Neely Wine is women-led, family-owned producer and grower of premium Chardonnay and Pinot Noir from an historic vineyard. In 1980, the Melchors hired Bob and Jim Varner to plant their estate to Chardonnay and Gewürztraminer. The Neelys took over ownership in 1995, adding Pinot Noir, and the Varner brothers stay until 2015, when Shalini Sekhar was hired as winemaker. Recently, Neely hired Sarah Green as their new winemaker. Sekhar is consulting winemaker. Kirk Neely and Holly Myers are owners, and Lucy Neely is Operations Manager.

VINEYARDS - The estate vineyard is 16 acres divided into two main vineyards: Spring Ridge, the original plantings of Chardonnay and Pinot, and Sausal Creek, newest plantings. Each vineyard is further subdivided into separate blocks from 500 to 1700 feet with various exposures, soils, and microclimates. The 230-acre property is less than 10 miles from the ocean and spans a large diverse landscape with native forests, creeks, grasslands, canyons, and redwoods. They farm sustainable using organic practices. Ken Swegles is viticulture advisor.

WINES - Neely produces single-vineyard, block-specific wines with low intervention that showcase their unique terroir.

● Santa Cruz Mountains Spring Ridge Vineyard Bee Block Estate Chardonnay 2019 O 595 cases; 50 $ - ▦ - A well-balanced Chardonnay with notes of Meyer lemon, pineapple, and vanilla from French oak (17% new) with good acidity and a smooth refined finish
Santa Cruz Mountains Spring Ridge Vineyard Picnic Block Estate Pinot Noir 2021 ● 133 cases; 60 $ - ▦ - Aromatic with notes of cranberry, raspberry, strawberry compote, red plum, rose, redwood, and brown spice with good acidity and fine grain tea tannin. 31% new French oak.
Santa Cruz Mountains Sausal Creek Vineyard Block Verde Estate Grüner Veltliner 2023 O 102 cases; 40 $ - ▢ - Clean and crisp with lime, green pear, green gage, white pepper, and saline, and a subtle rounded quality from partial malolactic fermentation.

acres 16 - cases 2,000
Fertilizers compost, cover crops, organic fertilizer
Plant protection organic
Weed control mechanical
Yeasts spontaneous fermentation, commercial cultured yeasts
Grapes 100% owned
Certification none

SOQUEL

REGAN VINEYARDS WINERY

3535 N Main Street - tel. (831) 475-2258
www.reganwinery.com - info@reganwinery.com

PEOPLE - The Regan Vineyards label is a spinoff from Bargetto Winery, founded by John Bargetto in 2022. The brand produces premium wines from the Bargetto estate vineyard. Bargetto is the vineyard manager, and Jesus Figueroa is the longtime vineyard foreman. Keegan Mayo is the winemaker.

VINEYARDS - Planted in 1992, the 40 acre Regan Vineyard consists of 12 grape varieties and clones, including Italian varietals. Seven miles from the Monterey Bay, the vineyard is in the Corralitos area on a hilltop at 600 feet with soil diversity, fog, and maritime breezes. Since 2017, Regan Vineyard has been certified sustainable by the CSWA. The property includes horses, chickens, organic vegetable gardens, olive trees and a large gazebo for wine tasting.

WINES - Wines are made with minimal intervention, unfiltered, with no additives, and are aged with in French oak (50% new) and sealed under wax.

● Santa Cruz Mountains Mt. Eden Clone Estate Pinot Noir 2021 ● 60 cases; 60 $ - ▦ - Bright red fruit, vanilla, cinnamon, earth and Chinese five spice meld with good acidity, fine tannin and a long finish.
Santa Cruz Mountains Mt. Eden Clone Estate Chardonnay 2021 O 58 cases; 40 $ - ▦ - Made from the Mt. Eden clone, this full bodied wine has tropical, stone, and citrus fruit notes, vanilla, sandalwood, ginger and toast with good acidity and a long, smooth finish.

acres 40 - cases 400
Fertilizers compost, biodynamic compost, cover crops, manure
Plant protection sulfur
Weed control animal grazing, mechanical, manual
Yeasts spontaneous fermentation, commercial cultured yeasts
Grapes 100% owned
Certification none

LOS GATOS

RHYS VINEYARDS

11715 Skyline Boulevard - tel. (866) 511-1520
www.rhysvineyards.com - info@rhysvineyards.com

 For farming organically, meticulous winemaking and exploring new frontiers in terroir.

PEOPLE - Smitten by Burgundy's Grand Crus, Silicon Valley venture capitalist Kevin Harvey pursues his dream of making world class Pinot Noir and Chardonnay, first in his backyard, and now over a wide ranging expanse of mountain vineyards. He's described the winery as "by wine geeks for wine geeks." The team is led by Jeff Brinkman, director of winemaking with winemaker Eric Prahl. Organic and biodynamic veteran vineyard manager Javier Tapia Meza oversees the vineyards.

VINEYARDS - The winery's pursuit of perfect spots includes a patchwork of tiny plots on ridgetops in the Santa Cruz Mountains, adjacent to the San Andreas fault. Each vineyard has its own unique geological characteristics. More than 16 clones are used. Plantings are high density and some are dry farmed. Two additional vineyards are in Mendocino, including Bearwallow, located in the Deep End of Mendocino's Anderson Valley.

WINES - The Pinots are foot trod in one ton stainless steel vessels, then basket pressed. Whole cluster is selectively used. Oak aging is light with 20-30 percent new oak used to showcase the natural expressiveness of the wines.

🔝 Santa Cruz Mountains Mt. Pajaro Pinot Noir 2021 SLOW WINE ● 300 cases; 79 $ - 🍷 - Aged 18 months in French oak (30% new). Delicate notes of red fruits, black raspberries and brambly flavors. Makes one wonder: is it really from California? Swoonworthy.

Santa Cruz Mountains Horseshoe Pinot Noir 2021 ● 600 cases; 89 $ - 🍷 - Aged 18 months in French oak (30% new). A deeper, darker, more concentrated expression with red fruits–cherries–and dark fruits. Beautifully focused. One for the cellar.

Santa Cruz Mountains Horseshoe Chardonnay 2021 ○ 450 cases; 89 $ - 🍷 - Aged 18 months in French oak (15% new). From heritage clones–Wente, Hyde and Mount Eden–planted in 2002 at 1,300 to 1,600 feet of elevation. Expressive with bright citrus and pear.

acres 120 - cases 5,000
Fertilizers compost, cover crops, manure, organic fertilizer
Plant protection sulfur, copper, organic
Weed control animal grazing, mechanical, manual
Yeasts spontaneous fermentation
Grapes 100% owned
Certification none

CUPERTINO

RIDGE VINEYARDS

17100 Monte Bello Road - tel. (408) 867-3233
www.ridgewine.com

PEOPLE - Ridge marked its 50th Lytton Springs vintage this year with the 2022 release of Dry Creek Valley Zinfandel by winemaker Shana Rosenblum. A second generation winemaker she is the daughter of Zinfandel icon Kent Rosenblum. Founder Paul Draper, who retired in 2016, is credited with helping rescue Zinfandel from obscurity and with jumpstarting interest in Rhone varieties in Sonoma county. John Olney oversees all the production at Monte Bello and Lytton Springs.

VINEYARDS - The winery has reduced its carbon footprint by 25 percent largely due to greener packaging–reducing bottle weight and switching to compostable boxes. Vineyard manager David Gates led a multiyear transition to organic certification. Now the winery is among the largest organic growers in Sonoma and the largest grower of organically certified grapes in the Santa Cruz Mountains. Some of the wines (not featured here) are grown with herbicides.

WINES - Red wine aging relies on air dried American oak that ranges in age from new to five years old. Winemaking adheres to the pre-industrial approach established by founder Paul Draper.

🔝 Dry Creek Valley Lytton Springs Zinfandel 2022 SLOW WINE ● 11,165 cases; 55 $ - 🍷 - The blend is Zinfandel (67%), Petite Sirah (19%), Carignane (11%) and Alicante Bouschet (3%), showing bright red and black berries, lavender, and tobacco on a medium-full body with elegant black currant and black pepper on the finish.

Paso Robles Grenache Blanc 2023 ○ 4,550 cases; 35 $ - 🍷 - A blend of Grenache Blanc (84%), Picpoul (14%) and Roussanne (2%) showing ripe pear, honeysuckle and a variety of citrus with a lush mouthfeel and lifted finish.

Santa Cruz Mountains Monte Bello Estate Cabernet Sauvignon 2021 ● 3,100 cases; 250 $ - 🍷 - Aged in new American oak (100%). A blend of Cabernet Sauvignon (64%), Merlot (31%) and Petit Verdot (5%) from an early, dry vintage that retained freshness. Bold, well framed by resolved tannins, mountain blackberries, cassis and tobacco.

acres 525 - cases 80,000
Fertilizers compost, biodynamic compost, cover crops, manure, organic fertilizer, synthetic fertilizer
Plant protection biodynamic preparations, synthetic pesticides, copper, organic
Weed control animal grazing, mechanical, manual
Yeasts spontaneous fermentation
Grapes 100% owned
Certification some of the vineyards are certified organic

PORTOLA VALLEY

SANDAR & HEM WINERY

111 Corte Madera Road - tel. (415) 341-4866
www.sandarandhem.com - info@sandarandhem.com

PEOPLE - Before starting Sandar & Hem with his wife Recha, owner and winemaker Robert Bergstrom worked at Rhys Vineyards and under Jeffrey Patterson of Mount Eden Vineyards. They founded the winery to explore the deep heritage of the Santa Cruz Mountains through its historical and important vineyards. The name Sandar & Hem is an homage to their family's Norwegian agricultural origins, with the home place (Sandar) and surname (Hem) of their ancestors.

VINEYARDS - Sandar & Hem works with some of the most historic vineyards in the Santa Cruz Mountains including Bald Mountain, Bates Ranch, Coast Grade, Mindego Ridge, Mountain Winery, Peter Martin Ray, others. They farm 15% of these vineyards. They showcase Chardonnay in particular, believing it gives the best expression of region's diverse terroir, but they also work with Grenache, Pinot Noir, Cabernet Sauvignon, and other Bordeaux varieties.

WINES - The wines are made with minimal intervention and aged 12 months in French oak (20% new) and 6 months in steel sur lie.

🔝 Santa Cruz Mountains Le Boeuf Vineyard Chardonnay 2022 O 50 cases; 52 $ - 🍷 - The vineyard, farmed with native cover crops, is in Wilder Ranch State Park near the Pacific Ocean. Tangerine, orange blossom, Asian pear, minerals, and good acidity. Only two barrels were made.

Santa Cruz Mountains Mountain Winery Vineyard Chardonnay 2022 O 100 cases; 52 $ - 🍷 - Citrus, white blossom, ocean spray, minerals with a kiss of French oak, the wine is zesty and refreshing. Made from an historic vineyard.

Santa Cruz Mountains Deerheart Vineyard Pinot Noir 2022 ● 100 cases; 58 $ - 🍷 - Whole cluster fermentation gives the wine bright raspberry and cherry notes with lavender, spice, earth, minerality and good tannin and acid balance.

acres 3.5 - cases 1,200
Fertilizers cover crops, manure, organic fertilizer
Plant protection sulfur, organic
Weed control mechanical, manual
Yeasts spontaneous fermentation, selected indigenous yeasts
Grapes purchase 85%
Certification none

SANTA CRUZ

SANTA CRUZ MOUNTAIN VINEYARD

334 A Ingalls Street - tel. (831) 426-6209
www.santacruzmountainvineyard.com - info@santacruzmountainvineyard.com

PEOPLE - Ken Burnap, a Santa Cruz Mountain Pinot Noir pioneer, founded the winery in 1975. In 1979, Jeff Emery started with Burnap and worked with him for 25 years. In 2004, Emery purchased the winery and brand from Burnap. The winery is in Westside Santa Cruz. Emery is starting his fifth decade with the winery and is a revered local expert on Pinot Noir and the AVA's history.

VINEYARDS - Ken Burnap bought the estate Jarvis Vineyard in 1974 from David Bruce. Jarvis Vineyard is one of the oldest continuously operated vineyards in California, originally established in 1863 as Jarvis Brothers Vineyard. Now Emery purchases grapes from sustainably grown vineyards, including the Zinfandel vineyard at Zayante (certified organic). Las Nietas is three years into converting to organic.

WINES - Emery makes wines with lower alcohol, good acidity and subtle oak. They are food friendly and ageworthy. Quinta Cruz, the winery's second label, features Iberian varieties.

🔝 Santa Cruz Mountains Zayante Vineyard Zinfandel 2021 SLOWWINE ● 127 cases; 44 $ - 🍷 - A rare, lower alcohol Zinfandel (13.2%), from own rooted vines planted in 1988 in rare "Zayante Sand" soils. Notes of brambles, wild blackberry, cocoa powder, hibiscus, cardamom, black pepper and spice.

Santa Cruz Mountains Las Nietas Vineyard Pinot Noir 2021 ● 144 cases; 35 $ - 🍷 - The light garnet color belies the complexity and ageability of this wine. Delicate aromas of tart cherry, cranberry, wildflowers and redwood. Good acidity, well integrated tannin, and a long finish.

Santa Cruz Mountains Luchessi Vineyard Cabernet Sauvignon 2018 ● 236 cases; 54 $ - 🍷 - Aged for 30 months. Black cherry, jalapeno pepper, mint, graphite, tobacco, garrigue and dusty plum with firm tannins.

acres 0 - cases 3,500
Fertilizers none
Plant protection sulfur, organic
Weed control mechanical, manual
Yeasts spontaneous fermentation, commercial cultured yeasts
Grapes purchase 100%
Certification some of the vineyards are certified organic, converting to organic

APTOS

SANTE ARCANGELI FAMILY WINES

154 Aptos Village Way C-1 - tel. (831) 207-6048
www.santewinery.com - aptos@santewinery.com

PEOPLE - The name is synonymous for evocative Pinot Noir from the Santa Cruz Mountains, where owner and winemaker John Benedetti has deep roots. He opened a second tasting room in 2021 in the Harley Farms Goat Dairy barn in Pescadero where guests can enjoy farmstead goat cheese paired with his wines. He is ramping up production, bringing back his very popular "Integrato" appellation cuvee, and has purchased concrete eggs.

VINEYARDS - Split Rail Vineyard is Benedetti's signature site and features 40 year old, dry farmed vines. As he is also the winemaker for the Lester label, he buys Lester fruit, too. Pinot Noir comes from Toulouse in Mendocino's Anderson Valley and Coast Grade Vineyard in the Ben Lomond Mountain AVA at the western edge of the Santa Cruz Mountains. New: the Sangiacomo family's Roberts Road Vineyard in the Petaluma Gap.

WINES - Benedetti wants his wines to be clean and precise and is very committed to showcasing the special sites he sources from.

Santa Cruz Mountains Lester Family Vineyard Pinot Noir 2021 ● 300 cases; 55 $ - From a great vintage. Savory aromas of bay leaf, damp earth and pomegranate, with lingering, textural flavor notes of crushed herbs and raspberry.

Santa Cruz Mountains Saveria Vineyard Pinot Noir 2022 ● 200 cases; 55 $ - Benedetti calls this wine a food chameleon. Aromatics reign. Structured, with a fruit forward core and nice acidity. Cherry, conifer needles and light spice notes on the nose, with flavors of tart red berries and a mouthfeel that lingers elegantly.

Santa Cruz Mountains Rosé of Pinot Noir 2023 ● 250 cases; 35 $ - A saignee with combined direct press juice. Slow, cold ferments. Vibrant aromas of flower blossoms and spiced watermelon, and flavors of saline, citrus and sage.

acres 7 - cases 2,200
Fertilizers compost, cover crops
Plant protection sulfur, synthetic pesticides, organic
Weed control mechanical, manual
Yeasts spontaneous fermentation, commercial cultured yeasts
Grapes purchase 90%
Certification none

SANTA CRUZ

SER WINERY

427 Swift Street, Suite B - tel. (831) 901-7806
www.serwinery.com - info@serwinery.com

PEOPLE - Ser, which means expressing identity or origin in Spanish, is an artisanal label started by owner/winemaker Nicole Walsh in 2012. Walsh honed her craft as longtime head winemaker for Bonny Doon Vineyard, working alongside Randall Grahm. Walsh also currently works with Maker Wine Co., a woman-owned canned wine producer that partners with a variety of small-lot winemakers.

VINEYARDS - Ser focuses on producing single vineyard, single varietal wines sourced from eclectic vineyards in several coastal influenced appellations, including Santa Cruz Mountains, Cienega Valley, Santa Lucia Highlands, and Edna Valley. She is a champion of Cabernet Pfeffer, a rare varietal that she sources from the decomposed granite and limestone soils of the 100-year-old Wirz vineyard and the nearby 130-year-old Gimelli vineyard. Both located in the Cienaga Valley AVA and both organically farmed.

WINES - Ser wines are terroir-focused, made with minimal intervention using a variety of techniques including foot treading, whole cluster fermentation, and native yeasts.

Cienaga Valley Wirz Vineyard Cabernet Pfeffer 2022 SLOW WINE ● 110 cases; 50 $ - Sourced from an ancient-vine, head-trained, dry-farmed vineyard and aged 16 months in neutral French oak. Bright red fruit with spice, rose hips, juniper, baking spice, and white pepper notes. Tannins are soft, complex and ageworthy.

Cienaga Valley Gimelli Vineyard Cabernet Pfeffer 2022 ● 72 cases; 50 $ - Sourced from the Gimelli vineyard (130 years old) showing cranberry, pomegranate, hibiscus tea, dusty earth, plum, cardamom and minerals.

San Benito County Siletto Vineyard Trousseau Gris 2023 ○ 60 cases; 30 $ - Aged 5 months in neutral puncheon showing a rounded texture and delicate notes of white flowers, white peach, grapefruit, wet stone, and flint.

acres 0 - cases 800
Fertilizers compost, cover crops
Plant protection sulfur, organic
Weed control mechanical
Yeasts spontaneous fermentation
Grapes purchase 100%
Certification converting to organic

SANTA CRUZ

SILVER MOUNTAIN VINEYARDS

1146 Soquel Avenue - tel. (408) 353-2278
www.silvermtn.com - info@silvermtn.com

PEOPLE - Jerold O'Brien founded the winery in 1979 and is a leader in organic farming in the Santa Cruz Mountains for over 40 years. Environmental stewardship is foremost with the certified organic estate vineyard, a large solar array, a vast rain catchment system, and a concrete wine cave for winemaking and barrel storage. Anthony Craig is winemaker.

VINEYARDS - The property was originally a vineyard from 1870 to 1920, then a fruit orchard. When O'Brien bought the estate in 1973, he replanted it to vines. In 1980, the estate vineyard earned organic certification from the CCOF. It is planted to Chardonnay (own rooted Mount Eden clones) and Pinot Noir (Swan clones). The vineyard faces southwest at 2,100 feet. A neighboring four acre vineyard is part of the estate and farmed by Silver Mountain.

WINES - Wines are made with minimal intervention and a gravity fed system and are released after at least three to six years bottle age.

TOP Santa Cruz Mountains Alloy Bordeaux Blend 2013 ● 800 cases; 44 $ - 🍷 - This Cabernet Sauvignon based Bordeaux blend is an elegant, perfectly aged, well balanced and rich red wine. Ripe blackberry, black plum, juniper, graphite, tobacco leaf, floral notes and brown spices. On the palate, even after 11 years, the wine is fruit driven with firm yet silky tannins. Awarded Best Bordeaux Red Blend in the state by the 2022 California State Fair Wine Competition.

Santa Cruz Mountains Estate Chardonnay 2021 ○ 300 cases; 40 $ - 🍷 - Aged in stainless steel and oak (20%). Elegant with notes of lemon, pineapple and minerality.

Santa Cruz Mountains Rosé of Pinot Noir 2022 ● 100 cases; 28 $ - 🍷 - Made in the saignée method, this wine has a pink salmon color and youthful flavors of strawberry, raspberry, watermelon and sour cherry.

acres 14 - cases 1,500
Fertilizers compost, cover crops
Plant protection synthetic pesticides, organic
Weed control mechanical
Yeasts selected indigenous yeasts
Grapes purchase 20%
Certification some of the vineyards are certified organic

APTOS

STORRS WINERY & VINEYARDS

1560 Pleasant Valley Road - tel. (831) 724-5030
www.storrswine.com - marketplace@storrswine.com

PEOPLE - Pamela and Stephen Storrs both studied winemaking at UC Davis then went on to consult at such wineries as Almaden, Domaine Chandon, Felton Empire, and as the first winemakers at Scheid Vineyards in Monterey. In 1988, they started Storrs Winery and eventually purchased their own estate in the Corralitos district of the AVA in 2001. Since then, Storrs Winery has won many prestigious awards for their terroir-driven wines, especially Chardonnay.

VINEYARDS - The Storrs labored for six years to convert their estate, Hidden Springs, to certified organic before planting Chardonnay and Pinot Noir. They work with several national organizations to implement sustainable practices. Since 2011, the Storrs have a flock of sheep who graze the weeds and provide biodiversity to the soils. The vineyard is under consideration for biodynamic and regenerative organic certifications.

WINES - The wines are complex and rich, showing the Storrs' depth of experience and their vineyards' terroir.

TOP Santa Cruz Mountains Hidden Springs Chardonnay 2019 SLOW WINE ○ 125 cases; 44 $ - 🍷 - The fruit for this elegant and complex Chardonnay comes from their certified organic estate vineyard and is a blend of clones (4 and 17). Perfectly balanced, the wine offers fresh pear and citrus notes along with vanilla and hazelnut.

Santa Cruz Mountains Rosé of Pinot Noir 2022 ● 200 cases; 26 $ - 🍷 - Bright salmon pink in the glass, this rosé has notes of strawberry, tart cherry, and cinnamon. Made in the saignée method.

Santa Cruz Mountains Hidden Springs Estate Pinot Noir 2021 ● 150 cases; 60 $ - 🍷 - This is Storrs' first Pinot from their organic estate vineyard and aged 16 months in French oak. Aromatic with notes of red and black fruit and violets, on the palate the wine is medium bodied with flavors of cherry, raspberry, cola, earth, and a touch of French vanilla.

acres 13 - cases 9,000
Fertilizers compost, biodynamic compost, cover crops, manure, organic fertilizer
Plant protection biodynamic preparations, organic
Weed control animal grazing, mechanical, manual
Yeasts selected indigenous yeasts, commercial cultured yeasts
Grapes purchase 70%
Certification organic

CORRALITOS

WINDY OAKS ESTATE 🍾

550 Hazel Dell Road - tel. (831) 724-9562
www.windyoaksestate.com - info@windyoaksestate.com

PEOPLE - Proprietors Jim and Judy Schultze developed their passion for wine, especially Pinot Noir, while living in France. After purchasing their home in the Corralitos area, neighboring land became available and they planted their vineyard. The first vintage was 1999. Since then Windy Oaks has gained a reputation for premium wines. The entire Schultze family is involved in winemaking, vineyard management and daily operations.

VINEYARDS - The estate is six miles inland, overlooking Monterey Bay at 1,000 feet. The altitude and cooling coastal influence give the vineyard a very long growing season—one of the longest of any Pinot Noir in California—with many microclimates within it. Only organic approved materials are used in the vineyard. They also work with five acres of non-estate vineyards that Schultze farms.

WINES - They use Burgundian techniques to make their wines—minimal intervention, no filtering, no fining, no racking, all gravity fed, and whole cluster fermentation.

🏆 **Santa Cruz Mountains Wild Yeast Estate Pinot Noir 2021** ● 219 cases; 64 $ - 🛢 - Aged 18 months in French oak (45% new). Highly aromatic, the wine is delicate and smooth with notes of cherry, rose, leather and cinnamon with a touch of earth. Very limited release.

Santa Cruz Mountains Estate Cuvée Pinot Noir 2022 ● 455 cases; 45 $ - 🛢 - A blend of estate vineyard parcels and clones, fermented mainly with native yeasts and partial whole cluster. Cherry, raspberry, rose, and licorice with wood notes, silky tannin and good acidity.

Santa Cruz Mountains One Acre Estate Chardonnay 2019 ○ 165 cases; 49 $ - 🛢 - Aged in French oak (25% new). The wine is elegant and balanced with lemon curd, dried pineapple, stewed apples, hazelnut and well integrated oak influences.

---

acres 27 - cases 5,000
Fertilizers compost, organic fertilizer
Plant protection sulfur, synthetic pesticides, organic
Weed control mechanical
Yeasts spontaneous fermentation, selected indigenous yeasts, commercial cultured yeasts
Grapes purchase 20%
Certification none

CENTRAL COAST
MONTEREY & OTHER

🍾 **Bottle**
112 Calera

$ **Coin**
114 Stirm Wine Co.

ACAMPO

ACQUIESCE WINERY & VINEYARDS

22353 N Tretheway Road - tel. (209) 333-6102
www.acquiescevineyards.com - whitewine@av-wine.com

PEOPLE - With a focus on white Rhone varieties, Acquiesce is a white wine producer in a land of red wines in Lodi. Sue and Rodney Tipton bonded over a Chateauneuf du Pape Blanc that set their course. Originally from Chicago, the couple bought their property in 2003. Sue started planting white Rhone grapes in 2008, including the first Picpoul in northern California. Christina Lopez makes the wines.

VINEYARDS - They grow nine Rhone varieties on the property. In 2022, a focus on soil health led to buying an under vine weedwhacker (instead of herbicides) and a roller crimper (instead of tilling or mowing). They also added an electric tractor. They planted pollinator habitat with milkweed plugs to attract monarch and have lots of native wildflowers. They also have bluebird boxes and are tracking wildlife.

WINES - They make Bourboulenc, Clairette Blanche, Cinsault, Grenache Blanc, Grenache, Grenache Gris, Picpoul and Viognier. Among the rarities–sparkling Clairette Blanc and sparkling Picpoul.

TOP Mokelumne River Bourboulenc 2022 ○ 381 cases; 36 $ - ⌀ - Sue was the first to plant Bourboulenc in Lodi. Aromatic, with a bright nose of floral, almond, and lemon-lime notes. It is fresh and textured with vibrant acidity.

Mokelumne River Picpoul 2023 ○ 367 cases; 36 $ - ⌸ - Whole cluster pressed and then cold fermented for 20-30 days before racking, fining, filtering and bottling. The wine is bright and fresh with green apple, melon, and lime notes and textured acidity.

Mokelumne River Viognier 2023 ○ 215 cases; 43 $ - ⌀ - An incredibly vibrant nose with notes of citrus flowers, pineapple, honeysuckle, and candied ginger, and a briny freshness on the finish.

acres 16 - cases 4,000
Fertilizers cover crops
Plant protection sulfur
Weed control mechanical, manual
Yeasts commercial cultured yeasts
Grapes purchase 1%
Certification none

HOLLISTER

CALERA

11300 Cienega Road - tel. (831) 637-9170
www.calerawine.com - info@calerawine.com

PEOPLE - Now owned by Duckhorn Wine Co., it was the late, great, Burgundy lover Josh Jensen (1944-2022), a true winemaking pioneer, who founded the iconic winery in the 1970's after finding limestone rich soil in remote San Benito County–a key element in his quest to make Pinot Noir in California. In 2007 he hired Hollister native Mike Waller (who had worked at nearby Chalone) as assistant. He became winemaker in 2009, a role Waller has continued in since Jensen sold the winery in 2017.

VINEYARDS - The estate sits on its own appellation, Mt. Harlan, east of Salinas in the Gavilan Mountains, once an historic wine growing region, as well as the site of a lime kiln. (Calera is Spanish for lime kiln). At 2,200 feet of elevation, the sparse, dry landscape is wild and untamed. Yields are low. The estate vines grow 22 percent of the wines. The winery also buys grapes from other vineyards. Some wines (not featured here) are grown with herbicides.

WINES - Waller continues to make the winery's two tiers–regional blends as well as single vineyard estate wines. Under Duckhorn, non estate single vineyard wines have been added to the brand.

TOP Mt. Harlan Ryan Vineyard Pinot Noir 2021 SLOW WINE ○ 1,100 cases; 95 $ - ⌸ - Aged 18 months in French oak (30% new). 100% whole cluster. Elegant, with dark currants, blackberries and wild strawberries on the palate.

Mt. Harlan de Villiers Pinot Noir 2021 ● 1,000 cases; 95 $ - ⌸ - Aged 18 months in French oak (30% new). 100% whole cluster. From Calera clones planted in 1996. Dark fruits galore. On the palate blackberry and black raspberry. Smooth tannins and an endless finish.

Mt. Harlan Chardonnay 2021 ○ 490 cases; 65 $ - ⌸ - Aged 15 months in French oak (30% new). Bright and lively. Some of the vines are own rooted and were planted in 1984. Dominated by tropical and lemon notes with key lime accents.

acres 65 - cases 35,000
Fertilizers compost, cover crops, organic fertilizer, synthetic fertilizer
Plant protection synthetic pesticides, organic
Weed control animal grazing, manual
Yeasts spontaneous fermentation
Grapes 100% owned
Certification some of the vineyards are certified organic

HOLLISTER

EDEN RIFT VINEYARDS

10034 Cienega Road - tel. (831) 636-1991
www.edenrift.com - tastingroom@edenrift.com

PEOPLE - The historic vineyard site is in a remote region. Christian Pillsbury purchased it in 2016 to make Eden Rift wines and also sold fruit to winemakers, including Seabold Cellars' Chris Miller. The winery spectacularly rose to become a Wine & Spirits Top 100 wineries in 2022 and 2023. Now Miller has become a partner at Eden Rift, moving to the site in 2023. Cory Waller makes the Eden Rift wines. Solar supplies all their power.

VINEYARDS - Located in the Gavilan Mountains at elevations of 1,200-1,600 feet, the property is 500 acres on varied terrain including some treasured limestone and terraces. In the vineyards, the team has dramatically reduced chemical inputs, tractor passes, soil compaction and carbon consumption. As a result, bird life is thriving. They've cut back on fungal sprays, trialing a new technology that enables them to target specific spots in the vineyard instead of treating the entire vineyard.

WINES - The team is bringing life and energy into the limestone soils on a site long recognized as a gem.

TOP **Cienega Valley Terraces Estate Pinot Gris 2022** ○ 250 cases; 46 $ - ⊞ - Grown on a terraced site. Aromas of peach skins, cinnamon and delicate vanilla notes. A food friendly wine that is very textured with full mouth acidity.
Cienega Valley Terraces Estate Chardonnay 2021 ○ 375 cases; 65 $ - ⊞ - Aged nine months in oak (20% new). Calcareous soils, whole cluster pressed, barrel fermented. A structured and linear wine with notes of apple skins, lemon, hazelnut, flint and spice and textured acidity.
Cienega Valley Estate Pinot Noir 2020 ● 200 cases; 48 $ - ⊞ - Aged 10 months in French oak (30% new). Whole cluster (30%). From granite and limestone soils. Red and dark fruit aromas of cranberry, cherry, pomegranate, blackberry, as well as violet, black tea, and spice notes. Medium bodied with fresh acidity and mineral notes.

acres 120 - cases 10,000
Fertilizers compost, cover crops, organic fertilizer
Plant protection sulfur, organic
Weed control mechanical
Yeasts spontaneous fermentation
Grapes purchase 3%
Certification none

HOLLISTER

SEABOLD CELLARS

10034 Cienega Road - tel. (831) 204-8364 - (831) 288-2730
www.seaboldcellars.com - wine@seaboldcellars.com

PEOPLE - A former somm, Chris Miller began working harvest in 2005 and started Seabold Cellars in 2017. In 2023 Miller partnered with Eden Rift and moved Seabold production there. Adam Geldmeier is his assistant winemaker. Miller has three tiers. Seabold Cellars is single varietal, single vineyard Burgundy and Rhone. Bold offers high quality for price single variety blends of vineyards. adroit (lower case a for informal brand) is good, natty wines.

VINEYARDS - Grapes come from inland and Central Coast growers. Pinot Noir and Chardonnay are from Eden Rift. Mourvedre, Pinot Blanc and Syrah come from Rodnick Farm (certified organic) in the Chalone AVA while Sauvignon Blanc comes from Zabala Vineyard (certified organic) in Arroyo Seco. Siletto Vineyard (certified organic) in San Benito grows Aglianico, Aligote, Cab Pfeffer, Falanghina, Mencia, Rondinella and Trousseau.

WINES - Miller prefers cool climate north Central Coast sources with a high proportion of limestone. His winemaking is very hands off as he listens to the vineyard and vintage.

TOP **Cienega Valley Eden Rift Pinot Noir 2022** ● 300 cases; 45 $ - ⊞ - Aged 16 months in oak (15% new). Half is partial whole cluster (30%). An inviting nose of black cherry, violets, plum and cinnamon. Lush on the palate. Elegant.
Monterey County Chardonnay 2021 ○ 300 cases; 25 $ - ⊞ - Aged in oak (10% new) with low lees stirring . Whole cluster. Aromas of citrus, stone fruits, and a hint of soft ripened cheese. Crisp yet rounded on the palate.
San Benito Siletto Vineyard Trousseau 2023 ● 120 cases; 35 $ - ⊞ - Aged in neutral oak. Made in a semi-carbonic style for 15 days followed by soft punchdowns and foot stomping. Aromas of wild strawberry and cherry, with a savory note. Fun and drinkable with a bitter orange rind note at the end.

acres 8 - cases 7,000
Fertilizers compost, biodynamic compost, cover crops, manure, organic fertilizer
Plant protection sulfur, biodynamic preparations, organic
Weed control animal grazing, mechanical, manual
Yeasts spontaneous fermentation
Grapes purchase 70%
Certification some of the vineyards are certified organic, some of the vineyards are certified biodynamic, converting to organic

WATSONVILLE

STIRM WINE CO. $

65 Rogge Lane - tel. (831) 854-7611
www.stirmwine.com - ryan@stirmwine.com

PEOPLE - Well known as an evangelist for California Riesling, Ryan Stirm is best known for his Kick On vineyard Riesling, making his first bottle from the Los Alamos region in 2013. He has also gone on to feature many new bottlings of obscure varieties. He champions Riesling for its climate change resilience—heat and drought tolerance, late ripening and high acid. He is also starting an affordably priced series honoring gemstones and minerals native to the San Benito region.

VINEYARDS - Ryan works with a few, old vine vineyards in warm, inland San Benito County, including the historic Wirz Vineyard and Gemelli Vineyard (next to Wirz). He buys rarely grown Cab Pfeffer from Wirz as well as from Siletto Vineyard. Stirm also planted his own vines at his winery in Aromas in 2021—mostly Vermentino (70%), Albarino (22%) and some Furmint (8%).

WINES - The style is to take a low intervention approach in the cellar, highlighting unique sites and varieties.

San Benito County Benitoite Red Blend 2022 EVERYDAY WINE ● 420 cases; 29 $ - A great weeknight wine but with special heritage fruit. A blend of Cab Pfeffer, Negrette and Zinfandel all planted in the mid 1800's. Benitoite, the state gem of California, found only in one specific mine here. Aromatic and light bodied with crushed herb, red berry and tannins on the palate.

Cienega Valley Wirz Vineyard Zinfandel 2021 ● 230 cases; 36 $ - Whole cluster. Old bush vines (1902). Co-fermented in redwood barrels with a bit of old vine Riesling (10%) from Wirz. Savory, red berry, spice and eucalyptus aromas. Strawberry jam, seed spices, crushed herbs and woody flavor notes prevail.

Cienega Valley Gemelli Vineyard Chardonnay 2022 ○ 140 cases; 29 $ - Aromas of pineapple sage, wet stone, hazelnut and toffee. Flavors of stone fruits, lovely acidity and a bit of salinity prevail with a lingering finish.

acres 2 - cases 3,300
Fertilizers compost
Plant protection sulfur, organic
Weed control mechanical, manual
Yeasts spontaneous fermentation
Grapes purchase 90%
Certification some of the vineyards are certified organic

CENTRAL COAST
SAN LUIS OBISPO

 Snail

121 Halter Ranch
125 Phelan Farm

Bottle

122 Lindquist Family Wines
127 Tablas Creek Vineyard
127 Tatomer

PASO ROBLES

ADELAIDA

5805 Adelaida Road - tel. (805) 239-8980
www.adelaida.com - info@adelaida.com

PEOPLE - Pioneers in Paso Robles' modern wine era, Don and Elizabeth Van Steenwyk began planting grapes on their Hilltop Ranch in 1973. Founding winemaker John Munch made the first vintage in 1981. Adelaida remains in the family and has steadily added estate vineyards and upgraded facilities over the years. A Napa Valley veteran (with enology and viticulture degrees from U.C. Davis and Fresno), Jeremy Weintraub is in his 12th year as winemaker.

VINEYARDS - The estate vineyards are in the coastal mountains of northwest Paso Robles where they are cooled by Pacific winds. The particular limestone soils there maintain unusually high acidity in the grapes (as seen in the Chardonnay below). Adelaida farms organically (certified), dry farms as possible and, if necessary, irrigates with recycled pond water. A thousand acres of their land remains natural habitat. Sheep are now part of the vegetation control program.

WINES - Winemaking and aging differs by site and variety: from neutral oak or concrete to 60 percent new oak.

Adelaida District HMR Vineyard Chardonnay 2023 ○ 512 cases; 50 $ - ⊞ - Aged nine months in French oak (25% new). Beautifully perfumed nose of yellow pear and apple, egg custard, delicate baking spice, lemon verbena and a soft kiss of oak. Lemon curd and tart apple with nuances of cream and spice on the extremely long, mouthwatering palate.

Adelaida District Anna's Estate Vineyard Counoise 2021 ● 292 cases; 40 $ - ⊞ - Aged 18 months in neutral French oak. Delicate, pretty, nuanced. Cranberry, raspberry, strawberry, red cherry, baking spice, wet clay. Lovely.

Adelaida District Anna's Estate Vineyard Signature Series Anna's Red 2021 ● 549 cases; 70 $ - ⊞ - Aged 18 months in French oak (30% new). Like a book you can't put down. Wonderfully balanced and complex. Plum, black cherry, spice, orange pith and garrigue. Fine, slightly chalky texture.

acres 160 - cases 12,000
Fertilizers compost, cover crops, organic fertilizer
Plant protection sulfur, organic
Weed control animal grazing, mechanical
Yeasts spontaneous fermentation, commercial cultured yeasts
Grapes 100% owned
Certification organic

TEMPLETON

AMBYTH ESTATE

510 Sequoia Lane - tel. (805) 319-8967
www.ambythestate.com - info@ambythestate.com

PEOPLE - The first biodynamic winery in Paso Robles, founded in 1998, AmByth is run today by Gelert Hart, the son of founders—his Welsh born father Philip (who grew up on a sheep farm) and his mother Mary—with his wife Robyn Hart. The founders were enthusiastic natural wine pioneers in the region and pioneered local use of amphorae. Philippe Armenier, native of the Rhone in France, was their first biodynamic consultant. Estate wines are certified biodynamic, a pure standard.

VINEYARDS - The dry farmed, head trained vines sit on steep slopes of Linne Calodo, sandy calcareous clay loam with rich shale and limestone, in Templeton Gap, where cool Pacific ocean breezes flow. Formerly all estate, Gelert today purchases grapes as the winery combats reduced yields in drought years and explores new flavors and cider making. They raise sheep, grow olive trees and make olive oil for sale.

WINES - Hart foot stomps the wines and ages them in neutral oak or terracotta amphorae, including California clay amphorae or white vitrified clay eggs.

Paso Robles Syrah and Roussanne Amphora 2019 ● 54 cases; 54 $ - ☾ - A blend of Syrah (77%) and Roussanne (23%). Aged 23 months in Italian terracotta amphora. No additives. Aromas of fresh red berries, fall leaves, florals; flavors of peppercorn, rich fruit. Round mouthfeel, medium acidity, firm tannins.

🔝 Paso Robles Adamo Red Rhone Blend 2017 SLOW WINE ● 231 cases; 66 $ - ⊞ ☾ - Grenache, Syrah, Mourvedre. Grenache aged in Italian terracotta amphora; others in French oak barrels. Aromas of savory, earth, mint, dried rose petals. On the palate, moderate tannins and acidity frame notes of dark plums, dark cherries, blueberries. Lingering finish.

Santa Ynez Valley Riesling Orange Wine 2022 ◎ 210 cases; 38 $ - ☾ - Grown at Coquelicot Vineyard (certified organic). Orange wine, unfined, unfiltered. On the nose, slightest hint of sweet, mint. Palate is tart with bright acidity, notes of dried apricot, leaves, orange.

acres 17 - cases 1,500
Fertilizers compost, biodynamic compost, manure, organic fertilizer
Plant protection biodynamic preparations, organic
Weed control animal grazing, mechanical, manual
Yeasts spontaneous fermentation
Grapes purchase 20%
Certification some of the vineyards are certified organic, some of the vineyards are certified biodynamic

PASO ROBLES

CAIRJN WINE CELLARS

2323 Tuley Road #120 - tel. (805) 423-9113
www.cairjnwinecellars.com - info@cairjnwinecellars.com

PEOPLE - Winemaker Andy Neja founded the winery in 2019, naming it Cairjn to honor Neja's family heritage of farming. The word "cairn" means "a heap of stones piled up as a memorial or as a landmark." Neja worked at Caliza Winery as associate winemaker for eight years before launching his own brand. Focused on the limestone rich terrain of West Paso, he makes his wines in Tin City. Many have received top scores.

VINEYARDS - Neja buys grapes from vineyards in five Paso Robles sub-AVAs–Adelaida, El Pomar, Geneseo, Templeton Gap and Willow Creek–each with different soil types. Duas Terras Vineyard in Geneseo is dedicated to Iberian varieties. Lopai Vineyard and Caliza are In Willow Creek, as is Jada (certified organic) which sits on hilltop terraces on fractured shale, rocks and limestone.

WINES - Fruit driven and food friendly, the wines are balanced, structured, refreshing and lively.

Paso Robles Willow Creek District Blend #2 2022 SLOW WINE ● 80 cases; 75 $ - Aged 14 months in French oak (85% new). A nearly 50/50 blend of Cabernet and Syrah. On the nose, raw meat, red fruit, herbs. Palate bursts with flavors of mocha, meet, red fruit, herbs, spice. Savory with moderate tannins and acidity.

Willow Creek Grenache 2021 ● 75 cases; 85 $ - Aged for 20 months in neutral French large oak barrels. From Lopai Vineyard. Cherries and red fruit on the nose. Palate of cherries, rich red fruit and spice was on a foundation of soft tannins and vibrant acidity. Layered and complex.

Paso Robles Geneseo District Duas Terras Vineyard Vermentino 2023 O 75 cases; 42 $ - Light and refreshing, citrus and mineral notes on the nose. Balanced with vibrant acidity, elements of umami, Italian herbs, summer tropical fruit tones on the palate.

acres 15 - cases 1,000
Fertilizers compost, cover crops, manure, organic fertilizer
Plant protection biodynamic preparations, organic
Weed control animal grazing, mechanical
Yeasts commercial cultured yeasts
Grapes purchase 100%
Certification some of the vineyards are certified organic

TEMPLETON

CLESI WINERY

1873 Templeton Road - tel. (805) 748-2779
www.clesiwines.com - info@clesiwines.com

PEOPLE - Founders Adrienne and Chris Ferrara, winemaker, focus on Italian varieties, with a special love for Sicily where Chris' family is from. The Clesi name honors his paternal great grandmother. The Ferraras met working at Ken Volk's Wild Horse Winery and Vineyards in 2002. In 2003, after new owners stopped making Italian varieties, Chris started Clesi with three barrels of Dolcetto in a leased building in San Luis Obispo.

VINEYARDS - In 2015, Chris and Adrienne bought a 30 acre goat ranch where they have an acre of vegetables, their winery, chickens and three children. In 2017 they planted six acres to Dolcetto, Montepulciano, Sangiovese and Sagrantino, adding Barbera and Nebbiolo in 2024. Plans are to expand acreage for heat tolerant, southern Italian varieties. Chris buys Aglianico, Malvasia Bianca, Negro Amaro and Nero d'Avola from growers who share the same chemical free ethos.

WINES - Oak use is light (around 20% new). Chris uses an Italian amphorae to age some of the wines.

Templeton Gap District Sagrantino 2021 ● 150 cases; 45 $ - Fresh and balanced. Aromas of earth, rich berries, spice led to flavors of black cherries, ripe blackberries bolstered by vibrant acidity and firm tannic structure. Lingering finish.

Templeton Gap District Ferrara Estate Dolcetto 2021 ● 125 cases; 45 $ - Aged 14 months in oak (20% new). Destemmed. The wine has lots of red fruit, cherry, and raspberry, with a touch of earthiness on the nose. On the palate, it has softly drying tannins with an elegant freshness.

Templeton Gap District Ferrara Estate Sangiovese 2021 ● 240 cases; 50 $ - Aged 17 months in 20% new oak, the wine has dark fruit, spice, and earthy aromas with dusty tannins and mouthwatering acidity.

acres 7 - cases 2,200
Fertilizers compost, cover crops
Plant protection organic
Weed control mechanical, manual
Yeasts spontaneous fermentation, commercial cultured yeasts
Grapes purchase 45%
Certification none

PASO ROBLES

COPIA VINEYARDS & WINERY

5076 Mustard Creek Road - tel. (805) 296-3000
www.copiavineyards.com - tastingroom@copiavineyards.com

PEOPLE - Anita and Varinder Sahi named their label Copia, meaning "abundance" in Latin. Raised in an Indian-Pakistani family in Chicago, Anita has hospitality experience. Punjabi born Varinder holds an MBA and U.C. Davis winemaking certificate. They have a 20 acre estate vineyard in the Willow Creek District and a second 20 acre estate in the Adelaida District. Their tasting room offers seasonal food and wine pairings.

VINEYARDS - Grapes come from the estate vineyards as well as from local growers. They grow red Rhone and Bordeaux varieties on steep slopes and limestone soils in Willow Creek District. Surrounded by oak forest, the estate uses organic approved materials. At their Adelaida District site, they grow red grape varieties, including their first Tempranillo and white Rhones.

WINES - Everything is fermented separately in small lots—like a spice box. One of their first wines was named Amrit, a Sanskrit word that means "immortality."

Central Coast The Source Syrah 2021 SLOW WINE ● 305 cases; 70 $ - ⊞ - A 50/50 blend of Willow Creek District vineyards (Denner, Copia) and cooler climate Syrah from Alisos Canyon (Thompson) and Santa Maria Valley (Bien Nacido Vineyard). Classic Syrah with aromas and flavors of peppercorn, smoked meat, blackberries, and violets. Mouthwatering. Ageworthy.

Willow Creek District The Cure Red Rhone Blend 2021 ● 380 cases; 65 $ - ⊞ - A GSM blend of Mourvedre (45%), Grenache (28%), and Syrah (27%). Textured and succulent with black fruit, herbes de Provence, and spice on the nose and palate with a long and elegant finish.

Central Coast The Story Grenache 2021 ● 330 cases; 65 $ - ⓘ - A blend of Grenache (92%) and Mourvedre (9%) with bright acidity and refined tannins. Aromas of sage, thyme, lavender. Flavors of black cherries, strawberries, spice, and flint with a lingering finish.

acres 40 - cases 2,000
Fertilizers compost, cover crops, organic fertilizer
Plant protection organic
Weed control animal grazing, mechanical, manual
Yeasts spontaneous fermentation, commercial cultured yeasts
Grapes purchase 30%
Certification none

PASO ROBLES

CORDANT WINERY

3310 Ramada Drive - tel. (805) 369-2313
www.cordantwinery.com - info@cordantwinery.com

PEOPLE - David, a Silicon Valley tech entrepreneur, and DeAnn Taylor founded Cordant Winery in 2014 to produce outstanding Rhone wines, Chardonnay and Pinot Noir from 20 celebrated Central Coast vineyard sites. Sites range from Monterey County, inland to the Santa Lucia Mountains and San Benito County, and as far south as Santa Barbara County. Southern California native Ryker Wall became the winemaker January 1, 2023.

VINEYARDS - The vineyard list reads like a wine lover's dream: Pinot Noir from Bien Nacido and Solomon Hills in Santa Maria Valley, Escolle Vineyard in the Santa Lucia Highlands and Radian in the Sta. Rita Hills. Rhones come from the Gabilan Mountains and Paso's Willow Creek and Adelaida Districts. The winery also makes Mourvedre from the historic Enz Vineyard in Lime Kiln Valley in San Benito County. (Some wines, not featured here, may be grown with herbicide.)

WINES - The wines provide a broad lens into the terroir of iconic vineyards.

Central Coast Hyperbole Pinot Noir 2022 ● 279 cases; 60 $ - ⊞ - A Central Coast regional blend from various vineyards. Intense floral notes on the nose, bright red fruit, savory spice.

Central Coast Maniacal GSM Red Rhone Blend 2021 ● 413 cases; 65 $ - ⊞ ⓘ - A GSM blend from mostly Paso Robles fruit with added cooler climate Monterey County and Santa Barbara fruit for increased texture and complexity. Lush notes of blackberry, black cherry, eucalyptus, spice, and toast. Florals lend a soft edge, while spice and toast bring a warmth to the glass. Moderate acidity and tannins.

Sta. Rita Hills Radian Vineyard Pinot Noir 2021 ● 228 cases; 70 $ - ⊞ - Textured with rusticity and depth as well as elegant, with moderate acidity and tannins, bright red fruit, florals, cedar.

acres 25 - cases 3,000
Fertilizers compost, biodynamic compost, cover crops, organic fertilizer, synthetic fertilizer
Plant protection sulfur, synthetic pesticides, organic
Weed control animal grazing, mechanical, manual
Yeasts spontaneous fermentation, selected indigenous yeasts
Grapes purchase 100%
Certification none

SAN LUIS OBISPO

DUNITES WINE CO.

1133 Garden Street - tel. (805) 858-8413
www.duniteswineco.com - info@duniteswineco.com

PEOPLE - Indie producers in the SLO Coast's blossoming natural wine scene, Tyler and Rachel Eck named their brand after a bohemian band of 1930s beach dune dwellers. Building out their SLO Coast range of wines, they doubled production this year. Tyler continues to work as the associate winemaker at Fess Parker and Rachel, who has a degree in viticulture, spends her time farming their small vineyard in the Edna Valley.

VINEYARDS - Rachel farms their 2.5 acre leased estate, Edna Valley Hi Kite Vineyard, planted to Grenache and Syrah. They also buy grapes from organic, biodynamic and regenerative vineyards as much as possible. They continue to work with the same vineyards and varieties. They purchase fruit from Bassi and Topatero (both practicing biodynamic) at Avila Beach, Marfarm, Rancho Arroyo Grande and Spanish Springs.

WINES - All wines are made in neutral oak without fining or filtering. There are no additions, no flavors added, and no flavors taken away to produce wines that express great minerality.

TOP SLO Coast Pinot Noir 2023 EVERYDAY WINE ● 600 cases; 32 $ - ⊞ - Aged eight months in neutral French oak. Partial whole cluster (26%) from coastal vineyards. Juicy and fresh with blackberry, black plum and sage aromas, textured tannins, and a mineral driven finish.
SLO Coast Dune Song Grenache 2023 ● 241 cases; 30 $ - ⊞ - Aged six months. Partial whole cluster (25%). A vibrant magenta color, it's fresh with plum, lavender, and wild herb aromas, lightly drying tannins, and crunchy acidity.
SLO Coast Moy Mell 2023 ○ 166 cases; 30 $ - ⊞ - A coastal white wine that's a unique blend of Pinot Noir Blanc (44%), Chardonnay (38%) and Albariño (18%). Fresh melon, white flowers, and lemon on the nose. On the palate, lovely fresh acidity, a rounded midpalate and a saline finish.

acres 2.5 - cases 3,000
Fertilizers compost, biodynamic compost, cover crops, manure
Plant protection sulfur, biodynamic preparations, organic
Weed control mechanical, manual
Yeasts spontaneous fermentation
Grapes purchase 80%
Certification some of the vineyards are certified organic, some of the vineyards are certified biodynamic

PASO ROBLES

DUNNING VINEYARDS

1953 Niderer Road - tel. (805) 704-3135
www.dunningvineyards.com - info@dunningvineyards.com

PEOPLE - Wine loving founders Robert and Jo-Ann Dunning were pioneers when they bought land in Paso in the 1980s. In 1991 they planted the vineyard, starting with Chardonnay cuttings from Paso's iconic James Berry, followed by Bordeaux blend essentials Cabernet Franc and Merlot. Their winery was bonded in 1994. They rent a one bedroom suite to wine club members and visitors with vineyard views.

VINEYARDS - The Dunnings were pioneers in what is now the Willow Creek District. Planted at 1,400' of elevation on calcareous rock soils, the estate vines produce low yields. Marked diurnal temperature shifts elongate the longer growing season, adding concentration and phenolic development in the grapes. They grow a wide variety of grapes, ranging from Bordeaux and Rhone varieties typical of the region, to Chardonnay and Pinot Noir as well as Petite Sirah and Zinfandel. They also purchase grapes.

WINES - Robert makes the wines in small lots, handcrafting each varietal to reflect estate terroir. Yeast choices depend on the variety.

TOP Willow Creek District Estate Cabernet Sauvignon Reserve 2021 SLOW WINE ● 84 cases; 85 $ - ⊞ - Aged in American and French oak. Produced only in the best vintages. Savory notes of violets, cherries, spice and rich red and black fruit, gripping tannins and vibrant acidity led to a lingering, lush finish.
Willow Creek District Forged By 2 Red Blend 2021 ● 125 cases; 65 $ - ◉ - A savory and balanced blend: Cabernet Sauvignon, Grenache, Petite Sirah and Zinfandel. Intense floral aromatics, spice, red fruit and a round mouthfeel, all lifted with moderate tannic structure and bright acidity.
Willow Creek District Estate Chardonnay 2022 ○ 210 cases; 42 $ - ⊞ - Barrel fermented. Ripe and creamy, showing soft acidity and notes of citrus, pear, subtle spice on the nose and palate. Delicate.

acres 16 - cases 1,800
Fertilizers cover crops
Plant protection synthetic pesticides, organic
Weed control mechanical
Yeasts spontaneous fermentation, selected indigenous yeasts, commercial cultured yeasts
Grapes purchase 20%
Certification none

PASO ROBLES

FIELD RECORDINGS WINE

3070 Limestone Way Suite C - tel. (805) 503-9660
www.fieldrecordingswine.com - sales@fieldrecordingswine.com

PEOPLE - Natural winemaker Andrew Jones began Field Recordings with Rhone varieties from tiny, assorted plots. Now he's bought vineyards and opened a tasting room and winemaking facility in hip Los Alamos and a tasting room in Tin City in Paso Robles. He's also innovated with his Boxie wines, natural wines sold in bag in box format. His popular orange wine, Skins, pioneered natural wine in boxed format. In 2024, he expanded his boxed wine lineup, adding more wines.

VINEYARDS - In 2018, Jones bought the Loomis Vineyard in west Paso Robles and certified it organic in 2021. He also has long term leases with vineyards in Edna Valley and Santa Maria Valley that he says he farms using only organic approved products. He buys from another 15 vineyards across the Central Coast, most of which he planted. (Some of the wines, not featured here, may be grown with herbicide.)

WINES - Jones sees the wines as casual wines, made for drinking not tasting. Tim Fulnecky is assistant winemaker.

Highlands District Shell Creek Valdigue 2023 ● 101 cases; 45 $ - Fermented via carbonic maceration. Bright, juicy. Intense bouquet, bright acidity, fresh strawberries, crunchy rhubarb, cinnamon, plums. Mouthwatering. Enjoy chilled.

Highlands District Shell Creek Chenin Blanc 2022 O 114 cases; 45 $ - A blend of Chenin Blanc from three old vine vineyards (Jurassic Park, planted 1978, and Shell Creek and Cat Canyon, both planted in 1972). Savory with bright acidity, vibrant notes of ripe orchard fruit, lemon, lime, spice on the finish. Aged for 6 months in 1000 L Hosch Fuder casks.

California Salad Days Pet Nat NV 624 cases; 25 $ - A white wine blend of Chardonnay, Chenin Blanc and Colombard from California vineyards. A sparkler to enjoy in warm weather. Snappy acidity and notes of golden apple, stone fruit and minerality.

acres 25 - cases 45,000
Fertilizers compost, cover crops, organic fertilizer
Plant protection sulfur, synthetic pesticides, copper, organic
Weed control animal grazing, mechanical, manual
Yeasts spontaneous fermentation
Grapes purchase 95%
Certification some of the vineyards are certified organic

PASO ROBLES

FOUR LANTERNS WINERY

2485 W Highway 46 - tel. (805) 226-5955
www.fourlanternswinery.com - info@fourlanternswinery.com

PEOPLE - Steve (formerly in finance) and Jackie GleGason unwittingly began a second career when they bought a home in Paso Robles in 2013. That turned into purchasing their first vineyard—Glass Hawk—which turned into building a winery and remodeling a tasting room. In 2024, they expanded the outdoor patio space, adding a pizza oven and grill. Big on hospitality, they also rent an Airbnb house and an RV spot on the property.

VINEYARDS - They grow a wide variety of grapes that includes Cabernet Sauvignon, Chenin Blanc, Merlot, Nebbiolo, Semillon along with Picpoul Blanc, Viognier, and other Rhones on two estate parcels in Templeton Gap District and the Willow Creek District. They harvested their first Cabernet Franc and Graciano in 2023 and their first Chenin Blanc and Mourvedre in 2024. Vineyard manager Jason Yeager is converting the vines to organic certification, a three year transition started in 2021.

WINES - Steve Gleason is the winemaker. Blending is a specialty. The winery is currently expanding its varietal diversity and also makes a sparkling wine.

Paso Robles Alma Paso 2023 SLOW WINE ● 65 cases; 49 $ - A 50/50 blend of Graciano and Tempranillo. Half was aged six months in neutral French oak. Light and refreshing with savory herbs, dried cranberries, dark cherries, pepper. Bright acidity and soft tannins. Serve chilled.

Paso Robles Viognier 2022 O 170 cases; 42 $ - Aromatic, bright and fresh, offers citrus, spice, herbs, lime, yellow florals, and grilled pineapple in aromas and on the palate. Moderate acidity and body with a snappy finish.

Paso Robles Rosado 2022 136 cases; 36 $ - A 50/50 blend of Tempranillo and Grenache. A snappy rosado with minerality, salinity, bright acidity and notes of strawberries and raspberries on the nose and palate.

acres 38 - cases 2,000
Fertilizers compost, cover crops, organic fertilizer
Plant protection organic
Weed control animal grazing, mechanical, manual
Yeasts selected indigenous yeasts, commercial cultured yeasts
Grapes purchase 5%
Certification converting to organic

PASO ROBLES

FULLDRAW VINEYARD

2660 Anderson Road - tel. (805) 712-4412
www.fulldrawvineyard.com - info@fulldrawvineyard.com

PEOPLE - Husband and wife Connor and Rebecca McMahon started Fulldraw in 2016 when, in 2012, they had a chance to buy a 30 acre parcel (which later expanded to 100). Connor had six years of winemaking and farming experience at the adjacent property, Booker Vineyard. Gary Irvin is the assistant winemaker. In 2020, the couple built a sleek, modern, architect designed winery. The new tasting room is a work in progress.

VINEYARDS - Their Willow Creek District estate is 45 planted acres with limestone soils and cooling maritime influences. Growers as well as vintners, they sell 60 percent of their Cabernet Sauvignon, Graciano and Rhone varieties. The oldest vines are from 2007. In 2012, Connor pulled out 15 acres of Cabernet and replanted in 2015. He also planted 15 new acres. Plantings are high density. He's farmed using only organically approved materials since 2012.

WINES - Connor uses very little whole cluster because he wants to showcase the purity of fruit and texture that come from the soils and microclimate.

⬤ Willow Creek District Chopping Block GSM 2020 ● 320 cases; 90 $ - 🛢 - Aged in neutral barrel puncheons of French oak. The blend is Syrah (49%), Grenache (30%) and Mourvedre (21%). Dark red fruits, menthol and spice on the nose. The density of fruit and tobacco are lifted by moderate acidity and firm tannins. Balanced and bold.

Willow Creek District Honey Bunny 2020 ● 250 cases; 90 $ - 🛢 - Their flagship wine. Syrah (92%) and Mourvedre (8%). Aromas of baking spices, rich red fruit. On the palate, juicy acidity and gripping tannins offered texture and complexity.

Paso Robles Hard Point Grenache 2019 ● 150 cases; 90 $ - 🛢 - Aged 16-18 months. A best barrels blend. Lush, dark red fruit and purple florals on the nose. Balanced palate expressing dense flavors is on a foundation of bright acidity and moderate tannins.

acres 45 - cases 2,000
Fertilizers biodynamic compost, cover crops, manure
Plant protection sulfur, organic
Weed control animal grazing, mechanical, manual
Yeasts spontaneous fermentation, selected indigenous yeasts, commercial cultured yeasts
Grapes 100% owned
Certification none

PASO ROBLES

GIORNATA WINES

470 Marquita Ave #A - tel. (805) 434-3075
www.giornatawine.com - info@giornatawines.com

PEOPLE - In the heart of Paso Robles, Stephy and Brian Terrizzi adventurously explore the potential of Italian varieties. Long a champion for under the radar, climate friendly wine grapes, Steph has been planting up a storm to increase the supply of Cesanese (from Lazio, outside Rome), Nerello Mascalese (from Etna) and more. The Terrizzi's also produce an aperitivo and a spectacular amaro (an herbal liqueur digestif uniquely infused with California natives) and own Etto Pastificio, an organic pasta company.

VINEYARDS - All of their vineyard sources are farmed organically. They have six acres on their home property, as well as chicken, goats, and sheep whose manure is what Stephy calls "poop soup." With five sticks with buds of Nero d'Troia, in 2019, she then grew 200 plants at the mother block over the hill from the house. She manages the organic Margett Vineyard and buys certified organic grapes when she can.

WINES - Made with minimal intervention, these are food friendly, balanced wines from wine varieties originating from the length and breadth of Italy. Look for pet nat, orange wine and sparkling, too.

⬤ Paso Robles Adelaida District Luna Matta Vineyard Nebbiolo 2020 ● 102 cases; 50 $ - 🛢 - Ages 10-12 months in neutral oak. Pretty notes of dried herbs, dried flowers, pomegranate, and cherry. Medium bodied and balanced with a combination of drying tannins and mouthwatering acidity at play on the palate.

Paso Robles Estate Bianco 2023 ○ 76 cases; 35 $ - 🏺 - Blend of Trebbiano (60%) and Friulano (40%) from their estate. Skin fermented in amphora for six weeks and then aged in amphora for seven months. Aromatic nose of pear, peaches, lemon with spicy savory notes and lots of acidity.

San Miguel District Margette Vineyard Montepulciano 2022 ● 105 cases; 40 $ - 🛢 🏺 - Aged in neutral oak and puncheon. Perfumed aromas with dark ripe juicy blackberry and black cherry, cocoa powder and velvety tannins.

acres 6 - cases 4,000
Fertilizers cover crops, manure, organic fertilizer
Plant protection sulfur, organic
Weed control animal grazing, mechanical, manual
Yeasts spontaneous fermentation
Grapes purchase 65%
Certification some of the vineyards are certified organic

PASO ROBLES

HALTER RANCH

8910 Adelaida Road - tel. (805) 226-9455
www.halterranch.com - info@halterranch.com

 For pioneering a holistic model of hospitality, ecofriendly production methods, organic farming and biodiversity preservation.

PEOPLE - Founded by Swiss entrepreneur Hansjorg Wyss, a philanthropist and leading conservationist, the 2,700 acre property with oak woodlands is mostly left wild. Wyss prioritizes energy efficiency, solar power, greenhouse gas reduction, and water conservation. Guests can dine at its restaurant on estate grown, organic meat and produce. Halter Ranch also has wineries in Texas (the first one in the state with certified organic vines) and Temecula.

VINEYARDS - Planted in 1996 along the westernmost boundaries of Paso Robles and the Santa Lucia Mountain Range, the vines sit on limestone parcels on steep, sunny south facing slopes at up to 1,950 feet. The team recently planted 75 new acres to Cabernet Sauvignon, Picpoul Blanc, and Tempranillo. They harvest honey from on site hives and make estate olive oil. A new trellis system will allow sheep to graze (controlling weeds) and fertilize the vines.

WINES - Longtime winemaker Kevin Sass makes six Bordeaux and Rhone wines using classic Old World techniques.

Adelaida District Block 22 Syrah 2021 ● 1,075 cases; 92 $ - ⊞ - Aged 18 months in French oak (50% new). Aromas of blueberry, blackberry, cassis, slate and cedar. A lush palate with flavors of raspberries and ripe plum leading to oak, spice and cocoa on the finish. Balanced with soft tannins and moderate acidity.

Adelaida District CDP Red Rhone Blend 2020 ● 2,024 cases; 55 $ - ⊞ - Aged in neutral oak and concrete (9%). A Grenache (70%) dominant blend. Aromas of raspberry, ripe plum and Provencal herbs. On the bright, fresh, savory palate, red and blue fruits, cherries and pomegranate. Moderate acidity and tannic structure. Chillable.

Adelaida District Libelle Picpoul Blanc 2020 ⊛ 216 cases; 85 $ - 🍾 - Traditional method sparkling wine. Fresh, lively aromas of crushed pineapple, lime, citrus and cream. Flavors of lemon and pear move into a balanced, clean finish.

acres 275 - cases 30,000
Fertilizers compost, biodynamic compost, cover crops, manure, organic fertilizer
Plant protection biodynamic preparations, organic
Weed control animal grazing, mechanical
Yeasts selected indigenous yeasts
Grapes 100% owned
Certification organic

PASO ROBLES

KUKKULA

9515 Chimney Rock Road - tel. (805) 227-0111
www.kukkulawine.com - info@kukkulawine.com

PEOPLE - Los Angeles transplants turned Rhone wine vintners, Kevin and Paula Jussila purchased the property in 2004, and over seven years, replaced 80 acres of walnuts and an acre of Cabernet with 30 acres of vines. After a career as a money manager, Kevin retired in 2024 and now dedicates all of his time to managing the vineyard and making the wine. They built their solar powered winery subterranean, with the south and west sides underground, saving energy.

VINEYARDS - kukkula has dry farmed and used only organic approved materials since day one. In addition to their estate, Kevin planted an additional 20 acres (for a friend) that he manages. After a difficult red blotch period—now eradicated—and massive replanting, Kevin is very vigilant, employing strict rules and not allowing outside equipment. He even bleaches cutters before use.

WINES - Of Finnish descent, Jussila named the winery kukkula, which means "the high place" in Finnish.

Adelaida District Sisu Red Rhone Blend 2021 ● 352 cases; 65 $ - ⊞ - Sisu (Se-Soo) is Finnish for patience, perseverance, and stamina. A blend of Syrah (46%), Mourvedre (30%), Grenache (20%), and Petit Sirah (4%). Savory and elegant with dark fruit and white pepper notes. Acid driven with a velvety midpalate. Finesse.

Adelaida District Aatto Red Rhone Blend 2021 ● 285 cases; 65 $ - - Aged 18-20 months in French oak (25% new). A blend of Counoise (44%), Mourvedre (36%), and Grenache (20%). Red fruit, floral, and cinnamon baking spice notes. Lovely texture and finish. Aatto means "eve" in Finnish (in honor of Kevin's father born on Christmas Eve).

Adelaida District Noir Syrah 2021 ● 306 cases; 65 $ - - Named for its inky color. Syrah (85%) and Petit Sirah (15%). Aromas of deep dark purple and black fruits, leather, and white pepper with a touch of floral notes. Voluptuous with grippy tannins.

acres 42 - cases 2,500
Fertilizers cover crops
Plant protection organic
Weed control mechanical, manual
Yeasts spontaneous fermentation
Grapes 100% owned
Certification converting to organic

ARROYO GRANDE

LINDQUIST FAMILY WINES

211 E Branch Street - tel. (805) 270-4900
www.verdadandlindquistfamilywines.com - info@lindquistwinesmo.com

PEOPLE - Renowned Rhone pioneer Bob Lindquist is a legend. He was the first to make Syrah in Santa Barbara County, as well as the first to produce Marsanne in California and Viognier and a red Rhone blend in Santa Barbara. For decades, Bob has made his wines in a winery he shared with Au Bon Climat, outside the Bien Nacido vineyard in the Santa Maria Valley. In 2024, the Arroyo Grande tasting room moved a few doors down to more spacious quarters in a Victorian.

VINEYARDS - A pioneer in biodynamic farming (but without vineyards of his own these days), he seeks out certified biodynamic growers including Christy & Wise (just outside the west end of Sta. Rita Hills) and Martian Ranch (Los Alisos). Other sources are Nolan Vineyard in Los Alamos and Reeves Vineyard in Arroyo Grand. He also gets fruit from choice blocks at Bien Nacido.

WINES - Lindquist is a master of Rhone varieties, and more, consistently making wines that are expressive and elegant. In addition, his Central Coast blends overdeliver on price and quality.

🔴 **Central Coast GSM 2021** ● 600 cases; 35 $ - 🍷 - A blend of Grenache (47%), Syrah (28%) and Mourvedre (25%). Transparent bright red color with lots of red fruit and white pepper notes on the nose and spice notes on the palate. Medium bodied and super fresh.

Santa Maria Valley Bien Nacido Vineyard Chardonnay 2022 ○ 800 cases; 30 $ - 🍷 - Aged one year in French oak (25% new). Lovely minerality comes immediately out of the glass. Apple and pineapple notes, following by textured and vibrant acidity.

Santa Maria Valley Bien Nacido Vineyard Z Block Syrah 2020 ● 100 cases; 65 $ - 🍷 - Aged 18 months in new oak (66% new). Original hillside planting from 1992. Partial whole cluster (33%). Dark fruits and violet flower aromas. At first opulent and juicy, then a fresh lift, followed by textured tannins and a long mouthwatering finish.

acres 5 - cases 3,000
Fertilizers compost, biodynamic compost, cover crops, manure
Plant protection sulfur, biodynamic preparations, organic
Weed control animal grazing, mechanical, manual
Yeasts spontaneous fermentation, commercial cultured yeasts
Grapes purchase 80%
Certification some of the vineyards are certified organic, some of the vineyards are certified biodynamic

PASO ROBLES

LXV WINE

1306-B Pine Street - tel. (805) 296-1902
www.lxvwine.com - info@lxvwine.com

PEOPLE - With Indian palates, and influenced by Super Tuscans and Bordeaux wines, Neeta and Kunal Mittal founded their winery with winemakers Jeff Strekas and consultant Frederick Ammons to make Bordeaux varietals which they uniquely source from both Paso Robles and Saint-Emilion. Their downtown Paso Robles tasting experience, lauded by Wine Enthusiast Magazine, offers Neeta's renowned wine and spice pairings. Their first vintage of estate grown Syrah was 2022.

VINEYARDS - Grapes come from celebrated Central Coast sites—Bien Nacido, G2 (north), Gateway, Portico Hills, and Vogelzang. The new Willow Creek District estate vineyard, Armaa.N, has eight acres of Cabernet Sauvignon, Cabernet Franc, Sangiovese and Syrah. They also have an additional 10 acres in Willow Creek District to plant Cabernet Franc and Merlot. Beginning in 2022, LXV will also produce wine from Saint-Emilion Grand Cru vineyard, Chateau Tour Perey.

WINES - The Mittals hired Frederick Ammons, formerly the winemaker at Napa's prestigious Cabernet producer, Rudd Estate, as consulting winemaker.

🔴 **Willow Creek District Meso Cabernet Sauvignon 2021** SLOW WINE ● 100 cases; 140 $ - 🍷 - From the low lying Gateway vineyard, sited on gravel, limestone, and clay soils. Savory, juicy, food friendly with age-ability. Balanced with dark red fruit, oak notes, brilliant acidity and tannic structure; textured, lasting finish.

Willow Creek District Cabernet Franc 2022 ● 100 cases; 150 $ - 🍷 - Sourced from G2North vineyard. Textured with intense aromas and flavors of lavender, plum, rich red fruit; firm tannins; vibrant acidity. Voluptuous with age-ability.

Willow Creek District Syrah 2022 ● 200 cases; 150 $ - 🍷 - First vintage of Syrah from Armaa.N estate vineyard. Savory aromas of juicy dark plum and dried leaves lead to a palate with round mouthfeel, rich red and black fruit; bright acidity; firm tannic structure.

acres 8 - cases 3,000
Fertilizers compost, cover crops, manure, organic fertilizer
Plant protection synthetic pesticides, organic
Weed control animal grazing, manual
Yeasts selected indigenous yeasts
Grapes 100% owned
Certification none

PASO ROBLES

MAHA

5995 Peachy Canyon Road - tel. (805) 712-8038
www.villacreek.com - info@mahaestatewine.com

PEOPLE - Before starting MAHA, Paso restauranteurs Cris and the late JoAnn Cherry made wine under the Villa Creek label, beginning in 2001 and using purchased fruit, until they launched their own estate vineyard and winery in 2006. In 2024, JoAnn Cherry died after a five year battle with colorectal cancer. She was widely admired by her community which held a celebration of life for her in August 2024. Cris and their family carry on.

VINEYARDS - Their all estate MAHA wines launched in 2019 and were focused at first on Grenache, their head trained vines sit at 1,500 to 1,800 feet in elevation with marine influences from the ocean 14 miles away. Calcareous soils retain water. In keeping with biodynamic principles, they integrate animal life with chickens, pigs and goats who wander pastures. In 2023, they achieved Regenerative Organic Certification (silver).

WINES - Oliver Mikkelsen is credited as the vineyard manager and winemaker. The wines have catapulted to the top of many wine critics' lists. Uniquely, they use Carignane as a blending grape in their reds.

Understory Red Rhone Blend 2021 ● 180 cases; 98 $ - ⊞ - Grenache, Mourvedre and Carignan. Aged 21 months in French oak (30% new). Aromas of ripe berries and cherries leads to bright red fruit and spice framed with firm tannins, vibrant acidity and aging potential.

Before Anyone Else Clairette Blanche 2021 ○ 130 cases; 98 $ - ⓦ - Aged 18-20 months in Hungarian oak foudres (30% new). Bright acidity with a creamy mouthfeel, tropical fruits, white peaches, jasmine, Meyer lemon and hint of marzipan.

Backlit Red Rhone Blend 2021 ● 150 cases; 98 $ - ⊞ - Aged 21 months in French oak (30% new). A lush blend of Syrah (50%), Carignan, Grenache and Mourvedre. Aromas and flavors of bing cherries, earth, sweet tobacco with soft acidity and tannins. Drink now.

acres 13 - cases 750
Fertilizers compost, biodynamic compost, cover crops, manure
Plant protection sulfur, biodynamic preparations, organic
Weed control animal grazing, mechanical, manual
Yeasts spontaneous fermentation
Grapes 100% owned
Certification biodynamic, organic, regenerative

PASO ROBLES

NINER WINE ESTATES

2400 Highway 46 West - tel. (805) 239-2233
www.ninerwine.com - info@ninerwine.com

PEOPLE - Niner was founded by Dick Niner, a self made man who worked his way out of the mines in West Virginia to put himself through college and graduate school before becoming a venture capitalist. He bought land Paso Robles in 2001, then the current location in 2003. Niner began farming in 2007 and built the winery and tasting room 2009. After he became ill in 2013, his son Andy took the helm in 2014.

VINEYARDS - Niner has three estate vineyards. Heart Hill (Willow Creek District), planted in 2007, is 113 planted acres on silicious shale, calcareous soil. Bordeaux varietals (but not Merlot), Syrah, Zinfandel, Carmenere are grown. Jespersen Ranch, purchased in 2011, is 30 miles south (Edna Valley, SLO Coast AVA). Windy, cool from Pacific Ocean influences, Albarino, Sauvignon Blanc, Chardonnay, Pinot Noir, Grenache, Syrah are grown on clay topsoil with sand/sandstone.

WINES - A recipient of the California Green Medal Award, the winery is LEED Silver Certified and solar powered. Some of the wines, not featured here, may be grown with herbicide.

Paso Robles Willow Creek and Geneseo Fog Catcher 2021 ● 980 cases; 150 $ - ⊞ - Cabernet Sauvignon (57%), Malbec (38%), Carmenere (5%) aged 28 months in 64% new French oak. Notes of coffee, serrano chili, blueberries, rich red fruit. Ageworthy.

Paso Robles Willow Creek and Geneseo Cabernet Sauvignon 2021 ● 3,385 cases; 60 $ - ⊞ - Cabernet Sauvignon (91%), Cabernet Franc, Malbec and Petit Verdot aged 21 months in 38% new French oak. Dark, blue fruit, cherries, red fruit, spice with a plush, round texture and lingering finish.

Paso Robles Edna Valley Chardonnay 2022 ○ 766 cases; 40 $ - ⓦ ⊞ - Chardonnay from single vineyard, fermented and aged for 16 months in 90% oak (25% new) and concrete. Balanced, round and fresh with a with Burgundian texture and flavors of apple, pear and citrus.

acres 285 - cases 20,000
Fertilizers compost, cover crops, manure, organic fertilizer
Plant protection sulfur, copper, organic
Weed control animal grazing, mechanical
Yeasts spontaneous fermentation, commercial cultured yeasts
Grapes 100% owned
Certification none

PASO ROBLES

ONX

2910 Limestone Way - tel. (805) 434-5607
www.onxwine.com - info@onxwines.com

PEOPLE - ONX (pronounced onyx) Estate Vineyard in the Templeton Gap AVA is a passion project and country escape for owners Steve and Brenda Olson of the Olson Company, a Seal Beach developer of housing in Orange and Los Angeles counties. The Olson's purchased 59 acres and planted a pilot vineyard in 2005. Jeff Strekas is director of winegrowing and Drew Nenow is winemaker. Nenow studied at Cal Poly SLO was an assistant winemaker at ONX until 2018, when he became head winemaker.

VINEYARDS - They have two estate vineyards—one in the Templeton Gap, one of the coolest areas in Paso Robles, and the Kiler Canyon Vineyard in the Willow Creek District. Soils are mostly the Linne-Calodo complex of alkaline clay loams on hillsides and river terraces and calcareous decomposed soil. Syrah, Mourvedre, Grenache and a small amount of Roussanne are cultivated and plantings have expanded to include 20 varieties. Both vineyards farm organically. The winery's first vintage was released in 2008.

WINES - Wines are layered, delicate, nuanced and complex with a typically long finish.

Paso Robles Templeton Gap Reckoning 2019 SLOW WINE
670 cases; 58 $ - Rich blend of 64% Syrah, 20% Petite Sirah, 8% Malbec, 8% Grenache aged in 35% new French barriques and puncheons. Savory with aromas of mushrooms, red fruit, earth, moss, anise. Showing flavors of dark red fruit, spice, chalk with a soft tannic structure and moderate acidity.

Paso Robles Templeton Gap Mad Crush 2020 390 cases; 48 $ - A flagship blend of 71% Grenache, 15% Mourvedre, 14% Tempranillo. Spice, cola, red fruit, cranberry, red fruit jam and blueberries framed with moderate tannins and bright acidity. Medium body with balanced, lasting finish.

Paso Robles Templeton Gap L'Autre Femme 2022 200 cases; 45 $ - Snappy blend of Picpoul Blanc (59%) and Viognier (41%). Aged in 60 gallon barrique on lees for 9 months. Intensely aromatic with bright citrus, a lean, refreshing texture with flavors of ripe citrus and vibrant acidity.

acres 90 - cases 8,000
Fertilizers biodynamic compost, cover crops
Plant protection sulfur, organic
Weed control mechanical
Yeasts selected indigenous yeasts, commercial cultured yeasts
Grapes 100% owned
Certification converting to organic

GROVER BEACH

OUTWARD WINES

965 Huber Street - tel. (805) 252-3441
www.outwardwines.com - hello@outwardwines.com

PEOPLE - Natalie Siddique and Ryan Pace started their label in 2016, named for their love of the outdoors and rock climbing. In 2023, they moved to Grover Beach and made their first full vintage. Starting as Rhone varietal producers, in 2023 they added Pinot Noir from the Bassi Vineyard in the SLO Coast and Grenache Rose from Two Wolves in Happy Canyon). In 2024, they added Falanghina from Stiletto in San Benito County and Sangiovese from their vineyard.

VINEYARDS - They buy most of the fruit from eight vineyards including Bassi, Presqu'ile, Rancho Arroyo Grande, Rivenrock in Cambria, Old Oak and Shell Creek. Certified organic sources include Siletto and Two Wolves. They also farm four vineyards, including three in Santa Ynez. The Pace Vineyard, at Ryan's dad's house, was planted to Syrah in 2000. Starfire Vineyard has 2.5 acres of Syrah that they will graft. Five Oaks Vineyard has one acre of Sangiovese.

WINES - They make single varietal, site specific wines that tell a story, speak of a place, time and the variety.

Carmel Valley Massa Vineyard Cabernet Sauvignon 2023 264 cases; 42 $ - Aged 10 months in neutral oak. Grown at 1,700 feet elevation on own rooted, dry farmed vines planted in 1968. Spends 30 days on skins. Aromas of dark red fruits with earthy and herbal notes. Fresh and juicy with soft tannins. A rethink of Cabernet Sauvignon.

Santa Maria Valley Presqu'ile Vineyard Gamay 2023 110 cases; 38 $ - Aged 6 months in neutral oak. Stem inclusion (30%). Bright fuchsia color, aromatic with herbal and earthy notes, concentrated on the palate with textured tannins and a juicy coating.

Paso Robles Highlands District Shell Creek Chenin Blanc 2023 240 cases; 34 $ - Aged 10 months on lees in neutral oak. From own rooted vines planted in 1972. Foot stomped, it spends 24 hours on skins. Aromas of stone fruits and mineral notes. Picked early for freshness and skin contact for texture. Light and textured with fresh acidity.

acres 6 - cases 2,800
Fertilizers compost, biodynamic compost, cover crops, manure, organic fertilizer
Plant protection sulfur, biodynamic preparations, organic
Weed control animal grazing, mechanical, manual
Yeasts spontaneous fermentation
Grapes purchase 75%
Certification some of the vineyards are certified organic

CAMBRIA

PHELAN FARM

3310 San Simeon-Monterey Creek Road
www.phelanfarm.com - team@phelanfarm.com

 Whether it is substituting ATVs for tractors to reduce soil compaction or consulting master pruners Simonit & Sirch, Phelan Farm is determined to support its natural systems.

PEOPLE - World famous sommelier and winemaker Raj Parr (Domaine de la Cote, Evening Land, Sandhi) devotes his attention to a cool climate, coastal Cambria farm where he pursues the mostly Jura and Savoie grapes which interest him (Jacquere, Savagnin, Trousseau, etc.). He recently acquired nearby Stolo Winery and its vineyards which he's incorporating into the 2024 vintage. His other brands, Brij and Scythians, rely on purchased grapes.

VINEYARDS - The leased estate hugs both sides of a creek and consists of sedimentary soils derived from a minerally convoluted bedrock called the Franciscan Mélange on one plot and a volcanic byproduct, Cambrian Felsite, on another. Farming continues the no till ethos of owner Greg Phelan, focusing on building soil mycorrhizae. Sprays consist of native plants, fermented herb teas, kelp and milk products. Roaming farm animals provide fertilizer.

WINES - Fresh and electric is the watchword here. No sulfur is used in the vineyard or winery.

SLO Coast Chardonnay 2022 ○ 140 cases; 65 $ - Green almond, pineapple and a hint of sweet spice on the nose. The palate is explosively tart and intense with Meyer lemon, lean orchard fruits and flinty reduction that is long lasting.

SLO Coast Pinot Noir 2022 ● 180 cases; 65 $ - Aromas of crushed leaves and grasses, dark cherry and rose merge into a palate of elegantly balanced dark cherry and savory herbal notes with hints of flavors to emerge in time.

SLO Coast Autrement 2022 ● 583 cases; 55 $ - A blend of Gamay and Mondeuse (40% each) and Pinot Noir (20%). Scents of crushed dried leaves and currant give way to a highly textured and fresh palate born of tart cranberry and red currant fruit, bitter herbal flavors and discreet tannins.

acres 11.2 - cases 1,000
Fertilizers compost, manure pellets
Plant protection organic
Weed control animal grazing, mechanical
Yeasts spontaneous fermentation
Grapes 100% owned
Certification none

PASO ROBLES

ROBERT HALL WINERY

3443 Mill Road - tel. (805) 239-1616
www.roberthallwinery.com - info@roberthallwinery.com

PEOPLE - Founded in 1999, B Corp certified O'Neill Vintners and Distillery bought this winery in 2016, and, in 2020, began a multi year research study comparing regenerative organic farming versus conventional and "sustainable." Managing director, New Zealand born Caine Thompson, is head of sustainability overseeing the study using carbon monitoring technology from Agrology. The team includes Amanda Gorter, director of winemaking, and Kirk Brown, head of viticulture.

VINEYARDS - One year into the study, originally on just 40 acres, the team saw rapid improvement in the regenerative and organic vines and immediately began to convert the remaining 70 acres to regenerative organic farming, keeping a five acre conventional vineyard as a control. They release mealybug predators (bred with a local supplier) via vineyard drones. Regenerative organic certification for the estate is being finalized in 2024. Some wines, not featured here, may be grown with herbicide.

WINES - The winery specializes in Bordeaux and Rhone varieties. It anticipates that in 2024 the estate vine wines will be organic and regenerative organic certified.

Estrella District Cavern Select Rosé 2023 EVERYDAY WINE 135 cases; 30 $ - A 50/50 blend of direct pressed Grenache and Syrah. Bright red fruit aromas of cherries and strawberries. Acidity hits both the front and back of the palate and the wine lingers with a midpalate weight.

Paso Robles Cavern Select Sparkling Grenache Blanc 2021 ✦ 460 cases; 40 $ - Aged 11 months in bottle. Whole cluster pressed. A Brut with 5 g/l residual sugar. Fresh notes of lemon peel, apple, and crush stone. Crisp and light bodied with a rounded midpalate and clean finish.

Paso Robles Cavern Select GSM 2020 ● 350 cases; 50 $ - Aged in a combination of French oak puncheons (50% new) and barrels (60% new). A Grenache dominant blend with Mourvedre (33%) and Syrah (14%). Aromas of lavender, cherry, plum, and spice, with a full midpalate.

acres 130 - cases 120,000
Fertilizers biodynamic compost, cover crops, manure, organic
Plant protection sulfur, biodynamic preparations, synthetic pesticides, organic
Weed control animal grazing, mechanical, manual
Yeasts spontaneous fermentation, selected indigenous yeasts, commercial cultured yeasts
Grapes purchase 50%
Certification converting to regenerative and organic

BAKERSFIELD

SAN RUCCI WINERY

1906 McIntosh Way - tel. (909) 837-8727
www.sanrucci.com - anthony.merz@sanrucci.com

PEOPLE - With family roots in Sicily and Central Italy, San Rucci combines the Sicilian and Tuscan family names San Filippo and Becherucci. Inspired by the family traditions of Francsico Becherucci and armed with a winemaking degree from the University of California Fresno, the father and son winemaking team of Bill and Anthony (Tony) Merz have years of experience to their credit. The team has expanded their portfolio with the addition of several Italian varieties.

VINEYARDS - San Rucci sources grapes from Cucamonga Valley, Paso Robles and San Benito County which includes all or parts of seven AVAs: Chalone, Cienega Valley, Lime Kiln Valley, Mt. Harlan, Pacheco Pass, Paicines, and San Benito. Soils in this landlocked AVA that has some of California's oldest producing vines are limestone and decomposed granite. The wines listed here were sourced from the Siletto Vineyard in hills outside of the small town of Tres Pinos.

WINES - Italian varieties show marked varietal character, modest amounts of new oak and a light touch in the cellar.

◉ San Benito County Family Ties Montepulciano 2021 ● 16 cases; 48 $ - 🍷 - Decanting is recommended but this youthful, structured vintage is approachable with pretty floral aromatics, moody black fruit and notes of tobacco leaf and hoarhound tea coating fine, dusty tannins.
San Benito County Falanghina 2023 ○ 61 cases; 36 $ - 🍷 - Bracing acidity and flinty notes of white peach and zippy citrus scented with dried thyme are a triumph for this inaugural release.
San Benito County Nebbiolo 2022 ● 60 cases; 48 $ - 🍷 - Aged in American oak for 14 months. Umami-laden aromas of red and black raspberry and ferrous earth with a leaner, focused palate showing well integrated oak and round tannins through a brief finish.

acres 0 - cases 2,400
Fertilizers compost, organic fertilizer
Plant protection organic
Weed control mechanical
Yeasts selected indigenous yeasts, commercial cultured yeasts
Grapes purchase 100%
Certification organic

CAMBRIA

STOLO VINEYARDS

3776 Santa Rosa Creek Road - tel. (805) 924-3131
www.stolovineyards.com - info@stolovineyards.com

PEOPLE - At the base of a sunny vineyard, the farmhouse and old dairy barn at Stolo Vineyards date from the late 1800s. Globally renowned sommelier turned vintner, Rajat Parr, now oversees farming and winemaking. His passion for cool climate wines led to Cambria where he's now leased the Stolo vineyards, tasting room and winery. He also produces wine under Sandhi, Domaine de la Cote, and Evening Land labels (listed separately in this guide).

VINEYARDS - Less than three miles from the Pacific Ocean, in Cambria's unique coastal microclimate, Parr grows Chardonnay, Gewürztraminer, Pinot Noir, Sauvignon Blanc, and Syrah using regenerative practices. The soil is mostly clay based with a small amount of limestone. He grows some of the grapes at his nearby (leased) Phelan Farm in San Simeon. Parr also purchases grapes from local growers. In 2024, the team planted 7.5 acres of Gamay, Gringet and Trousseau.

WINES - Parr favors cool climate, classic, French inspired wines that reveal the terroir of this specific area within the SLO Coast AVA. No sulfur is used in the vineyards or the wines.

◉ SLO Coast Creekside Chardonnay 2022 SLOW WINE ○ 100 cases; 49 $ - 🍾 - Aromas of spice, grilled pineapple, orchard fruit, spice, and oak waft from the glass, and continue on to the balanced, rich palate with vibrant acidity. Oak notes on the lingering finish.
SLO Coast Autrement Red Blend 2022 ● 600 cases; 55 $ - 🍾 - Aged 10 months in neutral oak. Blend of Gamay, Mondeuse and Pinot Noir. Intense floral nose of rose petals, savory palate with dried herbs, juicy fruit notes, high acidity, and a lasting finish.
SLO Coast Brij Wines Grenache Rosé 2023 ◐ 600 cases; 28 $ - 🍾 - From purchased grapes. Foot stomped for three hours, fermented in stainless steel and aged for 3-4 months in neutral oak. Light red fruit aromas, fresh and juicy raspberry flavors, lip smacking finish.

acres 22.5 - cases 2,000
Fertilizers compost, biodynamic compost, cover crops, manure, organic fertilizer
Plant protection sulfur, organic
Weed control animal grazing, mechanical
Yeasts spontaneous fermentation, selected indigenous yeasts
Grapes purchase 5%
Certification converting to organic

PASO ROBLES

TABLAS CREEK VINEYARD

9339 Adelaida Road - tel. (805) 237-1231
www.tablascreek.com - info@tablascreek.com

PEOPLE - A leader of the California Rhône movement and one of California's most acclaimed wineries, it was founded in 1987 by two families, the Perrins of Château de Beaucastel in Châteauneuf-du-Pape and their American distributor, the Haas family. Jason Haas, partner and general manager, runs the estate with the Perrins. Neil Collins is director of winemaking and vineyard manager. Chelsea Franchi is senior assistant winemaker.

VINEYARDS - Certified organic, biodynamic and regenerative organic, they grow 16 varieties from cuttings imported from the Perrin's French estate. At 1,500 feet the dry farmed vines grow on rolling hills with calcareous soils. They own 350 sheep to manage weeds, work the soil and fertilize. Starting with the 2024 vintage, Patelin wines (their second label, made from purchased grapes) will all be from certified organic vineyards.

WINES - Reds and Roussane based whites age in the Rhône tradition in large neutral oak foudres.

🔺 **Adelaida District Esprit de Tablas 2021** SLOW WINE ●
2,950 cases; 70 $ - 🍷 - This classic Mourvèdre based Rhône blend offers black cherry, mulberry, bay leaf, umami and dark chocolate notes with chewy tannin and a long finish. Ageworthy.
Adelaida District Dianthus Rosé 2023 ● 1,380 cases; 40 $ - 🍷 - Salmon color and notes of blood orange, juniper, pluot and minerality. Creamy texture and vibrant line of acidity. Made in the saignée method.
Adelaida District Côte de Tablas Blanc 2023 O 1,300 cases; 40 $ - 🍷 - A plush nose of white flowers, melon, lemon and crushed rock. The long finish shows lemongrass and mineral notes.

---

acres 140 - cases 32,000
Fertilizers compost, biodynamic compost, cover crops, manure
Plant protection sulfur, biodynamic preparations, synthetic pesticides, organic
Weed control animal grazing, mechanical, manual
Yeasts spontaneous fermentation, commercial cultured yeasts
Grapes purchase 40%
Certification some of the vineyards are certified organic, some of the vineyards are certified biodynamic, regenerative

LOMPOC

TATOMER

1299 W Laurel Avenue - tel. (805) 325-5612
www.tatomerwines.com

PEOPLE - As winemakers around him committed firmly to Pinot Noir and Chardonnay, Graham Tatomer, a cellar hand at Santa Barbara Winery, started producing his own Riesling and Sylvaner. After two years of interning at Weingut Knoll in Austria, he returned to the Santa Maria Valley where he has become the most committed producer of Grüner Veltliner and Riesling and (not to mention Pinot Noir) in the region, if not California.

VINEYARDS - Tatomer believes a cold climate presents Grüner and Riesling at their finest. He buys Grüner grown on Paragon Vineyard's marl, quartz and limestone soils. The Edna Valley site that receives the force of the cooling Pacific a few miles away. Much is the same with Kick On Ranch, the origin of Tatomer's signature Riesling and his Pinot Noir. The site, on sandy loam soils, is just west of the town of Los Alamos, fully blasted by Pacific winds.

WINES - Tatomer embraces the challenge of finding the savory flavors beyond the fruit with his Pinot Noir, while producing an unusually varied range of Grüner Veltliner and Riesling.

🔺 **Santa Barbara County Kick On Ranch Clone 239 Riesling 2021** O 96 cases; 50 $ - 🍷 - shows great concentration on the palate with potent grapefruit, orange and peach while delicate orange blossom and minerally diesel hover as aromas.
Edna Valley Paragon Vineyard Grüner Veltliner 2021 O 155 cases; 30 $ - 🍷 - Aged in both oak and stainless. Shows only vegetal aromas–hay, cucumber and sweet compost–while saving grapefruit, unripe pear and apricot for the palate. A wine very much of its site.
Santa Barbara County Kick On Ranch Pinot Noir 2021 ● 96 cases; 50 $ - 🍷 - A unique nose of strawberry eau de vie and dried strawberries buried in dried leaves and wood. The flavors are savory in the extreme, including amaro herbs and bitterness softened by strawberry and orange peel.

---

acres 0 - cases 4,500
Fertilizers compost, cover crops, organic fertilizer
Plant protection sulfur, synthetic pesticides, organic
Weed control mechanical
Yeasts selected indigenous yeasts
Grapes purchase 100%
Certification none

PASO ROBLES

THACHER WINERY & VINEYARD

8355 Vineyard Drive - tel. (805) 237-0087
www.thacherwinery.com - info@thacherwinery.com

PEOPLE - Thacher Winery is a family owned, boutique winery founded by Sherman and Michelle Thacher. They specialize in Rhône and Zinfandel varietals, along with unique blends. Sherman makes the wine and manages the vineyards. Breanna Hill has been assistant winemaker for three vintages. For single varietal wines, Thacher puts as much technical information on the back of the label as possible for transparency.

VINEYARDS - Their two Willow Creek District estate vineyards are Homestead Hill (16 acres), planted in 2018, and Kentucky Ranch Vineyard (5 acres). At the former, he grows Cab, Cinsault, Mourvedre, Syrah and a red field blend of 11 California heirloom varieties. Kentucky Ranch Vineyard (5) grows Alicante, Counoise, Mencia, Petite Sirah, Tempranillo, Viognier and a white field blend with 11 Mediterranean white varieties. They dry farm five acres of Carignan, Grenache and Zin.

WINES - The style emphasizes balance, depth and a sense of place, reflecting the terroir of Paso Robles.

TOP Willow Creek District Homestead Hill Vineyard Grenache 2022 ● 200 cases; 65 $ - Destemmed and fermented in concrete for 11 months for freshness. The transparent cherry red wine has a bright nose with red fruit, earth, and spice notes. Gentle on the palate with no over extraction. The wine is savory, elegant and very drinkable.

Willow Creek District Homestead Hill Vineyard Carignan 2021 ● 50 cases; 65 $ - Aged 18 months. Partial whole cluster (30%). Perfumed florals and red and purple fruit aromas, textured acidity and mouthwatering finish. Very pretty with velvety tannins.

Willow Creek District Homestead Hill Vineyard Syrah 2020 ● 247 cases; 65 $ - Aged 30 months in neutral barriques. Partial whole cluster (40%). Blackberry and meaty aromas with grippy tannins and mouthwatering acidity.

acres 21 - cases 5,000
Fertilizers compost, cover crops, manure, organic fertilizer
Plant protection sulfur, synthetic pesticides, organic
Weed control mechanical, manual
Yeasts spontaneous fermentation
Grapes purchase 35%
Certification some of the vineyards are certified organic

PASO ROBLES

THIBIDO WINERY

1350 Kiler Canyon Road
www.thibidowinery.com - gibsey@thibidowinery.com

PEOPLE - Seasoned, artisanal winemaker Josh Beckett, a Paso Robles native son—his parents started the local star Peachy Canyon where he serves as winemaker—together with his wife and co-owner Gibsey Beckett planted their eco-oriented Thibido label's vineyard in 2019. It's a winemaker's sandbox of blending varieties and flavors. Bottle labels indicate organic grapes. They participate in the 1% for the Planet program.

VINEYARDS - After five years of farming regeneratively, the vineyard was certified organic in 2024. They also buy grapes. The estate sits on chalky, rocky soils, with six varietals—Carignan, Grenache, Mourvedre, Petite Sirah, Syrah and Zinfandel. An irrigation system minimizes groundwater use. Geeky fact: Beckett is experimenting with a two acre block of own rooted Zinfandel, planted with the Uberoth clone on the western border of the vineyard.

WINES - Beckett uses a variety of small lot, handcrafted techniques including foot treading, hand punch downs, and whole cluster fermentations. One wine is carbonic.

TOP Willow Creek District Best Day Rosé 2023 ● 40 cases; 43 $ - Aged seven months in terracotta amphora. Aromas of ripe strawberries, juicy pears, stone fruit, crushed chalk rock. On the palate, notes of green apple, fresh strawberries, guava with vibrant acidity and minerality.

Willow Creek District Hippie Hill Red Rhone Blend 2022 ● 65 cases; 65 $ - Aromas of earth, sage, chocolate, dark cherries in this red blend. On the lush palate, spice, herbs, flint, dark plums, and dark cherries. Structured tannins and vibrant acidity. Ageworthy.

Willow Creek District The Bedfellow Syrah 2022 ● 50 cases; 65 $ - Aged 18 months in French oak. Elegance and finesse. Aromas of ripe stone fruit, red berries, cassis, and baking spice. Flavors: oak, leather, chalk, black olives. Elegant tannins and just-right acidity in this lush wine.

acres 10.6 - cases 400
Fertilizers compost, cover crops, manure, organic fertilizer
Plant protection organic
Weed control animal grazing, manual
Yeasts spontaneous fermentation
Grapes purchase 20%
Certification some of the vineyards are certified organic

ARROYO GRANDE

VERDAD WINE CELLARS

211 E Branch Street - tel. (805) 270-4900
www.verdadandlindquistfamilywines.com - info@lindquistwines.com

PEOPLE - The year 2025 marks the 25th anniversary of Louisa Lindquist's pioneering winery focused on Spanish varieties. She was one of the first people in California to make Albariño. This year, she released two new wines, Godello and Sauvignon Blanc. The Sauvignon Blanc is a good counterpoint to her best selling Paso Robles Cabernet Sauvignon. She shares a tasting room in Arroyo Grande with her husband Bob Lindquist and Lindquist Family Wines.

VINEYARDS - Louisa has a long term lease on four acre Reeves Vineyard in Edna Valley and makes a rose of Grenache from it. She buys Albariño and Tempranillo from Martian Ranch (certified biodynamic) in Alisos Canyon. She added Jack Ranch in Edna Valley in 2024 for two single vineyard Albariños. The year 2024 was the first bottling of 2022 Two Wolves Cabernet Sauvignon from Happy Canyon. Godello comes from Rancho Ontiveros and Sauvignon Blanc from Rusack (certified organic), both in Santa Ynez.

WINES - Verdad Wines puts an organic ingredient statement on label for their wines, including Cabernet Sauvignon and Sauvignon Blanc which come from certified organic vineyards.

🔴 Santa Maria Valley Ranchos Ontiveros Vineyard Godello 2022 ⭕ 57 cases; 35 $ - 🍷 - Aged 11 months. Fermented two thirds in one year old French barrels and one third in neutral barrels. Aromas of apricot, lemon curd, pineapple, honeysuckle and hazelnuts. Round and supple on the palate with good acidity.
Ballard Canyon Rusack Vineyard Sauvignon Blanc 2023 ⭕ 150 cases; 35 $ - 🍷 - Fermented on lees in stainless steel until bottling. Pretty aromas of stone fruits, tropical fruits, lemon curd and white flowers. Lush and round on the palate with a note of bitter almond and a long finish.
Alisos Canyon Martian Ranch Tempranillo 2022 ● 350 cases; 40 $ - 🍷 - Aged 18 months in French 500L puncheons. Syrah (10%) added for lift and lightness. Complex with dark red and black fruits, dried flowers, leather and tobacco with velvety tannins.

acres 5 - cases 2,000
Fertilizers compost, biodynamic compost, cover crops
Plant protection sulfur, biodynamic preparations, organic
Weed control mechanical, manual
Yeasts spontaneous fermentation, commercial cultured yeasts
Grapes purchase 80%
Certification some of the vineyards are certified organic, some of the vineyards are certified biodynamic

PASO ROBLES

VILLA CREEK CELLARS

5995 Peachy Canyon Road - tel. (805) 712-8038
www.villacreek.com - wine@villacreek.com

PEOPLE - Former restauranteurs, Cris Cherry, director of winemaking, and the late JoAnn Cherry started their winemaking career in 2001 making 300 cases of wine to serve at their restaurant in Paso. After their first vintage won a 93 point score from Wine Spectator, they expanded, launching the Villa Creek label with grapes from premium westside Paso vineyards. In 2006 they built their winery and, in 2019, launched a second, all estate Rhone label, MAHA.

VINEYARDS - Grapes come mostly from their own head trained vines at MAHA estate (certified organic and biodynamic) in the Adelaida District as well as from celebrated, local, iconic vineyards. These include the famed James Berry vineyard (Alban clones, farmed by Justin Smith of Saxum) in the Willow Creek District and Syrah from the celebrated Kirk Landry vineyard in the Adelaida District (certified organic).

WINES - Oliver Mikkelsen is credited as the vineyard manager and winemaker. The wines show ripeness and finesse.

🔴 Three Syrah 2022 ● 100 cases; 89 $ - 🍷 - From Adelaida District vines at MAHA and Kirk Landry. Aged 18 months in French oak. Big and juicy, this concentrated wine showed tobacco, red and black fruit and oak notes with chewy tannins and a lasting finish. Ageworthy.
Avenger Red Rhone Blend 2021 ● 530 cases; 69 $ - 🍷 - A blend of Carignan, Grenache, Mourvedre, Petite Sirah and Syrah. Aged 18 months in French oak. Approachable and food friendly. Firm tannins and moderate acidity framed notes of leather, tobacco, brioche, pepper, cocoa and spice.
Garnacha 2021 ● 200 cases; 72 $ - 🍷 - MAHA fruit. Aged 18 months in French oak puncheons and barrels. Balanced with black cherries, pomegranate, raspberries, anise and orange peel with bright acidity and moderate tannins leading to a lingering finish.

acres n/a - cases 2,500
Fertilizers compost, biodynamic compost, cover crops
Plant protection sulfur, biodynamic preparations, organic
Weed control animal grazing, mechanical, manual
Yeasts spontaneous fermentation
Grapes purchase 50%
Certification organic

CENTRAL COAST
SANTA BARBARA COUNTY

 Snail

137 Domaine de la Côte
139 Folded Hills
140 Grimm's Bluff
141 J. Dirt

Bottle

130 A Tribute to Grace
132 Au Bon Climat
134 Chanin Wine
142 Joy Fantastic & Holus Bolus
142 Kings Carey Wines
147 Montemar Winery
148 Piedrasassi
149 Refugio Ranch Vineyards
150 Roblar Winery & Vineyards
151 Sandhi Wines
156 The Brander Vineyard

$ Coin

136 Disko Wines
139 Entity of Delight
143 Land of Saints Wine Company
145 Lo-Fi Wines
154 Storm Wines

LOS ALAMOS

A TRIBUTE TO GRACE

490 Bell Street, #5 - tel. (805) 633-0598
www.gracewinecompany.com - angela@gracewinecompany.com

PEOPLE - The Grace in the title is Angela Osborne's late grandmother. But it is also the virtue, Grace, that is brought to the wine by Grenache, the most graceful grape. Her laser focus on multiple single vineyard Grenache bottlings through 16 vintages has not only proved her winemaking mastery, but arguably contributed to its current popularity as a category. Osborne, a New Zealand transplant, observes the biodynamic calendar when picking and bottling.

VINEYARDS - Osborne has done her diligence in finfding fine Grenache vineyards throughout the Central Coast and in the Sierra Foothills at Ann Kraemer's Shake Ridge Ranch where vines find iron and granite among volcanic soil. At Vie Caprice Vineyard in Santa Ynez there is sandy loam soil tended without any chemical inputs, while Dorigo Vineyard in Ballard Canyon plays against type with granite soils which Osborne's team farms with only approved organic materials.

WINES - With her multiple vineyard sites, the wines are a mosaic of California Grenache.

● **Amador County Shake Ridge Ranch Grenache 2022**
● 45 cases; 75 $ - 🛢 - A delicate nose of strawberry pastry and parsley, with a palate that delivers strawberry pastille, green almond and cut wood. Light but firm tannins.

Ballard Canyon Dorigo Vineyard Grenache 2022 ● 113 cases; 60 $ - 🛢 - A very perfumed nose of rose and violet, strawberry and graphite. On the palate, graphite informing strawberry and blackberry fruit with a vibrant shadow of firm, fine tannins.

Santa Ynez Valley Vie Caprice Vineyard Grenache 2022
● 215 cases; 55 $ - 🛢 - A rich nose of dried strawberry, currant and cut flower stem, with flavors of concentrated strawberry and green plum with plum skin tannins. 100% burly Alban clone.

---

acres 0 - cases 3,500
Fertilizers compost, cover crops, organic fertilizer
Plant protection sulfur, copper, organic
Weed control mechanical
Yeasts spontaneous fermentation
Grapes purchase 100%
Certification none

SANTA MARIA

ÂMEVIVE

2705 Aviation Way - tel. (209) 872-2420
www.amevivewine.com - alice@amevivewine.com

PEOPLE - Ecofriendly as ever, Alice Anderson continues to grow her brand with her love of nature at the foundation. To Alice, this year the work has been more intense than work done over the last 5 years. There are more beneficial species than before and more diversity, she says. She and her partner Topher De Felice hired Renee Berkus to assist with winemaking.

VINEYARDS - She now farms two estates in Los Olivos. Her first, acquired in 2020, is the 10 acre Ibarra-Young Vineyard, first planted in 1971. She now leases and farms the eight acre Mira Laguna Vineyard (certified organic since 2012) in Solvang and plans to add a hedgerow and pollinator habitat. She also buys Grenache from Martian Ranch in Los Alamos (certified biodynamic), Shokiran in Los Alamos and from Coquelicot (certified organic) in Santa Ynez Valley.

WINES - Focused mainly on Rhones, Alice personally farms all of her vineyard designate wines. "Soulful, lively soul, living soul" are the ideal words to describe Anderson and her wines.

Santa Barbara County Gamay 2023 SLOW WINE ● 305 cases; 32 $ - 🛢 - Aged seven months in neutral oak. All whole cluster. From grapes grown at Martian Ranch (certified biodynamic) in Los Alamos and Shokrian Vineyard. Harvested in three picks. The wine has a lovely earthiness with aromas of plum and tart red fruits.

Los Olivos District Ibarra-Young Vineyard Estate Périphérie 2023 ● 110 cases; 38 $ - 🛢 - Aged seven months in neutral barrels. A co-ferment of Marsanne, Syrah, and Mourvèdre from two peripheral rows from the original 1971 planting. A bright pomegranate color, the wine is clear and vibrant with notes of fresh red fruits. Fresh, fun, and drinkable.

Los Olivos District Ibarra-Young Vineyard Estate Marsanne 2022 ○ 110 cases; 38 $ - 🛢 - Aged in neutral barrel for one year. From old vines planted in 1973. Notes of apple and apple skins with mouthcoating acidity.

acres 18 - cases 3,000
Fertilizers compost, biodynamic compost, cover crops, manure, organic fertilizer
Plant protection biodynamic preparations, organic
Weed control animal grazing, mechanical, manual
Yeasts spontaneous fermentation
Grapes purchase 35%
Certification some of the vineyards are certified organic, some of the vineyards are certified biodynamic

LOMPOC

AMPELOS CELLARS

312 N 9th Street - tel. (805) 736-9957
www.ampeloscellars.net - rebecca@ampeloscellars.com

PEOPLE - Danish born Peter Work and his wife Rebecca are now excited about converting to Regenerative Organic certification. Ampelos has scaled back on production to focus more on its estate wines and high demand for the Funky Town Carignane. They've moved that wine from their Funky Town label to the main Ampelos brand label. The 20+ year old vineyard is in now its prime (and for sale).

VINEYARDS - The estate sits on tierra loam, tierra sandy loam and botella clay loam in a unique spot in the Sta. Rita Hills. Already certified organic, Ampelos is in the process of becoming Regenerative Organic. They have plans to expand their vineyard over the next couple of years. They continue to purchase fruit from Martian Ranch (certified biodynamic) in Los Alamos. Carignane comes from Santa Ynez Vineyard.

WINES - The two are enthusiastic about the extensive clone diversity on their 82 acre estate.

Sta. Rita Hills Rosé of Syrah 2023 EVERYDAY WINE ● 191 cases; 22 $ - 🍷 - A blend of Syrah (75%) with Grenache (18%) and Riesling (7%). Pretty pink color with strawberry, watermelon, and pomegranate notes and vibrant full mouth acidity.

Santa Barbara County Phi Viognier 2023 ○ 316 cases; 29 $ - 🍷 - Viognier from Martian Vineyard (89%) and the estate vineyard (11%) was picked late, allowing for good hang time. Vibrant and juicy with notes of peaches, pineapple, white flowers, and lime sorbet.

Sta. Rita Hills Delta Grenache 2020 ● 168 cases; 39 $ - 🛢 - Deep ruby red hues lead to strawberry, cherry, cinnamon, crushed granite, and floral notes. The wine has textured tannins and a juicy finish.

acres 25 - cases 5,000
Fertilizers compost, cover crops, manure, organic fertilizer
Plant protection sulfur, organic
Weed control animal grazing, manual
Yeasts spontaneous fermentation
Grapes purchase 10%
Certification some of the vineyards are certified organic, some of the vineyards are certified biodynamic

SANTA BARBARA

AU BON CLIMAT

813 Anacapa Street, Unit 5B - tel. (805) 963-7999
www.aubonclimat.com - tastingroom@aubonclimat.com

PEOPLE - Founded in 1982 by the legendary Jim Clendenen (1953-2021), the celebrated, iconic producer is known for Burgundian style Chardonnay and Pinot Noir. Isabelle and Knox, Jim's children, concentrate on sales and production. Jim Adelman has been the manager since the 1990s. Winemaker Sarah Atwood joined in 2022. All remain focused on creating signature wines, carrying on Clendenen's classic style.

VINEYARDS - The list of vineyards the winery buys grapes reads like a hit parade of Sta. Rita Hills and Central Coast sites. Star growers include Bien Nacido, its primary vineyard source. (Its block K is considered a California Grand Cru). Others are Sanford & Benedict, Solomon Hills, Talley and more. It sold its own 20 acre Le Bon Climat in 2022 (due to disease), preferring to buy from star growers in the region. It continues to own its 13 acre estate in Los Alamos Valley.

WINES - Au Bon Climat's four tiers use classic Old World techniques in the cellar, including François Frères barrels (popular in Burgundy) and hand punch downs. Whole cluster ranges from zero to 100 percent, depending on the wine.

Santa Maria Valley Knox Alexander Estate Bottled Pinot Noir 2021 ● 1,200 cases; 65 $ - ⊞ - Named after Knox, sourced from top lots in Santa Maria Valley. Aromas of Bing cherry, cranberry, rose hip, and dark chocolate, with Santa Maria spice.

Santa Maria Valley Nuits Blanches au Bouge Chardonnay 2022 ○ 1,000 cases; 50 $ - ⊞ - Aged two years in French oak. Whole cluster pressed, barrel fermented, 100% malo. From Bien Nacido's K Block. Find vibrant acidity, rich texture, and minerality. With lemon zest, grapefruit, and kumquat notes.

Santa Maria Valley La Bauge Au-dessus Pinot Noir 2020 ● 400 cases; 35 $ - ⊞ - From Bien Nacido and Le Bon Climat Vineyards. Red fruit, dried flowers, hibiscus, herbaceous, bright cherry notes. Offers great texture, balanced tannins, and acidity.

acres 13 - cases 65,000
Fertilizers organic fertilizer, synthetic fertilizer
Plant protection synthetic pesticides
Weed control n/a
Yeasts commercial cultured yeasts
Grapes purchase 70%
Certification some of the vineyards are certified organic

LOS OLIVOS

BECKMEN VINEYARDS

2670 Ontiveros Road - tel. (805) 688-8664
www.beckmenvineyards.com - info@beckmenvineyards.com

PEOPLE - Acclaimed for pioneering vineyards in Ballard Canyon specializing in Rhone varieties, Beckmen was also the first to bottle Grenache and Grenache Blanc in Santa Barbara County. Steve Beckmen manages the vineyard and makes the wine with a great team. Foreman Jorge Ruiz has led the crews for 27 years. As leaders in biodynamic farming (the first to be certified in Santa Barbara County), they offer a self guided tour to explain biodynamics.

VINEYARDS - They have two estates-one in Ballard Canyon and one in Los Olivos District. In Los Olivos, their first estate, with 24 acres planted, has gravelly clay loam soils. The Ballard Canyon Purisima Mountain (certified biodynamic), with 100 planted acres, is primarily clay and limestone with some sandy and gravel as well. They are adding more white varieties with an eye toward producing skin contact wines.

WINES - Their Cuvee le Bec, Syrahs and rosé are perennial favorites. This year, they released their first ever Graciano.

🔝 Santa Ynez Valley Sauvignon Blanc 2023 SLOW WINE ○ 1,400 cases; 30 $ - 🍽 - Sourced from an original block planted in 1997. From limestone soils in Ballard Canyon's Purisima Mountain. Vibrant tropical citrus aromatics with good acidity, lime skin texture, and good midpalate weight.

Santa Ynez Valley Grenache 2022 ● 705 cases; 39 $ - ⊞ - From three blocks on Purisima Mountain, including two from blocks planted in 1990. Transparent cherry red color with pretty cherry and red fruit aromas and a good acid/tannin structure. A very drinkable, enjoyable wine with a texture but fresh finish.

Ballard Canyon Purisima Mountain Vineyard Block 6 Syrah 2021 ● 503 cases; 85 $ - ⊞ - Block 6, planted in 1999, is at top of Purisima Mountain on a south, southwest facing slope. Small, intense berries. A structured wine with dark fruit aromas.

acres 130 - cases 16,000
Fertilizers biodynamic compost, cover crops, manure
Plant protection sulfur, biodynamic preparations, organic
Weed control animal grazing, mechanical, manual
Yeasts spontaneous fermentation, commercial cultured yeasts
Grapes purchase 3%
Certification biodynamic

SANTA MARIA

BIEN NACIDO

4705 Santa Maria Mesa Road - tel. (805) 318-6640
www.biennacidoestate.com - info@biennacidoestate.com

PEOPLE - Owned and operated by the Miller family, the world renowned, 500 acre Santa Maria Valley vineyard celebrated its 50th anniversary in 2023, and in 2024, opened the Gatehouse, inviting the public to visit for the first time. Winemaking under their own brand started in 2007. Anthony Avila has been the winemaker since 2019. Guests can now sit in the Adobe inspired tasting room and admire the legendary vineyards whose coveted grapes are made into A list wines.

VINEYARDS - After 25 years, long time vineyard manaager Chris Hammell announced his retirement following the 2024 harvest. Replanting is underway, targeting removal of blocks beginning with the benchland, where the original vines were planted. The 50 acres of old vine Chardonnay and six acres of X Block of Syrah, planted in the 1970s, are all still vibrant, as are the 20 acres of Z Block of Syrah planted in 1999.

WINES - The wines transparently express the varied sites, microclimates, elevations and exposures.

Santa Maria Valley Bien Nacido Estate Pinot Noir 2022 SLOW WINE ● 704 cases; 75 $ - Aged 16 months in French oak (45% new). 10% whole cluster. A blend of all the estate Pinot Noir blocks, including four soil types. Savory black cherry and raspberry aromas. On the palate, a briary character and textured tannins.

Santa Maria Valley Bien Nacido Estate Chardonnay 2022 O 436 cases; 60 $ - Aged 12 months in French oak and 5 five in stainless steel. From vines planted in 1973. Fresh acidity and notes of red apple, citrus, chamomile, and toasty minerality on the palate.

Santa Maria Valley Bien Nacido Estate Syrah 2022 ● 133 cases; 60 $ - Aged 16 months in oak (30% new) barrels and puncheons. Partial whole cluster (40%). Black fruits, leather, chocolate, and tobacco with a floral pop of white flowers on the nose. Mouthwatering acidity.

acres 500 - cases 1,250
Fertilizers compost, cover crops, organic fertilizer
Plant protection sulfur, organic
Weed control animal grazing, mechanical, manual
Yeasts spontaneous fermentation, commercial cultured yeasts
Grapes 100% owned
Certification none

LOMPOC

CAMINS 2 DREAMS

1520 E Chestnut Ct., Unit C & D - tel. (805) 741-7047
www.camins2dreams.com - info@camins2dreams.com

PEOPLE - Tara Gomez, the first Native American female winemaker, met Catalonian born Mireia Taribo at J.Lohr in Paso Robles. An immediate friendship blossomed into a romance. In 2017, they decided to launch their own project crafting small lot wines from the Sta. Rita Hills focusing on underrepresented varieties. They started working with Mencia in 2023 and are planning to work with Aligoté, Cabernet Pfeffer and Trousseau.

VINEYARDS - For years, Tara and Mireia have wanted to work with only organic vineyards and, beginning in 2024, they are. They work primarily with vineyards in the Sta. Rita Hills with its sandy silt and clay loam soils, including Christy & Wise (certified biodynamic), Donnachadh (certified organic), Fiddlestix and Hines on Mail Road. They also buy certified organic San Benito County grapes from Siletto and regeneratively farmed Paicines Ranch.

WINES - The two believe wine is made in the vineyard and terroir is expressed in their wines through minimal intervention.

Paicines Paicines Ranch Grenache 2023 SLOW WINE ● 75 cases; 38 $ - Aged 10 months in neutral French oak. A bright magenta color, the wine has aromas of candied fruits, candied orange, and violets. Grippy tannins. Finishes with a fresh lift.

Sta. Rita Hills Donnachadh Vineyard Syrah 2022 ● 120 cases; 46 $ - Aged 10 months in neutral French oak followed by a year in bottle. Aromas of dark fruit, dried herbs, hibiscus tea, baking spices and coffee. Medium bodied with rounded tannins.

Sta. Rita Hills Fiddlestix Vineyard Grüner Veltliner 2023 O 200 cases; 35 $ - Aged 10 months in neutral oak (80%) and stainless steel (20%). Aromas of ripe apple and an almost viscous Riesling like nose. In the mouth, round and juicy with good acidity.

acres 0 - cases 1,400
Fertilizers compost, biodynamic compost, cover crops, manure
Plant protection sulfur, biodynamic preparations, organic
Weed control animal grazing, mechanical, manual
Yeasts spontaneous fermentation
Grapes purchase 100%
Certification some of the vineyards are certified organic, some of the vineyards are certified biodynamic

BUELLTON

CENTRAL COAST GROUP PROJECT / SCOTTY BOY / L'ARGE D'OOR

53 Industrial Way - tel. (805) 874-2316
www.ccgpwines.com - info@ccgpwines.com

PEOPLE - When Scott Sampler started CCGP in 2021, the goal was to make vineyard designate, mostly single varietal wines with long extended maceration and ageing (four to eight years) in neutral oak. They now have 10 vintages from 2012 to 2023 in barrel. L'Arge d'Oor wines are only aged for one to three years. Scotty-Boy! Fine Wines & Super-Coolers are blends with long skin ferments and mixes of carbonic and barrel fermentations.

VINEYARDS - Scott sources from different vineyards, always looking for organically farmed vineyards or sustainable vineyards that do not use synthetic herbicides. After yields decreased due to drought at Las Hermanas Vineyard (certified organic), he got Grenache Blanc from Zaca Mesa. He also buys from Coquelicot, Larner and Spear Vineyards (all certified organic), as well as Shokrian Vineyard (in the three year process of becoming organic certified).

WINES - CCCP wines are vin de avant garde, extreme wines. L'Arge d'Oor wines are vin de garde, wines to keep. Scotty-Boy! Fine Wines & Super-Coolers are vin de soif, wines to drink now.

● Santa Barbara County Scotty-Boy! Klong Bursts & Fizz Fuzz Pet Nat of Pinot Grigio 2022 ⊛ 550 cases; 36 $ - 🍷 - Spends two weeks on the skins. Plum juice colored. Aromas of rhubarb and pomegranate. Super fresh and enjoyable.

Santa Barbara County L'Arge D'Oor Sangiovese 2019 ● 50 cases; 45 $ - 🍷 - Aged 42 months in neutral oak. From Coquelicot Vineyard. Spends 153 days on skins. This wine has character. Light yet complex with aromas of dark red and black fruits, and baking spice notes that continue on the palate.

Ballard Canyon CCGP Captain Kierk AKA the Knightwalker Syrah 2015 ● 22 cases; 129 $ - ⊞ - 30% whole cluster. From Larner Vineyard. 273 days on the skins and five years in barrel. Aromas of rose petals, blackberries, caramel, and warm brown spices. Flavors of spiced plum, lots of acidity, and lightly grippy tannins.

acres 0 - cases 4,500
Fertilizers compost, biodynamic compost, cover crops, manure, organic fertilizer
Plant protection sulfur, synthetic pesticides, organic
Weed control mechanical, manual
Yeasts spontaneous fermentation
Grapes purchase 100%
Certification some of the vineyards are certified organic

LOMPOC

CHANIN WINE

300 N 12th Street - tel. (805) 345-6544
www.chaninwine.com - info@chaninwine.com

PEOPLE - Learning from the masters, Gavin Chanin started as a harvest intern at celebrated Au Bon Climat (Burgundian) and Qupé (famous for Rhones) and rose to assistant winemaker. After these apprenticeships with star winemakers Jim Clendenen and Bob Lindquist, he launched his winery in 2007, focusing on single vineyard designate Chardonnay and Pinot Noir. In 2023, he won a prestigious top 100 winery in the world award from Wine and Spirits—for the seventh time.

VINEYARDS - The vineyards he buys from represent the region's finest. He seeks out old vines in coastal regions. The Los Alamos vines in Santa Barbara County are 25+ years old and sit on sandy soils at high elevation (900ft). The Bien Nacido vines in Santa Maria Valley were planted in 1973, and the Sanford & Benedict date from 1972. Each wine reflects its vineyard's unique terroir, emphasizing geography, geology, and climate.

WINES - Terroir driven and unfiltered, they express elegance and finesse, drawing upon classic winemaking techniques.

Santa Barbara County Los Alamos Chardonnay 2021 ○ 725 cases; 50 $ - ⊞ - Fermented and aged in French oak barrels (15% new). After 15 months on lees, they are racked, lightly fined, and bottled unfiltered. Find aromas of lemon, white flowers, grapefruit, and apricot, with almond flavor, texture, and finesse.

Sta. Rita Hills Zotovich Vineyard Pinot Noir 2022 ● 640 cases; 67 $ - ⊞ - Aged 16 months in French oak barrels (15% new). Grapes fermented (15% whole cluster) with twice daily punchdowns until dry. Fresh and bright. Presents light red and black cherry, rose petal, hibiscus tea, and white pepper.

Sta. Rita Hills Sanford & Benedict Vineyard Pinot Noir 2021 ● 1,900 cases; 70 $ - ⊞ - Grapes underwent a four day cold soak with 1-3 punch downs daily. 45% whole cluster. Aged 16 months French oak barrels (18% new). Bright and fresh with red fruits, blood orange, mint and sweet spice.

acres 0 - cases 5,500
Fertilizers compost, cover crops, manure, organic fertilizer
Plant protection sulfur, biodynamic preparations, synthetic pesticides
Weed control animal grazing, mechanical, manual
Yeasts spontaneous fermentation, selected indigenous yeasts
Grapes purchase 100%
Certification some of the vineyards are certified organic, some of the vineyards are certified biodynamic

LOS ALAMOS

CLEMENTINE CARTER WINES

388 Bell Street - tel. (805) 344-1900
www.clementinecarterwines.com - sonja@clementinecarterwines.com

PEOPLE - Winemaker Sonja Magdevski, a former Fulfbright scholar and journalist, has combined her two labels Casa Dumetz (Burgundian varieties) and Clementine Carter (Rhone varieties) under the Clementine Carter name. It's the name of her favorite Western character. In addition to making wine for 20 years, she hosts a long running speaker series every Friday night in her tasting room in Los Alamos.

VINEYARDS - Sonja works with 15 local vineyards, buying much fruit from certified organic vineyards including Christy & Wise, Kimsey, LaBarge, Larner, Robert Rae, and Two Wolves. Another source is her section at Zaca Mesa. New on her list: Syrah from Larner Vineyard and Roussanne from Robert Rae. Picpoul Blanc comes from Nolan and John Sebastiani Vineyards. Some of the wines (not featured here) are grown with herbicide.

WINES - Magdevski has four concrete eggs and enjoys exploring the textural effects they create.

Sta. Rita Hills Mourvedre 2022 ● 100 cases; 52 $ - ⊞ - Aged in old barrels for 10 months. Partial whole cluster (50%). From Robert Rae Vineyard. Her inaugural vintage. A lighter style of Mourvedre with chilled blueberry, earthy notes and savory freshness.

Santa Barbara County Grenache Blanc 2023 ○ 225 cases; 44 $ - ⌂ ⊞ - A blend from two vineyards–Kimsey and Zaca Mesa. Each was vinified differently–the Kimsey in concrete while the Zaca Mesa was skin fermented for two weeks. Pineapple citrus notes open to a wine with roundness on the palate but also bright acidity and a fresh finish.

Ballard Canyon Larner Vineyard Grenache 2022 ● 75 cases; 52 $ - ⊞ - Aged in neutral barrels for 10 months. Whole cluster (100%). The wine is a fuchsia color and offers a beautiful herbal bouquet of aromas and spice notes on the palate. Textured, lightly drying tannins and lingering acidity that tingles on the palate.

acres 0 - cases 3,000
Fertilizers biodynamic compost, cover crops, organic fertilizer
Plant protection sulfur, biodynamic preparations, synthetic pesticides, organic
Weed control animal grazing, mechanical, manual
Yeasts spontaneous fermentation
Grapes purchase 100%
Certification some of the vineyards are certified organic, some of the vineyards are certified biodynamic

LOS OLIVOS

COQUELICOT ESTATE VINEYARD

2884 Grand Avenue - tel. (805) 688-1500
www.coquelicotwines.com - info@coquelicotwines.com

PEOPLE - Inspired by the red poppies of France, hotelier restaurateur Bernard Rosenson founded Coquelicot ("Ko–Klee–Ko"), which is French for poppies. The all estate producer is now run by his children–sommelier Jonathan, Elissa, and Candice. The family also owns Mirabelle Inn and the Michelin recognized First & Oak restaurant in Solvang. Its tasting room is in Los Olivos. Veteran winemaker Mike Roth crafts handmade, limited production wines.

VINEYARDS - Established 1997, its 94 acre, Los Olivos District estate sits on Ballard gravelly, fine sandy loam soil, fostering deep roots and varietal character. Its temperate microclimate, shaped by coastal breezes from east-west mountain ranges, prolongs the growing season. Sustainable and organic methods enrich soil vitality and grape quality. The estate was certified organic in 2015. It also sells grapes to other wineries.

WINES - The wines are made with minimal intervention (and are aged in mostly neutral French oak), ensuring genuine, unmanipulated flavor.

Los Olivos District Estate Vineyard Reserve Cabernet Franc 2019 ● 125 cases; 75 $ - ⊞ - Aged two years in oak (10% new). Deep garnet in color with aromas of blackberry, violet, spice, and black cherry. On the palate, soft tannins, juicy blackberry and cherry, and a touch of spice.

Los Olivos District Estate Vineyard Carbonic Sangiovese 2022 ● 375 cases; 35 $ - ⊞ - Carbonic fermented whole cluster Sangiovese, aged for one year in neutral oak. With a light and chillable character, and aromas of a bowl of juicy ripe cherries. Good texture.

Los Olivos District Estate Vineyard Beton Blanc 2023 ○ 125 cases; 35 $ - ⊞ - A zippy blend of Grüner (40%) Riesling (40%) Sauvignon Blanc (20%). Aromatic wine with winter citrus, apple, and hints of minerality. On the palate, warm tropical fruit, apricot and citrus flavors, beautifully long aged on the skins. Good mouthfeel.

acres 58 - cases 4,000
Fertilizers cover crops, organic fertilizer
Plant protection organic
Weed control mechanical, manual
Yeasts spontaneous fermentation
Grapes 100% owned
Certification organic

LOS OLIVOS

DEMETRIA ESTATE

6701 Foxen Canyon Road - tel. (805) 471-6491
www.demetriaestate.com - inquiries@demetriaestate.com

PEOPLE - Rhone wine producers John and Sandra Zahoudanis bought the 213 acre property in 2005 to create a family winery honoring John's Greek heritage. They named it after their daughter, Demetria. (Demeter is the Greek goddess of agriculture.) Ryan Roark joined Demetria as vineyard manager in 2019 and became winemaker in 2021. Emily Myers is the assistant winemaker. The tasting room has a spacious, welcoming deck, an idyllic and relaxing spot, popular with visitors.

VINEYARDS - Pioneering Andrew Murray planted the original vines in 1990 at 1,100 to 1,450 feet of elevation. Former winemaker Mike Roth recommended converting to biodynamic farming, which was adopted in 2005 (though the estate is not certified). Grenache is planted along the long approach road to the winery. 2022 was a hot year but a good year for these blocks, so Roark, bottled the Grenache, calling it "O Dromos," which means "the road" in Greek.

WINES - Demetria specializes in small lot and limited release wines made from vines growing on hillsides at high elevation.

● Santa Ynez Valley Cuvée Constantine Red Rhone Blend 2021 ● 475 cases; 60 $ - 🍽 - A Grenache dominant GSM blend with Mourvèdre (10%), and Syrah (10%). Fermented in concrete. Aromas of blue and purple fruits, violets and lavender. Fresh with textured tannins and mouthwatering acidity.

Santa Ynez Valley Rosé of Grenache 2023 ● 898 cases; 35 $ - 🍽 - Sourced from a slope that ripens at different rates–hence, three to four different picks–all direct press. Light in color and high in acidity. Fresh and elegant with red fruit and stone fruit notes.

Santa Ynez Valley Cuvée Papou White Rhone Blend 2022 O White Rhone Blend; 528 cases; 45 $ - 🍽 - Papou (which means "grandfather" in Greek) is an homage to John's father. The blend is Roussanne (41%), Grenache Blanc (32%) and Marsanne (27%). Floral and stone fruit aromas, a full bodied, viscous mouthfeel, and intense acidity.

acres 42 - cases 9,000
Fertilizers compost, biodynamic compost, cover crops, manure
Plant protection sulfur, biodynamic preparations, organic
Weed control animal grazing, mechanical, manual
Yeasts spontaneous fermentation
Grapes purchase 30%
Certification none

SANTA MARIA

DISKO WINES $

5230 Tepusquet Road
www.diskowines.com - sean@diskowines.com

PEOPLE - Sean Hogan made his first wine while interning with his uncle, Mike Roth (Lo-Fi Wines), during a gap year. In 2015, after some college, Hogan became Roth's assistant at Coquelicot Wines (where Roth is the winemaker) and launched Disko wines in 2020. He's grown his brand to eight releases. He's thinking about a possible second label in the future for more ageworthy wines. Always cost sensitive, Hogan dropped some prices this year.

VINEYARDS - Hogan buys grapes for nearly all of his grapes from one site in the oak grasslands of Los Olivos District AVA. The vineyard is at a higher elevation than is typical in Los Olivos and benefits from a slightly cooler climate. Oak trees play a major part in the vineyard ecosystem. The soil is Chamise shaley loam. He also buys a small amount of grapes from a tiny vineyard called Old Oak Meadow that he farms himself. Both vineyards use only organic approved materials.

WINES - Hogan makes fun, easy going natural, drink now wines, mostly for young wine drinkers.

● Santa Barbara County Sangiovese 2022 EVERYDAY WINE ● 225 cases; 30 $ - 🍽 - An extravagant floral nose of dried rose and dark cherry go with a structured palate of gentian, dark cherry and cassis.

Santa Barbara County Chardonnay 2023 O 125 cases; 32 $ - 🍽 - Shows pear, apple and honeysuckle on the nose while the palate of green apple and grapefruit is set off nicely by a faint yeasty note.

Santa Barbara County Gamay Noir 2023 ● 275 cases; 28 $ - 🍽 - A generous nose of rose, red cherry and strawberry. The palate reveals loamy strawberry and red plum with plum skin tannins.

acres 0 - cases 1,200
Fertilizers organic fertilizer
Plant protection sulfur, organic
Weed control mechanical
Yeasts spontaneous fermentation
Grapes purchase 100%
Certification none

LOMPOC

DOMAINE DE LA CÔTE

1712 Industrial Way, Suite B - tel. (805) 695-4119
www.domainedelacote.com - wine@domainedelacote.com

 In a little more than a decade, the team has risen to prominence, producing wines of exceptional quality.

PEOPLE - The renowned collaboration of producers Sashi Moorman and Raj Parr is a benchmark in the region. Moorman planted the estate in 2007 for Evening Land Wines. In 2011, he partnered with star sommelier Raj Parr, to take over the unique cool climate site to make nuanced Pinot Noirs, planted at high density. A skilled crew oversees the vines, protecting them from weather and disease challenges. The team is also researching new robust clones from seed.

VINEYARDS - Moorman partnered with vineyardist Chris King to plant only California clones Mt Eden, Swan and Calera in five blocks which cascade down a steep hill on the chilly far western edge of the Sta. Rita Hills AVA. The plantings are southeast and south facing, winding around the hill to increased ocean effects from the nearby Pacific. Soils are diatomaceous earth and shale from a former seabed. The vines are planted at 4,000 to 7,000 vines per acre.

WINES - The five Pinot Noir bottlings, express their contiguous vineyards with tiny Sous Le Chêne being the most unique.

TOP Sta. Rita Hills Sous Le Chêne Pinot Noir 2023 ● 100 cases; 165 $ - ⊞ - On the nose, an effusive, complex nose of flowers, grass and herbs. The palate is graceful, showing slightly candied red cherry and strawberry in fine harmony with loam, oak, light spice and refined tannins. The wine is already fully formed.
Sta. Rita Hills La Côte Pinot Noir 2023 ● 661 cases; 155 $ - ⊞ - Shows intoxicating aromatics of dark cherry, red flowers and jasmine. On the palate, deep flavors of cherry, dried strawberry, dried herbs and licorice. The wine is earthy, saline, structured and surprisingly generous at this moment of release.
Sta. Rita Hills Memorius Pinot Noir 2023 ● 461 cases; 100 $ - ⊞ - Aromas of briny olive, dark cherry and smoked paprika. Flavors are bright of mulberry, bitter cherry and bay leaf with young stemmy tannins.

---

acres 25 - cases 2,576
Fertilizers compost, organic fertilizer
Plant protection sulfur, organic
Weed control mechanical
Yeasts spontaneous fermentation
Grapes 100% owned
Certification none

LOS OLIVOS

DRAGONETTE CELLARS

2445 Alamo Pintado Avenue - tel. (805) 693-0077
www.dragonettecellars.com - info@dragonettecellars.com

PEOPLE - The year 2025 marks the winery's 20th anniversary since the first commercial vintage. The team is solid with founding brothers John and Steve Dragonette and Brandon Sparks-Gillis, along with cellarmaster Brian Sparks (who has been there for a decade). Recently, they reduced the weight of their bottles, shaving 150 grams off for the 2022 vintages. They buy glass only from California suppliers, lowering their carbon footprint both in weight and in transportation.

VINEYARDS - The team buys grapes from 16 vineyards across the Santa Ynez Valley. For more than 12 years, they have been pushing vineyards to stop using herbicides and move towards organic farming. There are no herbicides in any of the blocks at any of the vineyards that Dragonette purchases. They have added more blocks at Bentrock Vineyard, Radian and Rita's Crown. After buying for 12 years from Stolpman Vineyard, they made their first single vineyard Stolpman Syrah in 2022.

WINES - Dragonette produces single vineyard designate wines, expressing the diversity of climate and soils in the Santa Ynez Valley.

TOP Sta. Rita Hills Sanford & Benedict Vineyard Pinot Noir 2022 ● 300 cases; 85 $ - ⊞ - Aged 17 months on the lees in oak (25% new). From blocks planted in 1971 and 1999, farmed organically since 2018. Partial whole cluster (10%). Cherry cola, as well as flowers, spice, and a subtle earth note.
Santa Barbara County Duvarita Vineyard Chardonnay 2022 ○ 95 cases; 55 $ - ⊞ - Aged 16 months on the lees with no stirring or sulfur. Whole cluster pressed. Certified biodynamic farming. The sandy soils of Duvarita add to the pretty aromatics of the wine which is light, delicate, elegant, and energetic.
Happy Canyon Grimms Bluff Vineyard Sauvignon Blanc 2022 ○ 150 cases; 60 $ - ⊞ - Aged on the lees in neutral cigar barrels. From head trained, biodynamic Sauvignon Blanc. Clean and vibrant with grapefruit and lemon notes. Textured with a long finish.

---

acres 0 - cases 6,500
Fertilizers compost, biodynamic compost, cover crops, manure, organic fertilizer
Plant protection sulfur, synthetic pesticides, organic
Weed control animal grazing, mechanical, manual
Yeasts spontaneous fermentation
Grapes purchase 100%
Certification some of the vineyards are certified organic, some of the vineyards are certified biodynamic

CAMARILLO

DUSTY NABOR WINES

1330 Flynn Road Unit E - tel. (818) 917-3716
www.dustynaborwines.com - dusty@naborwines.com

PEOPLE - A triathlete and former pro motocross racer, Dusty Nabor understands pushing it to extremes. But, as the sole employee of his winery, he knows that processing 35 tons of grapes and making 1,750 cases of wine is a lot. He makes single vineyard designates, zeroing in on vines in the southwest corner of the Sta. Rita Hills. There he buys Chardonnay, Grenache, Pinot Noir and Syrah. He still dabbles with vineyards in a few other areas of Santa Ynez Valley.

VINEYARDS - After a long wait, Dusty is getting access to the fruit that he wants. He returned to Bentrock, Fiddlestix, Peake Ranch and Radian vineyards. Grenache and Syrah from Peake Ranch are coming. He currently buys from J & K and Kimsey Vineyards (certified organic) in Ballard Canyon. (Kimsey recently sold so the future is unclear.) He returned to Vogelzang Vineyard in Happy Canyon in 2024 after his last vintage there in 2019.

WINES - Wines are mostly sold to his mailing list. Single vineyard designate wines made with minimal intervention that are nuanced and elegant.

🔝 Ballard Canyon Kimsey Syrah 2021 ● 100 cases; 45 $ - 🍷 - Aged 18-20 months in 500L puncheons. Whole cluster (100%). Dark fruit and floral aromas, as well as white pepper, spice, and herbal notes. The tannins are velvety. A long finish with lingering acidity.
Sta. Rita Hills Spear Vineyard Grenache 2022 ● 50 cases; 35 $ - 🍷 - Aged in barrel. Whole cluster (100%). Raspberry, blackberry, and violet aromas, followed by herbaceous and mineral notes on palate. A rich midpalate cut by a lifted note and juicy acidity. Texture and grip without being heavy.
Ballard Canyon J+K Vineyard Viognier 2022 ○ 50 cases; 33 $ - 🍷 - Aged 10 months in oak (25% new). Barrel fermented on the lees. Very bright with tropical citrus, white flowers, stone fruits, toasted almond and honey notes. Textured on the palate with chalky acidity and a long, mouthwatering finish.

acres 0 - cases 1,000
Fertilizers compost, cover crops, organic fertilizer, synthetic fertilizer
Plant protection sulfur, synthetic pesticides, organic
Weed control mechanical, manual
Yeasts spontaneous fermentation
Grapes purchase 100%
Certification some of the vineyards are certified organic

LOS OLIVOS

EISLYNN WINES

6701 Foxen Canyon Road - tel. (805) 364-4393
www.eislynnwines.com - emily@eislynnwines.com

PEOPLE - Assistant winemaker at Demetria Estate and Roark Wine Company, Emily Myers made the first vintage of her own wine in 2021, using her uncommon middle name, Eislynn, for the label. The origins of that name came from her mother, who, while pregnant with her, read a smutty romance with an Eislynn in it. Emily considers Eislynn her alter ego and a place to have fun with wine. She made Syrah in 2021, skipped 2022 and added Sauvignon Blanc in 2023.

VINEYARDS - Making a small amount of wine for a third label means access to fruit will come from vineyards Emily is already working with. For the Syrah, she got the grapes from Demetria Vineyard in Los Olivos and Alondra de los Prados in Santa Ynez. Ryan Roark farms both vineyards and is said to practice biodynamics. For the Sauvignon Blanc, the grapes come from White Barn Vineyard in Santa Ynez. For a third wine, Emily would like to find a variety she is not already working with.

WINES - Leveraging her connections to grapes in two winemaking day jobs, Myers makes low intervention wines that are affordable and fun to drink.

🔝 Santa Ynez Valley White Barn Vineyard Sauvignon Blanc 2023 EVERYDAY WINE ○ 90 cases; 29 $ - 🍷 - Aged for seven months in neutral oak. An entry level skin contact wine. The juice spends four days on the skins. The wine has a beautiful nose with big tropical, lime and floral aromatics. On the palate, the wine has chalky acidity and a very long finish.
Santa Ynez Valley Syrah 2021 ● 90 cases; 36 $ - 🍷 - Aged 11 months in neutral oak. Two thirds of the Syrah comes from Demetria and one third from Alondra de los Prados. The destemmed fruit, with 5%-10% stems added back, undergoes gentle fermentation in a one ton vessel with no pumpovers or punchdowns. The fresh wine has aromas of a fruit compote with notes of pomegranate, black cherry, and blackberry and fruit leather on leather on the palate.

acres 0 - cases 200
Fertilizers compost, biodynamic compost, cover crops, manure
Plant protection sulfur, biodynamic preparations, organic
Weed control animal grazing, mechanical, manual
Yeasts spontaneous fermentation
Grapes purchase 100%
Certification none

LOS ALAMOS

ENTITY OF DELIGHT $

PO Box 453 - tel. (707) 690-8184 - 707-690-8184
www.entityofdelight.com - crosby@entityofdelight.com

PEOPLE - Raised in Atlanta, natural winemaker Cro€sby Swinchatt spent five years working globally before starting his own label in 2022. His experience took him to Sea Smoke, Littorai, Pride Mountain Vineyards, and Lo-Fi in California and to Antica Terra in Oregon. He's also worked in New Zealand at Oyster Bay and Burn Cottage, and in Australia at Mt. Eden. Crosby's journey led him to create his own fun and enjoyable wines.

VINEYARDS - Seeking organic vineyards can be challenging, but Crosby sources exclusively from organically farmed vineyards along the Central Coast. He buys Chardonnay from the organically certified Spear Vineyards in Sta. Rita Hills. Organic and biodynamic vineyards (uncertified) include Bassi Vineyard (Pinot Gris and Pinot Noir) in Avila Beach in the SLO Coast AVA and Demetria (Grenache and Syrah) in the warmer Santa Ynez Valley AVA.

WINES - Crosby's wines, at around 12% ABV, have a light, bright structure. He aims to make acid driven wines that reflect their beautiful sites.

SLO Coast Bassi Pinot Noir 2022 ● 70 cases; 35 $ - From a beautiful vineyard tucked away in Avila Beach. Bright and lively. On skins for six days and fermented in barrel. With a bouquet of cherry, rose petal, and hints of leather.

Santa Maria Valley Rosata Pinot Gris 2022 170 cases; 30 $ - This rosé undergoes two weeks of skin contact during fermentation and aged 8 months in neutral barrels. An easy drinking wine with cherry, strawberry, citrus, and saline notes. Refreshing and fun, with a mouthwatering finish.

Sta. Rita Hills Spear Vineyard Chardonnay 2021 ○ 75 cases; 35 $ - White fruit and bright acid. Fermented and aged for 10 months in neutral oak. It's fresh and textured with aromas of fresh apple, stone fruits, and citrus.

---

acres 0 - cases 700
Fertilizers compost, biodynamic compost, cover crops, manure, organic fertilizer
Plant protection sulfur, biodynamic preparations, organic
Weed control animal grazing, mechanical, manual
Yeasts spontaneous fermentation
Grapes purchase 100%
Certification some of the vineyards are certified organic

GAVIOTA

FOLDED HILLS

2323 Old Coast Highway - tel. (805) 694-8086
www.foldedhills.com - wine@foldedhills.com

 A true farm to table winery, the Busch's have taken this property to new heights, with Osbourne's help.

PEOPLE - Rhone wine vintners and ranchers Kim and Andy Busch (of Anheuser-Busch) found their 600 acre heaven in the Santa Ynez Valley, north of Santa Barbara. The ranch is complete with a polo field (Andy's passion), year round animals, and solar powered, net positive operations. They have two tasting rooms—one on the Homestead ranch and another in Montecito. Kim's passion for Grenache rosé led to naming it in homage to Lilly Anheuser (1844-1928).

VINEYARDS - Planted in 2015, the certified organic estate spans two sites with 15 acres planted to vines. The Hillside vineyard sits on sandy loam soils and limestone and grows Grenache and Syrah. Creekside vineyard, with clay loam soils, grows whites—Clairette Blanche, Grenache Blanc, and Marsanne. Onsite compost supports vineyard fertilization needs. Sheep provide weed control. Another five acres grow row crops growing produce and fruit.

WINES - Renowned winemaker Angela Osbourne creates small lot wines using minimal intervention.

Santa Ynez Valley Lilly Rosé of Grenache 2023 900 cases; 35 $ - The wine, named in homage to Lilly Anheuser, is whole cluster (94%) and neutral French oak (67%) foot trod with native fermentation. It is pale pink with fresh aromas of nectarine, strawberry, and grapefruit. Plus a vibrant acidity.

Santa Ynez Valley August White Blend 2021 ○ 2,500 cases; 40 $ - This light-bodied wine, a blend of Grenache Blanc (86%) and Viognier (14%), is aged in neutral French oak and stainless steel. With citrus, honeysuckle, and pear aromas, and bright acidity and minerality.

Santa Ynez Valley Grant Vineyard Grenache 2021 ● 150 cases; 48 $ - Comes from the Golden Eagle and Ulysses estate blocks. It is 100% de-stemmed and foot-trod. Aged 12 months in French oak barrels (9% new). It has great texture and depth, with flavors of cranberry, pomegranate, dried herbs, and spice.

---

acres 15 - cases 6,000
Fertilizers biodynamic compost, cover crops, manure, organic fertilizer
Plant protection biodynamic preparations, organic
Weed control animal grazing, mechanical
Yeasts spontaneous fermentation
Grapes 100% owned
Certification organic

CAMARILLO

FUIL WINES

1330 Flynn Road, Unit E - tel. (818) 497-6151
www.fuilwines.com - info@fuilwines.com

PEOPLE - Actors by day and winemakers by night, Matt, a Wisconsin native, and Chilean born Carolina Espiro Jaeger started Fuil, pronounced "fool", in 2022. The name is a Gaelic word that means "blood, kindred, nature" as well as "fool." They've doubled production for the second year in a row, producing a total of five wines, three single vineyard wines and two wine blends.

VINEYARDS - Fuil works with three vineyards in the Santa Ynez Valley. In Ballard Canyon, J & K Vineyard practices biodynamic farming (not certified), growing Mourvèdre, Syrah and Viognier in sandy loam soils with limestone veins. In the Los Olivos District, Ryan Carr manages the Kaerskov Vineyard (the only Danish owned vineyard in Solvang) which just got certified organic. Other wines, not featured here, may be grown with herbicide.

WINES - Light, elegant, high acid wines utilizing whole cluster to add spice and oak to add roundness.

Santa Barbara County Tábla Solas Nua Chilled Red Wine 2023 ● 92 cases; 35 $ - ⊞ - A blend of Mourvèdre (70%) co-fermented with Syrah (5%); blended with Viognier (25%). Whole cluster. A wine originally made as an experiment with left over fruit, it is now made with intention. Raspberry and cherry notes, lightly textured tannins, and minerality on the finish.

Ballard Canyon J-K Vineyard Viognier 2023 ○ 74 cases; 42 $ - ⊞ - Aged in six months in neutral oak. Whole cluster pressed. Bright nose with crushed pineapple and tropical fruit notes. Clean and fresh with textured acidity and a mouthwatering finish.

Ballard Canyon J-K Vineyard Syrah 2022 ● 72 cases; 50 $ - ⊞ - Aged 18 months in oak (33% new). Whole cluster (100%). Notes of blackberry, black cherry, and menthol herbs. Elegant and structured, with fresh acidity.

acres 0 - cases 500
Fertilizers compost, biodynamic compost, cover crops, synthetic fertilizer
Plant protection sulfur, synthetic pesticides, organic
Weed control mechanical, manual
Yeasts spontaneous fermentation
Grapes purchase 100%
Certification none

LOS OLIVOS

GRIMM'S BLUFF

2445 Alamo Pintado Avenue #102 - tel. (805) 691-9065
www.grimmsbluff.com

 A winery committed to doing the utmost to farm beautifully and make exceptional wines.

PEOPLE - Owners Rick and Aurora Grimm transitioned from wine enthusiasts to vintners in 2012, acquiring a vast 240 acre rural estate with panoramic mountain views. The couple enlisted Provence born, biodynamic vigneron Philippe Coderey to plant the vineyard. Garrett Gamache is the onsite vineyard manager. Henry Grimm and his wife Samantha manage marketing with a tasting room in Los Olivos and offer spectacular ranch tours.

VINEYARDS - Perched 800' above the valley floor, the vines sit on rocky, mineral rich soils. Some reds grow in unilateral Guyot style, while most are head-trained Gobelet. Originally certified biodynamic, the vines are now certified organic, but the team continues to use biodynamic farming practices. The holistic farm includes Guinea fowl, cows, donkeys, sheep, and chickens among the vines, along with 500 olive trees and bee hives for sage honey.

WINES - Renowned winemaker Ernst Storm focuses on classic, Old World style wines, made with minimal intervention, producing complex wines with natural acidity.

Happy Canyon Contango Cabernet Sauvignon 2019 ● 150 cases; 105 $ - ⊞ - Exclusively from head trained vines, and made from four barrels, it's aged 18 months in French oak (75% new). It features notes of blackberries, slate, and stone, with smooth tannins and a succulent finish.

Happy Canyon Reserve Sauvignon Blanc 2020 ○ 100 cases; 58 $ - ⌕ - Primarily from head trained vines, it's whole cluster pressed. Offers vibrant aromas of lemon, peach, and chamomile. Aged on gross lees in a concrete egg for nine months, it achieves a complex character with fresh, crisp acidity.

Happy Canyon River Stone Cabernet Sauvignon Rosé 2023 ◐ 200 cases; 38 $ - ⌕ - Picked early and direct pressed. A pale salmon hue with ripe strawberry, melon and hints of Asian pear. Fresh and bright, with balanced acidity.

acres 16.8 - cases 2,000
Fertilizers compost, biodynamic compost, cover crops, manure, organic fertilizer
Plant protection sulfur, biodynamic preparations
Weed control animal grazing, mechanical, manual
Yeasts spontaneous fermentation, selected indigenous yeasts
Grapes 100% owned
Certification biodynamic, organic

LOMPOC

J. DIRT

2755 Purisima Road - tel. (805) 448-2148
www.jdirtwines.com - j.dirtwines@gmail.com

 A grower (and vintner) who cherishes his land and offers vineyard tours to help consumers learn more about exemplary farming and traditional techniques.

PEOPLE - As a grower, Brook Williams planted Duvarita Ranch in 2012, adding a second vineyard, Christy & Wise, in 2019. Brook developed the vines with Provence born, biodynamic guru Philippe Coderey. Williams sells most of his grapes to leading area wineries, including Dragonette Cellars. Curious to see for himself what his own grapes tasted like, Williams created his tiny J.Dirt label. The winery offers owner tours of its vineyards, located at the western edge of the Sta. Rita Hills.

VINEYARDS - Surrounded by 600 acres of wild land, the 80 acres of no till vines at Duvarita and Christy & Wise are certified organic and biodynamic. Helen Deneuve, who worked on a biodynamic estate in Languedoc, is the onsite vineyard manager. Duvarita grows Pinot Noir, Chardonnay, Syrah, and Viognier. Christy & Wise specializes in head trained Rhone varietals. Half of its acreage is an own rooted field blend of Carignane, Grenache, and Mourvèdre.

WINES - Aged in neutral oak, these exceptional wines highlight fruit and minerality. Vibrant salinity and pure flavors make them stand out.

Santa Barbara County Christy & Wise Grenache 2021 ● 98 cases; 55 $ - ▦ - Own rooted Grenache 362, Syrah Estrella, and Syrah 174. Aged 16 months in neutral French oak. Mulberry and dark berries mingle with lavender and bramble. Soft tannins and juicy acidity.

Santa Barbara County Duvarita Pinot Noir 2021 ● 58 cases; 60 $ - ▦ - Hand-picked clones 113, 667, and 777. Aged 17 months in neutral French oak. Notes of rose hips, Bing cherries, dried strawberries, olives, and black tea. Soft tannins, pronounced minerality.

Edna Valley Slide Hill Vineyard Syrah 2020 ● 105 cases; 60 $ - ▦ - Estrella selection. Minimal intervention. Aged 16 months in neutral oak. Bursting with mixed berries, violet, black olives, dried thyme, and cherry jam.

---

acres 80 - cases 500
Fertilizers compost, biodynamic compost, cover crops
Plant protection sulfur, biodynamic preparations, copper, organic
Weed control animal grazing, mechanical, manual
Yeasts spontaneous fermentation
Grapes 100% owned
Certification biodynamic, organic

SANTA BARBARA

JAFFURS WINE CELLARS

819 East Montecito Street - tel. (805) 962-7003
www.jaffurswine.com - info@jaffurswine.com

PEOPLE - Jaffurs focuses on single vineyard designates from Santa Barbara County. An urban winery, it is a premier producer in Santa Barbara's vibrant downtown, known for Rhône varieties, which make up 80 percent of its production. Half of its production is Syrah, with six single vineyard Syrahs. Founded in 1994 by Craig Jaffurs, Dan and Janelle Green bought it in 2016. Stephen Searle became head winemaker in 2017.

VINEYARDS - For 25+ years, Jaffurs has been buying grapes from the same blocks at their favorite vineyards in Santa Barbara County's Ballard Canyon, Los Alamos, Santa Maria Valley, Santa Ynez Valley and Sta. Rita Hills. Vineyards include Bien Nacido and Thompson and three certified organic vineyards in Ballard Canyon—Kimsey, Larner and Stolpman. Jaffurs works with their growers to limit yields, ensuring optimal farming practices.

WINES - Searle crafts 16 wines yearly, capturing each site's essence, using primarily neutral barrels. He recently added concrete tanks.

Ballard Canyon Larner Vineyard Syrah 2021 ● 200 cases; 55 $ - ▦ - Aged 22 months in oak (20% new). Structured yet elegant. Undergoes 2/3 whole cluster co-fermentation with 1% Viognier. It offers fresh red and blue fruits, crushed pepper, black fruit aromas, and chalky tannins.

Ballard Canyon Grenache 2021 ● 250 cases; 36 $ - ▦ - Aged 10 months in neutral oak. Made from Larner and Stolpman vineyards. It's 50% whole cluster. Ruby colored, medium bodied. Aromas of bright cherry, strawberry, gingerbread, rose petals, with fresh acidity, and elegant finish.

Ballard Canyon Roussanne 2022 ○ 150 cases; 42 $ - 🍷▦ - Aged 2/3 in concrete, 1/3 in barrel (17% new oak) and bottle aged one year. Fresh wine. With aromas of white flowers, orange zest, melon. Rich texture.

---

acres 0 - cases 5,000
Fertilizers compost, biodynamic compost, cover crops, manure, organic fertilizer
Plant protection sulfur, biodynamic preparations, synthetic pesticides, organic
Weed control mechanical, manual
Yeasts spontaneous fermentation, commercial cultured yeasts
Grapes purchase 100%
Certification some of the vineyards are certified organic

LOS OLIVOS

JOY FANTASTIC & HOLUS BOLUS

2902 San Marcos Street, Unit B - tel. (805) 637-1005
www.thejoyfantastic.com - peter@thejoyfantastic.com

PEOPLE - Amy Christine and Peter Hunken started their negociant brand 20 years ago while Hunken was an assistant winemaker at Stolpman Vineyards and Christine worked as a somm while studying for the Master of Wine. (She passed). In 2016, the couple assumed control of a five acre parcel in the Sta. Rita Hills which they named after a Prince album titled – The Joy Fantastic .

VINEYARDS - They buy grapes from John Sebastiano Vineyard in Sta. Rita Hills as well as Bien Nacido and cool climate Presqu'ile in the Santa Maria Valley (where soils are sandy). The Joy Fantastic estate site is on a steep plot in the western edge of Sta. Rita Hills, exposed to ocean effects, and sits on diatomaceous earth, shale and clay soils. The challenging climate produces grape concentration.

WINES - With their exacting palates, they make restrained, elegant examples of classic Burgundian and northern Rhone varietals.

🔝 **Santa Maria Valley Presqu'ile Vineyard Holus Bolus Syrah 2022** ● 220 cases; 45 $ - ⊞ - Highly expressive. Aromas of menthol and green olive with a sanguine touch. On the palate, earthy blackberry and dark cherries.

Sta. Rita Hills Joy Fantastic Gamay Noir 2022 ● 150 cases; 40 $ - ⊞ - Whole cluster (30%). Heady aromas of dried rose, strawberry and red plum fruit. On the palate, it shows earthy plum and red cherry. Juiciness from an adept balancing of acid and tannin.

Santa Maria Valley Bien Nacido Vineyard Holus Bolus Roussanne 2022 ○ 150 cases; 40 $ - ⊞ - The wine broadcasts yellow apple, honeysuckle and white flower aromas from the glass. A racy, lemon edged palate of green apple offers ripe tropical notes.

acres 5 - cases 2,500
Fertilizers compost, cover crops, manure, organic fertilizer
Plant protection sulfur, organic
Weed control mechanical
Yeasts spontaneous fermentation
Grapes purchase 70%
Certification none

SOLVANG

KINGS CAREY WINES

1210 Mission Drive, #103 - tel. (805) 680-7006
www.kingscarey.com - james@kingscarey.com

PEOPLE - James Sparks, a self taught winemaker, and Anna Ferguson-Sparks started their label in 2014 when they bought some Sta. Rita Hills Grenache from Spear Vineyard. Sparks is also the winemaker at Liquid Farm, the renowned Santa Ynez Valley label known for Chardonnay. For their own label, the couple moved into a new 1,600 square foot winery space for production and tastings and are launching a new sparkling wine project.

VINEYARDS - The couple works with five sites in four different AVAs. New additions include MiraLaguna (certified organic) in the Los Olivos District and Mar Farm in Edna Valley. The site for their signature Semillon, Star Lane Vineyard, is in the process of converting to organic certification, farming organically since 2021.

WINES - Early pick dates and low intervention methods balance freshness and ageworthiness, with a goal of offering accessibly priced wine.

🔝 **Los Olivos Dogged Vine Vineyard To Market Grenache 2022** ● 174 cases; 32 $ - ⊞ - Last vintage the Dogged Vineyard. A fresh and fun, chillable red. Super light ruby in color, full of brambly berry, strawberry, tarragon and black pepper aromatics. It is lush yet with lovely, long lasting acidity.

Sta. Rita Hills Valley Spear Vineyard Chardonnay 2022 ○ 48 cases; 48 $ - ⊞ - Extremely fresh and bright, aromatic with white pepper and spice, with savory, roasted stone fruit on the palate and a texturally appealing velvety quality.

Los Olivos District Mira Laguna Vineyard Cabernet Sauvignon 2022 ● 140 cases; 40 $ - ⊞ - A new release under their accessible "Pizza Joint" label. Very aromatic with blackberry, cocoa and black pepper. The palate of jerky, crushed oregano, dried fig and plum is savory, yet fruit forward. It is a wine to ponder awhile.

acres 0 - cases 1,200
Fertilizers cover crops, organic fertilizer
Plant protection sulfur, organic
Weed control mechanical, manual
Yeasts spontaneous fermentation
Grapes purchase 100%
Certification some of the vineyards are certified organic

SANTA BARBARA

L.A. LEPIANE WINES

P.O. Box 61803 - tel. (805) 451-1377
www.lepianewines.com - alison@lepianewines.com

PEOPLE - In 2023, Alison Thomson celebrated her winery's 10th anniversary. (The name is pronounced "Lay-pea-ah-nee.") She was inspired by her Calabrian great grandfather who moved to the Central Coast and established a winery in Hollister in 1935. That led to her focus on Italian varieties. Alison is also the co-wine-maker and general manager of Two Wolves Wines (owned by Pink). Thomson's own Nebbiolo's won high praise from top critics.

VINEYARDS - Finding the grapes she likes—Barbera, Malvasia Bianca and Nebbiolo— isn't easy. She works with three vineyards, each located in a different region—Mora (Los Olivos District), Rancho Sisquoc (Santa Maria Valley) and Santa Ynez Vineyard (Santa Ynez Valley), which has the largest planting of Italian varieties in Santa Barbara County. It's farmed by Juve Buenrostro whom Alison works with closely at Two Wolves. Some of the wines (not featured here) may be grown with herbicide.

WINES - Thomson makes single vineyard Barbera and Nebbiolo and also co-ferments the two varieties for her La Gaviota blend. She favors slow fermentations.

Alisos Canyon Nebbiolo 2019 ● 85 cases; 54 $ - ◐ - Aged 32 months in neutral puncheons. Final vintage before the Nebbiolo (from a certified organic vineyard) was pulled out. Fermented long and slow on skins for 35 days. Perfumed notes of dried flowers and dried herbs on the nose and on the palate.

Santa Ynez Valley Santa Ynez Vineyard Barbera 2022 ● 75 cases; 34 $ - ⊞ - Aged 22 months in neutral barrels for 22 months. Skin fermented for 25 days with gentle daily punch downs. Red currants, blackberry aromas and juicy acidity.

Santa Ynez Valley Malvasia Bianca 2023 ○ 50 cases; 30 $ - ⊞ - Aged in neutral barrels. Gently pressed and slowly fermented. Intense aromatics of orange blossom, lime zest and honeycomb. Bright with juicy acidity and a mineral backbone.

acres 0 - cases 500
Fertilizers compost, cover crops, organic fertilizer
Plant protection sulfur, synthetic pesticides
Weed control mechanical
Yeasts spontaneous fermentation
Grapes purchase 100%
Certification some of the vineyards are certified organic

ORCUTT

LAND OF SAINTS WINE COMPANY $

9550 San Antonio Road - tel. (805) 350-9638
www.loswines.com - info@loswines.com

PEOPLE - A partnership between Jason and Angela Osborne (of A Tribute to Grace) and Manuel Cuevas (the owner of C2 Cellars, a crush pad in Orcutt), the three identify superior grape sources nearby and create varietal bottlings at bargain prices. Cuevas makes the wine. With his custom crush vantage point, he has his finger on the pulse of what is available (as well as good farming practices). Recently Quinta de Mar Vineyard has become a regular grape source.

VINEYARDS - In order to maintain quality and low prices, their vineyard sources vary from year to year. Sauvignon Blanc comes from White Barn and Mesa Verde in Santa Ynez (overseen by organic specialist Chris King). They buy Pinot Noir from Quinta del Mar in SLO Coast AVA and GSM grapes from Osborne's Tribute to Grace sources at Santa Barbara Highlands, Dorigo in Santa Ynez (which they farm) and Syrah from Oak Savannah in the Los Olivos District.

WINES - The team does a superb job of making AVA varietal wines that express their place—at prices usually under $25.

SLO Coast Pinot Noir 2023 EVERYDAY WINE ● 640 cases; 24 $ - ⊞ - Whole cluster (25%). A wild herbal nose with effusive strawberry and red currant aromas. In the mouth, juicy strawberry is shaded with amaro and a very mineral buttressing.

Santa Barbara County GSM 2022 ● 2,210 cases; 24 $ - ⊞ - the nose is deeply floral with red fruit and a sanguine edge. Flavors include red and dark cherry, blackberry, tree bark and a fine hibiscus tannin. 25% whole cluster fermentation.

Santa Barbara County Sauvignon Blanc 2023 ○ 1,491 cases; 20 $ - ◯ - shows pleasant musk and green herb on the nose with a tangy and broad palate of grapefruit, lemon and red apple.

acres 0 - cases 18,000
Fertilizers cover crops, organic fertilizer
Plant protection sulfur, organic
Weed control mechanical
Yeasts spontaneous fermentation
Grapes purchase 100%
Certification none

LOS OLIVOS

LARNER VINEYARD & WINERY

2900 Grand Avenue - tel. (805) 688-8148
www.larnerwine.com - info@larnerwine.com

PEOPLE - After a 14 year struggle, Michael Larner is building a tasting room on his home property in Ballard Canyon to offer indoor and outdoor experiences. The dream started in 1995 when Steven and Christine purchased the property. Son Michael started making the wine. They also launched their Unconformity brand in 2017 showcasing co-fermented blends and released a new Viognier and Malvasia co-ferment.

VINEYARDS - A grower as well as a vintner, Larner sells 75 percent of its fruit to top producers in the Central Coast. Michael recently revamped 11 acres, changing them from vertical shoot positioning and widening the canopy width to get more air flow (for more even ripening and less mildew). He also brought in sheep and goats for the first time. He also buys grapes from Jamshid and SY Ranch in Los Olivos District. The estate has been certified organic since 2017.

WINES - With the beach like sand in the vineyard and a minimal intervention approach, Larner wines express minerality and a purity of fruit.

Ballard Canyon Estate Malvasia Bianca 2023 EVERYDAY WINE O 130 cases; 32 $ - Aged in concrete egg (50%), stainless steel (25%), and acacia barrels (25%) for four months on the lees. The grapes are destemmed, crushed, and spend 24 hours on the skins. Textured and lush with vibrant acidity and a richness on the back of the palate.
Ballard Canyon Unconformity Red 2021 ● 60 cases; 40 $ - Aged 15 months in Manetti amphora and then six months in bottle. Equal parts Grenache, Syrah, and Mourvedre co-fermented. Red and black fruit aromas and mineral elements.
Ballard Canyon Estate Syrah 2020 ● 140 cases; 45 $ - Aged 24 months in French oak (33% new). A blend of three Syrah clones. Bold blueberry, blackberry, mulled spices, crushed pepper and dusted cocoa notes.

acres 33 - cases 2,000
Fertilizers compost, cover crops, manure, organic fertilizer
Plant protection sulfur, organic
Weed control animal grazing, mechanical, manual
Yeasts spontaneous fermentation, commercial cultured yeasts
Grapes purchase 20%
Certification some of the vineyards are certified organic

SANTA BARBARA

LIEU DIT

23 E Canon Perdido - tel. (805) 225-3325
www.lieuditwinery.com - bonjour@lieuditwinery.com

PEOPLE - Lieu Dit [lyoo-dee] is a French wine term that means "named place" and for Justin Willett's Lieu Dit Wines the named place is Santa Barbara County. The focus is on Loire Valley varieties grown in the Santa Ynez Valley. They have their first tasting room, located in downtown Santa Barbara, in the same tasting room as Willett's other brand, Tyler. Wines are available to try in tasting flights or by the glass, paired with small plates.

VINEYARDS - Searching for vineyards that allow for the pure expression of the fruit, Justin finds the marine sediment and diatomaceous earth dominating Santa Barbara County is ideal for Loire varieties. He buys own rooted Cabernet Franc, Chenin Blanc and Sauvignon Blanc from Happy Canyon Vineyard. He gets Melon de Bourgogne from the North Canyon Vineyard in Santa Maria Valley. Some of the wines (not featured here) are grown with herbicide.

WINES - Willett's wines are bright, light and elegant, as well as low in alcohol. The wines show good acidity and texture.

Santa Ynez Valley Cabernet Franc 2023 ● 2,800 cases; 38 $ - From Happy Canyon Vineyard and Rock Hollow in Los Olivos District. A very pretty wine with violet and black cherry aromatics, soft texture, lightly drying fine tannins and a rush of acidity.
Santa Ynez Valley Chenin Blanc 2022 O 1,800 cases; 27 $ - Fermented and aged in both stainless steel and neutral barrel. From Happy Canyon Vineyard. Whole cluster pressed. Offers aromatics of stone fruits, mineral, citrus, and acacia honey. A textured wine, acidity coats the palate leaving a mouthwatering, mineral driven finish.
Santa Ynez Sans Soufre Cabernet Franc 2023 ● 150 cases; 38 $ - Six barrel selections remain in barrel for 8-10 months without racking without sulfur. Briary, black raspberry, pepper and earthy notes on the nose and sour cherry notes on the palate. Textured and savory with a fresh finish.

acres 0 - cases 15,000
Fertilizers compost, cover crops, manure, organic fertilizer, synthetic fertilizer
Plant protection sulfur, synthetic pesticides, copper, organic
Weed control mechanical
Yeasts spontaneous fermentation
Grapes purchase 100%
Certification none

LOS ALAMOS

LO-FI WINES $

448 Bell Street - tel. (805) 344-0179
www.lofi-wines.com - questions@lofi-wines.com

PEOPLE - Winemakers Mike Roth and Craig Winchester specialize in low intervention wines. Inspired by the Loire, their favored grapes are Chenin Blanc, Cab Franc and Gamay though their roster is wide. They keep acidity high which is crucial when avoiding additives. Their aesthetic is casual and unfussy in their wines, their labels—inspired by 60's records—and their vinyl powered tasting room. Lo-Fi is beloved for reasonable prices and OG ("Original Gangster") natural cred.

VINEYARDS - They have two estates. One is the Coquelicot Vineyard (certified organic) where Mike is the winemaker, in the Santa Ynez Valley AVA, on loam, clay and gravel. The other is Roth's own Clos Mullet (in Los Alamos) on shaley loam. They also buy from sites in Santa Maria Valley AVA and Los Olivos District AVA. All vineyards are said to use only organic approved materials (except Jurassic Park which eschews weed killer and gets a pass for fine Chenin Blanc).

WINES - Skin contact (in varying amounts) produces their textured whites, while carbonic maceration and whole cluster ferments create their juicy, aromatic reds.

TOP **Santa Barbara County Clos Mullet Cabernet Franc 2022** ● 97 cases; 32 $ - ▦ - Aromas of cherry, dried sappy leaf and black pepper. The palate is tart with mulberry and dark and maraschino cherry, leather and earth, bound with wiry tannins.
Santa Barbara County Clos Mullet Trousseau 2022 ● 176 cases; 30 $ - ▦ - A nose of fresh earth and red cherry/strawberry. A tangy, penetrating palate of earth, dried orange and strawberries.
Santa Barbara County Chenin Blanc 2022 ○ 200 cases; 26 $ - ▦ - A classic Chenin nose of lanolin and flint with pear and green apple notes which follow through on the palate, combining with Meyer lemon flesh for a tart satisfying finish.

---

acres 10 - cases 5,500
Fertilizers compost, cover crops, organic fertilizer
Plant protection sulfur, biodynamic preparations, synthetic pesticides, copper, organic
Weed control mechanical
Yeasts spontaneous fermentation
Grapes purchase 65%
Certification some of the vineyards are certified organic

SOLVANG

LUNA HART

Ballard Canyon - tel. (610) 880-6412
www.lunahartwines.com - gretchen@lunahartwines.com

PEOPLE - This year Gretchen Voelker celebrates her tenth year making artisanal boutique, small lot, handcrafted wines. With friend and business partner Tymari LoRe, she's doubled production in the last two years to 1,100 cases. Patty Emerson-Heery joined as assistant winemaker in 2023. In 2022, Luna Hart released the first traditional method sparkling Grüner Veltliner from Santa Barbara County.

VINEYARDS - Voelker buys from six vineyards. Organically farmed Grüner Veltliner comes from North Canyon vineyard (in transition to organic certification) in Santa Maria Valley for sparkling wine and Spear Vineyard (certified organic) in Sta. Rita Hills for still wine. She also buys from Coquelicot (certified organic). More grapes come from Ballard Adobes and Honeybear (both in Los Olivos District) and Hinnrichs Vineyard (Ballard Canyon).

WINES - Winemaking encompasses carbonic fermentation, skin contact and traditional method sparkling.

TOP **Los Olivos District Ballard Adobe Vineyard Sauvignon Blanc 2023** ○ 184 cases; 42 $ - ▯▦ - Fermented and aged six months in neutral oak (91%) and stainless steel (9%). Aromas of apricot and lime with hints of lemongrass and minerality. Fresh and bright with tart, textured acidity and a saline finish. A wine with purity of flavor.
Los Olivos District Coquelicot Vineyard Cabernet Franc 2023 ● 57 cases; 36 $ - ▦ - Aged six months in neutral oak after carbonic fermentation. Acid forward with raspberry, earthy minerality, pencil shavings and herbal notes. Lots of texture and flavor.
Ballard Canyon Hinnrichs Vineyard Syrah 2022 ● 110 cases; 45 $ - ▦ - Vinified three ways and then blended. Deep dark red fruit and cola notes, with anise, licorice and bay leaves. Intense aromas, but on the palate, the wine is medium bodied with a lovely freshness.

---

acres 0 - cases 1,100
Fertilizers compost, cover crops, organic fertilizer
Plant protection sulfur, biodynamic preparations
Weed control mechanical, manual
Yeasts spontaneous fermentation
Grapes purchase 100%
Certification some of the vineyards are certified organic

LOMPOC

MALLEA WINES

300 N 12th Street - tel. (805) 451-5893
erikmallea@gmail.com

PEOPLE - Started in 2018, star power collaborators Justin Willett and Eric Mallea make Rhones under this label. Mallea is a top vineyard manager farming big name vineyards—Sanford & Benedict, La Encantada, and La Rinconada—as well as vineyards associated with Willett's Tyler Wines. (The two run a vineyard management company together.) He also manages his family's grazing lands in the Gaviota Pass. Willett makes the wines.

VINEYARDS - Mallea farms four small vineyards (some sustainable, some organic) clustered in the Los Olivos District. Rancho Bernat (certified organic) was planted in 1998 with some Syrah. Other sources include the two acre Coteaux de Clair (organic materials only), planted in 2011 to Grenache and Mourvèdre and Tommytown (Los Olivos District), planted in 2011 to Syrah. The fourth vineyard, Rolling Vines, grows own rooted Counoise, Grenache and Syrah.

WINES - Long time vineyard experts, Willett and Mallea know where to get untapped fruit.

● Santa Barbara County Grenache Blanc 2023 ○ 500 cases; 25 $ - ⬜ - Grown at Coteaux de Clair, Whole cluster pressed to stainless tank. Vibrant aromas with notes of lime skins and passionfruit, the wine has textured acidity that coats the front of the palate and lingers with mouthwatering salinity.
Santa Barbara County Rose of Grenache 2022 ◐ 300 cases; 25 $ - ⊞ - Aged four months in neutral barrel. Whole cluster. Grown at Rolling Vines. Delicate, fresh and juicy with bright peach notes.
Santa Barbara County GSM 2022 ● 770 cases; 25 $ - ⊞ - Aged 22 months in neutral barrels. Aromatic aromas of wild strawberry, bramble, black pepper, sweet brown spices, and a fresh herbaceous notes. Soft tannins and a lovely midpalate texture that lingers.

acres 9 - cases 1,500
Fertilizers cover crops, manure, organic fertilizer
Plant protection none, organic
Weed control mechanical, manual
Yeasts spontaneous fermentation
Grapes 100% owned
Certification some of the vineyards are certified organic

LOMPOC

MELVILLE

5185 East Highway 246 - tel. (805) 735-7030
www.melvillewinery.com - info@melvillewinery.com

PEOPLE - Chad Melville calls himself the winegrower at the family winery established in the mid 1990s. Chad's philosophy is that everything starts in the vineyard and not a lot of winemaking is needed. He has 17 Pinot clones, six of Chardonnay and nine of Syrah. Six years ago, they planted Grenache and made rosé, adding a red Grenache wine this year. For the 2024 vintage, Garrett Adelman (formerly at Cakebread) joined the team as assistant winemaker.

VINEYARDS - The vines at Melville are healthy but live in stressful environments with high density spacing (2,000 vines per acre), low vigor rootstock and low nutrient soil. The vines have to work but the cool climate, sunshine and long growing season result in fruit that is concentrated and flavorful. Melville owns four vineyards—West Side (38 acres, 1997), East Block (41 acres, 1998), Rancho Nuevo (36 acres, 2006) and La Chapelle (24 acres, 1985).

WINES - Melville produces approachable wines, in price and style, from coastally influenced Sta. Rita Hills sites. Clonal diversity is a key element.

● Sta. Rita Hills Estate Chardonnay 2023 ○ 1,600 cases; 44 $ - ⊞ - A blend of eight clones. Whole cluster pressed. Vibrant, fresh and mineral driven with salinity and citrus blossom notes. Density of fruit on the palate surrounded by electric acidity. Very graceful.
Sta. Rita Hills Estate Pinot Noir 2022 ● 5,100 cases; 44 $ - ⊞ - Aged 11 months. Partial whole cluster (40%). Complexity comes from 21 blocks, 17 clones, six soils types and seven rootstocks, picked over eight weeks and fermented separately. Beautiful juicy cranberry and pomegranate notes, as well as dried herbs, cinnamon, black tea and ocean like saltiness. Elegant power.
Sta. Rita Hills Estate Syrah 2021 ● 1,200 cases; 44 $ - ⊞ - Partial whole cluster (40%). From seven clones. Dark red fruits, spice, green olives and green peppercorns. Textured tannins and bright acidity with an elegant finish.

acres 139 - cases 11,000
Fertilizers compost, cover crops, organic fertilizer
Plant protection sulfur, organic
Weed control mechanical, manual
Yeasts spontaneous fermentation, selected indigenous yeasts
Grapes 100% owned
Certification none

LOMPOC

MONTEMAR WINERY

1501 East Chestnut Court, Ste E - tel. (805) 735-5000
www.montemarwinery.com - info@montemarwinery.com

PEOPLE - In 1992 Steve Arrowood and friends from the aerospace industry began making wine in his Palos Verdes garage, naming their venture Montemar. In 2015, he moved to the Lompoc Wine Ghetto and opened a tasting room. After Steve fell ill, his son Kyle relocated to Santa Barbara in 2018. Following Steve's passing in 2020, Kyle and his fiancée Layne continued the business. Notably, the tasting room features friendly, cute animals to greet visitors.

VINEYARDS - Kyle buys grapes from up to 12 vineyards across the Santa Ynez Valley, sourcing fruit from varying microclimates. These include Chardonnay, Pinot Noir, and Rhône varieties from Sta. Rita Hills; Rhône varieties, Sangiovese and Tempranillo from Los Olivos Canyon; Bordeaux varieties and Graciano from Happy Canyon; and Rhône varieties from Alisos Canyon. The certified organic vineyards include Gnesa, Kimsey, Spear, and Two Wolves.

WINES - They produce wines that reflect the distinct characteristics of their specific vineyard sources and vintage years.

Alisos Canyon Watch Hill Vineyard Syrah 2015 ● 54 cases; 40 $ - ▦ - Aged in tight grained French oak barrels (35% new) in some double sized barrels to maintain freshness. Aged 24 months in barrel unfined, and unfiltered. Co-fermented with 3% Viognier. Red fruit, spice and a touch of toast.

Sta. Rita Hills La Encantada Vineyard Pinot Noir 2017 ● 48 cases; 54 $ - ▦ - Gently de-stemmed, then cold soaked for four days and fermented with gentle punchdowns. Aged for 24 months on lees in all tight grained French oak barrels (30% new). Fresh bright cherries on palate.

Tierra Alta Grenache Blanc 2022 ○ 48 cases; 28 $ - ▯ - This Grenache Blanc from was aged on the lees for 1yr in stainless steel. With flavors of green apple and stone fruit, with lush mouthfeel and great fresh acid.

acres 0 - cases 1,100
Fertilizers compost, cover crops, organic fertilizer
Plant protection sulfur, synthetic pesticides, organic
Weed control mechanical, manual
Yeasts spontaneous fermentation, commercial cultured yeasts
Grapes purchase 100%
Certification some of the vineyards are certified organic

SANTA MARIA

NATIVE9

6525 Dominion Road - tel. (805) 694-8882
www.ranchosdeontiveros.com - hello@native9.com

PEOPLE - Originally cattle farmers, ninth generation James Ontiveros planted Pinot Noir in 1997 at Rancho Ontiveros, a 1,000 acre ranch. He was inspired by meeting Mounir Saouma, a consultant from Lucien Le Moine in Beaune, and traveling to Burgundy in 2003 to learn about biodynamics. James started making wine in 2003, followed by Justin Willett in 2016. Wes Hagen has been the brand ambassador since 2022.

VINEYARDS - They grow Pinot Noir and Chardonnay on two vineyards on the Ontiveros property—Rancho Ontiveros (100 acres of Pinot Noirs and 30 acres of Chardonnay) and Rancho Viñedo (12 acres of Pinot Noir and Chardonnay). There are also a few acres of Syrah and Godello. Most of the fruit is sold to other winemakers and only a few acres are used for Native 9.

WINES - The team lowered the wine's carbon footprint, switching to lighter weight glass bottles that weigh 200 grams less.

TOP Santa Maria Valley Rancho Ontiveros Vineyard Pinot Noir 2021 ● 250 cases; 64 $ - ▦ - Aged 22 months in barrel, unfined and unfiltered. Partial whole cluster. Fermented in five ton fermenters with punchdowns and pumpovers for two weeks. A bright red berry color, with bright cherry and wild strawberry aromas but underneath are notes of molasses. Smooth with soft tannins, very elegant with ephemeral elegance.

Santa Maria Valley Rancho Viñedo Vineyard Doña Martina Chardonnay 2021 ○ 273 cases; 46 $ - ◍ - Aged one year in 500L puncheon and racked to tank for 6-7 more months on fine lees. From own rooted, old vine Chardonnay planted in 1973. Whole cluster. Apple, citrus, and ginger aromas followed by a full bodied wine. The wine is focused and structured and delicate acidity coats the entire palate. Fresh and elegant.

acres 58 - cases 750
Fertilizers compost, cover crops, organic fertilizer
Plant protection sulfur, organic
Weed control mechanical, manual
Yeasts spontaneous fermentation
Grapes 100% owned
Certification none

SOLVANG

PIAZZA FAMILY WINES

2825 Tapadero Road - tel. (805) 694-8046
www.piazzafamilywines.com - info@piazzafamilywines.com

PEOPLE - Vintners Nancy and Ron Piazza are growing their brand. The 2024 harvest marks the second vintage in their new Ballard Canyon winery, and they now have two bottle label designs—one with the vineyard image on the front and one with the Piazza label. (The goal is to be more recognizable.) They have also added a description of how the wine is made. Gretchen Voelcker makes the wines. The new assistant winemaker, Patty Emerson-Heery, joined in 2024.

VINEYARDS - They have two estate vineyards. Bella Vista (certified organic in 2022) in Ballard Canyon grows Bordeaux varieties (Cabernet, Merlot), Rhones (Grenache, Syrah) and Italian grapes (Montepulciano, Nebbiolo, and Sangiovese). Their Mount Carmel vineyard in the Sta. Rita Hills grows Burgundian grapes. Garrett Gamache began farming Bella Vista in 2023, which, coupled with the rains of the past year, led to explosive yields in the vineyard.

WINES - Voelcker spends much of her time in the vineyard. She produces minimal intervention wines that showcase the purity of the fruit.

🔝 **Ballard Canyon Bella Vista Vineyard Nancy's Cuvee 2021** ● 79 cases; 42 $ - 🍷 - A blend of Grenache (56%), Syrah (36%) and Graciano (14%). Grenache offers red fruit notes, Syrah dark fruit and herbaceousness and Graciano (a portion of which was carbonic) contributed intense primary fruit.
Ballard Canyon Bella Vista Vineyard Grenache 2022 ● 65 cases; 38 $ - 🍷 🔄 - Partial whole cluster (50%). The wine looks like pomegranate juice. Very floral and bright red fruits and crushed raspberry aromas. Textured with powerful tannins. A wine with aging potential but also with the freshness to enjoy now with food.
Ballard Canyon Bella Vista Vineyard Carbonic Graciano 2023 ● 104 cases; 30 $ - 🥂 - Fresh, fun and easy drinking with vibrant pomegranate, cherries and cranberry aromas. Cardamom spice notes on the nose and turmeric on the finish.

acres 26 - cases 1,400
Fertilizers cover crops, organic fertilizer
Plant protection sulfur
Weed control mechanical, manual
Yeasts spontaneous fermentation
Grapes 100% owned
Certification some of the vineyards are certified organic

LOMPOC

PIEDRASASSI

1501 E Chestnut Avenue - tel. (805) 736-6784
www.piedrasassi.com - melissa@piedrasassi.com

PEOPLE - Sashi Moorman and partner Melissa Soronr gon started Piedrasassi as a bakery featuring heritage grains and a winery making Syrah. Moorman's passion for cool-climate Syrah had him settling on four vineyard sites expressing cuvées from Sta Rita Hills, Santa Maria and Arroyo Grande as well a regional blend. Moorman employs whole cluster fermentation in the pursuit of powerful aromas while picking early, limiting his wines to 12.5% abv or so and a taut ripeness.

VINEYARDS - Moorman, himself farms the tiny Rim Rock Vineyard in Arroyo Grande Valley which consistently produces the most nuanced bottling. Organic practices and homeopathic sprays are employed in its farming. Organic blocks of Bien Nacido Vineyard constitute the Santa Maria Valley cuvée and a blend of grapes from Patterson (organic in practice) and the estate Hines Vineyard produce the Sta Rita Hills version.

WINES - A perennial survey of three Syrahs of specific AVAs as well as a regional blend reflecting the vintage. A rare Vin Santo is also produced in small amounts.

🔝 **Arroyo Grande Rim Rock Vineyard Syrah 2022** ● 132 cases; 65 $ - 🍷 - feels already almost fully formed with delicate violet and amaro cherry qualities pushing from the nose to the palate with hints of resin and seaweed. The palate balances tart freshness and ripe intensity. The long finish rewards with an elegant tannic button.
Santa Maria Valley Bien Nacido Vineyard Syrah 2022 ● 192 cases; 60 $ - 🍷 - on the nose, amaretto, black cherry and black olive. On the palate, black cherry and orange rind flavors are infused with resinous herbs.
Santa Barbara County PS Santa Barbara County Syrah 2022 ● 640 cases; 30 $ - 🍷 - from the glass, a blast of black cherry/berry with smoked meat, dark chocolate and iodine. The palate is fresh and tart showing blackberry and Seville orange and youthful fine tannins alloyed with a mineral streak.

acres 4 - cases 1,079
Fertilizers compost, manure
Plant protection sulfur, organic
Weed control mechanical
Yeasts spontaneous fermentation
Grapes purchase 85%
Certification none

LOS OLIVOS

REFUGIO RANCH VINEYARDS

2990 Grand Avenue - tel. (805) 697-5289
www.refugioranch.com - info@refugioranch.com

PEOPLE - Kevin Gleason purchased Refugio Ranch, a 415 acre former cattle ranch, in 2004 and in 2006 planted 28 acres of vines, prioritizing concentrated fruits. He also owns Roblar winery, sharing resources between his two wineries. Winemaker Max Marshak joined in 2020, making the Refugio wines at the Roblar facility. Vineyard manager Jesse Gal joined in 2023.

VINEYARDS - Farming is managed entirely in house. The vines sit on a north facing mountainside on the south side of the Santa Ynez River. The vines are primarily Rhône varieties–Syrah is the dominant variety– as well as Sauvignon Blanc. The site sits on hot, river flats with silty, alluvial soil, influenced by the marine layer and diurnal shift. They also sit on mountains with limestone under heavy clay soils and a gentler diurnal curve.

WINES - Concentrated Rhône varieties, with an eclectic selection of powerful wines and blends.

Santa Ynez Valley Tiradora Sauvignon Blanc 2023 O 38 cases; 38 $ - Barrel fermented and aged in neutral oak (40%) and stainless barrels (12%). Grown from a single block and clone–Clone 1. With aromas of white flowers, lime and white peach. Very fresh with bright acidity.

Santa Ynez Valley Escondrijo Grenache 2021 ● 250 cases; 50 $ - Aged in neutral French oak. High density head trained Grenache (70%) blended with Syrah (23%) and Petite Sirah (7%). Powerful, dense wine with notes of red and blue fruits, and a touch of sweetness on the finish.

Santa Ynez Valley Barbareño Red Blend 2021 ● 250 cases; 60 $ - Aged 18 months in French oak (10% new). A red blend of Syrah (92%), Petit Sirah (5%) and Grenache (3%). Some Syrah is whole cluster. A powerful wine with flavors of dark cherry, violets, plum, leather and dried herbs.

acres 27 - cases 3,500
Fertilizers compost, organic fertilizer
Plant protection sulfur, copper, organic
Weed control animal grazing, mechanical, manual
Yeasts commercial cultured yeasts
Grapes 100% owned
Certification none

LOS OLIVOS

ROARK WINE COMPANY

6701 Foxen Canyon Road
www.roarkwinecompany.com - ryan@roarkwinecompany.com

PEOPLE - Founded in 2009, Ryan is on his 15th vintage at his personal winery. His other job is managing the vineyard and winemaking at Demetria. Emily Myers is the assistant winemaker at both Roark and Demetria. At Roark, the two work with a wide spectrum of varieties. Their philosophy in the cellar is "naturally made, classically styled."

VINEYARDS - Many of the grapes for Roark come from vineyards he farms himself or in partnership with other growers. He grows Syrah at the one acre Alondra de los Prados Vineyard. In purchasing grapes, he seeks out growers with organic farming values. Merlot comes from C5 and Sauvignon Blanc from White Barn. Both are in Santa Ynez Valley. Zinfandel comes from the organically farmed Old Oak Vineyard in Paso Robles.

WINES - Roark makes low alcohol wines with minimal sulfur and no additives, aiming to highlight the natural expression of the fruit and terroir in each bottle.

TOP Santa Barbara County Pocket Full of Stones 2022 SLOW WINE O 185 cases; 28 $ - Aged 11 months in neutral oak with 10% in new acacia. A blend of Sauvignon Blanc (70%) and Chardonnay (30%). Direct press. Peach and pineapple aromas and lots and lots of bright acidity.

Santa Ynez Valley White Barn Vineyard Sauvignon Blanc 2022 O 70 cases; 36 $ - Aged 11 months in neutral oak and a little new acacia wood. Floral notes with stone fruit and muted citrus aromas. On the palate, the wine pops with lots of bright acidity and a saline finish.

Santa Ynez Valley Alondra de los Prados Syrah 2021 ● 82 cases; 58 $ - Nestled in a little nook down near the Santa Ynez River. Ten percent stem inclusion. Aromas of dark red and purple fruit and baking spice with textured, juicy tannins on the palate.

acres 1 acre - cases 700
Fertilizers compost, biodynamic compost, cover crops, manure, organic fertilizer
Plant protection sulfur, biodynamic preparations
Weed control animal grazing, mechanical, manual
Yeasts spontaneous fermentation
Grapes purchase 90%
Certification none

SANTA YNEZ

ROBLAR WINERY & VINEYARDS

3010 Roblar Avenue - tel. (805) 686-2603
www.roblarwinery.com - info@roblarwinery.com

PEOPLE - Owned by Gleason Family Vineyards since 2017, Roblar features scenic vineyards, a state of the art winery facility, a 5,000 square foot tasting room and a restaurant. Max Marshak became winemaker in 2020 and has been improving the vines, focusing on Bordeaux varieties. The property also offers a full restaurant serving lunch daily and supper Wednesday through Friday.

VINEYARDS - Located in Santa Ynez Valley, the vineyard, planted in 1999, grows Bordeaux varieties—Cabernet Franc, Cabernet Sauvignon, Petit Verdot—as well as Rhones (Grenache and Syrah)—along with Graciano and Sangiovese. Some blocks of Cabernet are high density plantings. The owners say the vines are farmed using only organic approved materials. The team recently added a new acre of Cab Franc vines.

WINES - Bordeaux varieties are their core focus. New oak use is minimal. The wines are fresh and complex.

Santa Ynez Valley Sangre de Dioses 2021 ● 500 cases; 68 $ - ⊞ - Aged 15 months in barrel (10% new oak). A unique take on a Super Tuscan, the blend is Sangiovese (60%), Petit Verdot (20%), Cabernet Sauvignon (10%) and Merlot (10%). The nose has dried mushrooms and umami flavors with raspberry jam. The palate has notes of cherry and dark cocoa, with pronounced tannin structure.

Santa Ynez Valley Cabernet Sauvignon 2021 ● 250 cases; 68 $ - ⊞ - Aged 18 months in French oak. A fresh, yet full bodied, dry red wine with dense color and flavor and grippy tannins. Deep, layered flavors of dark fruits and blackcurrant, with hints of green pepper and light oak. 15% ABV.

Roblar Cabernet Franc 2021 ● 350 cases; 70 $ - ⊞ - Age in French oak (40% new). A blend with Cabernet Sauvignon (13%). A dry red wine with medium body and tannins. Very good acid and freshness. It has flavors of blackberry, raspberry, bell pepper, and herbs.

acres 21 - cases 7,000
Fertilizers compost, cover crops, manure, organic fertilizer
Plant protection sulfur, synthetic pesticides, copper, organic
Weed control animal grazing, mechanical, manual
Yeasts commercial cultured yeasts
Grapes purchase 20%
Certification none

LOMPOC

RZN WINES

1225 W Laurel - tel. (805) 332-6354
www.rznwines.com

PEOPLE - Cutting his winemaking chops at Liquid Farm in 2019, Nate Axline's intense curiosity made him a quick study for the craft under winemaker James Sparks (Kings Carey). In 2020 he branched out, launching his wine brand RZN ("Reason") with an initial focus on white wine. An accomplished skateboarder, he integrates this love and aesthetic into his label's marketing.

VINEYARDS - He buys dry farmed, old vine Chenin Blanc from Santa Maria Valley's Tres Hermanas Vineyard (certified organic), a sandy site comprised of shale, sandstone and granite. Mencia and Clairette Blanche come from Nolan Ranch, a fairly new vineyard in Alisos Canyon. Soils there are also sandy with some limestone. Farming here is the same program as at Tres Hermanas (and by the same company, though without certification).

WINES - Axline is going for freshness in his young label. Relying on grape quality and picking on the edge of ripeness ensures that result.

Alisos Canyon Nolan Ranch Vineyard Clairette Blanche 2023 EVERYDAY WINE ○ 60 cases; 30 $ - ⊞ - Elegant on the nose with white flower, citrus and peach. A full, pure palate of red apple, lemon and clean minerality.

Santa Barbara County Tres Hermanas Vineyard Chenin Blanc 2023 ○ 90 cases; 30 $ - ⊞ - Aromas of yellow apple, pear and white flower. Ripe and racy, displaying pure apple and lemon flesh with a mineral streak on the palate.

Alisos Canyon Nolan Ranch Vineyard Mencia 2023 ● 85 cases; 35 $ - ⊞ - Smells of rose and cherry juice strained through cedar bark. On the palate, red and dark cherry, with hints of maraschino flavors are deeply informed by woodiness–surprising from this fresh, lighter style wine.

acres 0 - cases 240
Fertilizers compost, organic fertilizer
Plant protection sulfur, organic
Weed control mechanical
Yeasts spontaneous fermentation
Grapes purchase 100%
Certification some of the vineyards are certified organic

GOLETA

SAMSARA WINE CO.

6485 Calle Real Ste E - tel. (805) 845-8001
www.samsarawine.com - info@samSarawine.com

PEOPLE - Owners Joan and Dave Szkutak purchased the winery in 2017 that Chad and Mary Melville founded in 2002. Today the Szkutaks are on a path to reduce their carbon footprint. With winemaker Matt Brady, they switched to California made bottles that are 30 percent lighter. As of the 2021 vintage, they no longer use capsules. The SIP Certified winery in Goleta is powered by solar energy and they track all water and electricity usage.

VINEYARDS - SAMsARA works with numerous vineyards in the Sta. Rita Hills. Some are certified organic—Bentrock, Radian and Spear. Other wines, not featured here, may be grown with herbicide. They also source from two vineyards in Ballard Canyon—Larner and Kimsey (both certified organic) as well as Bien Nacido in Santa Maria Valley.

WINES - They bottled three new wines this year—a Mourvedre from Kimsey, a Syrah from Spear Vineyard, and a Chardonnay from Francesca Vineyard—as well as Blanc de Blanc, their first sparkling wine.

TOP Sta. Rita Hills Radian Vineyard Pinot Noir 2020 ●
164 cases; 74 $ - ⊞ - Aged in French oak (30%). Picked early. Stem inclusion: 30%. Spicy and savory with aromas of crushed red berries and rose petals. Initially light and ethereal on the palate, flavors develop.

Sta. Rita Hills Bentrock Vineyard Chardonnay 2021 ○ 138 cases; 64 $ - ⌀⊞ - Aged 15 months in French oak and then two months in tank. Picked early. Barrel fermented. Bright, fresh, and mineral driven. Aromas of apple, grapefruit, lemon, line, and crushed rock. Linear focus with a saline freshness on the finish.

Sta. Rita Hills Spear Vineyard Grenache 2021 ● 152 cases; 59 $ - ⊞ - Aged 18 months in neutral oak. Partial whole cluster (65%). Elegant with thyme, black cherry, cranberry aromas and textured acidity. Lovely savory notes on the palate.

acres 0 - cases 3,500
Fertilizers compost, cover crops, manure, organic fertilizer
Plant protection sulfur, synthetic pesticides, organic
Weed control animal grazing, mechanical, manual
Yeasts spontaneous fermentation
Grapes purchase 100%
Certification some of the vineyards are certified organic

LOMPOC

SANDHI WINES

1712 Industrial Way, Suite B - tel. (805) 500-8337
www.sandhiwines.com - tasting@sandhiwines.com

PEOPLE - Sandhi (Sanskrit for "collaboration") joins visionary winemaker Sashi Moorman and celebrated somm turned vigneron Raj Parr. They seek to elevate Sta Rita Hills Chardonnay to world class status. To this end, they make fine single vineyard cuveés and an AVA wine renowned for its character and value. This wine has been the company's calling card internationally and shows how dimensional (and obtainable) wine from the region can be.

VINEYARDS - Grapes from the duo's other local collaboration, Domaine de la Cote are leveraged as well as estate Hines Vineyard. Both are farmed with organic practice using fish and milk-based sprays. Single vineyard sources, Sanford & Benedict, Patterson and Rinconada use no synthetics. Jalama Canyon Ranch provides regeneratively farmed Pinot Noir. Grapes for the inexpensive Central Coast Chardonnay are mostly from San Luis Obispo County growers.

WINES - Sandhi shows the breadth and depth of Sta Rita Hills Chardonnay from excellent and affordable entry-level wines to extremes of concentration and refinement.

TOP Sta Rita Hills Patterson Vineyard Chardonnay 2022
○ 238 cases; 75 $ - ⌀⊞ - elegant citrus blossom, kumquat skin and yellow apple are on the nose with a hint of smokey reduction. Racy flavors of Meyer lemon, green pineapple and ripe nectarine are dialed up in concentration and rounded out with time in Stockinger puncheons.

Sta. Rita Hills Chardonnay 2022 ○ 4,198 cases; 32 $ - ⌀⊞ - shows refined white flower aromas along with spun sugar, yellow apple and hay. The palate is concentrated with tart Meyer lemon and nectarine with its skin. Lots of intensity in this flagship wine.

Santa Barbara County Jalama Canyon Ranch Pinot Noir 2022 ● 343 cases; 65 $ - ⊞ - has a generous nose showing rose petal, tobacco leaf and dark cherry giving way to rich flavors of dark plum and cherry as well as foresty humus and slightly chewy tannins.

acres 37 - cases 16,242
Fertilizers compost, biodynamic compost, cover crops, manure, organic fertilizer, synthetic fertilizer
Plant protection sulfur, biodynamic preparations, synthetic pesticides, copper, organic
Weed control mechanical
Yeasts spontaneous fermentation
Grapes purchase 61%
Certification none

LOS ALAMOS

SHOKRIAN VINEYARD

7910 Cat Canyon Road - tel. (805) 250-9363
www.shokrianvineyard.com - info@shokrianvineyard.com

PEOPLE - Film producer Babak Shokrian used to visit winemaker and friend Scott Sampler in Santa Ynez. In 2013, fed up with LA, he found the property on Cat Canyon in Los Alamos. It had fallen out of escrow, so he made an offer and became the owner of 100 acres with 50 planted acres. The first two years, Drake Whitcraft and Morgan Clendenen made the wines. Then Alice Anderson made the wines for three years before superstar Bob Lindquist became the winemaker in 2021.

VINEYARDS - Shokrian replanted 20 acres of Verna's Vineyard (formerly owned by Melville), adding Gamay, Grenache, Mencia, Mourvedre and Sangiovese. In 2018. he eliminated herbicides and in 2022 took over the farming. He has six cows, 40 goats, and 10 chickens for compost and weed control. There has been no tilling a few years. Instead he laid compost and wheat straws down to build a bed of mulch.

WINES - Complex, vibrant, and natural wines that emphasize a sense of place and minimal intervention.

🔝 Santa Barbara County Grenache Rose 2022 ● 75 cases; 38 $ - ⊞ - Direct to press, fermented in neutral barrel for five months, finished in tank. Lovely strawberry aromas, textured midpalate, and tart red fruit on the finish.
Santa Barbara County Syrah 2021 ● 100 cases; 60 $ - ⊞ - Aged 18 months. Partial whole cluster (50%). Estrella clone grown on a dry farmed, north facing hillside. Perfumed aromas of blackberry and earth. Rich midpalate with softly gripping tannins.
Santa Barbara County Red Blend 2020 ● 150 cases; 48 $ - ⊞ - Co-ferment of half Syrah and half Petite Sirah. Whole cluster (100%). Rich nose with dark boysenberry and wild raspberry aromas, hints of white pepper. Round on the palate with drying tannins with a layer of acidity on top.

acres 50 - cases 800
Fertilizers compost, cover crops, manure, organic fertilizer
Plant protection sulfur, organic
Weed control animal grazing, mechanical, manual
Yeasts spontaneous fermentation
Grapes 100% owned
Certification none

LOS OLIVOS

SOLMINER

2890 Grand Avenue - tel. (805) 691-9195
www.solminer.com - info@solminer.com

PEOPLE - Founders and winemakers David and Austrian born Anna deLaski are currently making more than 17 wines. After working with pet nats and carbonic fermentations, they are moving to more sulfite free wines—namely, a Blaufrankisch and a skin fermented Grüner Veltliner—to compare these bottlings over time with their other Blaufrankisch and their Grüner without skins. They are now making cider from the 60 apple trees on the estate, as well as olive oil.

VINEYARDS - Regenerative Organic Certified on their tiny estate for three years (and certified biodynamic since 2018), they're refining how they prevent mildew, build the microbiome and make compost tea sprays. They have 19 sheep along with donkeys (who provide compost) and chickens (who graze in the vines). They planted two acres of Blaufrankisch, Grüner Veltliner and Riesling on a new adjacent vineyard. Additional grapes come from local growers who are certified organic or biodynamic.

WINES - Solminer's philosophy is that when wine is well grown, there is no need to add anything. A low amount of sulfites are managed on a wine by wine basis.

🔝 Los Olivos District Pet Nat Rosé 2023 ⊕ 1,104 cases; 44 $ - ⌭ ⊞ - A half and half blend of estate grown Blaufränkisch and Syrah fermented in tank. Lovely ruby red grapefruit color, focused nose with lots of red fruit and blood orange notes, clean, precise and refreshing on the palate.
Los Olivos District Skin Fermented Field Blend 2022 ○ 84 cases; 36 $ - ⌭ ⊞ - Aged seven months in stainless and neutral oak barrels . A novel blend of Riesling (44%), Muscat (33%) and Grüner Veltliner (23%). Two weeks on skins. Elegant and serious with floral aromatics and juicy acidity.
Los Olivos District DeLanda Vineyard Curarse La Cruda Skin Fermented Grüner Veltliner 2023 ○ 56 cases; 36 $ - ⌭ ⊞ - Skin fermented and aged seven months in neutral oak and stainless steel without sulfur. Baked apple, citrus, and white tea notes, the wine is textured with intense acidity and a lovely juicy finish.

acres 5 - cases 1,800
Fertilizers biodynamic compost, cover crops, manure
Plant protection biodynamic preparations
Weed control animal grazing, mechanical, manual
Yeasts spontaneous fermentation
Grapes purchase 50%
Certification organic, some of the vineyards are certified biodynamic, regenerative

SANTA MARIA

SOLOMON HILLS ESTATE

3503 Rancho Tepusquet Road - tel. (805) 318-6503
www.solomonhillsestate.com - info@solomonhillsestate.com

PEOPLE - A highly regarded Santa Maria Valley vineyard, the Miller family, who famously own the acclaimed Bien Nacido Vineyard, bought it in 1999. In 2008, they launched it as a winery brand. Anthony Avila oversees the winemaking at both Solomon Hills and Bien Nacido. Chris Hammell manages the vines.

VINEYARDS - Solomon Hills Estate sits at the western edge of the valley, making it one of the closest vineyards to the Pacific Ocean, which brings cool, maritime influences, ideal for cultivating high quality Chardonnay and Pinot Noir. The soils on the estate consist of pure sand. Due to the proximity to the ocean, the vineyard is exposed to cold winds and fog, resulting in low yields.

WINES - The small clusters of berries have thin skins and produce concentrated, structured wines with high acidity.

⊙ Santa Maria Valley Belle of the Ball Chardonnay 2022 ○ 62 cases; 100 $ - ⊞ - Aged in oak (50% new). Dijon clone. Grown on a gentle slope with sandstone soils. An opulent and rich wine but also fresh and elegant. Acidity is so vibrant that it cuts through the richness of the wine.

Santa Maria Valley Estate Chardonnay 2022 ○ 243 cases; 60 $ - 🍷⊞ - Aged 12 months in French oak (40% new) and five months in tank. Barrel fermented. Vibrant aromas of tropical fruits, lemon curd and floral notes, rich on the palate with leesy notes and focused acidity.

Santa Maria Valley Solomon Hills Estate Pinot Noir 2022 ● 426 cases; 75 $ - ⊞ - Aged 16 months in French oak (45% new). Partial whole cluster (10%). A dark ruby red opaque color. Fresh and savory with herbal notes and structured tannins.

---

acres 20 - cases 1,250
Fertilizers compost, cover crops, organic fertilizer
Plant protection sulfur, organic
Weed control mechanical, manual
Yeasts spontaneous fermentation, commercial cultured yeasts
Grapes 100% owned
Certification none

LOMPOC

SPEAR VINEYARDS & WINERY

6700 E Highway 246 - tel. (805) 735-2190
www.spearwinery.com - visit@spearwinery.com

PEOPLE - Israeli born Ofer Shepher's dedication to quality viticulture has made Spear vineyard an acclaimed grower as well as popular vintner. Their elegant tasting room offers spectacular vineyard views, including views of the 500+ acre cattle ranch where Shepher raises grass fed, organic Black Angus. Spear started a sparkling wine program in 2018. They have hand disgorged a few bottles and are very happy with the results. James Sparks became winemaker in 2023.

VINEYARDS - Certified organic, Shepher sells more than half of his fruit to local winemakers. He planted three new acres of Grüner Veltliner in 2020 and 2024 was the first year for a full harvest. With five total acres of Grüner, Spear Vineyards has the largest organic Grüner planting in California. He also has five acres of organic Italian olives that were harvested for first time in 2023. There are plans to buy olive oil production equipment.

WINES - Spear Vineyard wines are known for their elegance, vibrant acidity and pure expression of Sta. Rita Hills terroir.

⊙ Sta. Rita Hills 943 Pinot Noir 2021 ● 96 cases; 70 $ - ⊞ - Aged 12 months in neutral oak. A single clone. Aromas of cherry and raspberry balanced with spice notes and floral notes. Rich on the palate with intense flavors and body, structured tannins and a long finish.

Sta. Rita Hills Estate Pinot Noir 2022 ● 480 cases; 55 $ - ⊞ - Aged 12 months in neutral oak. Partial whole cluster (30%). From six clones on six blocks. A vibrant garnet color, elegant with dark red fruit, dried herbs and brown spices. Textured tannins are balanced by fresh acidity.

Sta. Rita Hills Estate Chardonnay 2022 ○ 144 cases; 45 $ - ⊞ - Aged 12 months in neutral barrel. An equal blend of Wente and Mount Eden clones. Fresh and bright with citrus, red apple and white floral notes, the wine has delicate acidity and a mineral finish.

---

acres 42 - cases 1,500
Fertilizers compost, biodynamic compost, cover crops, organic fertilizer
Plant protection sulfur, organic
Weed control mechanical, manual
Yeasts spontaneous fermentation, commercial cultured yeasts
Grapes 100% owned
Certification organic

LOS OLIVOS

STOLPMAN VINEYARD

2434 Alamo Pintado Avenue - tel. (805) 688-0400
www.stolpmanvineyards.com - info@stolpmanvineyards.com

PEOPLE - Peter Stolpman manages the pioneering winery his father, L. A. attorney Tom Stolpman, started the 1990s. It was one of the first in Ballard Canyon—a region now known for Syrah. Spring 2025 releases will feature a new look—a black and white image of the vineyard and, on the back label, an ingredient list. Kyle Knapp is the winemaker while vineyard manager Ruben Solorzano oversees the vines. They reward vineyard workers annually with the profits from a select 10 percent of the vines.

VINEYARDS - The estate was certified organic in 2022 and biodynamic in 2023. They are currently planting a new 22 acre parcel for white varieties with a third each of Gewürztraminer, Pinot Gris and Tocai Friulano. They also have a new vineyard in the Los Olivos District (one hill over from Ballard Canyon), where they are planting three acres each of Chardonnay and Chenin Blanc and six acres of Sauvignon Blanc.

WINES - Bold, expressive wines as well as playful easy going wines. For fruit they purchase (labeled Santa Barbara County), they manage the farming and mandate no synthetics.

● **TOP** Ballard Canyon Unfiltered Sauvignon Blanc 2023 EVERYDAY WINE ○ 300 cases; 30 $ - ⓜ - Aged four months in neutral puncheons. From an own rooted, low yielding block. Green pineapple and passion fruit notes and intense acidity. A fun and delicious take on Sauvignon Blanc.
Ballard Canyon Estate Vin Gris 2023 ● 900 cases; 30 $ - ⓜ - Aged four months in neutral 500L puncheons. The first vintage of blend of Gamay (70%) and Trousseau (30%). No sulfur added. Translucent cherry color, fresh with bright fruit and earth notes, savory on the palate with herbal notes.
Ballard Canyon Estate Grown Originals Syrah 2022 ● 550 cases; 52 $ - ⓜ - From Stolpman's original vineyard blocks planted in 1993. Fermented in open top concrete and food tread. Fresh nose with a floral and dark red fruit perfume. Structured with elegant intensity.

acres 178 - cases 55,000
Fertilizers biodynamic compost, cover crops
Plant protection biodynamic preparations
Weed control mechanical, manual
Yeasts spontaneous fermentation
Grapes purchase 40%
Certification some of the vineyards are certified organic, some of the vineyards are certified biodynamic

SANTA MARIA

STORM WINES $

5069 Presqu'ile Drive - tel. (805) 350-9456
www.stormwines.com - info@stormwines.com

PEOPLE - Storm Wines, founded by South African Ernst Storm in 2006, considers itself a Pinot house, offering six single vineyard Pinot Noirs and one Santa Barbara County blend, but also makes many other wine varieties, producing them at Presqu'ile's facilities in Santa Maria Valley. Assistant winemaker Axel Kleemeier joined in 2020. Eighty percent of the wine is sold in Santa Barbara. Ernst also makes wine for Donnachadh and Grimm's Bluff.

VINEYARDS - Ernst chose the Santa Ynez Valley for its coastal influence. He works with 17 vineyards in Santa Barbara County, including Donnachadh, Duvarita, North Canyon, Presqu'ile, John Sebastiano, and Riverbench Vineyards (added in 2020). Storm has developed a deep understanding of each vineyard, securing long term contracts. Donnachadh is certified organic. Duvarita is certified biodynamic.

WINES - Nearly half of production is Sauvignon Blanc. All the wines are fresh wines, made with minimal intervention.

Santa Ynez Valley Sauvignon Blanc 2023 ○ 2,400 cases; 29 $ - ⓜ - Fermented in stainless steel and aged on lees for six months. It features lime, kumquat, and crushed rocks on the nose, with passionfruit, pink grapefruit, and citrus on a structured and vibrant palate.
Sta. Rita Hills Donnachadh Vineyard Pinot Noir 2021 ● 200 cases; 58 $ - ⓜ - Aged 18 months in neutral oak. Presents flavors of plum, fresh berries, and earthy undertones on the palate.
Santa Barbara County Pinot Noir 2022 ● 930 cases; 45 $ - ⓜ - Aged 10 months in French oak (10% new). A blend from different sites. It exudes wild strawberry, cherry, and tart pomegranate aromas, with hints of forest floor and dark spice. The palate offers vibrant berry fruit and spice.

acres 0 - cases 4,000
Fertilizers compost, cover crops, organic and synthetic fertilizer
Plant protection sulfur, biodynamic preparations, synthetic pesticides
Weed control animal grazing, mechanical, manual
Yeasts spontaneous fermentation, commercial cultured yeasts
Grapes purchase 100%
Certification some of the vineyards are certified organic, some of the vineyards are certified biodynamic

LOS OLIVOS

STORY OF SOIL WINE

2928 San Marcos Avenue - tel. (805) 686-1302
www.storyofsoilwine.com - info@storyofsoilwine.com

PEOPLE - Owner Jessica Gasca does not slow down. In addition to making single vineyard designates from Santa Barbara County for her label, she also makes wines for clients at her facility in Buellton. She also started making wine for Strange Family Vineyards. The owners also own Matti's Tavern and bought a vineyard six years go. They will be opening a tasting room in Los Olivos where Story of Soil has their tasting room.

VINEYARDS - Gasca works with more than a dozen sites. Ampelos, Bentrock, Donnachadh, Presqu'ile and Stolpman are all certified organic. Duvarita and Martian Ranch are certified biodynamic. Other sites include Fiddlestix, Gold Coast, Grassini, La Rinconada and Wild King Vineyard.

WINES - Gasca focuses on terroir driven wines that are elegant, balanced and express a sense of place.

Alisos Canyon Martian Ranch Gamay Noir 2023 ● 250 cases; 42 $ - 🛢 🔴 - Aged six months in neutral French puncheons. Partial whole cluster (50%). Fermented on the skins for three weeks. The nose is a mix of herbal, cherry, spice and floral notes. Savory and earthy yet fresh.

Sta. Rita Hills Ampelos Vineyard Pinot Noir 2022 ● 125 cases; 65 $ - 🛢 - Aged 18 months in neutral oak. Picked in three separate picks. Pretty red fruit and baking spices aromas, fresh on the palate with some spice notes, bright juiciness washes over the palate with textured tannins.

Sta. Rita Hills Duvarita Vineyard Syrah 2021 ● 150 cases; 55 $ - 🛢 - Aged 18 months in oak. Partial whole cluster (50%). Fresh nose of blue fruits, spice, and floral notes, the fruit is concentrated on the palate with soft tannins and a finish that leaves you salivating for more.

acres 0 - cases 3,000
Fertilizers compost, biodynamic compost, cover crops, manure, organic fertilizer
Plant protection sulfur, synthetic pesticides, organic
Weed control animal grazing, mechanical, manual
Yeasts spontaneous fermentation
Grapes purchase 100%
Certification some of the vineyards are certified organic, some of the vineyards are certified biodynamic

LOS OLIVOS

TERCERO WINES

2445 Alamo Pintado Drive, Suite 105 - tel. (805) 245-9584
www.tercerowines.com - larry@tercerowines.com

PEOPLE - For Larry Schaffer, winemaking was a second career. After his first (publishing), he fell in love with wine and went back to school, working at Fess Parker, after graduating from U.C. Davis. He started tercero wines in 2005, originally for Rhones, but broadened his offering in the 2020's, adding Cabernet Franc, Chenin Blanc, Pinot Noir and Petite Sirah. Full circle, he now teaches wine production for U.C. Davis's continuing professional education winemaking certificate program.

VINEYARDS - Larry would like all of his sources to be certified organic but that is challenging if he wants to stay within the Santa Barbara region, which is his first priority. He buys certified organic fruit from Larner Vineyard in Ballard Canyon and Spear Vineyard in Sta. Rita Hills. Some wines (not featured here) may be grown with herbicides. Since 2013, he's foot trod his red wines which are fermented whole cluster with stems.

WINES - His style relies on 100 percent stem inclusion, no new oak and extended barrel aging (up to 48 months). In 2024, he made his first multi-vintage wine of equal parts Carignan, Counoise, and Cinsault.

Sta. Rita Hills Spear Vineyard Grenache 2020 ● 75 cases; 45 $ - 🛢 - A Pinot drinkers' Grenache. Aromas of wild strawberries, wild berries, and floral notes and spice on the finish. Lively acidity with savory freshness.

Ballard Canyon Larner Vineyard Syrah 2015 ● 75 cases; 60 $ - 🛢 - Aged 40 months unracked on fine lees in neutral oak. Big structure but fresh. Initial aromas of dark red fruits, chocolate, and oak. The wine changes in the glass. Beautiful balance of acidity and softly textured tannins.

Santa Barbara County Santa Ynez Vineyard Picpoul Blanc 2023 ○ 120 cases; 35 $ - 🥛 - His second vintage of Picpoul, aka the "lip stinger," is fermented and aged in stainless steel. High acidity with citrus, stone fruit, and pineapple aromas, a fresh, crisp texture and a clean finish.

acres 0 - cases 2,000
Fertilizers compost, cover crops, manure, organic fertilizer
Plant protection sulfur, synthetic pesticides, organic
Weed control animal grazing, mechanical, manual
Yeasts spontaneous fermentation, commercial cultured yeasts
Grapes purchase 100%
Certification some of the vineyards are certified organic

SANTA YNEZ

THE BRANDER VINEYARD

2401 North Refugio Road - tel. (805) 688-2455
www.brander.com - office@brander.com

PEOPLE - Fred Brander, the "king of Sauvignon Blanc," produces up to 12 different Sauvignon Blancs annually. His flagship wine blends grapes from vineyards in Los Olivos District, an AVA he helped establish. Since 1977, he's specialized in Sauvignon Blanc, with the first vintage winning gold at the L.A. County Fair. Since that time he's mentored many winemakers. The first to grow and produce Sauvignon Blanc in the Santa Ynez Valley, he recently bottled their 47th vintage.

VINEYARDS - Brander's estate wines highlight Sauvignon Blanc, producing world-class wines including Pinot Blanc, Sauvignon Gris, Pinot Gris, Semillon, Muscat, and Riesling. The vineyard features 3.5 acres of 1975 ungrafted Cabernet. Fabian Bravo, winemaker since 2007, and Jim Stollberg of Hampton Farming, vineyard manager, work together to improve efficiency. Together, they've reduced irrigation, and use only organic approved materials in the estate vineyards.

WINES - Specialists in high quality, world class Sauvignon Blancs since the dawn of Santa Barbara wine country.

Los Olivos District au Natural Estate Sauvignon Blanc 2023 ○ 403 cases; 42 $ - ⃞ - Fruit from three lots, several pick days. Free run juice aged eight months on lees. Good texture from crushed de-stemmed fruit. Beautiful floral and tropical fruit aromatics. Fresh, bright, with roundness on the palate. Highlights the natural fruit of Santa Barbara.

Los Olivos District Cuvée Nicolas Estate Sauvignon Blanc 2022 ○ 146 cases; 38 $ - ⌸ - Free run juice aged in 100% French Oak (20% new) with lees stirring. With floral, melon, and delicate vanilla aromas, soft and lush on the palate with delicate persistent acidity.

Los Olivos District Estate Bordeaux Blend Bouchet 2020 ● 44 cases; 60 $ - ⌸ - The first meritage blend on the Central Coast, in 1984. Aged in 2yr old French Oak. A blend of Cabernet (50%), Cab Franc (50%). Smooth with flavors of red fruit, plum, boysenberry, and sweet spices. Fresh with nicely light tannins and acid.

acres 41 - cases 12,500
Fertilizers cover crops, manure, organic fertilizer
Plant protection sulfur, synthetic pesticides, organic
Weed control mechanical, manual
Yeasts spontaneous fermentation, commercial cultured yeasts
Grapes purchase 30%
Certification none

LOMPOC

TYLER WINERY

Mae Estate Vineyard House - tel. (805) 225-3395
www.tylerwinery.com - gabe@tylerwinery.com

PEOPLE - Santa Barbara native Justin Willett has established himself as one of the area's most prolific voices. Working with many Sta. Rita Hills vineyards, Justin has changed the label to focus on the vineyards. In 2024, he released his first sparkling wines, the 2020 Blanc de Noir and the 2020 Sparkling Rosé. His Mae Estate welcomes guests for tastings. He also opened a tasting room and wine bar with his sister label, Lieu Dit, in Santa Barbara.

VINEYARDS - There are two estate vineyards–Fiddled stix Vineyard and Mae Estate–both in the Sta. Rita Hills. Fiddlestix started its conversion to organic farming in 2021. Mae Estate is ideal for Chardonnay and Pinot Noir. It also has a new Syrah planting, grown in meter by meter spacing. First production is anticipated in 2024. Willett's partner Erik Mallea manages the farming. The winery also sources fruit from Sta. Rita Hills growers. Some wines (not featured here) may be grown with herbicide.

WINES - Tyler Winery focuses on elegance, restraint, and balance while expressing the terroir of Santa Barbara County's cooler-climate regions.

TOP Sta. Rita Hills Mae Estate Pinot Noir 2022 ● 400 cases; 75 $ - ⌸ - Partial whole cluster, aged 16 months in oak, then into ss for a few months. Beautifully elegant, aromas of crushed flowers, lavender, red fruits, dried herbs, black tea. Everything you want in a glass- structured, elegant, and delicious.

Sta. Rita Hills Mae Estate Chardonnay 2022 ○ 400 cases; 75 $ - ⌸ - Direct press, barrel fermentation, aged 11 months in neutral barrel, then tank. Bright and fresh, citrus peel, white peach, apple, white flower, crushed rock aromas, beautiful mineral-driven linearity followed by a rush of fresh acidity.

Sta. Rita Hills Fiddlestix Vineyard Pinot Noir 2022 ● 350 cases; 75 $ - ⌸ - Partial whole cluster, aged 16 months in oak, then tank, lots of red fruit aromas, bright on the palate with dusty tannins, rustic elegance with structure, depth. and length.

acres 130 - cases 15,000
Fertilizers compost, cover crops, manure, organic fertilizer
Plant protection sulfur, synthetic pesticides, copper, organic
Weed control mechanical, manual
Yeasts spontaneous fermentation
Grapes purchase 50%
Certification none

BUELLTON

VEGA VINEYARD & FARM

9496 Santa Rosa Road - tel. (805) 688-2415
www.vegavineyardandfarm.com - info@vegavineyardandfarm.com

PEOPLE - In 2022, Karen and Demetrios Loizides—he is from a Cypriot family—purchased the historic Mosby property to create their farm to table dream. It came with vineyards, a restaurant, tasting room and working farm. Hospitality pros, the couple added vineyard cabanas and let children feed the farm animals. They offer guests stays in their historic 1856 adobe or their modern, vineyard house. Local legend Steve Clifton oversees the vines and wines.

VINEYARDS - Clifton manages the three vineyards which are now In the second year of the three year transition to organic certification. They've added native cover crops and animals to mow and fertilize. They're also moving toward Italian varieties, grafting vines to Pinot Grigio as well as adding three new acres of Barbera and some Malvasia Bianca. Their four acre organic farm supplies Michelin starred Caruso at Rosewood Hotel as well as Vega's restaurant and farmstand.

WINES - With a new focus on Italian varieties, Clifton crafts approachable, well structured, ageworthy wines.

TOP Los Olivos District Malvasia Biana 2023 ○ 375 cases; 39 $ - 🍷 - From the Santa Ynez Ranch. Whole cluster pressed. Beautiful floral nose. Anticipating sweetness, but the wine is dry, fresh, vibrant and crisp with a long, lingering finish.
Santa Barbara County Pinot Grigio 2023 ○ 400 cases; 39 $ - 🍷 - Fruit from Santa Ynez Ranch. Lees stirred for mouthfeel and texture. Apple peel, citrus and almond peel aromas with a creamy midpalate and saline finish.
Santa Ynez Valley Barbera 2023 ● 400 cases; 47 $ - 🍷 - Aged in 500 liter puncheons (10% new) and stainless steel tank (25%). Elegant aromas of dark red and black fruits. Textured midpalate with lots of mouthwatering acidity with low tannin, mostly coming from the new oak.

acres 44 - cases 9,000
Fertilizers compost, cover crops, manure
Plant protection sulfur, synthetic pesticides, organic
Weed control animal grazing, mechanical, manual
Yeasts spontaneous fermentation, commercial cultured yeasts
Grapes purchase 15%
Certification converting to organic

SANTA BARBARA

WHITCRAFT WINERY

36 S Calle Cesar Chavez - tel. (805) 730-1680
www.whitcraftwinery.com - info@whitcraftwinery.com

PEOPLE - Drake Whitcraft worked in his family winery since his father started it in 1985, but took over in 2008 when his dad became ill. He switched from primarily Santa Maria fruit to Sta. Rita Hills grapes, adding varieties beyond Chardonnay and Pinot Noir. Today, he makes 10 vineyard designate Pinot Noirs. Within each variety, the wine is made in the same way: no new oak, no fining, no filtering—thereby showcasing terroir.

VINEYARDS - Whitcraft has a small quarter acre vineyard planted with Trousseau but primarily buys fruit from longstanding vineyard partners. He also explores new and interesting varieties. He buys Chardonnay, Gamay, Grenache, Pinot Noir, Syrah and Zinfandel mostly from Sta. Rita Hills. From these vineyards, he collects samples to inoculate his select indigenous yeast using a winery made fermentation starter from grapes, known as 'pied de cuve' (PdC).

WINES - Whitcraft's light touch creates fresh wines with short fermentations. There is no sorting table, pumps or filtration, yet the wines are clear.

Sta. Rita Hills Radian Vineyard Pinot Noir 2022 ● 157 cases; 90 $ - 🍷 - Aged 11 months in neutral oak with minimal sulfur. Whole cluster. Bright and fresh, with great acidity and elegance. With red fruit, floral, earthy, and minerality, with long lasting flavor. 13.0% ABV.
Sta. Rita Hills Pence Ranch Chardonnay 2021 ○ 110 cases; 55 $ - 🍷 - Aged 18 months in neutral barrels with no sulfur or stirring. Bright and mineral driven. Citrus, white flower, green apple and briny notes offer great acidity and a long, salty finish. 12.5% ABV.
Ballard Canyon Stolpman Vineyard Grenache 2022 ● 135 cases; 55 $ - 🍷 - Aged 11 months in neutral barrels. Whole cluster. Made Pinot Noir style. On the nose, a spicy, red fruit and lavender bouquet. Fresh red fruit and great acid.

acres 0.2 - cases 3,000
Fertilizers compost, cover crops, manure, organic fertilizer
Plant protection sulfur, biodynamic preparations, synthetic pesticides, copper
Weed control animal grazing, mechanical, manual
Yeasts selected indigenous yeasts
Grapes purchase 95%
Certification some of the vineyards are certified organic, some of the vineyards are certified biodynamic, converting to organic

VENTURA

WILDFLOWER WINERY

4517 Market Street, Suite 7 - tel. (805) 613-7036
www.wildflowerwineryventura.com - info@wildflowerwineryventura.com

PEOPLE - Living in Sicily for five years inspired Central Valley native Natalie Albertson's love of fresh, crisp wines, leading her to start her own winery in 2020. As a winemaker, she focuses on pet nats and carbonic wines as well as other minimal intervention wines. In 2023 she doubled her production and opened an urban tasting room in Ventura. She also makes keg wine for a local bar.

VINEYARDS - Albertson buys certified organic grapes from Coquliecot (Cinsault, Sangiovese and Syrah) in Santa Ynez Valley and Mira Luna (Sangiovese) in Los Olivos District. She also buys from La Quinta Norte and Zaca Mesa Vineyard. Primitivo comes from Rock Farms Vineyard in Joshua Tree, outside of Palmdale. The hot climate is out of her comfort zone, but she adapts by picking early.

WINES - Wildflower Winery makes playful wines including pet nats and carbonic wines. The wines are fresh, vibrant, and expressive of the terroir.

🔝 **Los Angeles County Rock Farms Vineyard Zee Rosso Bubbles Primitivo Pet Nat 2023** SLOW WINE ⊛ 55 cases; 34 $ - 🍷 - A vibrant ruby color with earthy, dark fruit notes. Lightly textured tannins and light bubbles that hit the front of the tongue.

Santa Ynez Valley Zaca Mesa Vineyard A Little Something Viognier 2023 ⭘ 55 cases; 26 $ - 🍷 - Whole cluster pressed and aged in tank. Aromas of white peach, citrus, and subtle honey notes. There is fresh acidity on the palate with minerality and salinity on the finish.

Santa Ynez Valley Sunshine Dry Riesling 2023 ⭘ 28 cases; 28 $ - 🍷 - The first vintage sourced from La Quinta Norte, a small, privately owned vineyard in Santa Ynez. Fresh aromas of stone fruits, apple, and tangerine. On the palate, tangy acidity and tart juiciness.

acres 2 - cases 750
Fertilizers compost, cover crops
Plant protection sulfur, organic
Weed control mechanical, manual
Yeasts spontaneous fermentation
Grapes purchase 100%
Certification some of the vineyards are certified organic

SOUTH COAST

$ Coin

159 Charlie & Echo
159 Herrmann York
160 J. Brix Wines
161 Los Pilares

SAN DIEGO

CHARLIE & ECHO $

8680 Miralani Drive #113 - tel. (877) 592-9095
www.charlieandecho.com - echo@charlieandecho.com

PEOPLE - Eric Van Drunen's mission is to make accessible wine and wine drinks in the fun spirit of his San Diegan clientele. In a region where craft beer rules, this means fruit spritzers and sparkling and still wine made from San Diego County grapes served at his casual wine bar. A physicist by training, his project has focused on pet nat of surprising variety and accomplishment. The "Charlie" is wife and partner Clara (retired Air Force service member).

VINEYARDS - Organic grapes are hard to come by in San Diego County. Van Drunen has settled on the Valentina Vineyard in Dulzura near the Mexico border which is said to use only organic approved materials. The vineyards are on granite and depleted limestone with native chapparal. Sapidity and aromatic undercurrents show throughout the wines. Under the relentless sun, ripeness descends quickly and must be monitored closely. Charlie & Echo is a member of 1% Percent for the Planet.

WINES - They're expanding and redefining San Diego wine culture with their creativity, making still and sparkling wines, along with their "Project X" (wine cocktails that release weekly).

TOP San Diego County Encounter Sauvignon Blanc 2021 EVERYDAY WINE 123 cases; 27 $ - Generous pine, apricot and beeswax aromas give way to an intense palate of dried apple and apricot, also showing a distinct texture from high acidity and nine days of skin contact.

San Diego County Two Tons Red Blend 2021 123 cases; 33 $ - A novel red blend of Nebbiolo (35%), Petit Sirah (24%), Syrah (21%) and Zinfandel (20%). Pretty aromas of rose, meat smoke and red and black fruits. Great juiciness with blackberry and red cherry and medium loamy tannins.

San Diego County Vigilant Fortified Wine 2017 34 cases; 33 $ - Fortified with neutral spirits to 18.1 ABV. Displays a nose of walnuts, yeast, and beeswax while on the palate is honey, dried orange and apricot .

acres 0 - cases 600
Fertilizers organic fertilizer
Plant protection sulfur, organic
Weed control mechanical
Yeasts spontaneous fermentation
Grapes purchase 100%
Certification none

REDLANDS

HERRMANN YORK $

570 Nevada Street, Ste M - tel. (951) 394-1755
www.herrmannyork.wine - taylor@herrmannyork.wine

PEOPLE - Brothers Garrett and Taylor York and friend Dustin Herrmann satisfied their fascination with wine by making it—in their own hometown of Redlands (an hour east of Los Angeles). Taking cues (and grapes) from the nearby Cucamonga Valley, they have reworked the traditions of mostly fortified wine production into distinctive table wines. They elevate "desert" wine at frequent bar takeovers, and their beautifully illustrated labels depict local history and legend.

VINEYARDS - Zinfandel's from Cucamonga's historic Lopez Vineyard (certified organic) on pure sand and silt. Grenache and Tempranillo come from the 15 acre Rock Farm Vineyard (using only organic approved materials) in the Antelope Valley at 2,500 feet, on rugged, granitic soils. Various Cabs and Zinfandels come from tiny vineyards in Yucaipa with granitic soils ranging from 2,200 to 4,200 feet, all well known to the winemakers for their responsible farming.

WINES - Adventurously discovering the potential for delicate wines from grapes grown in near desert conditions in southern inland California.

TOP San Bernardino Okneski Vineyard Zinfandel 2023 36 cases; 35 $ - Zinfandel showing lilac, red cherry and chipotle on the nose with a potent and juicy cherry palate.

Yucaipa Valley Red 2023 168 cases; 28 $ - From the country's newest AVA. A blend of Zinfandel (60%) and Cabernet (40%). Savory aromas of smoke, blackberry and dried leaf with young tannins/acids of green plum, cherry and mulberry. Should be formidable with time.

Antelope Valley of the California High Desert Rock Farm Red 2023 288 cases; 28 $ - A blend of Grenache and Tempranillo. Destemmed and whole cluster with four days skin contact. Shows subtle cherry, smoke and mulch on the nose with red cherry, cranberry, raw pear and a mineral streak on the palate. A wine whose flavors are infused not extracted.

acres 0 - cases 1,200
Fertilizers organic fertilizer
Plant protection sulfur
Weed control mechanical
Yeasts spontaneous fermentation
Grapes purchase 100%
Certification some of the vineyards are certified organic

ESCONDIDO

J. BRIX WINES $

298 Enterprise Street, Suite D - tel. (760) 994-8131
www.jbrix.com - emily@jbrix.com

PEOPLE - Wine lovers Jody and Emily Towe quickly segued from harvest interns to natural winemaking, while, at the time, maintaining careers in horticulture and design, respectively. Always advocates of non-synthetic farming in the grapes they buy, they have been attracted to lesser grown varieties including Carignan, Counoise, and Pinot Meunier. Their broad portfolio anticipated widely embraced wine styles such as pet nat, amphora aging and carbonic.

VINEYARDS - They buy Riesling from organically farmed vines at Kick On Ranch in the Los Alamos Valley. The site, an ancient seabed consisting of nutrient poor sandy loams, gets the full force of Pacific Ocean winds forcing quality from the vines. They buy Merlot and Syrah from Coquelicot (certified organic) in Santa Ynez Valley. The Solvang vineyard sits on sandy loam and gravel overlooking the Santa Ynez River. They also buy grapes from other local growers.

WINES - J. Brix can be counted on for experiments each vintage as well as classic styles at modest cost.

🔝 Santa Ynez Valley Défier Merlot 2021 ● 135 cases; 28 $ - ⊞ - Its fully carbonic treatment harkens to Cru Beaujolais and has a similar uplifted elegance. Red and dark plummy, mulchy aromas. On the palate, a bit of merlot cocoa, dark fruit and grown up tannins.
Santa Ynez Valley Coquelicot Vineyard La Belle Rêveuse Syrah 2021 ● 100 cases; 28 $ - ⊞ - Dark cherry, mulch and savory smoke from nose to palate with a bracing sweet tart texture interwoven with fine tannins.
Santa Barbara County Sunrise Over Skin Riesling 2021 ◎ 200 cases; 28 $ - ⊞ - Aromas of peach compote, beeswax and crushed leaves. The palate is dried apricot and orange. The texture is electric, fusing acidity to fine tannins resulting from seven days of skin contact.

acres 0 - cases 1,800
Fertilizers cover crops, organic fertilizer
Plant protection sulfur, organic
Weed control mechanical
Yeasts spontaneous fermentation
Grapes purchase 100%
Certification some of the vineyards are certified organic

LOS ANGELES

LOS ANGELES RIVER WINE CO.

2079 E 15th Street
www.scholiumwines.com

PEOPLE - Abe Schoener (of Scholium Project) came to southern California to find old vines, contributing to the "Cucamonga Revolution," a movement bringing recognition for historic Cucamonga Valley vines under a new generation of winemakers. (Like Schoener, the group prefers natural winemaking practices.) Schoener's winery in downtown L. A. frequently doubles as a salon for like minded vintners, sommeliers and aficionados.

VINEYARDS - Schoener's primary grape source is the historic Jose Lopez Vineyard (certified organic) planted mainly to Zinfandel and Palomino. It has been leased and farmed for 100 years by the Galleano family. Schoener also buys grapes from Francis Road Vineyard in Ontario, home to historic mixed red grapes. Both vineyards sustain old vines in pure sand. A small vineyard in Temecula, dating back to the 1890s, produces Zinfandel and Mission, some hybridized with wild grapes.

WINES - Wine is made simply–by foot treading, open top fermentation and pressing to tank or neutral barrel.

🔝 Cucamonga Valley Chiara 2023 SLOW WINE ○ 22 cases; 75 $ - ⊞ - is Palomino named after friend Chiara Pepe of esteemed producer Emidio Pepe. On the nose–white flower, yellow apple and the customary chapparal of the region. The palate is rich and racy with green apple, barely ripe pineapple and vadouvan.
Cucamonga Valley Lopez 2023 ● 24 cases; 50 $ - ⊞ - From two picks of Zinfandel. A potent nose of dried rose, red cherry, plum and chapparal. Tastes of tart, ripe cranberry and dark cherry with very fine and present tannins.
Cucamonga Valley Lopez Blanc 2023 ○ 162 cases; 36 $ - ⊡ ⊞ - A rosé with Palomino (70%), Zinfandel (20%) and Alicante Bouchet (10%). Shows a high toned floral aromas with a tart but candied palate of raspberry, unripe pear and salt.

acres 0 - cases 800
Fertilizers none
Plant protection none
Weed control mechanical
Yeasts spontaneous fermentation
Grapes purchase 100%
Certification some of the vineyards are certified organic

SAN DIEGO

LOS PILARES $

1477 University Avenue - tel. (619) 709-0664
www.lospilareswine.com - michael@lospilareswine.com

PEOPLE - Natural winemakers Michael Christian, Coleman Cooney and friends are out to promote San Diego County's unique terroir. Pioneers in natural wine before the category took off, they've practiced early harvesting and foot treading since the 2010s and produced one of the first American pet nats on the market. Low intervention wines are made in a scrupulously genuine fashion. They buried concrete and amphora fermenters on one of their vineyard sites.

VINEYARDS - They buy grapes from local growers including Highland Hills Vineyard (near Ramona) and the Hunter Mazetti Vineyard (on the Rincon Indian Reservation in northern San Diego County). At 2,000 feet, elevation and Pacific breezes keep nights cool, preserving acidity. Vineyard soils are mostly based on granite. Their own estate vineyard, further inland at 3800 feet, has just started producing Assyrtiko.

WINES - Muscat and Grenache are their signature grapes, producing distinctive, low alcohol wines.

San Diego County Grenache 2022 ● 64 cases; 30 $ - A combination of juice pressed to tank and long macerated in amphora. It smells of dried herbs, dried cherry and nuts. On the palate–fresh and dried dark cherries with a hint of chocolate.

BPN or Black Pét-Nat Grenache 2023 ● 62 cases; 30 $ - Has a brooding nose of dried flower, beeswax and strawberry hints. Very dry on the palate showing cranberry and strawberry with hibiscus tannin.

San Diego County La Dona Sparkling Muscat 2013 ● 125 cases; 26 $ - Shows pine sap, musky pollen and dried flower on the nose. Mineral and dried leaf flavors overlay muted dried fruit: apricot, mango, apple. A beautiful example of aged pet nat with its acidity and carbonation intact.

acres 2 - cases 275
Fertilizers compost
Plant protection sulfur, organic
Weed control mechanical
Yeasts spontaneous fermentation
Grapes purchase 100%
Certification none

OJAI

OJAI MOUNTAIN VINEYARD

7070 Sulphur Mountain Road - tel. (805) 669-2283
www.ojaimountainestate.com - info@ojaimountainestate.com

PEOPLE - After hedge fund executive Olga Chernova and her husband Mike Chernova, a UCLA finance professor, fell in love with Ojai, in 2015 she purchased a dramatic, high altitude (2,800 ft.) site on Sulphur Mountain. With the help of viticulturist Martin Ramirez, she set out to be a grower, but changed course, with the help of an A-team from Sonoma superstars organic viticulturalist Phil Coturri (consultant) and winemaker Erich Bradley who joined in 2020.

VINEYARDS - Growing above the fog in sunlit terraces, the high altitude vines sit on shallow shale soils. Paul Hofmeister is the on site vineyard manager, aided by master pruner Jacopo Miolo. The team initially planted 7.5 acres of Bordeaux, Nebbiolo, Rhone and Tempranillo, all of which are now dry farmed, regenerative and no till. Sheep and goats graze seasonally, and 150 chickens live on the property along with bees (for honey), citrus trees and a small garden.

WINES - The estate's high altitude yields grapes with thicker skins–they can create bold, rich wines. Purity comes from no cellar additions and neutral French oak.

Ventura County Estate Red Blend 2020 ● 264 cases; 60 $ - A blend of Grenache (30%), Syrah (25%), Cabernet Sauvignon (19%), Mourvèdre (18%) and Cabernet Franc (8%). A five day cold soak, open top fermentation. Blackberry, cassis and tart cherries. Fresh on the palate with supple tannins.

Ventura County Estate White Blend 2022 ○ 209 cases; 75 $ - A blend of Grenache Blanc (60%), Picpoul (34%) and Roussanne (6%). Candied citrus, green apple, and floral honey notes. Elegant with a rich midpalate, structured acidity and mineral finish.

Ventura County Estate Syrah 2021 ● 86 cases; 90 $ - Perfumed aromatics of dark fruits, spice, and dusted cocoa. The wine is powerful yet elegant with structured tannins and vibrant acidity.

acres 7.5 - cases 500
Fertilizers compost, biodynamic compost, cover crops, manure, organic fertilizer
Plant protection sulfur, biodynamic preparations
Weed control animal grazing, mechanical, manual
Yeasts spontaneous fermentation
Grapes 100% owned
Certification converting to biodynamic

TEMECULA

WILSON CREEK WINERY & VINEYARD

35960 Rancho California Road - tel. (951) 699-9463
www.wilsoncreekwinery.com - info@wilsoncreekwinery.com

PEOPLE - 2025 is the 25th anniversary of Wilson Creek Winery led by CEO Bill Wilson. The 14th winery in the hot, dry Temecula, it is now one of the largest producers in the area. It's also a regenerative pioneer in the region. An organic specialist, vineyard manager Greg Pennyroyal started there in 2012. Cucamonga raised Kristina Filippi, a Cal Poly grad, was promoted from assistant to head winemaker in 2023. Diego Aparicio has been with the company for 23 years and was promoted to vineyard foreman.

VINEYARDS - Pennyroyal, a medicinal plant geneticist, started a regenerative pilot program on the estate six years ago, initially converting 64 acres to no till farming using no herbicides or fungicides. Yields increased 28%, they reduced water use 40% and vine health improved (no Pierce's disease). Now all 286 acres are farmed this way. In 2023-2024, the team expanded their sheep flock from 50 to 500. They consult to other growers in the area to help them go regenerative.

WINES - Filippi now ferments regeneratively grown blocks of Cabernet and Syrah using only native yeasts. She lets the vineyard express itself.

Temecula Syrah 2022 ● 421 cases; 65 $ - ⊞ - Aged 20 months in French oak (20% new). Destemmed, fermented in stainless. Pretty aromas of red berries and dark cherry with notes of cedar and sweet spice. Medium bodied with good acidity and present tannins.

Temecula Valley Barbera 2022 ● 513 cases; 50 $ - ⊞ - Aged 18 months in French oak (15% new). Destemmed, fermented in stainless. Dark ripe fruit aromas of blackberry, plum, black cherry and spice. Ripe fruits notes on the palate with delicate acidity.

Temecula Valley GSM 2022 ● 728 cases; 50 $ - ⊞ - Aged 18 months in French and American oak (15% new). The blend is Grenache (55%), Syrah (32%) and Mourvedre (13%). Destemmed, fermented separately. Aromas of red currant, plum, raspberry and spice, medium-bodied with a balance of acid and tannin.

acres 286 - cases 45,000
Fertilizers compost, cover crops, organic fertilizer
Plant protection synthetic pesticides, organic
Weed control animal grazing, mechanical, manual
Yeasts spontaneous fermentation, commercial cultured yeasts
Grapes purchase 10%
Certification none

INLAND VALLEYS AND SIERRA FOOTHILLS

$ Coin

164 The End of Nowhere

PLYMOUTH

ANDIS WINES

11000 Shenandoah Road - tel. (209) 245-6177
www.andiswines.com

PEOPLE - Retiring from a career in finance, co-founders Janis Akuna, CEO, with her co-founder husband Andy Friedlander, found peace and rural life in the Sierra Foothills, where in 2010 they built a state of the art modern winery. Lorenzo Muslia, who worked in Italy, joined as a partner in 2015, bringing in an A-list team of winemaking consultants—Napa based Philippe Melka and his associate Maayan Koschitzky—to work with estate winemaker Mark Fowler.

VINEYARDS - At 1,500 feet, the estate vines sit on north facing, decomposed granitic and sandy loam soils, perfect for growing Barbera and Zin. They farm the estate only with organic approved materials. A new 15 acre vineyard parcel is being planted to Assyrtico, Clairette Blanc and Macabeo along with Bordeaux varieties. The winery adventurously experiments with varieties suggested by local wine expert, Darrell Corti, a renowned Sacramento grocer. Examples: Arinto and Schioppettino. (Some of the wines, not featured here, may be grown with herbicide.)

WINES - Andis is bringing a higher level of quality and craftsmanship to Amador County winemaking.

Sierra Foothills Barbera d'Amador 2022 EVERYDAY WINE
850 cases; 30 $ - Aged 18 months in French oak (15% new). Estate grown. Medium bodied. Bright notes of red cherry, cranberry and cedar. Easy drinking. Best decanted.
Sierra Foothills Sauvignon Blanc 2023 O 2,150 cases; 25 $ - Partially aged in concrete and barrel. Aromas of cut grass, lemon blossom, ripe passionfruit, and pineapple. On the palate, crisp, ripe citrus. Bright acidity.
Sierra Foothills Painted Fields Curse of Knowledge Cabernet Sauvignon 2021 ● 5,500 cases; 33 $ - Aged 14 months in French oak (25% new). A blend of Cabernet Sauvignon (77 %), Cabernet Franc (13 %), Merlot (7 %) and Petit Verdot (3 %). Aromas of dried violet, black cherry, fresh herbs and cocoa powder. Generous and round. A balanced midpalate, with a lingering finish of dark berries and black licorice.

acres 22 - cases 10,000
Fertilizers compost, cover crops, manure
Plant protection sulfur, synthetic pesticides, organic
Weed control mechanical, manual
Yeasts selected indigenous yeasts, commercial cultured yeasts
Grapes purchase 40%
Certification converting to organic

LODI

BOKISCH VINEYARDS

18921 Atkins Road - tel. (209) 642-8880 - (209) 642-8880
www.bokischvineyards.com - info@bokischvineyards.com

PEOPLE - Markus Bokisch's Catalan heritage is rooter here in Lodi in Spanish varieties and culture. After settling in Lodi, he and Liz have enjoyed success as consultants, producers and organic pioneers. They've grown a community of wine lovers who they take to Spain each year. In Lodi, they offer Spanish wine and food pairings. Now, in honor of Catalonia, they've planted Xarel-lo, Macabeo, and Paralleda to produce a Cava-style sparkling wine from Lodi. Elyse Perry is the winemaker.

VINEYARDS - They've focused their brand on their own certified organic vineyards—Terra Alta, Las Cerezas, and Miravet Vineyard—and have moved all Spanish varieties to the 14 acre Miravet (planted in 2019 and certified organic in 2025). The entire Spanish portfolio (Garnacha Blanca, Garnacha, Monastrell, Tempranillo, Verdejo and the three Catalan varieties) will now be sourced from their three organic vineyards. They also make wine from sustainably grown grapes.

WINES - Bokisch has been redefining Spanish wines in Lodi since 2000 and looks forward to celebrating the winery's 25th anniversary.

Mokelumne River Las Cerezas Vineyard Albariño 2023 O 168 cases; 31 $ - Grown on one acre planted in 1999 from cuttings brought from Spain. This is the oldest Albariño in the U.S. Crisp, clean, and fresh with bright stone fruit, citrus and floral notes. A saline finish.
Clements Hills Miravet Vineyard Verdejo 2023 O 224 cases; 29 $ - Aged in neutral French oak. Inaugural vintage from the Miravet Vineyard. The grapes spend 24 hours on the skin for phenolic texture. The nose has less primary notes and more Jazmin and green tea notes. A round midpalate and punchy acidity with a bitter almond finish.
Clement Hills Terra Alta Vineyard Graciano 2020 ● 336 cases; 36 $ - Aged 22 months in all French oak (20% new). Aromas of dark red fruits, baking spice, and leather. Savory on the palate with a soft juiciness. This is one of the few wineries to make Graciano, typically a blending grape.

acres 120 - cases 7,000
Fertilizers compost, cover crops, organic fertilizer
Plant protection sulfur, organic
Weed control mechanical, manual
Yeasts spontaneous fermentation, selected indigenous yeasts
Grapes 100% owned
Certification some of the vineyards are certified organic

PLYMOUTH

TERRE ROUGE/EASTON WINES

10801 Dickson Road - tel. (209) 245-4277
www.terrerougewines.com - info@terrerougewines.com

PEOPLE - A celebrated producer, Bill Easton was among the first wave of California winemakers drawn to Rhône varietals in the early 1980's. He has become a Sierra Foothills icon for seeing the region's ability to make terroir driven wines of distinction. In 2016 the Rhone Rangers honored him with its Lifetime Achievement award. The wines are very affordably priced for their (superb) quality.

VINEYARDS - The Rhones only label is Terre Rouge, or "red earth," named for the color of the soils in Easton's vineyards. Easton's three estate ranches in the Fiddletown and Shenandoah Valley AVAs sit on granitic and volcanic Sierra soils, well suited to southern Rhône varieties and Zinfandel. Due to consistent dry and breezy conditions, Easton dry farms and sprays on an as needed basis. Non estate wines (not featured here), may be grown with herbicide.

WINES - His Easton brand covers Zinfandel and other varietals. Wine lovers appreciate that Easton ages his red wines sufficiently (5-6 years) before releasing them.

TOP Fiddletown Easton "E" Zinfandel 2015 SLOW WINE ● n.a.; 38 $ - 🍷 - Aged 16 months in third and fourth use French oak. Savory blackberry and boysenberry scented with dried sage and sandalwood. Complex and velvety with a mineral freshness that is attributed to the schist-laden hillside.

Sierra Foothills Vin Gris d'Amador 2022 ● n.a.; 30 $ - 🍷 - A blend of Grenache (50%) 35% Mourvedre (35%), Grenache Blanc (6%) with Viognier and Roussanne (4.5% each).

acres 33 - cases 14,000
Fertilizers cover crops, organic fertilizer, synthetic fertilizer
Plant protection synthetic pesticides, organic
Weed control mechanical
Yeasts selected indigenous yeasts, commercial cultured yeasts
Grapes purchase 66%
Certification none

AMADOR CITY

THE END OF NOWHERE $

14204 Main Street - tel. (858) 342-8112
www.endofnowhere.wine - info@ljlwine.com

PEOPLE - Although local Amador County resident Chris Walsh grew up in Pioneer, like so many others he left home for college and stayed away for 15 years. In that time, a love of wine emerged while working in restaurants in New York City, so following an internship with pioneering natural wine brand Donkey and Goat in 2014, Walsh moved back home to establish a winery in his dad's old auto shop in Amador County in the Sierra Foothills.

VINEYARDS - His tiny estate vineyard has had many challenges due to frost, but 2024 was more promising. Walsh practices no till, no spray farming on the high elevation vineyard and winery located on the property that he grew up on. He also buys grapes from seven other vineyards from Amador, Clarksburg, El Dorado and Lodi counties. (Some wines, not featured here, come from unverified vineyards.)

WINES - The name for each wine comes from the songs he listens to while making them, music being part of the inspiration (and fun to listen to while drinking his wines).

TOP El Dorado County Camino Alto Vineyard Mind Over Matter 2023 EVERYDAY WINE ○ 96 cases; 30 $ - 🍷 - A blend of Pinot Gris and Arneis. Bright citrus, lemon zest and minerality on the nose. Flavors of stone fruit, pineapple and almond. A refreshing, lush mouthfeel and explosion of acidity.

Amador County D'Agostini Shenandoah Vineyard #1 Crush Rosé 2023 ● 100 cases; 30 $ - 🍷 - Dark pink in color and very aromatic with watermelon, strawberry and pink peppercorn. Flavor notes of brambly raspberries and spiced plum with an alluring finish.

San Joaquin County Fernow Ranch Dear Mr. Fantasy Counoise 2023 ● 125 cases; 36 $ - 🍷 - Partial carbonic maceration (30%). Woodsy aromatics of leather and blackberry. The powerful, yet medium light bodied red has flavors of black cherry compote and plum with nice tannic structure.

acres 3 - cases 1,800
Fertilizers compost, biodynamic compost, cover crops, organic fertilizer
Plant protection sulfur, organic
Weed control mechanical, manual
Yeasts spontaneous fermentation
Grapes purchase 75%
Certification some of the vineyards are certified organic

OREGON

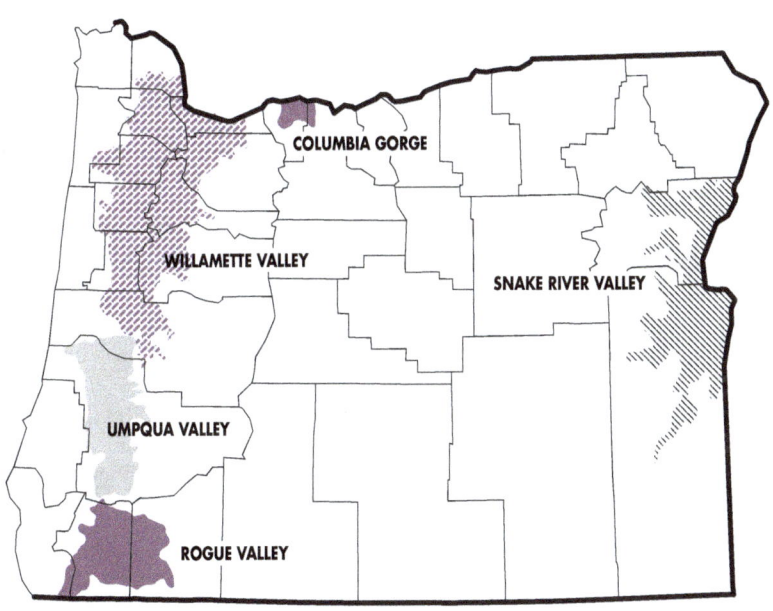

166 Willamette Valley
197 Southern Oregon
200 Columbia Gorge

WILLAMETTE VALLEY

🐌 Snail

- 167 Antica Terra Snail
- 167 Antiquum Farm
- 169 Beckham Estate Vineyard
- 169 Belle Pente Vineyard & Winery
- 172 Brick House Wines
- 175 Cooper Mountain Vineyards
- 177 Domaine Drouhin Oregon
- 182 J.K. Carriere
- 183 Johan Vineyards
- 185 Lemelson Vineyards
- 187 Lumos Wine Co.
- 188 Maysara Winery
- 189 Open Claim Vineyards
- 190 Résonance
- 193 Soter Vineyards
- 195 The Eyrie Vineyards
- 196 Youngberg Hill

🍾 Bottle

- 166 Abbott Claim
- 168 Authentique Wine Cellars
- 170 Bergström Wines
- 170 Bethel Heights Vineyard
- 171 Big Table Farm
- 172 Brooks Wine
- 177 Domaine Divio
- 178 Dominio IV
- 179 Evesham Wood
- 180 Flâneur Wines
- 182 J.C. Somers Vintner
- 184 King Estate Winery
- 186 Lingua Franca
- 188 Nicolas-Jay
- 192 Roserock Drouhin Oregon
- 192 Ruby Vineyard & Winery
- 193 Sokol Blosser Winery
- 195 WillaKenzie Estate
- 196 Winderlea Vineyard & Winery

$ Coin

- 171 Björnson Vineyard
- 176 David Hill Vineyards and Winery
- 181 Haden Fig
- 186 Longplay Wine
- 191 Ridgecrest

CARLTON

ABBOTT CLAIM

11011 NE Bayliss Road - tel. (503) 687-3893
www.abbottclaim.com - andrew@abbottclaim.com

PEOPLE - From a South African wine family, Antony Beck reassembled an 1855 land claim (with vineyards planted by Ken Wright) to create the estate. Acclaimed Burgundy trained winemaker Alban Debeaulieu leads production with assistant winemaker David Martinez. Viticulturist Heath Payne oversees the vines. Eco friendly measures include planting Oregon oak trees, cleaning wastewater naturally with worm bins, and using rooftop solar panels to power their electrical grid in summer.

VINEYARDS - The original Yamhill-Carlton vineyard, planted on marine sedimentary WillaKenzie soil, featured Pinot Noir only blocks in 2001-2007. In 2019 it added dry farmed Chardonnay. In 2021, the team planted an 80 acre Eola-Amity Hills vineyard to 12 coplanted clones of Pinot Noir and 14 coplanted clones of Chardonnay. The first harvest is expected in 2024. Payne works with OSU to monitor pollinator health. The team also buys grapes from local growers.

WINES - Partial whole cluster Pinot Noir with a varying range of new oak shows complexity, freshness and smooth texture.

🔺 **Yamhill-Carlton Abbott Claim Vineyard Pinot Noir 2021** ● 1,100 cases; 75 $ - 🍷 - Fermented with whole cluster (25%). Aromas of warm coffee, flashes of cherry, cinnamon and flowers. Palate is young but beautifully structured with silky tannins.

Yamhill-Carlton Orientate Pinot Noir 2021 ● 298 cases; 125 $ - 🍷 - Aged in oak (70% new). Fermented in concrete. Whole cluster (35%). Reductive aromas with dark fruit. Slightly grippier tannins yet crisp. Well structured for the long haul yet with an ethereal core and freshness in the finish.

Eola-Amity Hills Chardonnay 2021 ○ 550 cases; 75 $ - 🍷 - From four vineyards. Aged in oak (40% new) and on the lees. Aromas of toasted hazelnuts mingle with oak and roasted fowl. Floral notes intensify with air. Fresh entry, savory midpalate and a finish overlaid with lemon.

---

acres 30 - cases 1,900
Fertilizers compost, biodynamic compost, cover crops, organic fertilizer
Plant protection sulfur, biodynamic preparations, organic
Weed control mechanical
Yeasts spontaneous fermentation
Grapes purchase 25%
Certification none

DUNDEE

ANTICA TERRA

979 SW Alder St. - tel. (503) 244-1748
www.anticaterra.com - info@anticaterra.com

 Nature lovers with heart and soul and remarkably refined palates, this novel producer wows winelovers with the way it has reimagined wine, opening the door to a new aesthetic.

PEOPLE - Innovative, eclectic, artisanal and acclaimed, it began in 2005 when three friends–Scott Adelson, John Mavredakis, and Michael Kramer–bought a vineyard on a rocky hillside with Maggie Harrison, a visionary winemaker and novel blender (who previously worked under Manfred Krankl). Now hugely sought after for their wines, they've added intimate food and wine experiences, including pairing globally diverse selections as well as their own wines.

VINEYARDS - Over the years, they have transformed the original Eola-Amity Hills site, planted in 1989, dramatically. It sits on rocky soils with chunks of fossilized oyster shells and sandstone dotted by marine fossils. Exposed and raw, with westerly winds and marine inversion, it grows bonsaied vines with small, concentrated clusters with thick skinned berries. Biodynamic preparations evolve with the needs of the ecosystem. In 2023, they purchased the former Keeler Estate (certified biodynamic).

WINES - Relying on her palate and intuition, the whimsical, curious Harrison famously makes dazzling, unorthodox blends. Transparent, with a vast depth and focus, they showcase unique, historic geology and her intuitions.

🔴 **Eola-Amity Hills Antikythera Pinot Noir 2022** SLOW WINE ● 766 cases; 255 $ - Ⓑ - An ebullient bouquet of autumn leaves, black pepper and ink. Intensely infused with dark cherry, ripe plum, and juniper with structure, succulent tannins and saline, mineral persistence.

---

acres 50 - cases 4,000
Fertilizers compost, biodynamic compost, cover crops, manure, organic fertilizer
Plant protection biodynamic preparations, organic
Weed control mechanical, manual
Yeasts spontaneous fermentation
Grapes 100% owned
Certification some of the vineyards are certified organic, some of the vineyards are certified biodynamic

JUNCTION CITY

ANTIQUUM FARM

25075 Jaeg Road - tel. (541) 998-3153
www.antiquumfarm.com - info@antiquumfarm.com

 The Hagens showcase nature and its exceptional wines set the tone for what intricate and thoughtful farming can manifest.

PEOPLE - Stephen and Niki Hagen started the winery in 1996 as a self contained ecosystem celebrating the natural world. Leaders in "grazing based viticulture" and regenerative practices, they've transformed the 140 acre property into a diverse landscape that encompasses vineyards, forest, gardens, pasture and pond. Their dining and lodging offerings give guests the opportunity to be fully immersed in the unique expression of farming.

VINEYARDS - At 800 feet of elevation, the estate grows six acres of Pinot Gris and 14.5 acres of Pinot Noir on bellpine soils, a silty clay loam over sandstone. Hagen has enhanced the vineyard's soil microbiome, partially through integrating Katahdin/Dorper crossbred sheep, which inoculate the vineyard with their digestive gut fauna. The team integrates animals through careful canopy management. The unique closed system also includes chickens, geese, and pigs.

WINES - With the lush, exuberant fruit from their vibrant ecosystem, Stephen creates distinctive wines that are uniquely expressive and brimming with flavor.

🔴 **Willamette Valley Juel Pinot Noir 2022** SLOW WINE ● 1,600 cases; 50 $ - Ⓑ - Aged 10 months in French oak (28% new). A vibrant Pinot with pulsating acidity, ripe red raspberry, red currant, and herbaceous dried forest floor.
Willamette Valley Passiflora Pinot Noir 2022 ● 500 cases; 68 $ - Ⓑ - Aged 10 months in both new and neutral French oak. Crunchy pomegranate with zingy blood orange and wild blackberry and purple plum skin.
Willamette Valley Aurosa Pinot Gris Orange Wine 2023 ⊙ 250 cases; 38 $ - Ⓑ - Sits on the skins for 72 hours prior to malolactic fermentation with five months on lees to follow. A soft and rounded orange with layered tropical fruit, citrus, hibiscus and lavender.

---

acres 20.5 - cases 4,400
Fertilizers none, manure
Plant protection organic
Weed control animal grazing
Yeasts spontaneous fermentation
Grapes 100% owned
Certification biodynamic, organic, regenerative

NEWBERG

ARBORBROOK BY COOPER MOUNTAIN VINEYARDS

17700 NE Calkins Lane - tel. (503) 538-0959
www.arborbrookwines.com - info@arborbrookwines.com

PEOPLE - Longtime biodynamic producers, the pioneering Gross family, owners of Cooper Mountain Vineyards, bought this winery brand and land in 2021. The Gross family includes founder Bob Gross and his three children–Anne Branfman, David Gross and winery general manager Barbara Gross. After the purchase, they implemented organic and biodynamic farming. The former walnut barn is now an elegant tasting room that pays homage to its agricultural roots.

VINEYARDS - The Gross family has bought three vineyards in the Chehalem Mountains in recent years. Purchased in 2018, the family renamed the former Olenik vineyard (an historic site formerly owned by Oregon icon Dick Erath) the Corinne Vineyard in honor of the family matriarch and co-founder, the late Corinne Gross. The site, located two miles from Arborbrook, is a patchwork of soils. Half features volcanic fractured basalt, nicknamed "Anklebreaker Block" for its rocks.

WINES - French born Gilles de Domingo, their winemaker at Cooper Mountain Vineyards, makes the Arborbrook wines. He joined their Beaverton based winery in 2004. The original Arborbrook vines are expected to be certified organic and biodynamic in 2024 and will go into future vintages.

Chehalem Mountains Corinne Chardonnay 2021 ○ n.a.; 40 $ - ▦ - Half Wente clone and half Dijon Clone. Concentrated with topical fruits, ripe pears, lemon and lime with pleasingly tart notes and fresh acidity.

Chehalem Mountains Corrine Pinot Noir 2022 ● n.a.; 65 $ - ▦ - From a warm rocky site at 400 feet of elevation. Pommard clones on a south facing hillside with very varied soils. Notes of cherry, dark fruits and fresh berries.

acres 15 - cases 1,500
Fertilizers compost, biodynamic compost, cover crops, organic fertilizer
Plant protection biodynamic preparations, organic
Weed control mechanical
Yeasts spontaneous fermentation
Grapes 100% owned
Certification biodynamic, organic

AMITY

AUTHENTIQUE WINE CELLARS

5100 SE Rice Lane - tel. (503) 307-1593
www.authentiquewinecellars.com - nicholas@authentiquewinecellars.com

PEOPLE - U.C. Davis educated winemaker Nicholas Keeler has a long history in wine ranging from harvests with talented winemakers and selling French oak cooperage for Tonnellerie Allary. This combined experience informs his winemaking process from fermentation to vessels to aging. Over the years he has started working with numerous kinds of vessels to layer complexity into his wines.

VINEYARDS - Nicholas purchases fruit from his family's former home vineyard, Keeler Estate (certified biodynamic) and from other growers. With a focus on old vine Pinot Noir, he buys from a grower in Ribbon Ridge, whose vines were planted in the 1980's. In the Dundee Hills, he gets own rooted Pinot Noir from the historic Murto Vineyard, planted in 1978. Additionally, he purchases Pinot Noir from 37 year old vines at Temperance Hill (certified organic).

WINES - Fermented and aged in a variety of vessels–oak puncheons, Italian amphorae and concrete eggs–utilizing a combination of whole cluster and destemmed fruit.

Eola-Amity Hills Temperance Hill Vineyard Pinot Noir 2021 ● 200 cases; 75 $ - ⌾ - Offers up abundant blues and deep purples. Violet, blueberry and brambly fruit conserve meet earthy petrichor, warmed with gentle spice. Medium bodied with silky tannins.

Eola-Amity Hills Keeler Estate Pinot Noir 2021 ● 300 cases; 75 $ - ⌂⌾ - A long fermentation on skins occurs in a mix of oak and concrete with partial whole cluster (15%). Fresh and pure, with plenty of flavor packed into a medium body while remaining restrained and cool. Deep red berry fruit lifted with citrus and a stony minerality.

Eola-Amity Hills Bois Joli Chardonnay 2021 ○ 100 cases; 75 $ - ⌾ - Whole cluster pressed with pungent peach, vanilla, lemon curd and almond. A big character in a medium body, yet with an elegance that draws into a pleasant flinty undertone.

acres 15 - cases 2,000
Fertilizers biodynamic compost, organic fertilizer
Plant protection biodynamic preparations, organic
Weed control mechanical
Yeasts spontaneous fermentation
Grapes purchase 100%
Certification some of the vineyards are certified organic, some of the vineyards are certified biodynamic

SHERWOOD

BECKHAM ESTATE VINEYARD

30790 SW Heater Road - tel. (971) 645-3366
www.beckhamestatevineyard.com - annedria@beckhamestatevineyard.com

 Beckham is a highly unique estate, producing compelling and delicious wines with the handmade touch of estate made amphora.

PEOPLE - Amphora guru Andrew and his wife Annedria Beckham have been nurturing their estate since 2005, bringing their vision to life through the vineyard, ceramic studio, winery and tasting room. Beckham makes highly sought after amphora and uses them in his own winemaking as well, where they are a defining characteristic. Uniquely he is the only winemaker in the U.S. who makes amphora.

VINEYARDS - The 20 acres of dry farmed vines are uniquely planted to Aligoté, Gamay Noir, Pinot Noir, Riesling Sauvignon Blanc and Trousseau Noir. The estate has been organically farmed since 2005 and was certified organic in 2023. They have built up riparian zones for natural habitat, planted fruit trees and introduced beehives and sheep. The ecosystem is thriving with biodiversity.

WINES - A complete expression of Andrew's talents, from farming to the exclusive fermentation and aging in his handmade terracotta vessels.

Chehalem Mountains Creta Pinot Noir 2022 SLOW WINE
● 260 cases; 65 $ - ⓒ - Fermented and aged in Novum Amphora expresses bright strawberry and raspberry with baking spice and tea leaves. Beautiful texture and bright acidity.

Chehalem Mountains Sauvignon Blanc 2023 O 158 cases; 40 $ - ⓒ - Half fermented on skins for 10 days and half direct press give textured, tropical notes of ripe mango, passionfruit and pineapple along with aromatic honeysuckle, lime zest and dried orange.

Willamette Valley AD Beckham Gewürztraminer 2023
◉ 160 cases; 32 $ - ⓒ - Fermented on skins for 10 days. Pale straw in color. Aromas of Mandarin orange peel, rose hips and spicy ginger. Palate is layered with apricots, orange peel, lychee, ginger and wet slate. Sophisticated thirst quencher.

acres 20 - cases 2,800
Fertilizers compost, biodynamic compost, cover crops, organic fertilizer
Plant protection sulfur, biodynamic preparations, organic
Weed control animal grazing, mechanical
Yeasts spontaneous fermentation
Grapes purchase 20%
Certification organic

CARLTON

BELLE PENTE VINEYARD & WINERY

12470 NE Rowland Road - tel. (503) 852-9500
www.bellepente.com - wine@bellepente.com

 For three decades, Belle Pente has represented distinctive winemaking, careful stewardship of the land, and excellent value.

PEOPLE - Established in 1994, founders Brian and Jill O'Donnell are now working through a transition plan that will culminate in 2025—Brian's 30th harvest—and the promotion of associate winemaker Wes Dorlich to head winemaker. Since 2014, Brian and Marcial Gonzales, who manage the vineyard, have been modifying canopy management to mitigate the effects of warmer vintages. Livestock are integrated into the vineyard management.

VINEYARDS - The dry farmed estate sits at 240 to 500 feet on sedimentary WillaKenzie soils. Pinot Noir predominates. Chardonnay, Pinot Gris and Gamay Noir are also planted. Since 2000, the vineyard has used only organic approved materials (but is not certified). A unique Belle Pente block—named Riona's—features a vein of white volcanic ash embedded in sandstone.

WINES - Known for freshness, ageability and exquisite balance across the offerings. Moderately upping whole clusters in Pinot Noir.

Yamhill-Carlton Estate Reserve Pinot Noir 2019
SLOW WINE ● 190 cases; 60 $ - ⊞ - Fermented partially with whole clusters (13%). Red fruit nose with floral notes becomes delicately perfumed with a hint of spice with air. Bright acidity and medium long finish. Elegant.

Yamhill-Carlton Belle Pente Vineyard Pinot Noir 2021 ●
451 cases; 45 $ - ⊞ - Fermented partially with whole clusters (14%). Spicy dark fruit aroma with floral notes hint of chewing gum. Sweet entry, well balanced youthful palate medium finish.

Willamette Valley Belle Pente Vineyard Chardonnay 2021 O 146 cases; 45 $ - ⊞ - Aged in oak (30% new). Barrel fermented with full malolactic. Layered aromas of citrus over rich tropical fruit. Rounded entry with toasted nuts and creaminess, nice balance, good acidity and long finish.

acres 18 - cases 4,500
Fertilizers compost, cover crops, manure
Plant protection sulfur, copper, organic
Weed control animal grazing, mechanical, manual
Yeasts spontaneous fermentation, selected indigenous yeasts
Grapes purchase 20%
Certification none

DUNDEE

BERGSTRÖM WINES

8115 NE Worden Hill Road - tel. (503) 554-0468
www.bergstromwines.com - reservations@bergströmwines.com

PEOPLE - Oregon born and Beaune-educated Josh and Caroline Bergström (she is a native of Beaune) run the celebrated winery founded in 1999 by his parents, John and Karen Bergström. Josh is director of winemaking while Caroline oversees sales. Maddy Rausch is the winemaker. The winery is eliminating 200 grams of glass from each bottle and going for regenerative and B corp certifications. The winery has been a Wine & Spirits Top 100 Winery 11 times.

VINEYARDS - Nick Gianopoulos oversees the vines. The five estate vineyards sit in three AVAs. The Dundee Hills estate (1999) is on volcanic clay on basalt. Ribbon Ridge vineyards—Le Pré du Col vineyard (2006) and La Spirale (2005)—sit on marine sediments on shale and siltstone. In the Chehalem Mountains, Silice (2001-2006), and no till Winery Block planted (2002-2005) are on deep marine sedimentary sands on sandstone bedrock. Bergstrom farms their purchased grapes.

WINES - Chardonnays go through full malolactic fermentation and rest on a 14 year old lees solera. Pinot noirs are fermented whole cluster (up to 100%) to enhance structure and complexity.

● Ribbon Ridge Le Pre du Col Vineyard Pinot Noir 2022 ● 1,217 cases; 110 $ - ▦ - Evolving aromas feature floral notes, mushrooms, citrus, red fruit, and hints of spice. The well balanced palate is gorgeous, complex and waiting to mature.
Chehalem Mountains Silice Pinot Noir 2022 ● 1,192 cases; 100 $ - ▦ - Very citrusy on the nose with an earthy undertone, dark fruit and savory elements with a tight, tannic palate. Meatiness and some red fruit enter the olfactory mix with air.
Willamette Valley Sigrid Chardonnay 2022 ○ 604 cases; 125 $ - ▦ ⓞ - Toasty nutty nose with lemon emerging with air—a classic Willamette Valley Chardonnay aroma. On the palate, a burst of complex flavors highlighted by lemon and some serious juicy fruit and a lingering finish.

acres 70 - cases 10,000
Fertilizers compost, cover crops
Plant protection biodynamic preparations, organic
Weed control mechanical
Yeasts commercial cultured yeasts
Grapes purchase 40%
Certification none

SALEM

BETHEL HEIGHTS VINEYARD

6060 Bethel Heights Road NW - tel. (503) 581-2262
www.bethelheights.com - info@bethelheights.com

PEOPLE - A pioneering winery in Oregon's Willamette Valley, it was founded in 1977 by five members of the Casteel and Dudley families. Co-founder Terry Casteel passed away in November 2023 at the age of 81. He was head winemaker of the first commercial vintage in 1984 and continued until 2005. His son Ben Casteel carries on his legacy in the cellar. Ted Casteel is vineyard manager and Pat Dudley is president.

VINEYARDS - One of the oldest vineyards in the Eola-Amity Hills, the original Bethel Heights vineyard was planted in 1977. That vineyard and neighboring Lewman Vineyard, acquired in 2020, sit on volcanic soils. By contrast, marine sediments comprise the adjacent Justice Vineyard, planted in 1999. All are certified organic. An organic vegetable garden produces small bites to enhance special tastings. The winery employs a vineyard crew of 13 year round.

WINES - The estate produces serious wines with an emphasis on quality grapes over technique.

● TOP Eola-Amity Hills Aeolian Estate Pinot Noir 2022 SLOW WINE ● 1,000 cases; 50 $ - ▦ - Aged 10 months in French oak (25% new). From blocks planted in 2002. It's full of complex flavors of dusty fruit, violet, clove and vanilla penetrated by energetic acidity and supported by fine grained tannins.
Eola-Amity Hills Estate Chardonnay 2022 ○ 140 cases; 60 $ - ▦ - Aged 12 months in French oak (40% new). A graceful wine, it begins with a honeyed perfume, and then offers flavors of pineapple, yellow apple and Asian pear.
Eola-Amity Hills Estate Pinot Noir 2022 ● 4,550 cases; 36 $ - ▦ - Aged 11 months in French oak (30% new). A dazzling, easy drinking confection of red fruits.

acres 80.4 - cases 10,000
Fertilizers compost, cover crops
Plant protection sulfur, organic
Weed control animal grazing, mechanical, manual
Yeasts commercial cultured yeasts
Grapes 100% owned
Certification organic

GASTON

SALEM

BIG TABLE FARM

BJÖRNSON VINEYARD $

26851 NW Williams Canyon Road - tel. (503) 852-3097
www.bigtablefarm.com - bigtablefarm.appointments@gmail.com

3635 Bethel Heights Road NW - tel. (503) 687-3016
www.bjornsonwine.com - info@bjornsonwine.com

PEOPLE - The husband and wife team of Brian Marcy (winemaker) and Clare Carver, created their first small vintage in 2006. They continue to build a welcoming home and farm on the 70 acre estate that includes young vines, draft horses, sheep, pigs, bee hives and more. The regenerative estate utilizes solar power for their buildings and utility vehicles. A rainwater catchment system helps with vine irrigation.

VINEYARDS - They buy grapes from seven vineyards, including Belle Ponte in Yamhill-Carlton and Cattrall (certified organic) in the Eola-Amity Hills. After years of solely buying grapes, they've planted their own vines and are waiting for them to bear fruit. This year, they broke ground on a pond, which will expand the growing ecosystem and provide irrigation for the young vines as needed. They are also seeding new cover crops to build on soil composition.

PEOPLE - Formerly Minnesotans, Pattie and Mark Björnson (a retired healthcare executive) founded the winery in 2006. Scott Sabbadini is the head winemaker. Mark Thackaberry manages their two estate vineyards. In addition to the typical Burgundian wine grapes, they adventurously grow rare varieties. The estate tasting room, modeled on a French country stone farmhouse, opened in 2017. In 2024, they opened a second tasting room in McMinnville.

VINEYARDS - Their first site, the LIVE certified, Eola-Amity Hills AVA one, on volcanic Jory and Nekia soils, grows Chardonnay, Gamay Noir, and Pinot Noir. Their second, the Pamar Vineyard (planted in 2019) in the Van Duzer Corridor AVA, grows those plus Aligoté, Cabernet Franc, Chenin Blanc, Melon de Bourgogne, Pinot Blanc, Pinot Meunier, Sauvignon Blanc, and Trousseau. Rarities include Auxerrois (an Alsatian variety) and Gouias Blanc (an ancient variety) as well as Mondeuse Noir.

WINES - The wines are clean, vibrant expressions of Chardonnay and Pinot Noir that are lively, yet focused.

Eola-Amity Hills Cattrall Brothers Pinot Noir 2022 ● 64 cases; 72 $ - ⊞ - Warm strawberry rhubarb pie with complex, earthy dried leather, mushroom and thyme. A brightness of blood orange paired with desert spice. Funky, yet elegantly refined.

Willamette Valley Pinot Noir 2022 ● 2,139 cases; 50 $ - ⊞ - Aromatic dried roses, coriander and muddled raspberry. Candied bacon, anise and strawberry guava with a savory sweetness. Compelling with a lingering finish.

Willamette Valley Wild Bee Chardonnay 2022 ○ 1,222 cases; 34 $ - ⊞ - Vibrant with a white peach and grapefruit peel bouquet. Ripe pineapple with citrus zest and bright key lime melded with yellow cake and passionfruit jam. A hint of green apple.

WINES - Their diverse varietal plantings enable them to choose from a wide flavor spectrum. They prefer minimal intervention, yielding bright acidity and intense flavors.

TOP Eola-Amity Hills Viola Auxerrois 2023 ○ 124 cases; 32 $ - ⊡⊞ - Fresh aromas of sweet flowers and crisp apple with chalk emerging. Sur lie aging lends nice texture and full midpalate along with excellent length. With air, Asian pear with a tinge of citrus on the palate.

Van Duzer Corridor Pamar Vineyard Sauvignon Blanc 2023 ○ 124 cases; 32 $ - ⊡⊞ - Intense aromas typical of the variety with green notes and tropical fruit. Full flavors of citrus and guava are supported by sur lie induced texture. Finish is medium.

Eola-Amity Hills Isabel Pinot Noir 2022 ● 325 cases; 62 $ - ⊞ - Aged 13 months sur lie in oak (25% new). Attractive aromas of dark fruit, spice and flowers. A youthful delicate palate has gentler acidity and tannins and a long finish.

acres 8.5 - cases 4,800
Fertilizers biodynamic compost, cover crops, manure, organic
Plant protection sulfur, biodynamic preparations, synthetic pesticides
Weed control animal grazing, mechanical, manual
Yeasts spontaneous fermentation
Grapes purchase 100%
Certification some of the vineyards are certified organic, some of the vineyards are certified biodynamic

acres 60 - cases 6,000
Fertilizers compost, cover crops
Plant protection sulfur, synthetic pesticides, none
Weed control animal grazing, mechanical
Yeasts spontaneous fermentation, selected indigenous yeasts, commercial cultured yeasts
Grapes 100% owned
Certification none

NEWBERG

BRICK HOUSE WINES

18200 Lewis Rogers Lane - tel. (503) 538-5136
www.brickhousewines.com - info@brickhousewines.com

 For producing gorgeous wines from biodynamically farmed vineyards offered at fair prices for more than three decades.

PEOPLE - A beloved and now historic Willamette Valley producer, the winery is one of Oregon's most Burgundian in style, housed in a large, rustic barn. An Oregon native, Doug Tunnell founded it in 1990 after seeing, in 1987, that Burgundian royalty, the Drouhin family, was starting a Willamette Valley winery. Melissa Mills, his wife, joined in 1996. Doug's niece Savannah Mills is the associate winemaker. Wine is labeled Made with Biodynamic Grapes, a high standard.

VINEYARDS - A pioneer in ecofriendly farming and certification, Tunnell certified the vines organic in 1990 and added biodynamic certification in 2005. The estate grows Chardonnay, Gamay and Pinot Noir. They also farm Pinot Noir on the adjacent Halliday Hill vineyard (also certified organic and biodynamic). They recently planted 1.3 acres of Gamay, bringing the total for this variety to four acres.

WINES - Doug experimented with not cold soaking Pinot Noir and found that's reduced volatility.

⏺ Ribbon Ridge Les Dijonnais Pinot Noir 2022 ● 580 cases; 68 $ - ⊞ - From the oldest vines. Partial whole cluster (30%). Dark fruit, oak and warm spice on the nose with cinnamon. Young, but with complexity, nicely textured tannins, a rich mouthfeel and long finish. Aging recommended.

Ribbon Ridge Select Pinot Noir 2022 ● 680 cases; 46 $ - ⊞ - Aged in neutral oak. Partial whole clusters (30%). Offers seductive fragrances of flowers and cinnamon. With air, the aromas are highly perfumed and richer. Opens up on the palate to a lovely, approachable, well balanced Pinot with great acidity.

Willamette Valley Cascadia Reserve Chardonnay 2022 ○ 210 cases; 48 $ - ⊞ - Citrus aroma with some hay. Toasted hazelnut emerges. The entry is semi-rounded, crisp, with hints of toasted nuts and nice weight and texture. With air, richer and balanced.

acres 31 - cases 4,000
Fertilizers biodynamic compost, cover crops, organic fertilizer
Plant protection sulfur, biodynamic preparations, organic
Weed control mechanical
Yeasts spontaneous fermentation
Grapes 100% owned
Certification biodynamic, organic

AMITY

BROOKS WINE

21101 SE Cherry Blossom Lane - tel. (503) 435-1278
www.brookswine.com - info@brookswine.com

PEOPLE - A B corporation, this celebrated winery was voted Green Company of the Year by the Drinks Business. Jimi Brooks founded it in 1998. After he died of a brain tumor in 2004, his then young son Pascal became owner. Jimi's sister, managing director Janie Brooks Heuck, carries on Jimi's passions—Riesling and biodynamics. Jimi's friend (who took over midharvest when Jimi died in 2004) winemaker Chris Williams retired in 2024 and Claire Jarreau, his assistant for ten years, became head winemaker.

VINEYARDS - Brooks buys fruit from more than 15 vineyards. Some are certified organic (Johan, Temperance Hill). Jarreau oversees the 18 acre certified biodynamic estate with its historic Riesling and Pinot Noir vines dating back to the 1970's. Planted by the pioneering Don Byard, they're some of the oldest in the state. On their own biodynamic estate vines, they've farm meticulously, have been no till for five years, and, despite their low yields, treasure their old vines.

WINES - Elegant expressions to be enjoyed for many years to come. Transparently express their site and season.

⏺ Eola-Amity Hills Rastaban Pinot Noir 2022 SLOW WINE ● 500 cases; 80 $ - ⊞ - Heavenly rose aromatics. Polished and well balanced as layers of Bing cherries, exotic spice, earth, raspberries, mushrooms, orange peel and a twist of pink peppercorns interlace. Savory through the forever finish. Complex and ageworthy.

Eola-Amity Hills Brooks Estate Riesling 2022 ○ 150 cases; 40 $ - 🍶 - A brilliant Riesling, bursting with crisp pear, hints of peaches, lime zest, salinity, and a thread of minerality. Lively with classic tingling acidity, and zesty through the long lasting finish.

Eola-Amity Hills Old Vine Pommard Pinot Noir 2022 ● 300 cases; 65 $ - ⊞ - Scents of wild berries and spice. Silky on the palate as warm cherry pie, boysenberries, moist earth and brown spices unfold.

acres 18.5 - cases 17,000
Fertilizers biodynamic compost, cover crops
Plant protection sulfur, biodynamic preparations, organic
Weed control mechanical
Yeasts spontaneous fermentation
Grapes purchase 80%
Certification some of the vineyards are certified organic, some of the vineyards are certified biodynamic

SALEM

BRYN MAWR VINEYARDS

5935 Bethel Heights Road NW - tel. (503) 581 4286
www.brynmawrvineyards.com - info@brynmawrvineyards.com

PEOPLE - In 2009, vintners Jon and Kathy Lauer bought a four acre hilltop vineyard. With winemaker and vineyard director Rachel Rose, they expanded to 27 acres of vines, diversifying varietal selections and building a new winery and tasting room. The wine program includes sparkling wine, dry, aromatic whites, classic reds, and alternative varieties. A new culinary program offers locally sourced small plates and elevated pairings.

VINEYARDS - The Eola-Amity Hill estate sits on unweathered stony basalt and grows Chardonnay, Pinot Blanc, and Pinot Noir plus Dolcetto, Riesling and Tempranillo. Newly hired Jessica Cortell's Vitis Terra manages the vineyard. No till practices support beneficial mycorrhizal networks. The winery also buys from LIVE certified vineyards (herbicides permitted) and one biodynamic vineyard (Johan). (Some wines, not featured here, are grown with herbicide.)

WINES - Crafted from separately fermented microblocks to give complexity, the wines offer acidity and aromatics—the result of Van Duzer Corridor winds—and have plenty of structure to age well.

● Eola-Amity Hills Estate Pinot Noir 2021 SLOW WINE ●
900 cases; 50 $ - Partial whole cluster (35%). Pretty, complex aromas of cinnamon, forest floor, herbs dark cherry and a hint of violet. The youthful palate exhibits excellent balance and structure.

Eola-Amity Hills Reserve Pinot Noir 2021 ● 325 cases; 75 $ - Partial whole cluster (33%). A brooding nose with darker fruit and perfume. The palate is complex. Plenty of structure to age. The acidity is a bit lower and the tannins are firmer.

Eola-Amity Hills Estate Chardonnay 2021 ○ 125 cases; 50 $ - Aged 18 months sur lie in oak (20% new). Partial malo. Aromas of nuts, lemon and chalk with some creaminess emerging. Well balanced palate shows toasted nuts and a medium finish.

---

acres 27 - cases 7,500
Fertilizers cover crops, organic fertilizer
Plant protection sulfur, synthetic pesticides, organic
Weed control mechanical
Yeasts spontaneous fermentation, selected indigenous yeasts, commercial cultured yeasts
Grapes purchase 50%
Certification none, some of the vineyards are certified biodynamic

MCMINNVILLE

CELESTIAL HILL VINEYARD

1970 NW Garris Lane - tel. (503) 687-5770
www.celestialhillvineyard.com - chris@celestialhillvineyard.com

PEOPLE - Inspired by frequent trips to Burgundy, Chris and Melissa Thomas bought the former Falcon Glen vineyard in 2020, making their first vintage that year. Chris is the winegrower with Wynne Peterson-Nedry and Alisa Le in the cellar. Recently they moved the tasting room from Carlton to downtown McMinnville. They switched to lighter weight bottles without foil and now use sustainable corks. A winery built among the vines is expected to be completed in November 2024.

VINEYARDS - The 20 year old vineyard sits at 375-675 feet in the foothills of the Oregon Coast Range. Three of the four vineyards are named for the couple's three children—Benjamin, Kendall Grace, and Brady. The fourth is named for Glenn Howard, the previous owner. The soils are marine sedimentary and volcanic. (Some wines from purchased grapes, not featured here, may be grown with herbicide.) In 2024, the team planted 2,900 vines of multiple clones of Pinot Noir.

WINES - Chris is transitioning to becoming an all estate winery, releasing the first estate Chardonnay in 2024.

● Willamette Valley Benjamin Vineyard Pinot Noir 2021 2021 SLOW WINE ● 125 cases; 66 $ - Aged 18 months on lees in oak (40% new). Pommard clone. Sweet cherry with a whiff of flowers becoming more perfumed with air. Excellently structured palate, smooth tannins and a medium finish. Young but promising.

Willamette Valley Estate Pinot Noir 2021 ● 320 cases; 42 $ - Aged 18 months in oak (40% new). An estate vineyard blend. Shows it youth on both the red fruit, cherry, spice nose and light to medium palate. Acid driven and food friendly.

Willamette Valley Estate Barrel Select Chardonnay 2022 ○ 100 cases; 70 $ - Aged 18 months on lees in oak (50% new). Full malo. Rich, polished aromas of lemon with hints of cream, herbs and spice and an elusive whiff of honey. Crisp entry. A long well balanced finish featuring ample acidity.

---

acres 15 - cases 3,000
Fertilizers compost, biodynamic compost, cover crops, manure, organic fertilizer
Plant protection sulfur, synthetic pesticides, organic
Weed control animal grazing, mechanical, manual
Yeasts commercial cultured yeasts
Grapes purchase 17%
Certification none

NEWBERG

CHEHALEM WINERY

106 S Center Street - tel. (503) 538-4700
www.chehalemwines.com - visit@chehalemwines.com

PEOPLE - Oregon born proprietor Bill Stoller, a former HR management exec, and Stoller Wine Group president Gary Mortensen, an innovator, run this B Corp. certified winery founded in 2001. After co-owning it since 1993, Stoller purchased it outright in 2018. Jason Tosch is vice president of vineyard operations. Talented Head Winemaker Katie Santora has been making wine here for more than ten years.

VINEYARDS - At 850 feet of elevation, the estate vineyard grows a wide variety of clones and varieties: 17 Pinot Noir, six Chardonnay, four Pinot Gris, two Pinot Blanc, one Gamay, and one Grüner Veltliner. LIVE and Salmon Safe certified, they use mechanical weed control, keeping the vineyard herbicide free. Part of their vineyard properties are designated eco-zones, providing habitat for biodiversity, native plants and animals.

WINES - Chehalem is situated in the Laurelwood District AVA where their Chehalem Estate Vineyard is the coolest of their sites.

Laurelwood District Chehalem Estate Pinot Noir 2022 SLOW WINE ● 995 cases; 50 $ - 🍷 - Aged in French oak (20% new). Grown on the upper vineyard. Florals on the nose join sweetheart cherries, pomegranate, raspberries, exotic tea, and red currant jelly on the palate. Supple tannins and balancing acidity join the deep fruit profile as the wine flows elegantly across the palate to a finish of excellent length and verve.

Laurelwood District Chehalem Estate Pinot Blanc 2022 ○ 995 cases; 35 $ - 🍷 - Aged in stainless (58%), neutral oak (31%) and concrete egg (11%). The dazzling floral aroma is like strolling through a blooming garden. Notes of honeysuckle, peaches, hints of apricot and a twist of lemon intertwine, and the texture is sublime. Expresses the full potential of Pinot Blanc, shining all the way through the bright, uplifting finish.

acres 204 - cases 26,900
Fertilizers none, compost, cover crops, organic fertilizer
Plant protection sulfur, synthetic pesticides, organic
Weed control mechanical, manual
Yeasts commercial cultured yeasts
Grapes purchase 7%
Certification none

HILLSBORO

CHO WINES

24399 NE Albertson Road - tel. (503) 726-6466
www.getchowines.com - info@getchowines.com

PEOPLE - Industry innovators, Dave and Lois Cho founded the first Korean-American owned winery in Oregon in 2020 and opened a tasting room in 2024 on the vineyard site. Dave, an OSU graduate in vit and enology, makes the wines. They also started the Oregon Asian American and Pacific Island (AAPI) wine and food festival and specialize in wines that pair well with Asian flavors. The first crush on the home site will be in 2024.

VINEYARDS - The team planted eight acres of vines on the Chehalem Mountains estate on Bald Peak (1,000 feet) with the traditional Burgundian varieties. Currently they buy grapes from seven Oregon growers including Cancilla (certified organic) and one grower in Walla Walla. Eco-minded, during the fruitful fall season in 2023, they collected 15,000 acorns to be replanted by Willamette University. Some wines (not featured here) may be grown with herbicide.

WINES - They make still wine, pet-nat, and traditional method sparkling wines. The still wines tend to be acid driven with lower alcohol and gentle tannins, achieving delicacy over power.

Willamette Valley Dreamer's Reserve Pinot Noir 2022 ● 200 cases; 60 $ - 🍷 - Partial whole cluster (20%), 10 days of carbonic. Complex aroma of dark cherry, stem, hay and other savory notes. Hint of creaminess on the structured palate. Finishes with lingering fruit.

Chehalem Mountains LBP Aligoté 2022 ○ 160 cases; 55 $ - 🍷 - From the La Belle Promenade Vineyard, a rarely grown varietal. Shows white flowers on the nose.

The Rocks District of Milton-Freewater Rocks Syrah 2022 ● 250 cases; 75 $ - 🍷 - Partial whole cluster (50%). From the Hallowed Stones Vineyard (across from the famed Cayuse Vineyard) in Walla Walla. Distinctive Rocks gravelly nose with meat and funk. Finishes elegantly and long with great acidity and fine tannins.

acres 8.5 - cases 3,500
Fertilizers compost, biodynamic compost, cover crops, organic fertilizer
Plant protection sulfur, copper
Weed control mechanical, manual
Yeasts spontaneous fermentation, commercial cultured yeasts
Grapes purchase 100%
Certification some of the vineyards are certified organic

BEAVERTON

COOPER MOUNTAIN VINEYARDS

20121 SW Leonardo Lane - tel. (503) 649-0027
www.coopermountainwine.com - info@coopermountainwine.com

 Carbon neutral since 2010, this multigenerational family sets the bar for environmental leadership, organic and biodynamic farming and fine wines.

PEOPLE - A biodynamic leader in Oregon, the winery that Barbara Gross' father Dr. Robert Gross and her late mother Corinne began with their purchase of vines in 1978. In 1987 they opened the winery. Biodynamics, with its mineral and herbal sprays, aligned with Dr. Gross' view that homeopathic sprays were effective medicine for people and plants. Bordeaux native Gilles de Domingo has been the winemaker since 2004. Gerry Sanchez oversees the vines.

VINEYARDS - In the past several years, the winery has expanded from four vineyards to eight, buying and reuniting two vineyards in the Chehalem Mountains and purchasing Chehalem Mountain Vineyard and Arborbrook Vineyard (now their second label). Soils are volcanic, sedimentary, and windblown loess. In addition to the Willamette Valley mainstays, they also grow Gamay Noir, Gewürztraminer, and Tocai Friulano.

WINES - Its certified biodynamic wines meet a high purity standard for both winegrowing and winemaking. Macerations of 2-3 weeks followed by 10 months in oak preserve freshness.

⦿ **Willamette Valley Life Pinot Noir 2019** SLOW WINE ● 400 cases; 40 $ - 🍷 - A no added sulfite, translucent wine–a pure expression of the fruit. Vibrant and juicy, it transparently reflects terroir, with blue and black fruits. The finish lingers.
Willamette Valley Pinot Noir Old Vines 2019 ● 400 cases; 60 $ - 🍷 - From vines planted in 1978. Aromas and flavors of dark fruits–blackberries and black cherries–supported by roses and wet stone.
Willamette Valley Johnson Pinot Noir 2021 ● 400 cases; 65 $ - 🍷 - Gives voice to blackberry and blue fruit notes, supported by red fruits. Elegant and complex.

acres 200 - cases 20,000
Fertilizers biodynamic compost, cover crops, organic fertilizer
Plant protection sulfur, biodynamic preparations, organic
Weed control mechanical
Yeasts spontaneous fermentation
Grapes 100% owned
Certification biodynamic, organic

DUNDEE

CRAMOISI VINEYARD

8640 NE Worden Hill Road - tel. (503) 583-1536
www.cramoisivineyard.com - sofia@cramoisivineyard.com

PEOPLE - Former IT workers, Mexican born Sofía Torres McKay and her husband, Ryan McKay, an Oregonian, planted their vineyard in 2012. Jorge Chavez from Chavez Craft Vineyards oversees the vineyards. Jessica West and Drew Voit consult on winemaking and helped the white Pinot Noir. McKay also co-founded AHIVOY, a nonprofit organization advancing Hispanic vintners and workers in the Oregon wine industry.

VINEYARDS - The south facing Dundee Hills estate is planted to four Pinot Noir clones and one acre of Chardonnay. Their own vines, at 500-650 feet, sit on Jory soil. The vineyard has been seeded to native upland prairie cover crop. Sheep will be brought in for weed control and manure in 2025. They also buy Syrah from the celebrated Les Collines Vineyard in Walla Walla. The McKays are currently seeking biodynamic certification (expected in 2025), a three year process.

WINES - Stylistically, the Pinots are becoming more elegant, floral, and texturally interesting, through the judicious use of new oak and partial stem inclusion.

⦿ **Dundee Hills Reserve Pinot Noir 2021** ● 150 cases; 82 $ - 🍷 - Aged 18 months in oak (33% new). Partial stem inclusion; 13 to 18% is added back. A best barrel selection. Elegant nose. The palate is more perfumed and floral with a hint of citrus. Just lovely!
Dundee Hills White Pinot Noir 2022 ○ 100 cases; 82 $ - 🍷 - Inaugural vintage of this wine. Pretty, floral and tropical fruit, rich and complex, classy. Some citrus emerges with time. Less weighty than other examples but nicely textured.
Dundee Hills Sofía's Block Pinot Noir 2021 ● 200 cases; 70 $ - 🍷 - All Dijon 667 clone with about 13 to 18% stems added back in the fermentation. Intensely perfumed with integrated earth notes. Given the aromas, unexpectedly lighter on the palate but with great texture and a medium finish.

acres 7 - cases 1,000
Fertilizers compost, biodynamic compost, cover crops
Plant protection sulfur, biodynamic preparations, organic
Weed control mechanical
Yeasts spontaneous fermentation
Grapes purchase 10%
Certification converting to biodynamic, none

FOREST GROVE

DAVID HILL VINEYARDS AND WINERY $

46350 NW David Hill Road - tel. (503) 992-8545
www.davidhillwinery.com - mike@davidhillwinery.com

PEOPLE - An Oregon classic, it's managed by Mike Kuenz who oversees the two historic, acclaimed Charles Coury vineyards (planted in 1965 and Wirtz, planted in 1974), that he co-owns with Laurine and Tuscan born Alfredo Apolloni. Chad Stock has been the winemaker since 2019, using gentle vinification methods and atypical aging vessels—Acacia wood, Flex Cubes, concrete eggs—as well as large Austrian oak barrels.

VINEYARDS - Both estate sites are on loess soils and grow own rooted, heirloom selections. The Coury is the second oldest vineyard in the Willamette. It's grows Chasselas Doré, Gewürztraminer, Pinot Blanc, Pinot Noir, Riesling, Semillon, and Sylvaner. Chardonnay and Dijon clones of Pinot Noir were added. The no till Wirtz Vineyard, begun in 1974, grows 14 acres of heirlooms—Chardonnay (Draper clone), Gewürztraminer, Muscat, Pinot Gris, and Pinot Noir.

WINES - Stylistically cerebral yet elegant whites emphasize finesse over overt fruitiness. Pinot Noir from old vines intrigue with complex aromas and great texture.

TOP Tualatin Hills Whole Cluster Pinot Noir 2022 SLOW WINE ● 250 cases; 52 $ - ⓤ - Whole cluster (100%). Enticingly perfumed with floral, earth, stem and faint spice notes. Elegant acid driven palate, nicely textured and structured with silky tannins and medium finish.
Tualatin Hills Block 22 Pinot Blanc 2022 ○ 100 cases; 32 $ - ▦ - Aged in chestnut barrels. Bright aroma of citrus over guava. Soft entry blossoms into medium midpalate then proceeds to a refreshing burst of acidity in the long finish. With air, salinity apparent on the palate. Really nice.
Tualatin Hills Block 18 Melon de Bourgogne 2020 ○ 75 cases; 32 $ - ⓤ - Aged three years on lees. Floral aroma with savory and faint green notes. Rounded textured palate with hints of fruit but mostly savory and saline. Long finish.

acres 57 - cases 9,000
Fertilizers compost, cover crops, organic fertilizer
Plant protection sulfur, organic
Weed control mechanical
Yeasts spontaneous fermentation
Grapes 100% owned
Certification none

DUNDEE

DAY WINES

21160 N Highway 99 W - tel. (971) 832-8196
www.daywines.com - info@daywines.com

PEOPLE - Former waitress turned winemaker Brianne Day has a long history in food and wine, starting with the hospitality industry in Portland and extending to winemaking stints across three continents. Returning to Oregon, her first winemaking vintage was 2012. In recent years, she's focused more on Italian varieties—Arneis, Dolcetto, Nero d'Avola and Zibibbo—and exploring the nuances of fermentation of each.

VINEYARDS - Day works with as many as 30 different vineyards each year, prioritizing organic or biodynamic growers, including Johan Vineyards and Momtazi (both certified biodynamic). The diversity of vineyard sites from the Willamette Valley to the Applegate Valley bring many different varietals and terroirs into the cellar.

WINES - A creative and expressive lineup of minimal intervention, acid driven wines that showcase some single varietals unique to the region.

TOP Applegate Valley Four Diamonds Farm Nero d'Avola 2022 EVERYDAY WINE ⊛ 55 cases; 27 $ - ▦ - A playful and energetic sparkling wine. A rich nose of ripe blackberry, preserved cherry and rose. Bright and juicy palate of blackberry and red cherries. Bright acidity comes through in each refined bubble.
Chehalem Mountains Aurora Vineyard Arneis 2023 ○ 162 cases; 36 $ - ▦ ⓤ - Aromatic and floral notes of jasmine, gardenias and Asian pear. The juicy palate gives crunchy Bosc pear, ginger, honeycomb and olive oil with a thirst quenching minerality.
McMinnville Momtazi Vineyard Pinot Noir 2021 ● 193 cases; 58 $ - ⓤ - Partial whole cluster (25%) on skins for 23 days. Delicate and aromatic cherry, boysenberry and blueberry with hints of botanical herbs. Juicy, ripe berry notes have undertones of chocolate and coffee with a floral lift. Decidedly expressive.

acres - cases 20,000
Fertilizers biodynamic compost, cover crops, manure, organic
Plant protection sulfur, biodynamic preparations, synthetic pesticides, organic
Weed control none, animal grazing, mechanical, manual
Yeasts spontaneous fermentation
Grapes purchase 100%
Certification some of the vineyards are certified organic, some of the vineyards are certified biodynamic

NEWBERG

DOMAINE DIVIO

16435 NE Lewis Rogers Lane - tel. (503) 334-0903
www.domainedivio.com - info@domainedivio.com

PEOPLE - Dijon native Bruno Corneaux is a fourth generation grape grower from Burgundy. He participated in his first harvest in Oregon back in 1996 when his former high school classmate, Veronique Drouhin Boss of Domaine Drouhin, invited him to work crush. The area reminded him of Meloisey where he grew up. A sense of fellowship inspired him to found Domaine Divio with fellow Burgundian André Weil. They purchased the estate vineyard in 2014.

VINEYARDS - Most fruit is purchased from local growers. The soils at Clos Galia, their Ribbon Ridge estate, are reminiscent of those Bruno labored over in Burgundy—rich in marine sedimentary material. They originally planted Pinot Noir clones of Wadenswil, Dijon 777 and Dijon 115. Though not certified, they say they use biodynamic practices. The property boasts diverse tree plantings and wetlands that promote biodiversity.

WINES - Their wines pay homage to Burgundy through French tradition while embracing the essence of Oregon grapes and innovation.

Ribbon Ridge Clos Gallia Estate Pinot Noir 2022 SLOW WINE ● 290 cases; 65 $ - ⊞ - A representation of the best of the estate, this charming, complex wine is full of opulent fruit with a leather edge bringing together cherry, fresh fig and blueberry.

Ribbon Ridge Clos Gallia Estate Gabriel Block Pinot Noir 2021 ● 150 cases; 65 $ - ⊞ - Aged 11 months in oak (35% new). Its lavish fruit beauty highlights cherry front and center backed by silky tannins.

Ribbon Ridge Clos Gallia Estate Chardonnay 2022 ○ 180 cases; 65 $ - ⓠ - This wine is light on its feet with hints of pear and crisp Braeburn apple along accompanied by mouthwatering acidity.

acres 13 - cases 5,300
Fertilizers biodynamic compost, cover crops
Plant protection sulfur, biodynamic preparations, synthetic pesticides, organic
Weed control mechanical
Yeasts spontaneous fermentation
Grapes purchase 60%
Certification none

DAYTON

DOMAINE DROUHIN OREGON

6750 NE Breyman Orchards Road - tel. (503) 864-2700
www.domainedrouhin.com - info@domainedrouhin.com

 A superstar run by a renowned French family, it makes wines of elegance, balance and finesse and is now becoming certified organic.

PEOPLE - Convinced by the potential of the region, in 1987, the pioneering Drouhin family, Burgundy stars, bought land in the Dundee Hills. The winery's led today by siblings winemaker Véronique Boss-Drouhin and viticulturist Philippe Drouhin along with general manager David Millman. They also a have second winery, Roserock (see separate listing) and sell their French wines on their U.S. website.

VINEYARDS - Organic and biodynamic certified in Burgundy since 1993, the LIVE certified U.S. estate is transitioning to organic certification with the help of viticulturalist Leigh Bartholomew. The high density vines are planted at meter by meter spacing—popular in Burgundy but rare in the U.S. Inclusive, their long time Mexican American vineyard team is profiled on their website along with their tasting room staff and other employees.

WINES - The 2022 vintage was challenging due to an April frost, which resulted in lower yields, but the grapes were of exceptional quality.

Dundee Hills Cuvée Laurène Pinot Noir 2022 SLOW WINE ● 3,274 cases; 80 $ - ⊞ - Their top of the line wine. Spice and earth tones on the nose. On the palate, sumptuous layers of cassis, savory herbs, black cherries, exotic tea, hints of tobacco, understated French oak and tinges of orange zest. Fine grained tannins, lively acidity and a silky texture. Ageworthy.

Dundee Hills Origine 35 Pinot Noir 2022 ● 1,520 cases; 55 $ - ⊞ - The forest floor aroma tells you precisely what is in the glass. Mouthwatering on the palate as classic flavors of wild raspberries, Montmorency cherries, hints of nutmeg, mushrooms, subtle French oak nuances and a fresh grind of multi-colored peppercorns traverse the palate. Precisely balanced and ethereal through the heavenly finish.

acres 135 - cases 24,000
Fertilizers compost, cover crops, manure, organic fertilizer
Plant protection sulfur, organic
Weed control animal grazing, mechanical
Yeasts spontaneous fermentation, commercial cultured yeasts
Grapes 100% owned
Certification converting to organic

CARLTON

DOMINIO IV

11570 NE Intervale Road - tel. (971) 261-7781
www.dominiowines.com - info@dominiowines.com

PEOPLE - Viticulturalist Leigh Bartholomew and winemaker Patrick Reuter are the vintners behind the brand, founded in 2002. Ryan Kelly-Burnett is associate winemaker. With Megan Hattie Stahl, Reuter produced an audio documentary, "Sounds of Unknowing: the Making of an Oregon Sauvignon Blanc," about the process of producing the winery's Sauvignon Blanc. Bartholomew also farms for other wineries, including Domaine Drouhin.

VINEYARDS - The winery has two estate vineyards in markedly different regions—the 11 acre Shallow-bluesea in Yamhill-Carlton, growing mostly Burgundian varieties, and the 10 acre Three Sleeps Vineyard in the Columbia Gorge, where they grow Rhones and other varieties. They also buy grapes from Stermer Vineyard (Lemelson's certified organic vines in the Yamhill-Carlton AVA), Smith Vineyards and Wannamaker in the Gorge.

WINES - A range of graceful, kaleidolfactic (meaning "ever-changing aromas"), ageworthy varietal wines that are aromatically complex and well balanced with excellent acidity.

TOP Columbia Gorge The Tango Tempranillo 2017 SLOW WINE ● 148 cases; 42 $ - ⊞ - On the nose, dark fruit, forest floor and a hint of mint and leather emerging with air. Flavors are dark and varietally typical with leather notes. Tannins are abundant but medium fine adding to an intriguing texture.

Yamhill Carlton Rain on Leaves Pinot Noir 2016 ● 87 cases; 48 $ - ⊞ - From the Stermer Vineyard. Aromas of dark fruit, with whiffs of pine, mint, tarragon and wood. Well structured palate, initially youthful but opens with air.

Rogue Valley Still Life Viognier 2022 ○ 99 cases; 32 $ - ⌧ ⊞ - Intense floral perfume, a well balanced palate of delicate fruit, floral, and savory notes highlighting pineapple. Nice acidity. A lovely, refined rendition of this variety.

acres 21 - cases 4,000
Fertilizers compost, manure, organic fertilizer
Plant protection sulfur, biodynamic preparations, synthetic pesticides, organic
Weed control mechanical
Yeasts spontaneous fermentation, commercial cultured yeasts
Grapes purchase 35%
Certification some of the vineyards are certified organic, converting to organic, converting to biodynamic

DUNDEE

ÉLEVÉE WINEGROWERS

9653 NE Keyes Lane - tel. (503) 840-8448
www.eleveewines.com - tom@eleveewines.com

PEOPLE - Now Dundee Hills stars making top rated Pinot, Tom and France Fitzpatrick purchased their site back in 2008. Winemaker Tom, a UC Davis viticulture and enology graduate, had already worked in wine regions of Burgundy, Napa Valley and New Zealand. They're expanding in both vines (with a new Coast Range estate) and facilities, developing a new tasting room on their Dundee Hills property.

VINEYARDS - Their LIVE certified estate vineyard provides a third of the grapes. It sits at 540 feet and is no till, dry farmed and herbicide free. The Pinot Noir clones include Pommard, 115 and 777, growing on clay loam Jory soil, on a south facing slope with marine influence. Local growers provide two thirds of the grapes. Meredith Mitchell is certified biodynamic. They are also developing their 30 acre estate in the Coast Range located in the Willamette Valley's cooler northwestern edge.

WINES - The couple brings out the unique nuances of wines from the subappellations within the Willamette Valley AVA, striving for pure flavors in their wines.

TOP Eola-Amity Hills Björnson Vineyard Pinot Noir 2022 SLOW WINE ● 275 cases; 62 $ - ⊞ - Aged in French oak (30% new). A gem. Opens with a tantalizing savory aroma. On the palate, sumptuous flavors of black and red cherries, black tea, cherry cola, orange zest and a pinch of herbs.

Dundee Hills Élevée Vineyard Pinot Noir 2022 ● 225 cases; 62 $ - ⊞ - Aged in French oak (30% new). Perfumed aromas of cherries and spice at first swirl, mirrored on the palate. Sweetheart cherries, spiced raspberry coulis and sweet tobacco leaf interlace with underlying oak and anise accents. Satin smooth and elegant through the finish.

Ribbon Ridge Ridgecrest Vineyard Grüner Veltliner 2022 ○ 100 cases; 34 $ - ⌧ ⊞ - Wildly aromatic. Fresh and juicy with vivid layers of star fruit, classic white pepper, chamomile, lemon verbena and lively acidity. Oh so refreshing as it traverses the palate to a lingering finale.

acres 4 - cases 1,400
Fertilizers none, cover crops, synthetic fertilizer
Plant protection sulfur, synthetic pesticides, organic
Weed control manual
Yeasts spontaneous fermentation
Grapes purchase 64%
Certification none, some of the vineyards are certified biodynamic

DUNDEE

EVENING LAND VINEYARDS

1326 N Highway 99W, Suite 200 - tel. (503) 538-4110
www.elvwines.com - oregonhospitality@elvwines.com

PEOPLE - The esteemed Seven Springs Estate has been farmed and since 2022, is now owned by Sashi Moorman and reknowned somm-turned-vigneron Raj Parr. They continue the biodynamic practice established by previous consultant Dominique Lafon of Domaine Comte Lafon. The two address the challenge posed by the short, hot season in the Willamette Valley by minimizing harsh qualities in their grape must by gentle infusion techniques during fermentation.

VINEYARDS - The Seven Springs Vineyard is east-facing and in the path of the Van Duzer Corridor which channels cooling air from the Pacific. Soils are Jory and Nekia series volcanic with obsidian veins. Plantings are Pinot Noir and Chardonnay with a small amount of Gamay Noir. In recent replantings, fruit trees and biodynamic flora have been incorporated into the vineyard to establish sympathetic mycorrhizal networks as defense in the face of climate change.

WINES - The wines are bright, rich and fruited bearing the hallmark texture of their volcanic soil.

Eola-Amity Hills Summum Chardonnay 2022 O 347 cases; 100 $ - Aromas of honeysuckle and yellow apple emerge from the glass. There is acidic tension and a bit of grip on the palate with intense lemon curd, tangerine and apple fruit, though ripeness and harmony win out in this generous wine. Subtle oak and reduction effects add more depth of flavor.

Eola-Amity Hills Seven Springs Pinot Noir 2022 ● 564 cases; 80 $ - Aromas are earthy, floral and of a red fruit bowl. Flavors are rich yet without density, bright with red fruit, light spice and a long palate punctuated with very fine-grained tannins that connect to Seven Springs' volcanic soils.

Eola-Amity Hills Seven Springs Chardonnay 2022 O 2,732 cases; 40 $ - Shows a nose of white flower, yellow apple and bruléed custard giving way to a palate of apple, Meyer lemon and peach skin with both formidable tartness and welcoming fruit.

acres 85 - cases 11,477
Fertilizers compost
Plant protection biodynamic preparations
Weed control mechanical
Yeasts spontaneous fermentation
Grapes 100% owned
Certification none

SALEM

EVESHAM WOOD

3795 Wallace Road NW - tel. (503) 371-8478
www.eveshamwood.com - info@eveshamwood.com

PEOPLE - Erin Nuccio and his wife Jordan acquired the winery and pioneering organic Le Puy Sec Vineyard from founders Russ Rainey and his wife Mary in 2010. Nuccio keeps the winery, founded in 1986, true to the original vision and organic philosophies. A staunch advocate of dry farming, Nuccio is a member of the Deep Roots Coalition, which Rainey founded. Their Eola-Amity Hills site includes a charming tasting room as well as a gravity fed winery and wine caves.

VINEYARDS - The 13 acres of estate vines at Le Puits Sec and La Grive Bleue (certified organic since 2000) grow Pinot Noir and Chardonnay. Some Alsatian varieties are also planted. The Torres Brothers vineyard, purchased in 2022, is in transition to organic certification, as is Mahonia. They also buy grapes from Temperance Hill (certified organic) and other sites that share a similar farming philosophy including Illahe and Sojeau vineyards.

WINES - Winemaking with minimal intervention creates appealing, complex wines unmasked by oak.

Eola-Amity Hills Le Puits Sec Vineyard Pinot Noir 2022 SLOW WINE ● 400 cases; 56 $ - A sophisticated wine that reveals complexities of forest floor, baking spice, and black tea with brambly fruit in the background accompanied by vivid acidity and polished tannins.

Eola-Amity Hills Cuvee Pinot Noir 2022 ● 900 cases; 34 $ - Aged 18 months in French oak (15% new). A pretty perfumed nose of spring flowers leads to a juicy, energetic palate of cherry and raspberry with a cooling finish.

Willamette Valley Mahonia Vineyard Pinot Noir 2022 ● 200 cases; 48 $ - A pleasant wine showcasing flavors of black cherry, vanilla cola and raspberry.

acres 24.5 - cases 7,045
Fertilizers biodynamic compost, cover crops, manure
Plant protection sulfur, biodynamic preparations, organic
Weed control mechanical
Yeasts selected indigenous yeasts
Grapes purchase 66%
Certification some of the vineyards are certified organic, converting to organic

CARLTON

FLÂNEUR WINES

168 S Pine Street - tel. (503) 889-4121
www.flaneurwines.com - visit@flaneurwines.com

PEOPLE - After Marty Doerschlag left his family's Ohio based design firm, he ended up in Oregon where he started Flâneur Wines in 2013. In 2024, after two years as assistant winemaker, Anthony Sereni was appointed director of winemaking. Jaime Cantu is director of vineyards. A painstakingly restored grain elevator in Carlton is home to the tasting room, though guests may also schedule private tastings at the rustic barn located at La Belle Promenade vineyard.

VINEYARDS - The Flanerie Vineyard in the Ribbon Ridge AVA provides a bed of Willakenzie soil for the vines and eastern orientation. La Belle Promenade Vineyard in the Chehalem Mountains AVA sits at 820 feet with a cooler microclimate and forms a natural patchwork quilt of Aligote, Chardonnay, Grüner Veltliner, Pinot Meunier and Pinot Noir vines. Dry farming and organic practices aim to sustain the land for future generations.

WINES - The all estate wines celebrate each specific site and the characteristics of each vintage.

⓿ **Chehalem Mountains La Belle Promenade Pinot Noir 2021** SLOW WINE ● 785 cases; 60 $ - 🍽 - Aged one year in oak (16% new). This irresistible wine offers not only terrific depth but an approachable array of fresh fruitiness including plum and blackberry backed by moderate tannins.

Chehalem Mountains La Belle Promenade Extra Brut 2019 ✺ 399 cases; 65 $ - 🥂 - Aged en tirage for three and a half years. A blend of Pinot Noir (47%), Chardonnay (28%) and Pinot Meunier (25%). This festive sparkler showcases a delicate, fine mousse before hitting high notes of lemon curd moderated by classic brioche and a little beeswax on the finish.

Chehalem Mountains La Belle Promenade Chardonnay 2022 ○ 160 cases; 60 $ - 🍽 - Aged in French and Austrian oak (43% new). Whole cluster pressed. The result is an opulent palate coating wine that balances its weight with the vivacity of lemon curd and leaves behind a long, lingering finish of caramel toffee.

acres 50 - cases 5,000
Fertilizers compost, cover crops, manure, organic fertilizer
Plant protection sulfur, organic
Weed control mechanical, manual
Yeasts spontaneous fermentation
Grapes 100% owned
Certification none

MCMINNVILLE

GOODFELLOW FAMILY CELLARS

888 NE 8th Street - tel. (503) 939-1308
www.goodfellowfamilycellars.com - marcus@goodfellowfamilycellars.com

PEOPLE - Initially a restaurateur, Marcus Goodfellow did a stint at Evesham Wood and learned from Cristom's Steve Doerner, before making his first vintage in 2002 at Westrey Wine Company. His wife, Megan, joined him in 2011 as an intern, making their Matello brand wines. In 2014, after their child was born, they changed the name to Goodfellow Family. A new sparkling wine program just launched with three vineyard designate, traditional method wines.

VINEYARDS - Members of the Deep Root Coalition for dry farmed wines, grapes come from 21 acres of dry farmed, no till sites farmed by growers. That list includes Whistling Ridge in the Ribbon Ridge AVA (said to use only organic approved materials), Temperance Hill in the Eola-Amity Hills AVA (certified organic), Durant Vineyard in the Dundee Hills AVA, and Fir Crest Vineyard and Tsai Vineyard (in transition to organic certification), both in the Yamhill-Carlton AVA.

WINES - Minimal intervention. Shifting to larger vessels (500-820L). Elegant Pinot Noirs fermented with 75 to 100 percent whole cluster. Chardonnays age in puncheons for 20 months.

⓿ **Eola-Amity Hills Temperance Hill Vineyard Pinot Noir Heritage No. 20 2022** ● 115 cases; 80 $ - 🍽 - Fermented all whole cluster, which creates a pleasant stemminess on the nose. The rich palate is elegant, suave, and silky with lower acidity. Well structured.

Yamhill-Carlton Tsai Vineyard Chardonnay 2021 ○ 90 cases; 50 $ - 🍽 - Nutty aroma and nicely textured palate featuring great acidity. Warm nutty flavor and a long finish.

Yamhill-Carlton Tsai Vineyard Pinot Blanc 2023 ○ 113 cases; 27 $ - 🥂 - Aromas of pear with a hint of citrus on the nose and palate with bright acidity and a long finish.

acres 0 - cases 4,000
Fertilizers compost, cover crops, organic fertilizer
Plant protection sulfur, synthetic pesticides, organic
Weed control mechanical
Yeasts spontaneous fermentation, selected indigenous yeasts, commercial cultured yeasts
Grapes purchase 100%
Certification some of the vineyards are certified organic

DUNDEE

GRANVILLE WINE CO.

10464 Jory Lane - tel. (503) 435-8668
www.granvillewines.com - jackson@granvillewines.com

PEOPLE - High in the Dundee Hills, committed, second generation winegrowers, vigneron Jackson Holstein and his wife Ayla founded the winery in 2014, naming it for one of Jackson's ancestors who was a subsistence farmer. Ayla, also experienced in vit and winemaking, manages business operations and hospitality in their charming tasting room. Ruben Olmedo Lopez assists in the vineyard. The couple's son Louie and daughter O'Della lend their names to reserve bottlings.

VINEYARDS - Jackson grew up on their Holstein Estate Vineyard, originally planted in 1972, making it one of the earliest plantings in the Willamette. It sits on Jory soils at 615 and 740 feet and was replanted beginning in the 1990s. In 2019, the team planted a second Dundee Hills estate vineyard. They also buy from high elevation, volcanic soil sites including Koosah and Temperance Hill (both certified organic), Latchkey and Knudsen Vineyards.

WINES - Whole cluster fermentation for Pinot Noir and carefully modulated pressing to extract tannins for Chardonnay enhance ageability and complexity.

Eola-Amity Hills Temperance Hill Vineyard Pinot Noir 2022 ● 225 cases; 65 $ - Aged 12 months in French oak (30% new). Partial whole cluster (40%). A lovely nose with a stem base, floral perfume and spice. The palate is delicate with nicely textured tannins, intense acidity and a long finish.

Eola-Amity Hills Koosah Vineyard Chardonnay 2022 ○ 225 cases; 65 $ - Aged 12 months in French oak (15% new). Lees aging. Complex aromas of chalk and nuts with a hint of citrus. Palate is fresh. A long lemony finish and silky texture.

Willamette Valley O'Della Reserve Chardonnay 2022 ○ 175 cases; 95 $ - Aged 11 months in French oak (35% new). Intensely nutty on the nose giving way to lemon. Unexpectedly delicate entry on palate but long with silky texture emerging. Ageworthy.

acres 17 - cases 3,000
Fertilizers compost, biodynamic compost, cover crops, manure pellets
Plant protection sulfur, biodynamic preparations, synthetic pesticides, organic
Weed control mechanical, manual
Yeasts selected indigenous yeasts
Grapes purchase 50%
Certification some of the vineyards are certified organic

SALEM

HADEN FIG $

3795 Wallace Road - tel. (503) 371-8478
www.hadenfig.com - info@eveshamwood.com

PEOPLE - With a background in retail and distribution roles, Erin Nuccio made his way to Napa to study enology and viticulture. The call of the vineyards and Oregon Pinot Noir brought him to the Willamette Valley where he was mentored by Russ Rainey at Evesham Wood. Nuccio founded Haden Fig in 2008 as a way to experiment with spontaneous fermentation, barrel regime and elevage that deviate from the practices he employs for the Evesham Wood wines.

VINEYARDS - The winery relies on three vineyards in the Willamette Valley. Cancilla Vineyard (certified organic) sits at 500-600 feet in Melbourne soil with southeast exposure. Nuccio helped plant a portion of the vineyard. They also buy grapes from four blocks of Salmon Safe certified Croft Vineyard (certified organic). Freedom Hill Vineyard practices integrated pest management.

WINES - The goal is to create unmasked Chardonnay, Pinot Gris, Pinot Noir and Rosé using only minimal inputs, no stems and no yeast nutrients.

Willamette Valley Croft Vineyard Pinot Noir 2022 SLOW WINE ● 100 cases; 40 $ - A well structured energetic wine with enthralling depth that entices with dark cherry followed by cinnamon bark.

Willamette Valley Pinot Noir 2022 ● 1,465 cases; 26 $ - Aged in oak (15% new). The wine is an incredible value. Seamlessly unites the complexities of savory and fruit flavors. A cavalcade of eucalyptus, tamarind, cherry vanilla, cranberry and dried fig flavors are wrapped in approachable tannins.

Willamette Valley Cancilla Vineyard Pinot Noir 2022 ● 100 cases; 40 $ - Born out of Melbourne soils, the wine offers flavors of cherry, plum, hibiscus, prune and dried tobacco leaf.

acres 24.5 - cases 2,409
Fertilizers cover crops, manure
Plant protection sulfur, synthetic pesticides, organic
Weed control mechanical
Yeasts spontaneous fermentation
Grapes purchase 65%
Certification some of the vineyards are certified organic

NEWBERG

J.C. SOMERS VINTNER

1485 N Kilchis Avenue - tel. (503) 502-1641
www.jcsomers.wine - Jcsomersvintner@gmail.com

PEOPLE - Veteran Oregon vintner (and rock musician) Jay Somers has an intimate knowledge of the best regional growers as well as authentic winemaking. An Oregon native, he's made wine in the Willamette for 30 years. After working at J. Christopher, he became the winemaker at Anne Amie Vineyards and relaunched his own brand as well, using Anne Amie's facilities for both brands. His wife and partner, Ronda Newell-Somers managed the business and marketing.

VINEYARDS - He buys from three choice vineyards. Started in 1983, the family owned Croft Vineyard (certified organic), with ancient marine sediment soils, is one of the best white wine sites in the state and known for Sauvignon Blanc. He buys Pinot Noir from two premiere Dundee Hills sites planted on Jory soils–the iconic Abbey Ridge (Cloury clone) and the La Colina (Pommard and Wadenswil clones).

WINES - The whites exhibit varietal typicity with nice acid balance. Pinot Noirs are medium weight, complex, well balanced and capable of aging.

TOP **Dundee Hills La Colina Vineyard Pinot Noir 2022** SLOW WINE ● 100 cases; 40 $ - 🍷 - On the nose: classy, spice inflected, candied dark cherry notes. Approachable on palate with very fine tannins supporting the smooth texture and nice structure.

Dundee Hills Abbey Ridge Vineyard Pinot Noir 2022 ● 75 cases; 65 $ - 🍷 - On the nose: candied fruit with faint suggestion of mint initially, with more floral and cinnamon showing with air. Shy palate with muted fruit, nicely structured with paradoxically a long finish. Best cellared.

Willamette Valley Croft Vineyard Sauvignon Blanc 2022 ○ 150 cases; 30 $ - 🍷 - Forthright typical Sauvignon nose with some white flowers. Citrusy palate with classic Sauvignon fruit and floral overtones, lovely mouthfeel with good acidity and a medium finish.

acres 0 - cases 1,000
Fertilizers compost, cover crops
Plant protection sulfur, organic
Weed control mechanical
Yeasts spontaneous fermentation, commercial cultured yeasts
Grapes purchase 100%
Certification some of the vineyards are certified organic

NEWBERG

J.K. CARRIERE

9995 NE Parrett Mountain Road - tel. (503) 554-0721
www.jkcarriere.com - linda@jkcarriere.com

 Certified organic in 2022, the no till vineyard uses native cover crop, grazing sheep compost teas and is dry farmed, creating wines true to their terroir.

PEOPLE - An iconic Oregon Pinot guy, Jim Prosser is not only is a consummate winemaker but can also tell you a fascinating true story that you will never forget. (Ask him about the wasp that tried to kill him.) Jim, along with his general manager (and sister) Linda Crabtree, named the winery for their two grandfathers. They named their estate vineyard St. Dolores to honor to their mom. The two are passionate about being eco-friendly, organic and sustainable.

VINEYARDS - Most of the grapes come from their dry farmed St. Dolores estate (certified organic), planted in 2009. Chardonnay and some Pinot comes from the high elevation Temperance Hill Vineyard (certified organic) in the Eola-Amity Hills and Gemini Vineyard (which uses only organic approved materials) in the Chehalem Mountains. Prosser is also a board member of the Deep Roots Coalition, a dry farming group.

WINES - Ageworthy wines are the result of their regime for reds: cold soaks for six days with native fermentations (23-30 days) followed by wild malo in 18 months in barrel yields ageworthy wines.

TOP **Willamette Valley Vespidae Pinot Noir 2022** SLOW WINE ● 821 cases; 72 $ - 🍷 - Electrifying nose of cherries and spice broadens on the complex palate. A colorful kaleidoscope of Montmorency cherries, raspberry coulis, wild mushrooms and savoriness unfold. Pure and silky in texture.

Willamette Valley St. Dolores Estate Pinot Noir 2022 ● 190 cases; 72 $ - 🍷 - The herb tinged, wild cherry aromatics leads to layers of tropical mango and papaya and herb dusted cherry sauce. Allspice peeks through on the juicy, persistent finish.

Willamette Valley Lucidité Chardonnay 2021 ○ 184 cases; 38 $ - 🍷 - A delicate floral bouquet on the nose. Creamy pears, Meyer lemon, orange marmalade and pie spice create a breathtaking layer of flavors. Finely balanced, pure and complex. Brilliant.

acres 26 - cases 4,700
Fertilizers compost, cover crops, manure, organic fertilizer
Plant protection sulfur, organic
Weed control animal grazing, mechanical, manual
Yeasts spontaneous fermentation
Grapes purchase 20%
Certification some of the vineyards are certified organic

NEWBERG

JACHTER FAMILY WINES

21537 NE Kings Grade Road - tel. (971) 205-8310
www.jachterwine.com - hello@jachterwine.com

PEOPLE - Proprietors Dave Jachter, a former car dealer, and his wife Karen Jachter embarked on a new chapter of their lives in 2019, starting their family run winery in the heart of Oregon wine country. Son Aaron Jachter oversees the vineyards and his wife Candra manages production. Dave hired a name winemaker–Jared Etzel (also of Domaine Roy & fils) who is the son of acclaimed Oregon winemaking legend Michael Etzel of Beaux Freres–expecting great things to come.

VINEYARDS - The Jachters purchased 120 acres of land in 2019 and in 2020 cleared the blackberry bush covered site. They planted 18 acres of Chardonnay, Nebbiolo, Pinot Meunier and Pinot Noir on south facing slopes in well drained, red, volcanic Chehalem Mountains soils. They farm using only organically approved materials. While they wait for their own vines to grow, they buy herbicide free grapes from local growers.

WINES - Etzel's initial releases from local fruit show promise. Their inaugural estate vintage will be 2023. Wines are now in bottle or barrel, with releases expected soon.

 Chehalem Mountains Cuvée Karen Ann Pinot Noir 2021 ● 125 cases; 80 $ - ▥ - Tantalizing florals and red fruits on the nose. Well-defined and complex on the palate with layers of forest floor, red raspberries, anise, exotic tea, pomegranate, and French oak nuances supported by crisp acidity, polished tannins and a persistent finale.
Chehalem Mountains J Reserve Chardonnay 2021 ○ 125 cases; 80 $ - ▥ - Aged in French oak (50% new). Expressive aromas on the nose. The complex palate displays Crispin apples, white peaches, salinity, minerality, lemon herbs, spice accents and well integrated French oak (50% new). Beautifully textured with a long-lasting finish.

acres 18 - cases 2,400
Fertilizers manure, organic fertilizer
Plant protection sulfur, organic
Weed control animal grazing, mechanical, manual
Yeasts selected indigenous yeasts
Grapes purchase 85%
Certification none

RICKREALL

JOHAN VINEYARDS

4285 N Pacific Highway 99 W - tel. (503) 623-8642
www.johanvineyards.com - info@johanvineyards.com

 An outstanding team that sets the standard for regenerative biodynamic farming and expressive wines.

PEOPLE - When proprietor Mini (Banks) Byers bought the all estate winery in 2021 from its Norwegian family founders, she inherited a very talented team. (She also owns Cowhorn.) Morgan Beck is the longtime winemaker and general manager, while Nathan Wood is the vineyard manager. Drawing from a wide range of experience, they produce energetic and lively wines while offering exploratory tasting flights, wine club, a CSA farm share, and dining events set in the vineyard.

VINEYARDS - The 175 acre, certified biodynamic property grows 14 different varieties of grapes including some esoteric favorites like Blaufränkisch, Grüner Veltliner and Melon de Bourgogne, adding diversity within the vineyard and the broader Oregon wine landscape. They focus on regenerative farming, integrating a rotational grazing system and fertilizing with their 55 Katahdin sheep and 60 egg laying chickens that circulate through the vines and the oak savannas.

WINES - Expanding the Oregon palette through lively and focused expressions of Kerner, Melon de Bourgogne, Ribolla Gialla, Savagnin, Blaufränkisch and Zweigelt.

Van Duzer Corridor Drueskall Pinot Gris 2022 ◐ 276 cases; 40 $ - ▥ - A blend of destemmed, whole cluster and carbonic fermentations on skins for three to five weeks. Earth driven base notes with bright fruit and crunchy tannins. Juicy blood orange, savory herb garden and Chinese five spice.
Van Duzer Corridor Savagnin 2022 ○ 117 cases; 40 $ - ▥ - Dry with punchy acidity, this medium bodied Savagnin is full of lime leaf, herbaceous tarragon, white flower and wet stone that lingers for a persistent finish. Thirst quenching and fresh with layered complexity.
Van Duzer Corridor Murmuration Red Blend 2022 ● 510 cases; 30 $ - ▥ - A creative blend of Blaufränkisch, Cabernet Franc, Mondeuse, St. Laurent and Zweigelt. Nervy and delicious with notes of candied red fruit, roasted red pepper and fresh cracked black pepper.

acres 87 - cases 6,000
Fertilizers compost, biodynamic compost, cover crops, manure
Plant protection sulfur, biodynamic preparations, organic
Weed control animal grazing, mechanical, manual
Yeasts spontaneous fermentation
Grapes 100% owned
Certification biodynamic, regenerative

EUGENE

KING ESTATE WINERY

80544 Territorial Highway - tel. (541) 942-9874
www.kingestate.com - info@kingestate.com

PEOPLE - The largest organic and biodynamic grower in Oregon, it is aptly named. Founded by the late Ed King, Jr. and his son Ed King III in 1991, the property was a cattle ranch before they turned it into a powerhouse Pinot Gris and Pinot Noir producer with a large winery and a tasting room with panoramic views. Ed King III leads the team today with winemaker and co-COO Brent Stone. In 2023, in a carbon saving measure, they switched to bottles made in North America.

VINEYARDS - Director of viticulture Ray Nuclo and vineyard manager Meliton Martinez oversee the vines. In 2022, the winery added 70 planted acres at the Pfeiffer vineyard, a site it first bought grapes from in 1992. The purchase added 28 acres of Pinot Gris and 42 acres of Pinot Noir that were originally planted in the early 1980's. The new acres could be certified organic and biodynamic in time for the 2025 harvest. (Some wines, not featured here, may be grown with herbicide.)

WINES - The winery's known for well made Pinot Gris and Pinot Noir, but it also grows and makes lesser known Alsatian varieties and a sparkling wine.

● Willamette Valley Steiner Block Pinot Gris 2022 SLOW WINE O 150 cases; 28 $ - ⌆ - A top Pinot Gris from this Pinot Gris powerhouse. Whole cluster pressed and aged in concrete egg with weekly lees stirring. Own rooted grapes from 1992. Texture and minerality enhance its many delicate and nuanced charms. Ribbons of subtly shifting flavors on the palate.
Willamette Valley Domaine Pinot Gris 2022 O 2,400 cases; 30 $ - ⌆ - Aged eight months on lees to add texture and complexity. Varietal aromas of pear, apple and tropical and citrus fruits followed by green apple, pear and peach on the palate. Expressive.
Willamette Valley Domaine Pinot Noir 2021 ● 400 cases; 70 $ - ⌆ - Aged 18 months in French oak (30% new). Pommard and 115 clones. Partial whole cluster. Aromas of currant and plum with pronounced bramble berry on the palate.

acres 535 - cases 150,000
Fertilizers compost, biodynamic compost, cover crops, organic fertilizer
Plant protection sulfur, biodynamic preparations
Weed control mechanical
Yeasts spontaneous fermentation, commercial cultured yeasts
Grapes purchase 40%
Certification biodynamic, organic

NEWBERG

LACHINI VINEYARDS

18225 NE Calkins Lane - tel. (503) 864-4553
www.lachinivineyards.com - info@lachinivineyards.com

PEOPLE - Owners Ron and Marianne Lachini have owned the winery since 1998. making their first vintage in 2001. Florent Merlier is the winemaker. Ernesto Mendoza manages the vines. Their focus on their high end wines is structure, balance and long-term age worthiness.

VINEYARDS - On their estate, they grow 30 acres of Pinot Noir, three acres of Chardonnay and 10 rows of Muscat Canelli. Most of the vineyard is planted on grafted rootstock though ten acres are own rooted. On their own estate, they say they use only organic approved materials. They also buy fruit from local growers. (Some of the wines, not featured here, may be grown with herbicide.)

WINES - Powerful and complex Pinot Noir wines with expert use of oak create complexity and aging potential.

● Chehalem Mountains Cuvée Giselle Pinot Noir 2022 ● 138 cases; 95 $ - ⌆ - Aged 18 months in French oak (66% new). Aromas of black raspberry, black cherry, nutmeg, crushed granite and crab apple blossoms. The palate delivers layered structure with intense black cherry, coffee, mineral and plum skin.
Chehalem Mountains Family Estate Pinot Noir 2022 ● 510 cases; 75 $ - ⌆ - Aged 18 months in French oak (30% new). Aromas of white cherry, rose, raspberry and chocolate mint. The palate hits with intense minerality, black cherry, tool leather and red plum.
Willamette Valley Al di la Chardonnay 2022 O 148 cases; 50 $ - ⌆ - Aged in concrete egg for 9 months on lees and then aged in French oak puncheons and concrete eggs for 5 months. Aromas of subtle unripe pear and lemon with roundness on the palate and peach, yellow apple, wet basalt rock and brioche.

acres 33 - cases 9,000
Fertilizers compost, biodynamic compost, cover crops, manure, organic fertilizer
Plant protection sulfur, biodynamic preparations, synthetic pesticides, organic
Weed control animal grazing, mechanical, manual
Yeasts spontaneous fermentation, commercial cultured yeasts
Grapes 100% owned
Certification none

DUNDEE

LAFAYETTE AND WHITE CELLARS

240 SE Fifth St - tel. (503) 730-1757
www.lwcellars.com - lwcellars@gmail.com

PEOPLE - This young brand is a partnership between newly minted vintner and winemaker Danielle Lafayette and Andrew White. Both worked harvest at Antica Terra and were mentored by the renowned Maggie Harrison, famous for her originality in blending. Lafayette's passion for wine stems from her former work in Portland restaurants as a wine expert. White works at Walnut City Wineworks in both vineyard and cellar.

VINEYARDS - They buy grapes from growers across Oregon and from the lower Columbia Valley in Washington. In the Willamette Valley, these include Rocky Hill in Yamhill-Carlton, Sometimes a Grape Notion in Eola-Amity Hills and Confluence in the Willamette Valley. Crater View in the warm Rogue Valley in southern Oregon is another source. Some are LIVE certified. (Some wines, not featured here, may be grown with herbicide.)

WINES - Specializes in unusual blends and novel approaches—making skin contact wines, coferments and pet nat sparkling wine.

Yamhill-Carlton Eocene Rosé 2023 SLOW WINE · 25 cases; 25 $ - An atypical blend—Pinot Noir (80%), Pinot Gris (15%) and Cabernet Sauvignon (5%). The palate has suggestions of mint, watermelon, and watermelon rind. Great balance and texture.

Willamette Valley Echo Orange Wine 2022 · 50 cases; 30 $ - Novel and intriguing coferment of Pinot Gris (75%) and Gewürztraminer (25%) spent five days on skins. Savory aroma flirts with funk but never goes there. Bright orange aroma emerges. On the palate an impression of wood and juicy fruit.

Rogue Valley Eocene Grenache 2022 · 35 cases; 38 $ - Wild aroma of graphite over candied fruit with hint of earthy funk. Youthful palate offers savory elements, shy fruit, fine tannins and excellent acidity.

acres 0 - cases 500
Fertilizers compost, cover crops, manure
Plant protection sulfur, synthetic pesticides, organic
Weed control mechanical
Yeasts spontaneous fermentation
Grapes purchase 100%
Certification none

CARLTON

LEMELSON VINEYARDS

12020 NE Stag Hollow Road - tel. (503) 852-6619
www.lemelsonvineyards.com - info@www.lemelsonvineyards.com

 Ecofriendly from the start, Eric Lemelson and the entire team produce exceptional wines that express Slow Wine values.

PEOPLE - An environmentalist, climate change innovator and energy policy activist, Eric Lemelson, an organic advocate, first planted his vines in 1995, releasing its first vintage in 2001. Veteran winemaker Matt Wengel, who has been with the winery for 10 years, oversees winemaking. In August of 2024, Jillian Bradshaw joined the team as general manager.

VINEYARDS - Vineyard manager Rob Schultz oversees the vineyard. The six estate vineyards (certified organic since 2004) are located three AVAs—Stermer Vineyard, Johnson Vineyard and Rocky Noel Vineyard in the Yamhill-Carlton AVA, Meyer Vineyard in the Dundee Hills AVA and Chestnut Hill Vineyard in Chehalem Mountains. In a nod to inclusivity, the year round Mexican American vineyard stewards are profiled on the winery's website. In addition to Chardonnay and Pinot Noir, they grow Pinot Gris and Riesling.

WINES - Wines are crisp and focused on purity of fruit expression with low residual sugar. Made to age gracefully, they have great structure, focus and complexity.

Willamette Valley Thea's Selection Pinot Noir 2022 SLOW WINE · 9,554 cases; 40 $ - Fresh cherries and allspice rise from the glass. On the palate, Bing cherry, black tea, anise, pomegranate, dried herbs, sandalwood and exotic spices. Silken in texture, pure and polished with great balance.

Willamette Valley Tikka's Run Pinot Gris 2023 O 308 cases; 28 $ - A fragrant citrus and white floral bouquet aroma. A colorful pop of summer melon, tropical passion fruit and pears join sweet Meyer lemon accents. Fresh and mouthfilling.

Dundee Hills Dry Riesling 2023 O 312 cases; 32 $ - Classic wet stone aromas lead the way, followed by tropical star fruit, white peach, quince paste and crisp apple. Vibrant and mouthwatering with racy acidity. Electrifying through the persistent lime zest scented finish.

acres 125 - cases 20,000
Fertilizers compost, cover crops, organic fertilizer
Plant protection sulfur, organic
Weed control mechanical, manual
Yeasts spontaneous fermentation, selected indigenous yeasts
Grapes purchase 10%
Certification organic

SALEM

LINGUA FRANCA

9675 Hopewell Road NW - tel. (503) 687-3005
www.linguafranca.wine - hospitality@linguafranca.wine

PEOPLE - in 2022, Constellation Brands bought the acclaimed winery that Larry Stone, a Master Sommelier, founded in 2012. Setbacks due to twin challenges of Covid and wildfire catalyzed the sale, but Stone and co-owner Dominique Lafon, a celebrated Burgundy consultant, a founding investor with Stone, continue as advisors. Lafon's protege, French born Thomas Savre makes the wines. He formerly worked at Evening Lands and was once a cellar and harvest intern at DRC.

VINEYARDS - Brandon Hasart is the vineyard manager. Next to Evening Lands' Seven Springs, the estate vines (certified organic in 2022) are perched on a hillside. The soils are a combination of Witzel series on the steep slopes and Gelderman, Jory and Nekia series. Under the acquisition, they announced plans to vastly expand their Avni brand, which comes from purchased grapes, increasing production from 12,000 cases to 60,000. (Some Avni wines, not featured here, may be grown with herbicide).

WINES - As Stone has long said, Willamette Valley is "in its own way capable of making wines of the same finesse, structure and longevity that you find in great white Burgundy and red Burgundy."

TOP ● Eola-Amity Hills Estate Pinot Noir 2022 SLOW WINE ● 1,100 cases; 60 $ - ⊞ - Aged in French oak (21% new). Complex, finessed and ageworthy. Highly aromatic. On the palate, forest floor, pomegranate and Sweetheart cherry flavors with exotic spice, salinity, cola and minerality. One for the cellar.

Eola-Amity Hills Estate Chardonnay 2022 ○ 1,000 cases; 60 $ - ⊞ - Aged in French oak (27% new). Tantalizing citrus blossom and gardenia aroma followed by layers of white peach, Granny Smith apple, oyster shell salinity and Meyer lemon. Mouth filling and complex.

acres 75 - cases 60,000
Fertilizers compost, cover crops, manure, organic fertilizer
Plant protection sulfur, synthetic pesticides, organic
Weed control mechanical
Yeasts spontaneous fermentation
Grapes purchase 90%
Certification some of the vineyards are certified organic

NEWBERG

LONGPLAY WINE $

888 S Industrial Parkway - tel. (503) 489-8466
www.longplaywine.com - todd@longplaywine.com

PEOPLE - Winemaker Todd Hansen bought Lia's Vineyard in the Chehalem Mountains AVA in 2005, in anticipation of the birth of his daughter, Lia, in early 2006. He sold fruit to noted wineries, and then started working with Aron Hess, the former Rex Hill winemaker. He also worked with Jay Somers at J. Christopher, Todd Hamina at Biggio-Hamina and John Grochau at Grochau Cellars until he built his own winery in 2021.

VINEYARDS - In 2023, Hansen sold the dry farmed Lia's vineyard to Cooper Mountain (which will convert it to organic and biodynamic certification), but retained the right to purchase fruit from select blocks. First planted in 1990-1992 to own rooted Pommard and Wädenswil vines, a variety of grafted clones were planted in 1999, 2009, 2014 and 2015. Elevation is 280-560 feet with mostly southeast exposure. At the top, the soil is Jory transitioning to sedimentary soils.

WINES - Hansen highlights the distinctiveness of vintages and various blocks and barrels. Many are approachable young.

TOP ● Chehalem Mountains Hi-Tone Pinot Noir 2021 SLOW WINE ● 165 cases; 52 $ - ⊞ - Lovely complex aromas of spice and red fruit with intense floral note emerging with air. Palate lives up to the name "Hi Tone" but is also elegant elusive and nicely balanced with a medium finish.

Chehalem Mountains Experience Pinot Noir 2021 ● 111 cases; 52 $ - ⊞ - Aged in oak (20% new). All whole cluster. The nose is initially herbal with dark fruit, mint and spice emerging. The well balanced palate is well structured with more obvious tannins and acidity.

Chehalem Mountains Jory Slope Chardonnay 2021 ○ 31 cases; 35 $ - ⊞ - Mostly from the Wente clone. Concentrated aromas of juicy fruit gum and lemon cream. The palate is intensely saline and mouthwatering with balanced acidity and a very long finish.

acres 0 - cases 1,200
Fertilizers cover crops, organic fertilizer
Plant protection sulfur, biodynamic preparations
Weed control mechanical, manual
Yeasts spontaneous fermentation, commercial cultured yeasts
Grapes purchase 100%
Certification converting to organic, converting to biodynamic

PHILOMATH

LUMOS WINE CO.

24000 Cardwell Hill Drive - tel. (541) 929-3519
www.lumoswine.com - lumos@lumoswine.com

 An Oregon treasure, Dai Crisp, his wife PJK McCoy and their son make beautiful, affordable wines in paradise.

PEOPLE - Oregon wine growing icon Dai Crisp made waves in 2012 when he certified the acclaimed 100 acre Temperance Hill vineyard organic, a pioneering move. Farming is organic on his own estates further south, where he and his wife PK McCoy make their own wines. Founded in 2000, their sought after wines sell at consumer friendly prices. Their tasting room is surrounded by biodiversity, on a site overlooking a National Fender's Blue Butterfly and Kincaid Lupine Reserve.

VINEYARDS - Four vineyards provide a wide range of clones and microclimates. Their Wren Vineyard on the home ranch, originally planted in 1985 by Dai and his folks, grows 15 acres of Dijon clone Chardonnay, Pommard clone Pinot Noir and Pinot Gris. More Pinot Gris also comes from Logsdon Ridge Vineyard (near Corvalis). He also has his pick of choice blocks at Temperance Hill. New this year: Pinot Gris grown at Keeler.

WINES - Long time winemaker Julia Cattrall uses classic, Old World practices that showcase terroir and fruit purity.

Eola-Amity Hills Temperance Hill Vineyard Aligoté 2023 ○ 192 cases; 40 $ - 🍷 - Aged four months in French oak (neutral). Barrel fermented. White peach, elderflower and lemon notes.

Eola-Amity Hills Temperance Hill Vineyard Pinot Noir 2021 ● 336 cases; 52 $ - ⊞ - Aromas of cinnamon, marionberry and forest air on the nose. On the palate, cranberry, cherry, and amaro.

Eola-Amity Hills Pinot Noir Temperance Hill North Block Pinot Noir 2019 ● 75 cases; 62 $ - ⊞ - Aged in French oak. North is one of Temperance Hill's high elevation parcels (at 850 feet). Aromas of strawberry with plum and strawberry on the palate. Cellarworthy.

---

acres 26 - cases 3,000
Fertilizers compost, cover crops
Plant protection sulfur, copper, organic
Weed control mechanical
Yeasts spontaneous fermentation, selected indigenous yeasts, commercial cultured yeasts
Grapes 100% owned
Certification organic, some of the vineyards are certified biodynamic

FOREST GROVE

MALOOF

6200 NW Gales Creek Road - tel. (503) 217-4122
www.maloofwines.com - wine@maloofwines.com

PEOPLE - Maloof is a collaborative effort between Bee Maloof, Ross Maloof, and Perry Heistruman that began in 2015. Starting out as negociants, they now manage one of the oldest vineyards in the northern Willamette Valley, originally planted in 1972. They have injected life back into the estate, opening a seasonal restaurant on the vineyard. No Clos Radio Café is open on weekends from May to September, with a special Saturday night menu.

VINEYARDS - In 2020, they purchased their Tualatin Hills estate, originally planted in the 1970's, and now anticipate organic certification to be completed soon. They grow primarily white varietals that are own rooted and dry farmed in the Jory and Loess soils. In 2024, they planted a new five acre block of Gewürztraminer, propagated from their oldest vines. They also buy grapes from Johan (certified biodynamic), Nemarniki and Temperance Hill (certified organic).

WINES - Focuses on minimal intervention expressions of single vineyard, white varietals, playing with skin contact and sur lie aging.

Tualatin Hills No Clos Radio Pinot Gris 2022 ○ 200 cases; 28 $ - ⊞ - Fermented and aged 10 months on the lees. Bracing acidity with rich, custard like texture and notes of bruised apple, peach, zesty citrus and lemon curd.

Tualatin Hills No Clos Radio Gewürztraminer 2022 ◎ 50 cases; 29 $ - ⊞ - From own rooted vines planted in 1972. Macerated for 19 days. Old vines. Aromatic nose of bruised orchard fruit and basil. Grilled peaches, peach skin, lychee and basil.

Tualatin Hills No Clos Radio Riesling 2022 ○ 50 cases; 27 $ - 🍷 - From vines planted in 1972. Fermented and aged sur lie for eight months. A rich characteristic, like caramel dipped green apple lifted by aromatic white flowers. Good acidity.

---

acres 27 - cases 4,500
Fertilizers biodynamic compost, cover crops, manure, organic
Plant protection sulfur, biodynamic preparations, organic
Weed control mechanical, manual
Yeasts spontaneous fermentation
Grapes purchase 60%
Certification some of the vineyards are certified organic, some of the vineyards are certified biodynamic, converting to organic

MCMINNVILLE

MAYSARA WINERY

15765 SW Muddy Valley Road - tel. (503) 843-1234
www.maysara.com - tastingroom@maysara.com

 Maysara offers an impressive range of excellent age-worthy wines from its certified biodynamic vineyard and winery at remarkably reasonable prices.

PEOPLE - Certified biodynamic in both the vines and the winery, Maysara was founded by Iranian born Moe and Flora Momtazi when they planted their first vines in 1998. They now sell grapes to top tier vintners and make wine under their own brand. The eldest daughter, Tahmiene, has been the winemaker since 2007, while her sisters, Naseem and Hannah, manage sales. Uniquely, harvest interns get to produce a Pinot Noir, bottled as Zaal, named after an Iranian king.

VINEYARDS - The vines sit on a mixture of sedimentary and volcanic soils with an underlying layer of basalt. The vineyard grows Pinot Noir for itself and other wineries, who typically make it as a single vineyard designate. Maysara keeps its Chardonnay, Gamay Noir, Pinot Blanc, Pinot Gris, and Riesling for its own releases. They aim for a crop averaging two tons per acre, keeping quality high.

WINES - The wines are made under the "Biodynamic Wine" certification, a pure standard that transparently and faithfully transmits the vintage.

TOP ● **McMinnville Asha Pinot Noir 2013** SLOW WINE ● 450 cases; 58 $ - 🍷 - From the original vines planted in 1998. Bouquet is an interplay of dried prune plum and earth. A well balanced palate evolves quickly with a medium finish and fine acidity. A quiet thought provoking wine. Brightly contemplative.

McMinnville Arsheen Pinot Gris 2023 ○ 1,815 cases; 18 $ - 🍷 - A bit of reduction on the nose followed by floral notes. Citrus and nuts on the palate which share more savory than fruity. The finish is nicely textured with good acidity.

McMinnville Jamsheed Pinot Noir 2011 ● 3,494 cases; 32 $ - 🍷 - Deep earthy bouquet with subdued dried fruit. Delicate palate tapers off with a medium acidity which will ensure more years ahead. A bargain for a well aged example of a cool vintage, cool climate Pinot.

acres 260 - cases 8,000
Fertilizers compost, cover crops, manure
Plant protection sulfur, biodynamic preparations, organic
Weed control mechanical
Yeasts spontaneous fermentation, selected indigenous yeasts
Grapes 100% owned
Certification biodynamic

NEWBERG

NICOLAS-JAY

11905 NE Dudley Road - tel. (971) 412-1124
www.nicolas-jay.com - info@nicolas-jay.com

PEOPLE - Mentored by the iconic Burgundy winemaker Henri Jayer, winemaker Jean-Nicolas Méo (of Domaine Méo-Camuzet in Vosne-Romanée) founded the winery with Jay Boberg, a successful music entrepreneur, in 2012. The two had been friends for decades. Noah Roberts was appointed assistant winemaker in 2020. The gravity fed winery and tasting room—fashioned out of an old cow barn—opened in the Dundee Hills in 2021. The winery was a Wine & Spirits Top 100 winery in 2022.

VINEYARDS - The winery has two estate vineyards—Bishop Creek on sedimentary soils in Yamhill-Carlton (planted in 1987) and one on deep volcanic soils in the Dundee Hills (planted in 2021 and 2024). It also purchases fruit from leading sites including Hyland, Momtazi (certified biodynamic), Nysa, Pearlstead, Spirit Hill Vineyards, Temperance Hill (certified organic), Von Ohsen and Witness Tree. The estate vines are dry farmed and no till.

WINES - 100% destemmed with extended cold maceration. Picking early results in complex, savory, structured wines with high acidity, enhanced freshness and increased ageability.

TOP ● **Dundee Hills Nysa Vineyard Pinot Noir 2022** ● 166 cases; 95 $ - 🍷 - The nose exhibits creamy fruity floral notes, that are perfumed, with a hint of citrus emerging. The palate is savory with warm leather, silky texture, great balance and structure.

Eola-Amity Hills Temperance Hill Pinot Noir 2022 ● 97 cases; 100 $ - 🍷 - Initially, the nose leads with wood. Then some spice and dark fruit emerge with a hint of citrus. The palate shows leather, excellent acidity and well managed tannins.

Eola-Amity Hills Spirit Hill Chardonnay 2022 ○ 91 cases; 85 $ - 🍷 - Aged in oak (25% new). Lovely aromas of nuts, flowers and citrus with the impression of chalk. The palate is elegant and seductive with a medium finish.

acres 20 - cases 4,600
Fertilizers compost, biodynamic compost, cover crops, manure, organic fertilizer
Plant protection sulfur, biodynamic preparations, organic
Weed control mechanical
Yeasts spontaneous fermentation
Grapes purchase 66%
Certification some of the vineyards are certified organic, some of the vineyards are certified biodynamic

DALLAS

OPEN CLAIM VINEYARDS

2795 Ballard Road - tel. (949) 338-3343
www.openclaimvineyards.com - info@openclaimvineyards.com

 A tiny, all estate producer, with organic vines and exquisite wines.

PEOPLE - In 2012, proprietors Marnie and Brett Wall started planting grapes on a former Christmas tree farm Marnie's mother owned. Today, their tiny winery has taken off. Mark Bosko is the general manager. Tony Rynders makes the wines. They launched a new tasting house in Dallas with five course food and wine pairing followed by a second tasting room in Dundee to expand the private food and wine pairing experiences.

VINEYARDS - Vineyard manager Alex Cabrera, a graduate of Oregon State University's viticulture and enology program, oversees the vines. The 55 acre property is encircled by ancient oaks. Here marine sedimentary soils contain a significant number of volcanic rocks from ancient seabeds, unique in the Willamette Valley. Organic certified in 2022, they envision becoming Regenerative Organic certified as well.

WINES - Highly textured wines with great balance and sense of place through meticulous vineyard management, picking at optimal ripeness and extended elevage.

Mount Pisgah Estate Pinot Noir 2022 SLOW WINE ● 300 cases; 75 $ - 🍷 - An alluring spicy, earthy aroma. Multilayered and well defined as raspberries, olallieberries, plum sauce, truffles, subtle French oak spice and olive tapenade excite the palate. Smooth and complex with supple tannins and a hint of anise on the long, memorable finish. Ageworthy.

Mount Pisgah Estate Chardonnay 2022 O 297 cases; 75 $ - 🍷 - Aged in French oak (25% new). Tree fruits and citrus scents on the nose lead to a compelling palate of white peaches, creamy pears, bright acidity, lemon gelato, a whisper of herbs with nuances sitting pretty in the background. Smooth and graceful through the lip-smacking finish.

---

acres 21 - cases 800
Fertilizers compost, biodynamic compost, cover crops, organic fertilizer
Plant protection sulfur, biodynamic preparations, organic
Weed control mechanical
Yeasts spontaneous fermentation
Grapes 100% owned
Certification organic

CARLTON

RATIO:WINES

801 N Scott Street - tel. (503) 852-6100
www.ratiowines.com - anthony@rationwines.com

PEOPLE - Anthony King's spent years in the wine industry as winemaker at Acacia in Napa and in the same role at Lemelson in Oregon. Today he consults to wineries and is general manager at The Carlton Winemakers Studio, a cooperative winery and tasting room. At his own personal label, Ratio:Wines, a microwinery, he's a one man operation, with the freedom to make small lot, handcrafted wines as he chooses.

VINEYARDS - He buys Pinot Noir from the celebrated Temperance Hill Vineyard (certified organic) in the Eola-Amity Hills and Meredith Mitchell (certified biodynamic) in McMinnville. Both sit on volcanic soil. Pinot and Chardonnay come from three other Willamette Valley sites. Further south, Anya Vineyard in the warm Rogue Valley grows Albariño. Some wines (not featured here) are grown with synthetic herbicides.

WINES - Thoughtful and thought provoking, the wines are complex and attract attention through restraint rather than power. The aims are vibrant acidity and ageability.

Willamette Valley Retina Pinot Noir 2022 SLOW WINE ● 60 cases; 45 $ - 🍷 - Aged 16 months in neutral oak. Fermented whole cluster (100%). From Temperance Hill and Meredith Mitchell Vineyards. The nose is complex with aromas of cinnamon, lavender, red fruit and herbs. The youthful palate is delicate and understated with great acidity supported by smooth tannins. The medium finish is creamy.

---

acres 0 - cases 200
Fertilizers biodynamic compost, organic fertilizer
Plant protection biodynamic preparations, synthetic pesticides, organic
Weed control mechanical
Yeasts spontaneous fermentation
Grapes purchase 100%
Certification some of the vineyards are certified organic, some of the vineyards are certified biodynamic

DAYTON

REMY WINES

17495 NE McDougall Road - tel. (503) 864-8777
www.remywines.com - info@remywines.com

PEOPLE - Founded in 2006 by McMinnville native and winemaker Remy Drabkin, the winery produces Italian varieties, sparkling and Pinot Noir under the Remy Wines label, and other varietals under her Three Wives label. Remy is the mayor of McMinnville, the co-founder of nonprofit Wine Country Pride, and founder of the world's first Queer Wine festival. In 2022, her new winery facility was created with a carbon-neutral concrete formula bearing her name: the Drabkin-Mead Formulation.

VINEYARDS - The Three Wives estate vineyard, planted in 2009 to Pinot Noir and Lagrein, is being weaned from synthetic herbicides and is LIVE and bee friendly certified. Additional land is used for biodiversity. Remy sources grapes from Jubilee Vineyard and Zenith Vineyard, both in the Eola-Amity Hills AVA. The former consists of Jory and WillaKenzie soils and the latter sedimentary soils. Some wines (not featured here) are grown with herbicide.

WINES - Old World style wines made with minimal intervention and thoughtful use of new oak.

TOP Willamette Valley Unmet Desire Pinot Noir 2022
SLOW WINE ● 166 cases; 45 $ - 🍽 - Estate grown. Intensely floral with red fruit and herbal notes on the nose. Delicate yet confident entry with fine grained tannins and short finish. Lovely now with a long life ahead.

Dundee Hills Jules Pinot Noir 2019 ● 475 cases; 75 $ - 🍽 - Savory aroma with spice and floral notes emerging. Immature palate is more savory with medium tannins.

Eola-Amity Hills Jubilee Vineyard Dolcetto 2022 ● 240 cases; 35 $ - 🍽 - Tight spicy oak and dark fruit nose. Mouthwatering acidity with savory notes on the muted palate. Medium finish.

---

acres 8 - cases 2,500
Fertilizers compost, cover crops, organic fertilizer, synthetic fertilizer
Plant protection sulfur, synthetic pesticides
Weed control manual
Yeasts commercial cultured yeasts
Grapes purchase 60%
Certification none

CARLTON

RÉSONANCE

12050 NW Meadow Lake Road - tel. (971) 999-1603
www.resonancewines.com - info@resonancewines.com

 An iconic Oregon winery with a lengthy history of eco-friendly practices and renowned wines, now run by top tier Burgundian talent.

PEOPLE - Burgundy based Maison Louis Jadot bought the Oregon winery in 2013, sending its veteran winemaker Jacques Lardiere (winemaker for the company for 42 years) to make the wines initially. Now emeritus winemaker, he proclaims he "felt the energy" of this special site. Thibault Gagey is the director. The Wine Spectator declared 2021 Résonance Pinot Noir the 9th best of the top 100 wines of the world. The winery opened a second tasting room in 2023 in the Dundee Hills in addition to its Carlton tasting room.

VINEYARDS - All encompassing knowledge of each vineyard's terroir is key. They have four estate vineyards including two in the Dundee Hills and one each in the Eola-Amity Hills and Yamhill-Carlton. Dry farmed, the estate vineyards (certified organic) sit at elevations of 262-1,100 feet. These include Découverte, Jolis Monts, Koosah and Résonance.

WINES - French born Guillaume Large makes the wines. Each vineyard is vinified in separate tanks (brought over from France). They are committed to minimal intervention in the winery.

TOP Yamhill-Carlton Résonance Vineyard Pinot Noir 2021 SLOW WINE ● 1,700 cases; 75 $ - 🍽 - Expressive red cherry and earth aromas. Sweetheart cherries, raspberries, a pinch of herbs, minerality, earthiness and wild mushrooms join lively acidity on the palate. Complex with impressive finesse.

Yamhill-Carlton/Dundee Hills Découverte Vnyd Pinot Noir 2021 ● 540 cases; 50 $ - 🍽 - Compelling earth scented aromas. The palate showcases fresh Bing cherries, exotic spice, licorice, slight tobacco and savory raspberry coulis. Energy and purity shine through the long finish.

Dundee Hills Découverte Vineyard Chardonnay 2021 ○ 560 cases; 70 $ - 🍽 - Beautiful citrus blossom aromas. Honeycrisp apples and earthy notes join vanilla pastry cream with lemon herbs accents melding in harmony.

---

acres 140 - cases 20,000
Fertilizers cover crops, organic fertilizer
Plant protection organic
Weed control mechanical, manual
Yeasts spontaneous fermentation
Grapes 100% owned
Certification organic

NEWBERG

RIDGECREST $

20440 NE Ribbon Ridge Road - tel. (503) 789-4350
www.ridgecrestwines.com - jonf@rrwines.com

PEOPLE - Formerly known as Ribbon Ridge Winery, Ridgecrest started in 2002 as a side project of Harry Peterson-Nedry, who had founded Chehalem Winery in 1990 and sold it in 2018. His daughter, Wynne Peterson-Nedry, who eventually succeeded Harry as winemaker at Chehalem, joined the project in 2009 and is now winemaker and owner, making the wines at The Carlton Winemaker's Studio. For a small producer she is unusual for the number of white and red varieties she makes.

VINEYARDS - Harry Peterson-Nedry established Ridgecrest Vineyards in 1980 and planted the first vines 18 months later—the first on Ribbon Ridge. Today Chardonnay, Chenin Blanc, Gamay Noir, Grüner Veltliner, Pinot Gris, Pinot Noir and Riesling grow there. They have LIVE certified vineyards are on Willakenzie, an ocean sedimentary soil, which are dry farmed. The elevation ranges from 480-690 feet.

WINES - She makes bright, acid driven whites and well balanced Pinot Noirs with judicious use of new oak and whole cluster fermentation.

Ribbon Ridge RR Estate Reserve Riesling 2016 SLOW WINE ○ 102 cases; 30 $ - 🍷 - A poster child for how well Riesling ages. Intense petrol wrapped in tropical fruit in the nose. Rich entry lightens and finishes long with refreshing acidity. Midpalate shows fine tannins. Elegant.
Ribbon Ridge Ridgecrest Grüner Veltliner 2023 ○ 375 cases; 30 $ - 🍷 - Aromas of white flowers and pear with a citrus base. Palate builds to an acid driven crescendo with hints of juicy fruit and a medium finish.
Ribbon Ridge Ridgecrest Estate Pinot Noir 2021 ● 420 cases; 48 $ - - Fermented with partial whole clusters (21%). Aromas of dark cherry, cinnamon and cream. The well balanced palate is youthful with fruit and fine tannins. Medium finish with ample acidity.

acres 41 - cases 3,000
Fertilizers cover crops, organic fertilizer
Plant protection sulfur, copper, organic
Weed control mechanical
Yeasts spontaneous fermentation, commercial cultured yeasts
Grapes 100% owned
Certification none

YAMHILL

ROOTS WINE CO.

19320 NE Woodland Loop Road - tel. (503) 662-4652
www.rootswine.com - info@roots.wine

PEOPLE - In 2001, Chris and Hilary Berg started Roots, after following Chris' parents' move from Illinois to Oregon in 1999. Winegrower Chris makes no less than 11 Pinot Noirs, in addition to Pinot Gris and Chardonnay, as well as varieties less commonly found in the Willamette Valley, including Sauvignon Blanc and Trousseau. Chris plans to plant Mondeuse (a variety grown in the Savoy region of France) in the fall of 2024.

VINEYARDS - The original seven acre estate (said to use only organic approved materials) grows Pinot Noir and Pinot Gris. It tops out at 625 feet on WillaKenzie soil and has a broad vein of iron oxide. The Estate East has Pinot Noir (from Coury cuttings), Sauvignon Blanc and Trousseau. Purchased grapes come from two Chehalem Mountains sites, three Yamhill-Carlton sites and a Willamette Valley site. (Some wines, not featured here, may be grown with herbicide.)

WINES - Crisp, sometimes weightless bottlings of whites and complex, aromatic reds plus uncommon blends and treatments.

Yamhill-Carlton Roots Estate Racine Pinot Noir 2021 ● 25 cases; 95 $ - - A best barrel selection with a pretty, dark fruit nose that carries over to the well balanced palate. Medium long finish. Yummy now with a great future.
Yamhill-Carlton Roots Estate Pinot Noir 2022 ● 100 cases; 50 $ - - Dark fruit, oak and spice aromas. Young palate after the nose. With air, more dark fruit emerges.
Eola-Amity Hills Sauvignon Blanc 2023 ○ 48 cases; 30 $ - - Aged on the lees for six months. A mouthwatering wine with juicy fruit encased in white flowers on the nose. Youngish on palate with great balance.

acres 11 - cases 6,500
Fertilizers compost, cover crops, organic fertilizer
Plant protection sulfur, synthetic pesticides, organic
Weed control mechanical, n/a
Yeasts spontaneous fermentation
Grapes purchase 35%
Certification none

SALEM

ROSEROCK DROUHIN OREGON

4350 Gibson Road NW - tel. (503) 864-2700
www.roserockoregon.com - info@domainedrouhin.com

PEOPLE - Perched at the southern tip of the Eola-Amity Hills AVA, this is the famed Drouhin family's second Oregon winery. Planted began in 2004. The Burgundy based family purchased it in 2013 and it is already producing some of the top wines in Oregon. Just at their original Domaine Drouhin in the Dundee Hills (founded in 1987), viticulturist Philippe Drouhin, a sustainable agriculture advocate, oversees the vineyards, and Véronique Boss-Drouhin is in charge of winemaking.

VINEYARDS - Situated at the southern edge of the appellation on a south facing ridge, the estate vineyard sits on volcanic soils and benefits directly from the maritime influences via the Van Duzer corridor. The Drouhin Family's commitment to biodiversity, the absence of herbicides, and the property's LIVE certification underscores their dedication to sustainable agriculture.

WINES - Roserock's cool climate wines showcase depth, purity and lovely expression of the Eola-Amity Hills terroir.

TOP Eola-Amity Hills Zéphirine Pinot Noir 2022 SLOW WINE
● 2,518 cases; 75 $ - 🍷 - This gem has a gleaming personality starting with its expressive earthy, raspberry aroma. Exhilarating on the palate with juicy layers of marionberries, pomegranate seeds, savory strawberry sauce, earth tones, anise and well managed oak. Racy acidity creates brilliant balance, and fresh squeezed orange peeks through on the everlasting finish. Cellarworthy.

Eola-Amity Hills Chardonnay 2023 ○ 2,308 cases; 42 $ - 🍷 - The fragrance of citrus splashed tree fruits and shades of earthiness greets the nose. Crisp pears, Meyer lemon ice, kumquats, honeysuckle and chopped herbs join nicely integrated oak creating a vibrant blast of flavors dancing on the palate. Brisk acidity keeps the wine well-balanced, and there is good tension all the way through the enlivening finish.

acres 122 - cases 14,600
Fertilizers compost, cover crops, manure
Plant protection sulfur, organic
Weed control animal grazing, mechanical
Yeasts spontaneous fermentation, commercial cultured yeasts
Grapes 100% owned
Certification none

HILLSBORO

RUBY VINEYARD & WINERY

30088 SW Egger Road - tel. (503) 628-7829
www.rubyvineyard.com - info@rubyvineyard.com

PEOPLE - In 2012, co-owners Steve Hendricks and his wife Flora Habibi bought Chehalem Mountain's Beran Vineyards, in what is now the Laurelwood District subappellation. They had followed ancestral footsteps—Steve's great-great grandfather arrived in the Willamette Valley in 1843. Winemaker Andrew Kirkland made his first vintage here in 2015, and he remains Ruby's winemaker today.

VINEYARDS - Back in 1973, John and Beth Hiestand planted the first block of Wadenswil which go into Flora's Reserve. Today they grow Pinot Noir (8.1 acres) and Chardonnay (0.9 acres) in Laurelwood soil composed of millions of years old basalt topped with windblown loess. Their vineyards are LIVE certified, no till, dry farmed and herbicide free since 2017. They also buy grapes from local growers. (Some wines, not featured here, may be grown with herbicide.)

WINES - The Flora's Reserve showcases the oldest vines. Their first estate grown Chardonnay—the 2023 vintage—will be released in 2025.

TOP Laurelwood District Flora's Reserve Pinot Noir 2022 SLOW WINE ● 55 cases; 125 $ - 🍷 - Fragrant florals at first whiff, this divine Pinot Noir is mouthwatering. Black cherries, earthiness, anise, black raspberries, savory elements and cherry cola notes are supported by brisk acidity and supple tannins. Aging in once used French barrels contributes oak nuances, and the finish adds a kick of spice. Elegance and purity all the way through.

Laurelwood District Old Vine Estate Pinot Noir 2022 ●
550 cases; 65 $ - 🍷 - Aged in French oak (40% new). From own rooted vines and native yeast fermentation, this gem strikes a beautiful chord. Cherries on the nose are mirrored on the palate, joining brambleberries, savory cranberry/blueberry sauce and orange zest. Deep and well balanced with velvety tannins, it's finesse from irresistible start to lasting finish.

acres 9 - cases 4,500
Fertilizers compost, organic fertilizer
Plant protection sulfur, synthetic pesticides, organic
Weed control mechanical
Yeasts spontaneous fermentation
Grapes purchase 60%
Certification none

DAYTON

SOKOL BLOSSER WINERY

5000 NE Sokol Blosser Lane - tel. (503) 864-2282
www.sokolblosser.com - info@sokolblosser.com

PEOPLE - Founders Susan Sokol Blosser and Bill Blosser planted their first grapes in 1971, before most of the world knew that wine grapes were well suited to Oregon. They were passionate about sustainable farming practices from the start. Second generation family members now run things. Alex Sokol Blosser is the president, while Alison Sokol Blosser and Nik Sokol Blosser are winegrowers. The family is proud of their B Corp Certification.

VINEYARDS - Their estates are located in three sub-AVAs. Dundee Hills is home to 89 acres of planted grapevines. Another 16 acres of vine grow in their Blossom Ridge vineyard in the Eola-Amity Hills. Both are certified organic. Their newest acquisition, the bowl shaped hillside Kalita Estate Vineyard in the Yamhill Carlton AVA, has 22 planted acres. Already LIVE certified, they plan to certify it organic, too. They purchase fruit from local growers as well. Some wines, not featured here, may be grown with herbicide.

WINES - Robin Howell's made the wines since 2012. Organic pioneers, they first certified their estate vineyard organic back in 2010.

● **Dundee Hills Rosé of Pinot Noir 2023** SLOW WINE ●
5,400 cases; 28 $ - 🍷 - The expressive aroma knocks this thirst quencher out of the park. Fresh and vivacious layers of strawberries, sun kissed nectarines and fresh squeezed oranges entwine, and the acidity keeps it nicely balanced.

Yamhill-Carlton Kalita Vineyard Pinot Noir 2022 ● 2,915 cases; 45 $ - 🛢 - Aged in French oak (15% new). Earth tones, warm cherry turnovers, tayberries, savory spices and hints of tangerine are enhanced by the lively acidity and an edge of minerality. Juicy and silky through the dreamy finish.

Willamette Valley Sauvignon Blanc 2023 ● 300 cases; 35 $ - 🍷🫙 - Grown at Croft vineyard (certified organic). Citrusy aroma jumps from the glass. Time in stainless and concrete egg adds a nice textural quality. Juicy white grapefruit, lemon verbena and lemon-lime ice unfold.

acres 127 - cases 25,000
Fertilizers compost, manure, organic fertilizer
Plant protection sulfur, synthetic pesticides, organic
Weed control mechanical
Yeasts spontaneous fermentation, selected indigenous yeasts, commercial cultured yeasts
Grapes purchase 30%
Certification some of the vineyards are certified organic

CARLTON

SOTER VINEYARDS

10880 NE Mineral Springs Road - tel. (503) 662-5600
www.sotervineyards.com - info@sotervineyards.com

 Tony Soter's farsighted vision and commitment created this Oregon classic, exemplifying Slow Wine values.

PEOPLE - Oregon winemaking icon Tony and (the late) Michelle Soter created their winery in 1997. An early organic advocate in Napa (where he helped many, including Spottswoode, implement organic farming in the 1980's) and celebrated winemaking consultant, Tony wanted to return to his native state. Michele's legacy includes biodynamic farming. Soter purchased two more vineyards, adding other AVA diversity to make his Estates series launched in 2021.

VINEYARDS - Acquired in 1997, their biodynamic Mineral Springs Ranch, a 240 acre (40 acres planted) estate and farm, in the Yamhill-Carlton AVA, is farmed regeneratively, focusing on biodiversity, soil health and integration of plants and animals. The Estates series includes two vineyards (both certified organic)—18 acres in their Soter Ribbon Ridge vineyard, and 19 acres at their Tarren vineyard in Eola-Amity Hills. The company is also B Corp certified.

WINES - Soter's respectful farming, ancient, well drained sedimentary soils, and favorable climate create multi-layered, nuanced, compelling wines. Certifying the winery as well as the estate enables winemaker Chris Fladwood to make Demeter certified wines.

● **Willamette Valley Estates Pinot Noir 2022** SLOW WINE ●
3,473 cases; 50 $ - 🛢 - Aged in French oak (30% new). Expressive aromas of black cherries. Layers of Bing cherries, allspice, Black Splendor plums and dried herbs wrapped around supple tannins.

Willamette Valley Estates Chardonnay 2021 ○ 1,068 cases; 60 $ - 🛢 - A fragrant citrus driven aroma. Crisp Anjou pears, citrus blossom, Crispin apples, and Meyer lemon granita join chalky minerality and subtle toast from neutral oak aging. Precise, well defined and pure through the vivacious finish.

Willamette Valley 3rd Edition Brut Reserve Nonvintage ⊛ 325 cases; 70 $ - 🍷🛢 - Opens with a gorgeous citrus blossom fragrance. Crisp green apple, lemon gelato, flaky croissants, minerality and Marcona almonds dance on the palate.

acres 87 - cases 6,000
Fertilizers compost, biodynamic compost, cover crops
Plant protection sulfur, biodynamic preparations, organic
Weed control mechanical
Yeasts spontaneous fermentation, selected indigenous yeasts
Grapes 100% owned
Certification some of the vineyards are certified organic, some of the vineyards are certified biodynamic

JEFFERSON

ST. INNOCENT WINERY

10052 Enchanted Way SE - tel. (503) 378-1526
www.stinnocentwine.com - info@stinnocentwine.com

PEOPLE - Known for his single vineyard designates, Oregon winemaking legend Mark Vlossak learned about wine through his wine educator and importer father, and his mother, a trained chef who delighted in wine pairings. He founded his own winery in 1988 and quickly gained a solid reputation for well-crafted wines. Now the next generation winemaker is on the way. Mark's daughter Makenzie Holley's been working harvests in Oregon and Germany and made her first wine in 2021.

VINEYARDS - St. Innocent buys grapes from top vineyards, including Temperance Hill (certified organic) and Momtazi (certified biodynamic). In 2023 they were proud to have the first harvest from their own estate—Enchanted Way—planted in 2018, the same year they constructed a new winery and tasting room on the vineyard site. Vlossak is pleased to become a true vigneron, extending his reach into winegrowing after all these years.

WINES - Vlossak gives a unique voice to the single vineyard designates, capturing authentic characteristics of each site.

Yamhill-Carlton Shea Vineyard Pinot Noir 2021 SLOW WINE ● 1,094 cases; 75 $ - 🍷 - Aromas of earth and cherries. On the palate, Tulare cherries, exotic tea, allspice, raspberry coulis, hints of sassafras and a treasure trove of savory spice entwine. Supple tannins and lively acidity are spot on. Ageworthy.

Eola-Amity Hills Temperance Hill Vineyard Pinot Noir 2021 ● 1,071 cases; 55 $ - 🍷 - Silky and ethereal with layers of Bing cherries, anise seed, raspberries, forest floor and exotic spice traversing the palate. Pure and refined through the long lasting finale.

McMinnville Momtazi Vineyard Pinot Noir 2021 ● 1,047 cases; 55 $ - 🍷 - On the palate, Bing cherries, marionberries, blackberries, orange zest, minerality and anise seed intertwine in harmony. Firm tannins and balancing acidity enhance the package. Power and grace in a glass, and it promises years of ageworthiness.

acres 15.5 - cases 6,000
Fertilizers biodynamic compost, cover crops, manure, organic
Plant protection sulfur, biodynamic preparations, synthetic pesticides, organic
Weed control mechanical, manual
Yeasts spontaneous fermentation, commercial cultured yeasts
Grapes purchase 90%
Certification some of the vineyards are certified organic, some of the vineyards are certified biodynamic

DAYTON

STOLLER FAMILY ESTATE

16161 NE McDougall Road - tel. (503) 864-3404
www.stollerfamilyestate.com - tastingroom@stollerfamilyestate.com

PEOPLE - Eco-minded forward thinkers, owner Bill Stoller (a former HR firm exec who inherited a turkey farm in the Dundee Hills) and president Gary Mortensen manage this Oregon powerhouse. In 2024, OSU grad Ben Howe became vice president of winemaking, joining founding winemaker Melissa Burr. Stoller also owns Chehalem Winery (see separate listing).

VINEYARDS - At elevations of 210 to 650 feet, the vines grow in rich, well drained red Jory soils. Ten cultivars are planted including Pinot Noir (16 clones) and Chardonnay (5 clones). The LIVE certified vineyards are herbicide free. They promote biodiversity, hosting natural predators of pests and have acres of native perennial wildflowers and oak savannah. They buy a quarter of the grapes from local growers. (Some wines, not featured here, may be grown with herbicide.)

WINES - A certified B Corp, the winery was the first in the world to achieve LEED Gold certification.

TOP Dundee Hills Estate Reserve Pinot Noir 2021 SLOW WINE ● 3,500 cases; 60 $ - 🍷 - Aged in French oak (35% new). Earthy, berry aromas. The silky palate mirrors the forest floor and raspberry notes, with added layers of Bing cherries, anise, pomegranate and savory spice. Refined and graceful with fine tannins, excellent balance and a long lasting finish.

Dundee Hills Estate Reserve Chardonnay 2022 ○ 2,000 cases; 50 $ - 🍷 - The citrusy Kaffir lime nose is mouthwatering. Flavors of Sunrise pears, citrus-flecked Honeycrisp apples, and Meyer lemon join a thread of minerality and spice nuances dancing on the palate. Remarkably textured and the finish has you wanting more.

acres 225 - cases 80,000
Fertilizers compost, cover crops, organic fertilizer
Plant protection sulfur, synthetic pesticides, organic
Weed control mechanical, n/a
Yeasts spontaneous fermentation, selected indigenous yeasts
Grapes purchase 26%
Certification none

MCMINNVILLE

THE EYRIE VINEYARDS

935 NE 10th Avenue - tel. (503) 472-6315
www.eyrievineyards.com - info@eyrievineyards.com

 A venerated classic, and the first to produce the region's defining varieties, it is certified organic (since 2013), cares for its employees and supports biodiversity.

PEOPLE - Since 2005, Jason Lett, winegrower and winemaker, has managed the iconic, pioneering winery founded by his late parents, David and Diana, in 1965. They planted the first Chardonnay and Pinot Noir in the Willamette Valley that year, creating the now world famous Oregon Pinot Noir boom. Pinot Gris and Trousseau followed. The team includes assistant winemaker Julio Hernandez, vineyard manager José Garcia and a year round crew of seven, long time employees.

VINEYARDS - Five dry farmed, no till vineyards (all certified organic) produce the estate fruit. Fertilization is, as Lett says, from "a living carpet of native plants, kept lightly mowed." He describes the higher elevation vineyards as bonsai gardens for grapes. Clones include Pommard, Wadenswil, and Upright. The soils are Nekia and Jory. The vines live symbiotically with a rich community of native plants, surrounded by forests.

WINES - Gentle winemaking—minimal intervention, neutral oak, basket pressing and aging in large vessels—produce ethereally elegant wines with legendary ageability.

⊙ Dundee Hills The Eyrie South Block Reserve Pinot Noir 2019 ● 55 cases; 300 $ - 🍷 - From the oldest vines (50+ years old). Offers an elegant herbal citrus aroma with juiciness emerging. On the palate, a burst of sweet fruit, strawberries, finely textured tannins and gentle acidity. Pure class.

Dundee Hills Roland Green Pinot Noir 2022 ● 242 cases; 75 $ - 🍷 - Seductively perfumed with juicy red fruit. Young but approachable on the palate. Some retronasal floral notes. Full and round with a medium finish.

Dundee Hills Oregon Pinot Blanc 2022 ○ 30 cases; 36 $ - 🍷 - Restrained aromas of citrus with hints of almond and hay. Bold entry with lovely texture, nice balance and medium finish. At the beginning of a long life.

---

acres 57 - cases 9,000
Fertilizers none
Plant protection sulfur, organic
Weed control mechanical
Yeasts spontaneous fermentation, selected indigenous yeasts
Grapes 100% owned
Certification organic

YAMHILL

WILLAKENZIE ESTATE

19143 NE Laughlin Road - tel. (503) 662-3280
www.willakenzie.com - hospitality@willakenzie.com

PEOPLE - California based Jackson Family Wines purchased the all estate winery in 2016, expanding its Oregon holdings. The winery's founders, Burgundy born tech entrepreneur Bernard Lacroute and wife Ronni, cashed out of his high tech and venture capitalist Silicon Valley career, bought the land and planted the first vines in 1992. Today Erik Kramer makes the wines. The newly redesigned tasting room hosts visitors.

VINEYARDS - Named after the well-drained sedimentary WilaKenzie soil series, the Yamhill-Carlton estate has 100 planted acres on the 420 acre property in six distinct, terroirnamed vineyard sites. It also owns 92 acres in the Dundee Hills. The LIVE certified, herbicide free estates grow more than eight Pinot Noir clones. Most are Dijon clones. They also grow Chardonnay, Gamay Noir, Pinot Blanc, Pinot Gris and Pinot Meunier.

WINES - Known for texture driven wines. The higher end Pinot Noirs are characterized by new oak of around 60 percent.

⊙ Yamhill-Carlton La Crête Chardonnay 2021 SLOW WINE ○ 98 cases; 100 $ - 🍷 - Aged in French oak (35% new). From a single Chardonnay clone (76). Aroma of exotic flowers. Silky layers of honeysuckle, sautéed apples, salinity, Marcona almonds and lemon gelato. Crisp acidity. Pure and focused.

Yamhill-Carlton Triple Black Slopes Pinot Noir 2021 ● 434 cases; 80 $ - 🍷 - Aged in French oak (64% new). Aromas of cherries and earth rocks. Flavors of black cherry, licorice, raspberry, black truffles, hints of toffee and baking spices explode vividly onto the palate. Complex, satin smooth and nuanced.

Yamhill-Carlton Clairière Pinot Noir 2021 ● 333 cases; 80 $ - 🍷 - Aged in French oak (57% new). Forest floor aroma. The palate is brimming with Bing cherries, wild mushrooms, loganberries, raspberry tisane and subtle herbs. Fine grained tannins and classic acidity keep it bright and lively.

---

acres 100 - cases 13,000
Fertilizers compost, cover crops, synthetic fertilizer
Plant protection sulfur, synthetic pesticides, organic
Weed control mechanical, manual
Yeasts spontaneous fermentation, commercial cultured yeasts
Grapes 100% owned
Certification none

DUNDEE

WINDERLEA VINEYARD & WINERY

8905 NE Worden Hill Road - tel. (503) 554-9400
www.winderlea.com - info@winderlea.com

PEOPLE - Trading careers in Boston for a life of winemaking in Oregon, Bill Sweat and Donna Morris founded Winderlea with the purchase of an old vine, Dundee Hills estate vineyard in 2006 and built a solar powered, sustainable tasting room. Sweat makes the wines in consultation with Robert Brittan. Leigh Bartholomew oversees the two Dundee Hills estate vineyards. The company is a certified B corporation and supports local farmworker health initiatives.

VINEYARDS - They have three, certified biodynamic sites in two AVAs. Originally planted in 1974, the 18 acre Dundee Hills estate vineyard sits on Jory soils, growing Chardonnay and eight clones of Pinot noir. They lease and farm the 24 acre Worden Hill vineyard and buy grapes from the famed Meredith Mitchell vineyard. On their estates, heritage Shetland sheep mow and fertilize. Goats keep blackberries under control. They also buy grapes from six local growers.

WINES - Elegant Pinot Noirs emphasize delicacy and complexity with refreshing acidity and fine tannins. Ageable. Pinot Blancs have complex aromas and well balanced flavors.

Dundee Hills Imprint Pinot Noir 2022 ● 219 cases; 70 $ - From the 1974 plantings. A three clone blend fermented whole cluster (100%). Rich, deep aromas with some stem influence, with floral notes and chocolatey wood scents emerging. Palate is complex and well balanced with good acidity. Youthful tannins.

Dundee Hills Winderlea Vineyard Pinot Noir 2022 ● 484 cases; 80 $ - A clonal blend. Floral aromas mesh with cinnamon and roses which grow more intense over time. The palate is well balanced and smoothly textured. Attractive finish.

McMinnville Meredith Mitchell Pinot Blanc 2022 O 327 cases; 40 $ - Complex aromas of citrus, juiciness, and nuts which develop in intensity and include floral notes. The palate is lovely with juicy lemon and nice texture. Kaleidolfactic and yummy.

acres 42 - cases 6,000
Fertilizers compost, biodynamic compost, cover crops
Plant protection sulfur, biodynamic preparations, synthetic pesticides, organic
Weed control animal grazing, mechanical, manual
Yeasts spontaneous fermentation
Grapes purchase 27%
Certification biodynamic

MCMINNVILLE

YOUNGBERG HILL

10660 SW Youngberg Hill Road - tel. (971) 901-2177
www.youngberghill.com - wine@youngberghill.com

Diligent about sustainability and regenerative practices, their excellent wines reflect those efforts.

PEOPLE - Hospitality focused, Nicolette and Wayne Bailey established their vineyard in 1989, raising their three daughters here. They now have an event center and a bed and breakfast in addition to their winery and tasting room. Wayne oversees the vines and makes the wines.

VINEYARDS - The Baileys use regenerative practices and are herbicide free. Their vineyards have been no till for more than five years. Newborn baby kid goats, a brood of chickens and sheep join their Highland calves and cows in grazing on the 50 acre hilltop site. The four legged animals, help forage and fertilize their sizable wine country estate, with acres of biodiversity-grasses, herbs, and wildflowers.

WINES - Bright fruit, new clones, variations in fermentation and a variety of barrel cooperage create nuanced wines.

McMinnville YH J Block Pinot Noir 2019 SLOW WINE ● 213 cases; 65 $ - Aged in French oak (34% new). Berry and forest floor aromas. Black cherries, red plums, melted chocolate, olallieberries, and marry brilliantly. Pure, luscious and balanced. Cellarworthy.

Willamette Valley YH Pinot Noir Rosé 2023 ● 125 cases; 40 $ - An extraordinary rosé. Highly aromatic with dazzling scents and flavors of strawberries, raspberries, cranberry and orange sauce and a pinch of lemon herbs. Lively acids play off the juicy fruit and the bright finish is vibrant.

Willamette Valley YH Chardonnay 2022 O 151 cases; 45 $ - Honeysuckle on the nose. On the palate, juicy Yellow Delicious apples, creamy pears, spiced oak accents, seaside salinity and Meyer lemon meld in harmony. Precisely balanced.

acres 23 - cases 2,500
Fertilizers compost, cover crops, manure
Plant protection sulfur, synthetic pesticides
Weed control animal grazing, mechanical, manual
Yeasts selected indigenous yeasts, commercial cultured yeasts
Grapes purchase 5%
Certification none

SOUTHERN OREGON

 Snail

197 Cowhorn Vineyard & Garden **Snail**
199 Troon Vineyard
200 Upper Five Vineyard

JACKSONVILLE

COWHORN VINEYARD & GARDEN

1665 Eastside Road - tel. (541) 899-6876
www.cowhornwine.com - info@cowhornwine.com

 A biodynamic Rhone star in southern Oregon, it's a poster child for eco-friendly farming and elegant wines.

PEOPLE - A passionate eco-advocate, proprietor Mini Byers (neé Banks) runs what may be one of the greenest wineries in a state that has many contenders. Under her ownership (since 2021), she's integrated sheep and chickens. The certified biodynamic winery itself is a certified Living Building, achieving net zero energy status in 2022. Hospitality has expanded, too, with house-made, organic wood fired pizza on site, lodging, and a new fine dining restaurant in downtown Jacksonville.

VINEYARDS - Farmed with nature in mind, Cowhorn was one of the first in the U.S. to be certified biodynamic—back in 2006. It encompasses 117 acres along a river, including 25 planted to Rhone varieties. Domestic Katahdin lambs roam the property. The farm grows vegetables and fruits. Byers also owns biodynamic Johan Vineyards in the Willamette Valley.

WINES - Vince Vidrine makes the wines which are also certified biodynamic. From vibrant whites to electrifying rosés and sophisticated reds, the wines are complex and deeply layered.

Applegate Valley Syrah 2020 SLOW WINE ● 361 cases; 55 $ - A classic. On the nose, perfumed violets and roses captivate the senses. Lush and complex, while also pristinely balanced and elegant, it coats the mouth with black plum, blackberry, tobacco leaf, roasted meat and cacao nib flavors. The finish is long lasting. Ageworthy.

Applegate Valley Viognier 2022 ○ 224 cases; 40 $ - Whole cluster pressed and aged on the lees, this is a magical, highly aromatic Viognier. Layers of nectarine, lemon sorbet, a touch of fresh herbs and minerality entwine. Citrus blossom lingers on the long finish.

Applegate Valley Rosé 2023 ● 87 cases; 30 $ - This vivacious Grenache rosé crafted opens with a glorious floral aromatic. Fresh raspberries, strawberries and peaches intertwine with crushed herbs and crisp acidity through the mouthwatering finish.

acres 25 - cases 3,000
Fertilizers biodynamic compost, cover crops, manure
Plant protection biodynamic preparations, organic
Weed control mechanical
Yeasts spontaneous fermentation, selected indigenous yeasts
Grapes 100% owned
Certification biodynamic, organic

MEDFORD

DANCIN

4477 South Stage Road - tel. (541) 245-1371
www.dancin.com - info@dancin.com

PEOPLE - With a background as a chef in luxury fine dining, general manager Austin Marca, the youngest son of retired founders Dan and Cindy Marca, is bringing high level hospitality and culinary experiences to the winery. Executive chef Christopher Kempf offers fine cuisine and lovely views in the lower level tasting room and restaurant. The upper level, called "The Residence," hosts private events. Winemaker Chris Jiron completed his seventh harvest at the winery.

VINEYARDS - Their estate vineyard has been dry farmed and free of synthetic herbicides for more than six years. Surrounded by pine, cedar and oak trees, Chardonnay and Pinot Noir grow at 1,710-1,960 feet of elevation on northeast facing slopes. The team is in the process of to become LIVE certified. They also buy grapes from local growers who use a variety of products. (Some wines, not featured here, may be grown with herbicide.)

WINES - Healthy fruit is paramount. The team hand sorts multiple times for each vintage to bring forth wines of elegance and purity.

Rogue Valley Alto Pinot Noir 2022 SLOW WINE ● 98 cases; 45 $ - ⊞ - Expressive scents of cherries and earthiness. A well-defined and structured Pinot Noir rich in flavor while light on its feet. Notes of forest floor, pomegranate, anise, juicy red cherries, underlying oak and exotic spices marry in harmony.

Rogue Valley En L'air Rosé of Pinot Noir 2023 ● 210 cases; 35 $ - ⌀ - Pommard clone. Dry and beautifully aromatic and fresh, with aromas and flavors of cherry, raspberry chutney, a dash of spice and strawberry ice. Lively with brisk acidity through the uplifting finish.

Rogue Valley Capriccio Chardonnay 2022 ○ 47 cases; 35 $ - ⊞ - Aged in neutral French oak (which adds underlying barrel spice). Lifted aromatics and a round, smooth mouthfeel. Elegant and complex with honeysuckle, creamy Gala apples, Meyer lemon and pear tartine flavors entwine.

acres 35 - cases 3,500
Fertilizers compost, cover crops, organic fertilizer, synthetic fertilizer
Plant protection sulfur, synthetic pesticides, organic
Weed control mechanical, manual
Yeasts spontaneous fermentation
Grapes purchase 40%
Certification none

ROSEBURG

HILLCREST VINEYARD

240 Vineyard Lane - tel. (541) 673-3709
www.hillcrestvineyard.com - info@hillcrestvineyard.com

PEOPLE - Known internationally as the birthplace of Pinot Noir in Oregon, Richard Sommer, the "Father of Oregon Wine," planted the first Pinot here in the state in 1961. (The Willamette Valley followed in 1965). The DeMara's purchased the property in 2002. Today Dyson and Susan DeMara and their children preserve his legacy and expand upon it, making wines with friends in Priorat, Spain; Maury in the Languedoc-Roussillon in France; the Mosel Valley of Germany; and Caltagirone in Catania, Italy.

VINEYARDS - Dysons are passionate about wines with purity that reflect truth of terroir. Their motto is "Good wine tastes like a grape. Great wine tastes like a place." Located on a 100 acre property, their old vine, mountain vineyard is dry farmed and has been herbicide free for seven years.

WINES - Dyson uses old world style techniques and ferments in patented concrete fermenters, with 30 to 60 days of skin contact for the reds. Barrel aging is two to four years.

Umpqua Valley 50th Anniversary Pinot Noir 2017 SLOW WINE ● 110 cases; 75 $ - ⊞ - Aged in French oak (35% new). Elegant. An expressive nose leads to a palate with Bing cherries, boysenberries, black raspberries, spice box and wild mushrooms. The texture is satin smooth. Hints of caramel on the finish.

Umpqua Valley NONIHC Cabernet Franc 2018 ● 250 cases; 38 $ - ⊞ - Aged in French oak (20% new). Violets and berries on the nose. On the palate, juicy plums, subtle roasted red pepper, tayberries, graphite and cassis, wrapped around supple tannins. Bold and well structured.

Umpqua Valley Chardonnay 2017 ○ 100 cases; 38 $ - ⊞ - Highly expressive and fresh, with layers of Honeycrisp apples, hints of pineapple, honeysuckle and bright citrus accents.

acres 40 - cases 2,500
Fertilizers cover crops
Plant protection sulfur
Weed control mechanical
Yeasts spontaneous fermentation, commercial cultured yeasts
Grapes 100% owned
Certification none

JACKSONVILLE

QUADY NORTH

255 East California Street - tel. (541) 702-2123
www.quadynorth.com - info@quadynorth.com

PEOPLE - Herb Quady grew up at the family winery in California. After becoming enamored of Rhone varieties, he made his way to southern Oregon, where he and wife Meloney established Quady North, buying 100 acres in 2005. Associate winemaker Nichole Schulte fell hard for Rhone varieties while at the Université Jean Moulin in Lyon, France. Sustainably minded, the winery is among the first to use reusable Revino bottles.

VINEYARDS - Their LIVE and organic certified estate provides slightly less than half of the grapes. Five sheep graze there, fertilizing the soil and mowing cover crop. Mae's Vineyard grows Rhones—Grenache, Syrah, Tannat, Viognier—as well as Cab Franc, Malbec and Orange Muscat. Eevee's Vineyard grows more white Rhones—Grenache Blanc, Marsanne and Roussanne—along with Cab Franc and Malvasia Bianca. They also purchase fruit from Steelhead Run Vineyard and Layne Vineyard.

WINES - Herb crafts small lots using minimal handling to showcase the distinct terroir of southern Oregon.

Applegate Valley Mae's Vineyard Syrah 2019 SLOW WINE
● 100 cases; 39 $ - 🍽 - A deep dark fruit aroma wafts from the glass. Boysenberries, blackberries, cured meat, blackberries, dark plums, spice box and oak nuances intertwine. The long finish displays a nice touch of spice.

Applegate Valley Mae's Vineyard Bomba Grenache 2023
● 400 cases; 27 $ - 🍽 - A succulent Grenache (blended with 6% Syrah). Red fruits and spice on the nose lead to a flavorful palate of red cherries, cranberry sauce, fresh strawberries, and subtle spice. Bright, fresh and well balanced with an uplifting, persistent finish.

Applegate Valley Mae's Vineyard Ox Block Viognier 2023 ○ 200 cases; 27 $ - 🍽 - Expressive aromas of citrus blossom and delicate floral bouquet. Peaches and cream, honeysuckle, and Summer Kiss melons flow deliciously across the palate.

acres 25 - cases 7,000
Fertilizers compost, manure, organic fertilizer
Plant protection biodynamic preparations, synthetic pesticides, organic
Weed control mechanical, n/a
Yeasts commercial cultured yeasts
Grapes purchase 60%
Certification some of the vineyards are certified organic

GRANTS PASS

TROON VINEYARD

1475 Kubli Road - tel. (541) 846-9900
www.troonvineyard.com - tastingroom@troonvineyard.com

 For extraordinary achievement in raising the bar on farming, fruit, wines and climate resilience and serving as a role model for others.

PEOPLE - An eco leader for both farming and exceptional wines, Troon is certified both biodynamic and regenerative organic (ROC)—the only one in Oregon with all of those accolades. It's also one of only four farms in the world to achieve ROC's gold level, a very high bar that includes fair pay for workers and worker participation in decision making. Team leaders include owners Dr. Bryan and Denise White, winemaker Nate Wall, director of agriculture Garett Long, and general manager Craig Camp.

VINEYARDS - The team's planted 20 southern French varieties on their Kubli Bench estate, including Rhone mainstays as well as lesser known cultivars. That list includes Bourboulenc, Carignan, Cinsault, Clairette Blanche, Counoise, Grenache Blanc and Gris, Picpoul, Tannat and Tibouren. They also sell vegetables at their farm stand and produce honey and cider, following their whole farm strategy.

WINES - In 2023, the team integrated concrete eggs and tanks, preserving freshness in the expressive wines. Winemaking, too, is certified biodynamic, too, meaning the wines meet pure standards.

Applegate Valley Estate Syrah 2022 SLOW WINE ● 200 cases; 40 $ - 🍽 - Aged 18 month in French oak (neutral). Aromatic spice and black fruit lead to black plum, damp earth, savoriness, tobacco and black pepper spiced meat. Complex with a persistent finish.

Applegate Valley Vermentino 2023 ○ 460 cases; 35 $ - 🍽 - Citrus blossom and peaches on the nose. Mouth filling flavors of star fruit, white peach, faint herbs, and citrus splashed apples burst onto the palate. Precisely balanced with lively acidity through the saline tinged zesty finish.

Applegate Valley Ascendant Rosé 2023 ◐ 240 cases; 40 $ - 🥂 - A striking blend of Cinsault (38%), Mourvedre (33%), Grenache (11%), Counoise (10%) and Carignan (8%). Juicy flavors of raspberry, plum, strawberry ice and Sunkist orange burst onto the palate.

acres 50 - cases 6,000
Fertilizers biodynamic compost, cover crops
Plant protection biodynamic preparations, organic
Weed control animal grazing, mechanical, manual
Yeasts spontaneous fermentation
Grapes 100% owned
Certification biodynamic, organic, regenerative

TALENT

UPPER FIVE VINEYARD

1125 Morey Road - tel. (541) 285-8359
www.upperfivevineyard.com - terry@upperfivevineyard.com

 A small producer that adheres to Slow Wine values, epitomizing what exemplary farming and hands off winemaking can produce—and making exceptional wines that are affordable.

PEOPLE - Owner Terry Sullivan purchased the historic Bagley pear orchard in 1999. In 2003 he and co-owner Molly Morison planted the first grapevines on the upper five acres of the property—hence the winery's name. Both owners earned a Master of Science degrees—Terry's in ocean engineering and Molly's in botany and plant biology. They embrace a minimal manipulation winemaking style, including minimal (if any) use of new oak.

VINEYARDS - Certified organic since 2005 and Demeter certified biodynamic since 2018, the vines grow at an elevation of 1,920 feet, surrounded by biodiversity. They credit the elevation and northerly aspect "for good acid retention and distinctive complexity in our grapes."

WINES - They use clay amphora for Grenache to add further focus on fruit and minerality. Acacia puncheons for Sauvignon Blanc enhance brightness and textural qualities.

TOP Rogue Valley Rosé of Grenache 2023 SLOW WINE ● 120 cases; 20 $ - ⊞ - Expressive red fruit aromas. Reminiscent of a fine Provencal dry Rosé with flavors of fresh strawberries, raspberries, lemon herbs and juicy Friar plums are complemented by crisp acidity.
Rogue Valley Grenache 2022 ● 60 cases; 28 $ - ⊞ - Aromas of a basketful of fresh raspberries. On the palate, flavors of savory raspberry sauce join blueberries, black pepper tinges and a thread of minerality. Elegant and pure.
Rogue Valley Sauvignon Blanc 2023 ○ 80 cases; 22 $ - ⊞ - Expressive aromatics lead to fresh, lively citrus flecked green apples, lemon verbena and minerality quenching the palate. Aging in acacia puncheons rounds off any sharp edges, while crisp acidity ensures brilliant balance.

acres 3.5 - cases 650
Fertilizers compost, biodynamic compost, cover crops, manure, organic fertilizer
Plant protection sulfur, biodynamic preparations, organic
Weed control mechanical, manual
Yeasts spontaneous fermentation
Grapes 100% owned
Certification biodynamic, organic

COLUMBIA GORGE

🐌 **Snail**
201 Analemma Wines Snail

🍾 **Bottle**
202 EST

MOSIER

ANALEMMA WINES

1120 State Road - tel. (541) 478-2873
www.analemmawines.com - cellardoor@analemmawines.com

 For pioneering Spanish varieties in Oregon and for their commitment to eco-friendly winegrowing and their beautifully crafted wines.

PEOPLE - Co-founders Steven Thompson and Kris Fade started Analemma in 2011, focusing on developing a biodynamic estate at Mosier Hills. Analemma is the epitome of Slow Wine at its core, marrying a beautifully nourished estate with compelling wines and educational programming that offers insight into regenerative viticulture and winemaking. Beginning in 2023, they are all estate with grapes solely from their Mosier Hills estate where Iberian varieties predominate.

VINEYARDS - The certified biodynamic property consists of 52 acres set in the rain shadow of the Cascades on river stones and granitic glacial erratics from the Missoula Floods. The diverse site includes numerous Spanish varietals, wispy grasslands, Oregon white oaks, cherry trees, blue orchard bees and Jersey cows. Fostering conditions for strong microbial diversity in the soils translates into characterful fruit and expressive, elegant wines.

WINES - Iberian varieties-Godello, Mencia and Trousseau-with distinctive Gorge characteristics that are vibrant, fresh and complex.

Mosier Hills Trousseau 2023 ● 378 cases; 48 $ - Ethereal and expressive aromas of brambly raspberry, orange peel and wet stone. Light bodied on palate with flavors of pomegranate, red cherry and tomato vine. A Jura inspired varietal telling a Gorge story.

Mosier Hills Mencia 2022 ● 509 cases; 48 $ - An aromatic vintage with raspberry, lavender and bergamot. Lighter body yet maintains texture and distinctive tannins. Bright cherry, allspice and crushed gravel.

Mosier Hills Blanco 2023 ○ 300 cases; 40 $ - Gentle whole cluster press with 15 months on lees. Analemma's foundational white, the Godello dominant blend is aromatic with white flower, beeswax and Gorge minerality. Lively and textured palate with fresh lemon chiffon.

---

acres 17 - cases 3,000
Fertilizers biodynamic compost, organic fertilizer
Plant protection sulfur, biodynamic preparations, organic
Weed control animal grazing, mechanical, manual
Yeasts spontaneous fermentation
Grapes 100% owned
Certification biodynamic

CASCADE LOCKS

BUONA NOTTE

160 Herman Creek Lane, Suite 102 - tel. (303) 818-3525
www.buonanottewines.com - graham@buonanottewines.com

PEOPLE - Natural winemaker Graham Markel has been rooted in the Slow Food scene since childhood, growing up in his mother's cooking school in Tuscany. Eventually he ended up in the Pacific Northwest. After stints at Antica Terra and Hiyu, in 2016 he started his own label. His natural wines highlight the diversity of the Gorge with a big nod to Italy. He's integrated into the food and wine scene along the Columbia Gorge.

VINEYARDS - Graham co-manages eight different vineyard sites throughout the Gorge. Working in collaboration with multiple local farmers gives him the opportunity to influence how the broader viticulture landscape of the Gorge is managed while providing him with a diverse fruit to play with from varying soil compositions and microclimates. He also works with a few sites in the Columbia Valley AVA, buying grapes for his rustic Cento Per Cento Sangiovese there.

WINES - Markel makes Italian varietals in a minimal intervention style that lets the unique Gorge terroir shine, showcasing vibrant acidity and compelling profiles with occasional skin contact.

Columbia Valley Cento Per Cento Sangiovese 2022 ● 120 cases; 30 $ - Fermented partial whole cluster (25%) with 90 days on skins. Zingy cherry, red rose petal, tomato sauce and dusty sage brush. Juicy and savory.

Columbia Gorge Pianoforte Pinot Noir 2022 ● 200 cases; 35 $ - Partial whole cluster (20%) with 14 days on the skins. Compelling red fruit of Bing cherry, red plum flesh, and ripe raspberry with floral aromatics and refreshing acidity.

---

acres 17 - cases 2,500
Fertilizers compost, biodynamic compost, cover crops, organic fertilizer
Plant protection sulfur, biodynamic preparations, organic
Weed control mechanical
Yeasts spontaneous fermentation
Grapes purchase 100%
Certification some of the vineyards are certified organic, some of the vineyards are certified biodynamic

PORTLAND

EST

2419 SE 85th Ave - tel. (503) 522-2481
www.estwines.com - info@stateracellars.com

PEOPLE - Natural winemaker Meredith Bell established her label in 2014. Her background in enology and art paired with her previous experience in viticulture at U.C. Davis and Craft Wine Co. guide her creative process and allow her to play outside of the box, re-imagining wines through minimal intervention. Bell also makes wine under the Statera Cellars label.

VINEYARDS - The estate is the dry farmed Leland vineyard on the eastern slopes of the Willamette Valley (near Oregon City). The site was planted to own rooted Pinot Noir and Sauvignon Blanc in Jory soils in the 1980's by Bruce Weber. Bell farmed the site with Bruce for eight years prior to taking over in the last two years. The site is in organic conversion and expected to be certified by 2025.

WINES - Bright, acid driven wines that are juicy and easy to drink with layers of depth from creative combinations of whole cluster, skin contact and blends.

Willamette Valley EST Pinot Noir 2022 ● 102 cases; 31 $ - ⊞ - Whole berry fermented. Gentle extraction keeps the aromas and notes of dark cherry and raspberry fresh and delicate. Undertones of baking spice. Driven by bright acidity.

Willamette Valley EST Swirl 2022 ● 92 cases; 29 $ - ⊠ - Partial skin maceration. Pinot Noir blended with Sauvignon Blanc (100% whole cluster) after eight months of aging separately. Aromas of lychee and cherry with a grapefruit backbone. Bright, fresh and fun with nice phenolic tension on the palate.

Willamette Valley EST Sparkling Pinot Noir ⊕ 94 cases; 29 $ - ⊞ - A sparkling rosé wine blend of two vintages of Pinot Noir–partial whole cluster red (2021) and whole berry soaked((2022). Undisgorged bubbles in the method ancestral. Wildly juicy with ripe cherry and a hint of anise. Fine bubbles balance light tannins.

acres 4 - cases 350
Fertilizers organic fertilizer
Plant protection sulfur, organic
Weed control mechanical, manual
Yeasts spontaneous fermentation
Grapes 100% owned
Certification converting to organic

MOSIER

IDIOT'S GRACE

8450 Highway 30 - tel. (541) 399-5259
www.idiotsgrace.com - tastingroom@idiotsgrace.com

PEOPLE - A Gorge pioneer, this small, family owned estate was established by father and son Robert and Brian McCormick in 2006. Their thoughtful, yet minimal approach allows them to make expressive wines that showcase the diversity and range of possibilities in the Columbia Gorge AVA. Brian's background and nuanced approach helps him manage the organically farmed vines and fruit trees.

VINEYARDS - Idiot's Grace is tucked in the hills of Mosier at 300 feet. The 14 acre estate grows 20 different varietals, including Cabernet Franc, Chenin Blanc, Dolcetto and Gamay on sandy to clay loam soils. Cherry and pear trees add diversity to the vineyard. Alternate, higher elevation sites like Hamm, Hanna's Bench and Parker give certain varieties, like Grenache, more daytime sun exposure and cooler temps in the evening.

WINES - Minimal intervention wines with bright acidity, refreshing elegance and Old World flair that express site specific characteristics.

Columbia Gorge Gamay Noir 2022 ● 60 cases; 35 $ - ⊞ - It's the first red fruit harvested (by hand) each year. A mix of tart red and blue fruits, raspberry, cherry and black cherry lead a dry yet juicy palate with complex and earthy undertones of baking spice and a subtle umami.

Columbia Gorge Dryland Cabernet Franc 2021 ● 100 cases; 45 $ - ⊠ ⊞ - Head trained and dry farmed. Gives a nod to the Loire Valley while expressing Gorge. Black caps, charred red pepper and tart raspberry preserves meld with black pepper and nice minerality.

Columbia Gorge Chenin Blanc 2022 ○ 140 cases; 45 $ - ⊞ - Aged in a mix of new and old oak. Balanced palate of rich texture and bright acidity. Nectarine, apple, peach, zesty citrus and briny minerals.

acres 19.8 - cases 2,050
Fertilizers compost, cover crops, manure, organic fertilizer
Plant protection sulfur, organic
Weed control mechanical, manual
Yeasts selected indigenous yeasts
Grapes 100% owned
Certification organic

PORTLAND

STATERA CELLARS

2419 SE 85th Ave - tel. (503) 522-2481
www.stateracellars.com - info@stateracellars.com

PEOPLE - Friends Meredith Bell and Luke Wylde founded the Chardonnay focused label in 2014 playing with creative renditions. With backgounds at Craft Wine Company and Abbey Road Farm, the duo bring diverse winemaking experience to Statera, a great example of how a modern day negociant relationship can influence a concept for first generation winemakers.

VINEYARDS - Bell and Wylde buy fruit from multiple Oregon appellations. Working with top vineyards across the state gives them the opportunity to deepen their exploration of the regional intricacies of wine grapes, taking a creative and nuanced approach. They seek out vineyards farmed organically and biodynamically farmed (though most are not certified).

WINES - A lens focused on the spectrum of Willamette Valley Chardonnays, expressed through vineyard sites, vintages and playful creativity.

Willamette Valley Statera Cellars Remix Vol II 2021 ○ 98 cases; 29 $ - ⊞ - A 50/50 blend of whole cluster Chardonnay and Chenin Blanc left on the skins for three days. Bright nose of fresh green apple and pear with a touch of minerality lead into a juicy and plush palate full of peach and nectarine with a saline minerality. Lively acid.

Van Duzer Corridor Statera Cellars Johan Vineyard Chardonnay 2021 ○ 48 cases; 35 $ - ⊞ - Whole cluster fermented for 14 months with 16 months on the lees. Bright yet complex nose of lime and lime leaf matched by layers of stone fruit and stony minerality on the palate.

Willamette Valley Statera Unicus Chardonnay 2022 ◎ 98 cases; 29 $ - ⊞ - Half whole cluster fermented and half whole berry fermented. Compelling notes of hazelnut, dried orange peel and linseed oil with subtle tea leaf tannins and bright, citrus driven acidity.

acres 0 - cases 1,000
Fertilizers compost, biodynamic compost, cover crops, manure, organic fertilizer
Plant protection sulfur, biodynamic preparations, organic
Weed control animal grazing, mechanical, manual
Yeasts spontaneous fermentation
Grapes purchase 100%
Certification biodynamic, organic

WASHINGTON

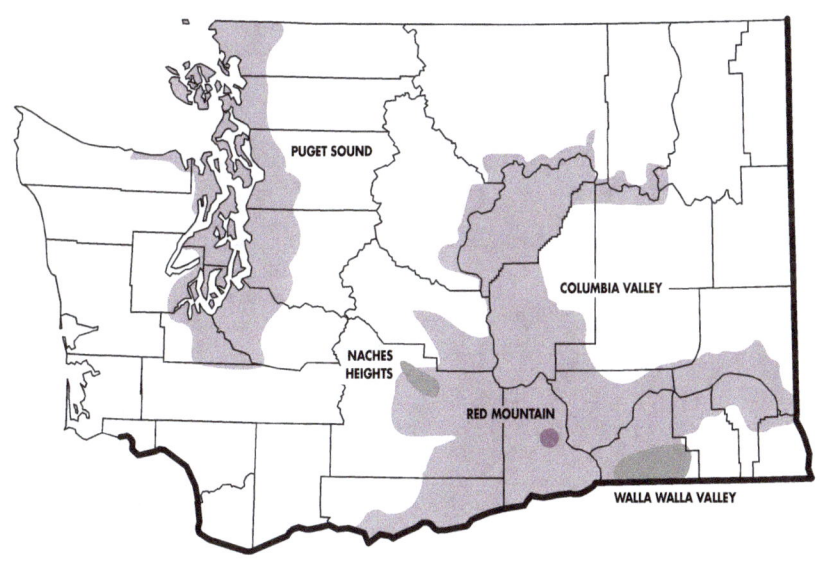

WASHINGTON

Snail

209 Domaine Magdalena **Snail**
217 Wilridge Vineyard, Winery & Distillery

Bottle

208 Caprio Cellars
208 Cayuse Vineyards & Bionic Wines
212 Hedges Family Estate
215 Savage Grace
216 Syncline

$ Coin

207 Badger Mountain Vineyard
216 Tagaris Winery

WALLA WALLA

AMAVI CELLARS

3796 Peppers Bridge Rd - tel. (509) 525-3541
www.amavicellars.com - reservations@amavicellars.com

PEOPLE - Known for top tier Syrah, the name Amavi Cellars means love (amor) and life (vita). Three pioneering Walla Walla families—the McKibbens, the Murphys, and the Pellets—own this powerhouse winery. McKibben retired to the region in 1991, becoming an early investor in Pepper Bridge winery in 1998 with Dennis Murphy and Swiss born winemaker Jean-François Pellet. They went on to found Amavi in 2001. Pellet, who formerly worked at Heitz in Napa, is the director of winemaking.

VINEYARDS - The team has seven vineyards and grows 11 varieties, selling grapes to other vintners and retaining a portion for their own production. Soils vary, but loess plays a major role. Named Washington Grower of the Year in 2021, Walla Walla native Sadie Drury manages the acclaimed 235 acre Seven Hills vineyard. Jared Brown manages the 170 acre Pepper Bridge vineyard, Brad Sorensen oversees the 290 acre Les Collines. Cover crop supports beneficial insects.

WINES - Wines are precision-made with light to medium intensity and concentration.

Walla Walla Valley Cabernet Sauvignon 2021 ● 3,337 cases; 40 $ - ▦ - Aged in mostly French oak (29% new). The blend includes Merlot (10%) and Malbec (6%). Nose of cocoa, saddle leather, black cassis and lilac. Supporting flavors of black plum, cinnamon and river stone. Loads of minerality and freshness.

Walla Walla Valley Syrah 2022 ● 1,617 cases; 42 $ - ⓜ - Aged in French oak (23% new) in 500L puncheons. The blend includes Grenache (11%). Aromas of blackberry, granite, black cherry and dried purple flowers. The palate is lean and slightly tannic with clove, under-ripe black plum, black olive and fungi. Tannins finish smooth.

Walla Walla Valley Semillon 2023 ○ 1,010 cases; 28 $ - ▦ - Aged in neutral oak. The blend included Sauvignon Blanc (15%). On the nose, lemon, white flowers, beeswax and terracotta. The palate is light and crisp with lifted notes of white peach, lemon rind, yellow apple and minerality.

---

acres 690 - cases 10,000
Fertilizers compost, cover crops, organic fertilizer
Plant protection sulfur, synthetic pesticides, copper, organic
Weed control mechanical
Yeasts selected indigenous yeasts
Grapes 100% owned
Certification none

KENNEWICK

SEATTLE

BADGER MOUNTAIN VINEYARD

CADENCE WINERY

1106 N Jurupa Street - tel. (800) 643-9319
www.badgermtnvineyard.com - info@badgermtnvineyard.com

9320 15th Avenue S unit CF - tel. (206) 381-9507
www.cadencewinery.com - info@cadencewinery.com

PEOPLE - Founded in 1982 by the late Bill Powers, the winery became the first in Washington state to obtain organic certification—back in 1990. Steve Rothwell, director of operations and winemaking, maintains the legacy with a watchful eye on quality in conjunction with winemaker Irving Mendoza. Green practices include solar panels on the facility, lighter weight glass bottles for single varieties and eco-friendly boxed wine blends.

VINEYARDS - Antonio Carreon joined the team in 2024 as vineyard manager. The vineyard (certified organic for 30+ years) is home to eight varieties rooted in soils composed of windblown loess and sandy loam. Though frost came through the area in the winter of 2024, the vines escaped major damage. In addition to their own estate, they buy grapes from other certified organic vineyards including a grower partner in Oregon.

PEOPLE - Acclaimed artisanal pioneers working in Red Mountain, the husband and wife team of Benjamin Smith, a former Boeing engineer, and Gaye McNutt, a lawyer, founded the winery in 1998 with the goal of making the state's first vineyard designated Bordeaux style blends. Smith is the winemaker. The wines all have names that are musical terms.

VINEYARDS - Their Cara Mia estate vineyard, which they planted in 2004, has unique and varied soil profile with deep cobblestone soils, clay, and fractured basalt sandy loams. Two of these soils, cobblestones and clay, have not been uncovered in any other Red Mountain vineyard sites. The physical makeup of the cobbles and clay are very similar to Pomerol and St. Emilion plateau in Bordeaux. Row spacing is a tiny four feet requiring all manual work.

WINES - The wines are certified as "organic wine"—therefore, no sulfites are added. Winemaking practices fend off oxygen to help the wines last longer in bottle. The goal is clean and pure wines with approachable fruit.

Columbia Valley Rivercrest Vineyard Organic Pinot Noir 2023 EVERYDAY WINE ● 1,700 cases; 18 $ - 🍷 - Faint licorice and cherry on the nose lead to a fruit forward and fresh example of the variety. Appealing flavors of cherry and a mild earthiness along with soft tannins.
Columbia Valley Organic Merlot 2023 ● 1,100 cases; 18 $ - 🍷 - This vintage comes entirely from the estate. Concentrated flavors of a plum tart intermingle with Bing cherry underlined by plush tannins.
Columbia Valley Badger Mountain Vineyard Organic Chardonnay 2023 ○ 1,100 cases; 18 $ - 🍷 - In order to retain acidity and a focus on fruit, there's no malolactic fermentation. The pale gold liquid reveals flavors of baked fruit along with ginger and cinnamon, evocative of spiced applesauce.

WINES - Elegant, terroir focused Cabernet and blends built for long aging.

TOP Red Mountain Coda 2022 EVERYDAY WINE ● 1,000 cases; 28 $ - 🍷 - Aged 16 months in French oak (50% new). The blend is Cabernet Franc (41%), Merlot (33%), Petit Verdot (17%), Cabernet Sauvignon (9%). Raspberry, red peppercorn, plum, cedar and sage on the nose. Good intensity with tightly wound black cherry, cardamon and crushed rocks. Very balanced. Pushes far above its price point.
Red Mountain Cara Mia Cabernet Sauvignon 2021 ● 300 cases; 50 $ - 🍷 - Aged 16 months in French oak (50% new). Bursting with red currant, plum, wet slate and cinnamon bark. Vibrant palate with high toned red and black fruit, nutmeg, plum and black olive.
Red Mountain Bel Canto Cara Mia Vineyard 2020 ● 300 cases; 70 $ - 🍷 - Aged 23 months in French oak (50% new). The blend is Cabernet Franc (73%) and Merlot (27%). Vibrant nose of black plum, dark chocolate, menthol and Sichuan pepper. Oak, fruit and zippy acidity in very nice balance. Flavors of ripe strawberry, white pepper and loads of minerality. Built for long term aging.

acres 73 - cases 35,000
Fertilizers compost, cover crops, organic fertilizer
Plant protection organic
Weed control mechanical, manual
Yeasts commercial cultured yeasts
Grapes purchase 50%
Certification organic

acres 10 - cases 1,200
Fertilizers compost
Plant protection sulfur, synthetic pesticides
Weed control manual
Yeasts commercial cultured yeasts
Grapes 100% owned
Certification none

WALLA WALLA

CAPRIO CELLARS

1603 Whiteley Road - tel. (509) 412-3054
www.capriocellars.com - info@capriocellars.com

PEOPLE - Winery owner and winemaker Dennis Murphy purchased the property in 2003 and transformed land growing wheat into a vineyard dedicated to Cabernet Sauvignon and Merlot. A sleek tasting room on the estate welcomes guests for tasting by appointment in order to provide top notch hospitality and masterful food pairings prepared in house free of charge. Philanthropy is also part of the philosophy—five percent of proceeds benefit nonprofits.

VINEYARDS - In October 2023, Dennis acquired ownership interest in Seven Hills Vineyard, one of the first commercial vineyards in the Walla Walla Valley. Currently the fruit is contracted out so the winery continues to focus on his own original three estate vineyards. Eleanor Vineyard, on a southwestern slope, sits on glacial loess soils. Octave Vineyard and Sanitella Vineyard reside on fractured basalt. Chris Banek oversees the three vineyards.

WINES - The winery concentrates on Bordeaux varieties and focuses on balance and depth to create wines that are harmonious pairing partners at the table.

🔴 **Walla Walla Valley Eleanor Estate Red Wine 2021** ● 1,378 cases; 68 $ - 🍷 - Aged 18 months in French oak (38% new). Fruit from all three estate vineyards, it's composed of Cabernet Sauvignon (60%), Cabernet Franc (16%), Malbec (15%), and Merlot (9%). An impeccable blend, it showcases a vibrant and well balanced core of cherry and plums dappled with cocoa and minerals.

Walla Walla Valley Red Label Cabernet Sauvignon 2021 ● 1,194 cases; 48 $ - 🍷 - Aged 18 months in French oak (30% new). This rousing cavalcade of juicy red fruit leads with cherries and raspberries.

Walla Walla Valley Sanitella Vineyard Estate Rosé 2023 ◐ 400 cases; 38 $ - 🍷 - The very pale salmon color suitably conveys an easygoing sipper that gives off refreshing flavors of watermelon and strawberries. A balanced and clean palate pleaser.

---

acres 25 - cases 3,800
Fertilizers compost, organic fertilizer
Plant protection sulfur, synthetic pesticides
Weed control mechanical, manual
Yeasts spontaneous fermentation
Grapes 100% owned
Certification none

MILTON-FREEWATER

CAYUSE VINEYARDS & BIONIC WINES

53863 Highway 332 - tel. (509) 526-0686
www.bionicwines.com - hello@cayusevineyards.com

PEOPLE - In 1997, Champagne native Cristophe Baron began planting vines in the Walla Walla Valley. He was first in the region to farm according to biodynamic principles and obtain certification. Baron's determination resulted in highly lauded award-winning wines and combined with his advocacy for the region, drew considerable attention to the area. In 2024 Baron was named Honorary Vintner for the Auction of Washington Wines in acknowledgement of his efforts.

VINEYARDS - When Baron first saw the property, its large stones covering the ground reminded him of the galets (rolled pebbles) in the Rhône region of France. Though the vineyard is no longer certified biodynamic, Baron says practices remain the same. The Hors Categorie vineyard has a 60 degree slope that necessitates farming with a winch. Baron also owns Horsepower Vineyards, famous for the draft horses that tend the land (see separate entry).

WINES - These standout wines, known for their characteristic smokiness and savoriness, are built for the long haul.

🔴 **Walla Walla Valley Hors Categorie Syrah 2021** SLOW WINE ● 291 cases; 280 $ - 🛢 - Offers aromas of leather and smoked meats that lead to a range of complex flavors. Blueberry, bacon and dark chocolate collide while wildly lively acidity pulsates before leading to a cooling herbal finish with a kiss of salinity.

Walla Walla Valley Impulsivo Tempranillo 2021 ● 402 cases; 107 $ - 🛢 - Aged 18 months in demi-muids (50% new). A complex wine rich in umami character with tobacco, soy sauce salinity, chocolate and a lengthy lingering mocha finish.

---

acres 54 - cases 8,400
Fertilizers compost, biodynamic compost
Plant protection sulfur, biodynamic preparations, organic
Weed control mechanical
Yeasts spontaneous fermentation
Grapes 100% owned
Certification none

ZILLAH

DINEEN VINEYARDS

2980 Gilbert Road - tel. (208) 928-6538
www.dineenvineyards.com - info@dineenvineyards.com

PEOPLE - Pat and Lanie Dineen purchased an apple orchard in Yakima Valley in 2001 and replanted it to wine grapes. They bought additional land in 2002 for the winery and tasting room. While working in Europe, daughter Marissa enrolled in the enology and viticulture programs at Washington State University and assumed leadership of the family business upon her return in 2020. Patrick Rawn is the vineyard manager. Samantha Mallery joined as winemaker in 2023.

VINEYARDS - Above the Missoula flood zone, the own rooted estate vines grow in silt loam soils and are planted mostly to red varieties (80 percent). The 1,200 foot elevation enables cool air to drain down the south facing slopes. One of the first to adopt the new Sustainable WA program, farming practices include cover crops of cheat grass to reduce the need to fertilize, owl boxes for pest control and beneficial insects dropped by drone to eat mealybugs.

WINES - All wines are handled with minimal intervention to represent the fruit in an elegant style. The 2023 vintage is Mallery's first at Dineen.

Yakima Valley Estate Syrah 2021 ● 200 cases; 42 $ - ⊞ - Whole clusters of Viognier (3%) co-fermented with Syrah in stainless steel. Enthralling fruit roars out of the glass followed by a whisper of smoked meat. The hard to resist combination judiciously balances fruit, acidity and fine grained tannins.

Yakima Valley Estate Semillon 2023 ○ 150 cases; 27 $ - ⊚ - Fermented and aged seven months sur lie in neutral French oak puncheons. The wine has some textural oomph. It offers apples, apricots, pear and honeysuckle and then finishes off with classic beeswax character.

Yakima Valley Estate Condriesque White Rhone Blend 2023 ○ 200 cases; 27 $ - ⊚ - Aged sur lie in neutral barriques for six months. This ode to the acclaimed French Rhône white, Condrieu, marries equal parts Viognier and Roussanne. A vivacious white, it flaunts peach and apricot and apricot tart with a bit of almond.

acres 76 - cases 2,500
Fertilizers compost, cover crops, organic fertilizer, synthetic fertilizer
Plant protection sulfur, synthetic pesticides, organic
Weed control mechanical, manual
Yeasts commercial cultured yeasts
Grapes 100% owned
Certification none

BENTON CITY

DOMAINE MAGDALENA

Benton City - 53222 N Sunset Road - tel. (509) 942-4204
www.domainemagdalena.com -

 Showcasing Red Mountain terroir in a fully biodynamic process is a top priority.

PEOPLE - As boutique and artisanal as one can get, this family run winery makes only Cabernet Sauvignon. It's the project of Maggie Hedges— and her husband Christophe. Maggie married into Christophe's winemaker family. The family owns Hedges Family Estate (see separate listing). The couple opted to spend their honeymoon budget planting their vines in 2005 and in 2014 produced their first vintage. Christophe's sister, Sarah Hedges Goedhart (the winemaker at Hedges) makes the wines.

VINEYARDS - The vineyard was certified organic and biodynamic in 2011. It is planted with own rooted Cabernet Sauvignon vines (clones 2, 4, 6, and 8) in high density blocks (at 5'x5' spacing) on vertical shoots and single cordon trained vines. Organic manure comes from local, certified organic dairy farms. They also grow locust trees, native wildflowers and sage and cultivate a near wild ecosystem.

WINES - There is a real clarity to the fruit profile that showcases balanced flavors and textures in spades—the priority is clearly on purity and precision of fruit. Oak use is restrained.

Red Mountain Cabernet Sauvignon 2019 ● 640 cases; 46 $ - ⊞ - Aged 16 months in French oak barrels (20% new). A clonal selection of clones 2 and 4. Evokes aromas and flavors of blackberry, blueberry, incense, black plum, black olive and cinnamon. Layers of fine grained tannin and structure give this wine a very sensual mouthfeel, a beautiful softness and persistent length.

Red Mountain Li'l Mag 2019 ● 50 cases; 34 $ - ⊞ - Aged seven months in French oak. Pure expression of bright ripe raspberries and mulberry notes. A low alcohol wine (11%), it's a delicate, easy going Cabernet even a Pinot Noir drinker might like. It possesses structure, but the tannins are silky and gentle. A focused Cabernet Sauvignon.

acres 4 - cases 690
Fertilizers compost, biodynamic compost, organic fertilizer
Plant protection sulfur, biodynamic preparations, organic
Weed control mechanical
Yeasts spontaneous fermentation
Grapes 100% owned
Certification biodynamic, organic

LYLE

DOMAINE POUILLON

170 Lyle-Snowden Road - tel. (509) 365-2795
www.domainepouillon.com - winery@domainepouillon.com

PEOPLE - In 2005, Alexis and Juliet Pouillon bought an abandoned alfalfa field 1,000 feet above the Columbia River in the rugged and windy Columbia Gorge AVA and set about establishing their small family winery. In November 2023, the couple opened the Domaine Pouillon Wine Bistro just four miles away, adjacent to the Columbia River. Wine tasting is available as are wines by the glass or bottle, and an expanded food menu.

VINEYARDS - In 2007, they planted Rhône varieties Marsanne, Roussanne, Viognier and Syrah. Vine material came from Paso Robles based Tablas Creek, due to their connection to Chateau de Beaucastel in Châteauneuf-du-Pape, where Alexis interned. Originally certified biodynamic, they switched to organic certification in 2022. They use compost teas and cover crops of clover and vetch help facilitate a healthy ecosystem. Some wines, not featured here, may be grown with herbicide.

WINES - Winemaking starts with a pied de cuve actively fermenting when the grapes are picked. The desire is to make something subtle and reflect the vintage.

⊙ Columbia Gorge Estate Syrah 2021 SLOW WINE ● 120 cases; 54 $ - 🍷 - The young wine rewards those who give it time to breath with enticing aromas of smoked meats and herbs along with captivating flavors of black pepper, currants, and plums enrobed in velvety tannins.

Columbia Gorge Pet-Nat of Pinot Noir 2023 ⊙ 178 cases; 31 $ - 🍷 - This clean, refreshing sparkler is a pale salmon hue with delicate fruit flavors in the glass including notes of pear, honeydew melon and almond. Grapes are from Jewett Creek Vineyard in nearby White Salmon and no sulfur is added.

Columbia Gorge Blanc du Moulin 2022 O 120 cases; 45 $ - 🛢 - A blend of Viognier (58%) and Roussanne (42%), each fermented separately in neutral barrel on the lees for 10 months. The harmonious blend offers pears, stone fruit and beeswax.

acres 2.5 - cases 2,200
Fertilizers compost, cover crops, organic fertilizer, synthetic fertilizer
Plant protection sulfur, biodynamic preparations, synthetic pesticides, organic
Weed control mechanical, manual
Yeasts spontaneous fermentation, commercial cultured yeasts
Grapes purchase 80%
Certification some of the vineyards are certified organic

WALLA WALLA

DUSTED VALLEY

1248 Old Milton HWY - tel. (509) 525-1337
www.dustedvalley.com - info@dustedvalley.com

PEOPLE - Wisconsin natives Corey Braunel and brother in law Chad Johnson, along with their wives Cindy and Janet, relocated to Walla Walla to pursue a dream of winery ownership. They established their family winery in 2003, putting their agricultural backgrounds to good use. Consumers may schedule a guided tasting and tour at the winery or visit the nearby tasting room. There are also outposts near Seattle in Woodinville and Edmonds.

VINEYARDS - There are three estates. The Sconni Block is on the Washington side of the Walla Walla Valley AVA adjacent to the winery. Soil is composed of silt loam above Missoula flood deposits. On the Oregon side of the valley, high elevation (1,000-1,430 feet) Southwind Vineyard is cobbly loam. Stoney Vine Vineyard in the Rocks District of Milton Freewater AVA is covered with cobblestones. (Some wines, not featured here, may be grown with herbicide.)

WINES - The ageworthy wines are of palate staining intensity. The oak program utilizes barrels not only from France but also from Wisconsin in a nod to the owners' roots.

⊙ Walla Walla Valley Sconni Block Estate BFM 2021 ● 175 cases; 55 $ - 🛢 - A blend of Merlot (66%), Cabernet Sauvignon (28%), and Petit Verdot (6%) is made to "Blow your Freaking Mind"! It leads with appealing aromatics of maraschino cherry, amaretto, high toned fruits and pencil lead. On the palate, bright cherry and blue fruits meet velvety lushness.

Walla Walla Valley Sconni Block Estate Vineyard Ramblin' Rosé Red Blend 2023 ⊙ 175 cases; 34 $ - 🍷 - A lively field blend that offers fresh watermelon and strawberry with an appealing chalky/mineral textural nuance backed by lingering acidity.

Walla Walla Valley Southwind Estate Vineyard Cabernet Franc 2021 ● 250 cases; 45 $ - 🛢 - Cab Franc typicity gushes from the glass starting with aromas of green pepper. Flavors of cocoa join raspberries and pomegranate wrapped up in dusty tannins balanced by acidity.

acres 55 - cases 6,000
Fertilizers compost, organic fertilizer
Plant protection sulfur, synthetic pesticides, organic
Weed control mechanical, manual
Yeasts spontaneous fermentation
Grapes purchase 50%
Certification none

WALLA WALLA

FOUNDRY VINEYARDS

1111 Abadie Street - tel. (509) 529-0736
www.foundryvineyards.com - info@foundryvineyards.com

PEOPLE - One of the few organic producers in Walla Walla, siblings Jay and Lisa Anderson operate the winery their parents established in 1998. Jay is Winemaker and Creative Director while Lisa is General Manager. The tasting room is also a renowned art gallery. All wines released since 2023 showcase organic grapes. In 2024 they closed their satellite tasting room in Seattle. Their other label is Pet Project (see separate listing).

VINEYARDS - In 2020 their estate Stonemarker Vineyard was the first in the Walla Walla AVA to be certified organic. Unfortunately, it's anticipated that the vineyard won't produce a crop in the 2024 vintage due to considerable damage from a bitter winter freeze. Grapes are also purchased from certified organic sites including Arete Vineyard, Hedges Family Estate, Paradisos del Sol, Red Boar Vineyard and Pear Ridge Vineyard.

WINES - From experimental skin contact wines to serious single vineyard bottlings, the wines highlight creativity and low intervention.

Red Mountain Hedges Cabernet Franc 2021 SLOW WINE
● 125 cases; 44 $ - ⓑ - The grapes are from a vineyard that is both certified organic and biodynamic. This heart pounding wine charms with flavors of strawberry crumble, baking spice and caramel. It's lovely.

Columbia Valley Conley Vineyard Chardonnay 2022 O
150 cases; 35 $ - ⊞ - The wine spent two years in neutral oak and 15% new American oak, and was blended with a small amount of the 2023 vintage to add freshness. It offers a nose of golden delicious apple with baked pear and ginger on the palate.

acres 3.5 - cases 1,500
Fertilizers compost, manure
Plant protection biodynamic preparations, organic
Weed control mechanical
Yeasts spontaneous fermentation
Grapes purchase 90%
Certification organic, some of the vineyards are certified biodynamic

MANSON

HARD ROW TO HOE VINEYARDS

300 Ivan Morse Road - tel. (509) 687-3000
www.hardrow.com - jumpintheboat@hardrow.com

PEOPLE - Judy and Don Phelps established their family winery on the north shore of Lake Chelan in 2004, five years before the Columbia Valley subregion was designated an AVA. With environmental backgrounds, they committed to farm the land responsibly and were the first in the area to be Salmon-Safe and LIVE certified. In 2024 they applied for organic certification. Julian Shaver is managing partner and head winemaker. A satellite tasting room is in Leavenworth, Washington.

VINEYARDS - The three estate vineyards are planted to fourteen varieties. Glacial Gravel Vineyard surrounds the tasting room. The southwest facing hillside is above the Missoula flood plain and composed of sandy loam, gravel and layers of volcanic pumice that reduce the need for irrigation. Syrah vines are head trained to better enable tending by hand and facilitate air flow to alleviate mildew pressure. Some wines, not featured here, may be grown with herbicide.

WINES - Single vineyard, single varietal wines that express fruit. The estate wines undergo spontaneous fermentation.

Lake Chelan Burning Desire Estate Cabernet Franc 2021 ● 166 cases; 59 $ - ⊞ - An enchantingly hedonistic combination of savories and fruits featuring smoked meats, cocoa, and dark plum, with a swath of fine grained tannins and a lingering finish. A dazzling wine.

Lake Chelan Estate Syrah 2021 ● 176 cases; 44 $ - ⊞ - A lively chorus of fruit and spice sings with tamarind and brambly fruit leading the way while tobacco and pepper hum in the background. Mouth tingling acidity accompanies a lingering finish.

Lake Chelan Glacial Gravels Vineyard Sandstone Riesling 2023 O 105 cases; 34 $ - ⓑ - Aged eight months in a sandstone jar. Bright and lifted flavors of pear, white peach and pineapple coarse across the tongue while a bit of residual sugar nicely balances the acidity. The lingering finish leaves behind a bit of chalky minerality.

acres 20 - cases 4,000
Fertilizers compost, manure, organic fertilizer
Plant protection sulfur, copper, organic
Weed control mechanical, manual
Yeasts spontaneous fermentation, commercial cultured yeasts
Grapes purchase 30%
Certification converting to organic

BENTON CITY

HEDGES FAMILY ESTATE

53511 N Sunset Road - tel. (509) 588-3155
www.hedgesfamilyestate.com - info@hedgesfamilyestate.com

PEOPLE - Before they became acclaimed Red Mountain pioneers, Tom and Anne-Marie Hedges (a native of Champagne) started American Wine Trade, brokering West Coast wines all over the world. In 1989 they purchased their own 50 acres in the new Red Mountain region and started their winery in 2001. Today their son Christophe Hedges manages sales. Their daughter Sarah Goedhart is director of winemaking and operations. Kayla Braich manages the vineyards.

VINEYARDS - They committed to both organic and biodynamic farming and certification on their estate wines early on. High winds and cold winters help reduce pest pressure. They do minimal mowing and use only organic approved products and biodynamic preparations to combat pests and mildew. They release beneficial insects to increase biodiversity. They also purchase fruit from certified organic growers for some of their non-estate wines.

WINES - The wines are complex and sturdy with good extraction and well suited to aging.

Red Mountain La Haute Cuvée Cabernet Sauvignon 2019 ● Cabernet Sauvignon; 650 cases; 75 $ - Aged 27 months in French and American oak (78% new). Added to the blend: Merlot and Petit Verdot (3.5% each). Aromas of clove, blueberry muffin, vanilla bean and black currant. A wine of great structure with black cherry, raspberry, black sesame seed and plum. Ageworthy.

Red Mountain Descendants Liégeois Dupont Syrah 2019 ● 736 cases; 40 $ - Aged 19 months in American and French oak (42% new). Aromas of blackberry, iron, violet and damp earth. Palate is robust with black plum, blackberry, orange rind and graphite.

Red Mountain Red Blend 2022 ● 8,500 cases; 30 $ - Aged 14 months in American and French oak (49% new). A blend of Cabernet Sauvignon (60%), Merlot (29%) and more. Aromas of spiced red currant, pumpkin pie and plum supported by flavors of red cherry, tobacco leaf, granite and cocoa.

acres 117 - cases 60,000
Fertilizers compost, cover crops, manure, organic fertilizer
Plant protection sulfur, biodynamic preparations, synthetic pesticides, organic
Weed control animal grazing, mechanical, manual
Yeasts spontaneous fermentation, selected indigenous yeasts, commercial cultured yeasts
Grapes purchase 30%
Certification some vineyards are certified organic or biodynamic

MILTON FREEWATER

HORSEPOWER VINEYARDS

53863 Highway 332 - tel. (509) 526-0686
www.horsepowervineyards.com - hello@bionicwines.com

PEOPLE - In 1997, the now renowned vintner Christophe Baron bought land in the Walla Walla Valley. In 2002, he was first in the area to implement biodynamic practices (initially being certified) including integrating animals into the farm. In 2008, inspired by traditions in his family's Champagne vineyards, Baron started using Belgian Percheron draft horses to till the high density vines. In 2021, long time assistant, Cal Poly educated Elizabeth Bourcier, was promoted to resident vigneronne.

VINEYARDS - The four, tiny estate vineyards—Sur Echalas, The Tribe, High Contrast and Fiddleneck—range in size from two to three acres each. Planted primarily to Syrah and Grenache, the vines are planted "sur echalas" (one vine per stake) with three feet between them, allowing them to achieve ripeness without off the charts levels of alcohol. Fiddleneck Vineyard is named after a flowering plant that grows in the area. Baron also owns Cayuse/Bionic Wines (see separate entry) and a Champagne label.

WINES - The unique character of the terroir is revealed through an exciting array of lively and distinct wines that offer savory/meaty and saline qualities. No new oak is used. The controversial wines are highly sought after.

Walla Walla Valley Fiddleneck Vineyard Grenache 2021 SLOW WINE ● 276 cases; 133 $ - A boldly expressive wine featuring a hedonistic combination of smoked meat (speck), chocolate and leather all wrapped up in velvety tannins and balanced by mouthwatering acidity. A memorable sip best described with a trail of exclamation points!!!

Walla Walla Valley The Tribe Vineyard Syrah 2021 ● 556 cases; 133 $ - The vineyard's telltale smoky meatiness leaps out of the glass. The intriguing wine leads with savory notes of tobacco, cured meats and bacon fat accompanied by red plum and pulsing acidity.

acres 18 - cases 1,880
Fertilizers compost, biodynamic compost
Plant protection sulfur, biodynamic preparations, organic
Weed control mechanical
Yeasts spontaneous fermentation
Grapes 100% owned
Certification none

UNDERWOOD

LOOP DE LOOP

541 Kramer Road - tel. (503) 298-9320
www.loopdeloopvintner.com - loopdeloopwines@gmail.com

PEOPLE - Founded by Julia and Scott Gulstine, the label focuses on high altitude, vintage specific wines. In the process of creating Loop de Loop, Julia has worked closely with Mimi Casteel, a mentorship that has influenced her focus on soil revitalization. Her low intervention winemaking and fluid approach allow her to guide the fruit and fermentations in a natural, expressive way that captures the characteristics of the unique sites.

VINEYARDS - Their Light Anthology estate sits at 1,250-1,350 feet on Underwood Mountain, on volcanic, ashy sandy loam soil on a 33 degree southeastern slope. They farm using regenerative practices, using diverse cover crops and native plantings, dry farming and incorporating compost teas and fish fertilizer. The site produces fruit with bright, focused, lithe, mineral personality. They also buy fruit from local growers.

WINES - The wines encapsulate the energetic, yet thoughtful approach in both the vineyard and cellar, full of structure, good acidity and finesse.

Columbia Gorge Light Anthology Vineyard Pinot Noir 2022 ● 50 cases; 50 $ - Partial whole cluster (35%). Perfumed notes of forest floor, rose petals and red fruit. Cranberry, tart red cherry and orange zest are highlighted with a bit of bergamot. Fine minerality and umami on the finish.

Columbia Gorge Light Anthology Vineyard Grüner Veltliner 2022 ○ 75 cases; 30 $ - Picked in two separate passes, two weeks apart. Overvintaged rendition highlights the minerality and savoriness. Ripe papaya, citrus marmalade, shitake mushroom, wet stone and pine forest floor. Velvety texture.

Columbia Gorge Light Anthology Vineyard Chardonnay 2021 ○ 50 cases; 35 $ - Aged 20 months on the lees after 12 hours on skins. A somewhat austere Chardonnay with pronounced aromatics of jasmine, beeswax, lemon and chamomile. Mouthwatering salinity, dry savory finish.

acres 9 - cases 4,500
Fertilizers compost, cover crops, manure, organic fertilizer
Plant protection synthetic pesticides, organic
Weed control none, n/a
Yeasts spontaneous fermentation
Grapes purchase 65%
Certification none

LYLE

LUSHINGTON WINES

170 Lyle-Snowden Road - tel. (804) 986-8476
www.lushingtonwines.com - lushingtonwine@gmail.com

PEOPLE - Teddi Fuller's work in wine took her from California to New Zealand and Australia before she landed in the Columbia Gorge. It was there as assistant winemaker at Domaine Pouillon, a role she maintains, that she worked with fruit from Hi Hill Vineyard. When an opportunity to lease the site arose, Fuller took it, and launched her own brand in 2021. With extremely limited production, wines are primarily available via the winery website.

VINEYARDS - The estate was planted in 1978 at an elevation of 1,880 feet in reddish volcanic soil on a south facing slope. Fuller farms the site using only organic approved materials. The locale's high acid Riesling and Pinot Noir (Roederer clone) are particularly suited to sparkling wine. Pinot Meunier was planted in 2019 and picked for its first bottling in 2023. Fuller also purchases Pinot Noir from nearby White Salmon Vineyard.

WINES - Fuller creates small batches of stylistically varied wines that are moderate in alcohol. Sparkling wines are meticulously hand riddled and disgorged.

TOP Columbia Gorge Hi Hill Vineyard Blanc de Noirs 2022 38 cases; 42 $ - Whole cluster pressed and fermented in neutral barrels with 16 months of tirage, hand riddled and disgorged. This delightful traditional method wine with a fine string of pearls is light and quaffable, offering honeydew melon and leesy complexity on the finish.

Columbia Gorge White Salmon Vineyard Pinot Noir 2022 ● 50 cases; 40 $ - Foot trod first, then gently pressed. An appealing example of the variety, showcasing fruity raciness with flavors of bright cherry and ripe blackberry.

Columbia Gorge Hi Hill Vineyard Rosé 2023 **40 cases;** 34 $ - A blend of Pinot Noir (75%) and Pinot Meunier (25%). Has an extremely pale tint. It saturates the palate with textural momentum accompanying flavors of star fruit, hibiscus and a kiss of lip tingling acidity.

acres 3 - cases 250
Fertilizers compost, biodynamic compost, cover crops, organic fertilizer
Plant protection sulfur, organic
Weed control mechanical, manual
Yeasts selected indigenous yeasts, commercial cultured yeasts
Grapes purchase 20%
Certification none

WASHINGTON

ZILLAH

PARADISOS DEL SOL WINERY & ORGANIC VINEYARD

3230 Highland Drive - tel. (509) 829-9000
www.paradisosdelsol.com - info@paradisosdelsol.com

PEOPLE - Paul Vandenberg, natural winegrower (formerly with Badger Mountain) and Barbara Sherman, president, started at this location in 2003—a new property where they could start from scratch with new cultivars, a new trellis system and a new irrigation system. The wines as well as the vines are certified organic and sulfite free. In addition, they list wine ingredients on their bottles.

VINEYARDS - Their certified organic estate sits on a ridge in the Yakima Valley with great air movement and high intensity sunlight at 1,000 feet elevation in a desert. They grow 15 varieties. The soil is a deep silt loam slack water deposit of the ice age Missoula Floods.

WINES - Vandenberg's hands off winemaking and aging practices emphasize long aging in barrel and in bottle before release.

Rattlesnake Hills Chenin Blanc Sève 2018 ○ 95 cases; 24 $ - ⊞ - Aged 11 months on lees in neutral oak. Barrel fermented. Aromas of lemon, white peach. Flavors of yellow apple, peach with braced acidity. Wine has good dimension and is well developed.

Rattlesnake Hills Oyster White Semillon 2017 ○ 96 cases; 24 $ - ⊞ - Aged in neutral oak. Barrel fermented. Aromas of honeyed yellow peach, lemon and yellow apple. Round, mature with dried apple and hay with depth and structure. Drink now.

Rattlesnake Hills Rojo Paradisos Red Blend 2014 ● 412 cases; 24 $ - ⊞ - Aged two years in neutral oak. Cabernet Sauvignon and Cabernet Franc with Sangiovese and Zinfandel. Robust aromas of spiced plum, blackberry, cranberry tea and cherry. Dark cherry, butterscotch, soy sauce, hazelnuts and mushrooms from bottle age.

acres 6 - cases 1,000
Fertilizers compost
Plant protection none
Weed control animal grazing
Yeasts spontaneous fermentation
Grapes 100% owned
Certification organic

WALLA WALLA

PEPPERBRIDGE WINERY

Washington - 1704 J B George Road - tel. (509) 525-6502
www.pepperbridge.com - info@pepperbridge.com

PEOPLE - Founded in 1998, its roots in the region run deep and spread across three owners. Norm Mckibben has been a cornerstone of Walla Walla region. since 1985. Co-owner and founding winemaker Jean-François Pellet and the Murphy family rounds out the ownership circle. Together they have elevated the Walla Walla Valley with innovation and quality benchmarks, including a gravity flow winery constructed in 2000. They were named one of Wine & Spirits Top 100 Wineries in 2021.

VINEYARDS - Pepper Bridge Vineyard began in 1991 and is primarily Walla Walla silt loam soil. Additional sites include Seven Hills Vineyards (1981) and Octave Vineyard (2007). Seven Hills has been named a top 10 vineyard in the world by Wine & Spirits magazine. Cover crop supports beneficial insects.

WINES - Wines are very structured, extracted and powerful. The winemaking approach optimized for long aging.

TOP Walla Walla Valley Red Blend Seven Hills 2021 ● 509 cases; 75 $ - ⊞ - Aged 19 months in oak (46% new). A Cab based blend (66%). Aromas of espresso, black plum, cardamom and vanilla bean. Black cherry, raspberry, mulberry and nutmeg on the palate. Ageworthy.

Walla Walla Valley Red Blend Pepper Bridge Vineyard 2021 ● 511 cases; 75 $ - ⊞ - Aged 20 months in oak (50% new). The blend is Merlot (34%), Malbec (33%), Cabernet Sauvignon (24%) and Petit Verdot (9%). Aromas of candied red cherry, plum and underbrush. A lifted midpalate with pomegranate and cherry flavors.

Walla Walla Valley Trine 2021 ● 719 cases; 75 $ - ⊞ - Aged 19 months in barrel (43% new). Cabernet Franc (42%) and Cabernet Sauvignon (36%) with Merlot (13%), Malbec (6%), Petit Verdot (3%). Nose of cranberry, plum and white pepper and dried herbs. Red cherry and baking spice on the palate.

acres 361 - cases 5,000
Fertilizers compost, cover crops, organic fertilizer
Plant protection sulfur, copper, organic
Weed control mechanical
Yeasts selected indigenous yeasts
Grapes 100% owned
Certification none

WALLA WALLA

PÉT PROJECT

1111 Abadie Street - tel. (509) 529-0313
www.petprojectwines.com - jay@petprojectwines.com

PEOPLE - Walla Walla native Jay Anderson founded this sister winery to Foundry Vineyards in 2019 to produce natural, sparkling wines, a departure from the still wines he makes for Foundry. His focus here is on low intervention, ancestral method sparklers, crafted with a diverse range of grapes, such as Muscat Ottonel, and only certified organic wine grapes. Wines are available at the Foundry Vineyards tasting room (see separate entry).

VINEYARDS - The estate vineyard, Stonemarker, earned organic certification in 2020 making it the only organic vineyard in Walla Walla at the time. Unfortunately, it's anticipated that the site won't produce a crop in 2024 due to damage from a bitter winter freeze. Grapes are also purchased from certified organic sites including Arete and Conley Vineyards in the Columbia Valley, Red Boar Vineyard in Walla Walla and Pear Ridge Vineyard in the Columbia Gorge.

WINES - Jay is committed to crafting sparkling wines, using only certified organic wine grapes, in order to create something complex.

Columbia Gorge Pear Ridge Vineyard Perpetual Cuvee 240 cases; 36 $ - A blend of Pinot Noir (52%) and Chardonnay (48%). This multi-vintage solera style wine is batch disgorged. In other words, after one batch sells out, the next is bottled. Its delicate pearls tickle the tongue with flavors of pear, almond and brioche. It's a polished sparkler with a lovely lingering finish.
Columbia Gorge Pear/Riesling Co-Ferment 90 cases; 28 $ - A blend of d'Anjou pear (60%) and Riesling (40%). It ferments in a pressure tank and is then bottled via counter pressure bottle filler. The delicate mélange is reminiscent of cream soda mingling with baked fruit, a refreshing quaff at just 9.5% ABV.

acres 3.5 - cases 600
Fertilizers compost, manure
Plant protection sulfur, biodynamic preparations, organic
Weed control mechanical
Yeasts spontaneous fermentation
Grapes purchase 90%
Certification organic

UNDERWOOD

SAVAGE GRACE

442 Kramer Road - tel. (206) 920-4206
www.savagegracewines.com - michael@savagegracewines.com

PEOPLE - Winemaker Michael Savage started his label in 2011 with Cabernet Franc. His enology background is infused with his artistic perspective as a musician, influencing the creative and exploratory paths he takes throughout the vinification process. Savage has prioritized the health of the Underwood Mountain Vineyard site, working to incorporate biodiversity throughout.

VINEYARDS - Certified organic in 2022, the estate provides a third of the fruit. The time and energy invested in soil health and regenerative practices are reflected in the health of the vines and the quality of fruit. Their newly planted vines, such as Chardonnay and Gamay, flourish while the old vine Gruner Veltliner is producing more consistent sized berries. He also buys fruit from local growers.

WINES - Clean minimal intervention wines that showcase various Washington sites through single varietals made in a Loire Valley style.

Oak Ridge Skin-Contact Gewürztraminer 2022 SLOW WINE 140 cases; 42 $ - Destemmed, whole berry fermented on the skins for 25 days. Full of fragrant orange blossom and jasmine, ripe apricot and a bit of spice characteristic. Refreshing, complex and clean with fine tannins on the finish.
Underwood Mountain Vineyard Grüner Veltliner 2022 200 cases; 42 $ - Whole cluster pressed with a small amount of skin contact. Complex notes of white pepper, honey, and lime zest acidity with refreshing salinity and wet stone.
Yakima Valley 'Cru Carbonic' Cabernet Franc 2023 125 cases; 35 $ - Whole cluster, carbonic maceration, pressed after three weeks. Juicy red raspberry grounded in earthy notes with a bit of young green pepper. The long finish and fine tannins balance the poppy fruit characteristics.

acres 17 - cases 3,500
Fertilizers compost, cover crops, organic fertilizer
Plant protection sulfur, organic
Weed control manual
Yeasts spontaneous fermentation
Grapes purchase 70%
Certification some of the vineyards are certified organic

LYLE

SYNCLINE

111 Balch Road - tel. (509) 365-4361
www.synclinewine.com - info@synclinewine.com

PEOPLE - After starting their family winery in 1998, James and Poppie Mantone purchased an old farm on fallow land and set to work transforming the property using sustainable practices. Based in the ruggedly wild landscape of the Columbia Gorge, they played a role in the AVA's formation in 2004. Guests to the site enjoy tasting in a beautiful outdoor setting adjacent to vines. An employee garden provides team members with fresh produce.

VINEYARDS - The estate is at 340 feet of elevation and grows Gruner Veltliner, Syrah and Viognier. In 2023 they had their first harvest of Furmint and planted new Grenache vines. James tends the land with Miguel Flores, incorporating compost and other eco-friendly practices. They purchase half the grapes from other growers, two of which they've convinced to go herbicide free. Some wines, not featured here, may be grown with herbicide.

WINES - Working with some thrillingly uncommon varieties, James crafts wines that are a little edgy.

Columbia Gorge Gamay Noir 2022 SLOW WINE ● 925 cases; 45 $ - Fermentation for the first picking begins with 60-80% of the grapes undergoing carbonic maceration. Then, a second picking is added, switching to a traditional fermentation for more ripeness and structure. Deep dark fruits meet an herbaceous character from the stems, accompanied by notes of slate. It's a fantastic expression of the site.

Columbia Gorge Steep Creek Ranch Red Blend 2021 ● 250 cases; 65 $ - A unique blend of Mondeuse (53%), Gamay (25%), Syrah (11%) and Grenache (11%). It's an irresistible black pepper, meaty, wild kind of wine with an olive brine finish and fine grained tannins.

Columbia Gorge Furmint 2023 ○ 45 cases; 40 $ - An exciting new variety in the lineup, aged in neutral barrels and bottled as a dry wine. Though it has a hushed nose, the wine is incredibly lively and energetic, loaded with zingy lemon.

acres 19 - cases 5,000
Fertilizers compost, manure
Plant protection sulfur, biodynamic preparations, organic
Weed control mechanical
Yeasts spontaneous fermentation
Grapes purchase 50%
Certification none

RICHLAND

TAGARIS WINERY $

844 Tulip Lane - tel. (509) 628-1619
www.tagariswines.com - info@tagariswines.com

PEOPLE - Michael Taggares founded Tagaris Winery in 1987. The winery name honors the proper Greek spelling of the family name whose members descend from the Greek royal family—and who first began growing grapes in the 15th century. The American winery has three generations of Columbia Valley grape growers. Winemaker Frank Roth has been at the helm for over 16 years. The winery is also certified organic so they can and do produce wines certified "Made with Organic Grapes."

VINEYARDS - The estate has 28 varieties on 750 acres of prime vineyard (400 organic acres used for Tagaris) in the Wahluke Slope region of the Columbia Valley. They sell grapes and bulk wine to other wineries. Most of their blocks are certified organic. Other certifications include Glyphosate Residue Free and Global G.A.P certified (a food safety standard). They use pollinators in the vines. Tagaris brand produces around 7000 cases per vintage and is all estate fruit.

WINES - Bright fresh fruit with clarity and precision is the main focus for their organically grown wines.

Columbia Valley Cote de la Rivière Red Blend 2022 ● 57 cases; 36 $ - The blend is Merlot (63%), Cabernet Sauvignon (23%) and Syrah (14%). Aromas of red plum, grape leaf, peony, and black cherry. The palate is supported by flavors of cherry, bramble berry, damp potting soil, cola nut and cocoa. Balanced acid and tannin integrate nicely in a very clean finish.

Wahluke Slope Syrah 2022 ● 57 cases; 36 $ - Nose of blackberry, sage, dried underbrush and lilac leading to flavors of black plum, boysenberry, crushed granite and traces of molasses. The wine is precise with tight knit skin tannins on the finish.

Washington Tagaris Late Harvest Chenin Blanc Made with Organic Grapes 2023 ● 115 cases; 26 $ - Aromas of candied lemon and honeydew; the palate is racy with white peach, Asian pear and lemon tart; the sweetness aligns well with the acidity for a balanced finish.

acres 750 - cases 34,000
Fertilizers compost, cover crops
Plant protection sulfur, organic
Weed control mechanical, manual
Yeasts commercial cultured yeasts
Grapes 100% owned
Certification organic, some of the vineyards are certified biodynamic

CLE ELUM

UPSIDEDOWN WINES

205 East 1st Street - tel. (541) 436-3851
www.upsidedownwine.com - info@upsidedownwine.com

PEOPLE - Seth and Audrey Kitzke courted in college and that led to marriage. Then they took an even bigger leap, in 2014, launching their own winery. Prior to that, Seth was introduced to agriculture on his family's farm and took on winemaking duties for the family winery, Kitzke Cellars. After living in Seattle, they left the city to take over the family vineyard. Wines are available at their tasting rooms in Cle Elum, Washington and Hood River, Oregon.

VINEYARDS - Dead Poplar Vineyard, the family's estate site, sits at 650 feet in elevation on sandy soils at the end of the Yakima Valley AVA. It has been pesticide and herbicide free since 2015 and they support native flora for biodiversity. High elevation vineyards are also sources for grapes including Konnowac Vineyard (certified organic) at 1,100 feet and LIVE certified Equus vineyard at 1,400 feet. Some wines, not featured here, may be grown with herbicide.

WINES - Seth's winemaking incorporates techniques (including carbonic maceration) to maintain freshness and highlight aromatics in the wines.

Yakima Valley Dead Poplar Vineyard Grenache 2022 ● 90 cases; 54 $ - Partial whole cluster (65%). The result is a compelling, complex wine with aromas of plums and cumin and flavors of darker toned fruit and dusty cocoa.

Columbia Valley Cluster F@*#!! Grenache 2022 ● 222 cases; 35 $ - Carbonic maceration (100%) followed by 10 months in neutral puncheons. A mouth tingling fusion of earthy richness and bright fruit showing flavors of plum, sweet tobacco and tamarind with approachable tannins.

Yakima Valley Konnowac Vineyard Viognier 2022 ○ 90 cases; 45 $ - Aged 10 months on the lees in French oak (30% new), giving it some textural heft. On the palate, it delivers white peach, mango, star fruit and honeycomb striking a lovely balance between fresh and opulent.

---

acres 5 - cases 2,500
Fertilizers compost, cover crops, organic fertilizer
Plant protection sulfur, synthetic pesticides
Weed control manual
Yeasts spontaneous fermentation
Grapes purchase 60%
Certification some of the vineyards are certified organic

YAKIMA

WILRIDGE VINEYARD, WINERY & DISTILLERY

250 Ehler Road - tel. (509) 966-0686
www.wilridgewinery.com - info@wilridgewinery.com

 For his dedication and pioneering vision in promoting the Washington wine industry, trialing under the radar varieties and being certified organic and biodynamic.

PEOPLE - Vintner Paul Beveridge, an attorney by trade, founded the first urban winery in Seattle in 1988 and continues to be a trailblazer in the Washington wine scene. In 2024, he became a mentor in the Northwest Transition to Organic Partnership Program (TOPP). The project aims to serve and grow the organic community by expanding organically grown wine grapes and wines sector and encouraging partners to pursue USDA organic certification.

VINEYARDS - Paul planted his vineyard in 2007, making it the certified first Salmon Safe, organic and biodynamic vineyard in the state. He grows 23 varieties. Chardonnay is his newest and is expected to be made as a 2024 inaugural vintage (thus eliminating the need to buy this from other vineyards). Based in the Naches Heights, the region was awarded AVA status in 2012 due to the petition Paul submitted. Abraham Gonzalez helps oversee vines.

WINES - The terroir driven wines are vibrant, due in part to his devotion to biodynamic farming. He also grows and makes many uncommon varietals-Nebbiolo, and Sagrantino, for example.

Naches Heights Estate Sagrantino 2018 SLOW WINE ● 117 cases; 40 $ - Deep garnet color, a dark and brooding well-structured wine from the first Sagrantino vines in Washington. Entices with a little coffee on the nose. On the palate it offers bramble berries, sweet tobacco and black tea with olive tapenade bringing up the rear.

Naches Heights Wilridge Vineyard Estate Rosé of Nebbiolo 2022 ● 107 cases; 32 $ - A delightfully refreshing wine that offers a bright pop of strawberry and plum sauce with a textured, minerally finish.

---

acres 15 - cases 6,000
Fertilizers biodynamic compost
Plant protection sulfur, biodynamic preparations, organic
Weed control manual
Yeasts spontaneous fermentation
Grapes 100% owned
Certification biodynamic, organic

NEW YORK

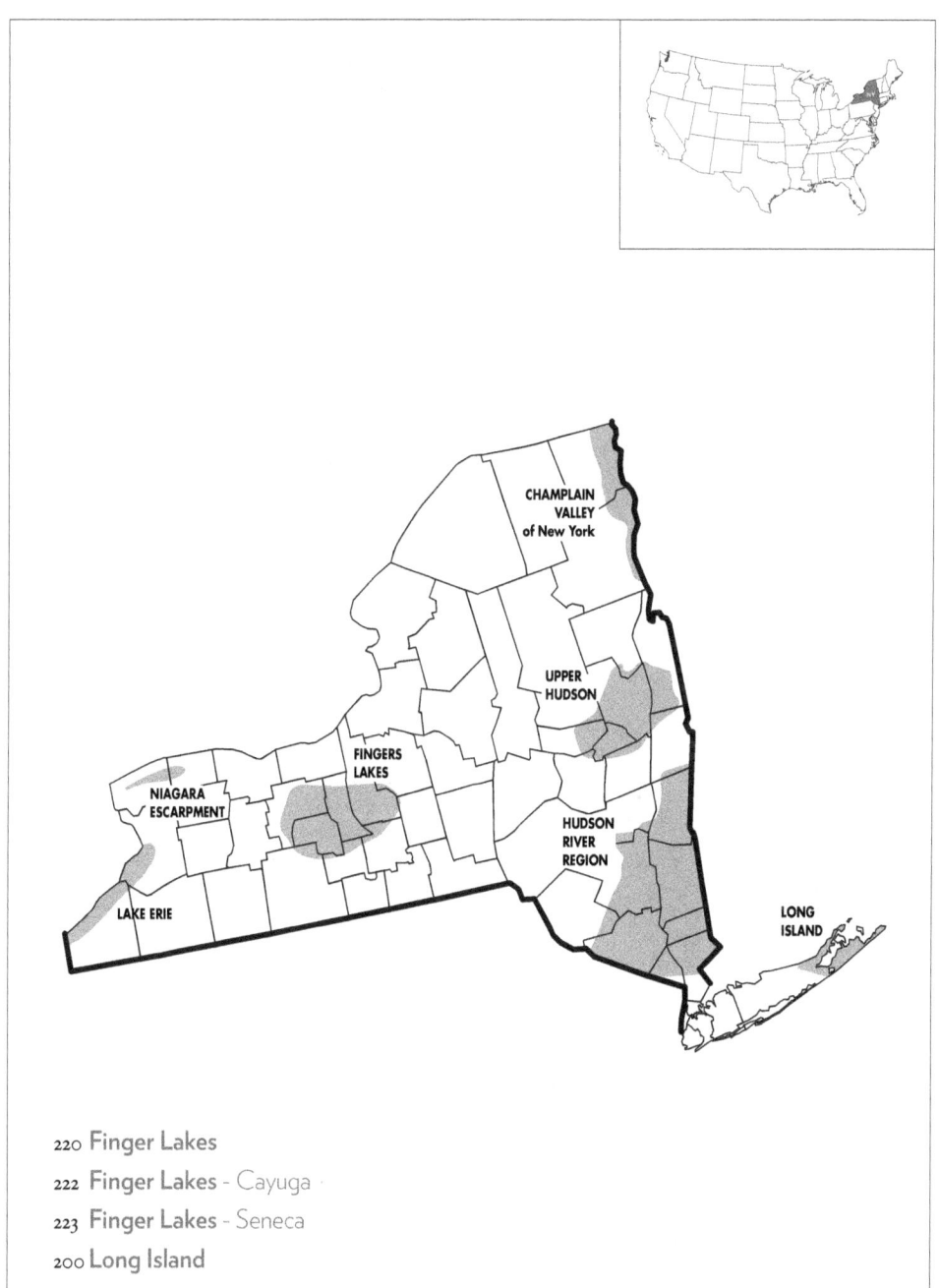

220 **Finger Lakes**
222 **Finger Lakes** - Cayuga
223 **Finger Lakes** - Seneca
200 **Long Island**

FINGER LAKES

HAMMONDSPORT

DR. KONSTANTIN FRANK WINERY

9749 Middle Road - tel. (800) 320-0735
www.drfrankwines.com - info@drfrankwines.com

PEOPLE - The pioneering Dr. Konstantin Frank, the "Father of Vinifera" in the Finger Lakes, revolutionized the industry when he planted the first vinifera—Pinot Noir and Riesling—here in 1958 and opened his winery in 1962. Third and fourth generation Fred and Meaghan Frank continue, celebrating 10 years of their HELM series (honoring Frank family women), growing their sparkling wine program and expanding their Georgian varieties Rkatsiteli and Saperavi.

VINEYARDS - The dry farmed estates (no herbicide) are located on Keuka (70 acres) and Seneca Lakes (65 acres) on steep slopes with high shale content. After 45 years, vineyard manager Eric Volz passed the baton to Jeff Zik and Brien Gardner. They grow 17 vinifera varieties and have some of the oldest Chardonnay, Pinot Noir and Riesling vines in the eastern U.S. They also buy fruit from local growers. Some of the wines, not featured here, may be grown with herbicide.

WINES - The team makes crisp aromatic white wines and rich red wines. Mark Veraguth is the head winemaker. Eric Bauman makes the acclaimed traditional method sparkling wines.

TOP **Finger Lakes Brut 2020** EVERYDAY WINE ○ Chardonnay, Pinot Noir, Pinot Meunier; 800 cases; 30 $ - 100% estate fruit. Three years minimum en tirage. Aromas of fresh green apple, nuanced brioche, and earth. Pure flavors of fresh green candied apple, elegant minerality and a clean finish.

Finger Lakes Margrit Dry Riesling (HELM Series) 2021 ○ 375 cases; 35 $ - Aged aromatics of petrol, stone, and lemon zest. On the palate, it begins with racy acidity of fresh lime, then rounds out to a softer, richer, and zesty palate. Engaging and complex.

Finger Lakes Saperavi 2022 ● 150 cases; 30 $ - 100% estate fruit. Aged 18 months in neutral French oak. Ripe black plum aromas and nuanced spice notes. The palate features concentrated black fruits with expressive herbs and spices. A long plum and vanilla finish.

acres 135 - cases 40,000
Fertilizers compost, cover crops, manure, organic fertilizer
Plant protection sulfur, synthetic pesticides, organic
Weed control mechanical, manual
Yeasts commercial cultured yeasts
Grapes purchase 35%
Certification none

HAMMONDSPORT

HERON HILL WINERY

9301 County Route 76 - tel. (607) 868-4241
www.heronhill.com - info@heronhill.com

PEOPLE - Owners John and Jo Ingle planted their first vineyards in 1972—more than 50 years ago. In 2000 they built an architecturally unique winery and tasting room on Keuka Lake and in 2010 opened a tasting room in a tastefully converted barn on Canandaigua Lake. Jordan Harris took over as winemaker (and COO) in 2020, moving to a more hands off approach. They host music concerts in summer and are expanding distribution to more states.

VINEYARDS - They have three vineyard sites located on Canandaigua and Keuka Lakes. The Ingle Vineyard on Canandaigua is their original homestead vineyard. With more than 50 years of conscious viticulture, they farm sustainably and do not use chemical fertilizers, herbicides or insecticides on the vines. John prefers hand maintenance over machinery. Wildflower gardens and cover crops were added in 2021. They also buy grapes from local growers.

WINES - Low-intervention wines representing what nature provides, with aromatic elegance and freshness that reflect terroir and varietal characteristics.

Finger Lakes Ingle Vineyard Blaufrankisch 2023 ●
150 cases; 40 $ - ⊞ - Extended skin maceration. Aged nine months in neutral French oak. It showcases earthy, spiced black plum aromas and flavors. Finger Lakes Blaufränkisch at its best.
Finger Lakes Ingle Vineyard Riesling 2023 ○ 300 cases; 30 $ - ⎕ - A five block blend from Canandaigua Lake. An elegant wine with notes of spicy ginger, grapefruit, and lime throughout the nose and palate. The finish is long, citrusy. Ageworthy.
Finger Lakes Ingle Vineyard Chardonnay 2023 ○ 350 cases; 30 $ - ⎕⎕ - From 35 year old estate vines. Fermented in two lots—one in stainless steel and one in Claver ceramic stoneware which are then blended in equal proportions. Aromas of guava, melon, and fresh herbs lead to tropical fruit, grapefruit, and lime flavors. Captivating through midpalate and finish.

acres 45 - cases 18,000
Fertilizers compost, cover crops, organic fertilizer
Plant protection sulfur, synthetic pesticides, organic
Weed control mechanical, manual
Yeasts spontaneous fermentation, commercial cultured yeasts
Grapes purchase 30%
Certification none

HAMMONDSPORT

LIVING ROOTS WINE & CO

8560 County Rd 87 - tel. (585) 383-1112
www.livingrootswine.com - info@livingrootswine.com

PEOPLE - A unique, intercontinental winery from husband and wife Seb and Colleen Hardy located in both New York and Australia. He comes from an historic Adelaide Hills wine family, she from Rochester. In the Finger Lakes, they have a tasting room in Rochester, and one on Keuka Lake that is powered by geothermal and solar energy and offers breathtaking lake views.

VINEYARDS - With family owned vineyards in two hemispheres, they work two harvests a year—one in the cool climate Finger Lakes and one in sun drenched Australia. At the Shale Creek estate vineyard overlooking Keuka Lake, they use no synthetic sprays, opting for natural pest control and clover cover crops. They also buy grapes from local growers (including hybrids Aramella, Cayuga, Traminette and Vidal). Some of the wines (not featured here) may be grown with herbicide.

WINES - Creatively made vinifera and hybrid based wines with a touch of whimsical experimentation, ranging from Charmat sparklings and pet nats to Riesling and Cab Franc.

Finger Lakes Shale Creek Chardonnay 2023 ○ 50 cases; 50 $ - ⊞ - Estate fruit. Fermented in old French oak. Fresh red apple and delicate creme fraiche aromas. Creamy mouthfeel with stone fruit flavors. Elegant and delicious.
Finger Lakes Session Sparkling White ○ 786 cases; 22 $ - ⎕ - A blend of native and hybrid varietals (Aromella, Cayuga White and Vidal Blanc) including the native estate grown Elvira (planted in 1945). Matchstick, fruity musk and floral aromatics. Fresh, herbaceous and fruit forward flavors with a stony saline finish.
Finger Lakes Session Gold ◉ 280 cases; 20 $ - ⎕ ⊞ - A blend of hybrids Cayuga White (fermented on Aromella skins) and Vidal Blanc (fermented on its own and Traminette skins). Expressive skin contact aromas of flowers, lychee, and apricot. Flavors of integrated tannins, tart and stone fruit flavors.

acres 13 - cases 4,000
Fertilizers compost, cover crops
Plant protection sulfur, synthetic pesticides
Weed control mechanical, manual
Yeasts spontaneous fermentation, selected indigenous yeasts
Grapes purchase 75%
Certification none

FINGER LAKES
CAYUGA

$ Coin

222 Buttonwood Grove Winery

ROMULUS

BUTTONWOOD GROVE WINERY $

Finger Lakes - 5986 State Route 89 - tel. (607) 869-9760
www.buttonwoodgrove.com - info@buttonwoodgrove.com

PEOPLE - David and Melissa Pittard are celebrating 10 years of operating this estate winery on Cayuga Lake. Dave leads the winegrowing team. Susan Passmore is the head winemaker. In 2024, they launched their new Farm Series line—novel blends of estate vinifera and hybrid grapes, representing the best that the farm can produce. They also have four comfortable lakeside cabins for visitors and host a summer music series on their property.

VINEYARDS - Buttonwood has two vineyard locations. Their 24 acres estate grows classic Finger Lakes vinifera varietals (traditional wine grapes) as well as two disease resistant hybrids that were developed at Cornell. The soils are mostly deep loam and clay with deep seated shale. Two other blocks down the road contain 50 year old plantings of Chardonnay and original plantings of Cayuga White, a hybrid.

WINES - Old World interpretations of classic Finger Lakes varietals and creative interpretations of Cabernet Franc and Riesling that showcase the versatility of these varietals.

TOP Cayuga Lake Sauvignon Blanc 2023 EVERYDAY WINE O 160 cases; 24 $ - 🍷 - Classic grassy and hay aromatics with subtle white grapefruit. Persistent acidity and minerality, lip smacking grapefruit and a bright lime finish.

Cayuga Lake Cabernet Franc Pet-Nat 2023 188 cases; 25 $ - 🍷 - Destemmed and soaked for three hours for color and flavor and then pressed. Cranberry, pomegranate and strawberry aromas with bright acidity and freshness. Produces lots of fizz.

Cayuga Lake The Farm Red 2022 ● Cabernet Franc, Cabernet Sauvignon; 390 cases; 20 $ - 🛢 - Aged 16 months in neutral oak. Both vinifera and hybrids, including Arandell, a Cornell hybrid. Aromas of bright red fruit, fresh herbs, and a touch of earth and oak. On the palate, crunchy red fruit, floral notes, and spice, with light tannins. Best served chilled.

acres 47 - cases 15,000
Fertilizers compost, cover crops, organic fertilizer
Plant protection sulfur, organic
Weed control mechanical
Yeasts spontaneous fermentation, commercial cultured yeasts
Grapes 100% owned
Certification none

OVID

SIX EIGHTY CELLARS

3050 Swick Road - tel. (315) 530-2663 - (917) 348-8258
www.sixeightycellars.com - info@sixeightycellars.com

PEOPLE - Established in 2020, this is a new winery from Buttonwood Grover owners Dave and Melissa Pittard on Cayuga Lake. They are adventurously exploring new directions in both wine grape varieties and winemaking techniques. Winemaker Ian Barry uniquely uses earthenware vessels for both fermentation and aging. In 2023, they opened a contemporary tasting room with expansive panoramic views.

VINEYARDS - In 2023, Dave planted European varieties not commonly grown in the Finger Lakes including Italian varieties—Nebbiolo and Primitivo, the hybrid Soreli— a close relative of Tocai Friulano, as well as Semillon— a native of Bordeaux. They also grow traditional cool climate varieties—Chardonnay, Grüner Veltliner, Pinot Meunier and Pinot Noir.

WINES - Imaginative and creative winemaking. Examples: a pet nat Merlot, a Riesling fermented in a sandstone egg, and a semi-carbonic Cabernet Franc.

🔝 **Cayuga Lake Concrete Diamond Pinot Noir Gewürztraminer Co-ferment 2023** EVERYDAY WINE ● 210 cases; 26 $ - 🏺 - 50/50 coferment of Gewürztraminer and Pinot Noir. Electric red hue. Aromas of spicy, floral sour cherry. Bright, candied fruit flavors of raspberry, sour cherry, cranberry, and rose. Low ABV. Lovely when served chilled.

Cayuga Lake Clay Claver Chenin Blanc 2023 ○ 84 cases; 30 $ - 🏺 - Inaugural vintage. Whole cluster. Aged eight months on lees with stirring. Tropical fruit aromas with stone and gooseberry. Fresh and juicy with nice acidity, balanced sweetness, and a crisp finish.

Cayuga Lake Sandstone Chardonnay 2022 ○ 110 cases; 32 $ - 🏺 - Aged eight months in a 1000L sandstone vessel. Beautiful blend of fruit and savory notes. Aromas of melon, raw honey and a touch of earth, then a round palate of savory herbs and lemon verbena.

---

acres 22 - cases 4,000
Fertilizers compost, cover crops
Plant protection sulfur
Weed control mechanical
Yeasts spontaneous fermentation, selected indigenous yeasts, commercial cultured yeasts
Grapes 100% owned
Certification none

FINGER LAKES
SENECA

 Snail

225 Hermann J. Wiemer Vineyard **Snail**
227 Red Tail Ridge Winery

 Bottle

226 Hillick & Hobbs
227 Silver Thread Vineyard

BURDETT

DAMIANI WINE CELLARS

4704 State Route 414 - tel. (607) 546-5757
www.damianiwinecellars.com - info@damianiwinecellars.com

PEOPLE - In 2003, founders Lou Damiani and Phil Davis set out to create noteworthy red wines from their east Seneca Lake vineyards. Today, with co-owner Glenn Allen, and winemaker Katey Larwood, they make award winning reds, as well as sparkling wine and nuanced whites. Katey's winemaking is vineyard focused—letting the fruit guide decision making. Native yeast fermentation creates refreshing and approachable wines that are lean, bright and lower in alcohol.

VINEYARDS - The two estate vineyards, Damiani and Davis, were planted in 1997 and 1998. West-facing, gravelly loam slopes in a "banana belt" microclimate capture extended sunlight and warmth. The vineyards have been herbicide free for decades, and the team incorporates a hybrid model of organic approved fungicides for disease control. They also buy grapes from local growers.

WINES - Premium wines thoughtfully made from vineyard to cellar. Wines of complexity and nuance, without pretense.

⬤ Seneca Lake Cabernet Sauvignon 2023 ● 300 cases; 33 $ - ⊞ - Estate fruit (64%) blended with purchased grapes. Native fermentation with stem inclusion (5%) and saignée (20%). Deep aromas of black currant, black pepper and tarragon. Highly structured with concentrated black fruit flavors. Excellent.

Seneca Lake Pinot Noir Damiani Vineyard 2022 ● 40 cases; 42 $ - ⓘ - Extended native fermentation with stem inclusion (20%) and saignée (20%) for flavor concentration. Nuanced cherry and purple blossom aromas. Soft tannins and fresh acidity allows the delicate cherry and pomegranate fruit to entice on the palate.

Seneca Lake Little Lotus Flower Sauvignon Blanc 2023 ○ 100 cases; 33 $ - ⊞ - From the Davis vineyard. Whole cluster pressed. Neutral oak with battonage. Delicate tangerine aromas. A dry wine with nuanced tropical notes and a long mineral finish.

acres 33 - cases 7,500
Fertilizers compost, manure
Plant protection sulfur, synthetic pesticides, copper, organic
Weed control mechanical, manual
Yeasts spontaneous fermentation, selected indigenous yeasts, commercial cultured yeasts
Grapes purchase 30%
Certification none

GENEVA

ELEMENT WINERY

Tasting Room: FLX Provisions, 18 Linden Street - tel. (315)730-3083
www.elementwinery.com - info@elementwinery.com

PEOPLE - In 2009, Christopher Bates, a chef, restauranteur and Master Sommelier, and Isabel Bogadtke started their winery to prove that pure, cool climate wines could be produced in the region. They have three brands—Element for single expression varietals with longer élevage; In Our Element for younger expressions and earlier drinking; and the newest, Colloquial (all estate), with small lot, terroir-driven wines. They also offer fine dining at their FLX Table.

VINEYARDS - The Equilibrium vineyard, on the east side of Seneca Lake, had been planted in 2000 to classic Bordeaux and Burgundy varietals, as well as Chardonnay and Syrah. Bates bought it in 2017, adding 10 French varietals, most of which are rarely grown in the region. After three years of yield restricting weather, including hail and frost, these vines are now producing exceptional fruit with few to no inputs. He also buys grapes from local growers.

WINES - Elegant, stunning wines created to redefine the potential of winegrowing in the Finger Lakes.

⬤ Finger Lakes Element Chardonnay 2017 ○ 45 cases; 55 $ - ⓘ - From their Equilibrium estate. Enticing aromas of white peach and clementine. On the palate, yellow apple and Bosc pear with creamy crème fraîche and honeysuckle. Layered elegance.

Finger Lakes In Our Element Can't Stop Won't Stop White 2022 ○ Chardonnay, Riesling; 160 cases; 20 $ - ⓘ - Entry level wine. A unique blend of Chardonnay and Riesling. Fine earth, stone and flint. Young and fresh expression with lemon and apple aromas. Round savory palate with a salty lime finish.

Seneca Lakes Colloquial From Now Forward Red Blend 2020 ● Cabernet Franc, Cabernet Sauvignon, Merlot, Syrah, Grenache; 71 cases; 125 $ - ⓘ - A stunning wine showing Finger Lakes expression of fruit and stone. A blend of Bordeaux and Rhone varieties. Dark fruit aromas with graphite and pencil shavings. Minerality. Black currant and plum on palate.

acres 16 - cases 1,500
Fertilizers compost, cover crops
Plant protection sulfur
Weed control mechanical, manual
Yeasts spontaneous fermentation
Grapes purchase 50%
Certification none

UNION SPRINGS

HEART & HANDS WINE COMPANY

4162 State Route 90 - tel. (315) 889-8500
www.heartandhandswine.com - info@heartandhandswine.com

PEOPLE - Producers Tom and Susan Higgins started their boutique winery in 2010. They make cool climate Chardonnay, Pinot Noir, Riesling and sparkling wines. Recently, they expanded their estate vineyards and launched a new ESO series (estate grown) that focuses on lesser known varieties not typically seen in the Finger Lakes–including Aligote and the Swiss variety Petite Arvine.

VINEYARDS - The estate is situated on a block of limestone bedrock that provides the foundation for producing exceptional Pinot Noir. In 2010, they planted a diverse clonal selection of Pinot Noir on a limestone slab with soil profiles varying from sandy to clay based. Meticulous vineyard management–from leaf pulling to cluster thinning, hand-picking, and optical sorting–ensures that only the best fruit is selected to make their wine. They also buy grapes from a local grower.

WINES - Exceptional wines crafted with low intervention winemaking that capture the essence of the land in each bottle.

Cayuga Lake Higgins Vineyard Reserve Estate Pinot Noir 2021 SLOW WINE ● 115 cases; 56 $ - Pinot grown on limestone bedrock. Hand-picked and optically sorted fruit. Aged 12 months in neutral French oak. Pronounced bing cherry aromatics and stoniness are emphasized in this elegant yet complex wine.
Cayuga Lake Estate Riesling 2022 ○ 35 cases; 30 $ - Estate fruit. Concentrated fruit aromatics of apple and white peach. Flavors of key lime, dried herbs, and honeysuckle, structured within crisp minerality and a long, elegant finish.
Cayuga Lake ESO Series Aligoté 2022 ○ 27 cases; 39 $ - Half fermented in tank and half in neutral oak. Delicate aromatics of orange and lemon cream, herbs, and a touch of salinity. The palate is soft and round, with fresh lemon curd and a brightly crisp, mineral finish.

acres 11 - cases 2,500
Fertilizers compost, cover crops, organic fertilizer
Plant protection sulfur, copper
Weed control mechanical, manual
Yeasts spontaneous fermentation, selected indigenous yeasts, commercial cultured yeasts
Grapes purchase 20%
Certification none

DUNDEE

HERMANN J. WIEMER VINEYARD

3962 State Route 14 - tel. (607) 243-7971 - (607) 703-9359
www.wiemer.com - shop@wiemer.com

 For making world class wines and farming biodynamically in a region where that is a tall order.

PEOPLE - Founded in 1979, Hermann J. Wiemer pioneered viticulture and winemaking in the Finger Lakes. Today's owners Oskar Bynke, Fred Merwarth, Maressa Tosto-Merwarth continue the pioneering legacy by being the first farm in New York State to earn Demeter Biodynamic Certification for their 33-acre HJW Vineyard. They view their work as essential for navigating the future of Finger Lakes wine growing. In their nursery, they experiment with potential varietals for the region.

VINEYARDS - The use of all herbicides and synthetic inputs were first eliminated in 2003. The certified biodynamic HJW vineyard (a decade-long process) is managed by Thijs Verschuuren. In the vineyard, you pass the chickens and geese (for pest control), and their organic-certified, pea and clover pollinator field. Their herd of sheep graze the cover crop and spread the seeds. Organic teas of horsetail and lavender are "brewed" and sprayed for fungal and insect control.

WINES - Premium wines with traditional roots and forward-thinking, which help pave the future of sustainable wine growing in the Finger Lakes.

Seneca Lake HJW Bio Riesling 2020 SLOW WINE ○ 350 cases; 45 $ - Whole cluster pressed. Aged half in stainless and half in large barrel. Complex aromas of lemon, clementine, and a touch of petrol and flint. On the palate, this stunning wine is bursting with stony minerality, followed by a soft and round mid-palate ending with show-stopping acidity in the finish.
Seneca Lake HJW Bio Chardonnay 2021 ○ 271 cases; 39 $ - A delicate, soft, and pure chardonnay from 44 year old vines. Aromas of lemon curd, honeydew, and fresh pear. Soft and inviting on the palate with perfectly balanced acidity. An excellent demonstration that the Finger Lakes is making world class chardonnay.
Seneca Lake HJW Flower Day Riesling 2023 ○ 500 cases, 27 $ - Aromas of honeysuckle, with flavors of lime, apricot and honey. Vey fresh and approachable.

acres 180 - cases 25,000
Fertilizers compost, biodynamic compost, cover crops, manure, organic fertilizer
Plant protection sulfur, biodynamic preparations, copper, organic
Weed control animal grazing, mechanical, manual
Yeasts spontaneous fermentation
Grapes 100% owned
Certification none, some of the vineyards are certified biodynamic, converting to biodynamic

BURDETT

HILLICK & HOBBS

3539 State Route 79 - tel. (607) 703-5999
www.hillickandhobbs.com - team@hillick-hobbs.com

PEOPLE - In 2013, renowned winemaker Paul Hobbs returned to his home state to make world class Riesling. Site selection focused on finding the optimal environment and soil to create Riesling wines with minimal intervention that truly showcase the essence of their environment. Together with winemaker Lynne Fahy, the wines have evolved from site discovery to highlighting specific site expression, culminating in the release of their first single vineyard wines.

VINEYARDS - Vineyard manager Sam Pulis meticulously manages the estate. Located on the east side Seneca Lake and high density planted, it incorporates three key elements Hobbs believes are necessary for optimal growing—deep slopes (with up to a 55-degree gradient), southwestern exposure, and shale dominant soil. East west row orientation promotes airflow, reducing frost risk and disease pressure. Year round cover crops and no till prevent erosion and promote soil health.

WINES - World class, ageworthy, site specific, and meticulously grown estate Riesling that pushes the boundaries of what is possible in the Finger Lakes.

TOP Seneca Lake Estate Dry Riesling 2023 O 2,000 cases; 35 $ - ⬚ - Concentrated aromas of fresh field herbs, wildflowers, and tropical fruit. Vibrant palate of salted papaya with a zesty lime finish. A highly distinctive and complex wine.

Seneca Lake Estate Dry Riesling 2022 O 1,200 cases; 35 $ - ⬚ - Whole cluster pressed and aged sur lie. Delicate aromas of white blossoms and salinity. Steely lime-driven flavors with a round midpalate and long mineral finish.

Seneca Lake Lower Terrace Riesling 2022 O 50 cases; 50 $ - ⊚ - Luminous jasmine and nectarine aromas introduce a steely, mineral driven midpalate of wet stone that softens into a lengthy peach and grapefruit finish.

acres 25 - cases 3,000
Fertilizers compost, cover crops, organic fertilizer
Plant protection sulfur, synthetic pesticides, organic
Weed control mechanical
Yeasts spontaneous fermentation
Grapes 100% owned
Certification none

GENEVA

RAVINES WINE CELLARS

400 Barracks Road - tel. (315) 781-7007
www.ravineswine.com - info@ravineswine.com

PEOPLE - A leading producer in the Finger Lakes, winemaker Morten and chef Lisa Hallgren founded the winery in 2001. Danish by birth yet raised in Provence by his winemaking family, Morten trained at Montpelier, a top wine school, and then worked in Bordeaux before coming to the Finger Lakes. He pioneered the bone dry, mineral driven Riesling style, now popular in the region. Sparkling wine production is expanding.

VINEYARDS - Their estate vineyards are meticulously managed to maintain balance and purity in the grapes. Limestone Springs Vineyard (59 acres), with its sloped soils and Onondaga limestone provides ideal conditions. The 16 Falls Vineyard (46 acres), on a steep slope and close to water, offers excellent temperature moderation. They also buy from the acclaimed Argetsinger vineyard.

WINES - Elegant, expressive wines—very dry and focused, driven by citrus and minerality.

TOP Seneca Lake Dry Riesling 2020 EVERYDAY WINE O 4,400 cases; 21 $ - ⬚ - An excellent value for a stunning Riesling. All estate fruit. Rich aromas of lime, pineapple pith, dry stone, and a touch of petrol from age. Bone dry on the palate, with penetrating minerality, deep citrus concentration, and a long lime peel finish.

Seneca Lake Sparkling Riesling 2019 ⊛ 968 cases; 35 $ - ⬚ - All estate fruit. Traditional method, en tirage for five years. Delicate aromas of stone, dried apricots and tarragon with minerality. Lime and dried peaches on the finish.

Seneca Lake Pinot Noir 2022 ● 794 cases; 29 $ - ⊞ - All estate fruit. Whole cluster (20%). Complex aromatics of black cherry, earth, herbs, and spice. Elegant and expressive on the palate with delicate tannins, bright fruit, and balanced acidity. Cellarworthy.

acres 137 - cases 25,000
Fertilizers compost, cover crops, manure, organic fertilizer, synthetic fertilizer
Plant protection sulfur, synthetic pesticides, copper
Weed control mechanical, manual
Yeasts spontaneous fermentation
Grapes purchase 20%
Certification none

PENN YAN

RED TAIL RIDGE WINERY

846 State Route 14 - tel. (315) 536-4580
www.redtailridgewinery.com - tastingroom@redtailridgewinery.com

 For their long-standing commitment to eco-friendly farming and building, and for making outstanding wines.

PEOPLE - Founded in 2005, owners Nancy Irelan, winemaker, and Mike Schnell, viticulturist, came from California with extensive, major league, wine industry experience. The two wanted to explore cool climate, minimal intervention winemaking. In 2009, they built their winery, the only LEED Gold certified winery in the state. In 2024, they opened a stunning tasting room, paneled in natural wood from trees on the property. They've also been James Beard Award semifinalists.

VINEYARDS - They planted their first vines in 2005, focused on the popular European varietals typically grown in the Finger Lakes. but adventurously expanded to growing atypical varieties including Blaufränkisch, Lagrein and Teroldego (which they make in a unique blend along with Cabernet Franc). The soils of glacial till and deep clay deposits help with water management. In 2023, they converted an acre of their estate to serve as a pollinator field.

WINES - Expressive wine with authentic character, lower alcohol and full phenolic ripeness and flavors.

Seneca Lake Sparkling Riesling Sekt Extra Brut 2019 SLOW WINE ⊛ 198 cases; 40 $ - ◯ - Four years en tirage, disgorged in small lots, with 4 g/L dosage. Aromas of lemon custard and subtle herbs. On the palate–pastry dough, anise spice, and saline minerality.

Seneca Lake Perpetual Change Cuvee No. 4 Sparkling Brut Nonvintage ⊛ Riesling, Chardonnay, Pinot Noir, Pinot Blanc, Zweigelt; 240 cases; 33 $ - ◯ ⊞ - A novel white blend aged in solera for three vintages. En tirage for six to ten months; no additional dosage. Dusty stone, honeyed earth and lime aromas, nuances of caramel and cherry on the palate.

Seneca Lake Lagrein 2020 ● 184 cases; 50 $ - ⊞ - Aged 21 months in neutral French oak. Beautiful black fruit with fresh herb aromatics and bright fruit clarity, integrated tannins, and a blackberry, vanilla, spice finish makes one wish there was more grown.

acres 30 - cases 4,900
Fertilizers compost, cover crops, manure
Plant protection n/a
Weed control manual
Yeasts spontaneous fermentation, selected indigenous yeasts, commercial cultured yeasts
Grapes 100% owned
Certification none

LODI

SILVER THREAD VINEYARD

9564 State Route 414 - tel. (607) 582-6116
www.silverthreadwine.com - info@silverthreadwine.com

PEOPLE - The winery was founded by a regional eco-pioneer in 1982. Winemaker Paul Brock, and General Manager Shannon Brock, both wine educators, purchased the winery in 2011. Today, as leaders for their sustainable practices, they helped to develop the New York State Sustainable Winegrowing certification program. The winery generates its energy from a solar array. They also make ecofriendly packaging decisions and are on the path to becoming zero waste.

VINEYARDS - Located on the east side of Seneca Lake, the vines grow in a temperate microclimate on shallow silt loam over shale rock. They describe their farming as biointensive viticulture , using free range chickens, compost and biochar to enrich the soil. They recently added a plot of hybrid varieties (including Regent) that enable them to farm those grapes organically. Thirty year old Chardonnay and Riesling vines were replanted. They also buy grapes from local growers.

WINES - Skillful, small lot winemaking and a commitment to showcasing what nature provides, creates wines of exceptional purity and expression.

Seneca Lake Estate Vineyard Riesling 2022 SLOW WINE ◯ 200 cases; 28 $ - ⊞ - Aged in neutral oak barrels (with some stainless steel). Dried thyme, apricot, lime, and stoniness with a soft, medium-bodied structure from the use of old barrels, lees contact, bottle aging, and just a touch of residual sugar.

Seneca Lake Dry Riesling 2023 ◯ 600 cases; 22 $ - ◯ - Some neutral barrel fermentation. Aromas of orange blossoms and orchard peach. The peach continues on the palate, accompanied by tart lime and minerality and a lingering stone fruit finish. Simply delicious.

Seneca Lake Petillant Naturel 2023 150 cases; 26 $ - ⊞ - A novel blend of Gewürztraminer, Pinot Noir, Riesling and hybrid Regent. Partially fermented on native yeast, then bottled. Gentle bubbles with strawberry, blood orange, flint and herbs and a touch of yogurt palate and a bright mineral finish.

acres 10 - cases 2,500
Fertilizers compost, cover crops, manure
Plant protection sulfur, biodynamic preparations, synthetic pesticides, copper, organic
Weed control mechanical, manual
Yeasts spontaneous fermentation, commercial cultured yeasts
Grapes purchase 25%
Certification none

HECTOR

STANDING STONE VINEYARDS

Finger Lakes - 9934 Route 414 - tel. (607) 583-6051
www.standingstonewines.com - ssvny@standingstonewines.com

PEOPLE - Hermann J. Wiemer partners Fred Merwarth, Maressa Tosto-Merwarth, and Oscar Bynke purchased Standing Stone Vineyards in 2017 for its treasure trove of old vines which includes the first plantings on Seneca Lake of Riesling and Chardonnay (now 50 years old), planted by Fournier and Devaux on Seneca Lake in 1974. The winery has 30 year old Gewürztraminer and Pinot Noir as well. The tasting room is beautiful and modern with expansive views.

VINEYARDS - The vines sit on deep shale on the southeast side of Seneca Lake in north-south rows. In addition to the celebrated historic vines, the site is unique for growing six acres of Saperavi (the largest planting of the Georgian variety in the U.S.) as well as a third of an acre of Sereksia, an Eastern European grape often blended with Saperavi. They aim for bio-intensive farming—without synthetic chemicals—with the goal of becoming Demeter certified biodynamic.

WINES - Reflects the pure vineyard expression of concentration and complexity from what many consider the best site in the Finger Lakes.

TOP Seneca Lake SSV Teinturier Dry Rosé 2023
EVERYDAY WINE ● Saperavi; 200 cases; 22 $ - ⃝ - An exceptional wine made from 100% direct press of early picked fruit. Aromas of intense floral and spice lead to flavors of strawberry, cherry, and allspice framed by beautiful minerality and acidity on the palate.

Seneca Lake Gewürztraminer 2021 ⃝ 125 cases; 1,950 $ - ⃝ - Vine age: 25-30 years. Classic Finger Lakes Gewürztraminer with significant floral and lychee aromas. Ripe and full without being heavy. Finishes clean and fresh.

Seneca Lake Farm White 2021 ⃝ Riesling, Gewürztraminer, Chardonnay; 250 cases; 22 $ - ⃝ - Three varietals fermented separately, then blended. (Riesling had 14 days on skins to add texture.) Aromas of citrus and earth. Complex fresh pear and stone fruit with a silky texture, subtle tannins and lots of acidity on the finish.

acres 42 - cases 5,000
Fertilizers compost, cover crops, manure, organic fertilizer, synthetic fertilizer
Plant protection sulfur, biodynamic preparations, synthetic pesticides, copper, organic
Weed control animal grazing, mechanical, manual
Yeasts spontaneous fermentation
Grapes 100% owned
Certification Converting to biodynamic

LONG ISLAND

Bottle
229 Channing Daughters Winery

BRIDGEHAMPTON

CHANNING DAUGHTERS WINERY

1927 Scuttlehold Road - tel. (631) 537-7224
www.channingdaughters.com - info@channingdaughters.com

PEOPLE - In 2001, winemaker Christopher Tracy left California for winemaking on Long Island, joining co-owners, veteran wine expert Larry Perrine and Allison Dubin, general manager, as a partner in the historic winery. The original founder, Walter Channing, planted a one acre experimental block in 1982. The halfacre of Chardonnay that remains is the oldest continuously farmed vineyard block on the south fork of Long Island.

VINEYARDS - Abel Lopez manages the vines. The team makes wine from 24 varieties, mostly from 10 blocks on the estate, each with their own history. One block is a field blend of French, Italian and Austrian varietals, including the rarely grown Blaufranksich and Teroldego. The vineyard also has Gewurztraminer, Muscat Ottonel, Ribolla Gialla and Tocai Friulano. Recently they planted Lagrein and Refosco del Pedunculo Rosso. They also buy from local growers.

WINES - Tracy uses multiple varietals, makes novel blends and likes whole cluster on the whites and foot treading on the reds.

Long Island Meditazione Orange Wine 2018 White Blend; 468 cases; 42 $ - Aged 26 months in oak (11% new). A novel white blend. Co-fermented on skins. Aromas of orange crème, toffee and vanilla cream. Baked fruit expression on the palate with a long finish. Complex and stunning.

Long Island L'enfant Sauvage Estate Chardonnay 2017 328 cases; 38 $ - Aged in Slovenian and French oak (100% new). Lemon, orange cream, vanilla and spice with an extensive finish. Exotic and delicious.

Long Island Bianco Cuvée Tropical Pet Nat 2022 Chardonnay, Muscat Ottonel ; 120 cases; 29 $ - Chardonnay (80%) and Muscat Ottanel (20%). Tropical notes of pineapple with earthy aromas. Fruity and tropical, with pineapple, orange and stone fruits on palate. Nice carbonation. A lovely summer wine.

acres 28 - cases 12,000
Fertilizers compost, cover crops
Plant protection sulfur, copper
Weed control mechanical, manual
Yeasts spontaneous fermentation, commercial cultured yeasts
Grapes purchase 30%
Certification none

MATTITUCK

MACARI VINEYARDS

150 Bergen Avenue - tel. (631) 298-0100 - (631) 831-4651
www.macariwines.com - info@macariwines.com

PEOPLE - Since 1995, three generations of Macari's have operated their estate winery on their 500-acre North Fork farm. Their Italian family winemaking origins date back to Queens where they sold homemade wine they made in their basement. In 2020, they hired U.C. Davis educated Byron Elmendorf as winemaker, incorporating native ferments, lees aging and more.

VINEYARDS - Inspired by his studies with biodynamic leaders Alan York from California and Alvaro Espinoza from Chile, Joe Jr. has developed and refined (over 30 years) their composting program with their herd of long horned cattle. He enhances the compost with kelp, a natural source of nitrogen and micronutrients. Over three decades, these practices have nurtured soils that are not just fertile but resilient, ensuring the longevity of their vineyards.

WINES - The main Marcari Line of wines showcase classic east coast maritime winemaking. The Lifeforce line ages wines in concrete vessels to highlight fruit purity and expression. Their Meadowlark line showcases small lot, fun, casual wines.

Long Island Lifeforce Sauvignon Blanc 2023 643 cases; 30 $ - Age six months, partly in concrete eggs and partly in stainless steel. Cold soaked for five days. Luscious tropical fruit aromas with a palate of ripe and green papaya. A voluptuously textured wine.

Long Island Sauvignon Blanc Katherine's Field 2023 1,994 cases; 28 $ - Aromas of subtle seagrass and fresh grapefruit. Palate is mineral driven with salinity, citrus and a delightfully crisp finish.

Long Island Cabernet Franc 2021 909 cases; 38 $ - Fermented and aged in neutral oak for 15 months. Brambleberry spice aromatics with a touch of dry herbs and dusty stone. A soft and silky medium bodied wine with savory red and black fruit and a fresh, spicy finish.

acres 150 - cases 12,000
Fertilizers compost, manure
Plant protection biodynamic preparations, synthetic pesticides, organic
Weed control mechanical, manual
Yeasts spontaneous fermentation, selected indigenous yeasts, commercial cultured yeasts
Grapes 100% owned
Certification none

SAGAPONACK

WÖLFFER ESTATE VINEYARD

139 Sagg Road Sagaponack - tel. (631) 537-5106 - (917) 435-4242
www.wolffer.com - info@wolffer.com

PEOPLE - Founded in 1988, the winery is owned by second generation siblings Marc and Joey Wölffer, along with head winemaker and partner Roman Roth. Their White Horse line features premium wine from estate grown fruit. The Cellar Series consists of small lot, limited release wines. Located in a popular summer watering hole, the winery make no less than six rosés. They also offer summer music concerts and yoga classes.

VINEYARDS - Vineyard Manager Richie Pisacano oversees 55 acres of vines on their main South Fork estate and 24 acres on the North Fork estate. Their estate vineyards, which sit on Bridgehampton loam soil, have been herbicide free since 2023, and they have been expanding their composting and cover crops. They uniquely planted Trebbiano, a fungal resistant Italian variety. They buy grapes from growers. Some of the wines (not featured here) may be grown with herbicide.

WINES - Using traditional techniques, they deftly create elegant, food friendly still and sparkling wines from classic varietals.

🔴 **Long Island White Horse Selection Antonov Sauvignon Blanc 2021** ⊙ 1,070 cases; 32 $ - 🗲 ⊞ - 100% estate. Intense aromas of grass, dried herbs, and ruby red grapefruit. A soft and delicate texture on the palate reveals tart gooseberry with a savory grapefruit pith finish.

Long Island White Horse Selection Grandioso Rosé 2022 ⚪ Merlot, Cabernet Franc, Chardonnay; 1,364 cases; 32 $ - 🗲 ⊞ - Estate fruit. Barrel fermented. Aged five months sur lie with a creamy texture. Aromas of chalky white strawberry and cherry blossoms. Flavors of delicate Rainier cherries and pink grapefruit.

Long Island White Horse Selection Christian's Cuvée Merlot 2019 ● Merlot, Cabernet Franc, Cabernet Sauvignon; 379 cases; 100 $ - ⊞ - Old vines. Aged 20 months in oak. Enticing black cherry and herb aromas. Soft, supple tannins and concentrated fruit, leading to a long cherry vanilla finish. Ageworthy.

acres 79 - cases 100,000
Fertilizers compost, cover crops, organic fertilizer
Plant protection sulfur, synthetic pesticides, copper
Weed control mechanical, manual
Yeasts spontaneous fermentation, selected indigenous yeasts, commercial cultured yeasts
Grapes purchase 75%
Certification none

INDEX OF WINERIES

A

Á Deux Têtes (CA)	48
A Tribute to Grace (CA)	130
Abbot's Passage (CA)	49
Abbott Claim (OR)	166
Acaibo (CA)	49
Accenti Wines (CA)	48
Acquiesce Winery & Vineyards (CA)	112
ADAMVS (CA)	26
Adastra (CA)	50
Adelaida (CA)	115
Alfaro Family Vineyard & Winery (CA)	100
Alta Orsa Wines (CA)	79
Amavi Cellars (WA)	206
AmByth Estate (CA)	115
âmevive (CA)	131
Amista Vineyards (CA)	50
Ampelos Cellars (CA)	131
Analemma Wines (OR)	201
Andis Wines (CA)	163
Antica Terra (OR)	167
Antiquum Farm (OR)	167
Arborbrook by Cooper Mountain Vineyards (OR)	168
Artevino (CA)	79
Ashes and Diamonds (CA)	27
Au Bon Climat (CA)	132
Authentique Wine Cellars (OR)	168

B

Badger Mountain Vineyard (WA)	207
Baldacci Family Vineyards (CA)	27
Bargetto Winery (CA)	100
BARRA of Mendocino (CA)	80
Beauregard Vineyards (CA)	101
Beckham Estate Vineyard (OR)	169
Beckmen Vineyards (CA)	132
Bedrock Wine Co. (CA)	51
Bee Hunter Wine (CA)	80
Belle Pente Vineyard & Winery (OR)	169
Benziger Family Winery (CA)	51
Bergström Wines (OR)	170
Bethel Heights Vineyard (OR)	170
Bien Nacido (CA)	133
Big Basin Vineyards (CA)	101
Big Table Farm (OR)	171
Birdhorse (CA)	52
Birichino (CA)	102
Björnson Vineyard (OR)	171
Blue Quail and McFadden Winery (CA)	81
Bokisch Vineyards (CA)	163
Bonterra Organic Estates (CA)	81
Brashley Vineyards (CA)	82
Brick House Wines (OR)	172
Brooks Wine (OR)	172
Bryn Mawr Vineyards (OR)	173
Buona Notte (OR)	201
Burgess Cellars (CA)	28
Buttonwood Grove Winery (NY)	222

C

Cadence Winery (WA)	207
Cain Vineyard And Winery (CA)	28
Cairjn Wine Cellars (CA)	116
Calera (CA)	112
Camins 2 Dreams (CA)	133
Campovida (CA)	82
Canihan Wines (CA)	52
Cantadora	Olivia Brion (CA)	29
Caprio Cellars (WA)	208
Carol Shelton Wines (CA)	53
CARY Q WINES (CA)	53
Cathiard Vineyard (CA)	29

Cayuse Vineyards & Bionic Wines (WA)	208	Dineen Vineyards (WA)	209
Celestial Hill Vineyard (OR)	173	Disko Wines (CA)	136
Central Coast Group Project / Scotty Boy / L'Arge d'Oor (CA)	134	Domaine Anderson (CA)	85
		Domaine de la Côte (CA)	137
Cesar Toxqui Cellars (CA)	83	Domaine Divio (OR)	177
Chance Creek Vineyards (CA)	83	Domaine Drouhin Oregon (OR)	177
Chanin Wine (CA)	134	Domaine Magdalena (WA)	209
Channing Daughters Winery (NY)	229	Domaine Pouillon (WA)	210
Chappellet (CA)	30	Dominio IV (OR)	178
Charlie & Echo (CA)	159	Dominus/Napanook (CA)	33
Chehalem Winery (OR)	174	Donkey & Goat (CA)	95
CHO Wines (OR)	174	Dr. Konstantin Frank Winery (NY)	220
Clay Shannon (CA)	84	Dragonette Cellars (CA)	137
Clementine Carter Wines (CA)	135	Drew Family Wines (CA)	85
Clesi Winery (CA)	116	DuMOL (CA)	57
Clif Family Winery (CA)	30	Duncan Peak (CA)	86
Comunitá (CA)	54	Dunites Wine Co. (CA)	118
Cooper Mountain Vineyards (OR)	175	Dunning Vineyards (CA)	118
Cooper-Garrod (CA)	102	Dusted Valley (WA)	210
Copia Vineyards & Winery (CA)	117	Dusty Nabor Wines (CA)	138
Coquelicot Estate Vineyard (CA)	135		
Cordant Winery (CA)	117	**E**	
Corison (CA)	31	Eden Rift Vineyards (CA)	113
Cormorant Cellars (CA)	54	Ehlers Estate (CA)	34
County Line Vineyards (CA)	55	Eislynn Wines (CA)	138
Covenant Wines (CA)	94	Element Winery (NY)	224
Cowhorn Vineyard & Garden (OR)	197	Élevée Winegrowers (OR)	178
Cramoisi Vineyard (OR)	175	Elizabeth Rose (CA)	34
Cricket Farms (CA)	84	Emme Wines (CA)	57
Crocker & Starr (CA)	31	Enfield Wine Co. (CA)	58
		Entity of Delight (CA)	139
D		Ernest Vineyards (CA)	58
Damiani Wine Cellars (NY)	224	EST (OR)	202
Dana Estates	Onda (CA)	32	Ettellia (CA)	96
DANCIN (OR)	198	Ettore (CA)	86
Dane Cellars (CA)	55	Evening Land Vineyards (OR)	179
Darling Wines (CA)	56	Everwild Wines (CA)	96
Dashe Cellars (CA)	95	Evesham Wood (OR)	179
DaVero Farms & Winery (CA)	56	Extradimentional Wine Co. Yeah (CA)	59
David Arthur Vineyards (CA)	32		
David Hill Vineyards and Winery (OR)	176	**F**	
Day Wines (OR)	176	Far Mountain (CA)	59
Demetria Estate (CA)	136	Ferrari Ranch Wines (CA)	103
Detert Family Vineyards (CA)	33	Fest Wine Co. (CA)	60

Field Recordings Wine (CA)	119
Flâneur Wines (OR)	180
Folded Hills (CA)	139
Foundry Vineyards (WA)	211
Four Lanterns Winery (CA)	119
Frey Vineyards (CA)	87
Frog's Leap (CA)	35
Fuil Wines (CA)	140
Fulldraw Vineyard (CA)	120

G

Gallica (CA)	35
Ghost Block (CA)	36
Giornata Wines (CA)	120
Gloria Ferrer (CA)	60
Goodfellow Family Cellars (OR)	180
Granville Wine Co. (OR)	181
Grgich Hills Estate (CA)	36
Grimm's Bluff (CA)	140
Guthrie Family Wines (CA)	61

H

Haden Fig (OR)	181
Halter Ranch (CA)	121
Handley Cellars (CA)	87
Hard Row to Hoe Vineyards (WA)	211
Heart & Hands Wine Company (NY)	225
Hedges Family Estate (WA)	212
Heitz Cellar (CA)	37
Hermann J. Wiemer Vineyard (NY)	225
Heron Hill Winery (NY)	221
Herrmann York (CA)	159
HillCrest Vineyard (OR)	198
Hillick & Hobbs (NY)	226
Horse & Plow (CA)	61
Horsepower Vineyards (WA)	212
House Family Vineyards (CA)	103
Hyde de Villaine - HdV (CA)	37

I

Idiot's Grace (OR)	202
Idlewild (CA)	62
Inman Family Wines (CA)	62

J

J. Brix Wines (CA)	160
J. Dirt (CA)	141
J.C. Somers Vintner (OR)	182
J.K. Carriere (OR)	182
Jachter Family Wines (OR)	183
Jaffurs Wine Cellars (CA)	141
Johan Vineyards (OR)	183
Jolie-Laide Wines (CA)	63
Joseph Jewell (CA)	63
Joy Fantastic & Holus Bolus (CA)	142

K

Kamen Estate Wines (CA)	64
Keplinger Wines (CA)	38
King Estate Winery (OR)	184
Kings Carey Wines (CA)	142
kukkula (CA)	121

L

L.A. Lepiane Wines (CA)	143
Lachini Vineyards (OR)	184
Lafayette and White Cellars (OR)	185
Land of Saints Wine Company (CA)	143
Larner Vineyard & Winery (CA)	144
Lasseter Family Winery (CA)	64
Lemelson Vineyards (OR)	185
Les Lunes Wine (CA)	97
Lester Estate Wines (CA)	104
Lichen Estate (CA)	88
Lieu Dit (CA)	144
Lindquist Family Wines (CA)	122
Lingua Franca (OR)	186
Littorai Wines (CA)	65
Living Roots Wine & Co (NY)	221
Lo-Fi Wines (CA)	145
Longplay Wine (OR)	186
Loop de Loop (WA)	213
Los Angeles River Wine Co. (CA)	160
Los Pilares (CA)	161
Lumos Wine Co. (OR)	187
Luna Hart (CA)	145
Lushington Wines (WA)	213
LXV Wine (CA)	122

M

Macari Vineyards (NY)	229
Madson Wines (CA)	104
MAHA (CA)	123
Maison Areion (CA)	105
Mallea Wines (CA)	146
Maloof (OR)	187
Marchelle Wines (CA)	65
Margins Wine (CA)	105
Mariah Vineyards (CA)	88
Martha Stoumen Wines (CA)	89
Massican (CA)	38
Maysara Winery (OR)	188
Melville (CA)	146
Merriam Vineyards (CA)	66
Merry Edwards (CA)	66
Mia Bea Wines (CA)	89
Miscreant Wines (CA)	97
Monte Rio Cellars (CA)	67
Montemar Winery (CA)	147
Moon Hollow (CA)	67

N

Native9 (CA)	147
Navarro Vineyards & Winery (CA)	90
Neal Family Vineyards (CA)	39
Neely Wine (CA)	106
Neotempo (CA)	39
Newfound Wines (CA)	40
Nicolas-Jay (OR)	188
Niner Wine Estates (CA)	123
North American Press (CA)	68

O

Oakville Ranch (CA)	40
Oakville Winery (CA)	41
Ojai Mountain Vineyard (CA)	161
Onx (CA)	124
Open Claim Vineyards (OR)	189
Opus One (CA)	41
Outward Wines (CA)	124
OVIS (CA)	90

P

Paradigm (CA)	42
Paradisos del Sol Winery & Organic Vineyard (WA)	214
Pax Wines (CA)	68
Pennyroyal Farm (CA)	91
Pepperbridge Winery (WA)	214
Pét Project (WA)	215
Phelan Farm (CA)	125
Piazza Family Wines (CA)	148
Piedrasassi (CA)	148
Porter Creek Vineyards (CA)	69
Pott Wines (CA)	42
Powicana Farm (CA)	91
Preston Farm & Winery (CA)	69
Purity Wines (CA)	98

Q

Quady North (OR)	199
Quintessa (CA)	43
Quivira Vineyards (CA)	70

R

Radio-Coteau (CA)	70
RAEN (CA)	71
Ram's Gate Winery (CA)	71
Ratio:Wines (OR)	189
Ravines Wine Cellars (NY)	226
Read Holland (CA)	72
Red Tail Ridge Winery (NY)	227
Refugio Ranch Vineyards (CA)	149
Regan Vineyards Winery (CA)	106
Remy Wines (OR)	190
Résonance (OR)	190
Rhys Vineyards (CA)	107
Ridge Vineyards (CA)	107
Ridgecrest (OR)	191
Roark Wine Company (CA)	149
Robert Hall Winery (CA)	125
Robert Sinskey Vineyards (CA)	43
Roblar Winery & Vineyards (CA)	150
Roots Wine Co. (OR)	191
Roserock Drouhin Oregon (OR)	192
Ruby Vineyard & Winery (OR)	192
Rudd Estate (CA)	44

Ruth Lewandowski Wine (CA) — 72
RZN Wines (CA) — 150

S

SAMsARA Wine Co. (CA) — 151
San Rucci Winery (CA) — 126
Sandar & Hem Winery (CA) — 108
Sandhi Wines (CA) — 151
Santa Cruz Mountain Vineyard (CA) — 108
Sante Arcangeli Family Wines (CA) — 109
Savage Grace (WA) — 215
Scribe (CA) — 73
Seabold Cellars (CA) — 113
Senses Wines (CA) — 73
Ser Winery (CA) — 109
Shokrian Vineyard (CA) — 152
Silver Mountain Vineyards (CA) — 110
Silver Thread Vineyard (NY) — 227
Six Eighty Cellars (NY) — 223
Small Vines (CA) — 74
Snowden Vineyards (CA) — 44
Sokol Blosser Winery (OR) — 193
Solminer (CA) — 152
Solomon Hills Estate (CA) — 153
Soter Vineyards (OR) — 193
Spear Vineyards & Winery (CA) — 153
Spottswoode Estate Vineyard & Winery (CA) — 45
St. Innocent Winery (OR) — 194
Staglin Family Vineyard (CA) — 45
Stags Leap Wine Cellars (CA) — 46
Standing Stone Vineyards (NY) — 228
Statera Cellars (OR) — 203
Stirm Wine Co. (CA) — 114
Stoller Family Estate (OR) — 194
Stolo Vineyards (CA) — 126
Stolpman Vineyard (CA) — 154
Stone Edge Farm (CA) — 74
Storm Wines (CA) — 154
Storrs Winery & Vineyards (CA) — 110
Story of Soil Wine (CA) — 155
Subject to Change Wines (CA) — 98
Surveyor (CA) — 75
Syncline (WA) — 216

T

Tablas Creek Vineyard (CA) — 127
Tagaris Winery (WA) — 216
Tatomer (CA) — 127
Terah Wine Co. (CA) — 99
Tercero Wines (CA) — 155
Terra Savia (CA) — 92
Terre Rouge/Easton Wines (CA) — 164
Testa Vineyards (CA) — 92
Thacher Winery & Vineyard (CA) — 128
The Brander Vineyard (CA) — 156
The End of Nowhere (CA) — 164
The Eyrie Vineyards (OR) — 195
The Grenachista (CA) — 75
Thibido Winery (CA) — 128
Trinafour (CA) — 93
Troon Vineyard (OR) — 199
Two Shepherds (CA) — 76
Tyler Winery (CA) — 156

U

Under the Wire (CA) — 76
Unti Vineyards (CA) — 77
Unturned Stone (CA) — 93
Upper Five Vineyard (OR) — 200
Upsidedown Wines (WA) — 217

V

Vega Vineyard & Farm (CA) — 157
Verdad Wine Cellars (CA) — 129
Villa Creek Cellars (CA) — 129
Volker Eisele Family Estate (CA) — 46

W

Ward Four Wines (CA) — 77
Whitcraft Winery (CA) — 157
Wildflower Winery (CA) — 158
WillaKenzie Estate (OR) — 195
Wilridge Vineyard, Winery & Distillery (WA) — 217
Wilson Creek Winery & Vineyard (CA) — 162
Winderlea Vineyard & Winery (OR) — 196
Windy Oaks Estate (CA) — 111
Winery Sixteen 600 (CA) — 78
Wölffer Estate Vineyard (NY) — 230

INDEX OF PLACES

A

Acampo (CA)	112
Alameda (CA)	60, 95
Amador City (CA)	164
Amity (OR)	168, 172
Angwin (CA)	26, 39
Aptos (CA)	104, 109, 110
Arroyo Grande (CA)	122, 129

B

Bakersfield (CA)	126
Beaverton (OR)	175
Benton City (WA)	209, 212
Berkeley (CA)	94, 95
Bonny Doon (CA)	101
Boonville (CA)	80, 88, 91
Boulder Creek (CA)	101
Bridgehampton (NY)	229
Buellton (CA)	134, 157
Burdett (NY)	224, 226

C

Camarillo (CA)	138, 140
Cambria (CA)	125, 126
Carlton (OR)	166, 169, 178, 180, 185, 189, 190, 193
Cascade Locks (OR)	201
Cle Elum (WA)	217
Corralitos (CA)	103, 111
Cupertino (CA)	107

D

Dallas (OR)	189
Dayton (OR)	177, 190, 193, 194
Dundee (OR)	167, 170, 175, 176, 178, 179, 181, 185, 196
Dundee (NY)	225

E

Elk (CA)	85
Escondido (CA)	160
Eugene (OR)	184

F

Forest Grove (OR)	176, 187
Forestville (CA)	63

G

Gaston (OR)	171
Gaviota (CA)	139
Geneva (NY)	224, 226
Glen Ellen (CA)	49, 51, 55, 64, 74
Goleta (CA)	151
Grants Pass (OR)	199
Grover Beach (CA)	124

H

Hammondsport (NY)	220, 221
Healdsburg (CA)	49, 50, 54, 56, 58, 62, 66, 69, 70, 72, 75, 77
Hector (NY)	228
Hillsboro (OR)	174, 192
Hollister (CA)	112, 113
Hopland (CA)	79, 81, 82, 86, 92

J

Jacksonville (OR)	197, 199
Jefferson (OR)	194
Junction City (OR)	167

K

Kennewick (WA)	207

L

Lakeport (CA)	84, 90
Lodi (CA)	163
Lodi (NY)	227
Lompoc (CA)	127, 131, 133, 134, 137, 141, 146-148, 150, 151, 153, 156
Los Alamos (CA)	130, 135, 139, 145, 152
Los Angeles (CA)	160
Los Gatos (CA)	107

Los Olivos (CA)   132, 135-138, 140, 142, 144, 149, 152, 154, 155

Lyle (WA)   210, 213, 216

M

Manchester (CA)   88
Manson (WA)   211
Mattituck (NY)   229
McMinnville (OR)   173, 180, 188, 195, 196
Medford (OR)   198
Milton Freewater (WA)   208, 212
Mosier (OR)   201, 202

N

Napa (CA)   27-29, 37-40, 42, 43, 46, 47, 50
Newberg (OR)   168, 172, 174, 177, 182-184, 186, 188, 191

O

Oakville (CA)   33, 34, 36, 41, 42, 44
Occidental (CA)   73
Ojai (CA)   161
Orcutt (CA)   143
Orinda (CA)   97
Ovid (NY)   223

P

Paso Robles (CA)   115-125, 127-129
Penn Yan (NY)   227
Philo (CA)   82, 85, 87, 90
Philomath (OR)   187
Plymouth (CA)   163, 164
Portland (OR)   202, 203
Portola Valley (CA)   106, 108

R

Redlands (CA)   159
Redwood Valley (CA)   80, 83, 87, 89, 91, 92
Richland (WA)   216
Richmond (CA)   96-99
Rickreall (OR)   183
Romulus (NY)   222
Roseburg (OR)   198
Rutherford (CA)   35, 36, 43, 45

S

Sagaponack (NY)   230
Salem (OR)   170, 171, 173, 179, 181, 186, 192

San Diego (CA)   159, 161
San Luis Obispo (CA)   118
Santa Barbara (CA)   132, 141, 143, 144, 157
Santa Cruz (CA)   102, 104, 105, 108-110
Santa Maria (CA)   131, 133, 136, 147, 153, 154
Santa Rosa (CA)   48, 53, 58, 62, 68, 72, 93
Santa Ynez (CA)   150, 156
Saratoga (CA)   102, 103
Seattle (WA)   207
Sebastopol (CA)   55, 57, 61, 65-68, 70, 71, 74, 89
Sherwood (OR)   169
Solvang (CA)   142, 145, 148
Sonoma (CA)   48, 51, 52, 56, 59-61, 63, 64, 67, 71, 73, 75-78
Soquel (CA)   100, 106
St. Helena (CA)   28-32, 34, 35, 37, 38, 40, 44-46
St. Saint Helena (CA)   31

T

Talent (OR)   200
Temecula (CA)   162
Templeton (CA)   115, 116

U

Ukiah (CA)   93
Underwood (WA)   213, 215
Union Springs (NY)   225

V

Ventura (CA)   158
Vineburg (CA)   52

W

Walla Walla (WA)   206, 208, 210, 211, 214, 215
Watsonville (CA)   100, 114
Windsor (CA)   54, 57, 76
Woodside (CA)   105

Y

Yakima (WA)   217
Yamhill (OR)   191, 195
Yorkville (CA)   79
Yountville (CA)   33

Z

Zillah (WA)   209, 214

www.ingramcontent.com/pod-product-compliance
Lightning Source LLC
LaVergne TN
LVHW020418070526
838199LV00055B/3655